SCOTT FORESMAN · ADDISON WESLEY

Mathematics

Authors

Randall I. Charles

Warren Crown

Francis (Skip) Fennell

Janet H. Caldwell
Mary Cavanagh
Dinah Chancellor
Alma B. Ramirez

Jeanne F. Ramos
Kay Sammons
Jane F. Schielack

William Tate
Mary Thompson
John A. Van de Walle

Consulting Mathematicians

Edward J. Barbeau
Professor of Mathematics
University of Toronto
Toronto, Ontario, Canada

David M. Bressoud
DeWitt Wallace Professor
  of Mathematics
Macalester College
Saint Paul, Minnesota

Gary Lippman
Professor of Mathematics
  and Computer Science
California State University
  Hayward
Hayward, California

PEARSON

Scott
Foresman

Editorial Offices: Glenview, Illinois • Parsippany, New Jersey • New York, New York

Sales Offices: Boston, Massachusetts • Duluth, Georgia • Glenview, Illinois
Coppell, Texas • Sacramento, California

Reading Consultants

Peter Afflerbach
Professor and Director of The Reading Center
University of Maryland
College Park, Maryland

Donald J. Leu
John and Maria Neag
 Endowed Chair in Literacy and Technology
University of Connecticut
Storrs, Connecticut

Reviewers

Mary Bacon
Mathematics Specialist
East Baton Rouge Parish School
 System
Baton Rouge, Louisiana

Cheryl Baker
Mathematics Teacher
Norton Middle School
Norton, Ohio

Marcelline A. Barron
Curriculum Leader Math and
 Science, K–5
Fairfield Public Schools
Fairfield, Connecticut

Mary Connery-Simmons
Mathematics Specialist
Springfield Massachusetts
 Public Schools
Springfield, Massachusetts

Anthony C. Dentino
Supervisor of Curriculum
Brick Township Schools
Brick, New Jersey

Dawn Evans
Mathematics Teacher
Bret Harte Elementary School
Chicago, Illinois

Sam Hanson
Teacher
Totem Falls Elementary
Snohomish, Washington

Allison Harris
Professional Development
 School Coach
Seattle Public Schools
Seattle, Washington

Pamela Renee Hill NBCT
Teacher
Durham Public Schools
Durham, North Carolina

Catherine Kuhns
Teacher
Country Hills Elementary
Coral Springs, Florida

Madeleine A. Madsen
District Curriculum Resource
Community Consolidated
 School District 59
Arlington Heights, Illinois

Lynda M. Penry
Teacher
Wright Elementary
Ft. Walton Beach, Florida

Deanna P. Rigdon
District Math Curriculum
 Specialist, Grades 3–4
Granite School District
Salt Lake City, Utah

Thomas Romero
Principal
Adams Elementary
Wapato, Washington

Wendy Siegel
Mathematics Coordinator K–12
Orchard Park Middle School
Orchard Park, New York

Sandra Smith
Teacher
Cheat Lake Elementary
Morgantown, West Virginia

Rochelle A. Solomon
Mathematics Resource Teacher
Cleveland Municipal School
 District
Cleveland, Ohio

Frank L. Sparks
Curriculum Design and Support
 Specialist, Secondary
 Mathematics
New Orleans Public Schools
New Orleans, Louisiana

Beth L. Spivey
Lead Teacher, Elementary
 Mathematics
Wake County Public
 School System
Raleigh, North Carolina

Paula Spomer
Teacher
Chisholm Elementary
Edmond, Oklahoma

Robert Trammel
Math Consultant
Fort Wayne Community Schools
Fort Wayne, Indiana

Annemarie Tuffner
Mathematics Lead Teacher,
 K–12
Neshaminy School District
Langhorne, Pennsylvania

Judy L. Wright
Curriculum and Staff
 Development Specialist
Columbus Public Schools
Columbus, Ohio

Theresa Zieles
Teacher
Indianapolis Public School 88
Indianapolis, Indiana

ISBN: 0-328-26366-4

Place Value and Money

Instant Check System
- Diagnosing Readiness, 2
- Warm Up, daily
- Talk About It, daily
- Check, daily
- Diagnostic Checkpoint, 17, 35, 47

Test Prep
- Mixed Review and Test Prep, daily
- Test Talk, daily, 48
- Cumulative Review and Test Prep, 54

eading For Math Success

Reading Helps!

- Reading Helps, 14, 32, 42
- Key Vocabulary and Concept Review, 50

Writing in Math

- Writing in Math exercises, daily

Problem-Solving Applications, 44

Discovery CHANNEL
SCHOOL   Discover Math in Your World, 21

Additional Resources
- Learning with Technology, 39
- Enrichment, 27, 31
- Chapter 1 Test, 52
- Reteaching, 56
- More Practice, 60

Time, Data, and Graphs

 Instant Check System
- Diagnosing Readiness, 190
- Warm Up, daily
- Talk About It, daily
- Check, daily
- Diagnostic Checkpoint, 203, 225, 241

Test Prep
- Mixed Review and Test Prep, daily
- Test Talk, daily, 242
- Cumulative Review and Test Prep, 248

Reading Helps!
- Reading for Math Success, 234
- Reading Helps, 216, 236
- Key Vocabulary and Concept Review, 244

Writing in Math
- Writing in Math exercises, daily
- Writing to Compare, 216

 Problem-Solving Applications, 238

Discovery CHANNEL SCHOOL Discover Math in Your World, 215

Additional Resources
- Learning with Technology, 195, 207, 231
- Practice Game, 221
- Enrichment, 211
- Chapter 4 Test, 246
- Reteaching, 250
- More Practice, 254

5 Multiplication Concepts and Facts

Instant Check System
- Diagnosing Readiness, 258
- Warm Up, daily
- Talk About It, daily
- Check, daily
- Diagnostic Checkpoint, 275, 297

Test Prep
- Mixed Review and Test Prep, daily
- Test Talk, daily, 298
- Cumulative Review and Test Prep, 304

Reading For Math Success
Reading Helps!
- Reading for Math Success, 268
- Reading Helps, 270, 284
- Key Vocabulary and Concept Review, 300

Writing in Math
- Writing in Math exercises, daily

 Problem-Solving Applications, 294

Discovery CHANNEL SCHOOL Discover Math in Your World, 279

Additional Resources
- Learning with Technology, 291
- Enrichment, 265
- Chapter 5 Test, 302
- Reteaching, 306
- More Practice, 310

More Multiplication Facts

Division Concepts and Facts

Instant Check System
- Diagnosing Readiness, 368
- Warm Up, daily
- Talk About It, daily
- Check, daily
- Diagnostic Checkpoint, 383, 395, 409

Test Prep
- Mixed Review and Test Prep, daily
- Test Talk, daily, 410
- Cumulative Review and Test Prep, 416

Reading For Math Success
Reading Helps!

- Reading for Math Success, 378
- Reading Helps, 380, 404
- Key Vocabulary and Concept Review, 412

Writing in Math

- Writing in Math exercises, daily

Problem-Solving Applications, 406

DISCOVERY CHANNEL
SCHOOL Discover Math in Your World, 377

Additional Resources
- Learning with Technology, 401
- Chapter 7 Test, 414
- Reteaching, 418
- More Practice, 422

8 Geometry and Measurement

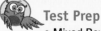

CHAPTER

10 Decimals and Measurement

11 Multiplying and Dividing Greater Numbers

Instant Check System
- Diagnosing Readiness, 610
- Warm Up, daily
- Talk About It, daily
- Check, daily
- Diagnostic Checkpoint, 625, 647, 661

Test Prep
- Mixed Review and Test Prep, daily
- Test Talk, daily, 662
- Cumulative Review and Test Prep, 668

Reading For Math Success
Reading Helps!
- Reading for Math Success, 642
- Reading Helps, 644, 656
- Key Vocabulary and Concept Review, 664

Writing in Math
- Writing in Math exercises, daily

Problem-Solving Applications, 658

Discover Math in Your World, 629

Additional Resources
- Learning with Technology, 621
- Practice Game, 635
- Enrichment, 615, 621, 655
- Chapter 11 Test, 666
- Reteaching, 670
- More Practice, 674

12 Measurement and Probability

✓ **Instant Check System**
- Diagnosing Readiness, 678
- Warm Up, daily
- Talk About It, daily
- Check, daily
- Diagnostic Checkpoint, 699, 713

Test Prep
- Mixed Review and Test Prep, daily
- Test Talk, daily, 714
- Cumulative Review and Test Prep, 720

Reading For Math Success
Reading Helps!
- Reading for Math Success, 686
- Reading Helps, 688, 708
- Key Vocabulary and Concept Review, 716

Writing in Math
- Writing in Math exercises, daily
- Writing to Explain, 708

Problem-Solving Applications, 710

Discovery CHANNEL SCHOOL
Discover Math in Your World, 707

Additional Resources
- Learning with Technology, 693
- Enrichment, 683
- Chapter 12 Test, 718
- Reteaching, 722
- More Practice, 726

What can help you get higher test scores?

Turn the page to find out.

Test-Taking Strategies

Remember these six test-taking strategies that will help you do well on tests. These strategies are also taught in the Test Talk before each chapter test.

Understand the Question

- Look for important words.
- Turn the question into a statement: "I need to find out..."

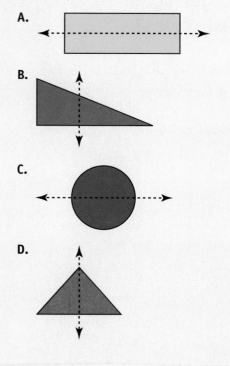

1. Which shape does NOT have a line of symmetry?

   A.

   B.

   C.

   D.

1. What are some important words in the problem that tell you what the problem is about?

2. What important word in the problem is highlighted using capital letters?

3. Turn the question into a statement that begins with "I need to find out..."

Get Information for the Answers

- Get information from text.
- Get information from pictures, maps, diagrams, tables, and graphs.

2. Ms. Hernandez needs 500 napkins. Circle packages to show 500.

4. What information from the picture is needed to solve the problem?

5. What information in the text is needed to solve the problem?

Plan How to Find the Answer

- Think about problem-solving skills and strategies.
- Choose computation methods.

3. The principal of Washington School unpacked a shipment of school supplies. There were 72 boxes of chalk, 24 library books, and 16 dictionaries. How many books were in the shipment?

   A. 8
   B. 30
   C. 40
   D. 112

6. Tell how you would use the following problem-solving skills and strategies as you solve the problem.

   - Identify extra or missing information.
   - Choose an operation.
   - Draw a picture.

7. Which of the following computation methods is best to use to solve this problem?

   - Place-value blocks
   - Paper and pencil
   - Calculator

Make Smart Choices

- Eliminate wrong answers.
- Try working backward from an answer.
- Check answers for reasonableness; estimate.

4. Cary can take 36 pictures with the roll of film in his camera. So far he has taken 19 pictures. How many more pictures can Cary take?

   A. 7 pictures
   B. 17 pictures
   C. 27 pictures
   D. 55 pictures

8. Which answer choices can you eliminate because you are sure they are wrong answers? Explain.

9. How could you use addition to work backward from an answer to see if it is correct?

10. How could you estimate the answer? Is the correct answer close to the estimate?

Use these two strategies when you have to write an answer.

Use Writing in Math

- Make your answer brief but complete.
- Use words from the problem and use math terms accurately.
- Describe steps in order.
- Draw pictures if they help you explain your thinking.

5. Jonah measured the length of a crayon. First he used Snap Cubes. Then he used paper clips.

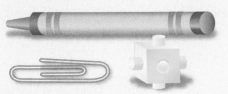

Did Jonah use more Snap Cubes or paper clips? Explain how you decided.

Work space

11. What words from the problem will you use in your response?

12. What steps could you describe in your response?

13. How can drawing a picture help you explain your thinking?

Improve Written Answers

- Check if your answer is complete.
- Check if your answer is clear and easy to follow.
- Check if your answer makes sense.

6. Look at the pattern in the chart.

1	2	3	4	5	6	7	8	9	10
11	12	13	14	15	16	17	18	19	20
21	22	23	24	25	26	27	28	29	30
31	32	33	34	35	36	37	38	39	40
41	42	43	44	45	46	47	48	49	50

What number comes next in the pattern? __28__

Explain how you found your answer.

I found the pattern and then I counted squares.

14. Is the answer that is given worth 4 points, using the rubric that is shown on the next page? Explain.

15. If the answer is not worth 4 points, tell how to improve the answer.

Scoring Rubric

4 points

Full credit: 4 points

The answer is correct. A full explanation is given as to how the answer is found.

3 points

Partial credit: 3 points

The answer is correct, but the explanation does not fully explain how the answer was found.

2 points

Partial credit: 2 points

The answer is correct or the explanation is correct, but not both.

1 point

Partial credit: 1 point

A solution is attempted, but the answer is incorrect. The explanation is unclear.

0 points

No credit: 0 points

The solution is completely incorrect or missing.

For more on Test-Taking Strategies, see the following Test Talk pages.

Test Prep

As you use your book, look for these features that help you prepare for tests.

Test Talk before each chapter test teaches Test-Taking Strategies.

Think It Through
- I will **check if the answer is complete.**
- I will **check if the answer makes sense.**

Test Talk: Think It Through within lessons helps you do the kind of thinking you need to do when you take a test.

Mixed Review and Test Prep

Mixed Review and Test Prep at the end of lessons gives you practice with the kind of items on tests.

Take It to the NET
Test Prep
www.scottforesman.com

Take It to the Net: Test Prep at the end of lessons offers online test prep.

Cumulative Review and Test Prep

Cumulative Review and Test Prep at the end of chapters helps you remember content you'll need to know when you take tests.

Place Value and Money

DIAGNOSING READINESS

A Vocabulary
(Grade 2)

Choose the best term from the box.

1. When you decide which number is greater, you are __?__ numbers.

2. The pattern 2, 4, 6, 8 shows __?__ by 2s.

3. The number 45 has four __?__ and 5 ones.

Vocabulary
- **tens** *(Gr. 2)*
- **comparing** *(Gr. 2)*
- **skip counting** *(Gr. 2)*
- **hundreds** *(Gr. 2)*

B Place Value
(Grade 2)

Write the number shown by the blocks.

4.    5.

Write each number.

6. seventy-two   7. fifteen

8. Kyle had 2 tens blocks and 3 ones blocks. He added 2 tens blocks. What number is he showing?

Which is faster, a white-tailed deer or a tiger?

You will find out in Lesson 1-15.

THE WORLD IN ONE DAY

Every day... 7 million pizzas are eaten in America... one human heart pumps enough blood to fill 170 bathtubs... lightning strikes Earth 8 million times...
by RUSSELL ASH, author of INCREDIBLE COMPARISONS

C Compare Numbers
(Grade 2)

Tell which number is greater.

9. 35 or 53 **10.** 24 or 19

Tell which number is less.

11. 15 or 19 **12.** 96 or 89

13. Write the numbers in order from least to greatest.

45 27 38

14. Jordan has 12 marbles. Kelly has 4 green marbles and 7 red marbles. Who has more marbles?

D Money
(Grade 2)

Write the value of each coin.

15.  cents

16. cents

17. cents

Key Idea
You can use numbers to locate things, to name things, to measure, or to count.

Vocabulary
• ordinal numbers

Ways to Use Numbers

LEARN

How do you use numbers?

You can use numbers to:

locate	**name**	**measure**	**count**
21 Elm Street	Route 66	1 pound	3 balls

You can use **ordinal numbers** to show the order of people or objects.

1st   2nd   3rd   4th   5th
first   second   third   fourth   fifth

Here are some more ordinal numbers.

6th	10th	12th	20th	21st	99th
sixth	tenth	twelfth	twentieth	twenty-first	ninety-ninth

✓ Talk About It

1. Why do you think houses have numbers on them?

2. How many children are in front of the 5th child in line?

Tell if each number is used to locate, name, measure, or count.

1.
12 Large Eggs

2. 10117 S. TRIPP AVENUE

3. Number Sense The students at the right are in gym class. If Alex gets in line behind Ben, what ordinal number tells his place in line?

Chris   Amy   Sam   Sue   Ann   Ben

PRACTICE

For more practice, see Set 1-1 on p. 60.

A Skills and Understanding

Tell if each number is used to locate, name, measure, or count.

4.

5.

For 6–9, use the picture of the children above. Who is

6. fifth in line?   **7.** first in line?   **8.** 2nd in line?

9. Write an ordinal number for Ben's place in line.

10. Number Sense What comes next? 81st, 82nd, 83rd, ▢

B Reasoning and Problem Solving

11. How many people are ahead of the 10th person in line?

12. <u>**Writing in Math**</u> Write directions for how to make your bed. Use the ordinal numbers *first, second,* and *third.*

🦉 Mixed Review and Test Prep

Take It to the NET
Test Prep
www.scottforesman.com

13. 3 + 6   **14.** 7 − 2   **15.** 13 − 4   **16.** 7 + 7

17. 8 cars + 5 cars = ▢ cars

A. 14   **B.** 13   **C.** 11   **D.** 3

Key Idea
You can use place value to read and write numbers in the hundreds.

Vocabulary
- digit
- place value
- expanded form
- standard form
- word form

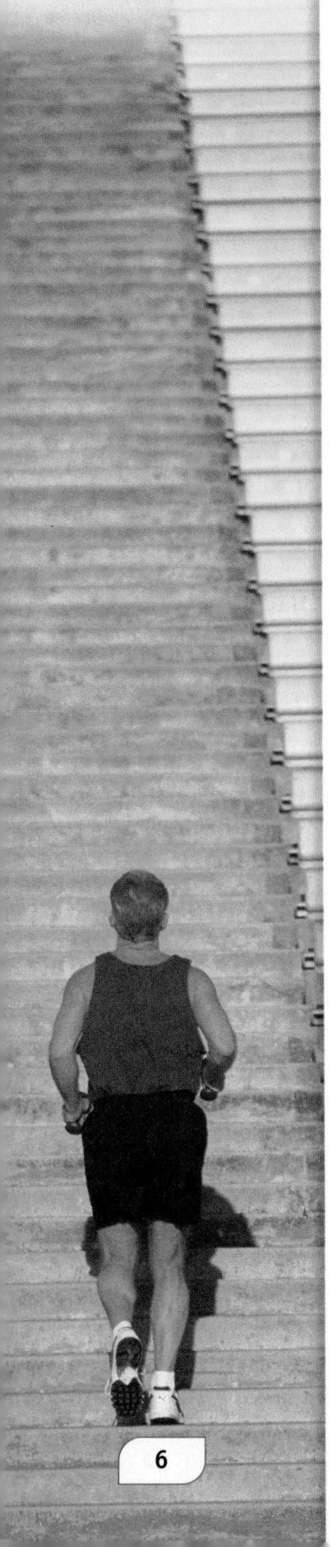

Numbers in the Hundreds

WARM UP

Copy and complete.

1. 23 = 2 tens ☐ ones
2. 52 = ☐ tens 2 ones
3. 37 = ☐ tens ☐ ones

LEARN

How can you read numbers using place value?

All numbers are made from the **digits** 0, 1, 2, 3, 4, 5, 6, 7, 8, and 9.

An athlete is training for endurance by running up 247 stairs. You can show 247 in different ways.

place-value chart:

hundreds	tens	ones
2	4	7
The value of the 2 is 2 hundreds, or 200.	The value of the 4 is 4 tens, or 40.	The value of the 7 is 7 ones, or 7.

place-value blocks:

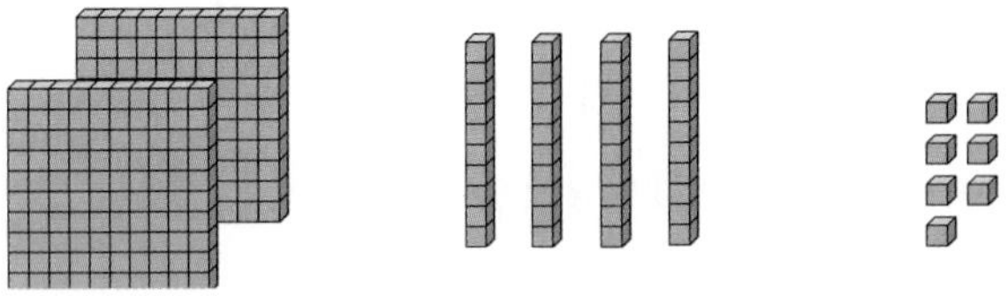

2 hundreds **4 tens** **7 ones**

expanded form: **200 + 40 + 7**

standard form: **247**

word form: **two hundred forty-seven**

Talk About It

1. How do you know that the value of the 4 in 247 is 40?

2. How could you show 305 in expanded form?

Write each number in standard form.

1.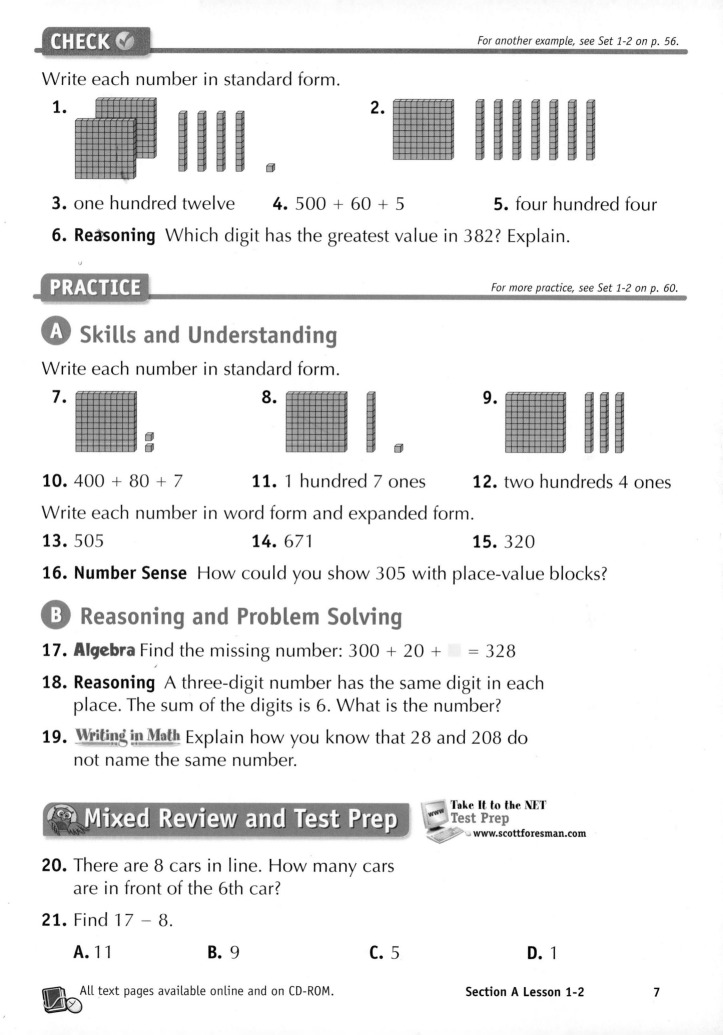

2.

3. one hundred twelve   **4.** 500 + 60 + 5   **5.** four hundred four

6. Reasoning Which digit has the greatest value in 382? Explain.

PRACTICE

A Skills and Understanding

Write each number in standard form.

7.   **8.**   **9.**

10. 400 + 80 + 7   **11.** 1 hundred 7 ones   **12.** two hundreds 4 ones

Write each number in word form and expanded form.

13. 505   **14.** 671   **15.** 320

16. Number Sense How could you show 305 with place-value blocks?

B Reasoning and Problem Solving

17. Algebra Find the missing number: 300 + 20 + ▮ = 328

18. Reasoning A three-digit number has the same digit in each place. The sum of the digits is 6. What is the number?

19. Writing in Math Explain how you know that 28 and 208 do not name the same number.

Mixed Review and Test Prep

Take It to the NET
Test Prep
www.scottforesman.com

20. There are 8 cars in line. How many cars are in front of the 6th car?

21. Find 17 − 8.

   A. 11   **B.** 9   **C.** 5   **D.** 1

Materials
• place-value blocks or  tools

Place-Value Patterns

LEARN

WARM UP
Copy and complete.
1. 10 = ☐ ones
2. 50 = ☐ tens
3. 100 = ☐ tens

Activity

How can you name the same number in different ways?

Our place-value system is based on groups of 10.

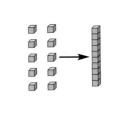

10 ones = 1 ten   10 tens = 1 hundred

These patterns of 10 can help you rename numbers.

Here's one way to show **134** with place-value blocks.

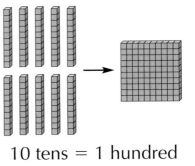

100 + 30 + 4 = 134
1 hundred 3 tens 4 ones = 134

Jen and Tucker found different ways to show 134.

Jen's Way   *Tucker's Way*

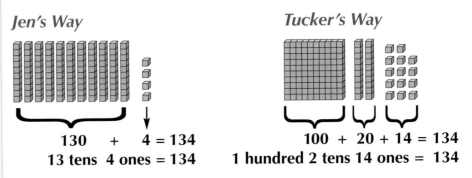

130 + 4 = 134   100 + 20 + 14 = 134
13 tens 4 ones = 134   1 hundred 2 tens 14 ones = 134

Use place-value blocks to show each number two ways. Draw the blocks you use for each answer.

a. 251   **b.** 122   **c.** 301   **d.** 180

e. How could you rename 200 using only tens?

Write each number in standard form.

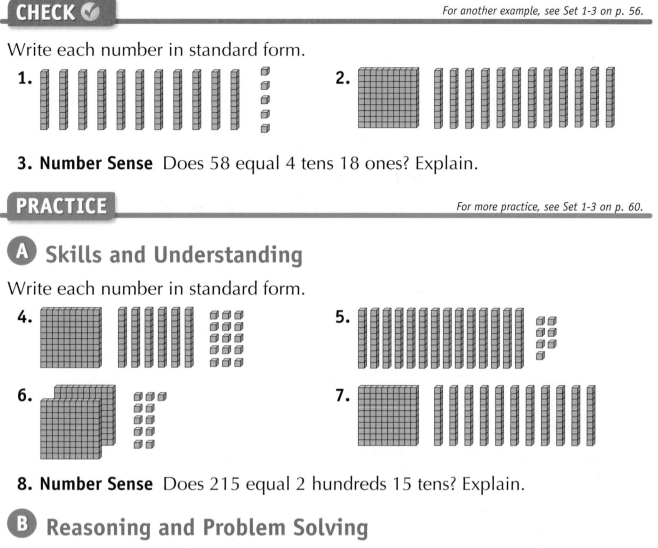

1.

2.

3. **Number Sense** Does 58 equal 4 tens 18 ones? Explain.

PRACTICE

For more practice, see Set 1-3 on p. 60.

Ⓐ Skills and Understanding

Write each number in standard form.

4.

5.

6.

7.

8. **Number Sense** Does 215 equal 2 hundreds 15 tens? Explain.

Ⓑ Reasoning and Problem Solving

9. How could you rename 320 using only tens?

10. **Reasoning** Two hundred eight people shopped at the Farmer's Market. Do you need any tens blocks to show that number? Explain.

11. **Writing in Math** Cindy has 20 tens blocks and 3 ones blocks. What other block does she need to show 213? Explain.

Mixed Review and Test Prep

Take It to the NET
Test Prep
www.scottforesman.com

12. Write 631 in expanded form.

13. Write the word name for 206.

14. Which has the same value as 13 − 6?

　A. 3 + 3　　　**B.** 14 − 7　　　**C.** 5 + 5　　　**D.** 15 − 9

Numbers in the Thousands

LEARN

How do you read and write 4-digit numbers?

A hotel chef made 1,345 pancakes. You can show 1,345 in different ways.

WARM UP

Copy and complete.

1. 303 = 3 hundreds ▢ ones

2. 129 = 1 hundred ▢ tens 9 ones

3. 250 = ▢ hundreds 5 tens

place-value chart:

thousands	hundreds	tens	ones
1,	3	4	5

1 thousand, or 1,000   3 hundreds, or 300   4 tens, or 40   5 ones, or 5

place-value blocks:

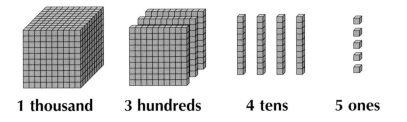

1 thousand   3 hundreds   4 tens   5 ones

expanded form: 1,000 + 300 + 40 + 5

standard form: 1,345

Write a comma between the thousands and the hundreds.

word form: one thousand, three hundred forty-five

✓ Talk About It

1. How many hundred blocks make a thousand block?

2. If you did not have any thousands blocks, how many hundreds blocks would you need to show 1,300?

For another example, see Set 1-4 on p. 57.

Write each number in standard form.

1.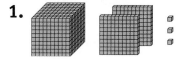

2. 5,000 + 300 + 20 + 3

3. six thousand, two hundred thirty

4. Write 4,005 in expanded form.

5. Reasoning Is one thousand, one hundred the same as eleven hundred? Explain.

For more practice, see Set 1-4 on p. 60.

Ⓐ Skills and Understanding

Write each number in standard form.

6.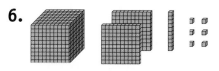

7.

8. 6,000 + 500 + 40 + 9

9. one thousand, two hundred fifty

10. Write 1,099 in expanded form.

11. Write 5,042 in expanded form.

12. Write the 4-digit number that has a tens digit of 3, a thousands digit of 2, and fives for the other digits.

Ⓑ Reasoning and Problem Solving

13. Reasoning Samir used place-value blocks to show the number 2,508. Then he added two more thousands blocks. What was the new number?

14. <u>Writing in Math</u> Explain the value of each digit in 4,063.

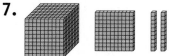 Mixed Review and Test Prep

Take It to the NET
Test Prep
www.scottforesman.com

15. 8 + 8   **16.** 8 + 3   **17.** 10 − 6   **18.** 9 + 4   **19.** 17 − 8

20. Which of these numbers is equal to 10 tens?

    A. 100   **B.** 110   **C.** 1,000   **D.** 10,000

Key Idea
Greater numbers have groups of 3 digits separated by commas.

Vocabulary
• period

Greater Numbers

LEARN

How do you read and write greater numbers?

A pet store filled a large aquarium with marbles and asked customers to guess how many were in it.

Zoe guessed that there were 157,103 marbles. Here are some ways to show this number.

place-value chart:

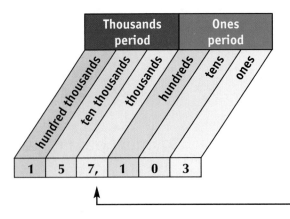

A **period** is a group of 3 digits in a number, starting from the right. Two periods are separated by a comma.

standard form:

157,103

expanded form:

100,000 + 50,000 + 7,000 + 100 + 3

word form:

one hundred fifty-seven thousand, one hundred three

✓ Talk About It

1. What is the value of the 8 in the number 287,051?

2. If a bag contains 1,000 marbles, how many marbles would be in 10 bags?

For over 2000 years, children all over the world have played with marbles.

For another example, see Set 1-5 on p. 57.

For 1–2, write each number in standard form.

1. two hundred ten thousand, six

2. 50,000 + 7,000 + 400 + 60 + 3

3. Number Sense Cari says the value of the digit 3 in 34,465 is 300,000. Do you agree or disagree? Explain.

PRACTICE

For more practice, see Set 1-5 on p. 61.

Ⓐ Skills and Understanding

For 4–7, write each number in standard form.

4. thirty-nine thousand, four hundred eighty-one

5. two hundred eleven thousand, five hundred thirty-six

6. 500,000 + 10,000 + 60 + 8 **7.** 40,000 + 3,000 + 200 + 10 + 9

8. Write 100,566 in expanded form. **9.** Write 48,755 in expanded form.

10. Number Sense If a six-digit number has a 7 followed by five 3s, what is the value of the 7 in this number?

Ⓑ Reasoning and Problem Solving

For 11–12, use the table at the right.

11. The number of different kinds of reptiles could be read as __?__ hundred.

12. <u>Writing in Math</u> Give the value of every 5 in the table. Explain why they are different.

Data File

Forms of Life	
Life Form	**How Many Kinds in the World**
Reptiles	More than 6,000 different kinds
Birds	More than 8,500 different kinds
Fish	More than 30,000 different kinds
Plants	More than 425,000 different kinds

👁 Mixed Review and Test Prep

Take It to the NET
Test Prep
www.scottforesman.com

Write the value of the underlined digit.

13. <u>4</u>,133 **14.** 2,0<u>7</u>6 **15.** 5,55<u>6</u> **16.** <u>9</u>87

17. Which is the standard form for six thousand, eleven?

A. 60,011 **B.** 6,111 **C.** 6,011 **D.** 611

Problem-Solving Skill

Reading Helps!

Identifying steps in a process

can help you with...

the *Read and Understand* phase of the problem-solving process.

Key Idea
Read and Understand is the first phase of the problem-solving process.

Read and Understand

LEARN

What steps can help you understand a problem?

Free Throws Marcy made 7 free throws out of 12 tries. Lila made 8 free throws out of 13 tries. How many free throws did they make together?

Read and Understand

Step 1: What do you know?

- Tell what you know in your own words.

  I know the number of free throws each girl made and tried.

- Identify key facts and details.

  Marcy: made 7, tried 12
  Lila: made 8, tried 13

Step 2: What are you trying to find?

- Tell what the question asks.

  The question asks how many free throws were made all together.

- Show the main idea.

?	
7	8
Marcy's total	Lila's total

✓Talk About It

1. How many free throws did they make all together? Use addition to find the answer.

$$7 + 8 = ?$$

Marcy's total   Lila's total   Total free throws made

2. Reasoning What information given in the problem is **not** needed to solve it?

For 1–3, use the Road Trip problem.

1. Step 1: What do you know?

   a. Tell what you know in your own words.

   b. Identify key facts and details.

2. Step 2: What are you trying to find?

   a. Tell what the question is asking.

   b. Show the main idea.

3. Solve the problem. Write the answer in a complete sentence.

| Ames | 50 miles |
| Traville | 90 miles |

Road Trip When Lucy's family gets to Ames, how many more miles will they have to travel to get to Traville?

PRACTICE

For more practice, see Set 1-6 on p. 61.

For 4–6, use the Bag of Bottles problem.

4. Step 1: What do you know?

   a. Tell the problem in your own words.

   b. Identify key facts and details.

5. Step 2: What are you trying to find?

   a. Tell what the question is asking.

   b. Show the main idea.

6. Solve the problem. Write the answer in a complete sentence.

Bag of Bottles Haley collected 17 clear bottles and 12 green bottles. She put 9 of the green bottles and 6 of the clear bottles in a bag. How many bottles were in the bag?

For 7–11, use the Sandwiches problem.

7. What facts are given?

8. What are you trying to find?

9. Draw a picture to show the problem.

10. How can you use your picture to solve the problem?

11. Write the answer in a complete sentence.

Sandwiches Jacob had 3 sandwiches. He cut 2 sandwiches into 2 pieces and 1 sandwich into 4 pieces. How many pieces of sandwich did he have?

Do You Know How?

Do You Understand?

Ways to Use Numbers (1-1)

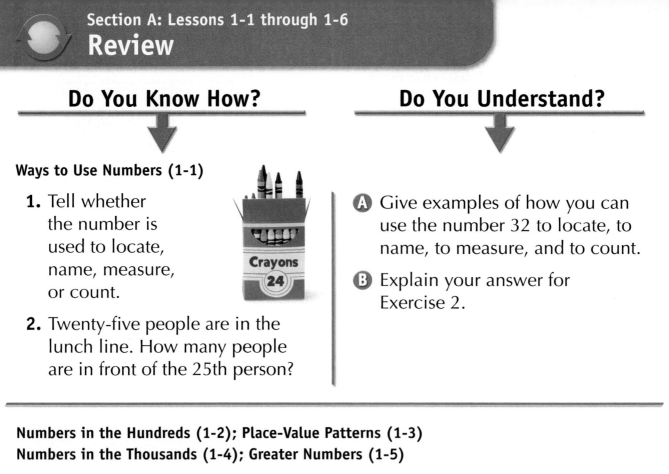

1. Tell whether the number is used to locate, name, measure, or count.

Crayons 24

2. Twenty-five people are in the lunch line. How many people are in front of the 25th person?

Ⓐ Give examples of how you can use the number 32 to locate, to name, to measure, and to count.

Ⓑ Explain your answer for Exercise 2.

Numbers in the Hundreds (1-2); Place-Value Patterns (1-3)
Numbers in the Thousands (1-4); Greater Numbers (1-5)

Write each number in standard form.

3. 4,000 + 900 + 50 + 1

4. three hundred sixteen

5. seven thousand, seven

6. 50,000 + 9,000 + 100 + 80 + 2

7. 300,000 + 60,000 + 200 + 40 + 5

8.

Ⓒ How do you know the number of zeros in the answer for Exercise 5?

Ⓓ What is another way to show the number in Exercise 8?

Problem-Solving Skill: Read and Understand (1-6)

9. Sam delivered 23 newspapers on Sunday. On Monday he delivered 14 newspapers. How many did he deliver in these two days?

Ⓔ For Exercise 9, tell what you know and what you need to find.

Ⓕ Explain why you chose to add or subtract to solve Exercise 9.

Diagnostic Checkpoint

Think It Through
I should eliminate wrong answers.

MULTIPLE CHOICE

1. How many cars are in front of the 22nd car in line? (1-1)

   A. 20   **B.** 21   **C.** 22   **D.** 23

2. The number 340 can be renamed as how many tens? (1-3)

   A. 3,400   **B.** 340   **C.** 34   **D.** 16

3. Which number has a 2 in the ten thousands place? (1-5)

   A. 210,365   **B.** 21,408   **C.** 92,570   **D.** 8,324

FREE RESPONSE

4. Tell if the number in the picture at the right is used to count, measure, name, or locate. (1-1)

For 5–6 write in standard form. (1-2, 1-4, 1-5)

5. 9,000 + 20 + 6

6. six hundred twenty thousand

For 7–8 write in expanded form. (1-2, 1-4, 1-5)

7. 693

8. seven thousand fifteen

For 9–11 use the Book Drive problem. (1-6)

Book Drive Pattie brought in 7 books for a book drive. Caleb and Susan each brought in 4 books, and Hal brought in 3. How many books did Pattie, Hal, Susan, and Caleb bring in all together?

9. What facts are given?

10. What are you trying to find?

11. Solve the problem. Write the answer in a complete sentence.

Writing in Math

12. Write directions for how to brush your teeth. Use the words *first*, *second*, and *third*. (1-1)

13. Draw two ways to show 308 with place-value blocks. Explain. (1-3)

Key Idea
You can use place value to help compare numbers.

Vocabulary
• compare
• number line

Comparing Numbers

LEARN

How do you compare numbers?

African lion
280 centimeters, including tail

Mountain lion
245 centimeters, including tail

You can **compare** 280 and 245 to find which lion is longer. When you compare numbers, you use these symbols.

$<$ $>$ $=$

is less than   **is greater than**   **is equal to**

You can use place-value blocks to compare 280 to 245.

 ← Same number → of hundreds
← More tens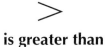

280   **245**

280 **is greater than** 245   245 **is less than** 280

280 > 245   245 < 280

You can also use a **number line** to compare 280 to 245.

245   280

200 210 220 230 240 250 260 270 280 290

280 is to the right of 245, so 280 is greater than 245.

The African lion is longer than the mountain lion.

How can you use place value to compare numbers?

Example

Compare 1,225 and 1,200.

Line up the numbers by place value.
Compare the digits starting from the left.

thousands	hundreds	tens	ones
1,	2	2	5
1,	2	0	0

    ↑   ↑   ↑

  same   same   different: 2 tens > 0 tens

So 1,225 **is greater than** 1,200.

1,225 > 1,200

✔ Talk About It

1. If the numbers in the Example were shown on a number line, which one would be farther to the right?

2. Number Sense Julie says that since 5 is greater than 3, the number 567 is greater than 3,098. Do you agree? Explain.

CHECK ✔

For another example, see Set 1-7 on p. 57.

Compare the numbers. Use <, >, or =.

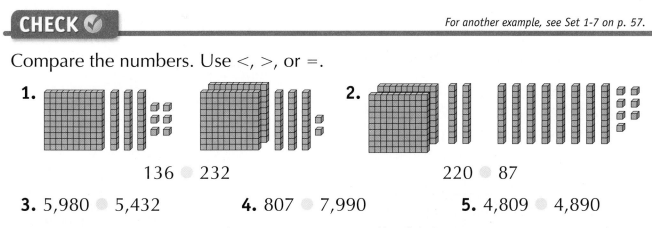

1.   136 ● 232   **2.**   220 ● 87

3. 5,980 ● 5,432   **4.** 807 ● 7,990   **5.** 4,809 ● 4,890

6. Reasoning For 304 and 3,217, can you tell which number is greater by comparing the first digit in each number? Explain.

A Skills and Understanding

Compare the numbers. Use <, >, or =.

7.

253 ○ 284

8.

220 ○ 87

9. 211 ○ 112

10. 436 ○ 467

11. 609 ○ 612

12. 1,203 ○ 1,302

13. 2,987 ○ 2,991

14. 3,001 ○ 776

15. Number Sense Draw a number line like the one at the right. Write the numbers 325 and 340 where they belong. Then tell which number is greater.

300 ———————————— 350

B Reasoning and Problem Solving

Math and Science

Use the table for 16–19.
For 16–18, write the lengths of the two animals in the order named and compare them. Use <, >, or =.

16. Blue whale ○ African elephant

17. Japanese spider crab ○ Ostrich

18. Asian saltwater crocodile ○ Whale shark

19. Writing in Math Here is how Nick and Ty read the length of a whale shark. Are both boys correct? Explain.

Data File

Longest Animal in its Class		
Class	Animal	Length in Centimeters
Fish	Whale shark	1,800
Land mammal	African elephant	400
Sea mammal	Blue whale	3,350
Reptile	Asian saltwater crocodile	1,000
Bird	Ostrich	275
Crustacean	Japanese spider crab	275

Nick: Eighteen hundred centimeters
Tyrone: One thousand, eight hundred centimeters

The Japanese spider crab lives about 1,000 feet below the surface in the ocean around Japan.

C Extensions

To compare numbers that are greater than 9,999, line up the numbers by place value and start comparing from the left. Use <, >, or =.

20. 15,278 ● 17,316

21. 803,410 ● 324,986

22. 243,156 ● 32,999

23. 96,273 ● 100,232

 **Mixed Review and Test Prep**

Take It to the NET
Test Prep
www.scottforesman.com

24. Kyle made 17 points. Kurt made 9. How many more points did Kyle make than Kurt? Show the main idea and solve the problem. Write the answer in a complete sentence.

25. Which has the same value as 40,000 + 600 + 70 + 9?

A. 479   **B.** 4,679   **C.** 40,679   **D.** 46,790

Discovery CHANNEL SCHOOL — Discover Math in Your World

The Manu Biosphere Reserve in Peru

The Manu Biosphere Reserve is the largest tropical park in South America. No other animal reserve on Earth contains as many kinds of birds.

1. Manu contains about 1,000 kinds of birds. How many groups of 100 kinds are in 1,000? How many groups of 10?

2. The Manu birds can enjoy 300 kinds of trees. Are there fewer kinds of birds or trees in the Manu reserve? Explain.

Take It to the NET
Video and Activities
www.scottforesman.com

Key Idea
Place value can help you put a list of numbers in order.

Vocabulary
• order

Ordering Numbers

LEARN

How can you order numbers?

When you **order** numbers, you write them from least to greatest or greatest to least.

The wingspans in inches of three large birds are shown on the number line below.

138 inches

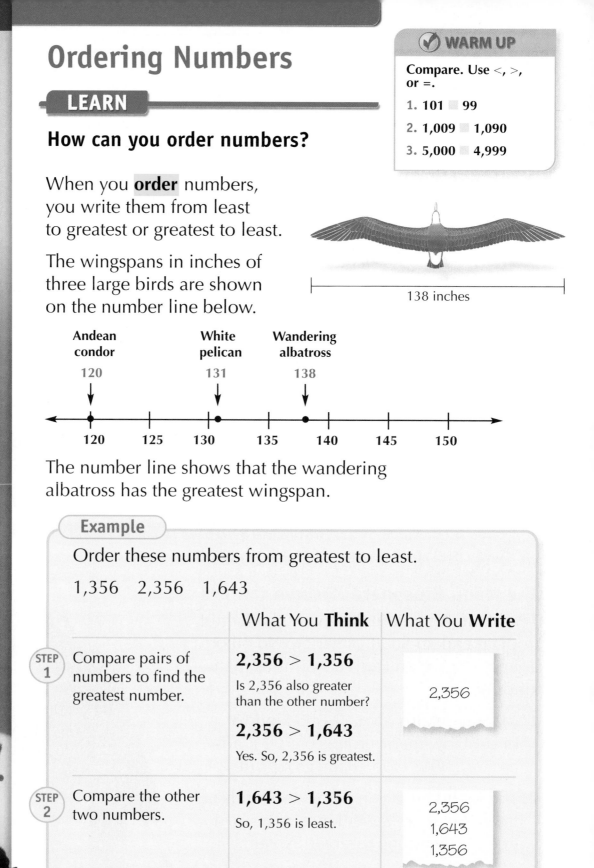

Andean condor — 120
White pelican — 131
Wandering albatross — 138

The number line shows that the wandering albatross has the greatest wingspan.

Example

Order these numbers from greatest to least.

1,356   2,356   1,643

	What You **Think**	What You **Write**
STEP 1 Compare pairs of numbers to find the greatest number.	**2,356 > 1,356** Is 2,356 also greater than the other number? **2,356 > 1,643** Yes. So, 2,356 is greatest.	2,356
STEP 2 Compare the other two numbers.	**1,643 > 1,356** So, 1,356 is least.	2,356 1,643 1,356

✔ **Talk About It**

1. How does the number line show that 120 is less than 138?

Order the numbers from least to greatest. You may use
a number line to help.

1. 122 114 190 　　　**2.** 150 105 200 　　　**3.** 99 122 188

Order the numbers from greatest to least.

4. 566 665 555 　　　**5.** 4,500 4,322 4,120 　　　**6.** 64 6,400 640

7. Reasoning Can a number with a 3 in the tens place be
greater than a number with an 8 in the tens place? Explain.

PRACTICE 　　　　　　　　　　　　　*For another example, see Set 1-8 on pg. 62.*

A **Skills and Understanding**

Order the numbers from least to greatest. You may use
a number line to help.

8. 3,900 3,401 3,788 　　**9.** 3,000 2,999 3,100 　　**10.** 4,000 3,655 3,887

Order the numbers from greatest to least.

11. 887 865 8,650 　　　**12.** 599 590 601 　　　**13.** 1,231 1,256 987

14. Representations Draw a number line showing 400
to 420. Write 412, 406, and 419 where they belong.

B **Reasoning and Problem Solving**

15. Which is higher, Angel Falls or
Tugela?

16. <u>Writing in Math</u> Write the names
of all four waterfalls in order of
their heights from least to greatest.

Data File

Heights of Waterfalls		
Waterfall	**Country**	**Height**
Angel Falls	Venezuela	3,212 feet
Mongefossen	Norway	2,540 feet
Tugela	South Africa	3,107 feet
Yosemite	USA	2,425 feet

Mixed Review and Test Prep

Take It to the NET
Test Prep
www.scottforesman.com

17. Compare. Write <, >, or =.
5,698 ● 5,677

18. Which is equal to 25 tens?

A. 25 　　　　**B.** 250 　　　　**C.** 2,500 　　　　**D.** 25,000

Algebra

Key Idea
You can use number lines and skip counting to find number patterns.

Vocabulary
• even number
• odd number

Number Patterns

LEARN

What is the pattern?

A chessboard has 64 squares. Sixty-four is an **even number**. An even number has a ones digit of 0, 2, 4, 6, or 8. An **odd number** has a ones digit of 1, 3, 5, 7, or 9.

You can use a number line to study even numbers, odd numbers, and other number patterns.

Example A

Are the red numbers on the number line even or odd?

The red numbers have 0, 2, 4, 6, and 8 in the ones place, so they are even.

Example B

Find the pattern. Then find the next three numbers.

1, 4, 7, 10, ▪, ▪, ▪

Look for the pattern on a number line.

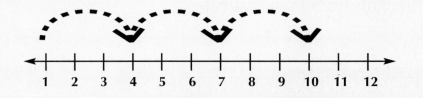

Each number is 3 more than the number before it. The next three numbers are 13, 16, and 19.

Chess is thought to have been invented in India or China about 600 A.D.

How can place-value patterns help you add?

Example C

Erica and Porter counted to 1,000 by tens and made this chart.

I see a pattern. Each number is 100 more than the number above it

I found 560 + 300 on the chart. I started at 560. Then I moved down three rows. 560 + 300 = 860

10	20	30	40	50	60	70	80		100
110	120	130	140	150	160	170	180	190	200
210	220	230	240	250	260	270	280	290	300
310	320	330	340	350	360	370	380	390	400
410	420	430	440	450	460	470	480	490	500
510	520	530	540	550	**560**	570	580	590	600
610	620	630	640	650	**660**	670	680	690	700
710	720	730	740	750	**760**	770	780	790	800
810	820	830	840	850	**860**	870	880	890	900
910	920	930	940	950	960	970	980	990	1,000

✔ Talk About It

1. Find the missing numbers in this pattern: 17, 15, 13, 11, ▮, ▮, ▮

2. Reasoning How would you use the chart in Example C to find 330 + 400? How could you find it by skip counting?

CHECK ✓

For another example, see Set 1-9 on p. 58.

Find the missing numbers in each pattern.

1. 5, 15, 25, ▮, ▮

2. 16, 12, 8, ▮, ▮

3. 14, 18, ▮, 26

Use place-value patterns to find each sum.

4. 500 + 220

5. 370 + 400

6. 250 + 700

7. Number Sense Is 700 even or odd? Explain.

Ⓐ Skills and Understanding

Find the missing numbers in each pattern.

8. 5, 10, 15, ▪, ▪   **9.** 18, 15, 12, ▪, ▪   **10.** 300, 350, ▪, ▪, 500

Use place-value patterns to find each sum.

11. 160 + 200   **12.** 500 + 500   **13.** 230 + 600

14. Number Sense Is 14,307 even or odd? Explain.

Ⓑ Reasoning and Problem Solving

Math and Social Studies

Use the time line to solve 15–16.

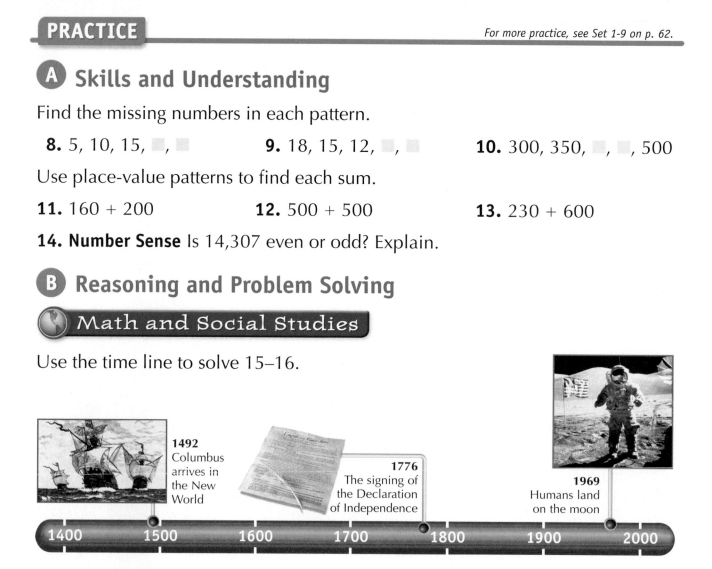

1492 Columbus arrives in the New World

1776 The signing of the Declaration of Independence

1969 Humans land on the moon

| 1400 | 1500 | 1600 | 1700 | 1800 | 1900 | 2000 |

15. Two hundred years after the Declaration of Independence was signed, the United States had a big celebration called the *bicentennial*. What year was that?

16. Three hundred years after Columbus arrived in the New World, the cornerstone of the United States Capitol was laid. What year was that?

17. Writing in Math How are even numbers and odd numbers alike? How are they different?

Ⓒ Extensions

You can use the chart on page 25 to subtract 560 − 400. Start at 560. Then move *up* four rows. 560 − 400 = 160.

Find each difference.

18. 490 − 200   **19.** 940 − 500   **20.** 1,000 − 600

Algebra Find the missing number.

21. $500 + \blacksquare = 800$ **22.** $310 - \blacksquare = 110$ **23.** $\blacksquare + 400 = 760$

Mixed Review and Test Prep

Take It to the NET
Test Prep
www.scottforesman.com

24. What is the value of the 8 in 4,890?

25. Which numbers are in order from greatest to least?

     A. 365   315   288   **C.** 288   315   365

     B. 288   365   315   **D.** 315   365   288

Enrichment

Roman Numerals

The numerals used by the ancient Romans are still seen today on some clock faces and buildings.

Roman numeral	I	V	X	L	C	D	M
Decimal value	1	5	10	50	100	500	1,000

Our number system is called the decimal system.

Roman numerals are not based on place value.
They are based on addition and subtraction.

VI = 5 + 1 = 6   When the symbol for the smaller number is written to the right of the greater number, add. No more than three symbols for smaller numbers are used in this way.

IV = 5 − 1 = 4   When the symbol for the smaller number is to the left of the greater number, subtract. No more than 1 symbol for a smaller number is used in this way.

For 1–5, write as Roman numerals.

1. 9   **2.** 60   **3.** 400   **4.** 90   **5.** 1,100

6. Write XLV as a decimal number.   **7.** Write MDL as a decimal number.

Key Idea
You can round numbers when you estimate to solve problems.

Vocabulary
• rounding

Rounding Numbers

LEARN

How do you use the number line to round numbers?

About how far is it from Philadelphia to Trenton? You can use **rounding** to tell about how many miles.

✓ WARM UP

Write each number in standard form.

1. 20 + 3
2. 100 + 60
3. 1,000 + 20 + 6

Data File

| Distance Between Some Eastern Cities | |
Cities	Miles
Philadelphia and Trenton	29
Baltimore and Washington	41
Camden and Princeton	45

Example A

Round 29 to the nearest ten.

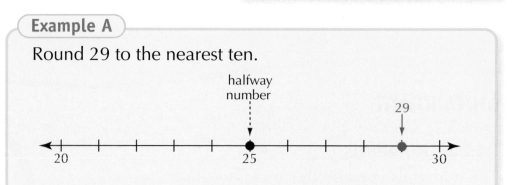

29 is closer to 30 than to 20, so **29 rounds to 30**.

It is about 30 miles from Philadelphia to Trenton.

Example B

Round 409, 470, and 450 to the nearest hundred.

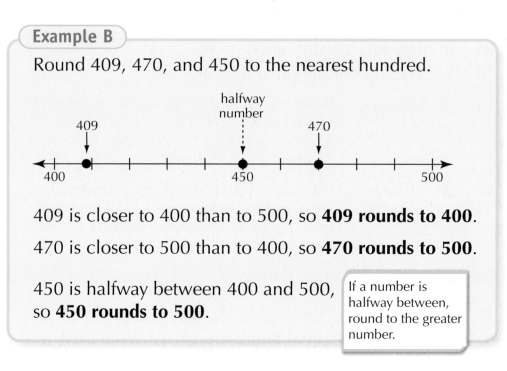

409 is closer to 400 than to 500, so **409 rounds to 400**.

470 is closer to 500 than to 400, so **470 rounds to 500**.

450 is halfway between 400 and 500, so **450 rounds to 500**.

If a number is halfway between, round to the greater number.

How do you use place value to round?

Here are the steps for rounding numbers.

Step 1   Find the digit in the rounding place.

Step 2   Look at the next digit to the right.

   If it is 5 or greater, increase the digit in the rounding place by 1.

   If it is less than 5, leave the digit in the rounding place alone.

Step 3   Change all the digits to the right of the rounding place to zeros.

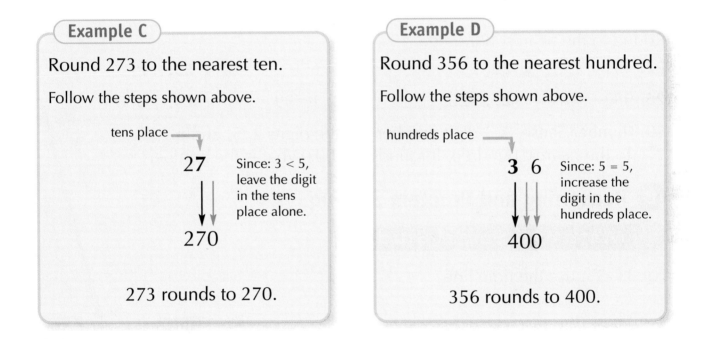

Example C

Round 273 to the nearest ten.

Follow the steps shown above.

tens place

27

Since: 3 < 5, leave the digit in the tens place alone.

270

273 rounds to 270.

Example D

Round 356 to the nearest hundred.

Follow the steps shown above.

hundreds place

3 6

Since: 5 = 5, increase the digit in the hundreds place.

400

356 rounds to 400.

✔ Talk About It

1. **Number Sense** What number is halfway between 140 and 150?

2. Give a number that rounds to 200 when it is rounded to the nearest hundred.

3. Explain the steps you would follow to round 356 to the nearest ten.

Round to the nearest ten.

1. 37 **2.** 73 **3.** 85 **4.** 427 **5.** 1,735

Round to the nearest hundred.

6. 166 **7.** 551 **8.** 309 **9.** 249 **10.** 4,032

11. Reasoning Round 988 to the nearest hundred. Explain your answer.

PRACTICE

For more practice, see Set 1-10 on p. 62.

Ⓐ Skills and Understanding

Round to the nearest ten.

12. 15 **13.** 86 **14.** 42 **15.** 55 **16.** 97

17. 154 **18.** 641 **19.** 901 **20.** 325 **21.** 1,508

Round to the nearest hundred.

22. 451 **23.** 203 **24.** 670 **25.** 448

26. 952 **27.** 926 **28.** 1,799 **29.** 1,008

30. Number Sense A 3-digit number has the digits 2, 5, and 8. To the nearest hundred, it rounds to 500. What is the number?

Ⓑ Reasoning and Problem Solving

Math and Social Studies

For 31–33, use the time line.

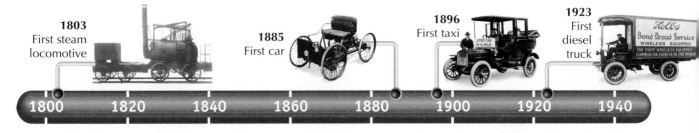

1803 First steam locomotive

1885 First car

1896 First taxi

1923 First diesel truck

1800 — 1820 — 1840 — 1860 — 1880 — 1900 — 1920 — 1940

31. Was the car invented in a year closer to 1800 or 1900?

32. Was the taxi invented about 10 or about 100 years after the car?

33. **Writing in Math** Would it make sense to say the taxi was invented in about the year 1800? Explain.

C Extensions

When you round or order larger numbers, use the same rules as for smaller numbers.

34. Round 27,573 to the nearest thousand.

35. Round 46,300 to the nearest thousand.

Write the numbers in order from least to greatest.

36. 10,276   24,324   10,129

37. 452,100   327,000   516,200

 **Mixed Review and Test Prep**

Take It to the NET
Test Prep
www.scottforesman.com

Order from least to greatest.

38. 343   509   124   **39.** 798   978   879   **40.** 2,098   2,077   1,399

41. Find the missing numbers in the pattern. 4, 7, 10, ■, ■,

   A. 13, 17, 20   **B.** 14, 18, 22   **C.** 13, 16, 19   **D.** 15, 20, 25

Practice Game

Make Ten

Number of Players: 2–4

Materials: number cube labeled 1–6
30 counters per player

5   6   7   8   9   **10**

1. Each player tosses the number cube and counts on from the number on the cube using counters to make a ten. For example, if a player tosses 4, the player counts on with counters: 5, 6, 7, 8, 9, 10.

2. The counters the player used to count on are placed in the center of the game area.

3. Play three rounds. The player with the *least* number of counters wins.

4. Variation: Play "Make Eight," "Make Nine," or "Make Eleven."

Problem-Solving Skill

Key Idea
Plan and Solve is the second phase of the problem-solving process.

Plan and Solve

LEARN

How can you make a plan to solve a problem?

Three-Legged Race Darrell used cones to mark off 50 feet for a race. He put one cone at the start, one at the finish, and one every 10 feet in between. How many cones did he use?

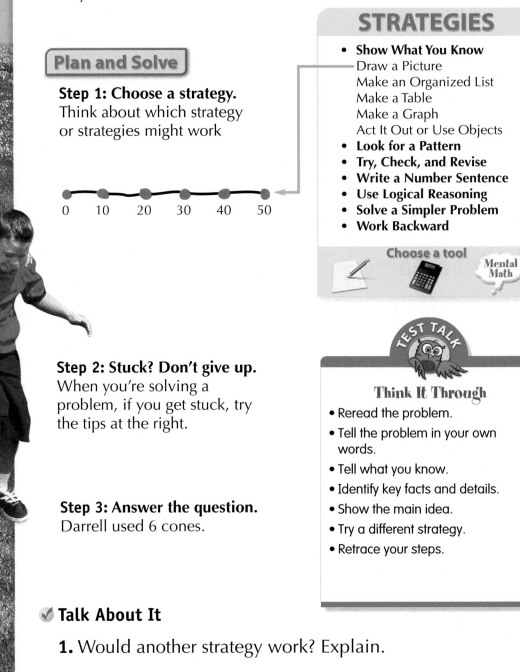

Plan and Solve

Step 1: Choose a strategy.
Think about which strategy or strategies might work

0   10   20   30   40   50

STRATEGIES

- **Show What You Know**
  Draw a Picture
  Make an Organized List
  Make a Table
  Make a Graph
  Act It Out or Use Objects
- **Look for a Pattern**
- **Try, Check, and Revise**
- **Write a Number Sentence**
- **Use Logical Reasoning**
- **Solve a Simpler Problem**
- **Work Backward**

Choose a tool

Mental Math

Step 2: Stuck? Don't give up.
When you're solving a problem, if you get stuck, try the tips at the right.

TEST TALK

Think It Through
- Reread the problem.
- Tell the problem in your own words.
- Tell what you know.
- Identify key facts and details.
- Show the main idea.
- Try a different strategy.
- Retrace your steps.

Step 3: Answer the question.
Darrell used 6 cones.

✔ **Talk About It**

1. Would another strategy work? Explain.

For another example, see Set 1-11 on p. 58.

CHECK ✓

For 1–3, use the Big Deal problem.

1. Copy and complete the list to help solve the problem.

> **Big Deal Lunches**
> 1) milk— hamburger
> 2) milk — hot dog
> 3) juice — hamburger
> 4) ?

2. What strategy was used?

3. Give the answer to the problem in a complete sentence.

Big Deal A Big Deal Lunch contains one drink and one sandwich. How many different Big Deal Lunches are possible?

PRACTICE

For another example, see Set 1-11 on p. 63.

For 4–7, use the Bead Bracelet problem.

4. Copy and complete the picture to help solve the problem.

r b b r b b r b b

5. What strategy was used to solve the problem?

6. Give the answer to the problem in a complete sentence.

7. Can you think of another strategy that would work? Explain.

8. **Writing in Math** For the Big Deal and Bead Bracelet problems, answer each of the questions below.

a. What do you know?

b. What are you trying to find?

Bead Bracelet
Chantelle put beads on a string to make a bracelet. She used a red bead, then two blue beads, then a red bead, then two blue beads, and so on, until she used 8 blue beads. How many beads did she use in all?

All text pages available online and on CD-ROM.

Section B: Lessons 1-7 through 1-11

Review

Do You Know How?

Do You Understand?

Comparing Numbers (1-7); Ordering Numbers (1-8)

Compare the numbers.
Use <, >, or =.

1. 327 ○ 346 **2.** 5,240 ○ 524

Order from greatest to least.

3. 128 491 326

4. 1,936 1,845 2,002

A In Exercise 2, what is the first step in comparing the numbers?

B In Exercise 4, how do you know which number is the greatest?

Number Patterns (1-9); Rounding Numbers (1-10)

Continue each pattern.

5. 1, 5, 9, ■, ■, ■

6. 18, 16, 14, ■, ■, ■

7. Round 56 to the nearest ten.

8. Round 850 to the nearest hundred.

C Explain the patterns in Exercises 5 and 6.

D In Exercise 8, how did you know whether to round to the lesser hundred or the greater hundred?

Problem-Solving Skill: Plan and Solve (1-11)

9. Copy and complete the list to solve the problem.

Kevin has 3 types of seashells. His display case can only hold 2 types at a time. How many different ways can he display his shells?

Types
1 and 2
2 and 3
?

E Give the answer to the problem in a complete sentence.

F What strategy was used to solve the problem?

MULTIPLE CHOICE

1. Which numbers are in order from greatest to least? (1-8)

A. 421 42 140   **C.** 104 42 421

B. 421 104 42   **D.** 42 104 421

2. Continue the pattern. 7, 12, 17, ▨, ▨, ▨ (1-9)

A. 27, 37, 47   **B.** 12, 27, 12   **C.** 22, 29, 33   **D.** 22, 27, 32

FREE RESPONSE

Compare. Use >, <, or =. (1-7)

3. 35 ● 350   **4.** 730 ● 730   **5.** 4,916 ● 4,216

Order the numbers from least to greatest. (1-8)

6. 356   306   530   **7.** 2,527   5,527   2,057

Round each number to the nearest ten. (1-10)

8. 32   **9.** 48   **10.** 757

Round each number to the nearest hundred. (1-10)

11. 6,444   **12.** 3,695   **13.** 426

For 14–16 use the Soccer Team problem. (1-11)

Soccer Team Pat, Ben, Pam, Liz, and Ken scored a total of 17 goals. Pat, Pam, and Ken each scored the same number of goals. Liz and Ben each scored one more goal than Ken. How many goals did Ben score?

14. Copy and complete the list to help solve the problem.

15. Give the answer to the problem in a complete sentence.

16. What strategy was used?

Pat	Pam	Ken	Liz	Ben	Total
1	1	1	2	2	7
2	2	2	3	3	12
3	3	3	?	?	?

Writing in Math

17. Explain how to round 648 to the nearest hundred. (1-10)

Counting Money

How do you count money?

Here are some familiar bills and coins.

5 dollars
$5 or $5.00

1 dollar
$1 or $1.00

half dollar
50 cents
50¢ or $0.50

quarter
25 cents
25¢ or $0.25

dime
10 cents
10¢ or $0.10

nickel
5 cents
5¢ or $0.05

penny
1 cent
1¢ or $0.01

A toy car costs one dollar and seventy-five cents.

$1.75

dollar sign ——————— **decimal point**

Example

Kendra has the money shown below. Does she have enough to buy the car?

Start with the bills.
Then count the coins starting with coins of the greatest value.

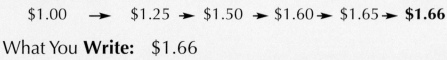

$1.00 → $1.25 → $1.50 → $1.60 → $1.65 → **$1.66**

What You **Write:** $1.66

What You **Say:**   one dollar and sixty-six cents

Kendra does not have enough money.

Activity

How can you show money amounts?

Here are two ways to show $1.32.

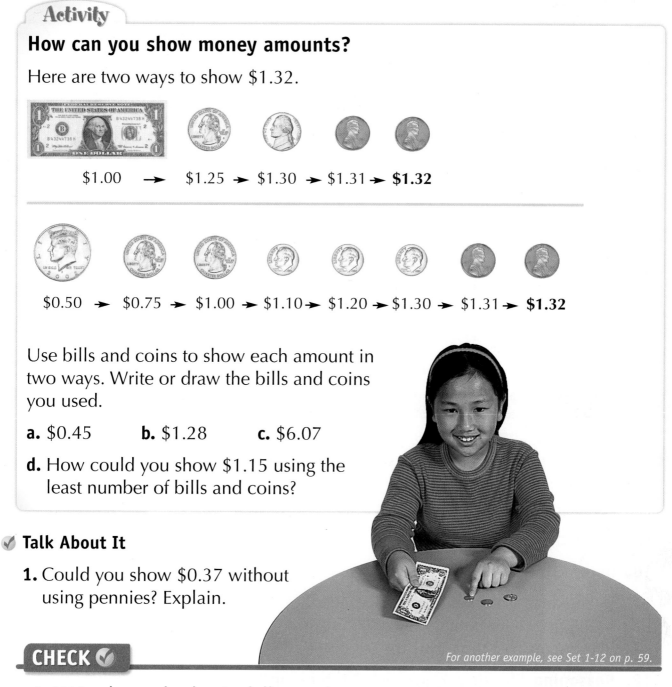

$1.00 → $1.25 → $1.30 → $1.31 → **$1.32**

$0.50 → $0.75 → $1.00 → $1.10 → $1.20 → $1.30 → $1.31 → **$1.32**

Use bills and coins to show each amount in two ways. Write or draw the bills and coins you used.

a. $0.45   **b.** $1.28   **c.** $6.07

d. How could you show $1.15 using the least number of bills and coins?

✔ Talk About It

1. Could you show $0.37 without using pennies? Explain.

CHECK ✔

For another example, see Set 1-12 on p. 59.

1. Write the total value in dollars and cents.

2. Tell what coins and bills you could use to show $3.80 in two ways.

3. Number Sense How could you make $1.43 using the least number of bills and coins?

TEST TALK

Think It Through
When I count money, I can **skip count** by 5s, 10s, 25s, and 50s.

A Skills and Understanding

Write the total value in dollars and cents.

4.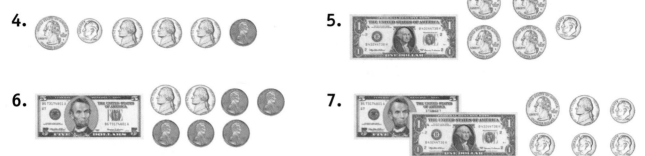

5.

6.

7.

8. **Number Sense** Tell what coins you could use to show $0.96 in two ways.

B Reasoning and Problem Solving

Math and Social Studies

The cost of a hamburger in the United States is about $2.54. In Switzerland, a hamburger costs about $3.65. What U.S. bills and coins could you use to show the cost of a hamburger

9. in Switzerland?

10. in the United States?

11. In England, a hamburger costs about $2.85. In which country does a hamburger cost the most? the least?

12. **Reasoning** Elise has 3 quarters, 2 dimes, and 1 penny. What coin does she need to make $1.06?

13. **Writing in Math** Are Jim's answers below correct? Explain.

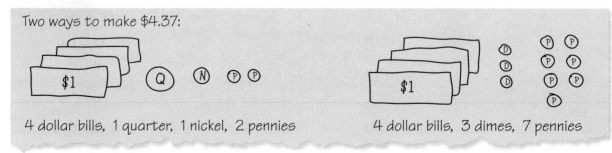

Two ways to make $4.37:

4 dollar bills, 1 quarter, 1 nickel, 2 pennies   4 dollar bills, 3 dimes, 7 pennies

C Extensions

14. Ana has six coins worth a total of $0.50. What coins are they?

15. Laura has $0.98 in her pocket. She has 3 quarters and 3 pennies. She has two other coins. What are they?

 **Mixed Review and Test Prep**

Take It to the NET
Test Prep
www.scottforesman.com

16. Solve the Paper Chain problem. Tell what strategy you used and write the answer in a complete sentence.

Paper Chain Al made a paper chain by connecting 1 yellow strip, then 2 green, then 1 yellow and 2 green. He continued until he used 10 green strips. How many yellow strips did he use?

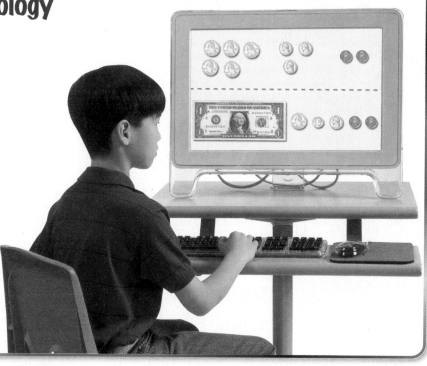

17. Round 75 to the nearest ten.

A. 50   **B.** 60   **C.** 70   **D.** 80

Learning with Technology

The Money eTool

With the parts screen and odometer selected, show each money amount in two ways. Use the bottom half of the screen to show the amount using the fewest number of bills and coins.

1. $1.48   **2.** $1.85

3. $5.77   **4.** $15.36

5. $20.11   **6.** $25.63

All text pages available online and on CD-ROM.

Making Change

LEARN

How do you count on to make change?

✓ WARM UP

Find the total value of each.

1. 4 dimes, 1 nickel
2. 1 quarter, 1 dime
3. 5 quarters, 3 pennies

The Booster Club sells balloons at the school fair.

Example A

Al bought a some balloons that cost $1.25. He paid with two $1 bills. How much change did he get?

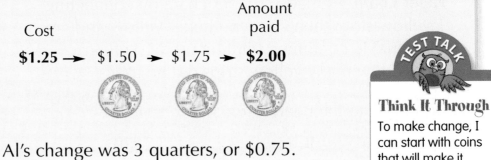

Cost | | | Amount paid

$1.25 → $1.50 → $1.75 → $2.00

Al's change was 3 quarters, or $0.75.

TEST TALK

Think It Through
To make change, I can start with coins that will make it easier to **skip count**.

Example B

Paul bought some snacks for $2.59. He paid with a $5 bill. How much change did he get?

Count on from $2.59.

Cost | | | | | | Amount paid

$2.59 → $2.60 → $2.70 → $2.75 → $3.00 → $4.00 → $5.00

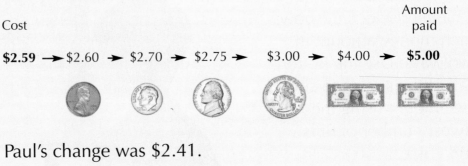

Paul's change was $2.41.

✓ **Talk About It**

1. Why does it make sense to start with pennies in Example B?

List the coins and bills you would use to make change.
Then write the change in dollars and cents.

1. Cost: $0.94
Amount paid: $1.00

2. Cost: $2.35
Amount paid: $5.00

3. Reasoning Christine bought a marker for $0.79 and paid with a $1 bill. Give two ways to make change.

PRACTICE

For more practice, see Set 1-13 on p. 63.

Ⓐ Skills and Understanding

List the coins and bills you would use to make change.
Then write the change in dollars and cents.

4. Cost: $3.21
Amount paid: $5.00

5. Cost: $1.09
Amount paid: $3.00

6. Reasoning Carlos bought crayons for $2.39. He used three $1 bills. Give two ways to show the change. Which uses the fewest coins?

Ⓑ Reasoning and Problem Solving

7. Algebra Keri bought a pen. She paid with a $1 bill. This is the change she got. How much did the pen cost?

8. Writing in Math Erica paid $1.00 for a balloon that cost $0.15. The change she received was all nickels. How many nickels did she get? How did you find the answer?

Mixed Review and Test Prep

Take It to the NET
Test Prep
www.scottforesman.com

9. Give the value of the 9 in 920,278.

10. How much money is shown?

A. $2.25 **B.** $5.26 **C.** $7.36 **D.** $15.26

Problem-Solving Skill

Reading Helps!

Identifying steps in a process **can help you with...**

the *Look Back and Check* phase of the problem-solving process.

Key Idea
Look Back and Check is the final phase of the problem-solving process.

Look Back and Check

LEARN

What are the last steps in solving a problem?

The Gettysburg Address In this famous speech, Abraham Lincoln began by saying, "Four score and 7 years ago, . . ." If a score is 20 years, how many years was President Lincoln talking about?

20 + 20 + 20 + 20 = 80   80 + 7 = 87   87 years

Look Back and Check

Step 1: Have you checked your answer?

- Did you answer the right question?

  Yes, I want to know the total number of years.

- Use estimation and reasoning to decide if the answer makes sense.

  Skip count by 20s four times: 20, 40, 60, 80. So *four score* is the same as 80.

Step 2: Have you checked your work?

- Compare your work with the information in the problem.

  I found the total number of years in 4 score and 7.

- Did you use the right operation?

  Addition is the right operation to find the total number of years.

✔ **Talk About It**

1. What strategy was used to solve the problem above?

The Lincoln Memorial was dedicated May 30, 1922.

For another example, see Set 1-14 on p. 59.

CHECK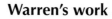

1. Look back and check Warren's work on the Gettysburg Address problem.

    a. Did he answer the right question? Explain.

    b. Is his work correct? Explain.

Warren's work

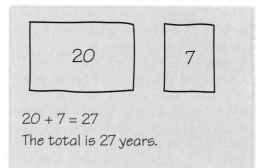

20 + 7 = 27
The total is 27 years.

PRACTICE

For another example, see Set 1-14 on p. 63.

Library Fine You pay 5 cents each day a library book is overdue. How much would you pay if the book were 6 days overdue?

Martha solved the Library Fine problem as shown at the right.

2. Look back and check Martha's work on this problem.

    a. Did Martha answer the right question? Explain.

    b. Is her work correct? If not, explain and give the correct answer.

Days overdue	You owe
1	5 cents
2	10 cents
3	15 cents
4	20 cents
5	30 cents
6	35 cents

You would pay 35 cents.

3. Solve the Sandwiches problem at the right. Look back and check your work.

Sandwiches Ellie has 3 sandwiches. She cuts each sandwich into 4 pieces. How many pieces of sandwich does she have?

4. <u>Writing in Math</u> Tell what strategy you used to solve Exercise 3 and explain how you solved it. How did you check that your answer makes sense?

DK Problem-Solving Applications

Animal Speeds Some animals can sprint very fast. Animals do this to capture prey or to avoid predators. To travel long distances, animals move at a much slower pace.

Trivia The spiny-tailed iguana now holds the speed record for land reptiles. It can run 21 miles per hour.

THE WORLD IN ONE DAY

Every day... 7 million pizzas are eaten in America... one human heart pumps enough blood to fill 170 bathtubs... lightning strikes Earth 8 million times...

By RUSSELL ASH, author of INCREDIBLE COMPARISONS

1 At a sprinting speed, a wildebeest would run more than 4,375 feet in 1 minute. What digit is in the hundreds place of 4,375? What digit is in the thousands place?

2 Pronghorns can run the length of a football field, 120 yards, in about 4 seconds. What is the greatest whole number that, when rounded to the nearest ten, would be 120?

3 At 43 miles per hour, a coyote could run 3,784 feet in 1 minute. Write the word form and expanded form of 3,784.

Using Key Facts

4 Daniella said that, when rounded to the nearest ten, the sprinting speeds shown in the Key Facts table would round to just two different numbers. Tony said that the speeds would round to three different numbers. Who is correct? What are the rounded speeds?

Key Facts

Animal	Sprinting Speed
•Elephant	25 mph
•Camel	20 mph
•White-tailed deer	30 mph
•Tiger	35 mph
•Rhinoceros	32 mph

5 **Writing in Math** One mile is a longer distance than one kilometer. A wildebeest can run 50 miles per hour. A crane can fly 50 kilometers per hour. Which animal can move faster? Explain.

6 Look at the Key Facts chart. Which animal is faster, a white-tailed deer or a tiger? Use > to compare the speeds of tigers and deer.

Good News/Bad News *The fast horses of the Pony Express delivered mail in record times, but the horses tired quickly. Riders had to change horses every 10 to 15 miles.*

7 **Decision Making** The animals pictured above are shown roughly in order of speed, with the slowest on the left and the fastest on the right. Choose four of the animals from the table at the right and draw your own diagram in the same style.

Animal	Speed
Chicken	9 mph
Cockroach	3 mph
Pig	11 mph
Sea turtle	22 mph
Squirrel	12 mph
Rabbit	35 mph

Do You Know How?

Do You Understand?

Counting Money (1-12)

Write the value in dollars and cents.

1.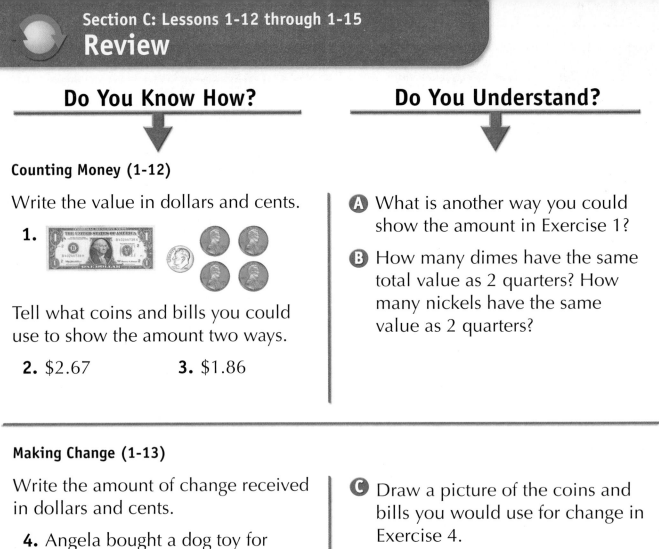

Tell what coins and bills you could use to show the amount two ways.

2. $2.67   **3.** $1.86

A What is another way you could show the amount in Exercise 1?

B How many dimes have the same total value as 2 quarters? How many nickels have the same value as 2 quarters?

Making Change (1-13)

Write the amount of change received in dollars and cents.

4. Angela bought a dog toy for $3.98. She paid with a $5 bill.

5. Evan bought a toy microphone for $2.75. He paid with three $1 bills.

C Draw a picture of the coins and bills you would use for change in Exercise 4.

D In Exercise 5, how much change would Evan get if he paid with a $5 bill?

Problem-Solving Skill: Look Back and Check (1-14)

6. Solve. Look back and check your work.

Robbie walks 4 blocks each way to and from school. Layla walks 5 blocks to school and 2 blocks from school to day care. Her father drives her home from day care. Who walks farther? Explain.

E Check your answer. Does it make sense? Did you answer the right question?

F Check your work. Did you use the right operations?

MULTIPLE CHOICE

1. Earl bought a puppet for $4.33. He paid with a $5 bill. How much change did he get? (1-13)

A. $0.67   **B.** $0.77   **C.** $0.87   **D.** $1.01

2. What is the least number of coins you need to show $0.31? (1-12)

A. 2   **B.** 3   **C.** 4   **D.** 7

FREE RESPONSE

Write the total value in dollars and cents. (1-12)

3.

4. What coins and bills you would use to show $3.87? (1-12)

5. Hanna bought a papaya for $1.43 and paid with two $1 bills. How much change did she get? (1-13)

6. Anton bought an apple for $0.68 and paid with 3 quarters. How much change did he get? (1-13)

Iris solved the problem below. Her work is shown at the right. (1-14, 1-15)

Each time you rent 3 videos, you receive a $1 coupon. How many videos would you need to rent to get 3 coupons?

7. Did Iris answer the right question? Explain.

8. Is her work correct? Explain.

Videos	$1 Coupon
1	NO
2	NO
3	YES
4	NO
5	NO
6	YES
7	NO
8	NO
9	YES

You need to rent 9 videos to get 3 coupons.

Writing in Math

9. Are 3 dimes, 2 nickels, and 1 penny the same as 1 quarter, 1 dime, and 1 penny? Explain (1-12)

Test-Taking Strategies

Understand the question.

Get information for the answer.

Plan how to find the answer.

Make smart choices.

Use writing in math.

Improve written answers.

Understand the Question

Before you can answer a test question, you have to understand it. The steps used with the problem below will help you understand what the question is asking.

1. The table shows distances from Tampa, Florida, to some other cities in Florida.

Distances from Tampa, Florida

City	Distance (in miles)
Daytona Beach	139
Key West	387
Miami	245
Naples	156

Which shows these distances in order from **least** to **greatest**?

A. 245 156 387 139

B. 139 156 245 387

C. 139 245 156 387

D. 387 245 156 139

Understand the question.

• Look for important words (words that tell what the problem is about and highlighted words).

• Turn the question into a statement that begins: "I need to find...."

I need to find the order of the numbers from least to greatest.

*The words **least** and **greatest** are bold. Least is written first, so I know that the least number in the list should come first. Then the greatest number should come last.*

2. What is the total value of these bills and coins?

A. $6.44   **C.** $6.74

B. $6.49   **D.** $6.89

Think It Through
*The words **total value** tell me that I should count the money. **I need to find** how much money is shown.*

Now it's your turn.

For each problem, identify important words. Finish the statement, "I need to find…."

3. Timothy made the greatest number using all four digits shown below. Which number did Timothy make?

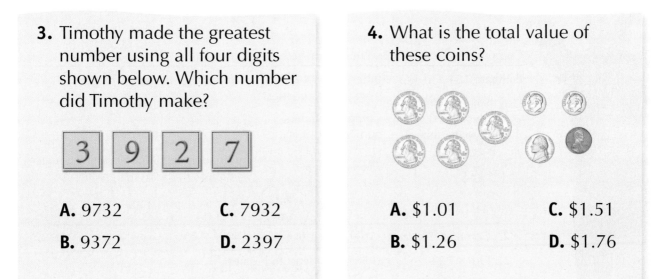

| 3 | 9 | 2 | 7 |

A. 9732   **C.** 7932

B. 9372   **D.** 2397

4. What is the total value of these coins?

A. $1.01   **C.** $1.51

B. $1.26   **D.** $1.76

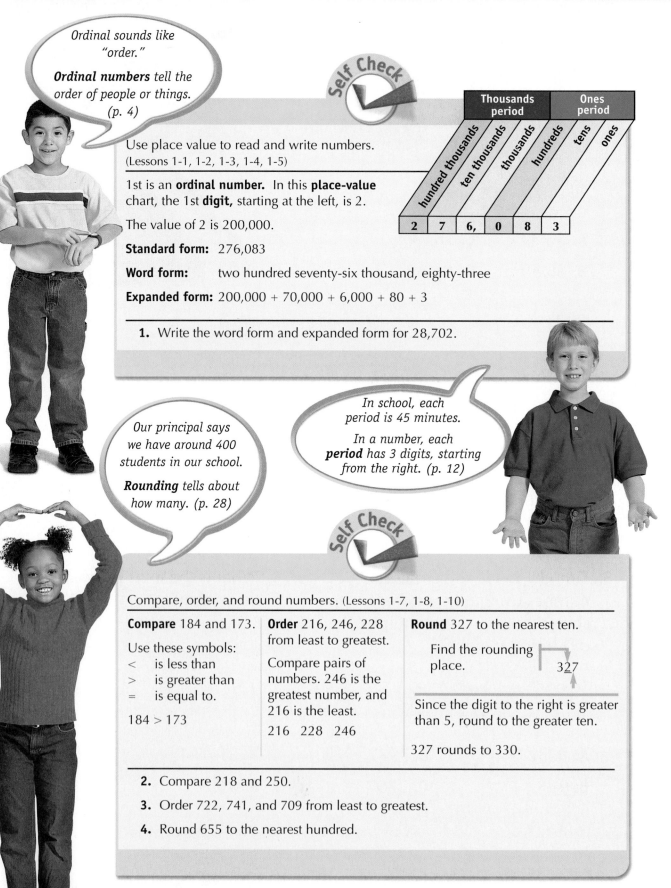

Ordinal sounds like "order."

Ordinal numbers *tell the order of people or things. (p. 4)*

Self Check ✓

	Thousands period			Ones period		
	hundred thousands	ten thousands	thousands	hundreds	tens	ones
	2	7	6,	0	8	3

Use place value to read and write numbers. (Lessons 1-1, 1-2, 1-3, 1-4, 1-5)

1st is an **ordinal number**. In this **place-value** chart, the 1st **digit,** starting at the left, is 2.

The value of 2 is 200,000.

Standard form: 276,083

Word form: two hundred seventy-six thousand, eighty-three

Expanded form: 200,000 + 70,000 + 6,000 + 80 + 3

1. Write the word form and expanded form for 28,702.

Our principal says we have around 400 students in our school.

Rounding *tells about how many. (p. 28)*

In school, each period is 45 minutes.

*In a number, each **period** has 3 digits, starting from the right. (p. 12)*

Self Check ✓

Compare, order, and round numbers. (Lessons 1-7, 1-8, 1-10)

Compare 184 and 173.

Use these symbols:
< is less than
> is greater than
= is equal to.

184 > 173

Order 216, 246, 228 from least to greatest.

Compare pairs of numbers. 246 is the greatest number, and 216 is the least.

216   228   246

Round 327 to the nearest ten.

Find the rounding place.   3$2\underline{7}$

Since the digit to the right is greater than 5, round to the greater ten.

327 rounds to 330.

2. Compare 218 and 250.

3. Order 722, 741, and 709 from least to greatest.

4. Round 655 to the nearest hundred.

A sign tells me information about something.

The **dollar sign** and **decimal point** tell me about money. (p. 36)

Self Check

Use counting with number patterns or money. (Lessons 1-9, 1-12, 1-13)

You can use **even numbers, odd numbers,** and skip counting to continue patterns.

21, 19, 17, 15, ■, ■

The next two numbers are 13 and 11.

Ben bought some ice cream for $3.59. He paid with a $5 bill. How much change did he get?

Count on from $3.59.

$3.59 $3.60 $3.70 $3.75 $4.00 $5.00

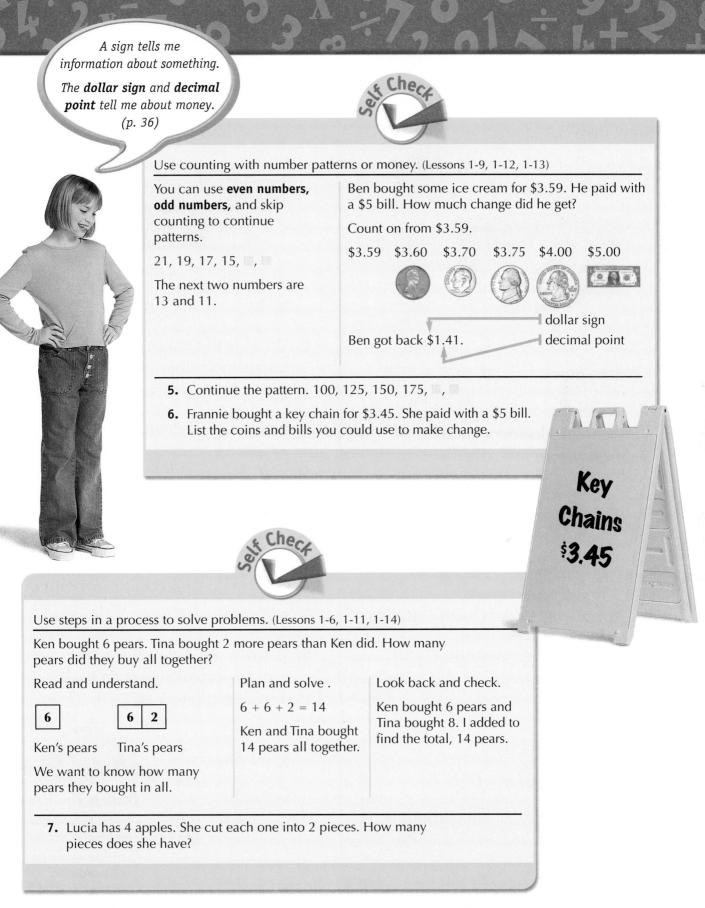

dollar sign

Ben got back $1.41.   decimal point

5. Continue the pattern. 100, 125, 150, 175, ■, ■

6. Frannie bought a key chain for $3.45. She paid with a $5 bill. List the coins and bills you could use to make change.

Key Chains $3.45

Self Check

Use steps in a process to solve problems. (Lessons 1-6, 1-11, 1-14)

Ken bought 6 pears. Tina bought 2 more pears than Ken did. How many pears did they buy all together?

Read and understand.

| 6 |

| 6 | 2 |

Ken's pears   Tina's pears

We want to know how many pears they bought in all.

Plan and solve .

6 + 6 + 2 = 14

Ken and Tina bought 14 pears all together.

Look back and check.

Ken bought 6 pears and Tina bought 8. I added to find the total, 14 pears.

7. Lucia has 4 apples. She cut each one into 2 pieces. How many pieces does she have?

Answers: 1. twenty-eight thousand, seven hundred two; 20,000 + 8,000 + 700 + 2 2. 218 < 250 3. 709, 722, 741 4. 700 5. 200, 225 6. Sample answer: 1 nickel, 2 quarters, 1 one-dollar bill 7. 8 pieces

Chapter 1 Key Vocabulary and Concept Review   51

MULTIPLE CHOICE

Choose the correct letter for each answer.

1. How is the following number used?

A. locate   **C.** measure

B. name   **D.** count

2. Which ordinal number describes the math book's position from the bottom?

A. 1st   **B.** 2nd   **C.** 4th   **D.** 5th

3. Find 5,603 in expanded form.

A. 500 + 600 + 3

B. 5,000 + 60 + 3

C. 5,000 + 600 + 3

D. 5,000 + 600 + 60 + 3

4. Find the numbers that continue the pattern: 21, 28, 35, ▩, ▢

A. 36, 37   **C.** 43, 51

B. 42, 49   **D.** 45, 55

5. Find the value of the money.

A. $5.58   **C.** $6.52

B. $6.27   **D.** $6.82

6. What is the value of the underlined digit in 3̲27,412?

A. 3   **C.** 3,000

B. 300   **D.** 300,000

7. How could you show $1.55 using bills and coins?

A. 1 half dollar, 55 pennies

B. $1 bill, 5 dimes, 5 nickels

C. $1 bill, 1 half dollar, 5 pennies

D. $1 bill, 5 nickels, 5 pennies

8. What is the greatest possible 5-digit number you can make from the digits 5, 3, 7, 9, 2?

A. 79,325

B. 97,532

C. 97,352

D. 79,523

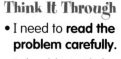

Think It Through

• I need to **read the problem carefully.**

• I should **watch for key words like greatest or least.**

FREE RESPONSE

Write each number in standard form.

9.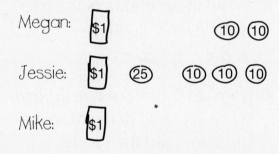

10. two hundred six

11. nine thousand seventeen

12. 600 + 90 + 8

13. 4,000 + 100 + 1

Write the value of the underlined digit.

14. <u>7</u>7,093   **15.** 19<u>3</u>,341

16. <u>6</u>81,924   **17.** 112,<u>8</u>40

Compare the numbers.
Use <, >, or =.

18. 367 ⬤ 483

19. 8,345 ⬤ 8,354

20. 1,048 ⬤ 983

Write from least to greatest.

21. 657   862   613

22. 1,543   1,254   1,765

Round to the nearest ten.

23. 35   **24.** 811

Round to the nearest hundred.

25. 321   **26.** 9,487

27. Roy bought a hamburger for $1.49. He paid with a $5 bill. How much change did he receive in dollars and cents?

Writing in Math

For 28–30, use the Plant Cost problem.

Plant Cost Megan and her friends want to buy a plant for their teacher. The plant will cost $4.59. Do they have enough money to buy the plant?

- Megan has a $1 bill and 2 dimes.

- Jessie has a $1 bill, 1 quarter, and 3 dimes.

- Mike has a $1 bill, 3 quarters, and 4 dimes.

28. Tell what you know and what you are trying to find.

29. Copy and complete the picture to solve the problem. Write the answer in a complete sentence.

Megan: $1   10 10

Jessie: $1   25   10 10 10

Mike: $1

30. Look back and check your work. How do you know your answer is correct?

Number and Operation

MULTIPLE CHOICE

1. How many tens make 100?

   A. 1,000   **C.** 10

   B. 100   **D.** 1

2. Which is NOT a way to show 361?

   A. 2 hundreds, 5 tens, 11 ones

   B. 2 hundreds, 16 tens, 1 one

   C. 3 hundreds, 6 tens, 1 one

   D. 3 hundreds, 5 tens, 11 ones

Think It Through
I should **watch for highlighted words** like NOT.

FREE RESPONSE

3. Write these numbers in order from least to greatest.

   3,465   3,546   3,245

4. Kara read 12 books. Josh read 9 books. How many more books did Kara read than Josh?

5. Round 2,583 to the nearest ten.

Writing in Math

6. Explain how you know that 64 is not the same as 640.

Geometry and Measurement

MULTIPLE CHOICE

7. How many feet are in one yard?

   A. 2   **B.** 3   **C.** 5   **D.** 6

8. Which shape would you make if you traced one side of the object?

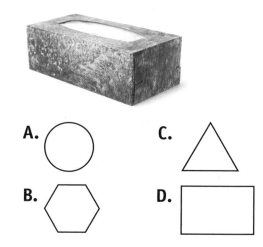

   A. ◯   **C.** △

   B. ⬡   **D.** ▭

FREE RESPONSE

9. About how long is the caterpillar?

Writing in Math

10. Would you go boating or sledding when the temperature is 28°F? Explain your answer.

Data Analysis and Probability

MULTIPLE CHOICE

Use the pictograph for 11 and 12.

Lemonade Sold

Saturday	🍋 🍋 🍋
Sunday	🍋 🍋 🍋 🍋 🍋
Monday	🍋

Each 🍋 = 2 glasses.

11. How many more glasses were sold on Sunday than on Saturday?

A. 1   **B.** 3   **C.** 4   **D.** 5

12. How many glasses were sold in all?

A. 9   **B.** 10   **C.** 17   **D.** 18

FREE RESPONSE

13. Use the bar graph below. On which day were the least number of students absent?

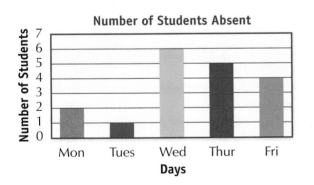

Number of Students Absent

Writing in Math

14. There are 10 red, 3 yellow, and 5 blue cubes in a bag. Which are you most likely to pick? Explain.

Algebra

MULTIPLE CHOICE

15. Which number completes the number sentence?

$$5 + \boxed{} = 8$$

A. 3   **B.** 5   **C.** 8   **D.** 13

16. Continue the pattern.

3, 6, 9, ▪, ▪, ▪

A. 10, 11, 12   **C.** 12, 16, 20

B. 11, 13, 16   **D.** 12, 15, 18

FREE RESPONSE

17. Kara bought a can of juice. She paid with a $1 bill. This is the change she got. How much did the juice cost?

18. Bill has 7 coins worth a total of $0.84 in his pocket. He has one half dollar and four pennies. What other two coins does Bill have in his pocket?

Writing in Math

19. Find the missing number in the pattern. Explain how you got your answer.

100, 90, ▪, 70, 60, 50

Set 1-1 (pages 4–5)

Find the 5th teacup from the bottom.

Start at the bottom of the stack.

Count up to the 5th teacup.

The dotted teacup is 5th from the bottom.

Remember that numbers are used to locate, name, measure, or count. Ordinal numbers show order.

1. Which teacup is 3rd from the bottom?

2. Write an ordinal number for the position of the red teacup from the bottom.

Set 1-2 (pages 6–7)

Write the number in expanded, standard, and word form.

Expanded form: 200 + 30 + 6

Standard form: 236

Word form: two hundred thirty-six

Remember that the digit 0 is needed to hold a place in a number.

Write each number in standard form.

1.   **2.**

3. 300 + 20 + 7

4. six hundred eighty-five

Set 1-3 (pages 8–9)

Write this number in standard form.

200 + 30 + 12 or 200 + 40 + 2

Standard form: 242

Remember that 1 ten = 10 ones and that 1 hundred = 10 tens.

Write each number in standard form.

1.

2.

3. Rename 300 using only tens.

4. Rename 540 using only tens.

Set 1-4 (pages 10–11)

Write four thousand, sixteen in standard form and expanded form.

thousands	hundreds	tens	ones
4,	0	1	6

Standard form: 4,016

Expanded form: 4,000 + 10 + 6

Remember to use a comma to separate thousands from hundreds.

Write each number in standard form and expanded form.

1. two thousand, one hundred four

2. six thousand, seventeen

Set 1-5 (pages 12–13)

Find the value of 4 in 847,191.

The 4 is in the ten thousands place.

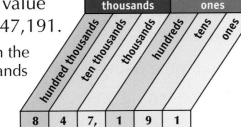

Its value is 40,000.

Remember that 10 thousands equal 1 ten thousand.

Write the value of each underlined digit.

1. 3̲41,791   **2.** 829̲,536

3. 570,89̲0   **4.** 31̲5,000

Set 1-6 (pages 14–15)

A family picture shows 4 children, 2 parents, and 4 grandparents. How many people are in the picture?

Step 1: Tell what you know.

Step 2: Tell what the question asks.

Remember, if you don't understand the problem at first, reread it.

1. What do you know about the family?

2. What does the problem asks?

3. Solve the problem.

Set 1-7 (pages 18–21)

Compare 7,948 and 7,682.

Line up the numbers by place value and start comparing from the left.

```
7, 9  4  8
7, 6  8  2
```
same ⬏ ⬑ different:
9 hundreds > 6 hundreds

7,948 > 7,682

Remember the symbol < means less than and the symbol > means greater than.

Compare. Use <, >, or =.

1. 479 ● 912   **2.** 820 ● 1,820

3. 7,222 ● 3,004

Set 1-8 (pages 22–23)

Order 7,268; 9,104; and 3,201 from greatest to least.

Compare pairs of numbers.

$7{,}268 < \mathbf{9{,}104}$

$3{,}201 < \mathbf{9{,}104}$ So **9,104** is greatest.

$\mathbf{3{,}201} < 7{,}268$ So **3,201** is least.

From greatest to least, the numbers are 9,104, 7,268, and 3,201.

Remember to compare only two numbers at a time.

Write the numbers in order from greatest to least.

1. 393 182 229

2. 1,289 2,983 1,760

3. 2,796 6,546 8,602

Set 1-9 (pages 24–27)

Continue the pattern.

51, 41, 31, ▨, ▨, ▨

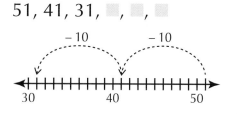

Subtract 10 to continue the pattern.

The pattern is 51, 41, 31, 21, 11, 1.

Remember that you can find patterns on a number line or a number chart.

Find the missing numbers.

1. 50, 55, 60, ▨, ▨, ▨

2. 7,200, 7,000, 6,800, ▨, ▨, ▨

3. 180, 190, 200, ▨, ▨, ▨

Set 1-10 (pages 28–31)

Round 867 to the nearest ten.

tens place

86   Since: 7 > 5, round to the greater ten.

870

867 rounds to 870.

Remember to think of the halfway point between tens or hundreds.

1. Round 61 to the nearest ten.

2. Round 259 to the nearest hundred.

Set 1-11 (pages 32–33)

Baseball caps come in two colors, yellow and green. The caps come in two sizes, medium and large. How many different types of caps are possible?

Remember to make a plan.

1. Make an organized list.

2. What strategy did you use?

3. Answer the problem in a complete sentence.

Write the total value in dollars
and cents.

$5.00, $5.25, $5.35, $5.40, $5.45, $5.46

The total is $5.46.

Remember to count bills first and
then count coins.
Write the total value in dollars
and cents.

1.

Set 1-13 (pages 40–41)

Derek paid for a $4.29 cap with a
$5 bill. How much change did
he get?

Count on from $4.29.

$4.29➤$4.30➤$4.40➤$4.50➤$4.75➤**5.00**

Derek got $0.71 in change.

Remember to use coins that will
make it easier to skip count.

How much change would you
receive from a $5 bill?

1. $4.86	**2.** $1.67
3. $1.19	**4.** $4.99

Set 1-14 (pages 42–43)

In the 2002 Olympics, Canada's
hockey team beat the United States'
team by 3 goals. A total of 7 goals
was scored in the game. What was
the final score?

Try: 1, 6   Check: 1 + 6 = **7**,
               but 6 − 1 = 5

Try: 2, 5   Check: 2 + 5 = **7**,
               5 − 2 = **3**

The final score was Canada 5 goals
and the United States 2 goals.

Remember to check your answer.

1. Does the answer match the
question?

2. Does the answer make sense?
Explain.

3. Is the work correct?

Set 1-1 (pages 4–5)

Write whether the number is used to locate, name, measure, or count.

1.

2.

3. Caitlin is 6th in line. How many people are in front of her?

Set 1-2 (pages 6–7)

Write each number in standard form.

1. seventy-one

2. one hundred one

3. 80 + 8

4. 600 + 20 + 4

5. Find the missing number. 200 + ▨ + 4 = 274

Set 1-3 (pages 8–9)

Write each number in standard form.

1. [base-ten blocks]

2. [base-ten blocks]

3. [base-ten blocks]

4. [base-ten blocks]

5. Riley has 14 tens blocks and 36 ones blocks. What other blocks does she need to show 276?

Set 1-4 (pages 10–11)

Write each number in standard form.

1. 4,000 + 600 + 10 + 4

2. 9,000 + 500 + 10

3. five thousand, five hundred seventeen

4. Write the 3-digit number that matches all the clues.

My tens digit is 3 more than my hundreds digit.
My ones digit is 1 less than the greatest digit possible.
My hundreds digit is 4.

Take It to the NET
More Practice
www.scottforesman.com

Set 1-5 (pages 12–13)

Write each number in standard form.

1. 20,000 + 8,000 + 200 + 20 + 7   **2.** 900,000 + 10,000 + 700 + 40

3. 300,000 + 20,000 + 6,000 + 400 + 30 + 7

4. 900,000 + 60,000 + 7,000 + 800 + 10 + 9

5. three hundred eighty-one thousand, four hundred thirty-seven

6. four hundred sixty thousand, eight hundred twenty-two

7. If a 5-digit number has a 3 followed by four 1s, what is the value of 3 in this number?

Set 1-6 (pages 14–15)

Mitchell's flight from San Francisco to Chicago made a stop in Phoenix. The flight from San Francisco to Phoenix took 2 hours. He had to wait in Phoenix for 4 hours. Then the flight from Phoenix to Chicago took 3 hours. How much time did the entire trip take?

1. What do you know?

2. What are you trying to find?

3. Solve the problem. Write the answer in a complete sentence.

Set 1-7 (pages 18–21)

Compare the numbers. Use <, >, or =.

1. 9,326 ⬤ 5,479   **2.** 1,906 ⬤ 1,906   **3.** 7,895 ⬤ 2,418

4. 5,132 ⬤ 1,340   **5.** 8,946 ⬤ 9,966   **6.** 4,600 ⬤ 4,825

7. 559 ⬤ 299   **8.** 5,370 ⬤ 678   **9.** 5,743 ⬤ 6,541

10. 214 ⬤ 549   **11.** 8,436 ⬤ 913   **12.** 724 ⬤ 724

13. Wally says that the number 9 is greater than the number 2, so 4,879 must be greater than 6,872. What is wrong with Wally's reasoning?

Set 1-8 (pages 22–23)

Write the numbers in order from least to greatest.

1. 175   157   179

2. 5,999   8,000   2,999

3. 175   75   1,750

4. 6,950   6,590   6,990

5. 6,897   6,561   6,134

6. 7,329   7,392   9,329

7. 475   455   745

8. 5,665   4,695   4,659

9. Eric collected 452 aluminum cans to be recycled, Bill collected 425, and Danielle collected 524. Who collected the most cans? Who collected the fewest cans?

Set 1-9 (pages 24–27)

Use place-value patterns to find each sum.

1. 200 + 300

2. 137 + 400

3. 489 + 100

4. 262 + 600

5. 853 + 100

6. 394 + 300

7. 213 + 200

8. 701 + 200

9. Rita's uncle was born exactly 200 years after the Declaration of Independence was signed. The Declaration of Independence was signed in 1776. What year was Rita's uncle born?

Set 1-10 (pages 28–31)

Round to the nearest ten.

1. 18

2. 92

3. 341

4. 204

Round to the nearest hundred.

5. 733

6. 185

7. 1,243

8. 3,690

9. What number is halfway between 50 and 60?

10. What number is halfway between 300 and 400?

11. What number is halfway between 9,700 and 9,800?

Take It to the NET
More Practice
www.scottforesman.com

Set 1-11 (pages 32–33)

Six people blew up some balloons. Each person blew up 1 blue and 2 red balloons. How many balloons were blown up in all? Copy and complete the picture to solve the problem.

1. What do you know?

2. What are you trying to find?

3. What strategy did you use?

4. Give the answer to the problem in a complete sentence.

Set 1-12 (pages 36–39)

Tell what coins and bills you could use to show each amount in two ways.

1. $0.06   **2.** $0.50   **3.** $1.41   **4.** $2.45

5. Ian says that two $1 bills, 3 quarters, and 2 pennies is equal to 5 half dollars, 1 dime, 2 nickels, and 2 pennies. Is he correct? Explain.

Set 1-13 (pages 40–41)

In 1–4, the cost of an item is given. List the coins and bills you would use to make change from a $5 bill.

1. $4.82   **2.** $3.33   **3.** $0.80   **4.** $4.05

5. Melissa bought a newspaper that was $0.35. She paid with a half dollar. Would two dimes be the correct change? Explain.

Set 1-14 (pages 42–43)

Mae, Ella, and Drew counted cars. Mae saw 4 more cars than Drew. Ella saw 3 fewer cars than Mae. If Ella saw 7 cars, how many cars did Mae and Drew each see?

1. Give the answer to the problem in a complete sentence.

2. Look back and check your work. Did you answer the right question? Is your work correct? Explain.

Addition and Subtraction Number Sense

DIAGNOSING READINESS

A Vocabulary
(Grade 2 and pages 6 and 28)

Choose the best term from the box.

1. In 3 + 5 = 8, the 8 is the __?__.

2. A __?__ number tells about how many.

3. In 348, the 4 is in the __?__ place, and the 3 is in the __?__ place.

Vocabulary

- **rounded** *(p. 28)*
- **sum** *(Gr. 2)*
- **hundreds** *(p. 6)*
- **tens** *(p. 6)*

B Addition Facts
(Grade 2)

4. 2 + 3	**5.** 5 + 5	**6.** 4 + 2
7. 6 + 4	**8.** 2 + 7	**9.** 3 + 3
10. 2 + 1	**11.** 6 + 5	**12.** 4 + 5

13. Bob has 3 apples. Terry has 5 apples. How many apples do they have in all?

14. Elaine bought 3 muffins on Monday and 2 on Tuesday. Write a number sentence to show how many muffins she bought in all.

Do You Know...

How much water can a fire truck spray in one minute?

You'll find out in Lesson 2-13.

Mighty Machines
FIRE TRUCK
And other emergency machines

C Subtraction Facts

(Grade 2)

15. 6 − 2   **16.** 8 − 5   **17.** 6 − 1

18. 7 − 4   **19.** 5 − 4   **20.** 9 − 2

21. 11 − 3   **22.** 9 − 7   **23.** 14 − 6

24. Lori had 12 grapes. She gave 7 to Al. How many grapes does Lori have left?

25. Carl has 9 hockey cards. David has 7 hockey cards. Write a number sentence to show how many more cards Carl has than David.

D Rounding

(pages 28–29)

Round each number to the nearest ten.

26. 21   **27.** 55   **28.** 97

Round each number to the nearest hundred.

29. 143   **30.** 151   **31.** 382

32. Ellen waited in line for 17 minutes to ride the roller coaster. Was her waiting time closer to 10 minutes or to 20 minutes?

Algebra

Key Ideas
Learning about properties can help you solve addition problems.

Vocabulary
- addends
- sum
- Commutative (order) Property of Addition
- Associative (grouping) Property of Addition
- Identity (zero) Property of Addition

Think It Through
If I have trouble remembering an addition fact, I can **change the order** of the addends.

$5 + 4 = 9$,
so $4 + 5 = 9$.

Addition Properties

LEARN

What is the Commutative Property?

At the fruit market, Alex bought 3 oranges first, then 4 apples. Jan bought 4 apples first, then 3 oranges. Did they buy the same number of pieces of fruit?

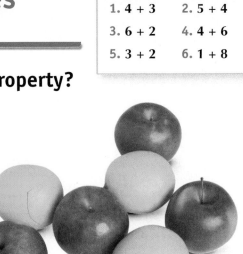

✔ WARM UP
1. 4 + 3   2. 5 + 4
3. 6 + 2   4. 4 + 6
5. 3 + 2   6. 1 + 8

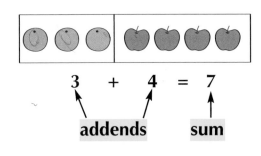

$$3 + 4 = 7$$

addends   sum

$$4 + 3 = 7$$

Addition properties are rules for addition that are always true. The **Commutative (order) Property of Addition** says that you can add numbers in any order and the sum will be the same.

So $3 + 4 = 4 + 3$.

Alex and Jan each bought 7 pieces of fruit.

Talk About It

1. Why does it make sense that the Commutative Property is also called the order property?

2. Draw a picture of how you could use counters to show that $5 + 6 = 6 + 5$.

3. If you know that $8 + 3 = 11$, how can you find $3 + 8$?

What is the Associative Property?

The **Associative (grouping) Property of Addition** says that you can group addends in any way and the sum will be the same.

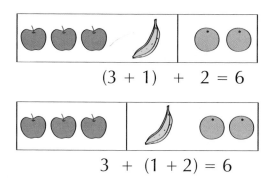

$(3 + 1) + 2 = 6$

$3 + (1 + 2) = 6$

So $(3 + 1) + 2 = 3 + (1 + 2)$.

> Grouping symbols, like parentheses, ( ), show which numbers to add first.

✔ Talk About It

4. Evan says, "You can rewrite $(5 + 3) + 2$ as $8 + 2$." Do you agree? Explain.

What is the Identity Property?

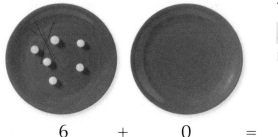

The **Identity (zero) Property of Addition** says that the sum of any number and zero is that same number.

$6 + 0 = 6$

✔ Talk About It

5. How could you use the Identity Property of Addition to find $536 + 0$?

CHECK ✔

For another example, see Set 2-1 on p. 116.

Find each sum.

1. $2 + (5 + 3)$　　　**2.** $3 + (1 + 4)$　　　**3.** $3 + 2 + 6$

Write each missing number.

4. $5 + 2 = 2 + \blacksquare$　　　**5.** $\blacksquare + 4 = 4$　　　**6.** $(1 + 4) + 3 = \blacksquare + (4 + 3)$

7. Number Sense What property of addition is shown in the following number sentence? Explain. $4 + (5 + 2) = (5 + 2) + 4$

A Skills and Understanding

Find each sum.

8. 3 + (1 + 5)   **9.** (5 + 4) + 3   **10.** (0 + 4) + 3

11. 6 + (1 + 1)   **12.** 7 + 4 + 2   **13.** 5 + 5 + 2

Write each missing number.

14. 0 + ▧ = 3   **15.** ▧ + 6 = 6 + 3   **16.** 13 = ▧ + (3 + 3)

17. 9 + 3 = ▧ + 9   **18.** 12 + ▧ = 12   **19.** (▧ + 2) + 1 = 7

20. (▧ + 1) + 4 = 5 + (1 + 4)   **21.** 6 + (2 + 6) = 6 + ▧

22. Number Sense Thomas said "2 + 3 = 5, so 3 + 5 = 2."
Do you agree? Explain.

B Reasoning and Problem Solving

Math and Everyday Life

In basketball, a shot inside the
three-point line is worth 2 points.
A shot outside the three-point
line is worth 3 points. A free throw
is worth 1 point.

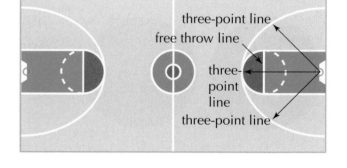

23. Jana made 2 three-point shots.
Then she made 1 free throw.
How many points did she score?

24. Darryl made 1 shot from outside the three-point line,
then missed a free throw. How many points did he score?

25. Algebra Rod made 2 free throws. Then he made one
more basket. He scored a total of 5 points. How many
points did he score on the last basket?

26. Writing in Math Two students gave different answers for the
following problem. Which is correct? Explain.

Find the missing number.   ▧ + 0 = ▧

▢ = 6 because 6 + 0 = 6   ▢ = 10 because 10 + 0 = 10

C Extensions

27. You know that 6 + 2 is the same as 2 + 6. Is 6 − 2 the same as 2 − 6? Explain.

28. You know that 6 + (5 + 2) = (6 + 5) + 2. Does 6 − (5 − 2) = (6 − 5) − 2? Explain.

Mixed Review and Test Prep

Take It to the NET
Test Prep
www.scottforesman.com

Solve the problem. Look back and check your answer.

29. Kyle walked 6 blocks from home to the library. Then he walked 3 blocks farther to the playground. Later he followed the same path home. How far did he walk in all?

30. If you spent $3.04 for a toy, how much change would you get back from $5?

    A. $0.96   **B.** $1.04   **C.** $1.96   **D.** $2.96

Enrichment

Venn Diagrams

A **Venn diagram** uses shapes like rings or circles to show how data belongs to groups. Each shape is named for the group it represents. If shapes overlap, or **intersect,** it is because some of the data belongs to more than one group.

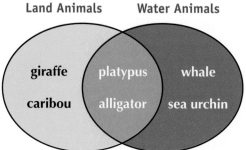

Land Animals   Water Animals

giraffe   platypus   whale

caribou   alligator   sea urchin

1. Which animals live only on land? Which live only in water?

2. Which animals live both on land and in water? How can you tell from the Venn diagram?

3. In what part of the Venn diagram would you place an octopus? a tortoise? a camel?

Algebra

Key Idea
Fact families show how addition and subtraction are related.

Vocabulary
• fact family
• difference

Think It Through

I can **draw a parts-whole picture** to show addition and subtraction.

Relating Addition and Subtraction

LEARN

How are addition and subtraction related?

✓ **WARM UP**
1. 2 + 5   2. 7 – 2
3. 3 + 9   4. 12 – 3
5. 4 + 7   6. 11 – 4
7. There are 9 red cars and 8 blue cars. How many cars in all?

You can think about parts and the whole to show how addition and subtraction are related.

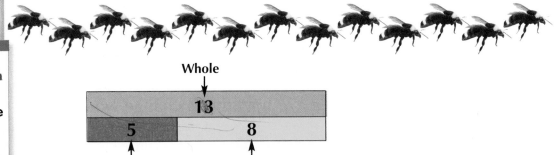

Whole

13	
5	8

Part   Part

You can write a **fact family** when you know the parts and the whole.

Fact family:

5 + 8 = 13   13 – 8 = 5

8 + 5 = 13   13 – 5 = 8

difference

Example

Find 12 – 7.

What You **Think**	What You **Write**
7 + ? = 12	12 – 7 = 5
7 + **5** = 12	

✓ **Talk About It**

1. What are the other three number sentences in the fact family with 6 + 3 = 9?

2. What addition fact can help you find 11 – 3?

Copy and complete each fact family.

1. $4 + 6 = $ ▢ $10 - $ ▢ $= 6$

▢ $+ 4 = 10$ ▢ $- 6 = 4$

2. $6 + 7 = $ ▢   ▢ $- 6 = 7$

$7 + 6 = 13$ $13 - 7 = $ ▢

Find each missing number.

3. $6 + $ ▢ $= 12$ **4.** $3 + $ ▢ $= 11$ **5.** $9 + $ ▢ $= 17$ **6.** $5 + $ ▢ $= 9$

7. Number Sense Haley says, "To find $8 - 6$, I can think of the addition fact $8 + 6 = 14$." Do you agree? Explain.

Ⓐ Skills and Understanding

Copy and complete each fact family.

8. $7 + 4 = $ ▢ $11 - $ ▢ $= 4$

▢ $+ 7 = 11$ ▢ $- 4 = 7$

9. ▢ $+ 9 = 12$ ▢ $- 9 = 3$

$9 + $ ▢ $= 12$ $12 - $ ▢ $= 9$

Find each missing number.

10. $5 + $ ▢ $= 7$ **11.** $8 + $ ▢ $= 16$ **12.** $6 + $ ▢ $= 10$ **13.** $7 + $ ▢ $= 16$

14. Number Sense Write the fact family for 3, 5, and 8.

Ⓑ Reasoning and Problem Solving

15. Write a subtraction fact for the story at the right. Then write an addition fact you could use to check it.

16. Writing in Math The fact family $4 + 4 = 8$ and $8 - 4 = 4$ has two number sentences. Write another fact family that has only two number sentences. Explain.

> Twelve bees are in the garden. Four of the bees are flying around. Eight of the bees are pollinating flowers.

🦉 Mixed Review and Test Prep

Take It to the NET
Test Prep
www.scottforesman.com

Write each missing number.

17. $6 + $ ▢ $= 8 + 6$ **18.** ▢ $+ 0 = 9$ **19.** $18 = $ ▢ $+ (7 + 3)$

20. Which shows the numbers in order from least to greatest?

A. 1,346, 1,436, 1,634   **C.** 1,436, 1,346, 1,634

B. 1,634, 1,436, 1,346   **D.** 1,346, 1,634, 1,436

All text pages available online and on CD-ROM.   **Section A Lesson 2-2**   **71**

Algebra

Key Idea
You can use a pattern to find an addition or subtraction rule.

TEST TALK

Think It Through
I can **look for a pattern** to find the rule that is used to change numbers in a table.

Find a Rule

LEARN

✓ WARM UP

Continue each pattern.

1. 6, 8, 10, ▢

2. 20, 25, 30, ▢

How can you find a rule?

In the picture at the right, two students are using a special machine that works with numbers. They put a number **In** the machine and look at the number that comes **Out.**

A rule describes what should be done to the **In** numbers to get the **Out** numbers. A table can be used to find a rule.

Examples

A.

In	4	7	1	6	9
Out	10	13	7	12	▢

Rule: **Add 6**

B.

In	10	4	6	8	12
Out	6	0	2	4	▢

Rule: **Subtract 4**

✓ **Talk About It**

1. What is the missing number in the table for Example A? for Example B?

2. **Reasoning** How could you tell if the rule for a table was "Add zero"?

Activity

How can you find a pattern in a table?

Copy and complete each table.

In	2	1	5	6	9
Out	6	5	9	10	

In	10	4	6	8	12
Out	7	1	3		

a. What pattern do you see in the first table? in the second table? Write each pattern as a rule, like "Add 2."

b. Does your rule for each table work for every **In** number?

Copy and complete each table. Then write a rule for the table.

1.

In	5	7	1	8	4
Out	10	12	6		

2.

In	7	6	9	11	14
Out	1	0	3		

3. Number Sense Sam uses the rule **subtract 9** for his table. If he puts in 11, what should he get out?

PRACTICE *For more practice, see Set 2-3 on p. 120.*

 **Skills and Understanding**

Copy and complete each table. Then write a rule for the table.

4.

In	5	9	6	8	2
Out	3	7	4		

5.

In	5	2	9	3	4
Out	13	10	17		

6.

In	9	5	8	6	1
Out	12		11	9	

7.

In	200	550	400	700	220
Out	100	450		600	

8. Number Sense Marissa uses the rule **add 5** for her table. If she puts in a zero, what should she get out?

B **Reasoning and Problem Solving**

9. If the hopscotch pattern shown continued to 16, what numbers would be in the diamond shapes? Draw a picture. What patterns do you see?

10. Writing in Math Make your own table with an In and Out pattern. Write the rule.

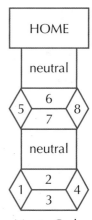

Monte Carlo
Hopscotch Pattern

Mixed Review and Test Prep

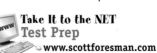 Take It to the NET
Test Prep
www.scottforesman.com

Find each missing number.

11. 8 + ▨ = 17   **12.** 5 + ▨ = 11   **13.** 6 + ▨ = 13   **14.** 7 + ▨ = 16

15. Tim had 16 spelling words to learn. He learned 8 on Monday. How many more does he have to learn?

A. 25   **B.** 15   **C.** 9   **D.** 8

All text pages available online and on CD-ROM.

Identifying the Main Idea

Identifying the main idea when you read in math can help you use the **problem-solving strategy, *Write a Number Sentence,*** in the next lesson.

In reading, identifying the main idea helps you know what the story is about. In math, the main idea for some word problems is **part-part-whole** with either a part or the whole unknown.

*The **main idea** here is part-part-whole, with the whole unknown.*

Ed spent $7 Monday and $6 Tuesday. How much did he spend in all on both days?

?	
7	6

Add to find the whole.

Part   Part   Whole
  7 + 6 = *n*

*The **main idea** here is part-part-whole, with one part unknown.*

Sue had $10. After she bought a book, she had $4 left. What did the book cost?

10	
?	4

Subtract to find a part.

Whole   Part   Part
 10 − 4 = *n*

*Each picture shows the main idea. The main idea helps you know what **number sentence** to write.*

1. In the first problem, the amount spent Monday is one of the parts. What is the other part?

2. Describe the two parts in the second problem.

For 3–6, use the information at the right.

Fifteen members of the third-grade swim team are girls. How many are boys?

Third-Grade Teams
Swim team: 28 members
Basketball team: 15 members
Soccer team: 14 members

3. What is the main idea for this problem?

4. Draw a picture to show the main idea.

5. Describe the part that is known in this problem.

6. **Writing in Math** What operation would you use to solve this problem? Explain how you know.

For 7–10, use the table at the right.

Mitch bought a cap and a pennant. How much did he spend altogether?

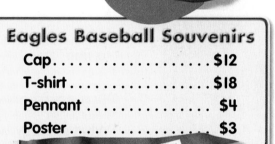

Eagles Baseball Souvenirs
Cap $12
T-shirt $18
Pennant $4
Poster $3

7. Identify the main idea.

8. Draw a picture to show the main idea.

9. Describe the two parts in this problem.

10. Write a number sentence for the problem.

For 11–15, use the table at the right.

Village Motors sold 9 used cars on Saturday. How many new cars did they sell on Saturday?

11. Identify the main idea.

12. Draw a picture to show the main idea.

13. Describe what is known in the problem.

14. Write a number sentence for the problem.

15. **Writing in Math** Write a part-part-whole problem about the number of cars sold on Thursday.

Village Motors Car Sales	
Day	**Cars Sold**
Monday	8
Tuesday	9
Wednesday	5
Thursday	11
Friday	16
Saturday	24

Problem-Solving Strategy

Algebra

Key Idea
Learning how and when to write a number sentence can help you solve problems.

Identifying the main idea
can help you with...
the problem-solving strategy, *Write a Number Sentence*.

Write a Number Sentence

LEARN

How do you write a number sentence to solve a problem?

Soccer Sale Suppose you had $15 to spend. How much money would you have left if you bought the soccer socks?

Soccer Gear Sale!

Soccer socks	$6
Goalie gloves	$8
Shinguards	$15

Read and Understand

What do you know?　　You can spend $15. The socks cost $6.

What are you trying to find?　　Find how much money you will have left.

Plan and Solve

What strategy will you use?

Strategy: Write a Number Sentence

To find the missing part, **subtract.**

n shows the money left over.

$$\$15 - \$6 = n$$
$$\$15 - \$6 = \$9$$
$$n = \$9$$

Answer: You will have $9 left.

How to Write a Number Sentence

Step 1　Show the main idea.
Step 2　Decide which operation fits the main idea.
Step 3　Use a letter to show what you are trying to find.
Step 4　Solve the number sentence.

Look Back and Check

Is your answer reasonable?　　$6 + 9 = 15$　Yes, it checks.

✔ **Talk About It**

1. Why is subtraction used for this problem?

Use the Soccer Gear Sale price list on page 76. Write a number sentence. Then solve.

1. Rachel bought soccer socks and goalie gloves. How much money did she spend?

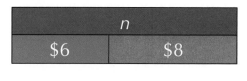

	n	
$6	$8	

Use the Soccer Gear Sale price list on page 76. Write a number sentence. Then solve.

2. Suppose you had $7 and wanted to buy shinguards. How much more money would you need?

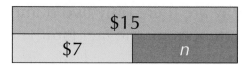

$15	
$7	n

3. How much more do the shinguards cost than the goalie gloves?

STRATEGIES

- **Show What You Know**
  Draw a Picture
  Make an Organized List
  Make a Table
  Make a Graph
  Act It Out or Use Objects
- **Look for a Pattern**
- **Try, Check, and Revise**
- **Write a Number Sentence**
- **Use Logical Reasoning**
- **Solve a Simpler Problem**
- **Work Backward**

Solve each problem. Write the answer in a complete sentence.

4. Lisa bought 3 blue buttons and 9 red buttons. She used 2 blue buttons for the eyes of a puppet. How many buttons did she buy in all?

5. Jon put beads on a string to make a bracelet. He put on a blue bead, then three white beads, then a blue bead, then three white beads, and so on, until he used 4 blue beads. How many beads did he use in all?

6. <u>Writing in Math</u> Write a word problem using the Soccer Gear Sale price list on page 76. Then solve your problem and explain how you know your answer is correct.

Think It Through

Stuck? I won't give up. I can:
- Reread the problem.
- Tell what I know.
- Identify key facts and details.
- Tell the problem in my own words.
- Show the main idea.
- Try a different strategy.
- Retrace my steps.

Do You Know How?

Do You Understand?

Addition Properties (2-1)

Find each missing number.

1. $7 + 9 = 9 + \square$

2. $2 + (8 + 16) = (2 + 8) + \square$

3. $\square + 0 = 27$

Ⓐ How does the Commutative (order) Property of Addition help you answer Exercise 1?

Ⓑ How does the Associative (grouping) Property of Addition help you answer Exercise 2?

Relating Addition and Subtraction (2-2)
Find a Rule (2-3)

Copy and complete each fact family.

4. $3 + 8 = \square$ $11 - \square = 3$

  $\square + 3 = 11$ $\square - 3 = 8$

5. $\square + 9 = 18$ $18 - 9 = \square$

6. Copy and complete the table. Then write a rule for the table.

In	12	15	11	10	6
Out	9	12	8		

Ⓒ Why are there only two number sentences for the fact family in Exercise 5?

Ⓓ If the next column in the table in Exercise 6 had a 0 in the **Out** box, what number would be in the **In** box? Explain how you know the answer.

Problem-Solving Strategy: Write a Number Sentence (2-4)

7. Write and use a number sentence to solve the Stamps problem.

   Stamps Calvin had 16 stamps in his collection. He gave 7 of them to his brother. How many stamps did Calvin have left?

Ⓔ For Exercise 7, tell what you know and what you need to find.

Ⓕ Explain why you chose to add or subtract to solve Exercise 7.

MULTIPLE CHOICE

1. Which number makes this number sentence true? (2-1)

$0 + \blacksquare = 18$

A. 0   **B.** 2   **C.** 10   **D.** 18

2. Which rule is used in this table? (2-3)

In	5	9	0	10	6
Out	10	14	5	15	11

A. Subtract 0   **B.** Add 5   **C.** Subtract 5   **D.** Add 10

FREE RESPONSE

3. Write the fact family for 9, 7, and 16. (2-2)

Find each missing number. (2-1)

4. $7 + \blacksquare = 4 + 7$ **5.** $8 + \blacksquare = 8$ **6.** $4 + (3 + 9) = (4 + 3) + \blacksquare$

Copy and complete each fact family. (2-2)

7. $6 + 5 = \blacksquare$ $11 - \blacksquare = 6$ **8.** $\blacksquare + 7 = 12$ $\blacksquare - 7 = 5$

    $\blacksquare + 6 = 11$ $\blacksquare - 6 = 5$ $7 + \blacksquare = 12$ $12 - \blacksquare = 7$

For 9–12 use the Coins problem. (2-4)

9. What facts are given?

10. What are you trying to find?

11. Write a number sentence.

12. Solve the problem and write the answer in a complete sentence.

> **Coins** Lucia counted the coins in her piggy bank. She has 12 quarters, 8 dimes, 9 nickels, and 16 pennies. How many more pennies than nickels does she have?

Writing in Math

13. In Su Ling's table, the **Out** number is always the same as the **In** number. Write two possible rules for her table. Explain your answer. (2-3)

In	3	9	12
Out	3	9	12

Mental Math: Break Apart Numbers

LEARN

How can you break apart numbers to add mentally?

A seamstress had 43 spools of thread. She went to a sewing shop and bought 25 more spools of thread. How many spools of thread does she have in all?

Show 2 ways to find 43 + 25 using mental math.

Think It Through

I can **use place value** to break apart numbers.

Alice's Way

First I broke apart both numbers into tens and ones.
43 = 40 + 3
25 = 20 + 5

Next I added the tens.
40 + 20 = 60

Then I added the ones.
3 + 5 = 8

Last, I put the tens and ones together.
60 + 8 = 68

So 43 + 25 = 68

The seamstress has 68 spools of thread.

Ethan's Way

I broke apart only the 25.
25 = 20 + 5

Then I added 20 to 43.
43 + 20 = 63

Next I added 5 to 63.
63 + 5 = 68

So 43 + 25 = 68.

The seamstress has 68 spools of thread.

✔ **Talk About It**

1. How did Alice break apart 43 and 25?

2. Is there another way to find 43 + 25, using the break-apart method? Explain.

Take It to the NET
More Examples
www.scottforesman.com

C Extensions

26. Reasoning You have learned to add 2-digit numbers mentally by breaking the numbers apart into tens and ones. How could you add 3-digit numbers using mental math? Try using your method to find 146 + 231.

27. Reasoning You have learned to add 9 to a number mentally by first adding 10 and then subtracting 1. How could you add 99 to a number using mental math? Try using your method to find 48 + 99.

Mixed Review and Test Prep

Take It to the Test Prep
www.scottf

Find each sum using mental math.

28. 15 + 23 **29.** 36 + 49 **30.** 28 + 19 3

32. The rule in Talia's table is **add 7.** What number will she get out if she puts in 9?

A. 2 **B.** 7 **C.** 16

Practice Game

Addition by Brain or Battery?
Number of Players: 3
Materials: number cards 1–20 (2 sets)
calculator

The dealer draws 2 cards from the deck and places both card face up at the same time, saying, "Go." One player uses the calculator to find the sum. The other player uses mental math to find the sum. The dealer decides which player is the first to say the correct sum and gives that player both cards. If the players disagree on the correct sum, the dealer should check it, using the calculator. The winner is the player with more cards when all the cards have been played.

✔ **Talk About It**

1. In Example A, why is 7 broken into 2 and 5 instead of 1 and 6?

2. In Example B, how does knowing 4 + 31 = 35 help you find 26 + 35 mentally?

3. In Example B, how was the Associative (grouping) Property of addition used?

How can you use tens to help add mentally?

Example C	Example D
Find 33 + 9.	Find 45 + 28.
You know that 9 is just 1 less than 10. Adding 10 is easier than adding 9.	You know that 28 is just 2 less than 30. Adding 30 is easier than adding 28.
To add 9:	To add 28:
First, add 10.	First, add 30.
33 + 10 = 43	45 + 30 = 75
Then subtract 1.	Then subtract 2.
43 − 1 = 42	75 − 2 = 73
So, 33 + 9 = 42.	So, 45 + 28 = 73.

TEST TALK

Think It Through
I can **make a simpler problem** by adding 10 or a group of tens. Then I can adjust by subtracting.

✔ **Talk About It**

4. Lynette says, "To add 43 + 8, I can find 43 + 10 then subtract 1." Do you agree? Explain.

5. To find 14 + 19, you could first find 14 + 20 = 34. Then what should you do?

CHECK ✓

For another example, see Set 2-6 on p. 117.

Find each sum using mental math.

1. 35 + 8 **2.** 25 + 9 **3.** 57 + 6 **4.** 38 + 7

5. Number Sense Emily says, "To find 36 + 18, I can think of 18 as 4 + 14." What should Emily do next?

A Skills and Understanding

Find each sum using mental math.

6. 66 + 8   **7.** 18 + 9   **8.** 7 + 54

10. 48 + 17   **11.** 36 + 55   **12.** 75 + 15

14. 49 + 9   **15.** 77 + 18   **16.** 68 + 6

18. Number Sense How does knowing 13 = 4 + 9 help you find 36 + 13?

19. Number Sense How does knowing 38 = 40 − 2 help you find 17 + 38?

B Reasoning and Problem Solving

Math and Social Studies

In many countries, people learn to speak two or more languages. English is the main language used in 57 countries.

20. How many countries use English or French as the main language?

21. How many countries use Spanish or Portuguese as the main language?

22. How many more countries use French than Arabic?

23. Which language is the main language of the most countries?

24. How many more countries use English than Portuguese?

25. **Writing in Math** Is Lara's work at the right correct? If not, tell why and write a correct answer.

Data File

Main Langu

Language
English
French
Arabic
Spanish
Portuguese

Find 45 + 8.

I'll think of
45 + 5 + 3 =
45 + 5 = 50
50 + 8 = 58
So, 45 + 8 =

Lesson 2-9

Key Idea
You can use a simpler problem to help you subtract mentally.

Think It Through
I can change numbers to **make a simpler problem** when subtracting mentally.

WARM UP

1. 12 − 3   2. 7 − 4
3. 15 − 8   4. 11 − 7
5. 18 − 9   6. 13 − 6
7. There are 16 cats and 9 dogs in a pet parade. How many more cats than dogs are there?

Mental Math: Using Tens to Subtract

LEARN

How can you use tens to make a subtraction problem simpler?

Hannah and Thad used different ways to find 53 − 17.

Hannah's Way	**Thad's Way**
53 − 17 =	53 − 17 =
It's easier to subtract 20!	I will make a simpler problem by adding the same amount to each number.
53 − 20 = **33**	
But, 20 is **3** more than 17, so I will add **3** to 33, because I subtracted **3** more than 17.	I will add **3** to each number because 20 is **3** more than 17. It's easy to subtract 20.
33 + 3 = 36	53 − 17 = ↓+3 ↓+3 56 − 20 = 36
53 − 17 = 36	53 − 17 = 36

✓ Talk About It

1. Why did Hannah add 3 after she subtracted 20?

2. Why did Thad add 3 instead of 2 to each number?

3. What number could you add to each number in 53 − 15, to subtract mentally?

Take It to the NET
More Examples
www.scottforesman.com

CHECK ✓

For another example, see Set 2-9 on p. 118.

Find each difference using mental math.

1. 29 − 18   **2.** 32 − 19   **3.** 71 − 15   **4.** 42 − 27

5. Number Sense Find 63 − 49 using one of the methods above. Explain your answer.

Ⓐ Skills and Understanding

Find each difference using mental math.

6. 47 − 19   **7.** 53 − 38   **8.** 77 − 28   **9.** 50 − 37

10. 92 − 56   **11.** 23 − 9   **12.** 32 − 24   **13.** 87 − 78

14. Number Sense To solve 37 − 18, Eric changed the problem to 39 − 20 and gave the answer 19. Do you agree? Explain.

Ⓑ Reasoning and Problem Solving

For 15–18, use the pictograph. Remember to count by twos.

15. How many students have cats?

16. How many more students have dogs than cats?

17. How many more students have cats than fish?

18. If none of the fish owners also have hamsters, how many students own fish or hamsters?

19. Writing in Math Bonnie found 81 − 36 as shown at the right. Is her work correct? If not, explain what she did wrong and solve the problem correctly.

Carter School Students Who Own Pets

Cat	
Dog	
Fish	
Hamster	

Each 🧍 = 2 students.

81 − 36 = ?
81 − 40 = 41
Add 6, since I subtracted 6 more than 36.
41 + 6 = 47
So, 81 − 36 = 47

🦉 Mixed Review and Test Prep

Find each sum using mental math.

20. 35 + 11   **21.** 43 + 14   **22.** 76 + 12   **23.** 25 + 14

24. Which is most reasonable to say about the sum of 28 and 57?

A. Less than 70   **C.** Less than 90

B. Greater than 90   **D.** Greater than 100

All text pages available online and on CD-ROM.   **Section C Lesson 2-9**   **95**

Mental Math: Counting On to Subtract

WARM UP

1. 3 + ■ = 7
2. 2 + ■ = 5
3. 6 + ■ = 10
4. ■ + 8 = 15
5. ■ + 7 = 12

LEARN

How can you count on to subtract?

Example A

Find 70 − 36.

Count on to subtract mentally.

Think: 36 + ■ = 70   Think of the problem as a missing addend number sentence.

36, **37, 38, 39, 40**   From 36, count up to the next 10.
36 + **4** = 40

40, **50, 60, 70**   Then count by tens up to 70.
40 + **30** = 70

You counted on: **4 + 30 = 34**.

So, 70 − 36 = 34.

Example B

Find 48 − 19.

Think: 19 + ■ = 48

19, **20**   From 19, count up to the next 10.
19 + **1** = 20

20, **30, 40**   Then count by tens up to 40.
20 + **20** = 40

40 + **8** = 48   Then count up to 48

You counted on: **1 + 20 + 8 = 29**.

So, 48 − 19 = 29.

50
40
30
20
10

Think It Through
I can **think addition** to subtract.

✔ **Talk About It**

1. In Example A, why do you first count on 4?

2. How could you write a missing addend number sentence to solve 54 − 39?

Count on to find each difference mentally.

1. $50 - 28$ **2.** $42 - 18$ **3.** $61 - 45$ **4.** $60 - 17$

5. Number Sense To find $41 - 27$ mentally, Alice thinks: $27 + 3 = 30$ and $30 + 11 = 41$. What does she need to do next to find the difference?

PRACTICE

For more practice, see Set 2-10 on p. 123.

A Skills and Understanding

Count on to find each difference mentally.

6. $54 - 29$ **7.** $88 - 68$ **8.** $65 - 38$ **9.** $40 - 37$

10. $63 - 28$ **11.** $72 - 45$ **12.** $40 - 21$ **13.** $88 - 45$

14. Number Sense What subtraction problem could be solved by thinking about $35 + \blacksquare = 61$? Find the difference.

B Reasoning and Problem Solving

Algebra Count on to find the value of the missing number.

15. $72 + n = 85$ **16.** $22 + x = 72$ **17.** $52 + y = 70$

18. Candace has made 24 muffins. She needs to make 60 altogether. How many more does she need to make?

19. Kent worked on math homework for 35 minutes and on science homework for 28 minutes. How much time did he spend on math and science homework altogether?

20. Writing in Math Write two numbers with a difference of 24. Explain how you chose the numbers.

🦉 Mixed Review and Test Prep

Take It to the NET
Test Prep
www.scottforesman.com

21. Use mental math to find $68 - 19$.

22. Which sentence is NOT true?

   A. $527 > 563$ **C.** $193 > 96$

   B. $432 < 478$ **D.** $700 < 705$

TEST TALK

Think It Through
I need to **watch for important words** like NOT.

Key Idea
When you estimate differences, you change to numbers that you can subtract mentally.

Vocabulary
- compatible numbers (p. 86)
- front-end estimation (p. 86)

Think It Through
Since I don't need to know exactly how many tickets were left, I can **estimate**.

Estimating Differences

LEARN

WARM UP
Round to the nearest hundred.
1. 543   2. 156

Exact answer or estimate?

Marcy and her brother have 291 prize tickets. If they use their tickets to get a glow bracelet, will they have enough left to get a stuffed animal?

Prize List

Stuffed animal	119 tickets
Yo-yo	217 tickets
Mood ring	97 tickets
Glow bracelet	126 tickets

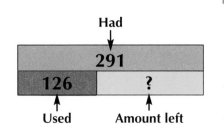

Had

291	
126	**?**

Used   Amount left

Estimate 291 − 126.

Then compare that estimate to 119.

How can you estimate differences?

Example A

Estimate 291 − 126.

One Way

Round each number to the nearest hundred.

$$\begin{array}{r} 291 \longrightarrow 300 \\ -126 \longrightarrow -100 \\ \hline 200 \end{array}$$

200 > 119

Another Way

Round each number to the nearest ten.

$$\begin{array}{r} 291 \longrightarrow 290 \\ -126 \longrightarrow -130 \\ \hline 160 \end{array}$$

160 > 119

Marcy and her brother have enough tickets.

Talk About It

1. Will you get a closer estimate of the difference if you round to the nearest ten or to the nearest hundred? Explain.

2. Estimate 148 − 89 by rounding to the nearest ten.

What are other ways to estimate differences?

Example B

Ella had 129 tickets. She bought a mood ring. Does she have enough tickets left for a glow bracelet?

Ramón used **compatible numbers.** Remember, these are numbers that are close but easy to subtract.

McKenzie used **front-end estimation.** She used the front digit of each number.

We agree! Ella does not have enough tickets for a glow bracelet.

$$\begin{array}{r} 129 \\ -\ 97 \\ \hline \end{array} \qquad \begin{array}{r} 125 \\ -100 \\ \hline 25 \end{array} \qquad \begin{array}{r} 129 \\ -\ 97 \\ \hline \end{array} \qquad \begin{array}{r} 100 \\ -\ 90 \\ \hline 10 \end{array}$$

$$25 < 126 \qquad\qquad 10 < 126$$

✔ Talk About It

3. In Example B, which method gives a closer estimate? How can you tell?

Take It to the NET
More Examples
www.scottforesman.com

CHECK ✔

For another example, see Set 2-11 on p. 119.

Round to the nearest hundred to estimate each difference.

1. 321 − 112   **2.** 255 − 189   **3.** 598 − 207   **4.** 277 − 111

Round to the nearest ten to estimate each difference.

5. 59 − 11   **6.** 163 − 47   **7.** 432 − 119   **8.** 225 − 98

Use any method to estimate each difference.

9. 102 − 76   **10.** 341 − 149   **11.** 312 − 105   **12.** 161 − 109

13. Reasonableness Jennifer estimated 312 − 197 and got 100. Is this reasonable? Explain.

A Skills and Understanding

Round to the nearest hundred to estimate each difference.

14. 168 − 86   **15.** 504 − 376   **16.** 655 − 376   **17.** 191 − 93

Round to the nearest ten to estimate each difference.

18. 88 − 32   **19.** 145 − 95   **20.** 361 − 117   **21.** 215 − 108

Use any method to estimate each difference.

22. 77 − 28   **23.** 202 − 144   **24.** 611 − 156   **25.** 312 − 205

26. Number Sense What compatible numbers could you use to estimate 342 − 153?

B Reasoning and Problem Solving

Math and Science

The Earth travels around the Sun in one year. The table shows the amount of time it takes six of the planets to orbit the Sun.

27. About how many more days does it take Mars to orbit the Sun than Earth?

28. Which of the 6 planets listed takes the longest to orbit the Sun?

29. About how many more days does it take Earth to orbit the Sun than Mercury?

30. About how much longer does it take Saturn to orbit the Sun than Jupiter?

Data File

Time it Takes for Planets to Orbit the Sun

Planet	How Long
Saturn	29 years
Jupiter	12 years
Mars	687 days
Earth	365 days
Venus	225 days
Mercury	88 days

A new planet called 2003UB313 was discovered October 21, 2003.

31. About how much longer does it take Mars to orbit the Sun than Venus?

32. Writing in Math Is Kevin's answer to the question below correct? If not, give a correct answer and explain.

> Is 700 − 215 greater than 500 or less than 500?
>
> I think 700 − 215 is greater than 500 because
> 700 − 200 = 500, and 215 is greater than 200.

C Extensions

33. Suppose you may spend $70 to buy school clothes. What three items could you buy without going over $70? Estimate to decide.

T-Shirt	$9
Jeans	$19
Zip Sweater	$28
Sneakers	$37
Hooded sweatshirt	$42

 Mixed Review and Test Prep

Take It to the NET
Test Prep
www.scottforesman.com

Count on to find each difference mentally.

34. 48 – 29   **35.** 63 – 37   **36.** 72 – 49   **37.** 56 – 28   **38.** 45 – 18

39. What is the value of the underlined digit?

2<u>8</u>4,649

A. 800   **B.** 8,000   **C.** 80,000   **D.** 800,000

Discovery CHANNEL SCHOOL™

Discover Math in Your World

Firefighters

The 3 ingredients for fire are fuel, oxygen, and heat. Firefighters know that they must remove a key ingredient to conquer a blaze. They usually try to get rid of the heat.

1. Suppose when it first bursts into flames, a fire is 580°F. After burning 5 minutes, the temperature of the fire is 1,190°F. Estimate the number of degrees the fire has increased.

2. To endure the heat, firefighters wear protective gear that weighs about 40 pounds. If a suited-up firefighter weighs 220 pounds, how can you use mental math to find the firefighter's weight without the gear?

Take It to the NET
Video and Activities
www.scottforesman.com

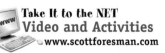

Problem-Solving Skill

Key Idea
There are specific things you can do to write a good explanation in math.

Think It Through
I should **identify steps in a process** and write the steps in order so my explanation is clear and easy to follow.

Writing to Explain

LEARN

How do you write a good explanation?

When you write to explain an estimate, you need to tell the reasons why you made your estimation.

Stamps To solve this problem you must ESTIMATE. Do NOT find the exact answer. If you bought two rolls of the stamps shown, would the cost be less than $100? Explain how you made your estimate.

Each roll of flag stamps: $37

Writing a Math Explanation

- Write your explanation in steps to make it clear.

- Tell what the numbers mean in your explanation.

- Tell why you took certain steps.

The cost would be less than $100.
Step 1   I rounded $37 to $40 and estimated the cost of 2 rolls.
          $40 + $40 = $80.
Step 2 $80 is less than $100.

✔ Talk About It

1. What numbers did you use to explain your estimate?

2. Explain why you can estimate to solve this problem.

1. Certain packages that weigh up to one pound can be mailed for $3.85. Wanda sent 3 of these packages and paid the postage with a ten-dollar bill and a five-dollar bill. Estimate to decide if she had enough money left for a $3 lunch. Explain how you made your estimate.

PRACTICE

For more practice, see Set 2-12 on p. 123.

Write to explain.

Menu	
Hamburger	$3.98
Drink	$0.85
Pie	$2.09

2. Elaine and two friends bought 3 hamburgers and 3 drinks. If they pay for the food with a $20 bill, will they receive change? Explain how you made your estimate.

3. Wilber has $6. Can he buy a hamburger, a drink and a piece of pie? Explain how you made your estimate.

4. Explain one way you can find 26 + 29 using mental math.

5. Explain why a 0 is needed to write the number shown by the place-value blocks.

6. Is Kelly's work correct? Explain.

> 124 is the same as
> 1 hundred, 2 tens, 4 ones
> or 12 tens, 4 ones

7. Children dressing in patriotic costumes for the 4th of July parade are grouped according to age. Norm is in Group D. How old might Norm be? How did you decide?

Section	Ages
A	2 to 4 years
B	5 to 7 years
C	8 to 10 years
D	?

For 8–9, use the Bottle Caps problem.

8. Explain why it would be better to round to the nearest ten than to the nearest hundred to solve this problem.

9. Give the estimated answer to the problem. Then use mental math to find the exact answer. Explain your methods for estimation and mental math.

Bottle Caps Ed collected 783 bottle caps. Jan collected 759 bottle caps. About how many more did Ed collect?

Problem-Solving Applications

Fire Trucks In colonial days, people fought fires with buckets of water. Modern firefighters have many types of equipment to use. The aerial-ladder truck is perhaps their most familiar and powerful tool.

Trivia Most fire stations no longer have poles because many firefighters were injured when they slid down the poles too quickly. Instead, most firefighters just use the stairs!

1 Ashley is 8 years old. In 8 more years she will be old enough to become a junior firefighter. How old must she be to become a junior firefighter?

2 A ladder truck may weigh 56,237 pounds. Write the word form of this number.

3 The first popular aerial ladder was 20 feet shorter than this modern 105-foot ladder. Use mental math to find the height of the early ladder.

Key Facts
Ladder Truck

• Truck width	8 feet
• Truck length	37 feet
• Maximum ladder height	105 feet
• Seating	6 people
• Water spray per minute	1,500 gallons
• Hose length	1,000 feet
• Hose width	5 inches

Good News/Bad News
Aerial-ladder trucks are quite useful in battling blazes, but they are very expensive. A new truck may cost as much as $850,000!

Using Key Facts

4 A hose runs along the ladder to a special nozzle at the top. How much water can the truck spray in one minute? Write the word form of this number.

5 Estimate the difference between the truck's length and width. Explain how you estimated.

6 <u>Writing in Math</u> Write your own word problem involving fire trucks. Write the answer in a complete sentence.

7 **Decision Making** Suppose you used a $20 bill to buy 2 models of fire-department vehicles. Which models would you buy? How much change would you get?

Model	Price
Pumper	$5
Aerial ladder	$8
Fire-chief car	$4
Rescue unit	$6

Do You Know How?

Do You Understand?

Mental Math: Using Tens to Subtract (2-9)
Mental Math: Counting On to Subtract (2-10)

Find each difference using mental math.

1. 65 − 29   **2.** 57 − 38

3. 90 − 35   **4.** 78 − 49

Ⓐ How can you use tens to solve Exercise 1?

Ⓑ Explain how you found your answer for Exercise 4.

Estimating Differences (2-11)

Round to the nearest hundred to estimate each difference.

5. 291 − 118   **6.** 627 − 483

Round to the nearest ten to estimate each difference.

7. 79 − 22   **8.** 375 − 219

Use any method to estimate each difference.

9. 495 − 326   **10.** 84 − 59

Ⓒ In Exercise 5, what would your estimate be if you rounded to the nearest ten?

Ⓓ In Exercise 8 what would your estimate be if you rounded to the nearest hundred?

Ⓔ What methods did you use for Exercises 9 and 10?

Problem-Solving Skill: Writing to Explain (2-12)

To solve this problem, estimate.

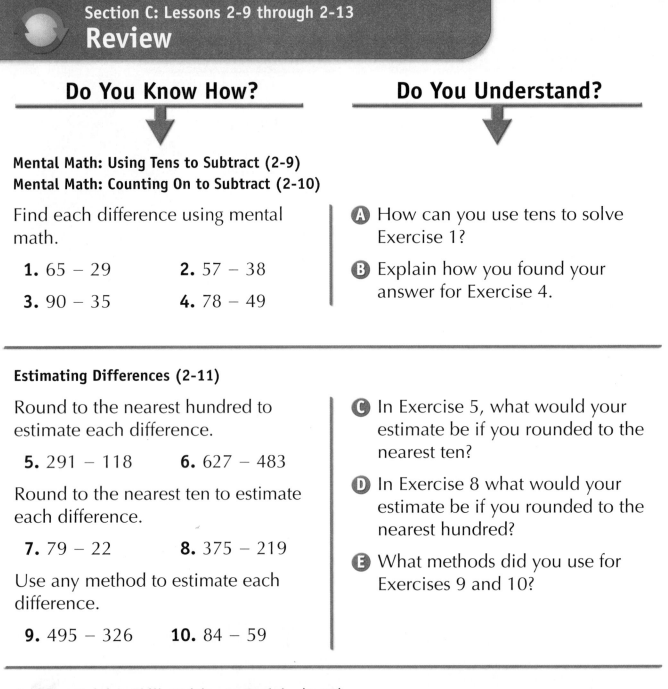

Baseballs: $6.99
Baseball bats: $11.95
Baseball gloves: $24.85

11. Tony wants a baseball, a bat, and a glove. Would the cost be less than $50? Explain how you made your estimate.

Ⓕ What numbers did you use to explain your estimate?

Ⓖ Tell what the numbers you used in your explanation mean.

MULTIPLE CHOICE

1. Laurie plans vacations for a travel agency. For the winter months, she has divided the United States into regions as shown in the table. Which of the following could be a temperature in Region 4? (2-12)

Region	Temperature
1	85° and above
2	65° to 84°
3	45° to 64°
4	?

A. 50°   **B.** 90°   **C.** 30°   **D.** 70°

2. On Tuesday, Cal spent 28 minutes on math homework and 43 minutes on science homework. How much more time did he spend on science than on math? Use mental math. (2-9)

A. 5 minutes   **B.** 15 minutes   **C.** 25 minutes   **D.** 71 minutes

FREE RESPONSE

Find each difference using mental math. (2-9, 2-10)

3. 80 − 27   **4.** 67 − 32   **5.** 90 − 56   **6.** 54 − 39

7. 63 − 18   **8.** 45 − 27   **9.** 82 − 63   **10.** 92 − 48

Round to the nearest hundred to estimate each difference. (2-11)

11. 398 − 129   **12.** 617 − 263   **13.** 924 − 705   **14.** 236 − 145

Round to the nearest ten to estimate each difference. (2-11)

15. 275 − 93   **16.** 48 − 19   **17.** 745 − 98   **18.** 173 − 85

19. 515 − 121   **20.** 39 − 17   **21.** 110 − 88   **22.** 403 − 367

Writing in Math

For 23–25, use the Hike problem. (2-12, 2-13)

Hike Two friends hiked alongside a waterfall. It took them 124 minutes to hike up and 105 minutes to hike down. About how long did they hike?

Think It Through
I need to give a **brief but complete explanation.**

23. Why can you estimate to solve this problem?

24. Estimate how long the friends hiked. Explain how you made your estimate.

25. What operation did you use when you estimated? Why?

Test-Taking Strategies

Understand the question.

Get information for the answer.

Plan how to find the answer.

Make smart choices.

Use writing in math.

Improve written answers.

Get Information for the Answer

After you understand a test question, you need to get information for the answer. Some test questions do not contain all the information you need in the text. You may need to look for more information in a picture, map, diagram, table, or graph.

1. Karen made this table to show the number of moons each planet has.

Planet Moons

Planet	Number of Moons
Mercury	0
Venus	0
Earth	1
Mars	2
Jupiter	16
Saturn	18
Uranus	21
Neptune	8
Pluto	1

Which of the following can be used to find out how many moons Jupiter and Saturn have all together?

A. 16 + 18 =

B. 18 − 16 =

C. 16 + 16 =

D. 16 − 18 =

Understand the question.

I need to choose the number sentence that can be used to find how many moons Jupiter and Saturn have in all.

Get information for the answer.

• Look for important information in the text.

In this problem, the text does not contain any numbers I need to find my answer.

• Look for important information in pictures, maps, diagrams, tables, or graphs.

The table shows me that Jupiter has 16 moons, and Saturn has 18 moons. I need this information to choose the correct number sentence.

2. The leaf is covering some of the acorns that are on the ground.

Which of the following could be a reasonable answer for the total number of acorns?

A. fewer than 10

B. more than 50

C. between 25 and 50

D. between 15 and 20

> **Think It Through**
> The **text** tells me that the leaf is covering some of the acorns. The **picture** shows that 10 acorns are not covered, so I know there are more than 10 acorns. The size of the leaf tells me that it is probably covering fewer than 10 acorns.

Now it's your turn.

For each problem, tell what information is needed to solve the problem.

3. The label is covering some of of the ants in the ant farm.

Which of the following could be a reasonable answer for the total number of ants?

A. about 15

B. about 25

C. fewer than 15

D. more than 50

4. Jake and some friends are canoeing the entire length of Moon Valley River. The first day they traveled 15 miles.

Which of the following could be used to determine how much farther they have to go?

A. $79 + 15 = $ ▨

B. $15 - 79 = $ ▨

C. $15 + 79 = $ ▨

D. $79 - 15 = $ ▨

Key Vocabulary and Concept Review

Self Check

Use properties and fact families to find sums and differences. (Lessons 2-1, 2-2, 2-3)

Use addition properties.

Commutative (order) Property of Addition

$2 + 7 = 7 + 2$

Associative (grouping) Property of Addition

$4 + (6 + 2) = (4 + 6) + 2$

Identity (zero) Property of Addition

$8 + 0 = 8$

Use a **fact family.**

$6 + 4 = 10$ $10 - 4 = 6$

$4 + 6 = 10$ $10 - 6 = 4$

addends   sum   difference

1. Copy and complete the table. Then write the rule.

In	5	4	8		6
Out	7	6	10	2	

> *My uncle takes the commuter train both ways to work.*
>
> The **Commutative (order) Property of Addition** *says you can add in any order (p. 66)*

Self Check

Use mental math to find sums and differences. (Lessons 2-5, 2-6, 2-9, 2-10)

Break apart numbers.

$47 + 8 = $ ▨   Break apart 8 to make a ten.

$47 + \mathbf{8}$

$47 + 3 + 5$

$50 + 5 = 55$

So, $47 + 8 = 55$.

Use tens.

$34 + 18 = $ ▨

$34 + \mathbf{20} = 54$ Add 20.

$54 - \mathbf{2} = 52$ Then subtract 2.

So, $34 + 18 = 52$.

Count on. $53 - 29 = $ ▨

29 30 40 50 51 52 53

1   10   10   1   1   1

You counted on
$1 + 20 + 3 = 24$.

So, $53 - 29 = 24$.

2. Use mental math to find $64 + 13$ and $78 - 25$.

> *My aunt belongs to a group called the Nurses Association.*
>
> The **Associative (grouping) Property of Addition** *says you can group addends in any way and the sum will be the same. (p. 67)*

People who are easy to get along with are compatible.

Compatible numbers are numbers that are easy to compute with. (p. 87)

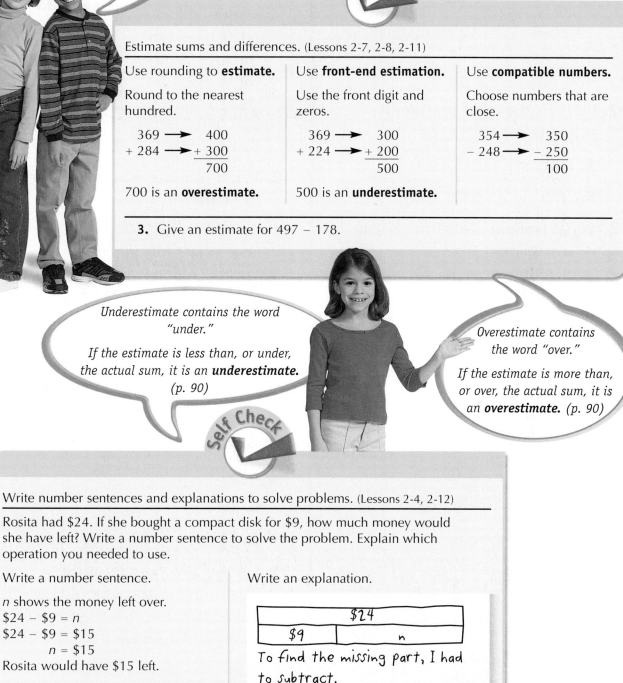

Estimate sums and differences. (Lessons 2-7, 2-8, 2-11)

Use rounding to **estimate.**	Use **front-end estimation.**	Use **compatible numbers.**
Round to the nearest hundred.	Use the front digit and zeros.	Choose numbers that are close.

Use rounding to **estimate.**

Round to the nearest hundred.

$$369 \longrightarrow 400$$
$$+ 284 \longrightarrow + 300$$
$$\overline{ 700}$$

700 is an **overestimate.**

Use **front-end estimation.**

Use the front digit and zeros.

$$369 \longrightarrow 300$$
$$+ 224 \longrightarrow + 200$$
$$\overline{ 500}$$

500 is an **underestimate.**

Use **compatible numbers.**

Choose numbers that are close.

$$354 \longrightarrow 350$$
$$- 248 \longrightarrow - 250$$
$$\overline{ 100}$$

3. Give an estimate for 497 − 178.

Underestimate contains the word "under."

If the estimate is less than, or under, the actual sum, it is an **underestimate.** (p. 90)

Overestimate contains the word "over."

If the estimate is more than, or over, the actual sum, it is an **overestimate.** (p. 90)

Write number sentences and explanations to solve problems. (Lessons 2-4, 2-12)

Rosita had $24. If she bought a compact disk for $9, how much money would she have left? Write a number sentence to solve the problem. Explain which operation you needed to use.

Write a number sentence.

n shows the money left over.
$\$24 - \$9 = n$
$\$24 - \$9 = \$15$
$\quad\quad n = \$15$
Rosita would have $15 left.

Write an explanation.

$24	
$9	n

To find the missing part, I had to subtract.

4. Joseph bought a new bike for $158 and a new helmet for $36. How much did Joseph spend in all?

Answers: 1. Table entries: 0, 8; Add 2. 2. 77; 53 3. Sample answer: 300 4. $194

MULTIPLE CHOICE

1. What is the missing number in 7 + ▢ = 15?

A. 5   **C.** 8

B. 7   **D.** 9

2. What is the most reasonable estimate for 612 − 390?

A. 100   **C.** 300

B. 200   **D.** 400

3. What is the missing number in 8 + ▢ + 3 = 12?

A. 1   **C.** 4

B. 3   **D.** 5

4. Find 29 + 45 using mental math.

A. 64   **C.** 74

B. 70   **D.** 75

5. Find 25 + 8 using mental math.

A. 28   **C.** 35

B. 33   **D.** 38

6. Round to the nearest ten to estimate 107 + 289.

A. 380   **C.** 400

B. 390   **D.** 410

7. Round to the nearest hundred to estimate 355 + 490.

A. 500   **C.** 850

B. 800   **D.** 900

8. Which number sentence is NOT a part of the fact family for 9 + 5 = 14?

Think It Through
- I'll **watch for words** like NOT.
- I need to **read each answer choice carefully.**

A. 14 + 5 = 19   **C.** 5 + 9 = 14

B. 14 − 5 = 9   **D.** 14 − 9 = 5

9. What number would complete the table?

In	6	8	2	7	5
Out	14		10	15	13

A. 0   **B.** 8   **C.** 12   **D.** 16

10. Kathleen has $13 to spend. She buys a T-shirt that costs $7. How much does she have left over? Find the number sentence you could use to solve the problem.

A. $13 + $7 = n

B. $13 − $7 = n

C. $7 − n = $13

D. $13 + n = $7

11. Lee had 15 pencils at the beginning of the school year. He gave away 6 to his friends. How many did he have left?

A. 9   **C.** 16

B. 10   **D.** 21

Estimate each sum. Then tell whether each estimate is an overestimate or an underestimate.

12. 34 + 51   **13.** 15 + 47

Find each sum using mental math.

14. 28 + 54   **15.** 19 + 48

Copy and complete each fact family.

16. 3 + 9 = ▨   12 − ▨ = 3

   ▨ + 3 = 12   12 − ▨ = 9

17. 2 + 7 = ▨   9 − 2 = ▨

   7 + ▨ = 9   9 − 7 = ▨

18. Write the fact family for 5, 6, and 11.

Find each difference using mental math.

19. 91 − 27   **20.** 48 − 32

21. 69 − 25   **22.** 77 − 50

Round to the nearest hundred to estimate each difference.

23. 166 − 97   **24.** 549 − 451

Round to the nearest ten to estimate each sum.

25. 9 + 82   **26.** 78 + 119

27. Bill and Molly are painting their house. The house has 13 rooms. Bill painted 6 rooms. How many rooms must Molly paint? Explain how you got your answer.

Writing in Math

28. Gail has $70. She wants to buy a pair of jeans for $37.99 and a pair of sneakers for $44.95. Does she have enough money? Estimate to decide. Explain how you estimated.

> **Think It Through**
> • I need to **explain how I solved the problem.**
> • My writing should be **brief but complete.**

29. Mary's class needs to raise $300 for a field trip. They held a bake sale that made $169. Then they raised $170 by washing cars. Do they have enough money? Estimate. Write a similar problem for a friend to solve.

30. Look for the pattern. Describe the rule and write the missing numbers to complete the table. Then create your own table that follows a rule.

In	12	5	16	9	13
Out	7		11		8

Number and Operation

MULTIPLE CHOICE

1. Round to the nearest ten to estimate 145 + 23.

   A. 100   **B.** 120   **C.** 160   **D.** 170

2. What is the value of the 6 in 375,609?

   A. 60   **C.** 6,000

   B. 600   **D.** 60,000

3. Use mental math to find 41 + 22.

   A. 19   **C.** 60

   B. 42   **D.** 63

   TEST TALK

   Think It Through
   I should **choose the most reasonable answer.**

FREE RESPONSE

4. Find 67 − 33 using mental math.

5. Fred bought a hot dog for $1.27. He gave the cashier $2.00. How much change did he get back?

6. Write 500 + 70 + 3 in standard form.

7. Round to the nearest hundred to estimate 576 − 390.

Writing in Math

8. Ann needs to practice the piano for 90 minutes total. She practices for 23 minutes on Monday and 38 minutes on Tuesday. Has she practiced long enough? Explain.

Geometry and Measurement

MULTIPLE CHOICE

9. Which object is more than 1 meter long?

   A. A pencil

   B. A car

   C. A grasshopper

   D. Your math book

10. What solid figure is shown at the right?

    A. cone   **C.** sphere

    B. cylinder   **D.** pyramid

FREE RESPONSE

11. How many quarts are in a gallon?

12. Name two objects you could use to trace a rectangle.

13. Name a shape that has fewer than 4 sides.

Writing in Math

14. Jeremy says the perimeter of this polygon is 18 cm. Is he correct? Explain.

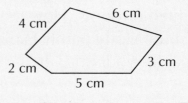

Data Analysis and Probability

MULTIPLE CHOICE

Use the bar graph for 15 and 16.

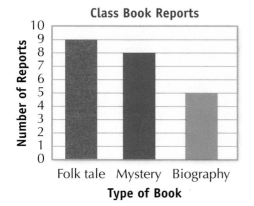

Class Book Reports

15. How many students wrote a report on a mystery book?

A. 5 **B.** 7 **C.** 8 **D.** 9

16. How many more reports were on folk tale books than biographies?

A. 1 **B.** 3 **C.** 4 **D.** 5

FREE RESPONSE

Use the pictograph for 17 and 18.

Science Fair Project

Weather	🗄️ 🗄️ 🗄️ 🗄️
Animals	🗄️ 🗄️
Insects	🗄️

Each 🗄️ = 1 project.

17. How many projects were about weather?

18. How many projects were in the science fair all together?

Writing in Math

19. Explain how you found the answer to Exercise 17.

Algebra

MULTIPLE CHOICE

20. Find the missing number:
$15 = \blacksquare + (4 + 5)$

A. 6 **B.** 9 **C.** 15 **D.** 23

21. Complete the pattern.

120, 115, 110, ▪, ▪, ▪

A. 115, 105, 90 **C.** 100, 85, 70

B. 105, 100, 95 **D.** 90, 85, 80

22. What is the rule for this table?

In	6	13	11	19
Out	13	20	18	26

A. Add 6 **C.** Subtract 7

B. Add 7 **D.** Subtract 8

FREE RESPONSE

23. Julie scored 76 in miniature golf on Saturday. She scored 63 on Sunday. How much lower was her score on Sunday than on Saturday? Write a number sentence and solve.

24. Brandon collected 15 stamps the first month. After the second month, he had 42 stamps. How many stamps did he collect in the second month?

Writing in Math

25. Create a table that shows a pattern. Then write the rule your table follows.

Set 2-1 (pages 66–69)

Find $(2 + 7) + 1$.

The Associative Property of Addition states that you can group addends in any way and the sum will be the same.

$(2 + 7) + 1 = 2 + (7 + 1)$

$9 + 1 = 2 + 8$

$10 = 10$

The Commutative Property of Addition states that you can add numbers in any order and the sum will be the same.

$4 + 6 = 6 + 4$

$10 = 10$

Remember that the sum of any number and zero is that same number.

Find each sum.

1. $4 + (8 + 3)$ **2.** $(1 + 3) + 0$

Write each missing number.

3. $9 + \blacksquare = 9$

4. $6 + 4 = \blacksquare + 6$

5. $(2 + 3) + 5 = 2 + (3 + \blacksquare)$

Set 2-2 (pages 70–71)

Copy and complete the fact family.

Think about parts and the whole.

$2 + \mathbf{8} = 10$ $10 - \mathbf{8} = \mathbf{2}$

$\mathbf{8} + 2 = 10$ $10 - \mathbf{2} = 8$

Find $10 - \blacksquare = 8$.

What You Think   What You Write

$8 + \blacksquare = 10$

$8 + \mathbf{2} = 10$ $10 - 2 = 8$

Remember you can use the related addition or subtraction facts you know to solve a problem.

Copy and complete the fact family.

1. $3 + 4 = \blacksquare$ $7 - \blacksquare = 3$

    $\blacksquare + 3 = 7$ $\blacksquare - 3 = 4$

Find each missing number.

2. $\blacksquare + 5 = 12$ **3.** $6 - \blacksquare = 1$

Set 2-3 (pages 72–73)

Copy and complete the table.

In	5	7	2	9	10
Out	9	11	6		

Look for a pattern.

$5 + \blacksquare = 9$ $5 + \mathbf{4} = 9$
$7 + \blacksquare = 11$ $7 + \mathbf{4} = 11$
$2 + \blacksquare = 6$ $2 + \mathbf{4} = 6$

Write the pattern as a rule. **Add 4.**

$9 + 4 = 13$

$10 + 4 = 14$

Remember that the rule must work for each pair of numbers in the table.

Copy and complete each table. Then write a rule for the table.

1.

In	13	10	7	9	12
Out	6	3	0		

2.

In	3	7	4	1	5
Out	11		12		13

When you write a number sentence to solve a problem, follow these steps.

Step 1: Show the main idea.

Step 2: Decide which operation fits the main idea.

Step 3: Use a letter to show what you are trying to find.

Step 4: Solve the number sentence.

Remember to look back and check to make sure your answer is reasonable.

Write a number sentence, then solve.

1. Carol had $25. She bought a compact disc for $13. How much money did she have left?

2. Glen washed 3 red shirts, 6 blue shirts, and 4 white shirts. How many shirts did he wash in all?

Use mental math to find $38 + 21$.

Break apart numbers into tens and ones.

$38 = 30 + 8$ $21 = 20 + 1$

Add the tens.   Add the ones.

$30 + 20 = 50$ $8 + 1 = 9$

Put the tens and ones together.

$50 + 9 = 59$

So $38 + 21 = 59$.

Remember to use place value when you break apart numbers.

Find each sum using mental math.

1. $30 + 56$	**2.** $45 + 19$
3. $83 + 11$	**4.** $39 + 31$
5. $25 + 16$	**6.** $66 + 33$
7. $79 + 15$	**8.** $27 + 17$
9. $54 + 27$	**10.** $19 + 13$

Find $48 + 9$ using mental math.

Make a ten.

Think of 9 as $2 + 7$.

$48 + 2 + 7$ is the same as

$\quad\downarrow$

$\quad 50 \quad + 7$

So $48 + 9 = 57$.

Remember that you can break numbers apart to make a ten.

Find each sum using mental math.

1. $35 + 7$	**2.** $68 + 5$
3. $78 + 6$	**4.** $14 + 9$
5. $26 + 18$	**6.** $45 + 12$
7. $58 + 7$	**8.** $37 + 18$

Set 2-7 (pages 86–89)

Estimate 478 + 134.

One Way:
Round to the nearest ten.

$$478 \rightarrow 480$$
$$+\ 134 \rightarrow +\ 130$$
$$610$$

Another Way:
Use front-end estimation.

$$478 \rightarrow 400$$
$$+\ 134 \rightarrow +\ 100$$
$$500$$

Third Way:
Use compatible numbers.

$$478 \rightarrow 470$$
$$+\ 134 \rightarrow +\ 130$$
$$600$$

Remember to think about which method would give the best estimate for each problem.

Use any method to estimate each sum.

1. 167 + 98   **2.** 211 + 164

3. 485 + 184   **4.** 362 + 615

5. 190 + 352   **6.** 572 + 125

7. 298 + 442   **8.** 701 + 110

Set 2-8 (pages 90–91)

Estimate 598 + 169 by rounding. Tell whether the estimate is an overestimate or underestimate.

Round to the nearest hundred to estimate the sum.

598 rounds to 600   600
169 rounds to 200   + 200
                            800

Each addend was rounded to the greater hundred, so the estimated sum, 800, is **greater than** the actual sum. It is an **overestimate**.

Remember that rounding each addend to the lesser ten or hundred means that your estimate will be an underestimate.

Estimate each sum by rounding. Then tell whether each estimate is an overestimate or an underestimate.

1. 34 + 71   **2.** 132 + 721

3. 476 + 587   **4.** 613 + 204

5. 207 + 819   **6.** 356 + 579

Set 2-9 (pages 94–95)

Use mental math to find 75 − 18.

Change numbers to make a simpler problem.

20 is 2 more than 18.

75 − 20 = 55.

Then add 2 because 2 too many were subtracted.

55 + 2 = 57.

So 75 − 18 = 57.

Remember that you can add the same amount to each number before subtracting.

Find each difference using mental math.

1. 56 − 14   **2.** 31 − 5

3. 74 − 12   **4.** 97 − 34

5. 73 − 67   **6.** 55 − 13

7. 99 − 53   **8.** 80 − 51

Find 80 − 34.

Count on to subtract mentally.

Think: 34 + ▨ = 80.

34 + 6 = 40

40 + 40 = 80

You counted on: 6 + 40 = **46**.

So, 80 − 34 = **46**.

Remember that you can think of addition when you subtract.

Count on to find each difference mentally.

1. 63 − 27 **2.** 81 − 22 **3.** 55 − 29

4. 80 − 46 **5.** 77 − 12 **6.** 98 − 64

7. 69 − 18 **8.** 50 − 35 **9.** 24 − 13

Estimate 486 − 177.

One Way

Round each number to the nearest hundred.

$$\begin{array}{r} 486 \longrightarrow 500 \\ -\ 177 \longrightarrow -\ 200 \\ \hline 300 \end{array}$$

Another Way

Round each number to the nearest ten.

$$\begin{array}{r} 486 \longrightarrow 490 \\ -\ 177 \longrightarrow -\ 180 \\ \hline 310 \end{array}$$

Remember to check place value when rounding to the nearest ten or hundred.

Round to the nearest hundred to estimate each difference.

1. 367 − 319 **2.** 732 − 110

Round to the nearest ten to estimate each difference.

3. 78 − 54 **4.** 932 − 27

When you explain your answer:

- Write your explanation in steps to make it clear.
- Tell what the numbers mean in your explanation.
- Tell why you took certain steps.

Remember that you should be able to explain each step you followed.

Katie sold 76 pizzas for a fund-raiser. Troy sold 59 pizzas. About how many more pizzas did Katie sell?

1. Is an exact answer or estimate needed? Explain.

2. What operation should you use? Why?

3. What is the answer? Explain how you found it.

Set 2-1 (pages 66–69)

Find each sum.

1. 4 + (2 + 6)　　　　**2.** (5 + 3) + 2　　　　**3.** 6 + (8 + 0)

4. 5 + 8 + 9　　　　　**5.** (0 + 8) + 7　　　　**6.** 1 + (2 + 5)

Write each missing number.

7. 0 + ▦ = 8　　　　**8.** ▦ + 2 = 2 + 6　　　　**9.** 19 = ▦ + (8 + 4)

10. 7 + 6 = ▦ + 7　　**11.** 5 + ▦ = 5　　　　**12.** (4 + ▦) + 6 = 11

13. (2 + 8) + 9 = 8 + (▦ + 2)　　　　**14.** 7 + (2 + 3) = 7 + ▦

15. Does (4 + 1) + 6 = 5 + 6? Explain.

Set 2-2 (pages 70–71)

Copy and complete each fact family.

1. 6 + 5 = ▦　　11 − ▦ = 6　　　**2.** ▦ + 3 = 12　　12 − ▦ = 9

　　　▦ + 6 = 11　　▦ − 6 = 5　　　　　3 + ▦ = 12　　12 − ▦ = 3

Find each missing number.

3. 6 + ▦ = 9　　　　**4.** ▦ + 8 = 8　　　　**5.** 5 + ▦ = 12

6. ▦ + 3 = 11　　　**7.** 18 − ▦ = 9　　　**8.** 10 − ▦ = 2

9. 0 + ▦ = 6　　　　**10.** ▦ + 7 = 13　　　**11.** 14 − ▦ = 7

12. ▦ + 2 = 11　　　**13.** 17 − ▦ = 8　　　**14.** 5 + ▦ = 12

15. Write the fact family for 4, 5, and 9.

Set 2-3 (pages 72–73)

Copy and complete each table. Then write a rule for the table.

1.

In	7	10	8	12	4
Out	3	6	4		

2.

In	20	15	30	25	5
Out	30	25	40		

3.

In	6	3	10	7	9
Out	15		19		18

4.

In	200	150	300	500	450
Out	150	100		450	

5. Paul put in 12 and got 6 out. Then he put in 10 and got 4 out. What rule was he using?

Take It to the NET
More Practice
www.scottforesman.com

Set 2-4 (pages 76–77)

Write a number sentence to solve each problem. Then write the answer in a complete sentence.

1. Jim has $12. If he buys a yo-yo for $5, how much money will he have left?

2. Phil caught 7 fish in the morning and 4 in the afternoon. How many fish did he catch in all?

3. Sue's basketball team scored a total of 57 points. Sue's team scored 21 points in the first half. How many points did Sue's team score in the second half?

4. There were 23 books on the shelf and 9 books on the table. How many books are there altogether?

5. Kathy ran for 5 minutes, walked for 2 minutes, ran for 5 minutes, walked for 2 minutes, and so on, until she had run for 20 minutes. How many minutes did she exercise in all?

Set 2-5 (pages 80–81)

Find each sum using mental math.

1. 45 + 19	**2.** 31 + 66	**3.** 56 + 13	**4.** 29 + 49
5. 16 + 50	**6.** 74 + 25	**7.** 75 + 22	**8.** 46 + 38
9. 24 + 61	**10.** 20 + 37	**11.** 63 + 32	**12.** 19 + 67

13. To add 47 + 26, Tom first thought, "47 + 20." What numbers should he add next?

Set 2-6 (pages 82–85)

Find each sum using mental math.

1. 9 + 28	**2.** 5 + 67	**3.** 14 + 74
4. 36 + 19	**5.** 77 + 55	**6.** 13 + 89
7. 8 + 65	**8.** 35 + 67	**9.** 58 + 12
10. 25 + 76	**11.** 43 + 58	**12.** 27 + 33
13. 19 + 72	**14.** 39 + 49	**15.** 32 + 18

16. How does knowing 26 = 30 − 4 help you find 7 + 26?

Set 2-7 (pages 86–89)

Round to the nearest hundred to estimate each sum.

1. 136 + 196   **2.** 408 + 67   **3.** 388 + 213

4. 544 + 381   **5.** 149 + 251   **6.** 716 + 199

Round to the nearest ten to estimate each sum.

7. 15 + 61   **8.** 37 + 89   **9.** 21 + 168

10. 361 + 566   **11.** 84 + 91   **12.** 218 + 315

Use any method to estimate each sum.

13. 150 + 65   **14.** 83 + 99   **15.** 425 + 79

16. 387 + 601   **17.** 291 + 223   **18.** 226 + 513

19. Olga estimated 86 + 221 and got 400. Is this answer reasonable? Explain.

Set 2-8 (pages 90–91)

Estimate each sum by rounding. Then tell whether each estimate is an overestimate or an underestimate.

1. 36 + 48   **2.** 14 + 22   **3.** 78 + 99

4. 44 + 104   **5.** 456 + 399   **6.** 151 + 821

7. Is it reasonable to say the sum of $104 and $121 is less than $200? Explain.

8. Karen's family is going to drive to Florida, 500 miles away. So far they have driven 383 miles. Karen estimates they have about 100 miles left to drive. Do you agree? Explain.

Set 2-9 (pages 94–95)

Find each difference using mental math.

1. 89 − 25   **2.** 26 − 14   **3.** 91 − 33

4. 69 − 31   **5.** 43 − 27   **6.** 77 − 52

7. 98 − 56   **8.** 64 − 17   **9.** 51 − 28

10. 36 − 15   **11.** 89 − 22   **12.** 73 − 27

13. To solve 54 − 26, Pat changed the problem to 58 − 30 and gave the answer 28. Do you agree? Explain.

Take It to the NET
More Practice
www.scottforesman.com

Set 2-10 (pages 96–97)

Count on to find each difference mentally.

1. $31 - 14$ **2.** $60 - 22$ **3.** $57 - 23$ **4.** $79 - 33$

Algebra Count on to find the value of the missing number.

5. $19 + n = 46$ **6.** $37 + y = 84$ **7.** $44 + x = 61$

8. What subtraction problem could be solved by thinking about $24 + \blacksquare = 53$?

Set 2-11 (pages 98–101)

Round to the nearest hundred to estimate each difference.

1. $214 - 171$ **2.** $688 - 232$ **3.** $310 - 198$ **4.** $673 - 355$

Round to the nearest ten to estimate each difference.

5. $67 - 11$ **6.** $64 - 23$ **7.** $191 - 38$ **8.** $356 - 141$

Use any method to estimate each difference.

9. $85 - 34$ **10.** $699 - 413$ **11.** $263 - 89$

12. What compatible numbers could you use to estimate $226 - 93$?

Set 2-12 (pages 102–103)

At T-shirts Galore, a sweatshirt costs $37 and a T-shirt costs $19. How much more does a sweatshirt cost than a T-shirt?

1. Is an exact answer or an estimate needed? Explain.

2. What operation is needed to solve this problem? Why?

3. What is the answer?

Bill collected 189 marbles. Linda collected 265 marbles. About how many more did Linda collect?

4. Explain why it would be better to round to the nearest ten than to the nearest hundred to solve this problem.

5. Give the estimated answer to the problem. Then use mental math to find the exact answer. Explain your methods for estimation and mental math.

CHAPTER 3

Adding and Subtracting

A Vocabulary
(pages 66, 70, and 86)

1. In 4 + 6 = 10, the 4 and 6 are __?__.

2. In 16 − 7 = 9, the 9 is the __?__.

3. In 9 + 8 = 17, the 17 is the __?__.

4. An __?__ will give you an answer that is close to the exact answer.

Vocabulary

- **difference** *(p. 70)*
- **sum** *(p. 66)*
- **addends** *(p. 66)*
- **estimate** *(p. 86)*

B Addition and Subtraction Facts
(Grade 2)

5. 3 + 9   **6.** 7 + 8   **7.** 5 + 5

8. 3 + 8   **9.** 6 + 6   **10.** 9 + 8

11. 12 − 4   **12.** 15 − 9   **13.** 11 − 3

14. 7 − 4   **15.** 13 − 8   **16.** 18 − 9

17. Katy has 17 blueberries. Rose has 8 blueberries. How many more blueberries does Katy have?

Do You Know...

When did monarch butterflies first appear in Hawaii?

You'll find out in Lesson 3-15.

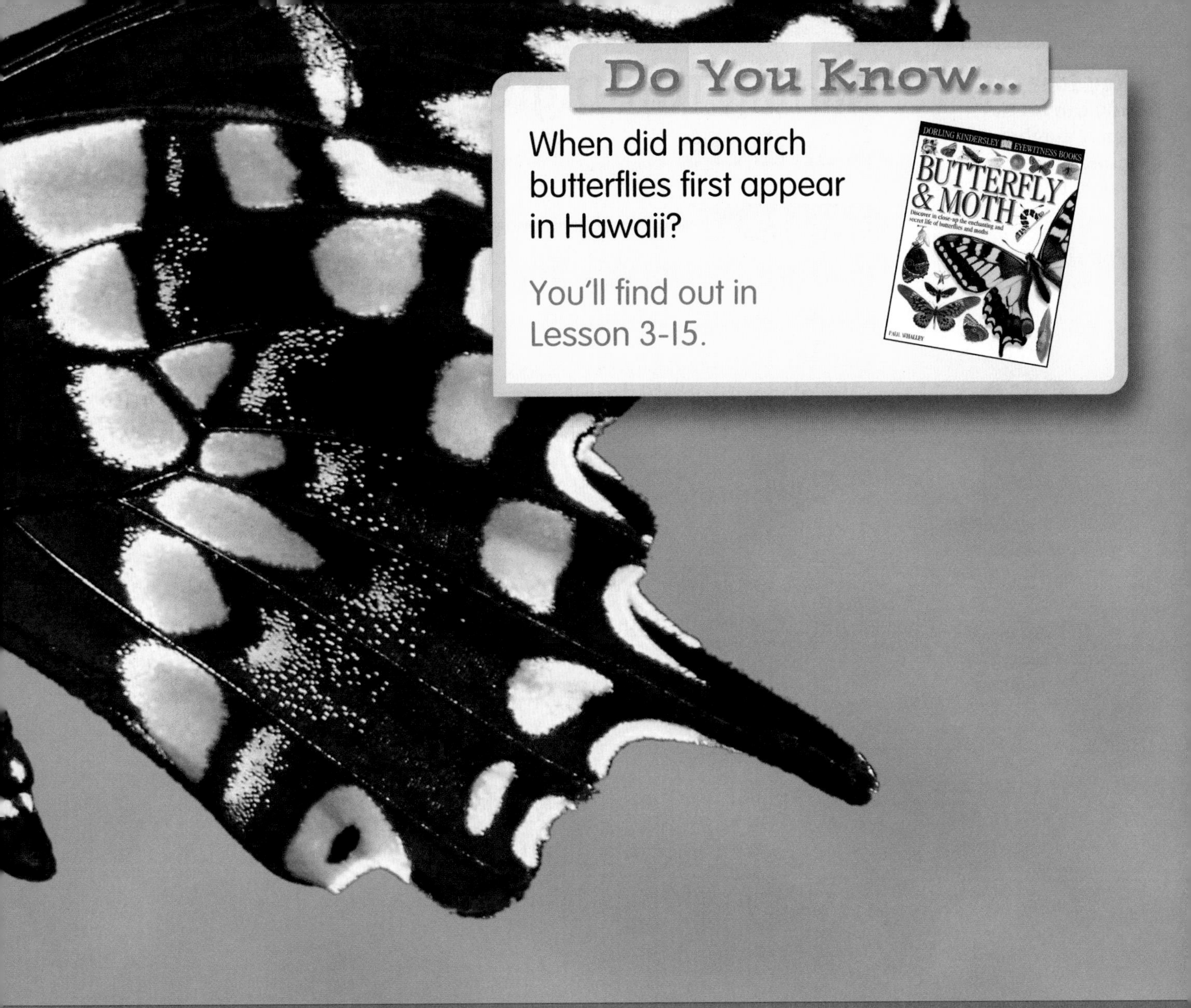

C Estimating Sums and Differences

(pages 86–89, 98–101)

Estimate each sum or difference.

18. 21 − 11

19. 19 + 39

20. 17 + 71

21. 82 + 38

22. 42 − 19

23. 58 − 29

24. 73 − 28

25. 61 − 18

26. Ron had 51 bottle caps. He gave 18 away. About how many does he have left?

D Comparing Numbers

(pages 18–21)

Compare. Write <, >, or =.

27. 81 ○ 80

28. 25 ○ 52

29. 34 ○ 40

30. 421 ○ 214

31. 1,456 ○ 1,527

32. 2,368 ○ 2,360

33. Jack had 3 pennies. He found 2 more. Elise has 7 pennies. Who has more pennies?

Key Idea
You can break apart numbers, using place value, to add.

Vocabulary
• regroup

Think It Through
• I should **estimate** so I will know if my answer is reasonable.
• I can **use place-value blocks** to show addition.

Adding Two-Digit Numbers

LEARN

How do you add two-digit numbers?

Example

Cal counted 46 ladybugs on a log and 78 more on some bushes. How many ladybugs did he count all together?

Find $46 + 78$.

Estimate: 46 rounds to 50. 78 rounds to 80.

$50 + 80 = 130$, so the answer should be about 130.

What You **Think**		What You **Write**

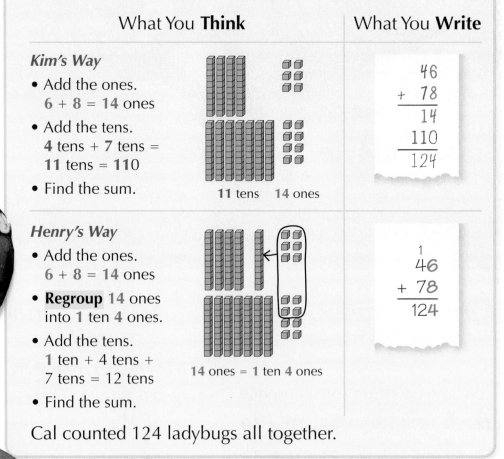

Kim's Way
• Add the ones.
  $6 + 8 = 14$ ones
• Add the tens.
  4 tens + 7 tens = 11 tens = 110
• Find the sum.

11 tens   14 ones

$$\begin{array}{r} 46 \\ +\ 78 \\ \hline 14 \\ 110 \\ \hline 124 \end{array}$$

Henry's Way
• Add the ones.
  $6 + 8 = 14$ ones
• **Regroup** 14 ones into 1 ten 4 ones.
• Add the tens.
  1 ten + 4 tens + 7 tens = 12 tens
• Find the sum.

14 ones = 1 ten 4 ones

$$\begin{array}{r} \overset{1}{}46 \\ +\ 78 \\ \hline 124 \end{array}$$

Cal counted 124 ladybugs all together.

✔ **Talk About It**

1. Why did Henry write a small 1 above the 4 in the tens place?

There are over 500 kinds of ladybugs in the United States.

2. Why should you estimate when adding two-digit numbers?

For another example, see Set 3-1 on p. 182.

1.   39
      + 42

2.   74
      + 12

3.   63
      + 38

4. 56 + 8

5. 67 + 39

6. Number Sense Mel added 48 and 27 and got 615. Is this answer reasonable? Explain.

PRACTICE

For more practice, see Set 3-1 on p. 186.

A Skills and Understanding

7.   68
      + 41

8.   29
      + 13

9.   43
      + 9

10.   83
      + 16

11.   35
      + 27

12. 42 + 54

13. 93 + 17

14. 26 + 67

15. 78 + 12

16. 19 + 32

17. Number Sense Eva added 39 and 12 and got 51. How can she estimate to check that her answer is reasonable?

B Reasoning and Problem Solving

18. An adult female ladybug can eat up to 75 aphids a day. An adult male ladybug can eat up to 40 aphids a day. How many aphids could a male and female pair eat in a day?

19. Bob had read 38 pages of his book. Then he read 17 more pages. How many pages has he read in all?

20. Writing in Math What is the largest sum you can get when you add two 2-digit numbers? Explain.

Mixed Review and Test Prep

Take It to the NET
Test Prep
www.scottforesman.com

21. Round to the nearest ten to estimate 58 − 27.

22. What is the value of the 6 in 26,489?

   A. sixty   **B.** sixty thousand   **C.** six thousand   **D.** six hundred

23. Writing in Math Write the standard form for the number shown at the right. Explain why two zeros are needed in the standard form.

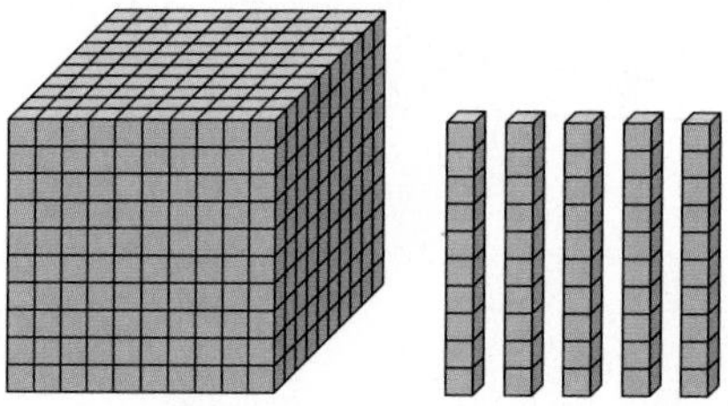

All text pages available online and on CD-ROM.

Key Idea
Add hundreds with hundreds, tens with tens, and ones with ones.

Materials
• place-value blocks
  or  tools

Think It Through
I can **show the two parts.** I need to find the total.

Models for Adding Three-Digit Numbers

LEARN

Why do you add?

Nancy has 135 shells in her collection. Mark has 247 shells. How many shells do they have in all?

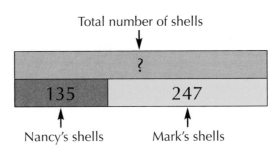

Total number of shells

?

| 135 | 247 |

↑ Nancy's shells   ↑ Mark's shells

Activity

How can you add with place-value blocks?

Find 135 + 247.

a. Show each number with place-value blocks.

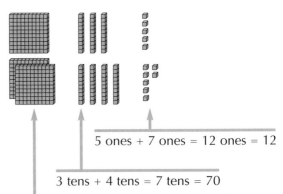

5 ones + 7 ones = 12 ones = 12

b. Combine the ones.

c. Combine the tens.

3 tens + 4 tens = 7 tens = 70

d. Combine the hundreds.   1 hundred + 2 hundreds = 3 hundreds = 300

e. Add each value to find the sum.

300 + 70 + 12 = 382

f. Use place-value blocks to find each sum.

132 + 218   244 + 39   138 + 25

g. To find 342 + 87, Cari began by combining 7 ones and 4 ones. What did she do wrong?

Activity

How can you record your work with place-value blocks?

Here is one way to record your work when you add.

Find 168 + 252.

| What You **Think** | What You **Show** | What You **Write** |

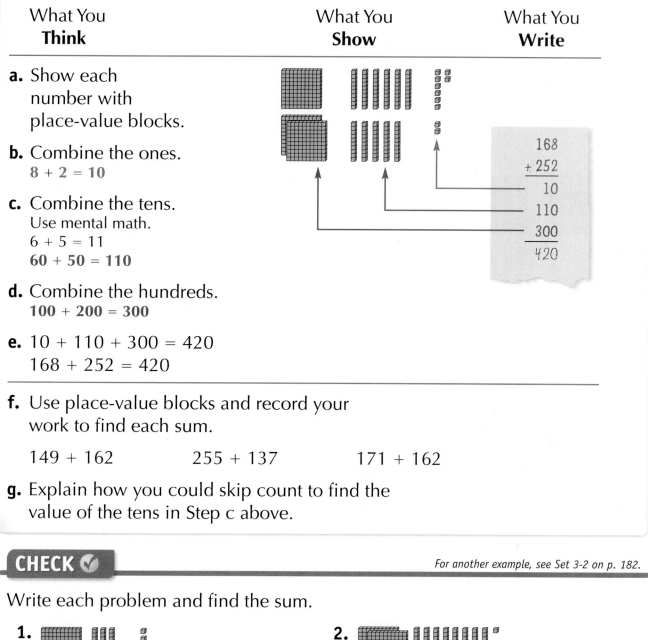

a. Show each number with place-value blocks.

b. Combine the ones.
8 + 2 = 10

c. Combine the tens.
Use mental math.
6 + 5 = 11
60 + 50 = 110

d. Combine the hundreds.
100 + 200 = 300

e. 10 + 110 + 300 = 420
168 + 252 = 420

$$\begin{array}{r} 168 \\ + 252 \\ \hline 10 \\ 110 \\ 300 \\ \hline 420 \end{array}$$

---

f. Use place-value blocks and record your work to find each sum.

149 + 162   255 + 137   171 + 162

g. Explain how you could skip count to find the value of the tens in Step c above.

CHECK ✓

For another example, see Set 3-2 on p. 182.

Write each problem and find the sum.

1.

2.

3. Number Sense Brenda wants to show 354 + 179. She has 13 ones blocks. Does she have enough ones? Explain.

For more practice, see Set 3-2 on p. 186.

A Skills and Understanding

Write each problem and find the sum.

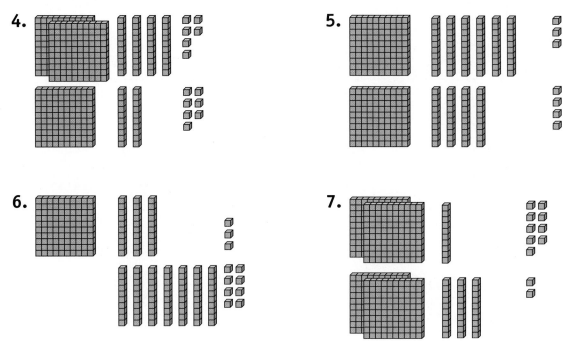

4.

5.

6.

7.

8. **Number Sense** Clark said that 168 + 252 is the same as 170 + 250. Is he correct? Explain. You can use or draw place-value blocks to help.

B Reasoning and Problem Solving

 Math and Science

The National Zoo in Washington, D.C., is home to the giant pandas Tian Tian and Mei Xiang. Zoo workers feed the pandas bamboo, apples, sweet potatoes, carrots, and biscuits. The tables show the weights of the pandas over three months.

9. In December, how much did Tian Tian and Mei Xiang weigh all together? in February?

10. In January, **about** how much more did Tian Tian weigh than Mei Xiang?

11. In one day, Tian Tian eats 850 grams of biscuits and 300 grams of apples. How many grams of these foods does he eat in all?

Tian Tian's Weight

Month	Weight
December	202 pounds
January	218 pounds
February	221 pounds

Mei Xiang's Weight

Month	Weight
December	135 pounds
January	141 pounds
February	145 pounds

12. Writing in Math Did Jack record the problem below correctly? If not, explain why and record it correctly. Find the sum.

$$\begin{array}{r} 149 \\ + 670 \\ \hline \end{array}$$

C Extensions

13. Jack used place-value blocks to solve an addition problem. He ended with 2 hundreds, 12 tens, and 7 ones. What might his addition problem be?

Mixed Review and Test Prep

Take It to the NET
Test Prep
www.scottforesman.com

Find each sum.

14. 45 + 45   **15.** 78 + 67   **16.** 89 + 34

17. What is 155 rounded to the nearest ten?

A. 150   **B.** 200   **C.** 160   **D.** 250

Learning with Technology
The Place-Value Blocks eTool

Before beginning, estimate each sum and record your estimate. With the odometer off, stamp each number in the problem. Then, regroup ones into tens and tens into hundreds. Check each sum against your estimate. Try different strategies to get your estimates and sums as close to each other as you can.

1. 26 + 18   **2.** 34 + 29

3. 47 + 36   **4.** 83 + 19

5. 78 + 22   **6.** 65 + 37

Think It Through
I can **do it another way** without regrouping.

```
   136
 + 288
 ─────
    14
   110
   300
 ─────
   424
```

Adding Three-Digit Numbers

LEARN

How can you regroup to add?

Example A

A gift store has 136 balloons on display and 288 in the warehouse. How many balloons does the store have?

Find 136 + 288.

Estimate: 136 rounds to 100. 288 rounds to 300.

100 + 300 = 400, so the answer should be about 400.

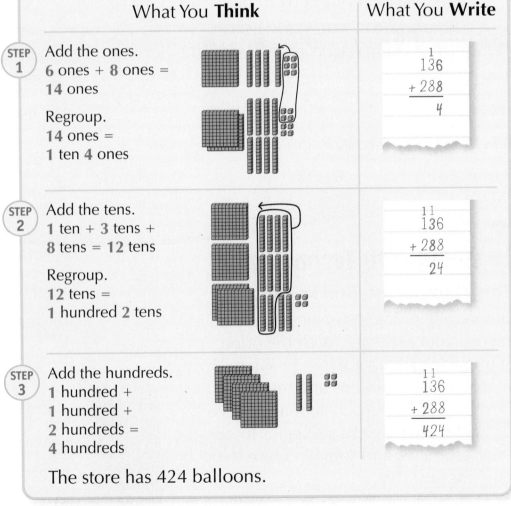

What You **Think**	What You **Write**
STEP 1 Add the ones. **6 ones + 8 ones = 14 ones** Regroup. **14 ones = 1 ten 4 ones**	``` 1 136 + 288 ───── 4 ```
STEP 2 Add the tens. **1 ten + 3 tens + 8 tens = 12 tens** Regroup. **12 tens = 1 hundred 2 tens**	``` 11 136 + 288 ───── 24 ```
STEP 3 Add the hundreds. **1 hundred + 1 hundred + 2 hundreds = 4 hundreds**	``` 11 136 + 288 ───── 424 ```

The store has 424 balloons.

✓ **Talk About It**

1. How can you use the estimate to check the answer in Example A?

How do you add with 2 regroupings?

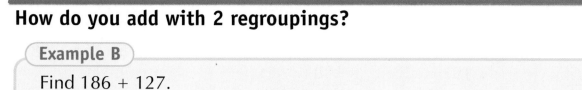

Example B

Find 186 + 127.

	What You **Think**	What You **Write**
STEP 1	Add the ones and regroup. 6 ones + 7 ones = 13 ones 13 ones = 1 ten 3 ones	$$\begin{array}{r} 1 \\ 186 \\ + 127 \\ \hline 3 \end{array}$$
STEP 2	Add the tens and regroup. 1 ten + 8 tens + 2 tens = 11 tens 11 tens = 1 hundred 1 ten	$$\begin{array}{r} 11 \\ 186 \\ + 127 \\ \hline 313 \end{array}$$
STEP 3	Add the hundreds. 1 hundred + 1 hundred + 1 hundred = 3 hundreds 186 + 127 = 313	$$\begin{array}{r} 11 \\ 186 \\ + 127 \\ \hline 313 \end{array}$$

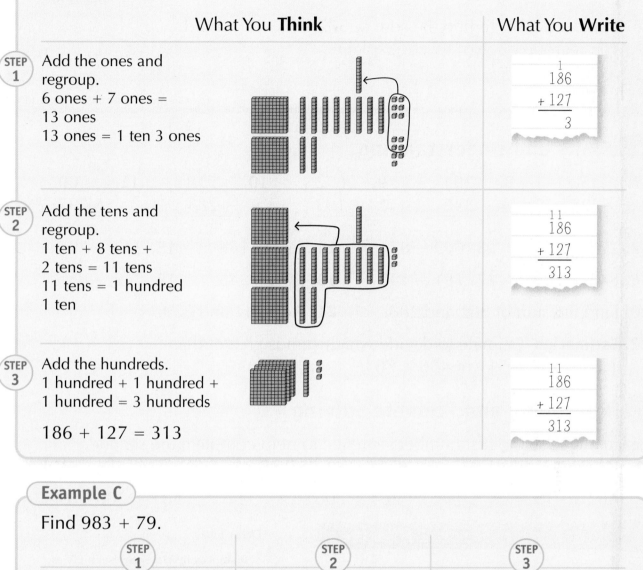

Example C

Find 983 + 79.

STEP 1	**STEP 2**	**STEP 3**
Add the ones. Regroup if needed.	Add the tens. Regroup if needed.	Add the hundreds.
$$\begin{array}{r} 1 \\ 983 \\ + \ 79 \\ \hline 2 \end{array}$$	$$\begin{array}{r} 11 \\ 983 \\ + \ 79 \\ \hline 62 \end{array}$$	$$\begin{array}{r} 11 \\ 983 \\ + \ 79 \\ \hline 1{,}062 \end{array}$$

983 + 79 = 1,062

✔ Talk About It

2. In Example C, why does the sum have a zero in the hundreds place?

For another example, see Set 3-3 on p. 182.

1. 127
+ 135

2. 351
+ 197

3. 833
+ 98

4. 207 + 188

5. 972 + 98

6. Number Sense To find the sum of 577 and 145, would you regroup once or twice? Explain.

PRACTICE

For more practice, see Set 3-3 on p. 186.

A Skills and Understanding

7. 456
+ 223

8. 295
+ 348

9. 672
+ 193

10. 718
+ 283

11. 509
+ 697

12. 275 + 38

13. 609 + 87

14. 927 + 156

15. 342 + 895

16. 842 + 189

17. 751 + 148

18. 279 + 345

19. 242 + 68

20. Find the sum of 862 and 288.

21. Add 544 and 129.

22. Estimation Estimate to decide which sum is greater than 1,000: 367 + 511 or 456 + 783.

B Reasoning and Problem Solving

Reasoning Use the first number sentence to help complete the second.

23. 462 + 375 = 837
462 + 475 = ▨

24. 289 + 706 = 995
284 + 706 = ▨

25. 537 + 246 = 783
537 + 206 = ▨

Math and Social Studies

Many ships carry cargo such as grain or iron ore over the Great Lakes.

26. A cargo ship travels from Duluth to Cleveland and back to Duluth. How far does it travel?

27. A ship carries grain from Chicago to Milwaukee and then to Buffalo. How far does it travel?

28. About how much greater is the distance by water from Duluth to Cleveland than from Chicago to Milwaukee?

Data File

Distances by Water Between Cities	
City	Distance
Duluth to Cleveland	833 miles
Chicago to Milwaukee	85 miles
Milwaukee to Buffalo	828 miles

29. <u>Writing in Math</u> Thomas used another way to add 999 + 98. Is he correct? Explain.

```
999   +1      1,000
+  98   −1    +   97
                1,097
```

C Extensions

30. Use each of the digits 1, 2, 3, 4, 5, and 9 once. Make an addition problem with the greatest sum possible.

Mixed Review and Test Prep

Take It to the NET
Test Prep
www.scottforesman.com

31. Write the problem and find the sum.

32. Continue the pattern:

41, 45, 49, ▉, ▉,

A. 53, 57, 61   **C.** 51, 53, 55

B. 59, 69, 79   **D.** 52, 56, 60

Practice Game

Cha-Ching

Number of Players: 2–4

Materials: number cube labeled 1–6

P	N	D	Q	Total	Change from $5

1. Each player copies the table at the right.

2. Each player tosses the number cube 4 times and records each toss in the table for any coin.

3. Each player totals the amount of money recorded and finds the amount of change they would get from $5, if they spent that amount. The player with the greatest amount of change wins the round.

4. Play 3 or more rounds. Discuss winning strategies.

Variation: The player with the least amount of change wins the round.

Think It Through

I should **look for extra information** that is not needed to solve the problem.

Adding Three or More Numbers

LEARN

How do you add more than two numbers?

Each year, millions of monarch butterflies migrate to Mexico for the winter. Many people enjoy watching this migration.

For 3 days in September, Molly counted and wrote down how many butterflies she saw in an hour. How many butterflies did she see?

Butterflies I Saw	
Day	Butterflies
Monday	125
Tuesday	96
Wednesday	109

The main idea is to find the total number of butterflies. You don't need to add the number of days.

Example

Find 125 + 96 + 109.

Estimate: 100 + 100 + 100 = 300

STEP 1

Line up the ones, tens, and hundreds.

```
  125
   96
+ 109
```

STEP 2

Add the ones. Regroup as needed.

```
   2
  125
   96
+ 109
    0
```

STEP 3

Add the tens. Regroup as needed.

```
  12
  125
   96
+ 109
   30
```

STEP 4

Add the hundreds.

```
  12
  125
   96
+ 109
  330
```

125 + 96 + 109 = 330

Molly saw 330 butterflies.

Talk About It

1. Why is there a small 2 above the tens place in Step 2?

Take It to the NET
More Examples
www.scottforesman.com

1. 47
   24
+ 66

2. 352
  673
   81
+ 98

3. 9 + 35 + 28

4. 375 + 150 + 32

5. Number Sense How can you tell that 55 + 60 + 35 is greater than 100 without solving the problem?

A Skills and Understanding

6. 35
  48
+ 79

7. 732
  265
+ 135

8. 408
  646
+ 12

9. 567
   42
  311
+ 728

10. 103
  242
  416
+ 352

11. 195 + 34 + 164

12. 21 + 63 + 95 + 72

13. 18 + 234 + 420

14. Number Sense Is 98 + 63 + 87 greater than or less than 300? How can you tell without adding?

15. Estimation Estimate the sum of 588 + 92 + 103.

16. Mental Math How can you use mental math to find 175 + 43 + 25?

B Reasoning and Problem Solving

17. Writing in Math Write an addition problem with three addends. Make the problem so the sum is greater than 300 but less than 500.

Mixed Review and Test Prep

Take It to the NET
Test Prep
www.scottforesman.com

Find each sum.

18. 372 + 81

19. 167 + 283

20. 927 + 106

21. 75 + 153

22. Robert had 12 goldfish and 5 guppies. He bought more fish with his birthday money. Then he had 18 goldfish and 9 guppies. How many goldfish did he buy?

A. 17   **B.** 7   **C.** 6   **D.** 4

Understand Graphic Sources: Pictures

Understanding graphic sources such as pictures when you read in math can help you use the **problem-solving strategy,** *Draw a Picture,* in the next lesson.

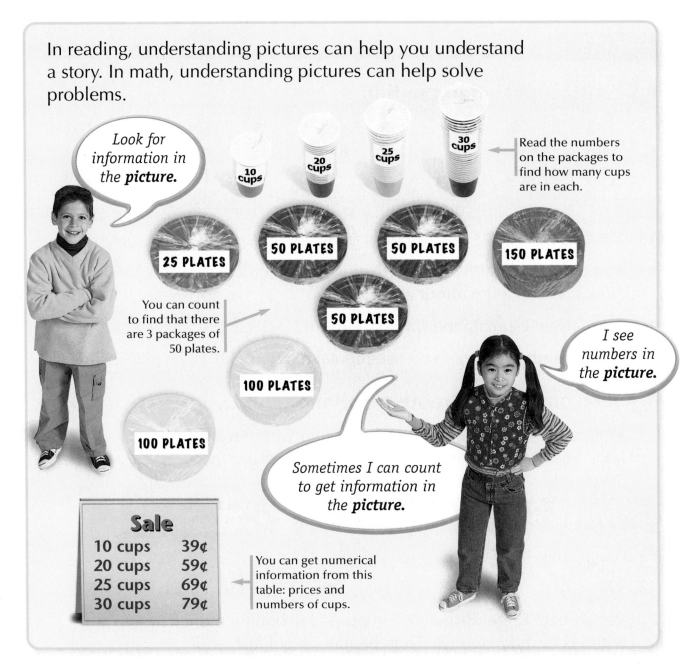

In reading, understanding pictures can help you understand a story. In math, understanding pictures can help solve problems.

Look for information in the **picture.**

Read the numbers on the packages to find how many cups are in each.

10 cups
20 cups
25 cups
30 cups

25 PLATES
50 PLATES
50 PLATES
150 PLATES
50 PLATES

You can count to find that there are 3 packages of 50 plates.

100 PLATES

100 PLATES

I see numbers in the **picture.**

Sometimes I can count to get information in the **picture.**

Sale

10 cups	39¢
20 cups	59¢
25 cups	69¢
30 cups	79¢

You can get numerical information from this table: prices and numbers of cups.

1. What is the price for a package of 30 cups?

2. There are how many packages of 100 plates?

3. What package costs 59¢?

For 4–7, use the picture at the right.

4. Describe the items in the picture.

5. How many 5-point balloons are in the picture?

6. How many balloons in all are in the picture?

7. **Writing in Math** With one toss of the dart, what is the highest score possible? Explain how you found your answer.

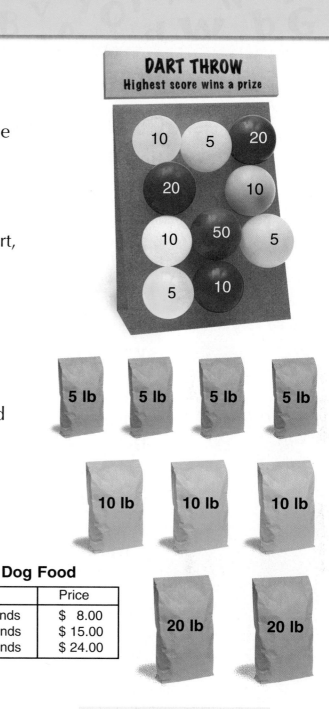

DART THROW
Highest score wins a prize

For 8–11, use the picture at the right. Remember, lb means pound, or pounds.

8. How many different sizes of dog-food bags are available?

9. **Writing in Math** What is the price of a 20-pound bag of dog food? Explain how you found your answer.

10. What size bag of dog food costs $15 per bag?

11. How many 5-pound bags of dog food are in the picture?

Dog Food

Size	Price
5 pounds	$ 8.00
10 pounds	$ 15.00
20 pounds	$ 24.00

For 12–15, use the picture at the right.

12. How many beads are in a package?

13. Which beads have the same price?

14. Does the necklace shown have more red beads or blue beads?

15. **Writing in Math** If you want to make a necklace like the one shown, would it cost the same to use green square beads instead of blue long beads? Explain.

Bead Prices
Packages of 100

Blue long	$3.89
Yellow round	$3.19
Red round	$3.19
Green square	$3.69

Problem-Solving Strategy

Key Idea
Learning how and when to draw a picture can help you solve problems.

Draw a Picture

LEARN

How do you draw a picture to solve a problem?

Snail in the Well A snail is at the bottom of a well that is 6 feet deep. Each day it climbs up 3 feet. Each night it slides back down 2 feet. If this pattern continues, how many days will it take the snail to get out of the well?

Read and Understand

What do you know?

The snail climbs 3 feet each day. It slides down 2 feet each night. The well is 6 feet deep.

What are you trying to find?

Find the number of days it will take to get out.

Plan and Solve

What strategy will you use?

Strategy: Draw a Picture

How to Draw a Picture

Step 1 Draw a picture to show the problem. Don't try to draw the real objects.

Step 2 Finish the picture to show the action in the problem.

Step 3 Use the picture to solve the problem.

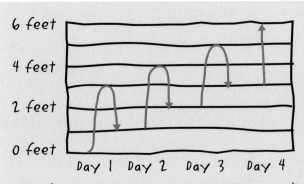

The picture shows that on Day 4 the snail has climbed 6 feet to get out of the well.

Answer: It will take 4 days.

Look Back and Check

Is your answer reasonable?

Yes, the pattern in the picture matches the pattern in the problem.

✔ Talk About It

1. In the picture, what does each arrow show?

2. Why does the last arrow go up but not back down?

When can you draw a picture?

School Photos Fred, Rhonda, Artie, and Vanessa each gave a photo to each of the others in the group. How many photos were given all together?

When To Draw a Picture

Think about drawing a picture when the story describes some action:
- Snail climbing out of a well
- People exchanging photos

F is Fred   R is Rhonda   A is Artie   V is Vanessa

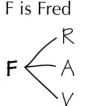

Answer: Twelve photos were given all together.

✔ Talk About It

3. Who did Fred give photos to? Who did Rhonda give photos to?

4. How many photos did Artie receive?

CHECK ✔

For another example, see Set 3-5 on p. 183.

1. Copy and finish the picture for the Sandwich problem. Write the answer in a complete sentence.

Sandwich Jeff can choose from white or rye bread. For the filling, he can choose from tuna, ham, or cheese. How many kinds of sandwiches can he choose from?

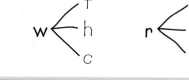

2. Draw and use a picture to solve the Necklace problem. Write the answer in a complete sentence.

Necklace Allie makes a necklace. She puts 4 red beads on the chain, then 2 blue beads, then 4 red beads, then 2 blue beads, and so on. If she uses 6 blue beads, then stops, how many red beads has she used?

A Using the Strategy

Completing a Picture to Solve a Problem Copy and complete the picture to solve the problem. Write the answer in a complete sentence.

Ted ||| |||

Ben || ||

3. Ted gives himself 3 carrot sticks for each 2 carrot sticks he gives Ben. If Ben has 6 carrot sticks, how many does Ted have?

Drawing a Picture to Solve a Problem Draw a picture to solve each problem. Write the answer in a complete sentence.

4. Karen puts 5 red beads after each white bead. If she uses 15 red beads, then stops, how many white beads has she used?

5. Tara, Anna, and Ellie each gave a friendship bracelet to each of the others in the group. How many bracelets were given in all?

6. Ryan was third in line. Jay was behind Emma. Lisa was behind Ryan. If Emma was first, who was second?

Math and Social Studies

The White House first became home to presidents and their families in the year 1800. It has gone through many changes since then. In 1879 the first telephone was put in for President Hayes. In 1942 President Roosevelt had a movie theater built. The first computer in the White House was hooked up for President Carter in 1978.

1891 electric lighting put in for President Harrison

1922 first radio installed for President Harding

1992 e-mail set up for President Bush

1860 1880 1900 1920 1940 1960 1980 2000

1994 President Clinton orders a White House web site

7. Draw a time line. Include the information given in the time line above and in the paragraph above the time line.

8. Which came first, electric lighting or the first telephone at the White House? Explain how you know.

9. How many years after the first radio was installed was e-mail set up in the White House?

B Mixed Strategy Practice

Solve each problem. Write the answer in a complete sentence.

10. In how many different ways can you use coins to make $0.12?

One Way

11. Tyler had 18 cookies. He gave 9 away. Then he ate 3 of the cookies he had left. How many cookies does he have left now?

12. <u>Writing in Math</u> Solve the Name Tags problem below. Explain how you know your answer is correct.

Name Tags Beth makes 2 name tags in the time it takes John to make 5 name tags. When John has made 15 name tags, how many has Beth made?

STRATEGIES

- **Show What You Know**
  Draw a Picture
  Make an Organized List
  Make a Table
  Make a Graph
  Act It Out or Use Objects
- **Look for a Pattern**
- **Try, Check, and Revise**
- **Write a Number Sentence**
- **Use Logical Reasoning**
- **Solve a Simpler Problem**
- **Work Backward**

TEST TALK

Think It Through
Stuck? I won't give up. I can:
- Reread the problem.
- Tell what I know.
- Identify key facts and details.
- Tell the problem in my own words.
- Show the main idea.
- Try a different strategy.
- Retrace my steps.

Mixed Review and Test Prep

Take It to the NET
Test Prep
www.scottforesman.com

Find each sum.

13.
```
  124
  112
+  17
```

14.
```
  105
   87
+  33
```

15.
```
   25
   58
+  75
```

16. What is the value of the underlined digit in 13,4<u>5</u>8?

A. 50,000 **B.** 5,000 **C.** 500 **D.** 50

17. <u>Writing in Math</u> Write a word problem that you could solve using the number sentence $17 - 9 = 8$.

Do You Know How?

Do You Understand?

Adding Two-Digit Numbers (3-1)

Find each sum.

1. 65
      + 18

2. 43
      + 81

3. 32 + 43

4. 54 + 68

A How can you regroup ones in Exercise 1?

B Roy says you can solve Exercise 4 by adding 12 and 110. Is he correct? Explain.

Models for Adding Three-Digit Numbers (3-2)
Adding Three-Digit Numbers (3-3)

5. Write the problem and add.

6. 599
      + 923

C How can you regroup 13 ones in Exercise 5?

D How could you estimate the sum in Exercise 6?

Adding Three or More Numbers (3-4)

7. 215 + 12 + 328

8. 75 + 53 + 25 + 7

E In Exercise 8, how could you tell that the sum is greater than 100 without adding?

Problem-Solving Strategy: Draw a Picture (3-5)

9. Draw and use a picture to solve the Raisins problem. Write the answer in a complete sentence.

Raisins Julio eats 6 raisins in the time Cari eats 4 raisins. When Julio has eaten 18 raisins, how many has Cari eaten?

F How do you know when to stop drawing Julio's raisins?

G If Cari and Julio both started with 18 raisins, how many does Cari have left when Julio has eaten all of his?

MULTIPLE CHOICE

1. Find the sum of 385 + 93. (3-3)

A. 3,178   **B.** 488   **C.** 478   **D.** 378

2. Mr. Peters drove 95 miles before lunch and 67 miles after lunch. How far did he drive in all? (3-1)

A. 1,512 miles   **B.** 162 miles   **C.** 152 miles   **D.** 142 miles

FREE RESPONSE

Find each sum. (3-1)

3. 22 + 13   **4.** 45 + 16   **5.** 76 + 39   **6.** 66 + 23

Write each problem and find the sum. (3-2, 3-3, 3-4)

7.

8.   420
     + 195

9.   139
     + 231

10.   786
      + 209

11. 43 + 589 + 15   **12.** 109 + 11 + 204   **13.** 150 + 81 + 50 + 19

Draw a picture for each problem. Write the answer in a complete sentence. (3-5)

14. Tessa makes a bracelet with 5 beads. She puts the blue bead first. The green bead is third. The silver bead comes after the green bead. If the white bead is last, where is the red bead?

15. Joanne, Teri, Grace, and Amber formed a cooking club. Each gave a recipe to each of the others in the group. How many recipes were given in all?

Writing in Math

16. Explain how to find 24 + 59 without regrouping. (3-1)

17. Sam thinks that 435 + 592 is less than 900. Is he correct? Explain. (3-3)

Think It Through
My answer should be **brief but complete.**

Key Idea
You can regroup
1 hundred as
10 tens and 1 ten
as 10 ones.

Materials
• place-value
  blocks
  or 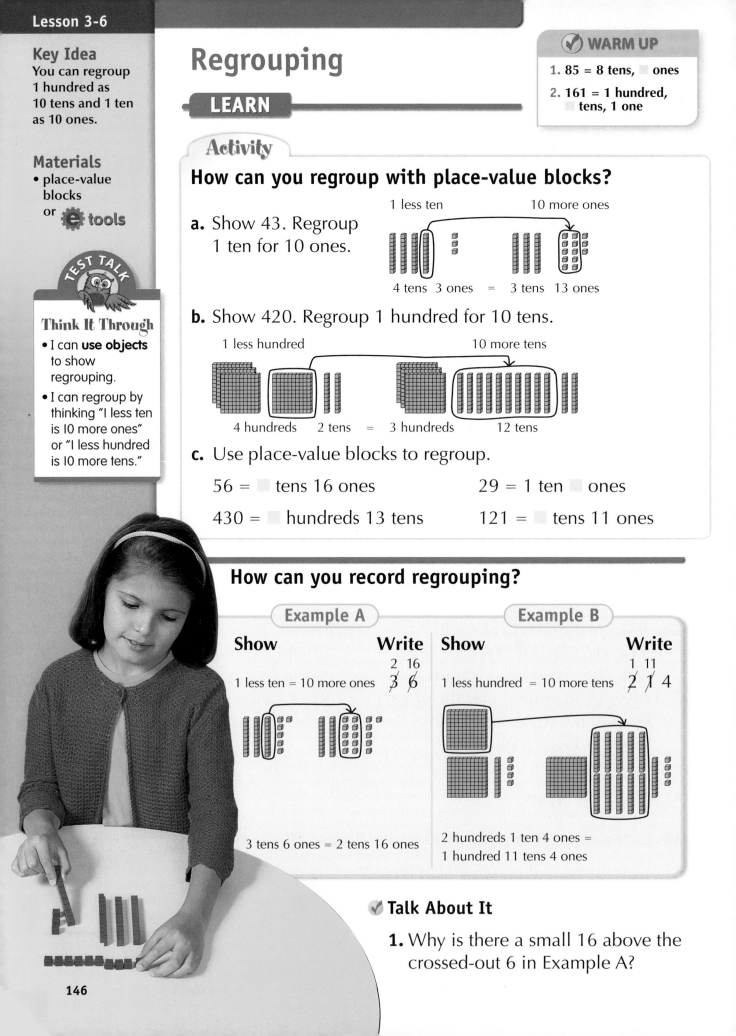 tools

TEST TALK

Think It Through
• I can **use objects**
  to show
  regrouping.
• I can regroup by
  thinking "1 less ten
  is 10 more ones"
  or "1 less hundred
  is 10 more tens."

Regrouping

LEARN

Activity

How can you regroup with place-value blocks?

a. Show 43. Regroup
1 ten for 10 ones.

1 less ten   10 more ones

4 tens 3 ones = 3 tens 13 ones

b. Show 420. Regroup 1 hundred for 10 tens.

1 less hundred   10 more tens

4 hundreds 2 tens = 3 hundreds 12 tens

c. Use place-value blocks to regroup.

56 = ☐ tens 16 ones   29 = 1 ten ☐ ones

430 = ☐ hundreds 13 tens   121 = ☐ tens 11 ones

How can you record regrouping?

Example A

Show   **Write**

                   2 16
1 less ten = 10 more ones   3̶ 6̶

3 tens 6 ones = 2 tens 16 ones

Example B

Show   **Write**

                        1 11
1 less hundred = 10 more tens   2̶ 1̶ 4

2 hundreds 1 ten 4 ones =
1 hundred 11 tens 4 ones

✔ Talk About It

1. Why is there a small 16 above the
crossed-out 6 in Example A?

Regroup 1 ten for 10 ones. You may use place-value blocks or draw a picture to help.

Think It Through
I can draw a simple picture to show blocks.
☐ = I hundred
| = I ten
● = I one

1. 55 = 5̸ tens 5̸ ones   **2.** 6 3̸ 7̸   **3.** 4 6

Regroup 1 hundred for 10 tens. You may use place-value blocks or draw a picture to help.

4. 274 = 2̸ hundreds 7̸ tens 4 ones   **5.** 8̸ 0̸ 3   **6.** 2 1 9

7. Number Sense Explain why 450 = 3 hundreds, 15 tens.

PRACTICE

For more practice, see Set 3-6 on p. 187.

Ⓐ Skills and Understanding

Regroup 1 ten for 10 ones. You may use place-value blocks or draw a picture to help.

8. 76 = 7̸ tens 6̸ ones   **9.** 2 2̸ 1̸   **10.** 3 6 2

Regroup 1 hundred for 10 tens. You may use place-value blocks or draw a picture to help.

11. 357 = 3̸ hundreds 5̸ tens 7 ones   **12.** 2̸ 4̸ 8   **13.** 4 3 4

14. Number Sense Explain why 153 = 1 hundred, 4 tens, 13 ones.

Ⓑ Reasoning and Problem Solving

15. Give two ways you could show $0.32 using dimes and pennies.

16. <u>Writing in Math</u> Draw 2 ways to show 121 using place-value blocks.

Mixed Review and Test Prep

Take It to the NET
Test Prep
www.scottforesman.com

17. Jan made a paper chain with the pattern red, white, blue, red, white, blue. What color was the 13th link? Draw a picture to solve.

18. Find 27 + 32 + 96.

   A. 155   **B.** 145   **C.** 128   **D.** 59

Key Idea
You can regroup
1 ten for 10 ones
to subtract
two-digit
numbers.

Think It Through
I should check the
ones first to **see if I
need to regroup.**

Subtracting Two-Digit Numbers

LEARN

How can you subtract two-digit numbers?

The Hubble telescope is a giant telescope in space. It is about 44 feet long. How much longer is the Hubble than a pickup truck that is 18 feet long?

Example

Find 44 − 18.

Estimate: 40 − 20 = 20

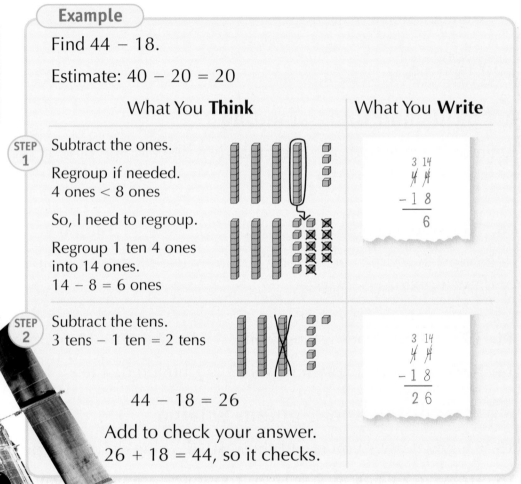

	What You **Think**	What You **Write**
STEP 1	Subtract the ones. Regroup if needed. 4 ones < 8 ones. So, I need to regroup. Regroup 1 ten 4 ones into 14 ones. 14 − 8 = 6 ones	3 14 / 4 4 / − 1 8 / 6
STEP 2	Subtract the tens. 3 tens − 1 ten = 2 tens. 44 − 18 = 26. Add to check your answer. 26 + 18 = 44, so it checks.	3 14 / 4 4 / − 1 8 / 2 6

The Hubble telescope is 26 feet longer than an 18-foot pickup truck.

✔ Talk About It

1. Do you need to regroup to find 37 − 14? Explain.

2. **Reasoning** Evan found 23 − 15 = 8. How can he add to check his answer?

1. 45
     − 28

2. 51
     − 16

3. 84 − 12

4. 37 − 9

5. 90 − 18

6. Number Sense Write a subtraction problem where you must regroup to solve.

PRACTICE

For more practice, see Set 3-7 on p. 187.

Ⓐ Skills and Understanding

7. 87
     − 22

8. 93
     − 15

9. 67
     − 43

10. 28
      − 9

11. 56
      − 48

12. 45
      − 16

13. 74
      − 7

14. 32
      − 27

15. 21
      − 14

16. 78
      − 38

17. 83 − 52

18. 62 − 25

19. 54 − 5

20. 93 − 47

21. 67 − 9

22. Number Sense Eva says that 71 − 28 = 57. Why is this answer not reasonable?

Ⓑ Reasoning and Problem Solving

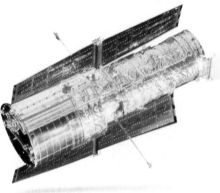

23. The Hubble telescope takes 97 minutes to orbit the Earth. How much more than 1 hour is this? Hint: 1 hour = 60 minutes.

24. Marcia read 32 pages on Monday, 54 on Tuesday, and 17 on Wednesday. How many pages did she read in the three days?

25. **Writing in Math** Brad wanted to find 78 − 19. He began by finding 9 − 8. What did he do wrong?

Mixed Review and Test Prep

Take It to the NET
Test Prep
www.scottforesman.com

Regroup 1 ten for 10 ones.

26. 68 = 6̸ tens 8̸ ones

27. 1 2̸ 6̸

28. 7 5

29. What is the value of 3 dimes, 2 nickels, and 1 penny?

   A. $0.31   **B.** $0.40   **C.** $0.41   **D.** $1.33

Key Idea
You can use blocks to show regrouping for subtraction.

Materials
• place-value blocks
  or 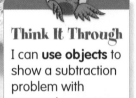 tools

TEST TALK

Think It Through
I can **use objects** to show a subtraction problem with regrouping.

Models for Subtracting Three-Digit Numbers

LEARN

Activity

How can you subtract with place-value blocks?

Find 255 − 163.

| | What You **Show** | What You **Write** |

a. Show 255 with place-value blocks.

$$\begin{array}{r} 2\,5\,5 \\ -\,1\,6\,3 \\ \hline \end{array}$$

b. Subtract the ones. Regroup if needed.

5 > 3. No regrouping is needed.

5 ones − 3 ones = 2 ones

$$\begin{array}{r} 2\,5\,5 \\ -\,1\,6\,3 \\ \hline 2 \end{array}$$

c. Subtract the tens. Regroup if needed.

5 tens < 6 tens.

So, regroup 1 hundred for 10 tens.

15 tens − 6 tens = 9 tens

$$\begin{array}{r} {}^{1}\;{}^{15} \\ \cancel{2}\,\cancel{5}\,5 \\ -\,1\,6\,3 \\ \hline 9\,2 \end{array}$$

d. Subtract the hundreds.

1 hundred − 1 hundred = 0 hundreds

$$\begin{array}{r} {}^{1}\;{}^{15} \\ \cancel{2}\,\cancel{5}\,5 \\ -\,1\,6\,3 \\ \hline 9\,2 \end{array}$$

e. Find the value of the remaining blocks in Step d: 9 tens 2 ones = 92, so 255 − 163 = 92.

f. In Step b, did you have to regroup to subtract the ones? Explain.

g. In Step c, did you have to regroup to subtract the tens? Explain.

h. Use place-value blocks to subtract.
243 − 72   145 − 126   223 − 156

Find each difference. You may use place-value blocks or
draw a picture to help.

1. 145
     − 37

2. 288
     − 194

3. 350 − 184

4. 265 − 63

5. Number Sense Frank says, "To find 432 − 193, you
need to regroup twice." Do you agree? Explain.

PRACTICE

For more practice, see Set 3-8 on p. 188.

Ⓐ Skills and Understanding

Find each difference. You may use place-value blocks or
draw a picture to help.

6. 231
     − 122

7. 367
     − 98

8. 228
     − 145

9. 227
     − 139

10. 212 − 75

11. 321 − 220

12. 450 − 233

13. 155 − 125

14. Number Sense Write a number you could subtract from
325 where you need to regroup hundreds. Then find
the difference.

Ⓑ Reasoning and Problem Solving

15. On a field trip, Andy counted 98 dandelions and
67 wild irises in a meadow. How many more
dandelions than irises did he count?

16. Writing in Math Kelly had 3 hundreds blocks, 4 tens
blocks, and 2 ones blocks. Give another way she
could use place-value blocks to show this number.

Mixed Review and Test Prep

Take It to the NET
Test Prep
www.scottforesman.com

17. 45 − 29

18. 78 − 65

19. 50 − 19

20. 81 − 9

21. Ernie has 67 baseball cards and 119 football cards.
How many cards does he have in all?

A. 52

B. 123

C. 186

D. 205

Key Idea
You can use what you know about regrouping to subtract 3-digit numbers.

Subtracting Three-Digit Numbers

LEARN

How can you record subtraction with regrouping?

Think It Through
- Before subtracting I should **check to see if I need to regroup.**
- I can **use estimation** to see if my answer is reasonable.

Example A

A diver is 341 feet below the surface of the water. A treasure box is directly below him at a depth of 532 feet. How far above the treasure box is the diver?

Find 532 − 341.

Estimate: 500 − 300 = 200

	What You **Think**	What You **Write**
STEP 1	Subtract the ones. You do not need to regroup. 2 ones − 1 one = 1 one	$\begin{array}{r} 532 \\ -341 \\ \hline 1 \end{array}$
STEP 2	Subtract the tens. Regroup 1 hundred for 10 more tens. 13 tens − 4 tens = 9 tens	$\begin{array}{r} ^{4\ 13}\\ \cancel{5}\cancel{3}2 \\ -341 \\ \hline 91 \end{array}$
STEP 3	Subtract the hundreds. 4 hundreds − 3 hundreds = 1 hundred	$\begin{array}{r} ^{4\ 13}\\ \cancel{5}\cancel{3}2 \\ -341 \\ \hline 191 \end{array}$

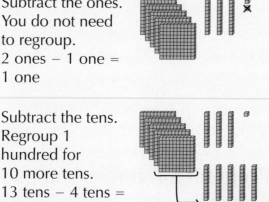

The diver is 191 feet above the treasure box.

✔ **Talk About It**

1. How can you use the estimate to check the answer above?

Use mental math, paper and pencil, or a calculator to solve.

1. 500
     − 270

2. 619
     − 387

3. $54.98
     + 37.86

4. 17,000
     + 2,100

5. Number Sense How could you use mental math to find 753 − 399?

PRACTICE

For more practice, see Set 3-13 on p. 189.

A Skills and Understanding

Use mental math, paper and pencil, or a calculator to solve.

6. 730
     + 230

7. 832
     − 691

8. 44,950
     + 4,962

9. 1,003
     − 999

10. 3,115 + 4,942 + 7,146   **11.** $215.98 + $45.02   **12.** $866.45 + $324.18

13. Number Sense To find 56 − 21 would you use paper and pencil, mental math, or a calculator? Explain why.

B Reasoning and Problem Solving

The book *A Symphony of Whales* is based on a true story. Late in 1984, about 3,000 whales were found trapped by ice in Siberia. It took 7 weeks to free the whales.

14. How many years ago were the whales found?

15. How many days did the rescue take? Remember, there are 7 days in each week. Use this number sentence:
(7 + 7) + (7 + 7) + (7 + 7) + 7 = ▨

16. Reasoning Ron added 326 + 175 as shown. Is his answer reasonable? Explain.

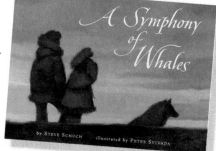

326 + 175 = 5,001

🦉 Mixed Review and Test Prep

Take It to the NET
Test Prep
www.scottforesman.com

17. $2.25
     + 1.75

18. $3.02
     + 3.48

19. $20.13
     − 2.31

20. $5.99
     + 4.65

21. $10.00
     − 6.36

22. Which shows 40,000 + 7,000 + 500 + 50 + 7 in standard form?

A. 74,557   **B.** 47,557   **C.** 45,750   **D.** 40,500

Algebra

Key Idea
You can use =, <, and > to compare sums and differences.

Vocabulary
• numerical expression
• equation
• inequality

Equality and Inequality

LEARN

More, less, or equal?

$5 + 3 = 10 − 2$ $5 + 1 < 10 − 1$ $3 + 4 + 1 > 12 − 6$

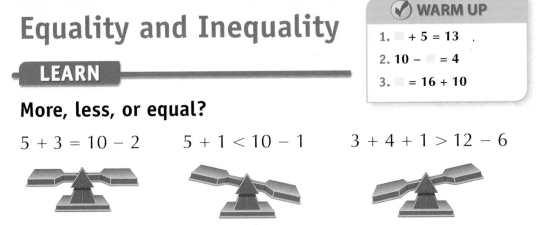

Each balance shows a **numerical expression** on each side of the =, <, or > sign in a number sentence. A numerical expression contains numbers and at least one operation. A number sentence that says two expressions are equal is an **equation.** A number sentence that uses < or > is an **inequality.**

You can add or subtract on each side of a number sentence to decide if the sentence is **true** or **false.**

$6 + 2 < 12 − 3$ $5 + 4 < 6 + 1$
$8 \quad < \quad 9$ **True** $9 \quad < \quad 7$ **False**

✓ **Talk About It**

1. Why is the first balance level? Why does the second tilt right and the third tilt left?

What could the hidden number be?

One of the numbers on the balance is hidden. Jerry says the hidden number is **6.** Yoko says it is **8.** Eric says it is **3.**

$5 + \;▢\; > 10$

Check: $5 + x > 10$

$5 + 6 > 10$	$5 + 8 > 10$	$5 + 3 > 10$
$11 > 10$	$13 > 10$	$8 > 10$
True	True	False

✓ **Talk About It**

2. What is another whole number that makes $5 + x > 10$ true?

3. Would 5 make $6 + ▢ < 10$ true? Explain.

Compare. Write <, >, or = for each ●.

1. 25 + 10 ● 50   **2.** 45 − 22 ● 35 + 11   **3.** 91 − 64 ● 19 + 8

Find three whole numbers that make each number sentence true.

4. 20 − ■ > 10   **5.** 250 + x < 350   **6.** 35 + 26 + n < 100

7. Number Sense Mel thinks there is only one whole number that will make 11 + x = 12 true. Do you agree? Explain.

PRACTICE

For more practice, see Set 3-14 on p. 189.

Ⓐ Skills and Understanding

Compare. Write <, >, or = for each ●.

8. 12 + 5 ● 20   **9.** 56 − 17 ● 15 + 20   **10.** 37 − 21 ● 6 + 19

11. 49 − 12 ● 27 + 10   **12.** 60 + 51 ● 25 + 79   **13.** 11 + 25 ● 78 − 42

Find three whole numbers that make each number sentence true.

14. 4 + ■ < 12   **15.** 16 − x > 10   **16.** 5 + n > 18

17. 33 − ■ < 12   **18.** 134 + y < 150   **19.** 66 + 104 + ■ > 200

20. Number Sense Is there any whole number that makes 9 − n > 9 true? Explain.

Ⓑ Reasoning and Problem Solving

21. The number sentence 6 + 12 = 19 is false. Find two ways you could change it to make a true sentence.

22. **Writing in Math** Write a number sentence that uses the expressions 10 + ■ and 18 − 6. Explain how you would find what numbers would make it true.

Mixed Review and Test Prep

Take It to the NET
Test Prep
www.scottforesman.com

Use mental math, paper and pencil, or a calculator to solve.

23. 3,564 + 4,589   **24.** 550 − 250   **25.** 301 − 299

26. What is the value of the underlined digit? 44,<u>5</u>63

   A. 50,000   **B.** 5,000   **C.** 500   **D.** 50

Problem-Solving Applications

Migrating Butterflies Like many birds, some butterflies and moths migrate. Surprisingly, these small insects have the energy to fly long distances without stopping to rest. They can even cross the Mediterranean Sea!

Trivia Without any guidance, monarch butterflies that are born in Canada are able to fly thousands of kilometers to the same forest groves in Mexico that their grandparents visited the previous year!

Monarch

❶ Airline pilots have reported seeing migrating monarch butterflies above an altitude of 3,219 meters (about 2 miles). What digit is in the tens place of 3,219? Round 3,219 to the nearest hundred.

❷ In 1884, monarch butterflies appeared in New Zealand. This was 39 years after they had first appeared in Hawaii. In what year did monarchs first appear in Hawaii?

Good News/Bad News Swarms of butterflies and moths can be a beautiful sight, but if they fly low over roads, they can clog radiators and coat windshields of passing cars!

Key Facts
Monarch Butterflies

- Wingspan   10 cm
- Weight $\frac{1}{5}$ oz.
- Typical speed   12 mph
- Lifespan   2-9 months

European Painted Lady

3 <u>Writing in Math</u> Write your own word problem involving butterflies. Write the answer in a complete sentence.

Using Key Facts

4 The cloudless sulfur butterfly has a wingspan of about 7 centimeters. How much longer is the wingspan of the monarch?

5 An African migrant butterfly's wingspan is 2 centimeters longer than that of a painted lady butterfly. The painted lady butterfly's wingspan is 4 centimeters shorter than that of a monarch butterfly. How long is the wingspan of an African migrant butterfly?

6 The monarch butterfly is the state insect of Alabama, Illinois, Texas, and Vermont. The swallowtail butterfly is the state insect of Florida, Georgia, Mississippi, Ohio, Oklahoma, Oregon, Virginia, and Wyoming. How many more states have the swallowtail butterfly as their insect than the monarch butterfly?

Cloudless Sulfur

7 **Decision Making** Suppose you wanted to draw life-size pictures of 3 different butterflies side-by-side with their wings spread out. Choose three of the butterflies mentioned in this lesson. How long does your paper need to be?

African Migrant

Do You Know How?

Do You Understand?

Problem-Solving Skill: Exact Answer or Estimate (3-11)

Decide if an exact answer is needed or if an estimate is enough. Solve.

1. Anna is making name tags for her club meeting. She must make tags for 13 girls and 11 boys. How many name tags must she make?

Ⓐ Can Anna estimate the number of name tags? Why or why not?

Ⓑ Do you need to add or subtract to solve this problem?

Adding and Subtracting Money (3-12)

Add or subtract.

2. $4.21
− 2.02

3. $7.32
+ 2.98

4. $3.14 + $4.89

Ⓒ In Exercise 3, how can you tell, before adding, that the sum will be more than $10?

Ⓓ Explain how to rewrite Exercise 4 before solving.

Choose a Computation Method (3-13)

Find each answer.

5. 30 + 50 + 9

6. 3,325
− 2,986

Ⓔ Explain why you would not use a calculator for Exercise 5.

Ⓕ Which method did you choose for Exercise 6? Explain.

Equality and Inequality (3-14)

Compare. Write <, >, or = for ●.

7. 17 + 10 ● 35 − 10

Give three whole numbers that make each statement true.

8. 15 + ■ > 20

9. 18 + ■ < 25

Ⓖ If the expressions in Exercise 7 were put on a balance, would it tilt down on the left or on the right?

Ⓗ Find a whole number that would make the number sentence in Exercise 8 false.

MULTIPLE CHOICE

1. Which number makes the statement true? (3-14)

45 − ■ = 55 − 20

A. 40   **B.** 30   **C.** 20   **D.** 10

2. Josiah bought a map for $12.50. The tax was $0.75. He paid with a $20 bill. How much change did he get back? (3-12)

A. $13.25   **B.** $11.75   **C.** $7.50   **D.** $6.75

FREE RESPONSE

Find each sum or difference. (3-12)

3. $2.56 − 1.06	**4.** $1.70 + 3.86	**5.** $5.76 − 0.97	**6.** $6.43 + 8.79	**7.** $1.50 − 0.75

Choose a computation method. Then solve. (3-13)

8. 4,327 + 3,009	**9.** 2,000 − 1,900	**10.** 2,761 + 2,258	**11.** 9,999 + 435	**12.** 5,088 − 4,307

Give three numbers that make each statement true. (3-14)

13. 12 + ■ > 20.   **14.** 12 − ■ < 10.

Compare. Write <, >, or = for each ●. (3-14)

15. 30 + 25 ● 10 + 35   **16.** 18 − 9 ● 9 − 0

Decide if an exact answer is needed or if an estimate is enough. Solve. (3-11, 3-15)

17. Tara had 301 stickers. She gave 29 to her sister. ABOUT how many stickers did she have left?

> **TEST TALK**
>
> **Think It Through**
> I should **watch for important words** like ABOUT.

Writing in Math

18. Write a word problem that needs an exact answer. Trade with a partner and solve. (3-11)

Test-Taking Strategies

Understand the question.

Get information for the answer.

Plan how to find the answer.

Make smart choices.

Use writing in math.

Improve written answers.

Plan How to Find the Answer

After you understand a test question and get needed information, you need to plan how to find the answer. Think about problem-solving skills and strategies and computation methods you know.

1. Tony noticed a number pattern written on some boxes.

If the pattern continues, what number will be written on the next box?

A. 16

B. 90

C. 100

D. 102

Understand the question.

I need to find the number that comes next in a pattern.

Get information for the answer.

I can get the numbers I need in the picture.

Plan how to find the answer.

- Think about problem-solving skills and strategies.

  I can look for a pattern by checking how to get the second number from the first, the third number from the second, and so on.

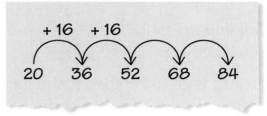

  Then I need to use the pattern to find the next number.

- Choose a computation method.

  I can use paper and pencil to get the next number from the last one shown, 84.

2. Look at the inequality below.

■ > 2

On the number line, draw dots to show all the whole numbers from 0 through 10 that would make the inequality true.

0 1 2 3 4 5 6 7 8 9 10

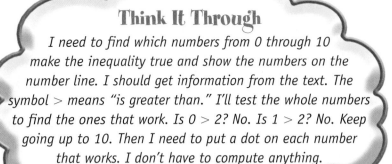

Think It Through

I need to find which numbers from 0 through 10 make the inequality true and show the numbers on the number line. I should get information from the text. The symbol > means "is greater than." I'll test the whole numbers to find the ones that work. Is 0 > 2? No. Is 1 > 2? No. Keep going up to 10. Then I need to put a dot on each number that works. I don't have to compute anything.

Now it's your turn.

For each problem, describe a plan for finding the answer.

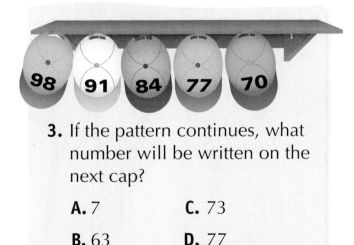

98 91 84 77 70

3. If the pattern continues, what number will be written on the next cap?

A. 7   **C.** 73

B. 63   **D.** 77

4. Look at the inequality below.

■ < 5

On the number line, draw dots to show all the whole numbers from 0 through 10 that would make the inequality true.

0 1 2 3 4 5 6 7 8 9 10

"Re-" means to do something again, as in "reread."

Follow steps when you add. (Lessons 3-1, 3-2, 3-3, 3-4, 3-12)

Add the ones. **Regroup** if needed.	Add the tens. Regroup if needed.	Add the hundreds.	Add money like whole numbers.
$\overset{1}{1}35$ 14 ones = $+\,16\mathbf{9}$ 1 ten, $\mathbf{4}$ 4 ones	$\overset{11}{1}35$ 10 tens = $+\,16\mathbf{9}$ 1 hundred, $\mathbf{04}$ 0 tens	$\overset{11}{1}35$ $+\,16\mathbf{9}$ 304	$\overset{1}{\$}7.04$ $+\quad 6.38$ $\$13.42$ Put \$ and . in the sum.

1. Find $94 + 182$, $\$6.75 + \$3.89$, and $248 + 161 + 703$.

You **regroup** when you group again by exchanging 10 ones for 1 ten or 10 tens for 1 hundred. (p. 126)

Follow steps when you subtract. (Lessons 3-6, 3-7, 3-8, 3-9, 3-10)

Subtract the ones. Regroup if needed.	Subtract the tens. Regroup if needed.	Subtract the hundreds.	Be careful when you subtract across zeros.

$6\,4\,8$ You do
 $-\,2\,5\,6$ not
 2 need to
      regroup.
	$\overset{5}{}\,\overset{14}{}$
	 $\cancel{6}\,\cancel{4}\,8$ Regroup
	 $-\,2\,5\,6$ 1 hundred
	 $9\,2$ for 10
	      more tens.
		$\overset{5}{}\,\overset{14}{}$
		 $\cancel{6}\,\cancel{4}\,8$
		 $-\,2\,5\,6$
		 $3\,9\,2$
			$\overset{}{}\overset{9}{}$
			 $\overset{4}{}\,\overset{10}{}\,\overset{16}{}$
			 $\cancel{5}\,\cancel{0}\,\cancel{6}$ Since there
			 $-\,3\,2\,7$ are no tens,
			 $1\,7\,9$ regroup the
			      hundreds
			      first to make
			      10 tens.

2. Find $97 - 48$, $803 - 385$, and $\$6.25 - \$1.77$.

Look at the silly expression on my face.

"9 + 7" and "18 − 3" are numerical **expressions.** Expressions do not contain >, <, or =. (p. 168)

Use >, <, and = to compare sums and differences. (Lesson 3-14)

Compare.

15 + 25 ⬤ 30 + 10

Add each **expression.**

15 + 25 = 40

30 + 10 = 40

So, 15 + 25 = 30 + 10.

An **equation** shows that the two expressions are equal.

Find three whole numbers that make the **inequality** 10 − n < 5 true.

Substitute whole numbers for n.

10 − 2 < 5	8 < 5	false
10 − 6 < 5	4 < 5	true
10 − 9 < 5	1 < 5	true
10 − 10 < 5	0 < 5	true

3. Compare. 24 − 16 ⬤ 53 − 47

4. Find three whole numbers that make the inequality 15 + x > 25 true.

"Complete" and "incomplete" are opposites.

Equation and **inequality** are opposites. (p. 168)

Look at a problem carefully to plan the solution. (Lessons 3-5, 3-11, 3-13)

Choose a computation method.

Find 430 + 140.

Use mental math.

400 + 100 = 500

30 + 40 = 70

So, the sum is 570.

Decide if the answer should be an estimate or an exact answer.

Al read 32 pages on Monday and 36 pages on Tuesday. Has he read at least 50 pages?

"At least" suggests an estimate.

32 + 36
↓   ↓
30 + 40 = 70

Al has read at least 50 pages.

Draw a picture to help you solve the problem.

Emily reads 3 books in the time Maya reads 1 book. If Emily has read 9 books, how many books has Maya read?

Maya has read 3 books.

5. Last year, Patty, Mark and Sondra each gave a birthday present to each of the others in the group. How many presents were given in all?

MULTIPLE CHOICE

Choose the correct letter for each answer.

1. Find 54 + 19.

A. 63   **B.** 64   **C.** 69   **D.** 73

2. Find the sum of 421 and 480.

A. 79   **C.** 901

B. 801   **D.** 921

3. Kelsey runs 4 laps in the time Brandon runs 3 laps. When Kelsey has run 12 laps, how many laps has Brandon run?

A. 3 laps   **C.** 9 laps

B. 6 laps   **D.** 12 laps

4. Find 623 − 418.

A. 205   **C.** 505

B. 228   **D.** 1,041

5. Find the difference of 900 and 371.

A. 271   **C.** 629

B. 529   **D.** 1,271

6. Which symbol makes this number sentence true?

4 + 8 ● 5

A. <   **B.** =   **C.** +   **D.** >

7. Jeff bought a cap for $3.75. He paid with a $5 bill. How much change did he get back?

A. $1.25   **C.** $3.05

B. $2.05   **D.** $4.80

8. Find the whole number that makes the number sentence below FALSE.

$12 - x > 5$

A. 2

B. 3

C. 6

D. 9

Think It Through
I need to **watch for important words** like FALSE.

9. Pam's family drove 365 miles the first day and 292 miles the second day to reach the campground. How many more miles did Pam's family drive the first day than the second day?

A. 73   **C.** 173

B. 133   **D.** 657

10. Find 118 + 89 + 56.

A. 263   **C.** 421

B. 307   **D.** 589

11. Which problem is shown by the place-value blocks below?

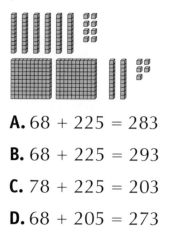

A. 68 + 225 = 283

B. 68 + 225 = 293

C. 78 + 225 = 203

D. 68 + 205 = 273

Write the problem and find the sum.

12.

Find each sum.

13. 104 + 54   **14.** 682 + 123

Regroup 1 ten for 10 ones.

15. 3 4   **16.** 7 8

Regroup 1 hundred for 10 tens.

17. 4 1 3   **18.** 2 8 2

Find each difference.

19. 61 − 23   **20.** 172 − 153

21.   501   **22.**   736
        − 331   − 297

Add or subtract.

23. $7.85   **24.** $9.89
        − 3.08   + 7.71

Use mental math or paper and pencil to solve.

25. 250 + 100 + 50

26. 534 − 144

Compare. Write <, >, or = for each ●.

27. 14 + 9 ● 12 + 5

28. 16 + 12 ● 37 − 9

29. Find 524 − 396. You may draw a picture to help.

30. Lydia read 100 pages of her book. Daryl read 78 pages of his book. How many more pages did Lydia read than Daryl?

Writing in Math

Think It Through
- Make your answer **brief but complete**.
- Check if your **answer makes sense**.

31. Do you need to regroup to solve 223 − 14? Explain.

32. Manuel needs 45 cookies for the club meeting. Each package has 24 cookies. If he has 3 packages, does he have enough cookies? Can you use an estimate to solve? Explain.

33. Tara, Lauren, Brent, and Will each gave a sticker to each of the others in the group. How many stickers were given all together? Draw a picture to help you solve. Explain how you know your answer is correct.

Number and Operation

MULTIPLE CHOICE

1. What is the value of the underlined digit in 50<u>7</u>,899?

   A. 7 ones   **C.** 7 thousands

   B. 7 hundreds   **D.** 7 ten thousands

2. Find 554 − 315.

   A. 235   **C.** 339

   B. 239   **D.** 345

3. Emily bought a sandwich with a $10 bill. She received $5.27 in change. How much did the sandwich cost?

   A. $4.27   **C.** $5.27

   B. $4.73   **D.** $5.73

FREE RESPONSE

4. Liz bought a box of pencils and two notebooks for $5.87. She paid with a $20 bill. How much change did she get back?

5. Use mental math to find 44 + 36.

6. Write 5 hundreds, 2 tens, and 4 ones in standard form.

Writing in Math

7. Clark subtracted 451 from 604 and got 249. How can you tell whether this answer is reasonable?

Geometry and Measurement

MULTIPLE CHOICE

8. What time does the clock say?

   A. 6:00

   B. 6:10

   C. 6:30

   D. 7:30

9. What shape has 4 equal sides?

   A. square

   B. triangle

   C. rectangle

   D. circle

FREE RESPONSE

10. Devon left his house at 6 P.M. He returned home at 9 P.M. How long was Devon gone from his house?

11. Draw a pattern using triangles and circles. Repeat the pattern 3 times.

12. Which is longer, a 1-inch piece of yarn, or a 1-foot piece of yarn?

Writing in Math

13. Explain what the hands of the clock look like when it is 12:15.

Find $10.00 − $3.86.

Estimate: $10 − $4 = $6

$$\begin{array}{r} \overset{9\ \ 9}{0\ \cancel{10}\ \cancel{10}\ 10} \\ \$\cancel{1}\ \cancel{0}.\cancel{0}\ \cancel{0} \\ -\ \ \ \ 3.8\ 6 \\ \hline \$6.1\ 4 \end{array}$$

Line up the decimal points. Add or subtract as with whole numbers. Write the answer in dollars and cents.

Remember to use a dollar sign and decimal point in the answer.

Add or subtract.

1. $2.57	**2.** $3.00	**3.** $7.56
− 1.39	− 0.78	+ 5.49

Use mental math, paper and pencil, or a calculator to add or subtract.

Find 300 − 260.

- This problem can be solved using mental math. Count up by tens.

- 270, 280, 290, 300
  4 tens = 40

300 − 260 = 40.

Remember to look at the problem first to see which method you want to use.

Use mental math, paper and pencil, or a calculator to add or subtract.

1. 3,965	**2.** 500
+ 2,588	− 50
3. 465	**4.** 630
− 227	+ 227

Find three whole numbers that make the number sentence true.

6 + ▨ > 23

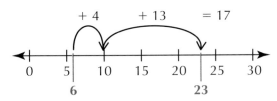

6 + 17 = 23

So the missing number must be greater than 17.
6 + 18 > 23 True
6 + 19 > 23 True
6 + 20 > 23 True

The three whole numbers could be 18, 19, and 20.

Remember you can try numbers until you find one that works.

Give three numbers that make each number sentence true.

1. 15 + ▨ > 22

2. 24 + ▨ < 34

Write <, >, or = for each ●.

3. 6 + 9 ● 7 + 8

4. 4 + 6 ● 3 + 5

5. 7 − 3 ● 12 − 5

6. 8 + 9 ● 7 + 6

Set 3-1 (pages 126–127)

Find each sum.

1. 23 + 65   **2.** 76 + 44   **3.** 51 + 57   **4.** 99 + 32

5. Jamie has 65 baseball cards and Monique has 39 baseball cards. How many do they have in all?

Set 3-2 (pages 128–131)

Write each problem and find the sum.

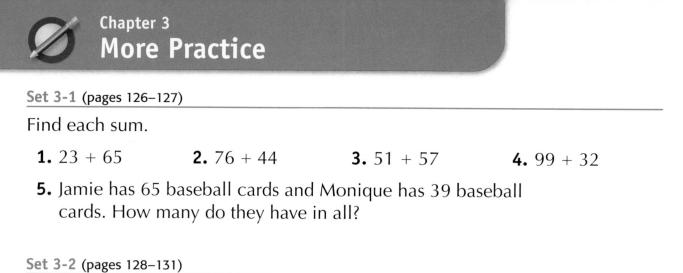

1.   **2.**   **3.**

4. Bill has 3 hundreds blocks, 14 tens blocks, and 5 ones blocks. He says this is the same as 445. Is he correct? Explain.

Set 3-3 (pages 132–135)

Add.

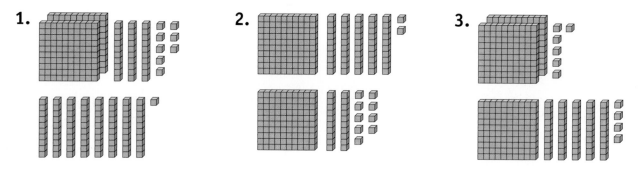

1. 165	**2.** 675	**3.** 490	**4.** 759	**5.** 983
+ 17	+ 541	+ 378	+ 357	+ 45

6. 84 + 250   **7.** 123 + 377   **8.** 271 + 721   **9.** 609 + 494   **10.** 532 + 389

11. Lars has 154 pennies in his bank. Reece has 278 pennies in his bank. How many pennies do they have in all?

Set 3-4 (pages 136–137)

Add.

1. 20 + 324 + 80   **2.** 404 + 345 + 118   **3.** 72 + 86 + 35 + 17

4. 74 + 308 + 36   **5.** 55 + 15 + 108   **6.** 98 + 141 + 376 + 75

7. Write a problem with 3 addends where the sum is less than 300 but greater than 200.

Take It to the NET
More Practice
www.scottforesman.com

Set 3-5 (pages 140–143)

Draw a picture for each problem. Write the answer in a complete sentence.

1. A snail is at the bottom of a 13-foot well. Each day it crawls up 3 feet. Each night it falls down 1 foot. How many days will it take the snail to get out?

2. Rudy makes 5 sandwiches in the time it takes Jeff to make 2 sandwiches. They each must make 10 sandwiches. When Rudy is done, how many more must Jeff make?

Set 3-6 (pages 146–147)

Regroup 1 ten for 10 ones.

1. 67 = 6̸ tens 7̸ ones　　**2.** 34̸5̸　　**3.** 2 2　　**4.** 4 3 1

5. Carol has 6 tens and 2 ones blocks. She regroups 1 ten for 10 ones. How many tens does she have now? How many ones?

Regroup 1 hundred for 10 tens.

6. 422 = 4̸ hundreds 2̸ tens 2 ones　　**7.** 5̸7̸1　　**8.** 6 3 0

9. Marlie has 1 hundreds block, 5 tens blocks, and 7 ones blocks. Jackie has 0 hundreds blocks, 14 tens blocks, and 2 ones blocks. Who is showing a greater number? Explain.

Set 3-7 (pages 148–149)

Subtract.

1. 50 − 25	**2.** 42 − 28	**3.** 65 − 61	**4.** 81 − 37	**5.** 33 − 16

6. 54 − 49　　**7.** 43 − 27　　**8.** 77 − 38　　**9.** 90 − 19　　**10.** 85 − 26

11. Carlo had 26 cookies. He gave 18 of them to his teachers. How many cookies did he have left?

Set 3-8 (pages 150–151)

Find each difference.

1. 176 − 28	**2.** 345 − 162	**3.** 520 − 317	**4.** 685 − 679	**5.** 259 − 163

6. 132 − 51   **7.** 165 − 128   **8.** 276 − 177   **9.** 343 − 52   **10.** 430 − 127

11. Rachel has 1 hundred, 2 tens, and 5 ones blocks. How can she regroup to subtract 31?

Set 3-9 (pages 152–155)

Subtract. Check each answer.

1. 298 − 127	**2.** 328 − 19	**3.** 513 − 155	**4.** 435 − 241	**5.** 637 − 375
6. 271 − 185	**7.** 342 − 78	**8.** 847 − 593	**9.** 715 − 617	**10.** 940 − 796

11. 421 − 287   **12.** 198 − 79   **13.** 322 − 106   **14.** 723 − 499   **15.** 443 − 356

16. Julia's family drove 245 miles on Saturday. They drove 139 miles on Sunday. How many more miles did they drive on Saturday?

17. Brian had $315 in his savings account. He spent $147 on sports equipment. How much money does he have left?

Set 3-10 (pages 156–157)

Subtract. Check each answer.

1. 204 − 21	**2.** 100 − 56	**3.** 308 − 188	**4.** 403 − 199	**5.** 600 − 305
6. 505 − 434	**7.** 308 − 179	**8.** 702 − 493	**9.** 500 − 56	**10.** 901 − 685

11. Harris has 100 marbles. Seventeen of them are red. How many marbles are not red?

12. Julie's friend Katy lives 108 miles away from Julie. Her friend Alice lives 97 miles away. How much farther away does Katy live than Alice?

Take It to the NET
More Practice
www.scottforesman.com

Set 3-11 (pages 160–161)

Decide if an exact answer is needed or if an estimate is enough.
Then solve. Write your answer in a complete sentence.

1. Rachel has 34 favors to make for a party. She has made 12. How many more must she make?

2. Jonah's family has driven 188 miles. They have 397 miles left to drive. Will they drive more than 500 miles? Explain.

Set 3-12 (pages 162–165)

Add or subtract.

1. $0.59
+ 0.78

2. $3.02
− 2.78

3. $1.25
− 0.32

4. $2.75
+ 0.50

5. Taylor had a $5 dollar bill. He bought a pencil for $0.43. How much change did he get?

Set 3-13 (pages 166–167)

Use mental math, paper and pencil, or a calculator to add or subtract.

1. 305
− 221

2. 976
+ 502

3. 1,986
+ 9,859

4. 1,500
− 250

5. Anna says she can use mental math to find 1,550 + 450. Explain how she can do this. Give the sum.

Set 3-14 (pages 168–169)

Compare. Write <, >, or = for each ●.

1. $5 + 8$ ● 12

2. $10 + 2$ ● 16

3. $15 - 9$ ● 9

4. Find a number that makes $40 + x = 54$ true. Is there more than one number that makes the number sentence true? Explain.

Find three whole numbers that make each number sentence true.

5. $9 + $ ▨ < 18

6. $14 - $ ▨ > 5

7. $24 + x < 30$

CHAPTER 4

Time, Data, and Graphs

 DIAGNOSING READINESS

A Vocabulary

(Grade 2 and page 18)

Choose the best term from the box.

1. A _?_ is a unit of time shorter than one _?_.

2. A _?_ can help you compare numbers.

3. A _?_ can help you compare information.

Vocabulary

- **minute** *(Gr. 2)*
- **hour** *(Gr. 2)*
- **pictograph** *(Gr. 2)*
- **number line** *(p. 18)*

B Time

(Grade 2)

Tell what time is shown on each clock.

4.    5.

6. How many minutes are in one hour?

7. List the days of the week in order starting with Sunday.

Do You Know...

How big were the giant drifts made by the blizzard of 1888?

You'll find out in Lesson 4-15.

DISASTER!
CATASTROPHES
THAT SHOOK
THE WORLD
DK

C Number Patterns

(pages 24–27)

Skip count to continue the pattern.

8. 15, 20, 25, 30, ▪, ▪, ▪

9. 40, 35, ▪, 25, ▪, 15, ▪

10. 10, 20, 30, ▪, ▪, 60, ▪

11. 0, 2, ▪, 6, ▪, ▪, ▪

12. 100, 98, ▪, 94, ▪, ▪

13. Tony stacked pennies in stacks of 10. He has 7 stacks. How many pennies does he have?

D Number Lines

(Grade 2)

Write the number for each point.

14. *A*　　　**15.** *B*　　　**16.** *C*

17. *D*　　　**18.** *E*　　　**19.** *F*

20. On a number line, what three whole numbers come between 5 and 9?

21. As you move to the right on a number line, do the numbers become greater or less?

191

Vocabulary
• hour
• minute
• half hour
• quarter hour
• second
• A.M.
• P.M.

Think It Through
I can **get information from a picture.**

Time to the Half Hour and Quarter Hour

LEARN

How do you tell time to the nearest half hour and quarter hour?

When reading a clock, we think in terms of **hours, minutes, half hours,** and **quarter hours.** Some clocks also show **seconds.**

The clocks below show the times of three daily shows at a zoo.

Data File

1 day	= 24 hours
1 hour	= 60 minutes
1 minute	= 60 seconds
1 quarter hour	= 15 minutes
1 half hour	= 30 minutes

Example A

What is the time of each show?

Zebra Show	Alligator Feeding	Leopard Show
10:30	1:15	3:45
What You Say	**What You Say**	**What You Say**
ten thirty or half past ten	one fifteen or 15 minutes after one or quarter past one	three forty-five or 15 minutes to four or quarter to four
What You Write	**What You Write**	**What You Write**
10:30	1:15	3:45

1. Where are the hour hand and minute hand on a clock when the time is 12:45?

How do you use A.M. and P.M. when saying the time?

The hours of a day are divided into A.M. and P.M. hours. The hours between midnight and noon are A.M. hours. The hours between noon and midnight are P.M. hours.

Example B	Example C
Would the leopard show more likely begin at 3:45 A.M. or 3:45 P.M.?	Would you more likely leave for school at 7:30 A.M. or 7:30 P.M.?
3:45 A.M. is very early in the morning. The zoo would not be open. 3:45 P.M. is in the afternoon.	7:30 P.M. is in the evening. Your school would not be open. 7:30 A.M. is in the morning.
The leopard show is more likely to begin in the afternoon, at 3:45 P.M.	You would more likely leave for school in the morning, at 7:30 A.M.

✔ Talk About It

2. Would the alligator feeding show more likely begin at 1:15 A.M. or 1:15 P.M.? Explain.

How do you estimate time?

Example D	Example E
Would it take closer to a minute or a second to wash your face?	Would it take closer to an hour or a day to cook dinner?
A second is a very short period of time. There are 60 seconds in one minute.	A day is 24 hours, much longer than the time needed to cook dinner.
It would take closer to a minute to wash your face.	It would take closer to an hour to cook dinner.

✔ Talk About It

3. Does it take closer to a minute or a second to close a door?

Write the time shown on each clock in two ways.

1.

2.

3.

4. Reasoning Would math class more likely begin at 10:00 A.M. or 10:00 P.M.? Explain.

A **Skills and Understanding**

Write the time shown on each clock in two ways.

5.

6.

7.

8. Brian said the movie began at 7:45 P.M. and Charles said it began at quarter to eight. Explain why they could both be right.

9. Number Sense Would it take closer to one minute or one hour to read a chapter of a book?

B **Reasoning and Problem Solving**

Math and Science

The Academy of Natural Sciences in Philadelphia contains the first dinosaur skeleton ever discovered in North America. Videos of this discovery are shown daily.

Video Show Times	
Weekdays	11:45, 1:15
Weekends	12:00
Holidays	12:00

10. Draw two clock faces with the hands showing the times the dinosaur video show begins on weekdays. Below each clock, tell if this is more likely to be an A.M. or P.M. time.

11. Draw a clock face with the hands showing the time you can see the video show on weekends. Do you think 12:00 here means noon or midnight?

PRACTICE

12. **Writing in Math** Is Jill's answer correct? Explain why or why not.

> How long does it take the minute hand to move all the way around from 12 to 12? The hour hand?
>
> *It takes the minute hand 60 minutes, or 1 hour.*
> *It takes the hour hand 12 hours.*

C Extensions

13. Number Sense How many times in an hour will the hour hand and the minute hand meet on a clock? How many times in a day?

Mixed Review and Test Prep

Take It to the NET
Test Prep
www.scottforesman.com

Compare. Write <, >, or =.

14. 7 + 8 ○ 20 **15.** 38 − 10 ○ 20 + 8 **16.** 45 + 14 ○ 58

17. Find 152 + 98.

A. 354 **B.** 250 **C.** 154 **D.** 54

Learning with Technology

Time eTool

Use the Time eTool to show time to the half hour and quarter hour. Set the hands of the clock to the correct time. Use the digital clock to check your answer. For each, tell if the digital clock should read A.M. or P.M.

1. half past twelve in the afternoon

2. quarter after eight in the morning

3. quarter to six in the afternoon

4. quarter after four in the afternoon

5. half past seven in the morning

6. quarter to one in the morning

TEST TALK

Think It Through
I can **skip count** by fives and then **count on** to tell time.

Time to the Minute

LEARN

How do you tell time to the nearest minute using a clock?

Big Ben is a famous clock in London. It has a minute hand that is 14 feet long.

Example A

What time is shown?

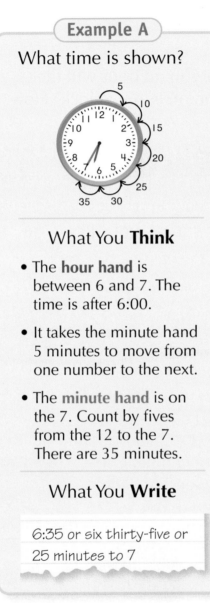

What You **Think**

- The **hour hand** is between 6 and 7. The time is after 6:00.

- It takes the minute hand 5 minutes to move from one number to the next.

- The **minute hand** is on the 7. Count by fives from the 12 to the 7. There are 35 minutes.

What You **Write**

6:35 or six thirty-five or 25 minutes to 7

Example B

What time is shown?

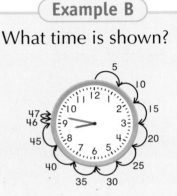

What You **Think**

- The **hour hand** is between 8 and 9. The time is after 8:00.

- It takes the minute hand 1 minute to move from one mark to the next.

- Count by fives from the 12 to the 9. Then count two more minutes. There are 47 minutes.

What You **Write**

8:47 or eight forty-seven or 13 minutes to 9.

✔ **Talk About It**

1. In Example A, is the time earlier or later than 6:45?

2. **Representations** What is another way to write eight minutes to nine?

Write the time shown on each clock two ways.

1.
2.
3.

4. Reasonableness Does Math class last about 1 hour or about 5 minutes?

PRACTICE   *For more practice, see Set 4-2 on p. 254.*

A Skills and Understanding

Write the time shown on each clock two ways.

5.
6.
7.

8. Number Sense Is twelve after five the same time as five after twelve? Explain.

B Reasoning and Problem Solving

Use the data file at the right for 9–11.

9. Draw a clock face showing the sunrise time.

10. Reasoning Is the sunset time closer to 5 P.M. or 6 P.M.?

11. _Writing in Math_ Write the moonrise time in two different ways using words.

Data File
Acadia National Park Weather Report 3/11/02

Temperature	34°F
Sunrise	5:52 A.M.
Sunset	5:28 P.M.
Moonrise	5:15 A.M.
Moonset	3:07 P.M.

Mixed Review and Test Prep

Take It to the NET
Test Prep
www.scottforesman.com

Write the time shown on each clock two ways.

12.
13.
14.

15. Round 653 to the nearest hundred.

   A. 500   **B.** 600   **C.** 700   **D.** 800

Vocabulary
• elapsed time

Think It Through
I can **draw a picture** of a clock to find the elapsed time.

Elapsed Time

LEARN

How do you find elapsed time?

In Sacramento, California, steam-powered train rides are available on summer weekends. The first train leaves at 11:00 A.M. and the last train returns at 5:40 P.M.

Elapsed time is the total amount of time that passes from the beginning time to the ending time.

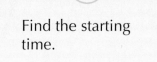

Find the elapsed time from the start of the first train ride to the end of the last train ride.

STEP 1	STEP 2	STEP 3
Find the starting time.	Count the hours.	Count the minutes.
Start at 11:00.	There are 6 hours from 11:00 A.M. to 5:00 P.M.	There are 40 minutes from 5:00 to 5:40.

The elapsed time is 6 hours 40 minutes.

✓ **Talk About It**

1. Why did you count by ones in Step 2 and by fives in Step 3?

2. **Number Sense** John arrived at the Sacramento Railroad Museum at 10:30 A.M. He stayed 5 hours 30 minutes. What time did he leave?

Find the elapsed time.

1. Start Time: 11:00 A.M.
   End Time: 6:00 P.M.

2. Start Time: 7:10 A.M.
   End Time: 8:00 A.M.

3. Start Time: 1:00 P.M.
   End Time: 6:47 P.M.

4. Reasoning Karen went to a movie that started at 5:00 P.M. The movie lasted 1 hour 50 minutes. What time did the movie end?

PRACTICE

For more practice, see Set 4-3 on p. 254.

A Skills and Understanding

Find the elapsed time.

5. Start Time: 4:00 P.M.
   End Time: 8:00 P.M.

6. Start Time: 10:00 A.M.
   End Time: 4:55 P.M.

7. Start Time: 5:40 P.M.
   End Time: 6:00 P.M.

8. Soccer practice lasted from 2:30 P.M. until 3:45 P.M. Did it last more than or less than one hour? Explain.

B Reasoning and Problem Solving

9. The Amtrak train leaves Baltimore at 9:25 A.M. and arrives in Washington, D.C., at 9:55 A.M. How long is the train ride?

10. When the bus arrived at 5:00 P.M., Rick had been at the station 45 minutes. When did he arrive at the station?

11. Reasoning The game started at 7:15 p.m. It lasted 2 hours 10 minutes. What time did the game end?

12. **Writing in Math** Which is longer, 90 minutes or 2 hours? Explain.

Mixed Review and Test Prep

Take It to the NET
Test Prep
www.scottforesman.com

13. 562 + 387　　**14.** 676 + 122　　**15.** 138 − 56　　**16.** 482 − 167

17. Which describes the time shown on the clock?

12:45

A. 15 minutes to twelve

C. 45 minutes before one

B. 45 minutes after one

D. 15 minutes to one

Vocabulary
• weeks
• months
• years
• leap years
• decades
• centuries
• ordinal numbers
(p. 2)

Think It Through
I can **use a calendar** to find days, weeks, and months.

Using a Calendar

LEARN

How do you use a calendar?

When reading a calendar, we think in terms of days, **weeks, months, years,** and **leap years.** Longer periods of time include **decades** and **centuries.**

The 13 colonies declared their independence from England on July 4, 1776. The date is shown on the calendar.

July 1776						
S	M	T	W	T	F	S
	1	2	3	4	5	6
7	8	9	10	11	12	13
14	15	16	17	18	19	20
21	22	23	24	25	26	27
28	29	30	31			

Data File

Time
1 week = 7 days
52 weeks = 1 year
1 year = 12 months
1 year = 365 days
1 leap year = 366 days
1 decade = 10 years
1 century = 100 years

Example A

On which day of the week did the 13 colonies declare their independence from England?

Look for the 4th day of July on the calendar at the right. Find the day of the week at the top of the calendar.

July 1776						
S	M	T	W	T	F	S
	1	2	3	4	5	6
7	8	9	10	11	12	13

The 4th of July was on a Thursday.

Example B

What is the fifth month of the year?

Fifth is an ordinal number. January is the first month of the year. Count five months starting with January.

The fifth month is May.

Order of the Months

January	July
February	August
March	September
April	October
May	November
June	December

✓ Talk About It

1. How could you use the calendar in Example A to find the day of the week for July 13, 1776?

2. What is the elapsed time, in days, from July 4 to July 10?

Use the calendar on page 200 to answer 1 and 2.

1. How many Sundays were there in July of 1776?

2. What date was the second Saturday in July in 1776?

3. Number Sense How many days are there in 4 weeks?

PRACTICE

For more practice, see Set 4-4 on p. 254.

A Skills and Understanding

Use the calendar on page 200 to answer 4 and 5.

4. How many Tuesdays were there in July of 1776?

5. Which day of the week was the 20th of July in 1776?

6. Write an ordinal number to describe the month of July when the months of the year are listed in order.

7. Number Sense How many days are there in two years if neither year is a leap year?

B Reasoning and Problem Solving

8. Reasoning How many decades are in a century? Hint: Think "How many 10s are in 100?"

9. Flag Day is a day to honor our flag. It is celebrated on June 14 each year. What is the elapsed time, in days, from June 14 to July 4?

10. <u>Writing in Math</u> Is Flag Day celebrated on the same day of the week every year? Explain.

June						
S	M	T	W	T	F	S
			1	2	3	4
5	6	7	8	9	10	11
12	13	**14**	15	16	17	18
19	20	21	22	23	24	25
26	27	28	29	30		

Mixed Review and Test Prep

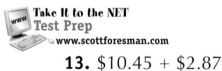

Take It to the NET
Test Prep
www.scottforesman.com

11. $2.15 + $8.93   **12.** $1.86 − $0.79   **13.** $10.45 + $2.87

14. How long did Lisa bake the cake?

Start Time: 2:10 P.M. ⟶ End Time: 2:45 P.M.

A. 30 minutes   **B.** 35 minutes   **C.** 40 minutes   **D.** 45 minutes

Do You Know How?

Do You Understand?

Time to the Half Hour and Quarter Hour (4-1)
Time to the Minute (4-2)

Write the time in 2 ways.

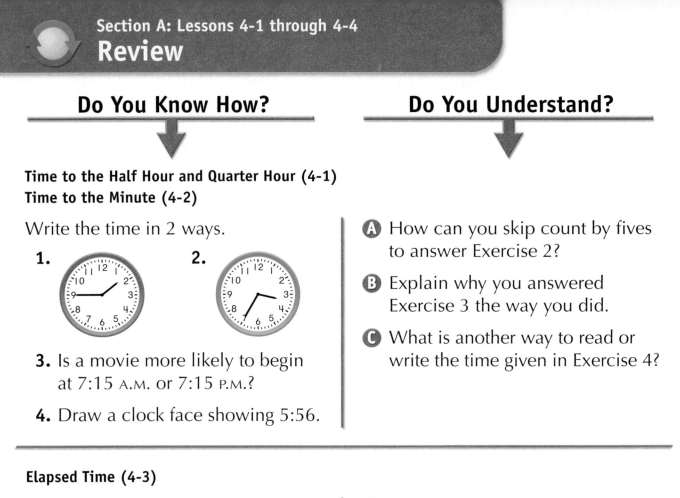

1.

2.

3. Is a movie more likely to begin at 7:15 A.M. or 7:15 P.M.?

4. Draw a clock face showing 5:56.

Ⓐ How can you skip count by fives to answer Exercise 2?

Ⓑ Explain why you answered Exercise 3 the way you did.

Ⓒ What is another way to read or write the time given in Exercise 4?

Elapsed Time (4-3)

5. Find the elapsed time.

Start time: 6:45 P.M.
End time: 8:00 P.M.

6. Joey started hiking at 11:20 A.M. and hiked for 1 hour and 15 minutes. What time did he stop?

Ⓓ In Exercise 5, was the elapsed time more than or less than 2 hours?

Ⓔ In Exercise 6, did Joey's hike end in the morning or afternoon?

Using a Calendar (4-4)

7. What date is the second Monday in December on this calendar?

December						
S	M	T	W	T	F	S
1	2	3	4	5	6	7
8	9	10	11	12	13	14
15	16	17	18	19	20	21
22	23	24	25	26	27	28
29	30	31				

Ⓕ How could you use the answer for Exercise 7 to find the date of the third Monday in December?

Ⓖ How many Saturdays are in December on the calendar shown? How many Sundays are there?

Think It Through
For multiple-choice questions, I need to **eliminate wrong answers.**

MULTIPLE CHOICE

1. How many days are there in 3 weeks? (4-4)

    A. 7 days   **B.** 10 days   **C.** 14 days   **D.** 21 days

2. Math class begins at 9:45 A.M. and ends at 10:35 A.M. How long is math class? (4-3)

    A. 1 hour 10 minutes   **C.** 40 minutes

    B. 50 minutes   **D.** 10 minutes

FREE RESPONSE

Write the time shown on each clock. (4-1, 4-2)

3.

4.

5.

6.

7.

8.

Find the elapsed time. (4-3)

9. Start Time: 2:10 P.M.
    End Time: 4:28 P.M.

10. Start Time: 11:05 A.M.
    End Time: 1:00 P.M.

Solve.

11. Earl began a bike ride at 10:00 A.M. He rode for 1 hour 40 minutes. At what time did his bike ride end?

Writing in Math

12. Write the months of the year in order and write the ordinal number for each month next to its name. (4-4)

13. If October fourth is a Tuesday, on what day of the week is October eleventh? Explain. (4-4)

Key Idea
Tally marks and frequency tables can help you organize data.

Vocabulary
• survey
• data
• tally chart
• tally mark

Think It Through
I can **make a table** to organize my data.

Using Tally Charts to Organize Data

LEARN

How can you collect and organize data?

When you take a **survey,** you collect information by asking a number of people the same question. The information you collect is called **data.** Data can be organized in a **tally chart,** like the one below.

Favorite Winter Olympic Sport to Watch

Sport	Tally	Number
Ice hockey	IIII	4
Figure skating	ⅢⅠ	5
Speed skating	ⅢⅠ III	8
Ski jumping	ⅢⅠ I	6

The survey asked the following question: "What is your favorite winter Olympic sport to watch?" Each sport that was named is listed, and a **tally mark** is recorded for each time that sport was given as an answer.

Example

Read the tally chart above.

STEP 1	The first column lists the answers given.	Ice hockey, figure skating, speed skating, ski jumping
STEP 2	The second column gives a tally mark for each time the sport was given as an answer.	Tally marks are used to keep track of the answers as they are given. Tally marks are grouped in fives. The group ⅢⅠ shows that five people chose figure skating.
STEP 3	The final column gives the number represented by the tally marks.	Four people chose ice hockey, five chose figure skating, eight chose speed skating, and six chose ski jumping.

✔ Talk About It

Use the tally chart on page 204.

1. Add the numbers in the *Number* column to find the total number of people who answered the survey. Does the total agree with the total number of tally marks? Explain.

2. Which sport is the most popular? How many more people voted for speed skating than for ski jumping?

How do you make a tally chart?

Activity

The data at the right was collected in a survey asking, "What is your favorite pizza topping?" The responses were listed in the order they were given. Use the data and follow the steps to make a tally chart.

Pepperoni, Ground beef, Pepperoni, Pepperoni, Vegetables, Ground beef, Pepperoni, Ground beef, Pepperoni, Vegetables, Ground beef, Ground beef, Vegetables, Pepperoni, Pepperoni, Ground beef, Vegetables, Pepperoni, Ground beef, Pepperoni, Vegetables, Pepperoni

a. Title the tally chart and label the columns.

Favorite Pizza Toppings
Topping	Tally	Number

b. List the toppings from the data above. Use tally marks to record how many times the answer pepperoni is given.

Favorite Pizza Toppings
Topping	Tally	Number
Pepperoni	⊬⊬ ⊬⊬	
Ground beef		
Vegetables		

c. Count the tally marks. Record the number.

d. How many people chose ground beef? How many chose vegetables? Complete the chart for the other toppings.

Favorite Pizza Toppings
Topping	Tally	Number
Pepperoni	⊬⊬ ⊬⊬	10
Ground beef		
Vegetables		

For 1–3, use the tally chart you made for the Activity on page 205.

1. What was the most popular pizza topping?

2. How many people all together answered the survey?

3. **Number Sense** What number is shown by 卌 卌 卌 卌 卌 ?

PRACTICE

For more practice, see Set 4-5 on p. 255.

Ⓐ Skills and Understanding

Use the data at the right to answer 4–7.

4. Make a tally chart to show the results.

5. How many people voted?

6. Which colors got the same number of votes?

7. How many more votes are for red than for green?

Favorite Color				
Red	Blue	Red	Red	Blue
Blue	Yellow	Blue	Green	Yellow
Red	Blue	Red	Blue	Green
Green	Blue	Yellow	Red	Yellow
Yellow	Green	Blue	Red	Green
Blue	Red	Yellow	Green	Blue

Ⓑ Reasoning and Problem Solving

Math and Art

The fourth-grade class voted for their favorite activities in art class.

8. Which art activity did the most people say was their favorite?

9. How many more people chose drawing as their favorite activity than using clay?

10. **Writing in Math** Do you agree with Jan's statement? Explain.

> If 7 more people voted for using clay, there would still be more votes for painting.

Favorite Art Activities

Activity	Tally	Number
Painting	卌 卌 卌	15
Drawing	卌 卌 I	11
Using clay	卌	5

C Extensions

11. Tally charts can be used to organize all kinds of data. List the letters *a, e, i, o,* and *u* on paper. Then choose a paragraph from this book and tally the number of times each letter is used in the paragraph. Complete the chart by writing the number for each.

Mixed Review and Test Prep

Take It to the NET
Test Prep
www www.scottforesman.com

12. If August 3 is the first Wednesday of the month, what is the date of the second Wednesday?

13. Find 17 + 23 + 46.

    A. 40   **B.** 69   **C.** 76   **D.** 86

14. **Writing in Math** Write a paragraph about the date of your birth. Include what day of the week it will be on this year. Also include what day of the week it was when you were born, if you know.

Learning with Technology

Spreadsheet/Data/Grapher eTool

Each block in a spreadsheet is called a *cell.* Cells are named by the column letter and row number. In the spreadsheet at the right, cell B3 is highlighted.

Create a spreadsheet from the flower data, entering the data in the order it appears.

	A	B
1	Flower	Total
2	Rose	2
3	Violet	11
4	Dandelion	1
5	Clover	8

1. What appears in cell A2? B2?

2. Name the cell that contains the clover total.

3. Enter a formula to find the total number of flowers.

All text pages available online and on CD-ROM.

Think It Through
I can use a line plot to **compare data.**

WARM UP

1. 24 – 12   2. 34 – 15
3. 56 – 11   4. 94 – 48
5. 42 – 17   6. 67 – 39

LEARN

How do you read a line plot?

Students in Ms. Ward's class listed how far each student lives from school. The results are recorded on the **line plot** below.

On the line plot, the number line shows the different distances between school and home. The *X*s represent how many students live that distance from school. Each *X* represents one student.

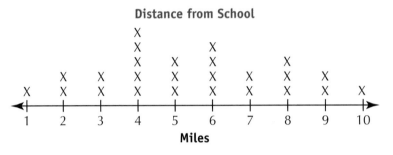

Distance from School

Miles

What information can you get from a line plot?

The **range** is the difference between the greatest and the least numbers in the data. The **mode** is the number that occurs most often in the data.

Example A	Example B	Example C
How many students live six miles from school?	What is the range for this set of data?	What is the mode for this set of data?
• Find 6 on the number line. • Count the *X*s above the 6. There are four.	The greatest number is 10. The least number is 1. **10 – 1 = 9**	On the line plot, the number 4 has the most *X*s above it.
Four students live six miles from school.	The range of the data is 9.	The mode of the data is 4.

208

✔ Talk About It

1. Do more students live one mile or two miles from school?

2. How many students live five miles or less from school?

3. **Reasoning** How many students are on the list that shows the distance from home to school? How did you find the total number of students?

For another example, see Set 4-6 on p. 251.

CHECK ✓

The height of each student in third grade was measured, and the data is shown in the line plot. Use the line plot to answer each question.

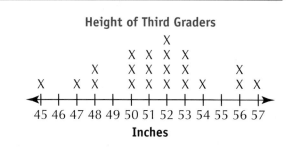

Height of Third Graders

Inches

1. What is the mode of the data? What does the mode tell you?

2. How many students are exactly 49 inches tall?

3. How many students are less than 51 inches tall?

4. **Reasoning** Three friends in the class are about the same height. How tall could they be? List all the possible heights.

PRACTICE

For more practice, see Set 4-6 on p. 255.

A Skills and Understanding

Each student in third grade performed the long jump. The results are shown on the line plot. Use the line plot to answer each question.

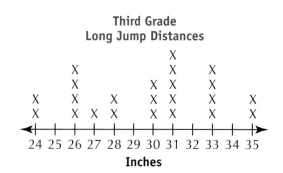

**Third Grade
Long Jump Distances**

Inches

5. How many students jumped 29 inches?

6. What is the range of the data?

7. How many students jumped 33 inches or less?

8. Which of the following statements best describes the data in the line plot? Explain your answer.

   • Most third graders can long jump at least 25 inches.
   • Most third graders can long jump at least 35 inches.

B Reasoning and Problem Solving

 **Math and Art**

Claude Monet was a successful painter. This line plot shows the number of paintings he finished each year for 4 years. Use the line plot to answer each question.

9. In which year shown did Monet finish the fewest paintings?

10. How many paintings did Monet finish from the beginning of 1903 through 1905?

11. **Writing in Math** Do you agree with Martin's statement below? Explain.

> Claude Monet finished as many pictures in 1903 as in 1904 and 1905 together.

Monet's *Waterlilies*

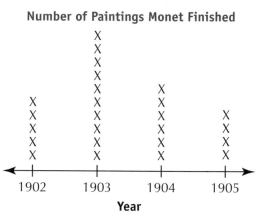

Number of Paintings Monet Finished

C Extensions

12. Line plots help us make conclusions about data. Describe the shape of the data on the line plot at the right. Hint: Does it look like a mountain or a valley?

13. **Writing in Math** Find the mode of the data. Explain what this tells you about running times for this group.

Time to Run 1 Mile

Mixed Review and Test Prep

 **Take It to the NET**
Test Prep
www.scottforesman.com

Compare. Write >, <, or =.

14. 24 ⬤ 17

15. 58 ⬤ 85

16. 21 ⬤ 19

17. Which shows 24 in tally form?

A. ⏦⏦ ⏦⏦ ⅠⅠⅠⅠ

C. ⏦⏦ ⏦⏦ ⏦⏦ ⏦⏦ ⅠⅠⅠⅠ

B. ⏦⏦ ⏦⏦ ⏦⏦ ⅠⅠⅠⅠ

D. ⏦⏦ ⏦⏦ ⏦⏦ ⏦⏦ ⏦⏦

Enrichment

Mean and Median

Materials: counters

A **mean** is a type of average. One way to find the mean is to rearrange the numbers from a group of data so that all the numbers are the same.

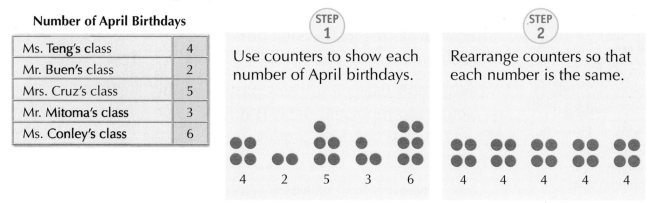

Number of April Birthdays

Ms. Teng's class	4
Mr. Buen's class	2
Mrs. Cruz's class	5
Mr. Mitoma's class	3
Ms. Conley's class	6

STEP 1
Use counters to show each number of April birthdays.

STEP 2
Rearrange counters so that each number is the same.

The mean number of April birthdays is 4.

If you order a group of data from least to greatest, the **median** is the middle number.

Number of June Birthdays

Ms. Teng's class	3
Mr. Buen's class	5
Mrs. Cruz's class	8
Mr. Mitoma's class	4
Ms. Conley's class	10

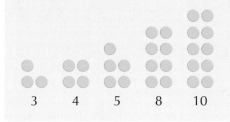

Order the counters for June birthdays from least to greatest.

The median number of June birthdays is 5.

For 1 and 2, use counters and the data above to find

1. the mean of June birthdays.

2. the median of April birthdays. What do you notice about the mean and median for this data?

3. Find the mode and the range for the data below. Use counters to find the mean and the median.

2, 3, 9, 5, 6, 5, 3, 3, 9

Key Idea
Pictographs use pictures to show data. Bar graphs use bars to show data.

Vocabulary
• pictograph
• key
• bar graph
• scale

Think It Through
I can use a pictograph to **compare data.**

Reading Pictographs and Bar Graphs

LEARN

How do you use a pictograph?

The pictograph below shows the number of ski resorts in each area of Michigan.

A **pictograph** uses pictures or parts of pictures to represent data. The **key** explains what each picture represents.

The U.S. National Ski Hall of Fame and Museum is located in Michigan.

Number of Major Ski Resorts in Michigan

Detroit area	✗ ✗ /
Grand Rapids and South	✗ ✗
Northern Lower Peninsula	✗ ✗ ✗ /
Upper Peninsula	✗ ✗ ✗ ✗ ✗

Each ✗ = 2 resorts. Each / = 1 resort.

Example A

How many resorts are in the Detroit area?

Use the key.

Each ✗ represents 2 resorts. Each / represents 1 resort. Count the ✗ and the /.

There are two ✗ and one /.

2 + 2 + 1 = 5

There are 5 resorts in the Detroit area.

✔ Talk About It

1. Are there more resorts in the Detroit area or the Upper Peninsula?

How do you use a bar graph?

Bar graphs use bars to compare information. The **scale** shows the units used on a bar graph.

Black diamond trails are trails that are difficult to ski. The bar graph shows the number of black diamond trails at 6 Michigan ski resorts.

On this graph, only the even-numbered grid lines are labeled. But, each grid line represents one trail. For example, the line halfway between 8 and 10 represents 9 trails.

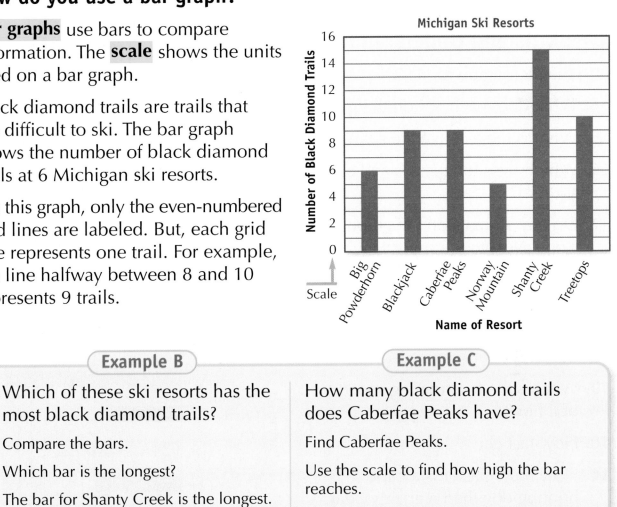

Michigan Ski Resorts

Example B

Which of these ski resorts has the most black diamond trails?

Compare the bars.

Which bar is the longest?

The bar for Shanty Creek is the longest.

Shanty Creek has the most black diamond trails.

Example C

How many black diamond trails does Caberfae Peaks have?

Find Caberfae Peaks.

Use the scale to find how high the bar reaches.

Caberfae Peaks has 9 black diamond trails.

✔ Talk About It

2. Which other resort has 9 black diamond trails?

3. Which resort has the fewest black diamond trails?

Take It to the NET
More Examples
www.scottforesman.com

CHECK ✅

For another example, see Set 4-7 on p. 251.

Use the pictograph on page 212 and the bar graph on this page for 1–3.

1. How many more resorts are there in the Detroit area than in the Grand Rapids and South area?

2. How many black diamond trails are there all together at Norway Mountain and Treetops?

3. What is the range of the data in this bar graph?

A Skills and Understanding

Use the pictograph for 4–7.

4. What does each 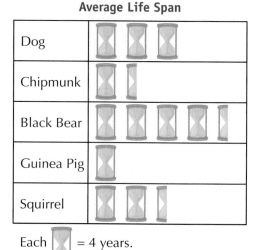 on the graph represent?

5. What is the average life span of a dog?

6. Which lives longer, a black bear or a squirrel?

7. Do any animals on the graph have the same average life span? How do you know?

Average Life Span

Dog	
Chipmunk	
Black Bear	
Guinea Pig	
Squirrel	

Each 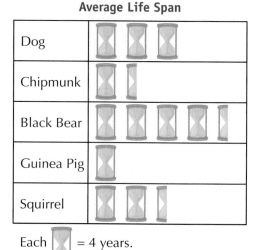 = 4 years.

Use the bar graph for 8–11.

8. Which animal on the graph has the fastest running speed?

9. What is the top running speed of a lion?

10. How fast can a zebra run?

11. How much faster is a cape hunting dog than a grizzly bear?

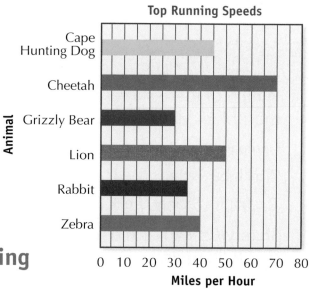

Top Running Speeds

B Reasoning and Problem Solving

Math and Music

Johann Sebastian Bach was a famous composer. He wrote many pieces of music. The bar graph shows how often he included each instrument.

12. What two instruments appear to have been used the same number of times?

13. Was the cello used more than or fewer than 50 times? the oboe?

14. Which instrument was used the greatest number of times? the fewest number of times?

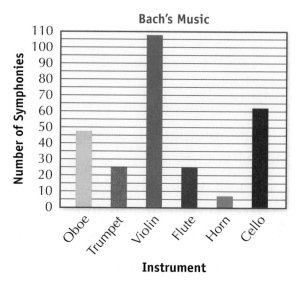

Bach's Music

15. <u>Writing in Math</u> Do you agree with Sam's statement? Explain. Use the graph at the top of page 214.

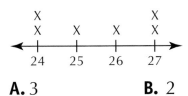
A squirrel lives for about 10 years.

Mixed Review and Test Prep

**Take It to the NET
Test Prep**
www.scottforesman.com

16. 28 − 19   **17.** 35 + 41   **18.** 71 − 25   **19.** 55 + 87

20. Find the range for the data on the line plot.

```
      X                 X
  X   X     X     X     X
 ←──┼─────┼─────┼─────┼──→
   24    25    26    27
```

A. 3   **B.** 2   **C.** 1   **D.** 0

Discovery CHANNEL SCHOOL

Discover Math in Your World

Snow Desert

Antarctica is the coldest place on Earth and the driest. When the air is very cold, there is not enough water vapor to create a lot of snow. Average amounts of snow are shown in the graph.

1. Which month shows the least amount of snowfall? the greatest amount?

2. Did any month shown in the graph have more than one inch of snow?

3. If March had $\frac{7}{10}$ of an inch of snow, would the bar for March be longer or shorter than the bar for April?

4. List the months February, April and June in order from least snowfall to greatest snowfall.

**Take It to the NET
Video and Activities**
www.scottforesman.com

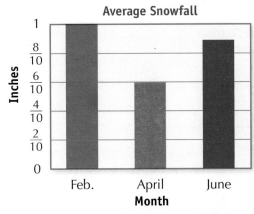
Average Snowfall

Problem-Solving Skill

Key Idea
There are specific things you can do to write a good comparison in math.

Writing to Compare

LEARN

How do you write a good comparison?

When you **write to compare,** you need to look closely at the information and tell how it is alike and different.

Most Admired Two groups of students were asked about their most admired professionals. The data for both groups is shown in the bar graphs below.

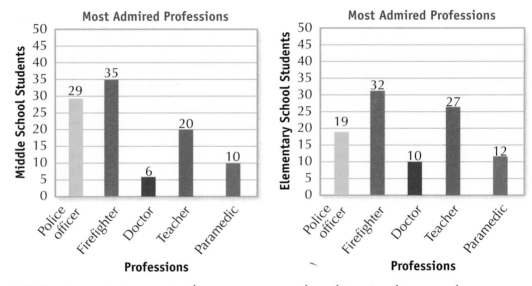

Write two statements that compare the data in the graphs.

Writing a Math Comparison

- Look closely at the data and tell how it is alike and how it is different.

- Use comparison words such as "most," "more," and "about the same."

Firefighters had the most votes in each group.

Elementary school students voted more for teachers than for doctors.

TEST TALK

Think It Through
I can use the graphs to find how the data about professions is **alike and different.**

✔ Talk About It

1. What other comparison statements can you make about the graphs? What comparison words did you use?

For another example, see Set 4-8 on p. 252.

Use the pictographs at the right.

1. Write two statements that compare the data on the graphs.

2. What comparison words did you use?

Favorite Pets of Mr. Day's Class

Dog	🧍 🧍 🧍 🧍
Cat	🧍 🧍 🧍 🧍 🧍 🧍
Gerbil	🧍 🧍
Goldfish	🧍 🧍
Parakeet	🧍

Each 🧍 = 2 votes.

Favorite Pets of Mrs. Lee's Class

Dog	🧍 🧍 🧍 🧍 🧍 🧍
Cat	🧍 🧍 🧍
Gerbil	🧍 🧍 🧍
Goldfish	🧍 🧍
Parakeet	🧍 🧍

Each 🧍 = 2 votes.

PRACTICE

For more practice, see Set 4-8 on p. 255.

3. Use the bar graphs at the right. Write two statements that compare the two girls' saving patterns. What comparison words did you use?

Amount Saved by Lupe

Amount Saved by Anita

4. The table at the right shows how long it takes Jamie to make bows for gift packages. If the pattern continues, how long will it take Jamie to make 6 bows?

Number of Bows	Number of Minutes
1	10
2	20
3	30
4	40

5. Jamie earned $12 by making bows and wrapping gifts last week. She spent $8.25 on toys and put the rest of the money into her piggy bank. How much money did she put in her piggy bank?

6. Explain what operations are needed to solve the Marathon Runners problem. Then solve the problem.

7. If 18 of the people who did not finish the marathon were men, how many were women?

Marathon Runners In a recent marathon, 465 men and 288 women ran in the race. All but 34 of the runners finished the race. How many people finished the race?

Algebra

Key Idea
Ordered pairs can help you locate points on a coordinate grid.

Vocabulary
- coordinate grid
- ordered pair
- plot

Materials
- first-quadrant grid or

  e tools

Graphing Ordered Pairs

LEARN

How can you name a point?

The Science Museum Visitors' Guide uses a **coordinate grid** to help people find points of interest. An **ordered pair** of numbers names the point on the grid.

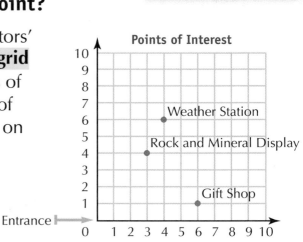

Points of Interest

Example A

Name the location of the rock and mineral display.

STEP 1 Put your finger on 0. Move it to the right until it is under the rock and mineral display. Count the number of spaces you moved.

3 spaces to the right

(3, ⬚)

STEP 2 Move your finger up until it reaches the rock and mineral display. Count the number of spaces you moved.

4 spaces up

(3, 4)

The rock and mineral display is at (3, 4).

Think It Through
- I can **act it out** by moving my finger along a grid to find a location.
- I need to **identify steps in the process.**

✔ Talk About It

1. **Reasoning** Would it be correct to say that the weather station's location is (6, 4)? Explain your answer.

2. Name the location of the gift shop.

How can you locate a point?

To **plot** a point, locate and mark the point using the given ordered pair.

Museum Exhibits	
Exhibit	**Location**
Sharks	(1, 2)
Rain forest	(2, 5)
Human body	(5, 4)
Planetarium	(2, 1)

Example B

Plot and label a point to locate the planetarium.

What You **Think**	What You **Write**

STEP 1 The planetarium is at (2, 1). Start at 0. Move 2 spaces to the right. Move 1 space up.

STEP 2 Make a point and label it *Planetarium*.

✔ Talk About It

3. How is the location of the shark exhibit different from the location of the planetarium?

 **Take It to the NET**
More Examples
www.scottforesman.com

For another example, see Set 4-9 on p. 252.

CHECK ✓

Write the ordered pair that describes the location of each point.

1. A   **2.** B   **3.** C   **4.** D

Give the letter of the point named by each ordered pair.

5. (3, 1)   **6.** (5, 5)   **7.** (0, 4)   **8.** (4, 0)

9. Number Sense If an object were located at (2, 3), would it be closer to an object at (2, 1) or an object at (4, 0)?

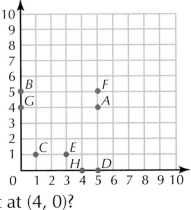

For more practice, see Set 4-9 on p. 256.

A Skills and Understanding

Write the ordered pair that describes the location of each point.

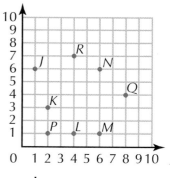

10. *J*   **11.** *K*   **12.** *L*   **13.** *M*

Give the letter of the point named by each ordered pair.

14. (4, 7)   **15.** (6, 6)   **16.** (2, 1)   **17.** (8, 4)

Draw a coordinate grid on a piece of grid paper. Mark each ordered pair on the grid.

18. *A* (3, 4)   **19.** *B* (2, 1)   **20.** *C* (4, 3)   **21.** *D* (5, 0)

22. Reasoning Describe the difference between locating a point at (5, 2) and a point at (2, 5).

B Reasoning and Problem Solving

Math and Social Studies

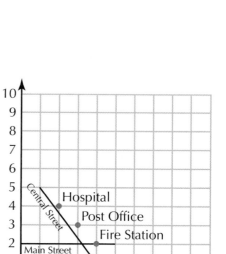

City maps sometimes use a grid system to show where places are located. Use the map at the right for 23–29. Tell what building is located at each point.

23. (2, 4)   **24.** (3, 3)

25. (4, 2)   **26.** (4, 1)

27. Give the ordered pair that names the location of the school.

28. If each space on the grid represents one block, how far is the school from the police station?

29. <u>Writing in Math</u> Do you agree with Marissa's answer below? If not, give the correct answer and explain her mistake.

> Between what two points does Main Street run?
>
> *Main Street runs between (2, 0) and (2, 5).*

C Extensions

30. Mark these 4 points on a coordinate grid: (2, 6); (4, 6); (4, 4); (2, 4). Connect the dots in order. What shape have you made?

Mixed Review and Test Prep

Take It to the NET
Test Prep
www.scottforesman.com

31. Which description is true for the season snowfall record in Thompson Pass, Alaska?

   A. Less than 900 inches

   B. Greater than 1,000 inches

   C. Less than 1,000 inches

   D. Exactly 1,000 inches

32. **Writing in Math** Write two comparison statements for the graph at the right.

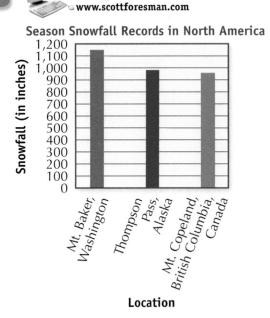

Season Snowfall Records in North America

Snowfall (in inches)

Location

Practice Game

Make a Rectangle

Number of Players: 2–4

Materials: 1 number cube labeled 0–5
   1 spinner with 6 sections, labeled 0–5
   coordinate grid numbered 0–5 for each player

1. Player 1 tosses the number cube for the first number in the ordered pair and then spins the spinner for the second number.

2. Player 1 plots the point for the ordered pair.

3. Each of the other players takes a turn, repeating Steps 1 and 2.

4. The first player to plot points that can be connected to make a rectangle is the winner.

Key Idea
The steps for reading a line graph are similar to the steps for finding points on a grid.

Vocabulary
• line graph

Reading Line Graphs

LEARN

✓ **WARM UP**
1. Explain how to find the ordered pair (5,4) on a grid.

How do you read a line graph?

A **line graph** shows how data changes over a period of time. The graph shows how the average temperature changes in Denver, Colorado, from September through January. Notice that it drops from about 62°F in September to 25°F in January.

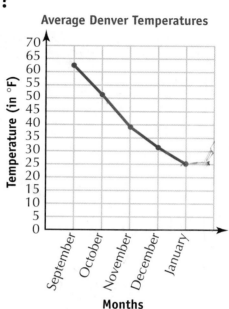

Average Denver Temperatures

Temperature (in °F)

Months

TEST TALK

Think It Through

I can **turn the question into a statement:** I need to find the average temperature for November.

Example

What is the average temperature for Denver, Colorado, in November?

	What You **Think**	What You **Do**
STEP 1	Find the month.	Move along the bottom of the graph until you get to November.
STEP 2	Where is the point?	Move up until you get to the point.
STEP 3	What number matches the point? What is the average temperature for November?	Move left to the scale. Read the numbers on the scale. The point is between 35° and 40°, but very close to 40°.

The average temperature in November is about 39°F.

✓ **Talk About It**

1. Of the five months shown, which month is the coldest in Denver? Which month is the warmest?

Take It to the NET
More Examples
www.scottforesman.com

Use the line graph on page 222 for 1–3.

1. What is the average October temperature for Denver?

2. How many months shown have an average temperature below 40°F?

3. Number Sense Is it correct to say that December is about 30° colder than September? Explain.

PRACTICE

For more practice, see Set 4-10 on p. 256.

A Skills and Understanding

Use the line graph for 4–7.

4. What data does the graph show?

5. How many students bought lunch on Tuesday?

6. On how many days did at least 200 students buy lunch?

7. Number Sense Is it correct to say that more than 250 students bought lunch on Monday? Explain.

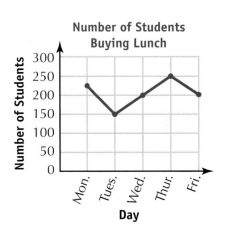

B Reasoning and Problem Solving

Use the line graph at the right for 8–11. Did Hank's practice time increase or decrease from

8. April to May?   **9.** May to August?

10. How much less was Hank's average daily practice time in August than in June?

11. Writing in Math Write a paragraph explaining possible reasons for the changes in Hank's practice time from April to September.

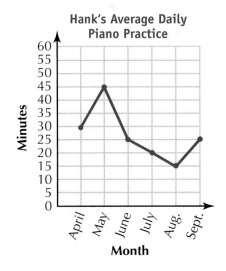

Mixed Review and Test Prep

Take It to the NET
Test Prep
www.scottforesman.com

12. Draw a coordinate grid and plot the ordered pair (3, 2).

13. Give the next three numbers in this pattern: 3, 8, 13, ▨, ▨, ▨

   A. 14, 16, 18   **B.** 16, 19, 22   **C.** 18, 23, 28   **D.** 18, 22, 26

Do You Know How?

Do You Understand?

Using Tally Charts to Organize Data (4-5); Using Line Plots to Organize Data (4-6)

1. Copy and complete the tally chart.

Favorite Meat

Meat	Tally	Number
Beef	⅏ IIII	
Chicken	⅏ ⅏	

Use the data at the left.

Weights of Puppies

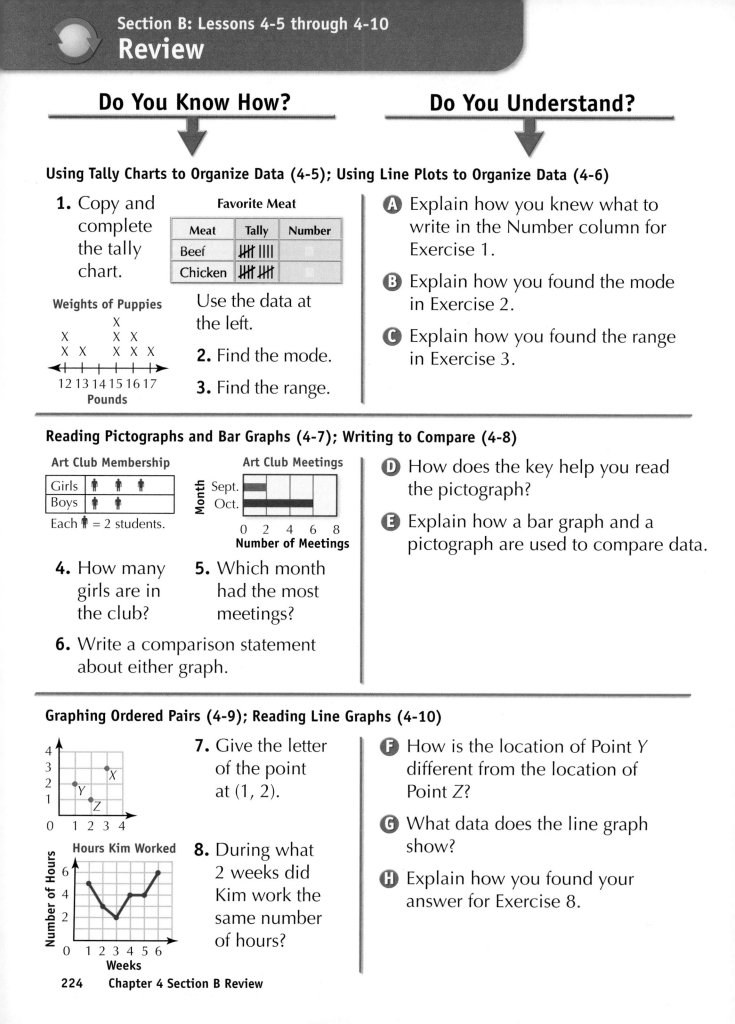

X
X   X X
X X   X X X
12 13 14 15 16 17
Pounds

2. Find the mode.

3. Find the range.

Ⓐ Explain how you knew what to write in the Number column for Exercise 1.

Ⓑ Explain how you found the mode in Exercise 2.

Ⓒ Explain how you found the range in Exercise 3.

Reading Pictographs and Bar Graphs (4-7); Writing to Compare (4-8)

Art Club Membership

Girls	🧍 🧍 🧍
Boys	🧍 🧍

Each 🧍 = 2 students.

Art Club Meetings

Month: Sept. / Oct.
0 2 4 6 8
Number of Meetings

4. How many girls are in the club?

5. Which month had the most meetings?

6. Write a comparison statement about either graph.

Ⓓ How does the key help you read the pictograph?

Ⓔ Explain how a bar graph and a pictograph are used to compare data.

Graphing Ordered Pairs (4-9); Reading Line Graphs (4-10)

4
3   •X
2   •
1   Y
      •Z
0 1 2 3 4

7. Give the letter of the point at (1, 2).

Hours Kim Worked

Number of Hours
6
4
2
0 1 2 3 4 5 6
Weeks

8. During what 2 weeks did Kim work the same number of hours?

Ⓕ How is the location of Point Y different from the location of Point Z?

Ⓖ What data does the line graph show?

Ⓗ Explain how you found your answer for Exercise 8.

Think It Through
I can try **working backward** from each answer choice.

MULTIPLE CHOICE

1. What number is represented by ||||| |||| ? (4-5)

A. 90   **B.** 14   **C.** 9   **D.** 8

2. What is the mode for the data below? (4-6)
3, 3, 4, 4, 4, 4, 5, 5, 6

A. 3   **B.** 4   **C.** 5   **D.** 6

3. Which point is at (3, 1)? (4-9)

A. N   **B.** K   **C.** L   **D.** M

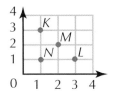

FREE RESPONSE

Use the bar graph for 4 and 5. (4-7)

4. How much taller is the giraffe than the lion?

5. List the 4 animals in order from shortest to tallest.

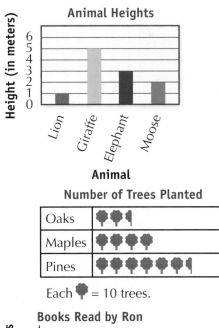

Use the pictograph for 6 and 7. (4-7)

6. How many oak trees were planted?

7. How many trees in all were planted?

Number of Trees Planted

Oaks	🌳🌳🌴
Maples	🌳🌳🌳🌳
Pines	🌳🌳🌳🌳🌳🌴

Each 🌳 = 10 trees.

Use the line graph for 8 and 9. (4-10)

8. What data does the line graph show?

9. How many books did Ron read when he was 10 years old?

Writing in Math

10. Write a comparison statement about the bar graph above. (4-8)

11. Explain how you would plot a point at (4, 5) on a coordinate grid. (4-9)

Key Idea
Making a pictograph is one way to display and compare data.

Think It Through
I can **draw a picture or symbol** to represent the key.

Making Pictographs

LEARN

WARM UP
1. Write ɪɪɪɪ as a number.
2. Write ɪɪɪɪ ɪɪɪɪ ||| as a number.
3. Write the missing numbers.
2, 4, 6, ▪, ▪, ▪

Activity

How do you make a pictograph?

Somerset Elementary had a Third Grade Family Math Night. The tally chart shows how many students from each class attended the Family Math Night.

Use the data in the chart to make a pictograph.

a. Copy the pictograph that has been started.

b. Write a title to explain what the pictograph shows.

c. Choose a symbol for the key. Notice that each symbol stands for 2 students.

d. Decide how many of your symbols are needed for each class. Draw them.

Data File

Class	Tally	Number
Mr. Ford	ɪɪɪɪ	5
Ms. Myers	ɪɪɪɪ ɪɪɪɪ ||||	14
Mrs. Wray	ɪɪɪɪ ɪɪɪɪ ||	11
Ms. Mercer	ɪɪɪɪ ||||	8

Mr. Ford	
Ms. Myers	
Mrs. Wray	
Ms. Mercer	

Each   = 2 students.

e. How many symbols did you draw for Mr. Ford's class?

f. Which class has 5 whole and 1 half of your symbols?

g. Explain why you chose the symbol you used in your pictograph.

h. How does the pictograph help you to compare the data?

i. Reasoning If the key was changed so that each symbol stood for 4 students, how many symbols would you use for the number of students from Ms. Myers' class?

Take It to the NET
More Examples
www.scottforesman.com

For another example, see Set 4-11 on p. 253.

Use the data in the table.

Suppose you are going to put the information in a pictograph. You would need to choose a symbol for your pictograph. Let each symbol stand for 5 books sold.

Data File	
Category of Book	**Number Sold**
Fiction	25
Nonfiction	40
Poetry	20
Dictionary	15

1. How many symbols would you draw for fiction?

2. Reasoning Why is 5 a good number to use in the key?

PRACTICE

For more practice, see Set 4-11 on p. 256.

Ⓐ Skills and Understanding

The data file shows how Susan's class voted on their favorite pet.

3. Copy and complete the table.

4. Copy the pictograph and insert the key. How many votes will each symbol stand for?

5. Complete the pictograph, including a title.

Data File		
Pet	**Tally**	**Number**
Dog	⊬⊬ IIII	
Cat	⊬⊬ ⊬⊬	
Fish	IIII	
Bird	⊬⊬ II	

Dog	
Cat	
Fish	
Bird	

Each ⬜ = 2 votes.

Ⓑ Reasoning and Problem Solving

6. <u>Writing in Math</u> Write the title you chose for the pictograph above. Explain why you chose that title.

Think It Through
A title should **tell the main idea** of the graph.

Mixed Review and Test Prep

Take It to the NET
Test Prep
www.scottforesman.com

Use the graph at the right.

7. How much did Kelly spend on Friday?

8. How much more did Kelly spend on Friday than on Tuesday?

A. $5   **C.** $15

B. $10   **D.** $20

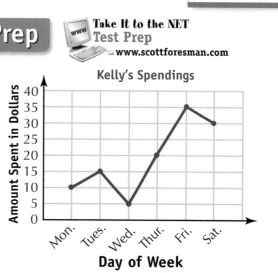

Kelly's Spendings

Key Idea
Making a bar graph is a way to display and compare data.

Materials
• grid paper
or  tools

Think It Through

• I must **use the scale** to determine the length of the bars.

• I must determine the title by **looking for the main idea.**

Making Bar Graphs

LEARN

Activity

How do you make a bar graph?

The table shows the number of points scored by a football team in their first six games of a season.

It will be easy to compare this data if you display it in a bar graph.

The first three games are already on the graph below.

Game	Points Scored
1	13
2	18
3	10
4	7
5	17
6	14

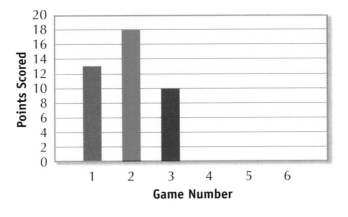

a. Copy the graph and make the bars for Games 4, 5, and 6.

b. Give the graph a title.

c. Where does the bar for Game 4 end? Game 5?

d. In which game did the team score the most points? How can you tell by looking at the bar graph?

e. Would it be easier to find the total number of points scored by using the graph or the table? Explain.

Take It to the NET
More Examples
www.scottforesman.com

For another example, see Set 4-12 on p. 253.

You will be using the data file at the right to make a bar graph.

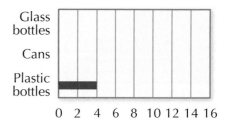

Data File

Trash Collection	
Type	**Number Collected**
Glass Bottles	6
Cans	12
Plastic Bottles	4

1. How many bars will be on your completed graph?

2. Copy the bar graph that has been started and make the rest of the bars. Give the graph a title and labels.

3. **Number Sense** If six more glass bottles were collected, which two bars would be the same length?

Glass bottles

Cans

Plastic bottles

0 2 4 6 8 10 12 14 16

For more practice, see Set 4-12 on p. 257.

A Skills and Understanding

You will be using the table at the right to make a bar graph.

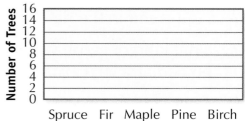

TREES PLANTED BY NATURE CLUB IN THE FALL	
KIND OF TREE	**NUMBER OF TREES**
SPRUCE	8
FIR	5
MAPLE	12
PINE	16
BIRCH	7

4. Which kind of tree will be represented by the longest bar?

5. Copy and complete the bar graph that has been started. Give the graph a title.

6. How many trees in all were planted?

7. **Number Sense** If the number of pine trees was decreased by 2 and the number of maple trees increased by 2, would there still be more pine trees than maple trees? Explain.

Number of Trees

16
14
12
10
8
6
4
2
0

Spruce Fir Maple Pine Birch

Kind of Tree

B Reasoning and Problem Solving

8. The Nature Club plans to plant 25 more trees in the spring. Including the ones from the fall, how many new trees will they plant this school year?

9. **Writing in Math** A bar graph helps to compare data. Which kind of graph shows change over time, a pictograph or a line graph? Explain your answer.

Math and Science

The table shows the average egg-hatching times for four different birds.

Egg-Hatching Times

Bird	Days
Chicken	21 days
Turkey	26 days
Duck	30 days
Pigeon	18 days

10. Copy and complete the bar graph.

11. How much longer does it take a duck egg to hatch than a pigeon egg?

12. List the birds in order of their egg-hatching times from least to greatest.

13. What is the range of the egg-hatching data?

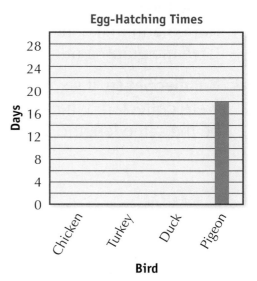

C Extensions

The tables at the right give information about the patients of two different kinds of doctors. The veterinarian's data compares numbers of patients of 4 different kinds. The pediatrician's data shows how one baby grew over time. Since the baby's height steadily increases, there is a **trend** in the data.

14. What kind of graph would best show the pediatrician's data?

15. What kind of graph would best show the veterinarian's data?

16. Make the graphs for the two sets of data. Remember to include a title and labels for each graph. Hint: Since the data for the pediatrician starts at 20, you can use a **broken scale,** as shown at the right for the numbers from 0 to 20.

Veterinarian's Data

Kind of Patient	Tally
Dogs	ⅢⅠ ΙΙΙ
Cats	ⅢⅠ ⅢⅠ
Birds	ΙΙΙ
Turtle	Ι

Pediatrician's Data

Age	Height
1 month	21 inches
3 months	23 inches
4 months	24 inches
6 months	26 inches

Mixed Review and Test Prep

Take It to the NET
Test Prep
www.scottforesman.com

17. If each symbol on a pictograph stands for 2 people, how many would you draw to show 8 people?

18. Connie had 12 carrot sticks. She ate 2 and gave 3 to her sister. How many were left?

19. Calvin's class has 23 students. Jordan's class has 17 students. How many more students does Calvin's class have?

20. Find 29 + 63.

A. 82   **B.** 90   **C.** 92   **D.** 93

Learning with Technology

Spreadsheet/Data/Grapher eTool

Make a list of colors. Then go around the room and ask ten classmates what their favorite color is. Put a tally mark next to the color chosen. Add up these tallies and enter your collected data into a spreadsheet.

Use the graphing tool to make a bar graph of your data.

1. How many colors are in the spreadsheet?

2. How many bars are in the graph?

3. Which color was chosen by the most classmates? by the fewest classmates?

	A	B
1	Color	Total
2		
3		
4		
5		

All text pages available online and on CD-ROM.

Materials
• grid paper
  or  tools

TEST TALK

Think It Through

• I can **get information from a table.**

• I can **make a line graph** to show how data changes over time.

Making Line Graphs

LEARN

Activity

How do you make a line graph?

The data file shows the daily high temperature for one city during the first week in January.

A line graph will show how the daily high temperature changed from day to day.

Data File

Week's High Temperatures	
Day	**Temperature**
Monday	45°F
Tuesday	50°F
Wednesday	40°F
Thursday	35°F
Friday	30°F

a. Copy the line graph that is started. The points for Monday and Tuesday are shown, with the line drawn between them.

b. Wednesday's high temperature was 40°F. Find Wednesday at the bottom of the graph and move up that grid line to 40. Draw a point and then connect it to the point for Tuesday with a line.

c. Complete the graph by plotting the points for Thursday and Friday and connect the points in order.

d. Why do you think the scale uses counting by 5s?

e. Describe how the temperature changed from Monday through Friday.

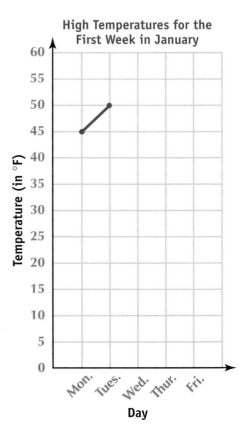

High Temperatures for the First Week in January

Copy the line graph that has been started.

1. Write the title and the labels where they belong.

Data File

Increase in Weight of Jim's Puppy

Puppy's Age	Weight
Birth	2 lb
6 months	10 lb
12 months	14 lb

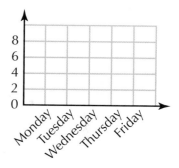

2. Reasoning Do you think the line will go higher or lower between the points for birth and 6 months?

3. Complete the graph.

PRACTICE

For more practice, see Set 4-13 on p. 257.

Ⓐ Skills and Understanding

4. Copy and complete the line graph that has been started.

5. On which 2 days did Laura bike the same number of miles? How does the graph show this?

Data File

Miles Laura Biked Each Day

Day	Miles
Monday	4
Tuesday	1
Wednesday	2
Thursday	2
Friday	3

Ⓑ Reasoning and Problem Solving

6. <u>Writing in Math</u> Suppose you made a line graph showing the changes in temperature from 5 P.M. to midnight in a desert area. Would the line more likely go up or down? Explain.

Mixed Review and Test Prep

 **Take It to the NET**
Test Prep
www.scottforesman.com

7. The third-grade students voted on their favorite color. In a bar graph, how would you show that red and blue had the same number of votes?

8. Find $20.00 − $13.99.

   A. $6.01   **B.** $6.99   **C.** $7.11   **D.** $9.11

 All text pages available online and on CD-ROM.

Understand Graphic Sources: Graphs

Understanding graphic sources such as graphs when you read in math can help you use the **problem-solving strategy, *Make a Graph,*** in the next lesson.

In reading, understanding graphs can help you understand what you read. In math, understanding graphs can help you solve problems.

How many cats are in the animal shelter?

A **pictograph** presents data by using pictures or symbols.

The key identifies what each symbol or picture represents.

Animals in the Animal Shelter

Rabbits	△ △
Lizards	△
Dogs	△ △ △ △ △
Cats	△ △ △ △ △ △ △
Birds	△ △ △

Each △ = 5 animals.

In this pictograph, each symbol represents 5 animals.

Count the △ next to *Cat.*
Skip count by 5s

5, 10, 15, 20, 25, 30, 35

There are 35 cats in the Animal Shelter.

1. How many more cats are in the animal shelter than dogs?

2. How many animals in all are in the animal shelter?

For 3–6, use the line plot at the right.

3. How many dogs in the animal shelter are 4 years old?

4. **Writing in Math** How many dogs in the animal shelter are 3 years old or younger? Explain how you found your answer.

5. How many more 2-year-old dogs are in the animal shelter than 1-year-old dogs?

6. How many dogs are in the animal shelter?

Ages of Dogs in the Animal Shelter

```
          X
          X   X
      X   X   X
      X   X   X
      X   X   X
      X   X   X           X
      X   X   X           X
      X   X   X   X       X
    +---+---+---+---+---+---+--->
      1   2   3   4   5   6
              Years
```

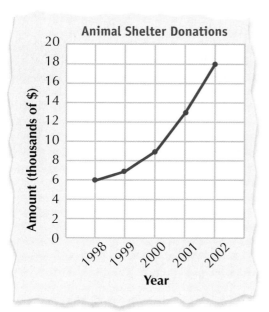

Animal Shelter Donations

For 7–10, use the line graph at the left.

7. How much money was donated in 1999?

8. During what year did the animal shelter collect $9,000?

9. **Writing in Math** How did the amount of donations change over the years? Explain how you know.

10. How much more money was donated to the animal shelter in 2002 than in 2001?

For 11–14, use the bar graph at the right.

11. How many dogs were adopted in 2002?

12. Which types of pets were adopted more often than rabbits?

13. Was the total number of pets adopted in 2002 less than or greater than 50?

14. **Writing in Math** Which bars are the same length? What does that mean?

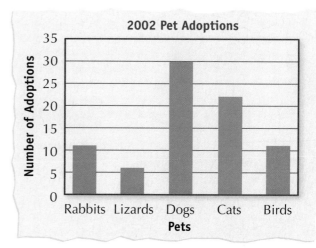

Problem-Solving Strategy

Understanding graphic sources such as graphs

can help you with...

the problem-solving strategy, *Make a Graph.*

Key Idea
Learning how and when to make a graph can help you solve problems.

Materials
• grid paper or  tools

TEST TALK

Think It Through
• I can solve the problem by **drawing a graph** about the bike riders.

Make a Graph

LEARN

How do you use a graph to solve problems?

Riding to School Mr. Lowe's class made a chart showing how many students rode their bikes to school each day for a week. How did the number change over the week?

Day	Riders
Monday	24
Tuesday	24
Wednesday	18
Thursday	10
Friday	2

Read and Understand

What do you know? You know how many rode each day.

What are you trying to find? Find how the number of riders changed over the five days.

Plan and Solve

What strategy will you use?

Strategy: Make a line graph.

Step 1 Make the line graph. Enter all known data.

Step 2 Read the graph. Look for a pattern.

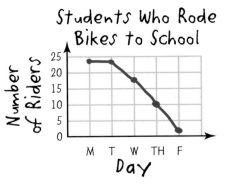

Students Who Rode Bikes to School

Answer: The most students rode on Monday and Tuesday. Then the number decreased each day. Only 2 rode on the last day.

Look Back and Check

Is your work correct? Yes, the graph shows the correct data.

✓ Talk About It

1. How can you tell just by looking at the graph that the number decreased each day after Tuesday?

Copy and complete the graph to solve each problem.

1. Which club has the most 3rd-grade members?

Reading Club	Computer Club	Bicycle Club	Art Club
12	10	16	8

3rd-grade Members in Elm School Clubs

Reading Club	
Computer Club	
Bicycle Club	
Art Club	

Each   = 2 students.

2. Who rode 20 miles more than Holly?

Member	Victor	Rosita	Gary	Holly
Number of miles	25	35	30	10

Miles Ridden by Bicycle Club Members

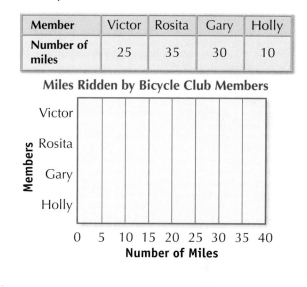

Members: Victor, Rosita, Gary, Holly

0 5 10 15 20 25 30 35 40
Number of Miles

Solve. Write each answer in a complete sentence.

3. Copy the line plot below. Then use the data at the right to complete the line plot. How many 3rd-grade Reading Club Members read 7 books in April?

Numbers of Books Read in April by 3rd-grade Reading Club Members

5	7	3
4	4	7
3	2	6
7	7	5

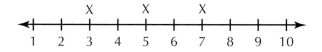

```
        X     X     X
◄─┼──┼──┼──┼──┼──┼──┼──┼──┼──►
  1  2  3  4  5  6  7  8  9  10
```

4. Use the bar graph to find how many people in all voted on their favorite type of exercise. Then give the graph a title.

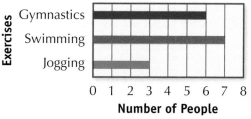

Exercises: Gymnastics, Swimming, Jogging

0 1 2 3 4 5 6 7 8
Number of People

5. Before the big race, Jose spent $12 on bicycle mirrors and $23 on a horn. How much did he spend in all?

6. At the farmer's market, Matt gives 2 free apples for every 6 apples you buy. If you buy 24 apples, how many free apples will you get?

7. <u>Writing in Math</u> Write a word problem that can be solved by reading the bar graph about favorite types of exercise.

DK Problem-Solving Applications

Blizzard of 1888 The word *blizzard* was first used to describe a snowstorm in Iowa around 1870. One of the worst blizzards hit New York City in 1888. The city was frozen by ice and 21 inches of snow. It took many days for normal city life to return.

Trivia During the Blizzard of 1888, winds created snowdrifts in New York City that were 20 feet high. Tunnels were dug to allow people to walk along the sidewalks.

❶ The Blizzard of 1888 blew down telegraph wires with gusts of over 70 miles per hour. A snowstorm is called a blizzard if it has winds of at least 35 miles per hour. How much faster than this were the winds in the Blizzard of 1888?

❷ Many trains became stuck in the snow. Some passengers were snowbound for about 2 days. How many hours are in two days?

Using Key Facts

③ List the cities in the Key Facts chart in order from most snowfall to least.

Key Facts
Blizzard of 1888

City	Snowfall
•Albany	47 in.
•Brooklyn	26 in.
•Middletown	50 in.
•New York City	21 in.
•White Plains	32 in.

④ Read the trivia. Snowdrifts in other parts of New England were estimated to be 30 feet higher than the largest drifts in New York City. How high were these giant drifts?

⑤ **Writing in Math** One writer reported that the storm became intense at 10 P.M. Sunday and did not ease until 6 A.M. Tuesday. For how many hours was the storm intense? Explain how you found your answer.

Good News/Bad News The Blizzard of 1888 caused much destruction, but it inspired the city to build subways and to bury utility wires. These improvements allow the city to function better during blizzards.

⑥ Decision Making What type of graph would best show the information in the Key Facts chart? Make that graph.

Do You Know How?

Do You Understand?

Making Pictographs (4-11); Making Bar Graphs (4-12); Making Line Graphs (4-13)

Copy and complete each graph.

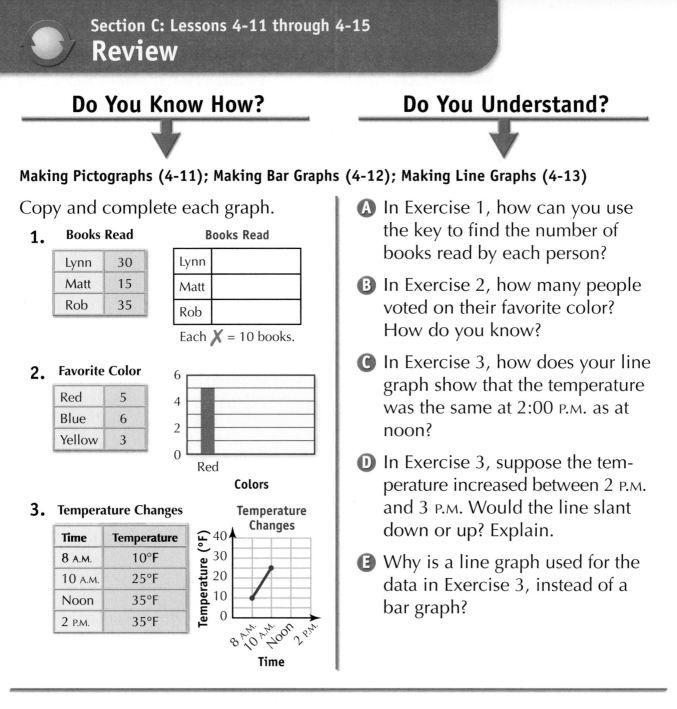

1. Books Read

Lynn	30
Matt	15
Rob	35

Books Read

Lynn	
Matt	
Rob	

Each ✗ = 10 books.

2. Favorite Color

Red	5
Blue	6
Yellow	3

3. Temperature Changes

Time	Temperature
8 A.M.	10°F
10 A.M.	25°F
Noon	35°F
2 P.M.	35°F

Temperature Changes

Ⓐ In Exercise 1, how can you use the key to find the number of books read by each person?

Ⓑ In Exercise 2, how many people voted on their favorite color? How do you know?

Ⓒ In Exercise 3, how does your line graph show that the temperature was the same at 2:00 P.M. as at noon?

Ⓓ In Exercise 3, suppose the temperature increased between 2 P.M. and 3 P.M. Would the line slant down or up? Explain.

Ⓔ Why is a line graph used for the data in Exercise 3, instead of a bar graph?

Problem-Solving Strategy: Make a Graph (4-14)

Copy and complete the graph.

4. Students in After-School Clubs

Day	Students
Mon.	10
Tues.	15
Wed.	20
Thur.	15
Fri.	10

Students in After-School Clubs

Number of Students

Ⓕ How can you tell from the data which bar will be the longest?

Ⓖ If you made a pictograph to show this same data, what number would you use in the key?

MULTIPLE CHOICE

1. If each symbol on a pictograph stands for 2 days, how many symbols would you draw to show 7 days? (4-11)

   A. 2 symbols

   B. 3 symbols

   C. 3 symbols and one half symbol

   D. 5 symbols

2. When you make a bar graph to show test scores for 10 students, how many bars should you make? (4-12)

   A. 2   **B.** 5   **C.** 8   **D.** 10

FREE RESPONSE

Copy and complete each graph. (4-11, 4-12, 4-13, 4-14, 4-15)

3.

Hockey Team

Month	Games Won
October	6
November	10
December	10
January	14

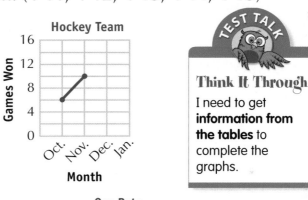

Test Talk

Think It Through

I need to get **information from the tables** to complete the graphs.

4.

Our Pets

Type	Number
Dog	16
Cat	12
Bird	2

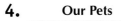

5.

Art Club Projects

Project	Number
Paper folding	13
Collage	8
Mobile	7

Art Club Projects

Paper folding	
Collage	
Mobile	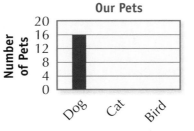

Each ◯ = 2 projects.

Writing in Math

6. Explain how the line graph above shows that the same number of games were won in November and December. (4-13)

CHAPTER 4
Test Talk

Test-Taking Strategies

Understand the question.
Get information for the answer.
Plan how to find the answer.
→ Make smart choices.
Use writing in math.
Improve written answers.

Make Smart Choices

To answer a multiple-choice test question, you need to choose an answer from answer choices. The steps below will help you make a smart choice.

1. Barbara's soccer practice lasted 2 hours. The clock shows the time when it started. At what time did Barbara's soccer practice end?

A. 2:00

B. 5:00

C. 7:00

D. 9:00

Understand the question.

I need to find when the soccer practice ended.

Get information for the answer.

*The **text** says the practice lasted 2 hours. The **picture** shows the starting time, 5:00.*

Plan how to find the answer.

I should count 2 hours after 5:00. First I'll look at the choices and eliminate those that do not make sense.

• Eliminate wrong answers.

The practice could not start and end at the same time. Answer choice B, 5:00, is wrong.

The practice could not end earlier than it started. Answer choice A, 2:00, is wrong.

Check answers for reasonableness.

Answer choices C and D are both reasonable. I'll count to make the right choice.

5:00→6:00→7:00

The correct answer is C, 7:00.

2. Four students volunteer at their local animal shelter. The bar graph shows how many hours they each volunteered last month.

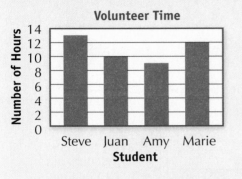

Volunteer Time

What is the total number of hours Steve and Marie volunteered?

A. 6   **B.** 12   **C.** 18   **D.** 25

Think It Through

I need to find out how many hours Steve and Marie together volunteered. The bar graph shows how many hours they each volunteered. The answer has to be greater than either Steve's hours or Marie's hours. So answer choices A and B are wrong. They each volunteered more than 10 hours, so the total has to be more than 20.

That makes answer choice C wrong. That leaves answer choice D for the correct answer. I can check with addition.

13 + 12 = 25

Now it's your turn.

For each problem, give the answer and explain how you made your choice.

3. Donato went to a party for 5 hours. The clock shows the time he arrived. At what time did he leave the party?

A. 3:00

B. 5:00

C. 6:00

D. 8:00

4. Goldie, Ginger, and Cleo had kittens. The pictograph shows how many kittens each cat had.

Newborn Kittens

Goldie	▲ ▲ ▲
Ginger	▲ ▲ ◢
Cleo	▲ ▲

Each ▲ = 2 kittens.

How many kittens were born in all?

A. 4   **B.** 10   **C.** 15   **D.** 30

I wake up around 7:00 A.M. and I go to bed around 9:30 P.M.

***A.M.** includes times from midnight until noon. **P.M.** includes times from noon until midnight. (p. 193)*

There are 4 quarters in a dollar.

*There are 4 **quarter hours** in an hour. (p. 192)*

Self Check

Use clocks and calendars to measure time. (Lessons 4-1, 4-2, 4-3, 4-4)

Find the elapsed time.

Start Time: End Time:
10:00 A.M.   1:48 P.M.

10:00 A.M. to 1:00 P.M.:
3 hours
1:00 P.M. to 1:48 P.M.:
48 minutes

The elapsed time is
3 hours and 48 minutes

What day of the week is May 18th?

MAY						
S	M	T	W	T	F	S
		1	2	3	4	5
6	7	8	9	10	11	12
13	14	15	16	17	18	19
20	21	22	23	24	25	26
27	28	29	30			

May 18th is on Friday.

1 day = 24 hours
1 hour = 60 minutes
1 minute = 60 seconds
1 quarter hour =
15 minutes
1 half hour = 30 minutes

1 week = 7 days
52 weeks = 1 year
1 year = 12 months
1 year = 365 days
1 leap year = 366 days
1 decade = 10 years
1 century = 100 years

1. Find the elapsed time from 9:00 P.M. to 1:35 A.M.

2. Using the calendar above, what date is the fourth Monday in May?

Ordered pair contains the word "order."

*The order of the numbers in an **ordered pair** is very important. (6, 2) is not the same as (2, 6). (p. 218)*

Self Check

Locate points on a coordinate grid. (Lesson 4-9)

Ordered pairs are used to name locations and **plot** points on a **coordinate grid.**

Start at (0, 0).   Point *D* is at (5, 3).

Move 5 spaces   Move 3
to the right.   spaces up.

3. Give the letter of the point named by (1, 4).

4. Write the ordered pair that describes the location of point *C*.

My talents range from soccer to singing.

*The **range** of a set of data tells how spread out the data is. (p. 208)*

Display and describe survey results. (Lessons 4-5, 4-6)

Ages of Choir Members

Age	Tally	Number
7	ⵑⵑⵑ	5
8	ⵑⵑⵑⵑ IIII	9
9	III	3
10	ⵑⵑⵑ II	6

The tally chart at the left and the line plot on the right show the same **data.** Each person in the **survey** is represented by one **tally mark** in the tally chart or one X in the line plot.

range: 10 – 7 = 3
mode: 8

Ages of Choir Members

```
        X
        X
        X
        X           X
X       X           X
X       X           X
X       X     X     X
X       X     X     X
X       X     X     X
←---+---+---+---+→
    7   8   9   10
```
Age in Years

5. How many choir member are 9 years old?
   How many are more than 7 years old?

Our bathroom scale has lots of numbers.

*There are numbers on the **scale** of a graph. (p. 213)*

Make, read, or compare graphs to help solve problems. (Lessons 4-7, 4-8, 4-10, 4-11, 4-12, 4-13, 4-14)

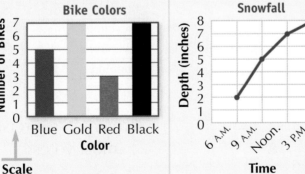

Pictograph
Baseball Wins

Mt. Gale	⚾ ⚾ ⚾ ⚾
Kellsburg	⚾ ⚾ ⚾
Solaria	⚾ ⚾ ⚾ ⚾

Each ⚾ = 2 wins.

↑
key

Bar Graph
Bike Colors

Number of Bikes / Color (Blue, Gold, Red, Black)

↑
Scale

Line Graph
Snowfall

Depth (inches) / Time (6 A.M., 9 A.M., Noon, 3 P.M.)

6. How many wins did Mt. Gale have? Solaria?

7. Why are two of the bars in the bar graph the same length?

8. How much snow had fallen by noon?

Answers: 1. 4 hours 35 minutes 2. May 28th 3. A 4. (3, 3) 5. 3; 18 6. 8; 7 7. There are the same number of gold bikes as there are black bikes. 8. 7 inches

MULTIPLE CHOICE

Choose the correct letter for each answer.

1. What date is the third Wednesday in March?

March						
S	M	T	W	T	F	S
	1	2	3	4	5	6
7	8	9	10	11	12	13
14	15	16	17	18	19	20
21	22	23	24	25	26	27
28	29	30	31			

   A. March 10   **C.** March 18

   B. March 17   **D.** March 24

2. Larry has 7 poetry books in his library. Which shows how the poetry bar on a graph would look?

   A.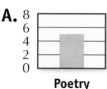
   Poetry

   B.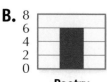
   Poetry

   C.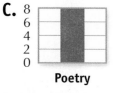
   Poetry

   D.
   Poetry

TEST TALK

Think It Through
- I need to **read each answer choice carefully.**
- I can **eliminate unreasonable answer choices.**

3. Which house is located at (5, 2) on the grid?

   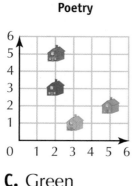

   A. Red   **C.** Green

   B. Blue   **D.** Orange

4. How would you show the number 6 on a tally chart?

   A. ⅢⅠ   **C.** ⅢⅠ ‖

   B. ⅢⅠ Ⅰ   **D.** ‖‖ ‖‖

5. The clock shows the time that soccer practice began. What time did soccer practice begin?

   A. 3:00   **C.** 6:15

   B. 3:30   **D.** 6:30

6. Use the clock in question 5. If soccer practice lasted 1 hour 30 minutes, what time did soccer practice end?

   A. 7:00   **C.** 8:00

   B. 7:30   **D.** 8:30

For 7–8, use the pictograph below.

Favorite Exercise

Rowing	🚶
Bicycling	🚶 🚶 🚶
Swimming	🚶 🚶 🚶 🚶 🚶
Running	🚶 🚶 🚶

Each 🚶 = 2 votes.

7. Which exercise received the most votes?

   A. Running   **C.** Swimming

   B. Bicycling   **D.** Rowing

8. If walking got 4 votes, how many symbols would you draw?

   A. 1   **B.** 2   **C.** 4   **D.** 9

Write the given time in two ways.

9.
10.

Find the elapsed time.

11. Start Time: 5:00 P.M.
End Time: 7:25 P.M.

12. Start Time: 11:30 A.M.
End Time: 11:55 A.M.

For 13–15, use the line plot below.

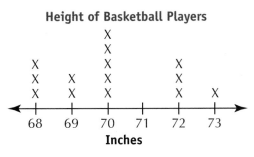

Height of Basketball Players

13. Find the mode.

14. Find the range.

15. How many basketball players are at least 70 inches tall?

For 16–17, use the line graph below.

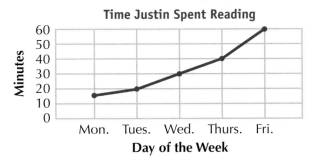

16. How many minutes did Justin read on Wednesday?

17. How many more minutes did Justin read on Thursday than on Tuesday?

Writing in Math

18. Explain how to plot a point at (7, 11) on a coordinate grid.

19. Use the graphs below. Write two statements that compare the average daily temperatures in January and February.

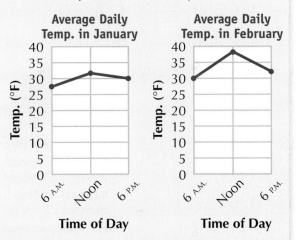

20. Copy and complete the bar graph. Which type of tree appears most often in the orchard? Explain how the graph shows this.

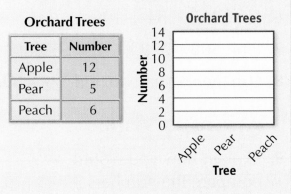

Orchard Trees

Tree	Number
Apple	12
Pear	5
Peach	6

Number and Operation

MULTIPLE CHOICE

1. Rose has 2 quarters and a nickel. Jack has 3 dimes. How much more money does Rose have?

   A. $0.25   **C.** $0.50

   B. $0.35   **D.** $0.85

2. Round 6,812 to the nearest hundred.

   A. 6,000   **C.** 6,900

   B. 6,800   **D.** 7,000

3. Find $9.27 – $3.95.

   A. $5.32

   B. $6.32

   C. $6.72

   D. $13.22

   TEST TALK

   Think It Through
   I need to **subtract money as I would subtract whole numbers.**

FREE RESPONSE

4. Find 675 – 398.

5. Round to the nearest ten to estimate 45 + 12.

6. Find 217 + 54 + 199.

7. Find 508 – 279.

8. Use mental math to find 127 – 99.

Writing in Math

9. Explain how you would compare the numbers 3,548 and 3,812.

Geometry and Measurement

MULTIPLE CHOICE

10. How many corners does this shape have?

    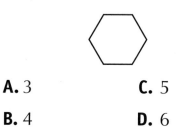

    A. 3   **C.** 5

    B. 4   **D.** 6

11. Which solid figure does the roll of paper towels look like?

    A. Rectangular prism

    B. Cylinder

    C. Pyramid

    D. Sphere

FREE RESPONSE

12. How many sides does a pentagon have?

Writing in Math

13. Would you measure your shoe in inches or yards? Explain.

14. Can you draw a triangle with 4 sides? Explain.

Data Analysis and Probability

MULTIPLE CHOICE

Use the bar graph for 15 and 16.

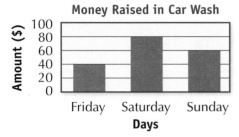

15. How much more money was raised on Saturday than on Sunday?

    A. $10 **B.** $20 **C.** $30 **D.** $90

16. How much money was raised in all?

    A. $100   **C.** $180

    B. $130   **D.** $200

FREE RESPONSE

Use the line graph for 17 and 18.

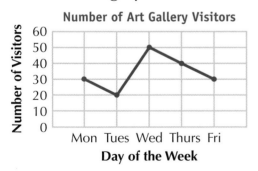

17. Which two days had the same number of visitors?

Writing in Math

18. How can you tell without looking at any numbers that fewer people visited on Tuesday than on Monday?

Algebra

MULTIPLE CHOICE

19. Find the number that makes the number sentence below true.

    $6 + n < 14$

    A. $n = 5$ **C.** $n = 10$

    B. $n = 9$ **D.** $n = 14$

20. Find the missing number.

    $20 = \blacksquare + (5 + 6)$

    A. 8   **B.** 9   **C.** 10   **D.** 19

21. Solve $31 + \blacksquare = 52$.

    A. 21   **B.** 22   **C.** 31   **D.** 83

22. Continue the pattern.

    25, 34, 43, 52, $\blacksquare$, $\blacksquare$

    A. 60, 70   **C.** 61, 70

    B. 63, 74   **D.** 61, 72

FREE RESPONSE

Find three whole numbers that make each number sentence true.

23. $12 - x > 8$

24. $\blacksquare + 10 < 18$

Writing in Math

25. Write a word problem for the number sentence $6 + \blacksquare = 9$. Solve the problem.

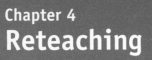

Set 4-1 (pages 192–195)

What is the time?

6:45, 15 minutes to 7, or quarter to seven

Remember that an hour can be divided into half hours and quarter hours.

Write the time shown.

1. **2.**

Set 4-2 (pages 196–197)

What is the time?

12:37, twelve thirty-seven, or twenty-three minutes to one

Remember it takes the minute hand 5 minutes to move from one number to the next.

Write the time shown.

1. **2.**

Set 4-3 (pages 198–199)

Find the elapsed time.

Start Time: 4:00 P.M.
End Time: 8:15 P.M.
There are 4 hours from 4:00 P.M. to 8:00 P.M.
There are 15 minutes from 8:00 P.M. to 8:15 P.M.
The elapsed time is 4 hours 15 minutes.

Remember that you can draw a picture of a clock to help you count the hours and minutes.

1. Start Time: 3:00 P.M.
   End Time: 8:20 P.M.

2. Start Time: 8:00 A.M.
   End Time: 12:30 P.M.

Set 4-4 (pages 200–201)

What day of the week did astronauts first land on the moon?

| July 1969 | | | | | | |
S	M	T	W	T	F	S
		1	2	3	4	5
6	7	8	9	10	11	12
13	14	15	16	17	18	19
20	21	22	23	24	25	26
27	28	29	30	31		

July 4: Independence Day
July 20: First Moon Landing

July 20 was on Sunday.

Remember that when reading a calendar, think of days, weeks, months, and years.

1. What day of the week was Independence Day in 1969?

2. What date was the second Monday in July 1969?

Read the tally chart below.

Favorite Season

Season	Tally	Number
Spring	ЖЖ	5
Summer	ЖЖ |||	8
Fall	||||	4
Winter	|||	3

The chart shows students' favorite seasons. Spring got 5 votes and winter got 3 votes.

Remember that when you take a survey, you collect information by asking a number of people the same question.

1. Which season had the most votes?

2. How many more people voted for summer than for winter?

3. How many people were surveyed?

How many students read 4 books?

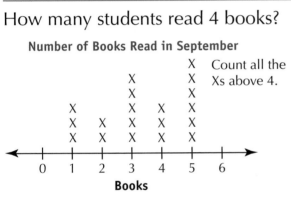

Number of Books Read in September

Count all the Xs above 4.

Three students read 4 books.

Remember that the mode is the number that occurs most often.

1. What is the mode of the data?

2. What is the range of the data?

3. How many students read **at least** 3 books in September?

How many students are in 3rd grade?

Number of Students at Westlake Elementary

Kindergarten	🧍 🧍 🧍
1st Grade	🧍 🧍 🧍 🧍 🧍
2nd Grade	🧍 🧍 🧍
3rd Grade	🧍 🧍 🧍 🧍
4th Grade	🧍 🧍 🧍 🧍
5th Grade	🧍 🧍 🧍 🧍 🧍

Each 🧍 = 10 students.

There are 35 students in 3rd grade.

Remember to use the key to find out what each symbol shows.

1. How many more students are in 5th grade than in 3rd grade?

2. Which has more students, 1st grade or 5th grade?

3. How many students all together attend Westlake Elementary?

Set 4-8 (pages 216–217)

Use the bar graphs. How is the data alike? How is it different?

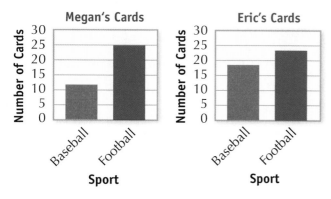

Megan's Cards

Eric's Cards

Remember Use comparison words such as "most," "least," and "about the same" when you compare.

1. Write a statement about how the card collections are alike.

2. Write a statement about how the card collections are different.

Alike: Each has cards for two sports.
Different: Eric has more cards than Megan.

Set 4-9 (pages 218–221)

Write the ordered pair that describes the location of point C.

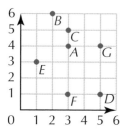

Point C is 3 spaces to the right from 0 and 5 spaces up.

Point C is located at (3, 5).

Remember to move right for the first number and up for the second number.

Write the ordered pair for each point.

1. A   2. B   3. D

Give the letter of each point.

4. (3, 1)   5. (5, 4)   6. (1, 3)

Set 4-10 (pages 222–223)

How much did the lamb weigh when it was 4 weeks old?

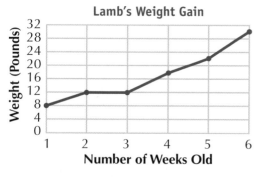

Lamb's Weight Gain

Remember a line graph shows change over time.

1. Between which two weeks did the lamb's weight stay the same?

2. How many pounds did the lamb gain between the 1st week and the 6th week?

The lamb weighed 18 pounds when it was 4 weeks old.

Copy and complete the pictograph.

Books Read During the Summer

Student	Tally	Number
John	IIII	4
Krista	IIII II	7
Alan	III	3
Akihiko	IIII	5

Remember to include a key and a title.

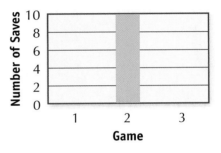

John	
Krista	
Alan	
Akihiko	

Each = 2 books.

Copy and complete the bar graph.

Saves Made by the Goalie

Game	Saves
1	8
2	10
3	6

Remember to include labels, a scale, and a title.

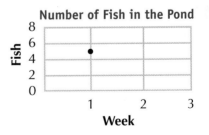

Copy and complete the line graph.

Number of Fish in the Pond

Week	Number
1	5
2	4
3	8

Remember to plot each point and connect them with a line.

Number of Fish in the Pond

Copy and complete the graph to solve the problem. Who lost the most pencils?

Pencils Lost

Student	Number of Pencils
Sarah	IIII I
Fred	IIII III
Lance	III

Remember that making a graph can help you solve problems.

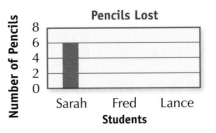

Pencils Lost

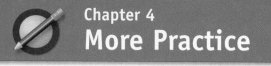
Set 4-1 (pages 192–195)

Write the time shown on each clock.

1. **2.** **3.** **4.**

5. Write three different ways you could say 9:45.

Set 4-2 (pages 196–197)

Write the time shown on each clock.

1. **2.** **3.** **4.**

5. At which time would it probably be dark outside: 2:40 A.M. or 2:40 P.M.?

Set 4-3 (pages 198–199)

Find the elapsed time.

1. Start Time: 6:30 A.M.
    End Time: 1:35 P.M.

2. Start Time: 12:45 P.M.
    End Time: 10:45 P.M.

3. Start Time: 5:25 A.M.
    End Time: 6:30 A.M.

4. Start Time: 2:20 P.M.
    End Time: 8:40 P.M.

5. Start Time: 9:15 P.M.
    End Time: 12:30 A.M.

6. Start Time: 11:50 P.M.
    End Time: 12:05 A.M.

7. The hockey game began at 8:30 P.M. and ended at 10:55 P.M. How long was the hockey game?

Set 4-4 (pages 200–201)

Use the calendar to answer the questions.

1. How many Sundays are in February?

2. What date is the third Monday in February?

3. What day of the week is Valentine's Day?

February						
S	M	T	W	T	F	S
		1	2	3	4	5
6	7	8	9	10	11	12
13	14	15	16	17	18	19
20	21	22	23	24	25	26
27	28					

February 14: Valentine's Day
February 21: President's Day

Take It to the NET
More Practice
www.scottforesman.com

Set 4-5 (pages 204–207)

1. Make a tally chart to show the results.

2. How many students were surveyed?

3. Which activity got the most votes?

4. How many more students voted for basketball than volleyball?

Favorite Gym Activities

basketball, volleyball, floor hockey, volleyball, basketball, floor hockey, volleyball, volleyball, basketball, floor hockey, basketball, basketball

Set 4-6 (pages 208–211)

The number of pencils each student has in Mrs. Kerr's class is shown on the line plot.

1. What is the mode of the data?

2. How many students have exactly 1 pencil?

3. How many students have fewer than 4 pencils?

Number of Pencils Students Have

```
                X
        X   X
        X   X
        X   X   X
        X   X   X           X
        X   X   X   X   X   X
        X   X   X   X   X   X               X
    <---+---+---+---+---+---+---+---+---+---+---+--->
        0   1   2   3   4   5   6   7   8   9   10
```
Pencils

Set 4-7 (pages 212–215)

1. What does each butterfly on the graph represent?

2. How many butterflies were in the garden on Day 3?

3. On which day were more butterflies seen in the garden, Day 1 or Day 4?

Butterflies in the Garden

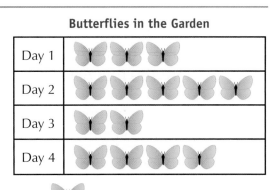

Each 🦋 = 3 butterflies.

Set 4-8 (pages 216–217)

1. Write a statement about how the groups are alike.

2. Write a statement about how the groups are different.

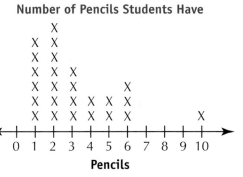

Set 4-9 (pages 218–221)

Use the coordinate grid to answer the questions.

Write the ordered pair that describes the location of each point.

1. A **2.** B **3.** C

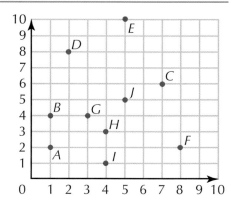

Give the letter of the point named by each ordered pair.

4. (2, 8) **5.** (4, 1) **6.** (3, 4)

7. Explain how to plot the point (6, 7) on the coordinate grid.

Set 4-10 (pages 222–223)

Use the line graph to answer the questions.

1. What data does the graph show?

2. How long did it take Laura to run a mile on the third day?

3. How many days shown did she take less than 10 minutes to run a mile?

4. Is it correct to say that Laura improved her time over the five days? Explain.

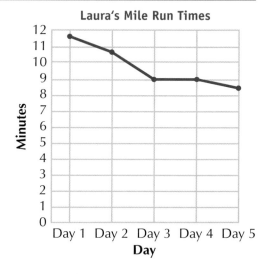

Laura's Mile Run Times

Set 4-11 (pages 226–227)

The table shows how many students from third grade attended Family Fun Night.

1. Copy and complete the table.

2. Copy and complete the pictograph. Include a title.

Class	Tally	Number
Ms. Pickert	卌 卌 IIII	
Mr. Gregorits	卌 卌 卌 II	
Mrs. McKillan	卌 卌 II	
Mr. Eaves	卌 卌 卌 IIII	

Ms. Pickert	🚹🚹🚹🚹🚹🚹🚹
Mr. Gregorits	🚹🚹🚹🚹🚹🚹🚹🚹
Mrs. McKillan	
Mr. Eaves	

Each 🚹 = 2 students.

Take It to the NET
More Practice
www.scottforesman.com

Set 4-12 (pages 228–231)

1. Copy and complete the bar graph.

2. Give your graph a title.

3. How many students all together are in the band?

Students in the School Band

Grade	Number of Students
3	31
4	28
5	42

Set 4-13 (pages 232–233)

Copy the line graph that has been started.

1. Write the title and labels where each belongs.

2. Plot the points for the number of laps Michael swam each day.

3. On which two days did Michael swim the same number of laps?

Laps Michael Swam

Day	Laps
Monday	12
Tuesday	15
Wednesday	19
Thursday	17
Friday	15

Set 4-14 (pages 236–237)

1. How many more third-grade students play the clarinet than the trumpet? Copy and complete the bar graph to solve.

Third-Grade Band Members

Flute	Clarinet	Trumpet	Drums
8	9	5	6

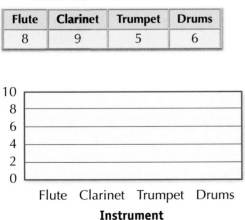

2. How many clarinet players practice more than 30 minutes each day? Copy and complete the line plot to solve.

Average Number of Minutes Clarinet Players Practice Each Day

30	60	45	15	60
30	30	60	60	45
45	15	45	45	30

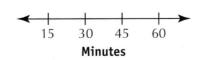

Minutes

Multiplication Concepts and Facts

 DIAGNOSING READINESS

A Vocabulary
(Grade 2 and page 24)

Choose the best term from the box.

1. You __?__ when you put groups together to find how many in all.

2. In __?__ numbers the ones digit is 0, 2, 4, 6, or 8.

3. When finding the value of a bag of nickels, you can __?__ by fives.

Vocabulary
- **odd** *(p. 24)*
- **skip count** *(Gr. 2)*
- **add** *(Gr. 2)*
- **even** *(p. 24)*

B Adding Equal Groups
(Grade 2)

4. 6 + 6

5. 8 + 8 + 8

6. 3 + 3 + 3

7. 1 + 1 + 1 + 1

8. 7 + 7 + 7

9. 5 + 5 + 5 + 5

10. Katie has 2 bags of oranges. Each bag has 4 oranges. How many oranges does she have in all?

11. Draw a picture showing 3 plates with 4 carrots on each plate. How many carrots are there in all?

Do You Know...

What is the greatest speed that anyone has reached on a bicycle?

You will find out in Lesson 5-12.

MACHINES and HOW THEY WORK

C Skip-Counting Patterns
(pages 24–27)

Find the missing numbers in each pattern.

12. 3, 6, 9, ▢, ▢, ▢

13. 2, 4, ▢, 8, ▢, 12, ▢

14. 10, 20, 30, ▢, ▢, ▢

15. 30, 25, 20, ▢, ▢, ▢

16. Leslie has 4 nickels. How much money does she have?

17. Use skip-counting to find the value of 3 quarters.

D Arrays
(Grade 2)

Use the array above to answer 18–20.

18. How many dots are there in each row?

19. How many rows of dots are there?

20. How many dots are there in all?

Algebra

Key Idea
Multiplying is a quick way of adding equal groups.

Vocabulary
• multiplication
• factor
• product

Materials
• counters
or  tools

Think It Through
I can **use objects** to show equal groups.

Multiplication as Repeated Addition

LEARN

Activity

How can you find the total?

There are **4 groups of** 3 paintbrushes.

You can use addition to put together groups.

$$3 + 3 + 3 + 3 = 12 \quad \text{Addition sentence}$$

When you put together **equal groups,** you can also use **multiplication.**

What You **Say:**   4 times 3 equals 12

What You **Write:**   4   ×   3   =   12   **Multiplication sentence**
                       ↑   ↑   ↑
                    factor factor   product

a. Write an addition sentence and a multiplication sentence to show the total number of counters below.

b. Use counters and draw a picture to show the groups described below. For each picture, write an addition sentence and a multiplication sentence to show how many counters in all.

5 groups of 2
4 groups of 5
3 groups of 3

Take It to the NET
More Examples
www.scottforesman.com

For another example, see Set 5-1 on p. 306.

CHECK ✓

Copy and complete.

1.

3 groups of ▨
2 + 2 + 2 = ▨
3 × ▨ = ▨

2.

▨ groups of 3
▨ + ▨ + ▨ + ▨ + ▨ = 15
5 × ▨ = ▨

3. Number Sense Can you write 3 + 4 + 5 = 12 as a multiplication sentence? Explain.

PRACTICE

For more practice, see Set 5-1 on p. 310.

A Skills and Understanding

Copy and complete.

4.

2 groups of ▨
▨ + ▨ = 14
2 × ▨ = ▨

5.

▨ groups of 6
▨ + ▨ + ▨ = 18
▨ × 6 = ▨

6. Number Sense Can you write 9 + 9 + 9 = 27 as a multiplication sentence? Explain.

B Reasoning and Problem Solving

7. Draw a picture that shows equal groups. Then write an addition sentence and a multiplication sentence for your picture.

8. **Writing in Math** Tara says, "When you put together any groups, you can add or multiply." Is she correct? Explain.

Mixed Review and Test Prep

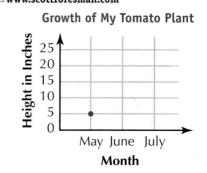

Take It to the NET
Test Prep
www.scottforesman.com

9. Copy and complete the line graph to show a height of 10 inches in June and 20 inches in July.

10. How much did the plant grow from May to July?

A. 5 inches   **C.** 15 inches

B. 10 inches   **D.** 20 inches

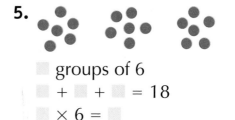

Growth of My Tomato Plant

All text pages available online and on CD-ROM.

Algebra

Key Idea
You can show multiplication by making equal rows.

Vocabulary
• array
• Commutative (order) Property of Multiplication

Materials
• counters
  or  **e tools**

Think It Through
I should **keep my drawings simple.** I can draw an x for each object in an array.

Arrays and Multiplication

LEARN

Activity

How does an array show multiplication?

An **array** shows objects in equal rows. This array shows 3 rows of 5 tulips.

To find the total number of tulips, you put together equal groups. So you can add or multiply.

3 rows

5 in each row

Add:

5 + 5 + 5 = 15

Multiply:

3 × 5 = 15

↑ Number of rows   ↑ Number in each row

a. Write an addition sentence and a multiplication sentence for each array below.

b. Use counters and draw an array to show each multiplication fact below. Use your drawing to find the product.

5 × 3   4 × 2   6 × 4   3 × 4   2 × 5

Take It to the NET
More Examples
www.scottforesman.com

Does it matter in what order you multiply?

Lynn multiplies two different ways to find how many squares are in her quilt.

First she holds her quilt like this.

$$X\ X\ X\ X$$
$$X\ X\ X\ X \Big\} \begin{array}{l} \textbf{3 rows} \\ \textbf{4 in each row} \end{array}$$
$$X\ X\ X\ X$$

$4 + 4 + 4 = 12$

$3 \times 4 = 12$

Then she holds the quilt like this.

$$X\ X\ X$$
$$X\ X\ X \Big\} \begin{array}{l} \textbf{4 rows} \\ \textbf{3 in each row} \end{array}$$
$$X\ X\ X$$
$$X\ X\ X$$

$3 + 3 + 3 + 3 = 12$

$4 \times 3 = 12$

There are 12 squares in Lynn's quilt.

The **Commutative (order) Property of Multiplication** says you can multiply in any order and the product is the same.

So, $3 \times 4 = 4 \times 3$.

a. Make two arrays with counters to show that 3×2 has the same product as 2×3. Write a multiplication sentence for each array you made.

b. How do the arrays below show the Commutative Property of Multiplication?

Think It Through

I can **use objects** to show that I can multiply in any order.

Draw an array to find each multiplication fact. Write the product.

1. 4×2 **2.** 3×6 **3.** 2×8 **4.** 6×4 **5.** 3×3

Copy and complete. You may use counters or draw an array to help.

6. $4 \times 2 = 8$
$\blacksquare \times 4 = 8$

7. $5 \times \blacksquare = 10$
$2 \times \blacksquare = 10$

8. $2 \times 8 = \blacksquare$
$8 \times 2 = \blacksquare$

9. Number Sense How does an array show equal groups?

A Skills and Understanding

Draw an array to show each multiplication fact. Write the product.

10. 2×2 **11.** 6×5 **12.** 1×4 **13.** 7×2 **14.** 4×3

Copy and complete. You may use counters or draw an array to help.

15. $5 \times 3 = 15$
$\blacksquare \times 5 = 15$

16. $7 \times \blacksquare = 14$
$2 \times \blacksquare = 14$

17. $1 \times 6 = \blacksquare$
$6 \times 1 = \blacksquare$

Write a multiplication sentence for each array.

18. ●●●●●●●●
●●●●●●●●
●●●●●●●●

19. ●●●●
●●●●

20. ● ● ●
● ● ●
● ● ●

21. Number Sense Explain why the Commutative Property of Multiplication is sometimes called the *order property*.

B Reasoning and Problem Solving

Math and Everyday Life

Stamps are often sold in sheets or rolls of 100 or in small booklets of 20.

A "pane" of stamps has 4 rows of 5 stamps.

22. Use the picture of the stamps. Write an addition sentence to show the total number of stamps.

23. Write a multiplication sentence to show the total number of stamps.

24. Representations Draw a picture to show another way the stamps could be arranged in equal rows. Write a multiplication sentence for your picture.

25. <u>Writing in Math</u> Elise wrote an addition sentence and a multiplication sentence for the array shown. Find her mistake and write the sentences correctly.

$6 + 6 = 12$
$6 \times 6 = 12$

Mixed Review and Test Prep

Take It to the NET
Test Prep
www.scottforesman.com

26. Copy and complete.

2 groups of ▨
▨ + ▨ = 8
2 × ▨ = ▨

27. $123 - 57$

   A. 180   **B.** 96   **C.** 66   **D.** 45

Enrichment

Using Objects to Solve Problems

Materials: Counters or small squares of paper in 2 different colors

You can use objects to help find missing addends or missing factors.

A. Kate had 12 pennies. After her brother gave her some more, she had 21 pennies. How many pennies did her brother give her? $12 + ▨ = 21$

Put down 12 red counters. Then count on from 12, and put down enough yellow counters until you have a total of 21 counters. There are 9 yellow counters. $12 + 9 = 21$

B. Al is setting up 36 chairs, with 9 chairs in each row. How many rows will there be? $▨ \times 9 = 36$

Put down a row of 9 counters. Repeat until you have 36 in all. There are 4 rows of counters. $4 \times 9 = 36$

Use objects to solve each problem.

1. There are 15 girls in a class of 28 students. How many boys are there? $15 + ▨ = 28$

2. An orchard has 4 equal rows of trees. There are 24 trees in all. How many trees are in each row? $4 \times ▨ = 24$

Think It Through
- I should always end my story with a **question**.
- I can **draw a picture** to show the main idea.

Writing Multiplication Stories

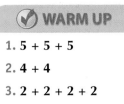

LEARN

What is a multiplication story?

Example A

Maria wrote a multiplication story for $4 \times 3 = $ ▨.

A girl had 4 cats. Her cats liked to run, jump, and play with toys. The girl bought 3 toys for each cat. How many toys did she buy?

$4 \times 3 = 12$
She bought 12 toys.

Example B

Roy wrote a story for $3 \times 3 = $ ▨.

Ron Rabbit planted 3 rows of carrots in his garden. He planted 3 carrots in each row. How many carrots did Ron plant?

$3 \times 3 = 9$
Ron planted 9 carrots.

✓ **Talk About It**

1. How do you know that each example is a multiplication story?

2. How does each picture help you solve the multiplication story?

3. How would Maria's story change if the multiplication sentence was $5 \times 3 = $ ▨?

Write a multiplication story for each. Draw a picture to find each product.

1. 6×2 **2.** 5×6 **3.** 1×7

4. Number Sense How can you tell without finding the product that 4×8 is greater than $4 + 8$?

PRACTICE   For more practice, see Set 5-3 on p. 310.

A Skills and Understanding

Write a multiplication story for each. Draw a picture to find each product.

5. 3×6 **6.** 5×5 **7.** 9×2

8. Number Sense Is the Eggs story a multiplication story? Explain. Write a number sentence for the story.

Eggs

Julio had 12 eggs. He used 3 eggs to make muffins. How many eggs does he have left?

B Reasoning and Problem Solving

9. Algebra Rachel bought some packs of plums. Each pack had 4 plums. She had 12 plums in all. Draw a picture to find how many packs of plums Rachel bought.

10. Writing in Math Draw a picture to show $3 \times 5 = 15$. You may draw an array or equal groups of objects. Write about your picture using the words **factors** and **product.**

Mixed Review and Test Prep

Take It to the NET
Test Prep
www.scottforesman.com

Write a multiplication sentence for each array.

11. ●●
●●
●●
●●
●●

12. ●●●
●●●

13. ●●●●
●●●●
●●●●
●●●●

14. Amy's soccer practice starts at 3:00 and lasts 45 minutes. When does it end?

A. 2:45   **B.** 3:45   **C.** 4:00   **D.** 4:15

Understand Graphic Sources: Tables and Charts

Understanding graphic sources such as tables and charts when you read in math can help you use the **problem-solving strategy, Make a Table,** in the next lesson.

In reading, understanding tables can help you understand what you read. In math, understanding tables can help you solve problems.

The title of the **table** *or* **chart** *tells you in general what it is about.*

This title tells you the table is about the prices of flowers at Greene's Nursery.

The entries in the **table** *give specific pieces of information.*

Greene's Nursery Flower Prices

Number of flower packets	1	2	3	4	5
Price	$3	$6	$9	$12	$15

These headings tell you that the information gives the number of flower packets and their prices.

The entry $9 is in the column for 3 flower packets and the row for price. So, 3 flower packets cost $9.

The headings describe the different types of information in the **table**. *The headings can go either across or down.*

1. What is the cost of 5 flower packets?

2. How many flower packets can you buy with $6?

For 3–5, use the Edgeview Cinema schedule at the right.

3. What information is presented in the schedule?

4. Which movies start at 7:10?

5. <u>Writing in Math</u> How many times is *English Mansions* shown? How do you know?

Edgeview Cinema Movie Schedule

Movie	Theater	Times
Rover & Pixie	1	4:30; 6:15 8:00; 10:00
Jazzy City	2	5:00; 7:10; 9:20
Giants of the Ballpark	3	4:50; 7:10; 9:30
English Mansions	4	4:45; 6:35 8:30; 10:30

For 6–8, use the Green Mountain Amusement Park table at the left.

6. How many people visited the Green Mountain Amusement Park in 2001?

7. In which year(s) did adults pay $24 for admission?

8. <u>Writing in Math</u> Tell all the information in the table about the year 2000.

Green Mountain Amusement Park

Year	Number of Rides	Number of Visitors	Adult Admission	Child Admission
2003	33	1,230,052	$24.00	$14.00
2002	31	987,086	$24.00	$14.00
2001	31	970,248	$22.00	$12.00
2000	30	964,779	$22.00	$12.00
1999	26	855,768	$20.00	$10.00

For 9–12, use the Golden Fruit Punch table at the right.

9. What information is presented in the table?

10. How many cups of orange juice are needed if you want to make 3 quarts of punch?

11. If you use 4 cups of pineapple juice, how many cups of orange juice should you use?

12. <u>Writing in Math</u> Write a sentence that tells the information given in the shaded row.

Golden Fruit Punch

Number of Quarts	Cups of Orange Juice	Cups of Pineapple Juice
1	3	1
2	6	2
3	9	3
4	12	4
5	15	5

Problem-Solving Strategy

Key Idea
Learning how and when to make a table can help you solve problems.

Make a Table

 **LEARN**

How do you make a table to solve a problem?

Bridges Matt built these bridges using toothpicks. If he continues the pattern, how many triangles are needed to build the 4th bridge? the 5th bridge?

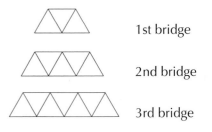

1st bridge

2nd bridge

3rd bridge

Read and Understand

What do you know?

The number of triangles in each of the first 3 bridges is given.

What are you trying to find?

Find the number of triangles needed for the 4th and 5th bridges.

Plan and Solve

What strategy will you use?

Strategy: Make a Table

How to Make a Table

Step 1 Set up a table with headings.

Step 2 Enter the information you know in the table.

Step 3 Look for a pattern in the table. Continue the pattern.

Step 4 Find the answer in the table.

Bridge number		
Number of triangles		

Bridge number	1	2	3
Number of triangles	3	5	7

Bridge number	1	2	3	4	5
Number of triangles	3	5	7	9	11

Bridge number	1	2	3	4	5
Number of triangles	3	5	7	9	11

Answer: He will need 9 triangles for the 4th bridge and 11 for the 5th bridge.

Look Back and Check

Is your work correct?

Yes. Each bridge gets 2 more triangles. $7 + 2 = 9$, $9 + 2 = 11$.

B Mixed Strategy Practice

Solve each problem. Write the answer in a complete sentence.

8. Justine was in line with 3 other students. Max was second. Tom was last. If Justine was first, what place in line was Lydia?

9. Roberto went to camp for 2 days during the summer. He rode the bus with 12 other campers on Monday and 15 other campers on Tuesday. How many more campers were there on Tuesday than on Monday?

10. **Writing in Math** Keiko wants to make 4 rows of this bead pattern. How many beads will she need in all? Explain how you know.

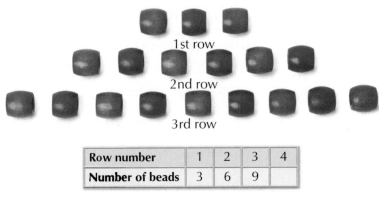

1st row

2nd row

3rd row

Row number	1	2	3	4
Number of beads	3	6	9	

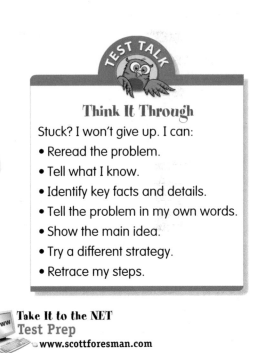

STRATEGIES

- **Show What You Know**
  Draw a Picture
  Make an Organized List
  Make a Table
  Make a Graph
  Act It Out or Use Objects
- **Look for a Pattern**
- **Try, Check, and Revise**
- **Write a Number Sentence**
- **Use Logical Reasoning**
- **Solve a Simpler Problem**
- **Work Backward**

TEST TALK

Think It Through

Stuck? I won't give up. I can:
- Reread the problem.
- Tell what I know.
- Identify key facts and details.
- Tell the problem in my own words.
- Show the main idea.
- Try a different strategy.
- Retrace my steps.

Mixed Review and Test Prep

Take It to the NET
Test Prep
www.scottforesman.com

Write a multiplication story for each. Use counters or draw a picture to find each product.

11. 4×7 **12.** 3×4 **13.** 8×3

14. Which amount shows the value of 2 quarters and 5 dimes?

    A. $1.25   **B.** $1.00   **C.** $0.75   **D.** $0.50

15. **Writing in Math** Write an addition problem with 2 three-digit numbers that you could solve without regrouping.

All text pages available online and on CD-ROM.

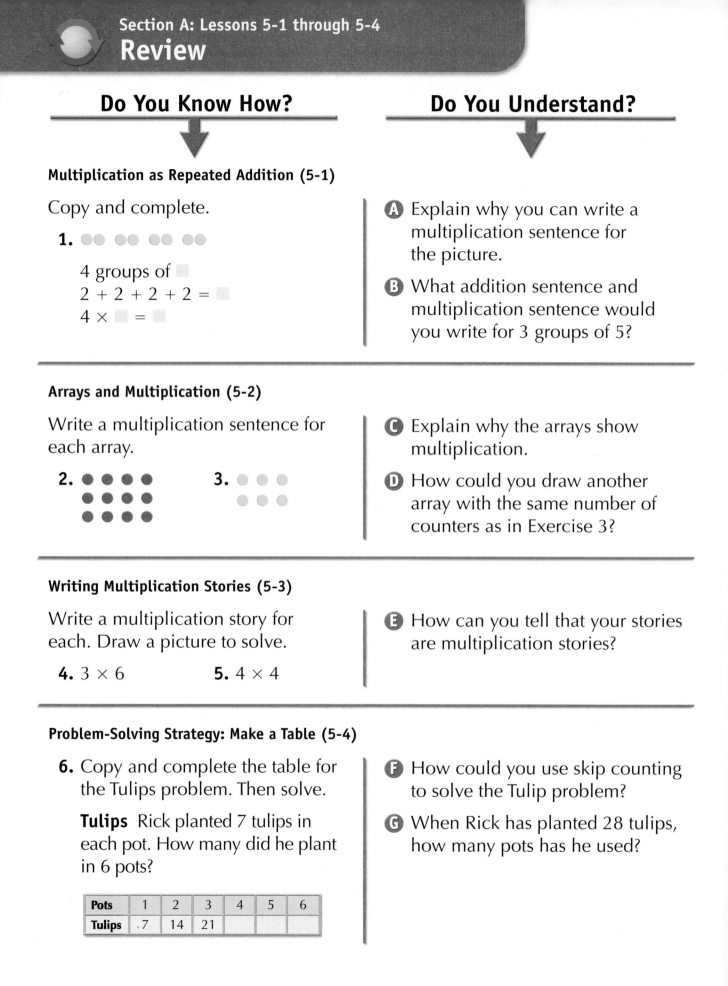

Do You Know How?

Do You Understand?

Multiplication as Repeated Addition (5-1)

Copy and complete.

1. ●● ●● ●● ●●

4 groups of ▨
2 + 2 + 2 + 2 = ▨
4 × ▨ = ▨

Ⓐ Explain why you can write a multiplication sentence for the picture.

Ⓑ What addition sentence and multiplication sentence would you write for 3 groups of 5?

Arrays and Multiplication (5-2)

Write a multiplication sentence for each array.

2. ● ● ● ●
● ● ● ●
● ● ● ●

3. ● ● ●
● ● ●

Ⓒ Explain why the arrays show multiplication.

Ⓓ How could you draw another array with the same number of counters as in Exercise 3?

Writing Multiplication Stories (5-3)

Write a multiplication story for each. Draw a picture to solve.

4. 3 × 6　　　**5.** 4 × 4

Ⓔ How can you tell that your stories are multiplication stories?

Problem-Solving Strategy: Make a Table (5-4)

6. Copy and complete the table for the Tulips problem. Then solve.

Tulips Rick planted 7 tulips in each pot. How many did he plant in 6 pots?

Pots	1	2	3	4	5	6
Tulips	7	14	21			

Ⓕ How could you use skip counting to solve the Tulip problem?

Ⓖ When Rick has planted 28 tulips, how many pots has he used?

MULTIPLE CHOICE

1. Which has the same value as 3×2? (5-2)

   A. $3 + 3 + 3$ **B.** $3 + 2$ **C.** 2×3 **D.** $2 + 2$

2. Which has the same value as $7 + 7$? (5-1)

   A. 3×7 **B.** 2×7 **C.** 7×1 **D.** 7×7

FREE RESPONSE

Copy and complete. (5-1)

3.

5 groups of ▨
$5 + 5 + 5 + 5 + 5 =$ ▨
$5 \times$ ▨ $=$ ▨

4.

4 groups of ▨
$2 + 2 + 2 + 2 =$ ▨
$4 \times$ ▨ $=$ ▨

Draw an array to find each multiplication fact. Write the product. (5-2)

5. 3×5 **6.** 4×2 **7.** 1×9 **8.** 4×4

Write a multiplication story for each. Draw a picture to find each product. (5-3)

9. 2×2 **10.** 3×7 **11.** 4×2

Copy and complete the table to solve the problem. Write the answer in a complete sentence. (5-4)

12. Joe rented a video. He must pay $2 for each day it is late. How much must he pay if he returns it 5 days late?

Days late	1	2	3	4	5
Money owed	$2	$4			

Writing in Math

13. Draw two arrays to show that 5×4 has the same product as 4×5. Explain your arrays. (5-2)

14. Can you write $3 + 8 + 5$ as a multiplication sentence? Explain. (5-1)

Think It Through

I should make my answer **short** but **complete**.

Key Idea
You can use addition doubles and patterns to multiply by 2.

Vocabulary
• multiple
• even number (p. 24)

Think It Through
When **groups are equal**, I can **multiply** to find the total.

2 as a Factor

LEARN

WARM UP
1. 6 + 6   2. 4 + 4
3. 9 + 9   4. 3 + 3

How can you use addition doubles to multiply by 2?

How many legs are on 2 spiders?	How many legs are on 2 beetles?	How many legs are on 2 frogs?
2 groups of 8	2 groups of 6	2 groups of 4

Since you are putting together equal groups, you can multiply. To find 2 groups of 8 legs, write 2×8.

Example A

Find 2×8.

When you multiply with 2, you can think of an addition doubles fact.

2×8 is the same as 2 groups of 8, or $8 + 8$.

○○○○○○○○ Addition   Multiplication   2
○○○○○○○○ sentence: sentence: × 8
                $8 + 8 = 16$ $2 \times 8 = 16$ or   16

There are 16 legs on 2 spiders.

Legs on 2 Beetles	Legs on 2 Frogs
2 groups of 6	2 groups of 4
$2 \times 6 = $ ▧	$2 \times 4 = $ ▧
Think: $6 + 6 = 12$	Think: $4 + 4 = 8$
$2 \times 6 = 12$	$2 \times 4 = 8$

Example B		Example C	
Find 2 × 5.		Find 2 × 7.	
What You **Think**	What You **Write**	What You **Think**	What You **Write**
2 groups of 5 5 + 5 = 10 ●●●●● ●●●●●	2 x 5 = 10	2 groups of 7 7 + 7 = 14 ●●●●●●● ●●●●●●●	2 x 7 = 14

✔ **Talk About It**

1. How could you write 2 × 9 as an addition sentence?

2. How could you use addition doubles to find 6 × 2?

How can you use patterns to help multiply by 2?

Here are the multiplication facts for 2. The products are also called **multiples** of 2. All multiples of 2 are **even numbers**.

	0 × 2	1 × 2	2 × 2	3 × 2	4 × 2	5 × 2	6 × 2	7 × 2	8 × 2	9 × 2
Multiples of 2 →	0	2	4	6	8	10	12	14	16	18

*Each multiple of 2 ends in **0, 2, 4, 6,** or **8.***

Each multiple of 2 is 2 more than the one before it.

✔ **Talk About It**

3. Is 63 a multiple of 2? Explain how you know.

4. **Reasoning** How can you skip count to find 2 × 9?

1. 2×6 **2.** 2×7 **3.** 5×2 **4.** $\begin{array}{r} 4 \\ \times\ 2 \\ \hline \end{array}$ **5.** $\begin{array}{r} 2 \\ \times\ 8 \\ \hline \end{array}$

6. Number Sense Use the patterns you see on page 277 to find 2×10.

PRACTICE

For more practice, see Set 5-5 on p. 311.

A Skills and Understanding

Find each product.

7. 2×3 **8.** 2×2 **9.** 9×2 **10.** 1×2 **11.** 2×8

12. $\begin{array}{r} 5 \\ \times\ 2 \\ \hline \end{array}$ **13.** $\begin{array}{r} 2 \\ \times\ 6 \\ \hline \end{array}$ **14.** $\begin{array}{r} 7 \\ \times\ 2 \\ \hline \end{array}$ **15.** $\begin{array}{r} 2 \\ \times\ 2 \\ \hline \end{array}$ **16.** $\begin{array}{r} 3 \\ \times\ 2 \\ \hline \end{array}$

17. Find the product of 2 and 4.   **18.** Find 2 times 5.

19. Multiply 8 and 2.   **20.** Multiply 2 and 1.

21. Reasoning Draw a picture to show that $6 \times 2 = 2 \times 6$.

B Reasoning and Problem Solving

Math and Everyday Life

During play, there are 6 hockey players on the ice for each team.

22. If the equipment manager sharpens 8 pairs of skates, how many skates does he sharpen?

23. How many hockey players in all are on the ice while 2 teams are playing?

24. Professional hockey players sometimes lose 7 pounds during a game. If a player loses 7 pounds in one game and 5 pounds in the next, how many pounds has he lost?

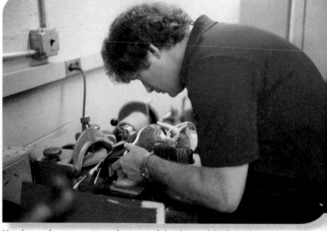

Hockey players wear skates with sharp blades that allow players to turn and stop quickly.

25. Writing in Math Sarah wrote these number sentences to show two ways she could find the number of eyes on 3 cats. Do you agree? Explain.

$2 + 2 + 2 = 6$
$3 \times 2 = 6$

C Extensions

26. Number Sense Explain how you could find the product of 2 and 25 by adding.

Mixed Review and Test Prep

Take It to the NET
Test Prep
www.scottforesman.com

27. Ernie made 10 cents for each can he recycled. How much did he make for recycling 4 cans? Copy and complete the table to solve. Write the answer in a complete sentence.

Number of cans	1	2	3	4
Money	10¢	20¢		

28. Which is another way to show 3×3?

A. $3 + 3$ **B.** 2×3 **C.** $3 + 3 + 2$ **D.** $3 + 3 + 3$

Discovery
CHANNEL
SCHOOL™

Discover Math in Your World

Reinventing the Wheel

In the late 1960s, skateboards had clay roller-skate wheels. Clay wheels did not grip the road well and skaters were thrown by every little rock or surface crack. The ride got better a decade later when larger polyurethane wheels were introduced.

Draw a picture or make a table to help you solve each problem.

1. Each skateboard has four wheels. How many wheels are needed for 4 skateboards? For 8 skateboards?

2. One store sells wheels for $6 each. Another store sells sets of 4 wheels for $28. Which is the better buy? Explain how you know.

Take It to the NET
Video and Activities
www.scottforesman.com

Think It Through

When **putting together equal groups,** I can **multiply** to find the total.

5 as a Factor

LEARN

When do you multiply?

Kim will make a bracelet for each of her 5 cousins. Each bracelet will have 4 beads.

To show 5 groups of 4 beads, write 5 × 4.

How can you multiply by 5?

Example A

How many beads will Kim need for 5 bracelets with 4 beads on each?

Find 5 × 4.

You can count by 5s until you have said 4 numbers.

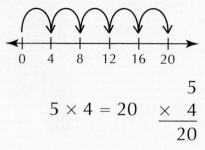

$$5 \times 4 = 20 \qquad \begin{array}{r} 5 \\ \times\ 4 \\ \hline 20 \end{array}$$

Kim will need 20 beads.

Example B

Find 5 × 6.

You can use patterns.

5s Facts	
5 × 0 = 0	5 × 5 = 25
5 × 1 = 5	5 × 6 = 30
5 × 2 = 10	5 × 7 = 35
5 × 3 = 15	5 × 8 = 40
5 × 4 = 20	5 × 9 = 45

Pattern: Each multiple of 5 ends in **0** or **5**.

$$5 \times 6 = 30 \qquad \begin{array}{r} 5 \\ \times\ 6 \\ \hline 30 \end{array}$$

✔ Talk About It

1. How could you skip count to find 5 × 5?

2. Reasoning Use a pattern in the table to find 5 × 10.

Take It to the NET
More Examples
www.scottforesman.com

1. 5×6 **2.** 5×2 **3.** 8×5 **4.** $\begin{array}{r} 1 \\ \times\ 5 \\ \hline \end{array}$ **5.** $\begin{array}{r} 5 \\ \times\ 5 \\ \hline \end{array}$

6. Number Sense Toby has a handful of nickels and no other coins. Could he have exactly 42 cents? Explain.

PRACTICE

For more practice, see Set 5-6 on p. 312.

Ⓐ Skills and Understanding

7. 5×3 **8.** 5×4 **9.** 7×5 **10.** 3×2 **11.** 5×9

12. $\begin{array}{r} 5 \\ \times\ 1 \\ \hline \end{array}$ **13.** $\begin{array}{r} 9 \\ \times\ 2 \\ \hline \end{array}$ **14.** $\begin{array}{r} 6 \\ \times\ 5 \\ \hline \end{array}$ **15.** $\begin{array}{r} 5 \\ \times\ 8 \\ \hline \end{array}$ **16.** $\begin{array}{r} 2 \\ \times\ 2 \\ \hline \end{array}$

17. Number Sense How could you skip count to find 11×5?

Ⓑ Reasoning and Problem Solving

18. Algebra What two 1-digit factors could you multiply to get a product of 45?

19. Lila has 6 nickels in her pocket. Write a multiplication sentence that shows how much money she has.

20. Erin bought 5 red pens and 9 blue pens. How many pens did she buy?

21. Writing in Math What multiplication sentence is shown by the array of buttons at the right? Explain.

🦉 Mixed Review and Test Prep

Take It to the NET
Test Prep
www.scottforesman.com

Find each product.

22. 2×4 **23.** 1×2 **24.** 2×9 **25.** 2×7 **26.** 8×2

27. Continue the pattern. 4, 8, 12, 16, ▨, ▨

     A. 18, 20   **B.** 20, 24   **C.** 20, 25   **D.** 32, 64

Key Idea
You can use patterns to multiply by 10.

Materials
• hundred chart

Think It Through
I can **use a pattern** to continue shading multiples of ten.

10 as a Factor

LEARN

Activity

How does a hundred chart show 10s facts?

1	2	3	4	5	6	7	8	9	10
11	12	13	14	15	16	17	18	19	20
21	22	23	24	25	26	27	28	29	30
31	32	33	34	35	36	37	38	39	40
41	42	43	44	45	46	47	48	49	50
51	52	53	54	55	56	57	58	59	60
61	62	63	64	65	66	67	68	69	70
71	72	73	74	75	76	77	78	79	80
81	82	83	84	85	86	87	88	89	90
91	92	93	94	95	96	97	98	99	100

a. Use a hundred chart. Skip count by 10s. Shade each multiple of 10 blue.

b. Copy and complete the multiples of 10.

$0 \times 10 = 0$ $5 \times 10 = $
$1 \times 10 = 10$ $6 \times 10 = $
$2 \times 10 = 20$ $7 \times 10 = $
$3 \times 10 = 30$ $8 \times 10 = $
$4 \times 10 = 40$ $9 \times 10 = $

c. Explain how you can use a pattern to find 10×10.

I see! The number you are multiplying by 10 goes in the tens place.

Right! Just place a zero after the number you multiply by 10.

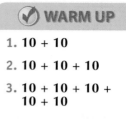

282

1. 10×5 **2.** 4×10 **3.** 10×6

4. $\begin{array}{r} 4 \\ \times\ 2 \\ \hline \end{array}$ **5.** $\begin{array}{r} 10 \\ \times\ 3 \\ \hline \end{array}$

6. Number Sense Roberto has only dimes in his pocket. Could he have exactly 35 cents? Explain.

PRACTICE

For more practice, see Set 5-7 on p. 312.

Ⓐ Skills and Understanding

7. 1×10 **8.** 10×7 **9.** 10×9 **10.** 10×10 **11.** 5×5

12. $\begin{array}{r} 10 \\ \times\ 1 \\ \hline \end{array}$ **13.** $\begin{array}{r} \$10 \\ \times\ 9 \\ \hline \end{array}$ **14.** $\begin{array}{r} 10 \\ \times\ 8 \\ \hline \end{array}$ **15.** $\begin{array}{r} 0 \\ \times\ 10 \\ \hline \end{array}$ **16.** $\begin{array}{r} 9 \\ \times\ 5 \\ \hline \end{array}$

17. Number Sense Is 72 a multiple of 10? Explain.

Ⓑ Reasoning and Problem Solving

18. Reasoning List the multiples of 2 from 0 through 30. Then list the multiples of 5 from 0 through 30. Circle the numbers that are in both lists. What pattern do you notice?

19. Booker had 3 packs of pencils. Each pack had 10 pencils. He gave 5 pencils to Julie. How many pencils does he have left?

20. Gary says 20 is a multiple of 10. Jen says 20 is a multiple of 5. Who is right? Explain.

21. Writing in Math Write a multiplication story about the picture of T-shirts. Trade with a partner and solve.

$10.00 $10.00 $10.00 $10.00 $10.00

🦉 Mixed Review and Test Prep

Take It to the NET
www Test Prep
www.scottforesman.com

Find each product.

22. 6×5 **23.** 5×9 **24.** 3×5 **25.** 5×0 **26.** 8×5

27. Find $400 - 199$.

A. 201 **B.** 198 **C.** 101 **D.** 100

Problem-Solving Skill

Key Idea
Identifying hidden questions helps you solve multiple-step problems.

Think It Through
To find hidden questions, I should figure out **what happened first, then next,** and so on.

Multiple-Step Problems

LEARN

How do you find hidden questions?

Some word problems have hidden questions that must be answered before you can solve the problem.

At the pet store, Kim and Myra bought small water bottles for their hamsters' cages. Myra bought 4 bottles and Kim bought 5. The water bottles cost $2 each. How much did they spend?

One Way	*Another Way*

Read and Understand

One Way

Find the **hidden question:**

How many water bottles did they buy in all?

5 + 4 = 9

They bought 9 water bottles.

Solve the problem:

How much money did they spend?

9	×	$2	=	$18
Water bottles		Cost of each		Total spent

They spent $18.

Another Way

Find two **hidden questions:**

1. How much did Myra spend?

4	×	$2	=	$8
Water bottles		Cost of each		Amount Myra spent

2. How much did Kim spend?

5	×	$2	=	$10
Water bottles		Cost of each		Amount Kim spent

Solve the problem:

How much money did they spend?

$8 + $10 = $18

They spent $18.

✔ Talk About It

1. What are the differences between the two ways of solving the problem?

For 1 and 2, use the price list. Write and answer the hidden question or questions. Then solve the problem.

Snack Bar Prices
Soft pretzel . $2
Pizza slice . . $3
Hamburger . $5
Juice $1

1. Marley ordered 3 soft pretzels and 1 slice of pizza. How much money will she need?

2. Hank's dad bought 3 hamburgers and paid with a $20 bill. How much change will he get?

PRACTICE

For more practice, see Set 5-8 on p. 312.

Write and answer the hidden question or questions. Then solve the problem. Use the picture at the right for 3 and 4.

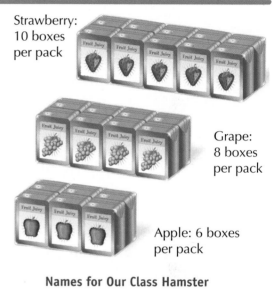

Strawberry: 10 boxes per pack

Grape: 8 boxes per pack

Apple: 6 boxes per pack

3. Terese needs to buy 20 juice boxes. If she buys one grape pack, one strawberry pack, and one apple pack, how many extra juice boxes will Terese have?

4. Jerry bought 5 grape packs and 2 strawberry packs. How many juice boxes did he buy all together?

For 5 and 6, use the graph.

5. How many students voted for the name Beanie or Lassie?

6. How many more students voted for Smokey than voted for Hammie?

7. **Writing in Math** Write a word problem that has a hidden question. Use the data below about carnival rides. Solve your problem.

Names for Our Class Hamster

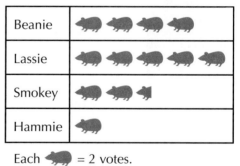

Each 🐹 = 2 votes.

Carnival Prices	Under 10 Years Old	Over 10 Years Old
Ferris Wheel	$1	$2
Roller Coaster	$2	$4
Bumper Cars	$0.50	$0.75

 All text pages available online and on CD-ROM.

Algebra

Key Idea
You can use a pattern to multiply with 0 and 1.

Vocabulary
• Identity (one) Property of Multiplication
• Zero Property of Multiplication

Materials
• counters or

 tools

TEST TALK

Think It Through
I can **use objects** to see a pattern when I multiply with 1.

Multiplying with 0 and 1

LEARN

Activity

Can you find patterns with multiples of 1 and 0?

This array shows $1 \times 7 = 7$.

● ● ● ● ● ● ●   1 row
7 counters in a row

a. Use counters. Make an array to show each multiplication fact. Write each product.

$1 \times 5 = $◻ $1 \times 8 = $◻ $1 \times 10 = $◻
$6 \times 1 = $◻ $9 \times 1 = $◻ $4 \times 1 \ = $◻

b. Write a pattern you see when you multiply with 1.

c. How many cherries are there in the 3 bowls below?

d. What multiplication sentence can you write to show how many cherries are in the bowls?

What's the rule?

Example A

Identity (one) Property of Multiplication: When you multiply a number and 1, the product is that number.

$1 \times 8 = 8$ $245 \times 1 = 245$

Example B

Zero Property of Multiplication: When you multiply a number and 0, the product is 0.

$0 \times 8 = 0$ $0 \times 389 = 0$

✓ **Talk About It**

1. Explain how you can use the properties above to find 456×1 and 0×554.

1. 1×5 **2.** 0×9 **3.** 8×1 **4.** $\begin{array}{r} 6 \\ \times\ 0 \\ \hline \end{array}$ **5.** $\begin{array}{r} 1 \\ \times\ 1 \\ \hline \end{array}$

6. Number Sense Draw a picture to show $1 \times 4 = 4$.

PRACTICE

For more practice, see Set 5-9 on p. 313.

Ⓐ Skills and Understanding

7. 0×10 **8.** 4×1 **9.** 0×0 **10.** 3×1 **11.** 1×7

12. $\begin{array}{r} 0 \\ \times\ 5 \\ \hline \end{array}$ **13.** $\begin{array}{r} 2 \\ \times\ 1 \\ \hline \end{array}$ **14.** $\begin{array}{r} 6 \\ \times\ 1 \\ \hline \end{array}$ **15.** $\begin{array}{r} 0 \\ \times\ 4 \\ \hline \end{array}$ **16.** $\begin{array}{r} 2 \\ \times\ 0 \\ \hline \end{array}$

17. $\begin{array}{r} 9 \\ \times\ 1 \\ \hline \end{array}$ **18.** $\begin{array}{r} 3 \\ \times\ 0 \\ \hline \end{array}$ **19.** $\begin{array}{r} 0 \\ \times\ 7 \\ \hline \end{array}$ **20.** $\begin{array}{r} 10 \\ \times\ 1 \\ \hline \end{array}$ **21.** $\begin{array}{r} 8 \\ \times\ 0 \\ \hline \end{array}$

22. Number Sense Explain how you can find the missing number in $4 \times \blacksquare = 4$.

Ⓑ Reasoning and Problem Solving

Copy and complete. Write $<$, $>$, or $=$ for each ●.

23. 0×9 ● 1×9 **24.** 1×8 ● 329×0 **25.** 1×0 ● 0×27

Copy and complete. Write $\times$ or $+$ for each ●.

26. 3 ● $1 = 3$ **27.** 3 ● $0 = 0$ **28.** 3 ● $1 = 4$ **29.** 3 ● $0 = 3$

30. Cindy bought a pen for $2 and 3 notebooks for $2 each. How much did she spend?

31. **Writing in Math** Write a multiplication sentence that uses the Identity (one) Property of Multiplication. Explain why it shows this property.

Mixed Review and Test Prep

Take It to the NET
Test Prep
www.scottforesman.com

32. 10×7 **33.** 10×4 **34.** 3×10 **35.** 5×6 **36.** 2×8

37. Gary paid $2 each for 9 hamburgers. He paid with a $20 bill. How much change did he get?

A. $20   **B.** $18   **C.** $12   **D.** $2

Key Idea
Patterns can help you remember multiplication facts with 9 as a factor.

TEST TALK

Think It Through
I can **look carefully at the table** to see the patterns.

9 as a Factor

LEARN

What's the pattern?

Chico and Eddie must find 8×9. They look for patterns in the table to help.

9s Facts

$0 \times 9 = \ 0$
$1 \times 9 = \ 9$
$2 \times 9 = 18$
$3 \times 9 = 27$
$4 \times 9 = 36$
$5 \times 9 = 45$
$6 \times 9 = 54$
$7 \times 9 = 63$
$8 \times 9 = \ ?$

*The **ones** digit goes down by 1 each time. So the next ones digit is 2.*

*The **tens** digit goes up by 1 each time. So the next tens digit is 7.*

So, $8 \times 9 = 72$.

I see a different pattern. The tens digit is 1 less than the first factor.

The digits of the product add to 9.

$8 - 1 = 7$
$8 \times 9 = 72$
$7 + 2 = 9$

✔ **Talk About It**

1. How can you use a pattern to find 9×9?

2. Explain how $2 \times 9 = 18$ can help you find 3×9.

Are there more patterns with 9?

You can use your fingers to help find 9s facts!

Put both hands on your desk, palms down. Mentally number your fingers from left to right.

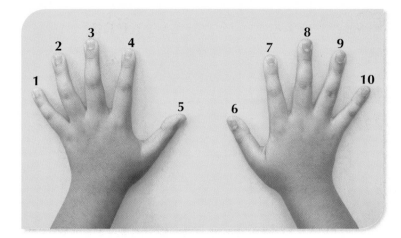

To find 4 × 9, bend down finger number 4.

Fingers to the left of the bent finger show the number of tens in the product.

Fingers to the right of the bent finger show the number of ones in the product.

4 × 9 = 36

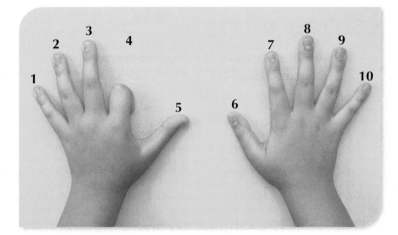

✔ Talk About It

3. How can you use the finger pattern to find 6 × 9?

4. When you bend down one finger, how many fingers are left? How does this relate to the sum of the digits in the product of a 9s fact?

5. Try using the finger pattern to find 7 × 9 and 8 × 9. Do your answers fit the patterns that Chico and Eddie found on page 288?

CHECK ✔

For another example, see Set 5-10 on p. 309.

1. 9 × $5   **2.** 4 × 9   **3.** 9 × 0   **4.** $2 × 6   **5.** 7 × 9

6.   5
   × 5

7.   2
   × 9

8. $3
   × 9

9.   6
   × 9

10.   1
   × 5

11. Number Sense Darcy thinks that 4 × 9 is 24. Use a 9s pattern to show that she is wrong.

Ⓐ Skills and Understanding

12. 1×9 **13.** 6×9 **14.** 9×8 **15.** $\$2 \times 2$ **16.** 7×5

17. 9×9 **18.** 9×3 **19.** $\$10 \times 4$ **20.** 4×9 **21.** 9×10

22. $\begin{array}{r} 7 \\ \times\, 9 \\ \hline \end{array}$ **23.** $\begin{array}{r} 5 \\ \times\, 5 \\ \hline \end{array}$ **24.** $\begin{array}{r} \$9 \\ \times\, 8 \\ \hline \end{array}$ **25.** $\begin{array}{r} 1 \\ \times\, 4 \\ \hline \end{array}$ **26.** $\begin{array}{r} 6 \\ \times\, 2 \\ \hline \end{array}$

27. $\begin{array}{r} 10 \\ \times\, 7 \\ \hline \end{array}$ **28.** $\begin{array}{r} 5 \\ \times\, 9 \\ \hline \end{array}$ **29.** $\begin{array}{r} 0 \\ \times\, 1 \\ \hline \end{array}$ **30.** $\begin{array}{r} 3 \\ \times\, 2 \\ \hline \end{array}$ **31.** $\begin{array}{r} 9 \\ \times\, 2 \\ \hline \end{array}$

32. Multiply 9 and 3.   **33.** Find the product of 9 and 7.

Ⓑ Reasoning and Problem Solving

🦋 Math and Science

Polar bears love water and are found in Arctic regions.

Of all the kinds of bears in the world, the sun bear weighs the least. The polar bear weighs the most. Sun bears live in trees and are found in Asia. Sun bears can weigh up to 145 pounds. They have claws up to 5 inches long to help them climb.

34. A polar bear might weigh as much as 1,760 pounds. How much more can a polar bear weigh than a sun bear?

35. Bears that live in cold places take a long winter nap. During this time, a bear's heart slows to about 9 beats per minute. About how many times will its heart beat in 5 minutes?

36. <u>Writing in Math</u> Kayla used a pattern to find 9×9. Her work is shown below. Change Kayla's work so it is correct.

> $\underline{9} \times 9 \longrightarrow$ The tens digit of the product
>   must be 8.
> $8 + \underline{1} = 9 \longrightarrow$ The ones digit of the
>   product must be 1.
>   So, $9 \times 9 = 18$.

C Extensions

Algebra In the number sentences below, each letter represents a number less than 10. Find each number.

37. $a \times b = 72$
$a + b = 17$

38. $c \times d = 35$
$c + d = 12$

39. $e \times f = 54$
$e + f = 15$

Mixed Review and Test Prep

Take It to the NET
Test Prep
www.scottforesman.com

Copy and complete. Write <, >, or = for each ●.

40. 1×6 ● 0×6

41. 7×0 ● 47×0

42. 1×22 ● 22×1

43. Find $75 + (25 + 90)$.

A. 100   **B.** 115   **C.** 190   **D.** 290

Learning with Technology

Double the Cost!

Jack's sister, Beth, said he could borrow her roller blades, just for today, for a $1 charge. For every day he keeps them after today, she will double the charge. A rental store would charge $10 for today, plus $5 for each extra day. Jack thinks Beth's offer sounds better. If he keeps the roller blades for 10 days after today, which is the better deal?

Doubling is the same as multiplying by 2. You can use the Constant key, **Cons**, on a calculator to double numbers or to add the same number over and over.

Copy the table.

1. To find Beth's charges, first press × 2 **Cons**.

2. The charge for today is $1, so enter 1 **Cons**. Record the amount. Then, for each day in the table, press **Cons** and record the amount. Clear the calculator display.

3. To find the store's charges, press + 5 **Cons**.

4. Enter 10 **Cons**. Record the amount. Continue to press **Cons** once and record for each day in the table.

5. Was Jack right about Beth's offer? Explain.

Days Used	Beth's Charge	Store's Charge
Today	$1	$10
+ 1 day		
+ 2 days		
+ 3 days		
+ 4 days		
+ 5 days		
+ 6 days		
+ 7 days		
+ 8 days		
+ 9 days		
+ 10 days		

Key Idea
Playing a game
can help you
remember
multiplication
facts.

Materials
• number cards
  labeled 0, 1, 2,
  5, 9, and 10
• number cards
  labeled 1–10
• counters
• game board

TEST TALK

Think It Through
I can **write a
number sentence**
using each number
card as a factor.

Practicing Multiplication Facts

LEARN

Activity

How can you practice basic facts?

Play the Product Game with a partner.

Place both piles of number cards face down.

Player 1:

a. Take the top number card from each pile.

b. Find the product of the numbers.

c. On the game board, cover the product
with a yellow counter.

$$2 \times 6 = 12$$

$$9 \times 3 = 27$$

d. Replace each card in its original pile.
Shuffle both piles of cards.

Player 2:

e. Repeat Steps a and b above.

f. Place a red counter on the product.

g. Repeat Step d above.

Continue to play until one player covers 3 products in a row
(across, up, down, or diagonally). A free space counts as a
covered fact.

0	1	2	3	4	5
6	7	8	9	10	12
14	Free Space	15	16	18	20
25	27	30	35	36	Free Space
40	45	50	54	60	63
70	72	80	81	90	100

h. What strategies did you use to help remember
multiplication facts?

For another example, see Set 5-11 on p. 309.

1. 5×5 **2.** 9×6 **3.** 7×2 **4.** 4×1 **5.** 9×8

6. Number Sense Tiffany says that $7 \times 9 = 65$. What pattern could you use to show her that her answer is not correct?

PRACTICE

For more practice, see Set 5-11 on p. 313.

A Skills and Understanding

7. 2×3 **8.** 7×0 **9.** 8×10 **10.** 2×6 **11.** 5×2

12. 2×2 **13.** 5×3 **14.** 8×5 **15.** 8×2 **16.** 9×9

17. $\begin{array}{r} 9 \\ \times\, 5 \\ \hline \end{array}$ **18.** $\begin{array}{r} 4 \\ \times\, 5 \\ \hline \end{array}$ **19.** $\begin{array}{r} 2 \\ \times\, 9 \\ \hline \end{array}$ **20.** $\begin{array}{r} 10 \\ \times\, 1 \\ \hline \end{array}$ **21.** $\begin{array}{r} 5 \\ \times\, 6 \\ \hline \end{array}$

22. $\begin{array}{r} 10 \\ \times\, 10 \\ \hline \end{array}$ **23.** $\begin{array}{r} 3 \\ \times\, 9 \\ \hline \end{array}$ **24.** $\begin{array}{r} 7 \\ \times\, 5 \\ \hline \end{array}$ **25.** $\begin{array}{r} 4 \\ \times\, 9 \\ \hline \end{array}$ **26.** $\begin{array}{r} 2 \\ \times\, 4 \\ \hline \end{array}$

27. Number Sense Nathan thinks $8 \times 5 = 42$. What pattern shows that his answer is not correct?

B Reasoning and Problem Solving

Algebra Write the missing number.

28. $9 \times \boxed{} = 63$ **29.** $3 \times \boxed{} = 30$ **30.** $\boxed{} \times 5 = 35$

31. An octet has 8 musicians. A quartet has 4 musicians. How many people are in a group of 3 octets and 2 quartets?

32. **Writing in Math** Write a multiplication problem about the cherries at the right. Trade problems with a partner and solve.

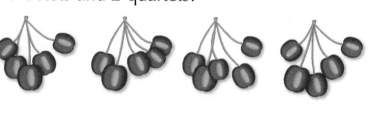

Mixed Review and Test Prep

Take It to the NET
Test Prep
www.scottforesman.com

33. 6×9 **34.** 9×9 **35.** 8×9 **36.** 7×9 **37.** 5×9

38. Which has the same value as 8×2?

    A. $8 + 2$ **B.** $2 + 2$ **C.** 2×8 **D.** 8×8

All text pages available online and on CD-ROM.

Problem-Solving Applications

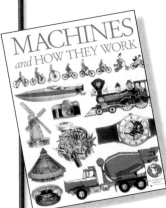

Bicycles Bicycles are not just sources of fun. In many places today, a bicycle is an important means of travel. Worldwide, there are more bicycles purchased each year than cars!

Trivia The introduction of the Rover safety bicycle in 1885 made bicycling popular. People finally had fast transportation that was easy to use and maintain. Bikes even affected clothing styles!

1 Many bicycles have 4 brake shoes. How many brake shoes are needed for 9 of these bikes?

2 On one type of bicycle, each of the 5 gears on the rear wheel can be used with each of the 3 gears that are turned by the pedals. How many different combinations of gears does this bicycle have?

3 How many wheels are there on 8 bicycles?

Using Key Facts

4 Order the countries from which the U.S. imported small bicycles in 2001 from lowest to highest value.

5 Writing in Math Read the trivia. Estimate how long ago the Rover safety bicycle made bicycling popular. Explain how you estimated.

Key Facts U.S. Imports of Small Bicycles, 2001	
Country	**Value**
•Italy	$58,000
•Japan	$152,000
•Germany	$64,000
•United Kingdom	$112,000

6 The first bicycle with steering was shown in Paris in 1818. This was 48 years before a bicycle with pedals was patented in the U.S. When was the bicycle with pedals patented? Read the trivia. How many years passed after this patent before Rover bicycles made bicycling popular?

7 In the 1870s, bicycles with high front wheels were the fastest bicycles. They could go about 23 miles per hour. The greatest speed anyone has reached on a bicycle is at least 144 miles per hour faster than this. What is this speed?

8 **Decision Making**
Suppose you had $20 to spend at a bike shop. Which accessories would you purchase? How much change would you get back?

Good News/Bad News Since bicycles do not pollute or require fuel, riding one is a great way to commute to work. Unfortunately, many towns were built with only cars in mind. Many people live too far from work and many roads are not safe for bicyclists.

Item	Cost
Horn	$3
Bell	$4
Pegs (1 pair)	$15
Water bottle	$3
Headlight	$12
Decals	$1

Do You Know How?

Do You Understand?

2 as a Factor(5-5)
5 as a Factor (5-6)
10 as a Factor (5-7)

1. 2×3 **2.** 5×4 **3.** 5×2

4. 10×5 **5.** 6×2 **6.** 5×5

7. 2×8 **8.** 7×5 **9.** 10×7

Ⓐ Tell a pattern you can use to help remember 2s facts and 10s facts.

Ⓑ How could you skip count to find 5×8?

Multiple-Step Problems (5-8)

10. Jen had 5 bags. She put 3 apples in each bag. Then she gave 1 bag of apples away. How many apples did she have left?

Ⓒ What is the hidden question in this problem? What is the answer to the hidden question?

Multiplying with 0 and 1(5-9)
9 as a Factor (5-10)

11. 9×7 **12.** 6×9 **13.** 4×9

14. 0×9 **15.** 9×3 **16.** 5×9

17. 2×9 **18.** 8×9 **19.** 9×9

Copy and complete. Write $\times$ or $+$ for each ●.

20. $12 \; ● \; 1 = 12$ **21.** $4 \; ● \; 0 = 4$

Ⓓ Explain what happens when you multiply any number and 1.

Ⓔ Explain what happens when you multiply any number and 0.

Ⓕ What patterns can you use to find 6×9?

Practicing Multiplication Facts (5-11)

Find each product.

22. 2×7 **23.** 5×3 **24.** 6×5

25. 8×10 **26.** 2×4 **27.** 0×7

Ⓖ Brad says that 2×7 is 15. What pattern shows that he is not correct?

MULTIPLE CHOICE

1. Which number is NOT a multiple of 2? (5-5)

    A. 5   **B.** 4   **C.** 12   **D.** 18

2. What is the product of 5 and 8? (5-6)

    A. 3   **B.** 13   **C.** 20   **D.** 40

FREE RESPONSE

Find each product. (5-5, 5-6, 5-7, 5-10, 5-11)

3. 2×2 **4.** 2×7 **5.** 8×2 **6.** 2×4 **7.** 9×2

8. 5×8 **9.** 4×5 **10.** 7×10 **11.** 9×5 **12.** 10×6

13. $\begin{array}{r} 2 \\ \times 9 \\ \hline \end{array}$ **14.** $\begin{array}{r} 4 \\ \times 9 \\ \hline \end{array}$ **15.** $\begin{array}{r} 7 \\ \times 9 \\ \hline \end{array}$ **16.** $\begin{array}{r} 9 \\ \times 8 \\ \hline \end{array}$ **17.** $\begin{array}{r} 9 \\ \times 6 \\ \hline \end{array}$

18. $\begin{array}{r} 2 \\ \times 6 \\ \hline \end{array}$ **19.** $\begin{array}{r} 10 \\ \times 5 \\ \hline \end{array}$ **20.** $\begin{array}{r} 9 \\ \times 9 \\ \hline \end{array}$ **21.** $\begin{array}{r} 3 \\ \times 9 \\ \hline \end{array}$ **22.** $\begin{array}{r} 5 \\ \times 7 \\ \hline \end{array}$

23. Find the product of 10 and 2.   **24.** Find 5 times 2.

Write and answer the hidden question or questions. Then solve the problem. (5-8, 5-12)

25. Tara bought 2 stuffed animals for $3 each. She paid with a $10 bill. How much change did Tara get?

26. Eli bought 2 packages of muffins. Each package had 6 muffins. After he ate 2 muffins, how many did Eli have left?

Copy and complete. Write $\times$ or $+$ for each ⬤. (5-9)

27. $7 \,⬤\, 0 = 7$ **28.** $7 \,⬤\, 1 = 7$ **29.** $7 \,⬤\, 0 = 0$ **30.** $7 \,⬤\, 1 = 8$

Writing in Math

31. Rachel says that any number multiplied by 2 ends in a 5 or a 0. Do you agree? Explain. (5-5)

32. Explain how you could use the Identity Property of Multiplication to find the product of any number and 1. (5-9)

Test-Taking Strategies

Understand the question.

Get information for the answer.

Plan how to find the answer.

Make smart choices.

→ Use writing in math.

Improve written answers.

Use Writing in Math

Sometimes a test question asks for a written answer, such as an explanation, a description, or a comparison. See how one student followed the steps below to answer this test item by writing in math.

1. To solve this problem, you must ESTIMATE. Do NOT find the exact answer.

ESTIMATE the number of flowers in the vases.

Estimate: _____

On the lines below, explain how you made your estimate.

_____

_____

Understand the question.

I need to estimate the number of flowers in the vases and explain how I made my estimate.

Gather information for the answer.

I'll need to get information from the text and the picture.

Plan how to find the answer.

Each vase has about the same number of flowers. So I can use multiplication.

Use writing in math.

• Make your answer brief but complete.

• Use words from the problem and use math terms accurately.

• Describe steps in order.

Estimate: _40 flowers_

On the lines below, explain how you made your estimate.

First, I counted 10 flowers in one of the vases. Next, I counted 4 vases. Then I multiplied 4 x 10. I got the estimate of 40 flowers.

• Is the question completely answered?

• Is the answer clear?

• Are the steps explained in order?

2. The table below shows the number of strawberries needed to make strawberry tarts. Complete the pattern in the table to find how many strawberries are needed for 6 tarts.

Strawberry Tarts

Number of tarts	1	2	3	4	5	6
Number of strawberries	3	6	9	12	15	

Answer: <u>18 strawberries</u>

On the lines below, explain how the number of strawberries changes as the number of tarts changes.

<u>The number of strawberries</u>

<u>increases by 3 for each tart.</u>

Think It Through

I have found the pattern: the missing number is 18. Now I need to explain or describe the pattern in the table. The problem asks me to tell how the number of strawberries changes as the number of tarts changes. I will begin by using words from the problem. The number of strawberries increases by 3 for each tart.

Now it's your turn.

For each problem, give a complete response.

3. To solve this problem, you must ESTIMATE. Do NOT find the exact answer.

ESTIMATE the number of bugs on the leaves. Then explain how you found your estimate.

4. The table below shows the number of bandages in first-aid kits.

First-Aid Kits

Number of kits	1	2	3	4	5
Number of bandages	4	8	12	16	

Find the number of bandages in 5 first-aid kits. Then explain how the number of bandages changes as the number of kits changes.

Self Check

When my dad commutes to work, he takes the same route there and back.

*The **Commutative (order) Property of Multiplication** says you can multiply in any order. (p. 263)*

Draw an array, use repeated addition, or multiply in any order. (Lessons 5-1, 5-2)

Multiply 3×6.

Draw an **array.**

3 rows of 6

$$\underset{\text{factor}}{3} \times \underset{\text{factor}}{6} = \underset{\text{product}}{18}$$

Use repeated addition.

3 groups of 6

$6 + 6 + 6 = 18$

Use the **Commutative Property.**

$3 \times 6 = 6 \times 3$

1. Find 6×7 and 4×4.

My mom planted a nice array of flowers in the garden.

*An **array** is an arrangement of objects in equal rows. (p. 262)*

Self Check

Write a story to show a multiplication problem. (Lessons 5-3, 5-4)

Write a multiplication story for 5×2. Then solve the problem.

Becky bought 5 packs of pens. Each pack contained 2 pens. How many pens did Becky buy?

You can make a table to solve the problem.

Number of packs	1	2	3	4	5
Number of pens	2	4	6	8	10

Becky bought 10 pens.

2. Write a multiplication story for 7×3. Make a table to find the product.

I can use a copy machine to make multiple copies.

A **multiple** of 5 is the product of 5 and a whole number. (p. 277)

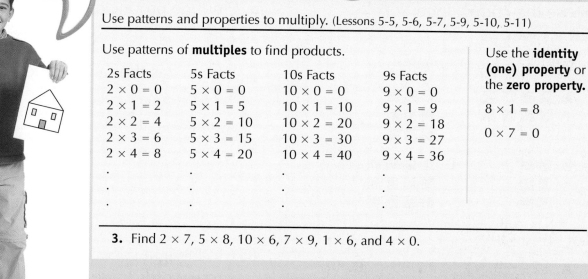

Use patterns and properties to multiply. (Lessons 5-5, 5-6, 5-7, 5-9, 5-10, 5-11)

Use patterns of **multiples** to find products.

2s Facts	5s Facts	10s Facts	9s Facts
$2 \times 0 = 0$	$5 \times 0 = 0$	$10 \times 0 = 0$	$9 \times 0 = 0$
$2 \times 1 = 2$	$5 \times 1 = 5$	$10 \times 1 = 10$	$9 \times 1 = 9$
$2 \times 2 = 4$	$5 \times 2 = 10$	$10 \times 2 = 20$	$9 \times 2 = 18$
$2 \times 3 = 6$	$5 \times 3 = 15$	$10 \times 3 = 30$	$9 \times 3 = 27$
$2 \times 4 = 8$	$5 \times 4 = 20$	$10 \times 4 = 40$	$9 \times 4 = 36$

Use the **identity (one) property** or the **zero property**.

$8 \times 1 = 8$

$0 \times 7 = 0$

3. Find 2×7, 5×8, 10×6, 7×9, 1×6, and 4×0.

Identical things look the same.

The **Identity (one) Property of Multiplication** says that when you multiply a number by 1, you get that same number. (p. 286)

The zero property must be about the number 0.

The **Zero Property of Multiplication** says that when you multiply a number by 0, you get 0. (p. 286)

Look for hidden questions when you solve problems. (Lesson 5-8)

Clark bought 5 packs of rubber stamps. Each pack contained 6 stamps. He gave 8 of his stamps to his friend. How many stamps does Clark have left?

First find the hidden question.

What is the total number of stamps Clark bought?

5	×	6	=	30
Packs		Stamps in each pack		Stamps Clark bought

Then solve the problem.

$30 - 8 = 22$

Clark has 22 stamps left.

4. Each pack of rubber stamps cost \$9. Jessica bought 3 packs of rubber stamps and Flora bought 4 packs. How much money did they spend in all?

3	6	9	12	15	18	21
1	2	3	4	5	6	7

Answers: 1. 42; 16 2. Stories will vary; 3. 14; 40; 60; 63; 6; 0 4. \$63

Chapter 5 Vocabulary and Concept Review

MULTIPLE CHOICE

Choose the correct letter for each answer.

1. Which array shows 3×4?

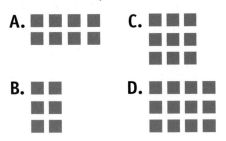

2. Find 8 times 9.

A. 17   **B.** 72   **C.** 89   **D.** 98

3. Larry bought 9 boxes of cards. Each box had 6 cards in it. Which number sentence can be used to find the total number of cards Larry bought?

A. $9 \times 6 = \blacksquare$

B. $3 \times 9 = \blacksquare$

C. $3 + 9 + 6 = \blacksquare$

D. $3 + 9 - 6 = \blacksquare$

4. Which is NOT a multiple of 2?

A. 4   **B.** 8   **C.** 9   **D.** 10

5. Josh had 5 carrots. He cut each into 3 pieces. How many carrot pieces does he have?

A. 2   **C.** 10

B. 8   **D.** 15

Think It Through
- I should **choose an operation** before I solve.
- I can **draw a picture** to help.

6. Find the product of 8 and 2.

A. 6   **B.** 10   **C.** 16   **D.** 28

7. Which has the same value as 4×5?

A. $4 + 4 + 4 + 4$

B. $5 + 5 + 5 + 5$

C. $4 + 5$

D. $2 + 2 + 5$

8. Mr. Dwight gave 5 students some words to define. Each student got 10 words. How many words were there in all?

A. 15   **B.** 20   **C.** 50   **D.** 70

9. Which multiplication fact matches the picture below?

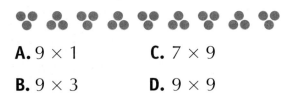

A. 9×1 **C.** 7×9

B. 9×3 **D.** 9×9

10. Phil bought 5 comic books that cost $2 each. How much did he spend?

A. $2   **B.** $10   **C.** $15   **D.** $25

11. Mrs. Kenneth bought 5 packs of erasers. Each pack had 4 erasers. She gave 6 erasers to Mr. Kern. How many erasers does Mrs. Kenneth have left?

A. 1   **B.** 4   **C.** 14   **D.** 28

Copy and complete.

12.

5 groups of ▨
▨ + ▨ + ▨ + ▨ + ▨ = 15
5 × ▨ = ▨

Draw an array to show each multiplication fact. Write the product.

13. 5 × 6   **14.** 2 × 4

Copy and complete. Write <, >, or = for each ●.

15. 0 × 7 ● 7 × 1

16. 3 × 2 ● 2 × 3

17. 5 × 1 ● 9 × 0

Find the product.

18. 2 × 8   **19.** 9 × $4

20. 6 × 1   **21.** 4 × 0

22. 4 × 5   **23.** 7 × 10

24. 5   **25.** 2
       × 9   × 6

26. 10   **27.** 2
       × 1   × 8

28. Write a multiplication story for 3 × 2. Find the product.

29. Mrs. O'Hanlon teaches 7 ballet classes. She has 10 students in each class. How many ballet students does she have in all?

Writing in Math

30. The lemonade stand charges $3 for a large lemonade. Copy and complete the table to show how much it would cost to buy 5 large lemonades. Explain the pattern in the table.

Number of lemonades	1	2	3	4	5
Cost	$3				

31. For the problem below, write and answer the hidden question or questions. Then solve the problem.

TEST TALK

Think It Through
Some problems have **hidden questions** that I need to solve first.

Anthony bought a box of golf balls. He gave 5 golf balls to each of his 3 friends, and he had 6 golf balls left over. How many golf balls were in the box?

32. Candi sold 6 cans of popcorn and Rick sold 4 cans. Each can of popcorn cost $9. Explain what Rick did to find out how much money they earned in all.

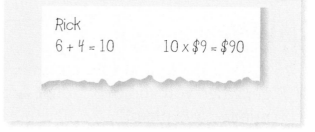

Rick
6 + 4 = 10   10 × $9 = $90

Number and Operation

MULTIPLE CHOICE

1. Dana bought a jump rope for $1.59. She gave the cashier a $5 bill. How much change should she receive?

   A. $3.41

   B. $3.51

   C. $4.41

   D. $4.59

TEST TALK

Think It Through
I should **look for key words** that tell me which operation to use.

2. Find the sum of 431 + 58.

   A. 427   **B.** 479   **C.** 489   **D.** 589

3. Which array shows 3 × 6?

   A.   **C.**

   B.   **D.**

FREE RESPONSE

4. Find 9 × 6.

5. Write 6,792 in expanded form.

6. Find 105 − 75 using mental math.

Writing in Math

7. What is the largest sum you can get when you add two 3-digit numbers? Explain.

Geometry and Measurement

MULTIPLE CHOICE

8. How many sides does the figure have?

   A. 4   **C.** 6

   B. 8   **D.** 14

9. Choose the best estimate for the length of a marker.

   A. 1 inch

   B. 2 feet

   C. 8 inches

   D. 24 inches

FREE RESPONSE

10. How long is the eraser to the nearest inch?

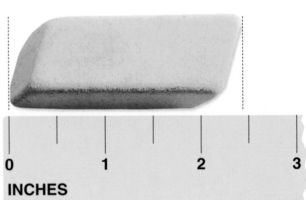

11. Draw a picture of a house using at least 3 different shapes. Name each shape you used.

Data Analysis and Probability

MULTIPLE CHOICE

Use the line plot for 12 and 13.

30-Minute Running Distance

```
              X
              X   X
              X   X
              X   X   X
      X   X   X   X       X
      X   X   X   X       X
   ←──┼───┼───┼───┼───┼──→
      1   2   3   4   5
            Miles
```

12. How many students ran 3 miles **or more** in 30 minutes?

A. 5   **B.** 8   **C.** 10   **D.** 13

13. What is the mode of the data?

A. 1   **B.** 2   **C.** 3   **D.** 5

FREE RESPONSE

Students at Summer Camp

1st Grade	🧍 🧍 🧍 🧍 🧍 🧍
2nd Grade	🧍 🧍 🧍 🧍 🧍 🧍 🧍
3rd Grade	🧍 🧍 🧍 🧍 🧍 🧍 🧍 🧍
4th Grade	🧍 🧍 🧍 🧍 🧍 🧍 🧍
5th Grade	🧍 🧍 🧍 🧍

Each 🧍 = 2 students.

14. How many more 3rd grade than 1st grade students are at camp?

15. How many students in fourth grade are at camp?

Writing in Math

16. Explain how you can use multiplication and addition to find how many 4th graders are at camp.

Algebra

MULTIPLE CHOICE

17. What two factors could you multiply to get a product of 18?

A. 2, 9   **B.** 3, 8   **C.** 2, 6   **D.** 3, 9

18. Which number makes the number sentence true?

$6 + \blacksquare < 14$

A. 7

B. 8

C. 12

D. 14

TEST TALK

Think It Through
I can **try different answer choices** to find which one is correct.

19. Solve $53 + \blacksquare = 70$.

A. 7   **B.** 17   **C.** 27   **D.** 123

FREE RESPONSE

20. Jamie's brother is 17 years old and his sister is 15 years old. The total of all three of their ages is 40. How old is Jamie?

21. Chris has 5 photos in his photo album. His photo album can hold 12 photos. How many more photos can Chris put in his album?

Writing in Math

22. Complete the table. Write the rule for the table, and explain how you found it.

In	1	2	3	4	5
Out	5	10	15		

Set 5-1 (pages 260–261)

Find the total number of counters.

There are 3 groups of 2.

Use addition to put together groups.

2 + 2 + 2 = **6**

You can also multiply.

3 × 2 = **6**

Remember that multiplication is a quick way of adding equal groups.

Copy and complete.

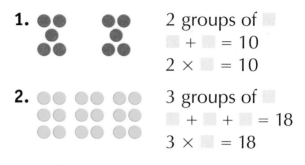

1. 2 groups of ▨

▨ + ▨ = 10

2 × ▨ = 10

2. 3 groups of ▨

▨ + ▨ + ▨ = 18

3 × ▨ = 18

Set 5-2 (pages 262–265)

Draw an array to show 2 × 3. Then write the product.

Show the objects in equal rows.

2 rows ◼◼◼ This array shows
3 in each row ◼◼◼ 2 rows of 3.

3 + 3 = **6** or 2 × 3 = **6**

3 rows ◼◼ This array shows
2 in each row ◼◼ 3 rows of 2.
◼◼

2 + 2 + 2 = **6** or 3 × 2 = **6**

Because of the Commutative Property, 2 × 3 = 3 × 2.

Remember that you can multiply in any order and get the same product.

Draw an array to show each multiplication fact. Write the product.

1. 5 × 4   **2.** 8 × 4

Write a multiplication sentence for each array.

3. ★★★★★   **4.** ●●●●
     ★★★★★   ●●●●
                          ●●●●

Set 5-3 (pages 266–267)

Write a multiplication story for 3 × 5.

Draw a picture to show the main idea.

Jessica had 3 bags of pretzels. She had 5 pretzels in each bag. How many pretzels did Jessica have in all?

Jessica had 15 pretzels.

Remember that your multiplication story should always end with a question.

Write a multiplication story for each. Use counters or draw a picture to find each product.

1. 3 × 9   **2.** 5 × 6

3. 7 × 2   **4.** 4 × 4

When you make a table to solve a problem, follow these steps.

Step 1: Set up a table with labels.

Step 2: Enter the information you know in the table.

Step 3: Look for a pattern. Continue the pattern.

Step 4: Find the answer in the table.

Remember it can help to make a table when you are looking at two or more things, or the amounts change according to a pattern.

Copy and complete the table to solve the problem. Write the answer in a complete sentence.

Emily wants to give 3 party favors to each guest at her party. If she has 5 guests, how many favors will she need?

Number of guests	1	2	3	4	5
Number of favors	3	6	9		

Set 5-5 (pages 276–279)

Find 2×9.

2×9 is the same as 2 groups of 9, or $9 + 9$.

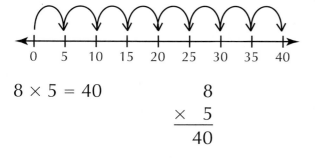

Addition sentence:
$9 + 9 = 18$

Multiplication sentence:
$2 \times 9 = 18$

Remember that you can use addition doubles and patterns to multiply by 2.

1. 2×7 **2.** 5×2

3. 3×2 **4.** 2×8

5.   6   **6.**   2
      $\times\ 2$ $\times\ 2$

Set 5-6 (pages 280–281)

Find 8×5.

You can skip count to multiply by 5.

$5 + 5 + 5 + 5 + 5 + 5 + 5 + 5 = 40$

```
 ⌢  ⌢  ⌢  ⌢  ⌢  ⌢  ⌢  ⌢
◄─┼──┼──┼──┼──┼──┼──┼──┼──►
  0  5  10 15 20 25 30 35 40
```

$8 \times 5 = 40$ 8
                      $\times\ 5$
                      ────
                        40

Remember it can be helpful to make a table and use a pattern to multiply by 5.

1. 5×9 **2.** 4×5

3. 6×5 **4.** 10×5

5.   5   **6.**   5
      $\times\ 7$ $\times\ 5$

Set 5-7 (pages 282–283)

Find 10 × 9.

Use a pattern.

Step 1: Put the number you are multiplying by 10 in the tens place.

10 × **9** = **9**

Step 2: Put a zero in the ones place.

10 × 9 = 9**0**

Remember that you can use a hundred chart to find multiples of 10.

1. 10 × 7   **2.** $5 × 10

3. 10 × 2   **4.** 10 × 8

5. 3 × $10   **6.** 10 × 10

7. 4 × 10   **8.** 10 × 6

Set 5-8 (pages 284–285)

Write and answer the hidden question or questions. Then solve the problem.

Jeff's Summer Jobs

Lawn Mowing	$9
Car Washing	$10
Dog Walking	$7

During one week, Jeff washed 6 cars and walked one dog. How much money did Jeff earn that week?

Find the hidden questions:
How much money did Jeff earn washing 6 cars?
6 × $10 = $60

How much money did Jeff earn walking one dog?
$7

Solve the problem:
How much money did Jeff earn in all?
$60 + $7

Jeff earned $67.

Remember it can help to carefully read the order in which things happen, to solve the problem.

Ticket Prizes

Whistle	5 tickets
Rubber ball	8 tickets
Pencil	6 tickets
Spider ring	2 tickets

Write and answer the hidden question or questions. Then solve the problem.

1. Bonnie wants to get 2 rubber balls and 1 pencil. How many prize tickets will she need?

2. Mark got 4 whistles and 2 rubber balls. How many prize tickets did Mark use?

3. Kerra got 5 pencils and Lucy got 10 spider rings. How many more tickets did Kerra use than Lucy?

Set 5-9 (pages 286–287)

The **Identity Property of Multiplication** says that when you multiply a number and 1, the product is that number.

$1 \times 6 = 6$

$12 \times 1 = 12$

The **Zero Property of Multiplication** says the product of 0 and any number is 0.

$0 \times 6 = 0$

Remember that you can think about an array with 1 row when you multiply by 1.

1. 7×0

2. 1×10

3. 0×9

4. 3×1

5. $\begin{array}{r} 14 \\ \times\ \ 0 \\ \hline \end{array}$

6. $\begin{array}{r} 5 \\ \times 1 \\ \hline \end{array}$

Set 5-10 (pages 288–291)

Find 9×6.

Use a pattern.

The tens digit is 1 less than the second factor.

$6 - 1 = 5 \quad 9 \times 6 = \mathbf{5}$

The digits of the product add to 9.

$5 + \mathbf{4} = 9 \quad 9 \times 6 = 54$

Remember that you can also use your fingers to find 9s facts.

1. 9×5

2. 7×9

3. 10×9

4. $\$9 \times 4$

5. $\begin{array}{r} 9 \\ \times 1 \\ \hline \end{array}$

6. $\begin{array}{r} \$8 \\ \times\ \ 9 \\ \hline \end{array}$

7. $\begin{array}{r} 9 \\ \times 9 \\ \hline \end{array}$

8. $\begin{array}{r} 3 \\ \times 9 \\ \hline \end{array}$

Set 5-11 (pages 292–293)

Find 7×5.

$7 \times 5 = 5 \times 7$

or $5 + 5 + 5 + 5 + 5 + 5 + 5 = 35$

$7 \times 5 = 35$

Remember that you can play a game to help you remember multiplication facts.

1. 2×6

2. 9×8

3. 5×1

4. 5×7

5. 9×9

6. 0×4

7. $\begin{array}{r} 10 \\ \times 10 \\ \hline \end{array}$

8. $\begin{array}{r} 4 \\ \times 9 \\ \hline \end{array}$

9. $\begin{array}{r} 8 \\ \times 2 \\ \hline \end{array}$

Set 5-1 (pages 260–261)

Copy and complete.

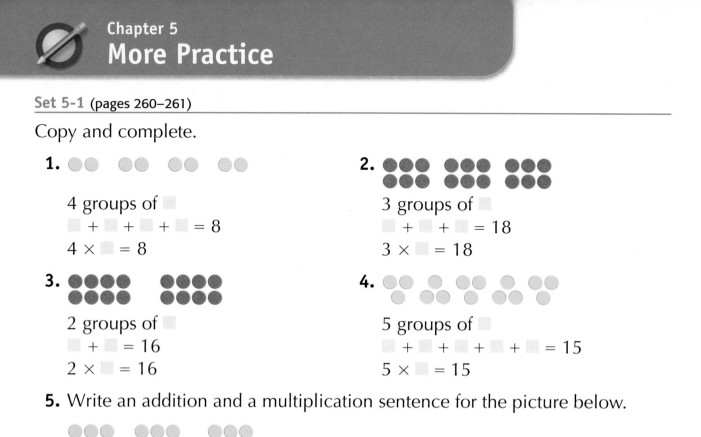

1.

4 groups of ▢
▢ + ▢ + ▢ + ▢ = 8
4 × ▢ = 8

2.

3 groups of ▢
▢ + ▢ + ▢ = 18
3 × ▢ = 18

3.

2 groups of ▢
▢ + ▢ = 16
2 × ▢ = 16

4.

5 groups of ▢
▢ + ▢ + ▢ + ▢ + ▢ = 15
5 × ▢ = 15

5. Write an addition and a multiplication sentence for the picture below.

Set 5-2 (pages 262–265)

Draw an array to show each multiplication fact. Write the product.

1. 4 × 3   **2.** 5 × 6   **3.** 1 × 7

Write a multiplication sentence for each array.

4. ⠿   **5.** ★ ★ ★   **6.** ▲▲▲▲▲▲▲▲
                          ★ ★ ★   ▲▲▲▲▲▲▲▲
                          ★ ★ ★   ▲▲▲▲▲▲▲▲
                                                ▲▲▲▲▲▲▲▲

7. Paula says 3 × 7 is the same as 7 × 3. Is she correct? Explain.

Set 5-3 (pages 266–267)

Write a multiplication story for each. Use counters or draw a picture to find each product.

1. 2 × 6   **2.** 5 × 4   **3.** 4 × 3   **4.** 3 × 9

5. Amy gave 3 stickers to each of her 4 friends. Draw a picture to show how many stickers Amy gave away.

Take It to the NET
More Practice
www.scottforesman.com

Set 5-4 (pages 270–273)

Copy and complete the table to solve the problem. Write the answer in a complete sentence.

1. Beth ran 2 laps on her first visit to the gym. She increased the number of laps she ran each visit by 2 laps. Beth is now on her 7th visit to the gym. How many laps will Beth run?

Visit	1	2	3	4			
Laps	2	4	6				

2. The symphony gives 1 adult ticket free for every 4 student tickets that are purchased for the school show. Mrs. Morton has 28 students in her class. How many adult tickets will Mrs. Morton's class receive free if every student buys a symphony ticket?

Number of adult tickets	1	2	3	4	5		
Number of student tickets	4	8	12	16			

3. Jason's mom will buy him 1 book for every 6 books he reads from the library. Jason wants to buy a book series that is made up of 5 books. How many books from the library does Jason have to read in order to get the whole book series?

Number of library books read	6	12	18		
Number of books bought	1	2			

Set 5-5 (pages 276–279)

1. 2×6

2. $\$2 \times 9$

3. 5×2

4. $\$8 \times 2$

5. 10×2

6. 2×2

7. $\begin{array}{r} 2 \\ \times \$7 \\ \hline \end{array}$

8. $\begin{array}{r} 4 \\ \times 2 \\ \hline \end{array}$

9. $\begin{array}{r} 2 \\ \times 1 \\ \hline \end{array}$

10. Find 2 times 4.

11. Find the product of 2 and 8.

12. Multiply 3 and 2.

13. Multiply 6 and 2.

14. Draw a picture to show that 2×7 is the same as 7×2.

15. On the first day of drawing class, each student is given 2 new pencils to sharpen. If there are 9 students in the class, how many pencils get sharpened?

Set 5-6 (pages 280–281)

1. 3×5 **2.** 5×8 **3.** $5 \times \$5$ **4.** 2×5 **5.** $\$6 \times 5$ **6.** 5×9

7. $\begin{array}{r} 1 \\ \times\ 5 \\ \hline \end{array}$ **8.** $\begin{array}{r} 5 \\ \times\ 4 \\ \hline \end{array}$ **9.** $\begin{array}{r} 7 \\ \times\ \$5 \\ \hline \end{array}$

10. Todd has 10 nickels in his money jar and no other coins or bills. Write a multiplication sentence that shows how much money Todd has in his money jar.

Set 5-7 (pages 282–283)

1. $\$10 \times 5$ **2.** 6×10 **3.** $9 \times \$10$ **4.** 10×4 **5.** $10 \times \$2$ **6.** 7×10

7. $\begin{array}{r} 10 \\ \times\ 3 \\ \hline \end{array}$ **8.** $\begin{array}{r} 10 \\ \times\ 2 \\ \hline \end{array}$ **9.** $\begin{array}{r} 10 \\ \times\ \$8 \\ \hline \end{array}$

10. Candace baked 5 trays of cookies with 10 cookies on each tray. She baked a sixth tray with only 4 cookies. How many cookies did Candace bake in all?

Set 5-8 (pages 284–285)

Write and answer the hidden question or questions. Then solve the problem.

For 1 and 2, use the price list.

1. Tara bought 2 T-shirts. She gave the clerk a $20 bill. How much change did she get?

T-shirt $8 Shoes $10 Jeans $20 Socks $3

2. Dave wants to buy 2 pairs of shoes and 5 pairs of socks. How much money will he need?

For 3 and 4, use the graph.

3. How many more students voted for Anne than for Charles?

4. How many students voted for class president?

Votes for Class President

Ben	✓✓✓✓✓
Melissa	✓✓✓
Anne	✓✓✓✓✓✓✓
Charles	✓✓✓

Each ✓ = 5 votes.

Take It to the NET
More Practice
www.scottforesman.com

Set 5-9 (pages 286–287)

1. $0 \times \$6$ **2.** 4×1 **3.** 0×8 **4.** 1×9 **5.** 10×0 **6.** 1×7

7. $\begin{array}{r} 5 \\ \times 1 \\ \hline \end{array}$ **8.** $\begin{array}{r} 3 \\ \times 0 \\ \hline \end{array}$ **9.** $\begin{array}{r} 1 \\ \times \$2 \\ \hline \end{array}$ **10.** $\begin{array}{r} 1 \\ \times 1 \\ \hline \end{array}$ **11.** $\begin{array}{r} 0 \\ \times 0 \\ \hline \end{array}$ **12.** $\begin{array}{r} 12 \\ \times 0 \\ \hline \end{array}$

Copy and complete. Write <, >, or = for each ●.

13. 5×0 ● 1×5 **14.** 0×8 ● 79×0 **15.** 24×0 ● 4×1

16. Explain how you can find the missing number in ■ $\times 6 = 0$.

Set 5-10 (pages 288–291)

1. 9×1 **2.** 3×9 **3.** 9×7 **4.** 5×9 **5.** 4×9 **6.** 9×2

7. $\begin{array}{r} 6 \\ \times \$9 \\ \hline \end{array}$ **8.** $\begin{array}{r} 9 \\ \times 8 \\ \hline \end{array}$ **9.** $\begin{array}{r} 10 \\ \times 9 \\ \hline \end{array}$ **10.** $\begin{array}{r} 9 \\ \times 9 \\ \hline \end{array}$ **11.** $\begin{array}{r} 0 \\ \times 9 \\ \hline \end{array}$ **12.** $\begin{array}{r} 7 \\ \times 9 \\ \hline \end{array}$

13. Find 9 times 9.   **14.** Find the product of 2 and 9.

15. Multiply 6 and 9.   **16.** Multiply 9 and 4.

17. Jeremy drinks 9 glasses of water each day. How many glasses of water does Jeremy drink in a week?

Set 5-11 (pages 292–293)

1. 3×2 **2.** 5×7 **3.** 9×3 **4.** 6×1 **5.** 0×5 **6.** 3×5

7. $\begin{array}{r} 9 \\ \times 0 \\ \hline \end{array}$ **8.** $\begin{array}{r} 4 \\ \times 5 \\ \hline \end{array}$ **9.** $\begin{array}{r} 10 \\ \times 6 \\ \hline \end{array}$ **10.** $\begin{array}{r} 4 \\ \times 5 \\ \hline \end{array}$ **11.** $\begin{array}{r} 2 \\ \times 9 \\ \hline \end{array}$ **12.** $\begin{array}{r} 5 \\ \times 5 \\ \hline \end{array}$

13. $\begin{array}{r} 8 \\ \times 1 \\ \hline \end{array}$ **14.** $\begin{array}{r} 3 \\ \times 10 \\ \hline \end{array}$ **15.** $\begin{array}{r} 2 \\ \times 7 \\ \hline \end{array}$ **16.** $\begin{array}{r} 9 \\ \times 8 \\ \hline \end{array}$ **17.** $\begin{array}{r} 6 \\ \times 5 \\ \hline \end{array}$ **18.** $\begin{array}{r} 9 \\ \times 4 \\ \hline \end{array}$

Write the missing number.

19. ■ $\times 4 = 40$ **20.** ■ $\times 9 = 54$ **21.** $2 \times$ ■ $= 14$

22. Valerie says that $8 \times 2 = 12$. How could you show her that her answer is not correct?

DIAGNOSING READINESS

A Vocabulary
(pages 66, 260)

Choose the best term from the box.

1. In the number sentence
$2 \times 7 = 14$, the number
2 is a __?__.

2. In the number sentence
$2 \times 7 = 14$, the number
14 is the __?__.

Vocabulary

- **product** *(p. 260)*
- **addend** *(p. 66)*
- **factor** *(p. 260)*

B Arrays
(pages 262–265)

Draw an array to find each
multiplication fact. Write the product.

3. 5×3 **4.** 1×4

5. 2×4 **6.** 6×2

7. Draw two arrays to show that
3×2 has the same product as
2×3.

8. How many counters are in an
array that has 5 rows with 2 in
each row?

Do You Know...

How long can an earthworm grow to be?

You will find out in Lesson 6-12.

SHORELINE
See the natural world of a shoreline as never before!

C Multiplication Facts
(pages 276–283, 286–291)

9. 7×2 **10.** 5×2 **11.** 3×9

12. 4×2 **13.** 3×5 **14.** 6×0

15. 3×10 **16.** 6×2 **17.** 4×9

18. Aaron has 3 apples. He cuts each into 2 pieces. How many apple pieces does he have?

19. Each package of juice has 5 cans. How many cans of juice are in 6 packages?

D Using a Table
(pages 270–273)

Use the table to solve.

Packages	1	2	3	4
Bagels	9	18	27	

20. How many bagels are in each package?

21. How many bagels are in 4 packages?

22. What pattern do you see in the table?

3 as a Factor

LEARN

Buttons are often used as decorations. The star-shaped buttons shown here are arranged in an array.

Activity

How can you break apart arrays to multiply with 3?

Use **1**s facts and **2**s facts to help multiply with **3**.

Find 3×6.

What You **Show**	What You **Think**
●●●●●● ●●●●●● } $2 \times 6 = 12$ ●●●●●● $1 \times 6 = 6$ $12 + 6 = 18$	$3 \times 6 = 3$ groups of 6. That's 2 sixes plus 1 more six. So, $3 \times 6 = 18$.

a. Use counters. Make an array for each multiplication sentence. Copy and complete each sentence.

$2 \times 4 = $ ▯

$1 \times 4 = $ ▯

b. How can you use your arrays to find 3×4?

c. Draw an array or use counters to show 2×8 and 1×8. Label each array. What 3s fact is shown by these arrays together?

d. Copy and complete each multiplication sentence. You may use counters or draw a picture to help.

$3 \times 3 = $ ▯ $3 \times 7 = $ ▯ $3 \times 9 = $ ▯ $3 \times 5 = $ ▯

CHECK ✓

For another example, see Set 6-1 on p. 360.

1. 3×8 **2.** 3×4 **3.** 3×1 **4.** $\begin{array}{r} 3 \\ \times 9 \\ \hline \end{array}$ **5.** $\begin{array}{r} 6 \\ \times 3 \\ \hline \end{array}$

6. Number Sense How can you use $2 \times 9 = 18$ to find 3×9?

A Skills and Understanding

7. 3×3 **8.** 5×9 **9.** 3×10 **10.** 4×2 **11.** 7×3

12. 3×2 **13.** 0×3 **14.** 5×2 **15.** 3×8 **16.** 4×9

17. 0×5 **18.** 9×3 **19.** 2×7 **20.** 5×3 **21.** 10×2

22. $\begin{array}{r} 3 \\ \times 2 \\ \hline \end{array}$ **23.** $\begin{array}{r} 3 \\ \times 0 \\ \hline \end{array}$ **24.** $\begin{array}{r} 5 \\ \times 3 \\ \hline \end{array}$ **25.** $\begin{array}{r} 3 \\ \times 6 \\ \hline \end{array}$ **26.** $\begin{array}{r} 8 \\ \times 3 \\ \hline \end{array}$

27. Number Sense Which multiplication fact is the same as 2×8 plus 1×8?

B Reasoning and Problem Solving

28. Copy and complete the table. Write a pattern you see.

Stools	0	1	2	3	4	5	6	7	8	9
Legs	0	3			12				24	

29. A musical group with 3 people is called a trio. How many people are in 4 trios?

30. One card of buttons has 6 rows with 3 buttons in each row. Another card has 5 rows with 4 buttons in each row. How many buttons are on these two cards all together?

31. <u>Writing in Math</u> Cooper drew these arrays to show 3×5. Explain what he did wrong. Draw the correct arrays and label them.

```
x x x x x          2 x 5 = 10
x x x x x

x x x               1 x 3 = 3

10 + 3 = 13, so 3 x 5 = 13.
```

Mixed Review and Test Prep

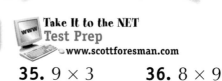

Take It to the NET
Test Prep
www.scottforesman.com

32. 2×10 **33.** 5×5 **34.** 6×2 **35.** 9×3 **36.** 8×9

37. Kendra had $0.58 in her pocket and $1.22 in her bank. How much money did she have?

     A. $0.64   **B.** $0.88   **C.** $1.80   **D.** $18

Materials
• counters
  or  tools

TEST TALK

Think It Through
• I can break
  4 × ■ into a
  double double :
  2 × ■ and 2 × ■.

• I can **use objects**
  to show why this
  works.

4 as a Factor

LEARN

WARM UP
1. 2 × 5   2. 2 × 3
3. 2 × 4   4. 2 × 7
5. 2 × 8   6. 2 × 9

Activity

How can you use doubles to multiply with 4?

To multiply by 4, you can think of a **2s** fact, then **double it.**

Find 4×6.

What You **Show**	What You **Think**
⚪⚪⚪⚪⚪⚪ ⚪⚪⚪⚪⚪⚪ } $2 \times 6 = 12$ ⚪⚪⚪⚪⚪⚪ ⚪⚪⚪⚪⚪⚪ } $2 \times 6 = 12$ $12 + 12 = 24$	4×6 is the same as 2 sixes plus 2 sixes. First, find $2 \times 6 = 12$. Then, double the product. So, $4 \times 6 = 24$.

a. Use counters to make an array for 2×7.

b. How can you use your array to find 4×7?

c. Use counters to make an array for each 2s fact. Then
double the 2s fact to find each 4s fact.

$2 \times 8 = ▇$ $2 \times 4 = ▇$ $2 \times 9 = ▇$

$4 \times 8 = ▇$ $4 \times 4 = ▇$ $4 \times 9 = ▇$

d. Copy and complete each multiplication sentence. You
may use counters or draw a picture to help.

$4 \times 3 = ▇$ $4 \times 7 = ▇$ $4 \times 4 = ▇$

$4 \times 2 = ▇$ $4 \times 8 = ▇$ $4 \times 6 = ▇$

CHECK ✓

For another example, see Set 6-2 on p. 360.

1. 4×2 **2.** 5×4 **3.** 4×8

4.   2   **5.**   1
       × 2   × 4

6. Number Sense If you know $2 \times 5 = 10$, how can you
find 4×5?

A Skills and Understanding

7. 4×6 **8.** 9×8 **9.** 4×7 **10.** 10×4 **11.** 3×6

12. 4×5 **13.** 0×5 **14.** 9×4 **15.** 3×8 **16.** 8×4

17. 0×4 **18.** 7×4 **19.** 6×3 **20.** 1×4 **21.** 2×8

22. $\begin{array}{r} 4 \\ \times 4 \\ \hline \end{array}$ **23.** $\begin{array}{r} 4 \\ \times 0 \\ \hline \end{array}$ **24.** $\begin{array}{r} 2 \\ \times 4 \\ \hline \end{array}$ **25.** $\begin{array}{r} 3 \\ \times 4 \\ \hline \end{array}$ **26.** $\begin{array}{r} 4 \\ \times 9 \\ \hline \end{array}$

27. Number Sense Terrence said, "I can find 4×7 by finding 3×7 and doubling it." Do you agree? Explain.

B Reasoning and Problem Solving

28. Continue each pattern.

   a. 12, 16, 20, ▨, ▨, ▨   **b.** 0, 4, 8, ▨, ▨, ▨   **c.** 40, 36, 32, ▨, ▨, ▨

29. In the book *Grandfather's Journey*, the writer's grandfather crossed the Pacific on a great ship. He did not see land for 3 weeks. For how many days did he not see land?

30. Alex has 4 bags with 8 cookies in each. How many cookies does he have in all?

31. James had 2 dozen eggs. He made four 3-egg omelets for his family. How many eggs did he have left? Remember, 1 dozen = 12.

32. **Writing in Math** Write a multiplication story about the oranges inside the crate at the right. Make sure you end your story with a question.

Mixed Review and Test Prep

Take It to the NET
Test Prep
www.scottforesman.com

33. 3×7 **34.** 8×3 **35.** 3×3 **36.** 3×6 **37.** 2×5

38. Which shows the Zero Property of Multiplication?

   A. $3 \times 1 = 3$ **B.** $0 + 3 = 3$ **C.** $3 \times 0 = 0$ **D.** $3 - 0 = 3$

Key Idea
You can use a 5s fact to multiply with 6 or 7.

Think It Through
I can **use facts I already know** to multiply with 6.

6 and 7 as Factors

LEARN

When can you multiply?

Tasha wants to make 6 muffins. Each muffin needs 8 raisins on top. How many raisins does she need?

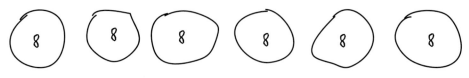

Since I'm putting together equal groups, I can multiply.

To find the total of 6 groups of 8, find 6 × 8.

How can you break apart arrays to multiply with 6?

Example A

Find 6 × 8.

Use **5**s facts and **1**s facts to help multiply with **6**.

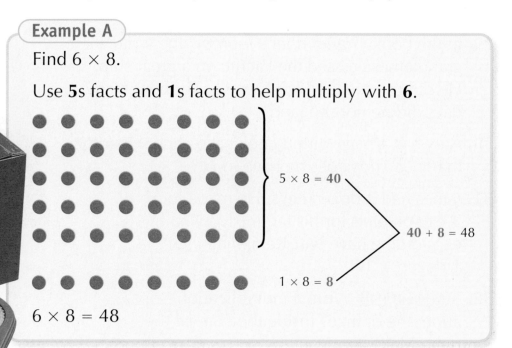

$5 \times 8 = 40$

$1 \times 8 = 8$

$40 + 8 = 48$

$6 \times 8 = 48$

Tasha needs 48 raisins.

✓ Talk About It

1. Can you think of another way to find 6 × 8?

2. How could you use 5 × 6 = 30 to find 6 × 6?

3. Joseph says, "I can find 6 × 7 by adding 5 × 6 and 1 × 6." Do you agree? Explain.

How can you break apart arrays to multiply with 7?

Example B

Ethan is selling granola bars for his scout troop. There are 6 granola bars in each box. If he sold 7 boxes, how many granola bars did Ethan sell?

Find 7×6.

Use **5**s facts and **2**s facts to help multiply with **7**.

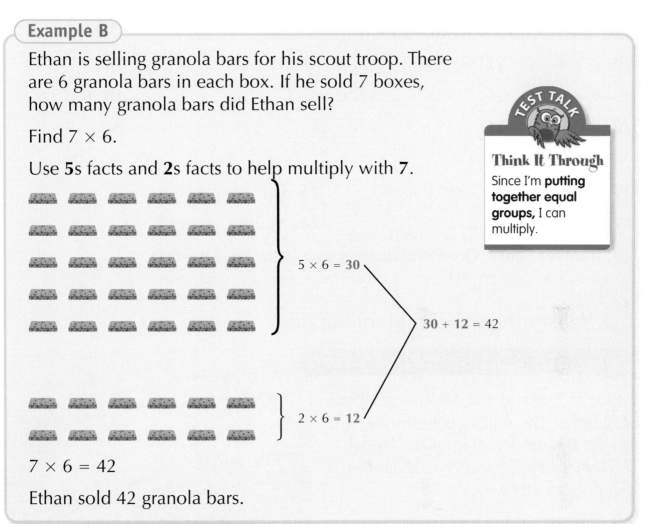

Think It Through
Since I'm **putting together equal groups**, I can multiply.

$5 \times 6 = 30$

$30 + 12 = 42$

$2 \times 6 = 12$

$7 \times 6 = 42$

Ethan sold 42 granola bars.

✔ Talk About It

4. Can you think of another way to find 7×6?

5. How could you use $5 \times 8 = 40$ to find 7×8?

6. How could you use 5×5 and 2×5 to find 7×5?

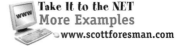
Take It to the NET
More Examples
www.scottforesman.com

For another example, see Set 6-3 on p. 360.

CHECK ✓

1. 7×5 **2.** 7×7 **3.** $4 \times \$6$ **4.** $\begin{array}{r} 6 \\ \times\,7 \\ \hline \end{array}$ **5.** $\begin{array}{r} 9 \\ \times\,6 \\ \hline \end{array}$

6. Find the product of 6 and 8.

7. Find 4 times 7.

8. Multiply 6 and 5.

9. Number Sense How can you use the Commutative Property to find 7×5?

A Skills and Understanding

10. 7×4 **11.** $6 \times \$6$ **12.** 4×3 **13.** 10×7 **14.** 2×6

15. 9×5 **16.** 7×9 **17.** 6×5 **18.** 7×8 **19.** 6×1

20. $\begin{array}{r} \$6 \\ \times\ 8 \\ \hline \end{array}$ **21.** $\begin{array}{r} 3 \\ \times 3 \\ \hline \end{array}$ **22.** $\begin{array}{r} 2 \\ \times 7 \\ \hline \end{array}$ **23.** $\begin{array}{r} 5 \\ \times 5 \\ \hline \end{array}$ **24.** $\begin{array}{r} 7 \\ \times 3 \\ \hline \end{array}$

25. Find the product of 10 and 6.   **26.** Find 1 times 7.

27. Multiply 3 and 6.   **28.** Multiply 5 and 3.

29. Number Sense Draw a picture of two arrays to show that 6×3 is the same as 5×3 plus 1×3. Explain your drawing.

B Reasoning and Problem Solving

Math and Social Studies

Made in England, the *Mallard* reached a speed of 126 miles per hour in 1938. The fastest modern train is the French *TGV.* It reached a speed of 320 miles per hour in 1990.

30. If there were 6 rows with 4 passengers in each row in a car of the *Mallard,* how many passengers were in the car?

31. Three families with 4 people each bought tickets on the *TGV.* How many tickets did they buy in all?

The Mallard is the fastest steam train ever built.

32. How much faster in miles per hour is the *TGV* than the *Mallard*?

33. **Writing in Math** Charlie made the two arrays at the right to find 6×3. Explain how you could change his drawing to find 7×3. Draw a picture to help.

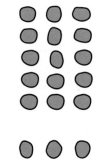

C Extensions

34. Todd says he can double 3×5 to find 6×5. Do you agree? Explain.

35. How could you skip count to find 3×7?

 **Mixed Review and Test Prep**

Take It to the NET
Test Prep
www.scottforesman.com

36. 2×4 **37.** 4×8 **38.** 7×4 **39.** 6×4 **40.** 4×10

41. $\begin{array}{r} \$3 \\ \times\ 3 \\ \hline \end{array}$ **42.** $\begin{array}{r} 3 \\ \times\ 8 \\ \hline \end{array}$ **43.** $\begin{array}{r} 7 \\ \times\ 3 \\ \hline \end{array}$ **44.** $\begin{array}{r} 3 \\ \times\ 9 \\ \hline \end{array}$ **45.** $\begin{array}{r} 4 \\ \times\ 4 \\ \hline \end{array}$

46. Which is the missing number?
$12 + n = 20$

A. 32   **C.** 10

B. 22   **D.** 8

47. How many days are in 5 weeks?

A. 5 days   **C.** 28 days

B. 7 days   **D.** 35 days

Discovery CHANNEL SCHOOL

Discover Math in Your World

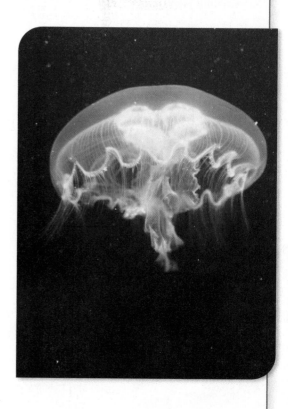

No Bones About It

Jellyfish can be tiny or huge, but no jellyfish has a skeleton. They also have no brain, heart, eyes, or ears! Jellyfish have tentacles that sting their prey. They also have feeding arms. Scientists estimate there may be 2,000 kinds of jellyfish.

1. Most jellyfish have between 4 and 8 feeding arms. If 5 jellyfish each have 8 feeding arms, how many feeding arms are there in all?

2. Only about 70 of the 2,000 kinds of jellyfish can seriously harm people who are stung by them. How many kinds can not seriously harm people?

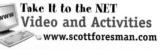 Take It to the NET
Video and Activities
www.scottforesman.com

All text pages available online and on CD-ROM.

Vocabulary
- Commutative Property of Multiplication (p. 262)
- square number

Think It Through
To find $8 \times$ ▪, I can find $4 \times$ ▪ and **use doubles.**

8 as a Factor

LEARN

Is there extra information?

Danielle went to soccer camp for 5 days. She bought 8 key chains for her friends. How much did the key chains cost in all?

The price list shows that each key chain costs $3. I do not need to know how many days Danielle went to camp.

To find 8 groups of $3, find $8 \times \$3$.

⚽ **Camp Store** ⚽
— Price List —

Key chain	$3
Bracelet	$5
T-Shirt	$8
Shoelaces	$4

How can you multiply with 8?

Example

Find 8×3.

One Way

You can double a 4s fact to multiply with 8.

First, find $4 \times 3 = 12$. Then, double the product.

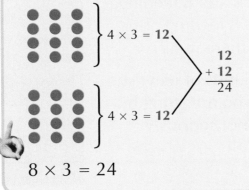

$4 \times 3 = 12$

$\begin{array}{r} 12 \\ + 12 \\ \hline 24 \end{array}$

$4 \times 3 = 12$

$8 \times 3 = 24$

Another Way

Use the **Commutative Property of Multiplication** to change the order.

$8 \times 3 = 3 \times 8$

I know $3 \times 8 = 24$, so $8 \times 3 = 24$.

The eight key chains cost $24.

1. How could you use 5 × 8 to help you find 8 × 5?

2. How can you use 4 × 7 to find 8 × 7?

What is a square number?

The product of a number multiplied by itself is called a **square number** because the array forms a square.

The product of 8 × 8 is a square number. You can double a 4s fact to find 8 × 8.

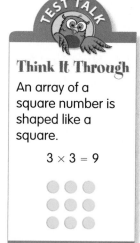

TEST TALK

Think It Through
An array of a square number is shaped like a square.

3 × 3 = 9

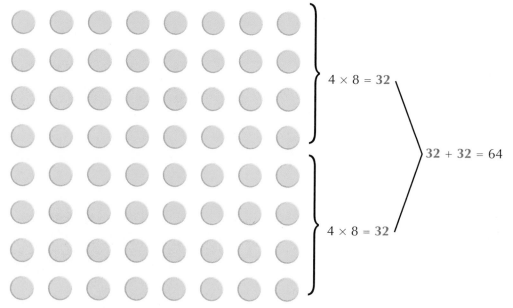

4 × 8 = 32

32 + 32 = 64

4 × 8 = 32

8 × 8 = 64

✔ **Talk About It**

3. What are two other multiplication sentences that have a square number as a product?

4. How could you use 8 × 8 = 64 to find 9 × 8?

CHECK ✔

For another example, see Set 6-4 on p. 361.

1. 8 × 6   **2.** 8 × 2   **3.** 7 × 8   **4.** 8 × 9   **5.** $5 × 8

6. $1   **7.**   8   **8.**   4   **9.**   8   **10.**   0
     × 8   × 3   × 8   × 8   × 8

11. Number Sense Jackie says, "To find 8 × 8, I can find 2 × 8 and double it." Do you agree? Explain.

A Skills and Understanding

12. 1×8 **13.** $8 \times \$8$ **14.** 7×6 **15.** 8×10 **16.** 5×5

17. 8×3 **18.** 7×7 **19.** 4×8 **20.** 6×4 **21.** 8×0

22. $\begin{array}{r} \$9 \\ \times\ 8 \\ \hline \end{array}$ **23.** $\begin{array}{r} 4 \\ \times 7 \\ \hline \end{array}$ **24.** $\begin{array}{r} 8 \\ \times 7 \\ \hline \end{array}$ **25.** $\begin{array}{r} 3 \\ \times 2 \\ \hline \end{array}$ **26.** $\begin{array}{r} 9 \\ \times 6 \\ \hline \end{array}$

27. Number Sense How can knowing $4 \times 9 = 36$ help you find 8×9?

B Reasoning and Problem Solving

Math and Art

The Castle del Monte is known for its unusual architecture. It has 8 towers and 8 sides. Inside, there are 8 rooms of the same size, and an inner courtyard.

28. Each side of the castle has 2 windows. Write a multiplication sentence to show how many windows are in the castle. Then solve.

29. The outside walls of the Castle del Monte are about 100 inches thick. The inside walls are about 94 inches thick. How much thicker are the outside walls than the inside walls?

30. **Writing in Math** Brendan's work is shown at the right. Is it correct? If not, find his mistake and write a correct answer. If his work is correct, draw the arrays that show how he used doubling.

The Castle del Monte is located in Apulia, Italy.

To find 8×7, I can first find:
$4 \times 7 = 24$
Then double it:
$24 + 24 = 48$.
So, $8 \times 7 = 48$.

C Extensions

31. Algebra Is 49 a square number? Explain how you know.

32. Draw an array to show any square number you choose. Label the array with the multiplication sentence it shows.

Mixed Review and Test Prep

Take It to the NET
Test Prep
www.scottforesman.com

Find each product.

33. 2×7 **34.** 7×8 **35.** 3×7 **36.** 7×9 **37.** 7×7

38. 3×3 **39.** 2×2 **40.** 4×4 **41.** 9×9 **42.** 5×5

43. Round 1,254 to the nearest hundred.

    A. 1,000   **B.** 1,200   **C.** 1,300   **D.** 2,000

Learning with Technology

Counters eTool—Array Workspace

You can use the Counters eTool to find factors of a number.

To find all the factors of 12, stretch the array until it can hold 12 counters. Find all the ways you can hold 12 counters in an array.

1. How many factors does 12 have?

A number that has only 2 factors is called a **prime** number. A number with more than 2 factors is called a **composite** number.

5 is a prime number because it has only 2 factors, 1 and 5. There are only 2 ways you can show 5 counters in an array.

• • • • • 1×5

5×1

2. Stretch the array to find factors for 11, 6, 13, 4, 16, and 23. Write *prime* or *composite* for each number.

This is one way to make an array with 12 counters. The array shows that 3 and 4 are factors of 12.

Vocabulary
• Commutative Property of Multiplication (p. 262)

Think It Through
If one strategy is too difficult, I can **choose a different strategy.**

Practicing Multiplication Facts

LEARN

What strategies do you know?

Students in Ms. Ramsey's class each think of a different way to find 8×7.

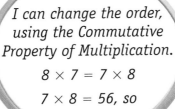

I can change the order, using the Commutative Property of Multiplication.

$8 \times 7 = 7 \times 8$

$7 \times 8 = 56$, so
$8 \times 7 = 56$.

I can use doubling to multiply by 8.

$4 \times 7 = 28$
$28 + 28 = 56$
So, $8 \times 7 = 56$.

*I can use **5s** facts and **3s** facts to multiply with 8.*

$5 \times 7 = 35$
$3 \times 7 = 21$
$35 + 21 = 56$
So, $8 \times 7 = 56$.

✔ **Talk About It**

1. Think of a fact that is hard for you to remember. What strategy can you use to help remember this fact?

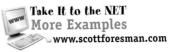

Take It to the NET
More Examples
www.scottforesman.com

1. 6×7 **2.** 8×9 **3.** 3×8 **4.** $\begin{array}{r} 5 \\ \times\ 3 \\ \hline \end{array}$ **5.** $\begin{array}{r} 7 \\ \times\ 4 \\ \hline \end{array}$

6. Number Sense Jane knows that $3 \times 7 = 21$. How can she use that fact to find 4×7?

PRACTICE
For more practice, see Set 6-5 on p. 365.

A Skills and Understanding

7. 8×8 **8.** 2×9 **9.** 5×5 **10.** 6×4 **11.** 8×7

12. 7×9 **13.** 4×8 **14.** 5×7 **15.** 8×6 **16.** 0×9

17. 6×9 **18.** 7×3 **19.** 7×7 **20.** 8×2 **21.** 9×3

22. 6×2 **23.** 8×5 **24.** 6×5 **25.** 7×0 **26.** 4×4

27. $\begin{array}{r} 9 \\ \times\ 9 \\ \hline \end{array}$ **28.** $\begin{array}{r} 6 \\ \times\ 6 \\ \hline \end{array}$ **29.** $\begin{array}{r} 9 \\ \times\ 5 \\ \hline \end{array}$ **30.** $\begin{array}{r} 7 \\ \times\ 2 \\ \hline \end{array}$ **31.** $\begin{array}{r} 3 \\ \times\ 6 \\ \hline \end{array}$

32. Number Sense Could you multiply a number by 2 and get a product of 29? Explain.

B Reasoning and Problem Solving

For 33–35, use the price list at the right.

33. How many erasers are in 4 packs?

34. How many pencils are in 3 packs?

35. Reasoning How many crayons could you get for 50 cents?

36. <u>Writing in Math</u> Draw an array to show a multiplication sentence. Explain how the array shows the multiplication sentence.

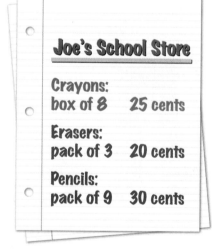

Joe's School Store

Crayons:
box of 8   25 cents

Erasers:
pack of 3   20 cents

Pencils:
pack of 9   30 cents

Mixed Review and Test Prep

Take It to the NET
Test Prep
www.scottforesman.com

37. 8×8 **38.** 8×6 **39.** 8×7 **40.** 3×8 **41.** 9×8

42. Find $450 - 74$.

A. 524 **B.** 376 **C.** 324 **D.** 154

Predict and Generalize

Predicting and generalizing when you read in math can help you use the **problem-solving strategy, *Look for a Pattern,*** in the next lesson.

In reading, predicting and generalizing can help you figure out what comes next in a story. In math, predicting and generalizing can help you figure out what comes next in a pattern.

First figure out how to get the second picture from the first picture.

How many circles will be in the 4th picture?

Next figure out how to get the third picture from the second picture.

1st   2nd   3rd

Add 2 circles to the first to get the second.

Add 2 circles to the second to get the third.

***Generalize* to describe the pattern:** *The number of circles increases by 2 each time.* Then **predict.** *The fourth picture will have 8 circles.*

1. Predict the number of circles in the fifth picture.

2. If the pattern were the same but the first picture had 12 circles, how many circles would be in the second picture?

For 3–6, use the picture at the right.

3. How can you get the second row from the first row?

★ ★ ★   1st row

★ ★ ★ ★ ★ ★   2nd row

★ ★ ★ ★ ★ ★ ★ ★ ★   3rd row

4. How can you get the third row from the second row?

5. **Writing in Math** Generalize by describing the pattern.

6. Predict the number of stars that will be in the fourth row.

For 7–10, use the picture below.

7. Starting at the left, how you can get the number of the second car from the number of the first car?

8. How can you get the number of the third car from the number of the second car?

9. **Writing in Math** Generalize by describing the pattern.

10. Predict what number will be on the next car.

For 11–14, use the picture below.

11. How can you get the second jar from the first jar?

12. How can you get the third jar from the second jar?

13. **Writing in Math** Generalize by describing the pattern.

14. Predict the marbles that will be in the fourth and fifth jars.

Problem-Solving Strategy

Key Idea
Learning how and when to look for a pattern can help you solve problems.

Look for a Pattern

LEARN

How can you find a pattern?

Towers Stacey built a pattern with blocks. How many blocks will be in the fourth and fifth towers?

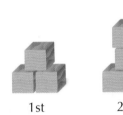 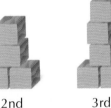

1st   2nd   3rd   4th   5th

Read and Understand

What do you know?   The number of blocks in the 1st, 2nd, and 3rd towers.

What are you trying to find?   The number of blocks for the 4th and 5th towers.

Plan and Solve

What strategy will you use?   **Strategy: Look for a Pattern**

How to Look for a Pattern

Step 1 Show what you know.

Step 2 Look for what repeats or changes.

Step 3 Check that what repeats or changes works for all cases.

Step 4 Describe the pattern or patterns.

1st: 3 blocks **2nd:** 4 blocks **3rd:** 5 blocks

There is 1 more block in the 2nd tower than in the 1st tower.

There is 1 more block in the 3rd tower than in the 2nd tower.

The 1st tower has 3 blocks. Then, the number of blocks increases by 1 each time.

Answer: There are 6 blocks in the 4th tower and 7 in the 5th tower.

Look Back and Check

Is your work correct?   Yes. The "increases by 1" pattern works for all the towers shown.

✔ Talk About It

1. How does the picture help you find a pattern in the towers?

2. Do you see any other patterns in the Towers problem? Explain.

When might you look for a pattern?

House Numbers The house numbers on Forest Street change in a planned way. Describe the pattern. Tell what the next two house numbers should be.

> **When to Look for a Pattern**
>
> Think about looking for a pattern when something repeats or changes in a predictable way.
>
> • Number of blocks increases by one in each tower.
>
> • Numbers on the houses are multiples of 3.

✔ Talk About It

3. Callie says that each house number increases by 3. Do you agree? Explain.

4. Jon says the house numbers are multiples of 3. Do you agree? Explain.

5. What are the next two house numbers?

CHECK ✔

For another example, see Set 6-6 on p. 361.

Describe patterns you see. Write the answer in a complete sentence. Use the picture of corn plants for 1 and 2.

1. Jane planted corn in these rows. How many corn plants will be in the 4th and 5th rows?

2. How many corn plants would be in the 8th row?

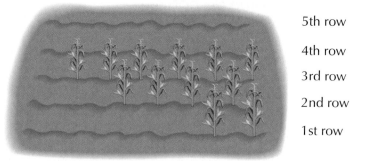

5th row

4th row

3rd row

2nd row

1st row

3. What are the next two numbers in the pattern below?

35, 30, 25, 20, ▒, ▒

4. List the even numbers from zero through 10. Write a pattern you see.

Ⓐ Using the Strategy

Describe patterns you see. Write the answer in a complete sentence.

5. Michele made a pyramid with blocks. How many blocks will be in the 4th row?

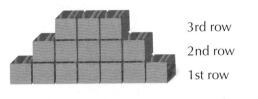

3rd row
2nd row
1st row

6. Tod arranged his pennies in these stacks. How many pennies will be in the next stack?

7. What are the missing numbers in the pattern below?

24, 31, ▢, 45, 52, ▢, ▢

4   8   12   16

8. Sam's soccer team took numbers that follow a pattern. What are the numbers on the muddy jerseys?

Math and Science

Don't touch this plant! Poison ivy has an oil on its leaves that can cause a very itchy rash. This is a picture of poison ivy in the summertime. Notice some of its natural patterns. Each cluster has 3 leaves. New leaves are shiny. Older leaves are duller. Some leaves have notches. Some do not.

9. How would you count by 3s to find the number of leaves on a plant with 9 clusters?

10. If a poison ivy plant has 7 clusters, how many leaves does it have?

11. Algebra Megan found a poison ivy plant with 12 leaves. How many clusters did it have? You may draw a picture to help.

B Mixed Strategy Practice

Solve each problem. Write the answer in a complete sentence.

12. Ralph made a bracelet with beads that spelled his name. He made the bracelet using the pattern shown. If he used 6 purple beads, how many red beads did he use?

13. Domingo spent $1.25 on lemonade mix. He sold 7 cups of lemonade for a quarter each. How much more money did Domingo make than he spent?

14. __Writing in Math__ Greg had 40 tiles when he started making this pattern. He wants to continue the pattern until all the tiles are gone. How many rows will there be in all? Explain. You may draw a picture to help.

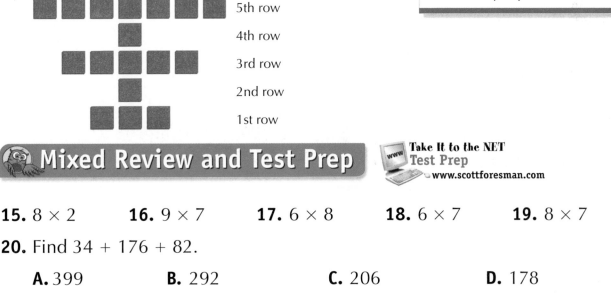

6th row
5th row
4th row
3rd row
2nd row
1st row

STRATEGIES

- **Show What You Know**
  Draw a Picture
  Make an Organized List
  Make a Table
  Make a Graph
  Act It Out or Use Objects
- **Look for a Pattern**
- **Try, Check, and Revise**
- **Write a Number Sentence**
- **Use Logical Reasoning**
- **Solve a Simpler Problem**
- **Work Backward**

Think It Through

Stuck? I won't give up. I can:
- Reread the problem.
- Tell what I know.
- Identify key facts and details.
- Tell the problem in my own words.
- Show the main idea.
- Try a different strategy.
- Retrace my steps.

Mixed Review and Test Prep

Take It to the NET
Test Prep
www.scottforesman.com

15. 8×2 **16.** 9×7 **17.** 6×8 **18.** 6×7 **19.** 8×7

20. Find $34 + 176 + 82$.

A. 399   **B.** 292   **C.** 206   **D.** 178

21. __Writing in Math__ How can you tell without subtracting that $411 - 187$ is greater than 211?

Do You Know How?

Do You Understand?

3 as a Factor (6-1)
4 as a Factor (6-2)

1. 3×9 **2.** 3×5 **3.** 7×3

4. 4×7 **5.** 6×4 **6.** 8×4

7. 4×3 **8.** 4×9 **9.** 3×8

Ⓐ How can you use 2×7 to find 3×7?

Ⓑ Draw an array to show 4×6. Write the product.

6 and 7 as Factors (6-3)
8 as a Factor (6-4)

10. 6×9 **11.** 7×5 **12.** 7×7

13. 6×8 **14.** 3×7 **15.** 3×6

16. 7×9 **17.** 6×5 **18.** 7×8

19. 8×8 **20.** 8×9 **21.** 4×8

Ⓒ How can you use a 5s fact and a 2s fact to find 7×4?

Ⓓ If you know $5 \times 3 = 15$, how can you find 6×3?

Ⓔ How can use $4 \times 3 = 12$ to find 8×3?

Practicing Multiplication Facts (6-5)

22. 7×4 **23.** 8×6 **24.** 6×6

25. 9×8 **26.** 9×9 **27.** 6×7

28. 9×3 **29.** 3×9 **30.** 5×8

Ⓕ Explain a strategy you could use to find 7×5.

Ⓖ Could you double a 2s fact to find 3×5? Explain.

Problem-Solving Strategy: Look for a Pattern (6-6)

Describe a pattern you see. Write the answer in a complete sentence.

31. What are the missing numbers in the pattern below?

36, 30, 24, ▪, ▪, ▪

Ⓗ How can you use subtraction to find a pattern in the numbers in Exercise 31?

Ⓘ Jordan says the numbers in Exercise 31 are multiples of 5. Do you agree? Explain.

Think It Through

For multiple-choice items, I should first **eliminate wrong answers.**

MULTIPLE CHOICE

1. Find the product of 4 and 7. (6-2)

A. 14   **B.** 21   **C.** 28   **D.** 36

2. Jackie has 3 baskets of muffins. Each basket contains 4 muffins. How many muffins are there? (6-1)

A. 7   **B.** 10   **C.** 12   **D.** 24

FREE RESPONSE

Find each product. (6-1, 6-2, 6-3, 6-4, 6-5)

3. 3×7 **4.** 8×7 **5.** 9×6 **6.** 6×6 **7.** 4×8

8. 6×3 **9.** 8×5 **10.** 7×4 **11.** 9×4 **12.** 6×7

13. 8×9 **14.** 7×5 **15.** 3×9 **16.** 4×6 **17.** 3×8

18. $\begin{array}{r} 4 \\ \times 4 \\ \hline \end{array}$ **19.** $\begin{array}{r} 3 \\ \times 4 \\ \hline \end{array}$ **20.** $\begin{array}{r} 2 \\ \times 6 \\ \hline \end{array}$ **21.** $\begin{array}{r} 8 \\ \times 8 \\ \hline \end{array}$ **22.** $\begin{array}{r} 8 \\ \times 6 \\ \hline \end{array}$

23. $\begin{array}{r} 7 \\ \times 7 \\ \hline \end{array}$ **24.** $\begin{array}{r} 7 \\ \times 9 \\ \hline \end{array}$ **25.** $\begin{array}{r} 4 \\ \times 2 \\ \hline \end{array}$ **26.** $\begin{array}{r} 3 \\ \times 3 \\ \hline \end{array}$ **27.** $\begin{array}{r} 5 \\ \times 6 \\ \hline \end{array}$

28. Find the product of 7 and 2.   **29.** Multiply 4 and 5.

Describe patterns you see. Write the answer in a complete sentence. (6-6)

30. Emma made this pattern with tiles. How many tiles will be in the next figure?

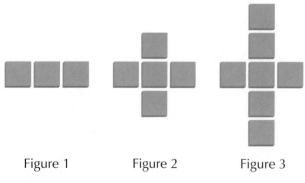

Figure 1   Figure 2   Figure 3

Writing in Math

31. Explain how you can use a 2s fact to find 3×6. (6-1)

32. Explain how you can find 8×4 if you know 4×8. (6-2)

Key Idea
Multiplication can be used to compare the size of two groups.

Vocabulary
• twice

Think It Through
I can **draw a picture** to show a comparison.

Using Multiplication to Compare

LEARN

What does *times as many* mean?

Max has 7 plastic dinosaurs. He has 2 times as many, or **twice** as many, plastic horses as dinosaurs. How many horses does he have?

| dinosaurs | | → Number of dinosaurs |
| horses | horses | → 2 times as many horses as dinosaurs |

To find *2 times as many*, or *twice as many*, multiply by 2.

| 7 | | → 7 dinosaurs |
| 7 | 7 | → 2 × 7 = 14 horses |

Max has 14 plastic horses.

✓ Talk About It

1. Suppose Max has 4 times as many toy trucks as dinosaurs. What multiplication sentence could you write to find how many toy trucks he has?

2. If Max has 3 times as many marbles as dinosaurs, how many marbles does he have?

For another example, see Set 6-7 on p. 362.

1. Margie is three times as old as Jordan. Jordan is 8. How old is Margie?

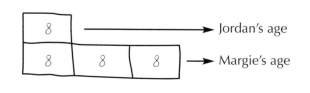

2. Ramona made 4 bracelets. Tara made 5 times as many bracelets. How many bracelets did Tara make?

3. **Number Sense** Jackie has 6 dolls. Anne has twice as many dolls as Jackie. How many dolls do they have all together?

PRACTICE

For more practice, see Set 6-7 on p. 366.

A Skills and Understanding

4. Harry has 3 times as many crayons as Jill. Jill has 7 crayons. How many does Harry have?

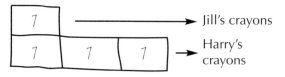

5. Kevin has 9 goldfish. Jeff has twice as many goldfish. How many goldfish does Jeff have?

6. **Number Sense** Gordon has twice as many beads as Julie. Gordon has 10 beads. How many beads does Julie have?

B Reasoning and Problem Solving

Use the recipe for banana bread for 7 and 8.

7. Maria used twice as many bananas as the recipe asks for. How many bananas did she use?

8. **Writing in Math** Write a multiplication story about the bread recipe. Use the words "4 times as many" in the story.

Banana Bread
you will need:

3 cups flour   2 bananas   4 eggs

Mixed Review and Test Prep

Take It to the NET
Test Prep
www.scottforesman.com

9. What are the next two numbers in the pattern?

32, 132, 232, ▪, ▪

10. Find 33 + 56 + 22.

    A. 111   **B.** 132   **C.** 321   **D.** 350

 All text pages available online and on CD-ROM.

Materials
• blank multiplication chart

TEST TALK

Think It Through
If I come to a fact I don't know, I can **use a pattern** to help fill in the fact.

Patterns on a Table

LEARN

Activity

Can you find product patterns?

The table shows multiplication facts. The shaded boxes show how to find 6 × 3 = 18.

×	0	1	2	3	4	5	6	7	8	9	10	11	12
0	0	0	0	0	0	0	0	0				0	
1	0	1	2	3	4	5	6					11	
2	0	2	4	6	8	10		14		18		22	24
3	0	3	6	9	12				24		30	33	36
4	0	4	8	12		24				36	40	44	48
5	0	5	10	15	20							55	
6	0	6	12	18					48		60		72
7												77	
8						48	56						96
9													108
10		10	20		40		70					110	
11		11	22	33		55		77		99			132
12		12	24		48		72		96			132	

a. Copy and complete the table.

b. How can skip counting help you fill in the row of facts for 6?

c. Look at the row that shows 11s facts. Write a pattern you see.

d. If you know 11 × 5 = 55, how can you find 12 × 5?

e. If you know 2 × 12 = 24, how can you find 3 × 12?

f. Describe two patterns you see in the table.

1. 7×3 **2.** 4×4 **3.** 8×3 **4.** 9×4 **5.** 6×11

6. Number Sense Gordon knows that $5 \times 12 = 60$. How can he use this fact to find 6×12?

PRACTICE   *For more practice, see Set 6-8 on p. 366.*

Ⓐ Skills and Understanding

7. 8×2 **8.** 11×9 **9.** 6×12 **10.** 6×6 **11.** 7×8

12. 12×4 **13.** $\$7 \times 6$ **14.** 9×8 **15.** 10×9 **16.** 8×6

17. 2×7 **18.** 5×10 **19.** 11×8 **20.** 3×9 **21.** 11×10

22. $\begin{array}{r} 5 \\ \times\ 3 \\ \hline \end{array}$ **23.** $\begin{array}{r} \$2 \\ \times\ 9 \\ \hline \end{array}$ **24.** $\begin{array}{r} 11 \\ \times\ 3 \\ \hline \end{array}$ **25.** $\begin{array}{r} 12 \\ \times\ 3 \\ \hline \end{array}$ **26.** $\begin{array}{r} 10 \\ \times\ 4 \\ \hline \end{array}$

27. Number Sense Explain why 75 cannot be on the 11s row on the multiplication table.

Ⓑ Reasoning and Problem Solving

28. Joe cut 2 bananas into 6 slices each. He cut 3 more bananas into 8 slices each. How many banana slices did Joe have?

29. Hannah bought 2 bags of marbles for $0.25 each. Each bag contained 12 marbles. How many marbles did she buy?

30. **Writing in Math** Jordan explained how to use 11×4 to find 12×4. Explain how you could use an 11s fact to find 12×3.

> 12×4 is the same as
> 11×4 plus one more 4.
> $11 \times 4 = 44$
> $44 + 4 = 48$.
> So, $12 \times 4 = 48$.

🦉 Mixed Review and Test Prep

Take It to the NET
Test Prep
www.scottforesman.com

31. Joy's age is 4 times Sue's age. Sue is 2 years old. How old is Joy?

32. Which shows the Zero Property of Multiplication?

A. $23 \times 1 = 23$ **B.** $23 \times 0 = 0$ **C.** $23 + 0 = 23$ **D.** $23 - 0 = 23$

Algebra

Key Idea
When multiplying 3 numbers, you can start with any 2 of the numbers.

Vocabulary
• Associative (grouping) Property of Multiplication

Think It Through
I should always check if there's a way to **make a computation easier.**

Multiplying with Three Factors

LEARN

How can you multiply 3 numbers?

When you multiply 3 or more numbers, you can choose which 2 numbers you want to multiply first.

The **Associative (grouping) Property of Multiplication** says that you can change the grouping of the factors, and the product will be the same.

Show three ways to find $3 \times 2 \times 4$.

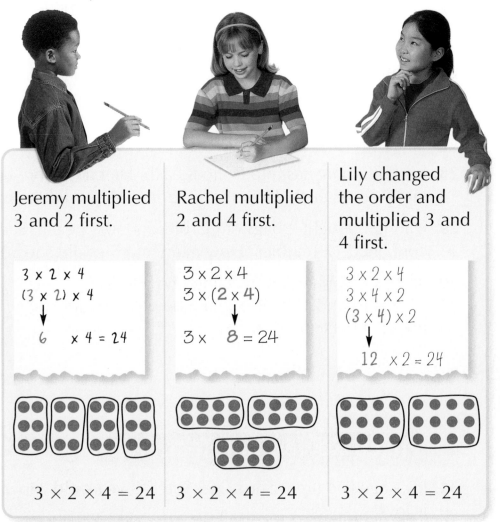

Jeremy multiplied 3 and 2 first.

$3 \times 2 \times 4$
$(3 \times 2) \times 4$
$\downarrow$
$6 \quad \times 4 = 24$

$3 \times 2 \times 4 = 24$

Rachel multiplied 2 and 4 first.

$3 \times 2 \times 4$
$3 \times (2 \times 4)$
$\downarrow$
$3 \times \quad 8 = 24$

$3 \times 2 \times 4 = 24$

Lily changed the order and multiplied 3 and 4 first.

$3 \times 2 \times 4$
$3 \times 4 \times 2$
$(3 \times 4) \times 2$
$\downarrow$
$12 \times 2 = 24$

$3 \times 2 \times 4 = 24$

✔ Talk About It

1. Whose way do you think is easiest? Explain.

For another example, see Set 6-9 on p. 362.

CHECK ✓

1. $2 \times 5 \times 2$ **2.** $3 \times 1 \times 7$ **3.** $3 \times 2 \times 4$ **4.** $2 \times 2 \times 3$

5. Number Sense Greg says that $3 \times 6 \times 2$ is the same as 6×6. Do you agree? Explain.

PRACTICE

For more practice, see Set 6-9 on p. 367.

A Skills and Understanding

6. $1 \times 6 \times 3$ **7.** $3 \times 3 \times 2$ **8.** $0 \times 8 \times 6$ **9.** $4 \times 2 \times 2$

10. $2 \times 4 \times 5$ **11.** $4 \times 1 \times 7$ **12.** $3 \times 4 \times 2$ **13.** $4 \times 5 \times 0$

14. Number Sense Nita says that $5 \times 2 \times 3$ is greater than $2 \times 3 \times 5$. Do you agree? Explain.

B Reasoning and Problem Solving

15. A crate of oranges contains 2 boxes. Each box has 3 layers of oranges. Each layer has 9 oranges. How many oranges are in the crate?

16. Write three ways to find $2 \times 5 \times 1$.

17. Algebra Write a multiplication sentence with three factors that has a product of 48.

18. Writing in Math The grocer put 2 of the juice box packages shown in each bag. She filled 4 bags. How many juice boxes were there? Write a multiplication sentence to solve this problem.

Mixed Review and Test Prep

Take It to the NET
Test Prep
www.scottforesman.com

Multiply.

19. 4×8 **20.** 7×2 **21.** 8×8 **22.** 7×6 **23.** 10×5

24. Max collected 12 green bottles, 8 clear bottles, 13 cans, and 15 milk cartons. How many bottles and cans did he collect?

     A. 33   **B.** 28   **C.** 21   **D.** 20

Algebra

Key Idea
You can find a rule for patterns in a table.

Materials
• counters
or 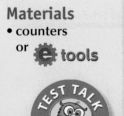 tools

Find a Rule

LEARN

Think It Through
• I can **look at the table** to see a number pattern with cars and wheels.

• I can **use objects** to help decide how many wheels are needed for each number of cars.

Activity

How can you find a rule for a pattern?

Candace wants to put together 5 model cars. Each car has 4 wheels. How many wheels does she need?

1 car   2 cars   3 cars   4 cars

Number of cars	1	2	3	4	5
Number of wheels	4	8	12	16	

The rule for the table is:
Multiply the number of cars by 4.

5 × 4 = 20, so the missing number is 20.

a. Look for patterns in the table below. Tell the rule.

Number of stools	1	2	3	4	5
Number of legs	3	6	9		

1 stool   2 stools   3 stools

b. Use your rule to complete the table.

c. Use counters to show how many legs are in 4 stools and 5 stools.

d. Give a rule for the table below. Complete the table.

In	3	4	5	6	7
Out	15	20	25		

Write a rule for each table. Complete the table.

1.

Number of cookies	1	2	3	4	5
Number of raisins	2	4	6	8	

2.

Number of packages	1	2	3	4	5
Number of fruit cups	7	14	21		

3.

In	4	6	5	7	8
Out	32	48	40		

4. Number Sense Carole's table has a rule of *Multiply by 7*. If the **Out** number is 21, what is the **In** number?

PRACTICE

For more practice, see Set 6-10 on p. 367.

Skills and Understanding

Write a rule for each table. Complete the table.

5.

Number of boxes	1	2	3	4	5
Number of crayons	8	16	24		

6.

Number of lanes		3	6	2	5	9
Number of bowling pins		30	60	20		

7.

In	1	2	3	4	5
Out	9	18	27		

In 1903, a box of crayons with 8 colors cost a nickel.

8. Number Sense Ryan's mom said she will give him $15 if he works for 3 hours. How much will she give him for 1 hour?

 Reasoning and Problem Solving

9. Writing in Math Write an addition rule for this table. Then write a multiplication rule for it. Copy the table twice and complete it for each rule.

In	4	5	6	7	8
Out	8				

Mixed Review and Test Prep

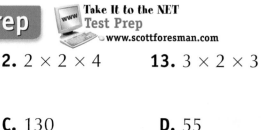
Take It to the NET
Test Prep
www.scottforesman.com

10. $1 \times 10 \times 3$ **11.** $0 \times 7 \times 9$ **12.** $2 \times 2 \times 4$ **13.** $3 \times 2 \times 3$

14. Find $400 - 255$.

  A. 265   **B.** 145   **C.** 130   **D.** 55

Problem-Solving Skill

Reading Helps!
Identifying the main idea
can help you with...
choosing an operation.

Key Idea
Understanding when to choose a particular operation can help you solve problems.

Think It Through
• Since the **most important idea** is equal groups of food, I should multiply to find the amount for one week.

Choose an Operation

LEARN

How can you find the main idea?

You can draw a picture of the action in a problem. The picture shows the main idea and helps you know whether to add, subtract, or multiply.

Sea Otters California sea otters became protected by a law in 1911. This was 170 years after the start of commercial hunting of sea otters. There are fewer than 2,000 sea otters off the California coast.

	Example A	**Example B**
	Some aquariums take care of sea otters. If a sea otter is fed 8 pounds of food each day, how much is it fed in a week?	When did the commercial hunting of sea otters start?
Read and Understand **Show the main idea.**	⑧ ⑧ ⑧ ⑧ ⑧ ⑧ ⑧	? ⟵——┃————1911———┃——⟶ 170 years
Plan and Solve **Choose an operation.**	Multiply to find the total when you put together equal groups. $7 \times 8 = 56$	Subtract to take 170 away from the later year, 1911. $1911 - 170 = 1741$

✔ **Talk About It**

1. Answer each question above in a complete sentence.

2. **Number Sense** Could you solve Example A with addition? Explain.

Take It to the NET
More Examples
www.scottforesman.com

For another example, see Set 6-11 on p. 363.

CHECK

The picture shows the main idea. Use the picture to choose an operation and solve the problem.

| 5 | 5 | 5 |

1. An aquarium worker recorded that a sea otter spent 5 hours a day grooming. How many hours did the sea otter spend grooming in 3 days?

PRACTICE

For more practice, see Set 6-11 on p. 367.

Draw a picture to show the main idea. Then choose an operation and solve the problem.

2. Use the data at the right. Were more tickets sold on Monday and Tuesday together or on Wednesday? Explain.

3. Use the data at the right. Three times as many tickets were sold on Saturday as on Monday. How many tickets were sold on Saturday?

4. Harry made 42 pancakes. He used 7 eggs and 5 cups of milk. Twelve of the pancakes were blueberry. The rest were banana. How many banana pancakes did he make?

5. Mandy earns $4 for an hour of babysitting. She earns $6 for washing her aunt's car. How much will Mandy make if she babysits for 3 hours?

6. **Writing in Math** Write a word problem for the picture at the right. Explain what operation you would use to solve the problem.

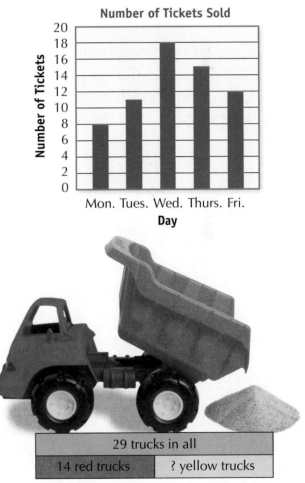

Number of Tickets Sold

29 trucks in all

| 14 red trucks | ? yellow trucks |

DK Problem-Solving Applications

Sandworms Worms squirm in many different shapes and sizes. The worms shown here are certainly not a pleasant sight! They are known as ragworms, clamworms, or sandworms.

Trivia The jaws of the sandworm move side-to-side. They are powerful enough to crush small clams and oysters!

1 Each segment of a sandworm's body has 2 paddle-like features. How many of these features are on 7 body segments?

2 Each body segment has 4 bundles of stiff bristles that grip surfaces. How many bundles are on 3 body segments?

Using Key Facts

3 Sandworms may have 5 times as many teeth as eyes. They have twice as many eyes as antennae. How many teeth do sandworms have?

4 Earthworms can grow to be more than 7 times the length of the largest sandworm. How long can an earthworm grow to be?

⑤ Decision Making What bait would you like to use to catch fish? How much would it cost to buy 4 packages of your choice ?

Bait	Cost per Package
Sandworms	$3
Earthworms	$2
Plastic worms	$4

⑥ Writing in Math One sandworm has 32 segments. Another has 88 segments. Explain how you could estimate the difference in the number of segments.

Key Facts
Sandworms

- Up to 3 feet long
- 2 antennae
- 8 tentacle-like cirri near the mouth
- Eat plants and animals
- Live along coastlines
- Burrow 4 inches deep

Good News/Bad News
Sandworms can be raised on farms to supply the fishing industry, but normally the worms will reproduce only in the spring.

Do You Know How?

Do You Understand?

Using Multiplication to Compare (6-7)

1. Ed is 3 years old. Ryan is twice as old as Ed. How old is Ryan?

2. Nando has 2 eggs. He needs 3 times this many to make breakfast for his family. How many eggs does he need?

A What is another way to say *twice as many*?

B Draw a picture to show the problem in Exercise 2.

Patterns on a Table (6-8)

3. 11×3 **4.** 8×10 **5.** 6×7

6. 10×5 **7.** 12×2 **8.** 4×9

C Is 42 on the 5s row of the multiplication table? Explain.

Multiplying with Three Factors (6-9)

9. $2 \times 3 \times 3$ **10.** $1 \times 4 \times 8$

11. $3 \times 3 \times 3$ **12.** $3 \times 5 \times 2$

D Write two ways to multiply for Exercise 12.

Find a Rule (6-10)

13. Write a rule. Complete the table.

In	1	2	3	4	5
Out	4	8	12		

E Use the rule you found for the table in Exercise 13. If the **Out** number is 24, what is the **In** number?

Problem-Solving Skill: Choose an Operation (6-11)

Choose an operation and solve.

14. Mandy raked 4 yards. She spent 2 hours on each yard. How many hours did she rake?

F Could you use a different operation than the one you chose to solve Exercise 14? Explain.

MULTIPLE CHOICE

1. Which has the same value as $2 \times 6 \times 3$? (6-9)

   A. $2 + 3 + 6$ **B.** $2 \times 3 \times 12$ **C.** 8×3 **D.** 6×6

2. Darian bought 4 times as many apples as Sally. If Sally bought 6 apples, how many did Darian buy? (6-7)

   A. 8   **B.** 10   **C.** 12   **D.** 24

FREE RESPONSE

Solve. (6-7)

3. Jana had 9 carrot sticks. She cut each in half, so now she has twice as many carrot sticks. How many does she have now?

4. **Reasoning** Mia's recipe makes 6 biscuits. She must make 18 biscuits. Should she multiply the recipe by 2 or by 3? Explain.

Multiply. (6-8)

5. 11×4 6. 10×8 7. 12×3 8. 7×9 9. 2×11

10. How can you find 12×8 if you know $11 \times 8 = 88$?

11. How can you skip count to find 4×9?

Find each product. (6-9)

12. $2 \times 3 \times 5$ 13. $4 \times 7 \times 1$ 14. $3 \times 2 \times 2$

Write a rule for each table. Complete the table. (6-10)

15.

In	1	2	3	4	5
Out	6	12	18		

16.

In	3	7	4	6	8
Out	15	35	20		

Choose an operation and solve the problem. (6-11, 6-12)

17. Ann made 3 sandwiches. She put 4 ham slices on one, 2 ham slices on another, and 1 ham slice on the third sandwich. How many ham slices did she use?

TEST TALK

Think It Through

I should **identify the main idea** before I choose an operation.

Writing in Math

18. Explain how you would multiply to find $3 \times 5 \times 3$. (6-9)

Test-Taking Strategies

Understand the question.

Get information for the answer.

Plan how to find the answer.

Make smart choices.

Use writing in math.

→ **Improve written answers.**

Improve Written Answers

You can follow the tips below to learn how to improve written answers on a test. It is important to write a clear answer and include only information needed to answer the question.

The rubric below is a scoring guide for Test Question 1.

Scoring Rubric

4 points

Full credit: 4 points

The table and rule are correct.

3 points

Partial credit: 3 points

Only one of the two table entries is correct, and the rule is correct.

2 points

Partial credit: 2 points

Either the table is correct, or the rule is correct, but not both.

1 point

Partial credit: 1 point

Only one of the two table entries is correct, and the rule is incorrect.

0 points

No credit: 0 points

The table and rule are both incorrect.

1. The table below shows how many awards a student can earn and how many books the student has to read to earn those awards. Complete the table to tell how many books have to be read to earn 5 awards and 6 awards.

Number of awards	1	2	3	4	5	6
Number of books read	5	10	15	20		

On the lines below, tell a rule for finding the number of books read for a certain number of awards.

_____

_____

Improve Written Answers

• Check if your answer is complete.

*In order to **get as many points as possible,** I must complete the table and write a rule.*

• Check if your answer makes sense.

*I need to **check the numbers** I have written in the table. **Does my rule hold** for all the numbers in the table?*

- Check if your explanation is clear and easy to follow.

*I should reread my rule to check that I have **accurately and clearly described** how to get the numbers in the table and that I haven't included unnecessary information.*

Ken used the scoring rubric on page 352 to score a student's answer to Test Question 1. The student's paper is shown below.

Think It Through
The student forgot to fill in the last number in the table. The student should have put 30 in the last box. The other number in the table is correct and so is the rule. So this student gets 3 points.

Number of awards	1	2	3	4	5	6
Number of books read	5	10	15	20	25	

On the lines below, tell a rule for finding the number of books read for a certain number of awards.

<u>Multiply the number of awards</u>

<u>by 5 to get the number of</u>

<u>books read.</u>

Now it's your turn.

Score the student's paper. If it does not get 4 points, rewrite it so that it does.

2. The table below shows the number of students in different classes and the number of hot dogs ordered for a class picnic in those classes. Complete the table to tell how many hot dogs are needed for classes with 22 and 27 students.

Number of students	18	25	28	24	22	27
Number of hot dogs	20	27	30	26	24	29

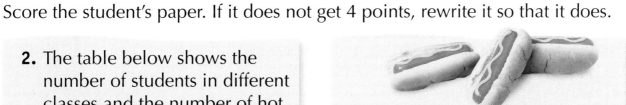

On the lines below, tell a rule for finding the number of hot dogs that should be ordered for certain classes.

<u>Subtract 2 from the number of</u>

<u>students in the class to get</u>

<u>the number of hot dogs.</u>

All the sides of a square are the same.

*A product is a **square number** if both factors are the same. (p. 325)*

Self Check ✓

Use facts you know to help multiply. (Lessons 6-1, 6-2, 6-3, 6-4, 6-5)

Find 3 × 7.

Use 1s facts and 2s facts.

$2 \times 7 = 14$
$1 \times 7 = 7$ 2 sevens plus
$14 + 7 = 21$ 1 more seven
So, $3 \times 7 = 21$.

Find 4 × 7.

Think of a 2s fact. Then double the product.

$2 \times 7 = 14$
$14 + 14 = 28$ 2 sevens plus 2 sevens
So, $4 \times 7 = 28$.

Find 8 × $8.

Think of a 4s fact. Then double the product.

$4 \times 8 = 32$
$32 + 32 = 64$ 64 is a
So, $8 \times \$8 = \$64$.   **square number.**

Find 6 × 4.

Use the **Commutative Property of Multiplication.**

$6 \times 4 = 4 \times 6$ $4 \times 6 = 24$
So, $6 \times 4 = 24$.

1. Find 3×9 and $6 \times \$6$.

My dad commutes an hour to and from work.

*Remember, the **Commutative Property of Multiplication** says you can multiply in either order. (p. 263)*

Self Check ✓

Find patterns in tables. (Lesson 6-8, 6-10)

Look for patterns in a fact table.

X	0	1	2	3	4	5	6
0	0	0	0	0	0	0	0
1	0	1	2	3	4	5	6
2	0	2	4	6	8	10	12
3	0	3	6	9	12	15	18
4	0	4	8	12	16	20	24
5	0	5	10	15	20	25	30
6	0	6	12	18	24	30	36

$5 \times 4 = 20$

Write a rule for the table below. Complete the table.

In	1	2	3	4	5
Out	6	12	18	24	

The rule is: Multiply by 6.

In	1	2	3	4	5
Out	6	12	18	24	30

$5 \times 6 = 30$

2. Write a rule for the table. Complete the table.

In	1	2	3	4	5
Out	8	16	24		

When you multiply 3 numbers, start with any 2 of them. (Lesson 6-9)

Find $6 \times 5 \times 2$.

Use the **Associative (grouping) Property of Multiplication.** Here are 3 ways.

$6 \times 5 \times 2$	$6 \times 5 \times 2$	$6 \times 5 \times 2$ Switch the 5 and 2.
$(6 \times 5) \times 2$ Multiply 6 and 5 first.	$6 \times (5 \times 2)$ Multiply 5 and 2 first.	$6 \times 2 \times 5$
$\downarrow$	$\downarrow$	$(6 \times 2) \times 5$ Multiply 6 and 2 first.
$30 \times 2 = 60$	$6 \times 10 = 60$	$\downarrow$
		$12 \times 5 = 60$

3. Find $2 \times 3 \times 7$.

When my teacher assigns group work, all the members need to associate with one another.

*The **Associative (grouping) Property of Multiplication** says you can change the way factors are grouped and the product will be the same. (p. 342)*

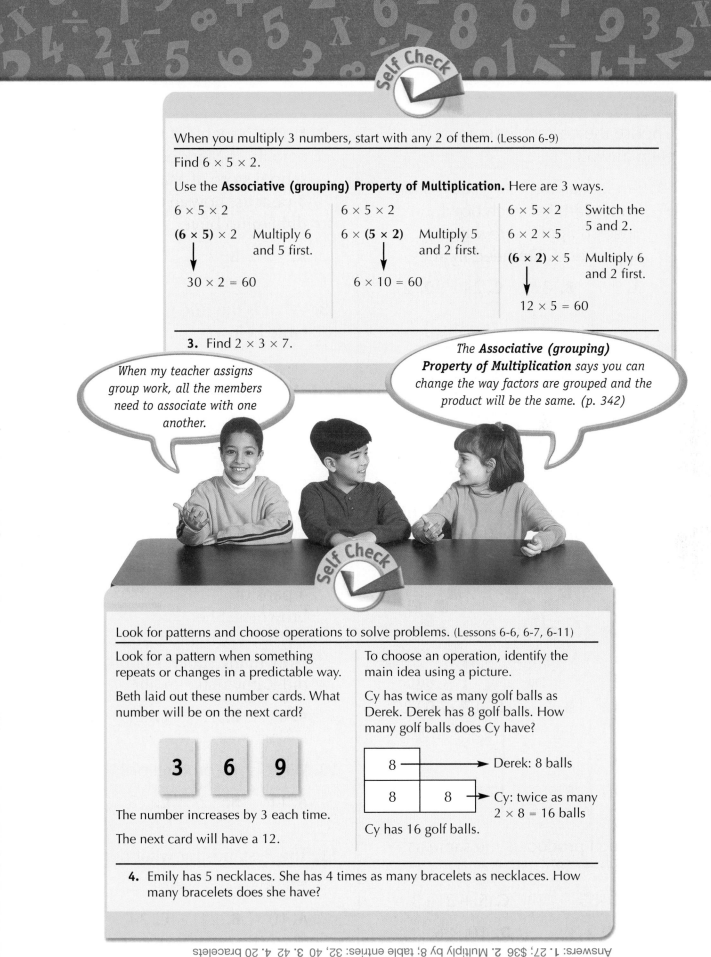

Look for patterns and choose operations to solve problems. (Lessons 6-6, 6-7, 6-11)

Look for a pattern when something repeats or changes in a predictable way.

Beth laid out these number cards. What number will be on the next card?

3 **6** **9**

The number increases by 3 each time.

The next card will have a 12.

To choose an operation, identify the main idea using a picture.

Cy has twice as many golf balls as Derek. Derek has 8 golf balls. How many golf balls does Cy have?

| 8 | | → Derek: 8 balls |
| 8 | 8 | → Cy: twice as many $2 \times 8 = 16$ balls |

Cy has 16 golf balls.

4. Emily has 5 necklaces. She has 4 times as many bracelets as necklaces. How many bracelets does she have?

Answers: 1. 27; $36 2. Multiply by 8; table entries: 32, 40 3. 42 4. 20 bracelets

MULTIPLE CHOICE

Choose the correct letter for each answer.

1. Jim is making 3 large bowls of fruit salad. For each bowl, he needs 8 apples. How many apples does Jim need in all?

   A. 3 **B.** 8 **C.** 24 **D.** 27

2. Find the product of 7 and 4.

   A. 11 **B.** 21 **C.** 24 **D.** 28

3. Multiply 9 and 6.

   A. 48 **B.** 54 **C.** 56 **D.** 64

4. Lynn made this pattern with tiles. How many tiles will be in the fourth figure?

   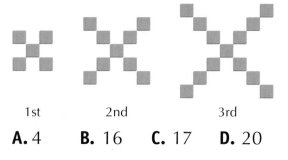

   1st   2nd   3rd

   A. 4 **B.** 16 **C.** 17 **D.** 20

5. Find 5×8.

   A. 40 **B.** 45 **C.** 50 **D.** 80

6. Which product is the same as $5 \times 2 \times 3$?

   A. 5×5 **C.** $5 + 2 + 3$

   B. 10×3 **D.** 10×6

7. Emilio bought 3 times as many pencils as Mark bought at the school store. If Mark bought 3 pencils, how many pencils did Emilio buy?

   A. 1 **B.** 3 **C.** 6 **D.** 9

8. What is the rule for the table below?

In	2	3	4
Out	12	18	24

   A. Multiply by 6.

   B. Add 6.

   C. Multiply by 8.

   D. Add 10.

Think It Through
- I need to **eliminate wrong answers.**
- I can **try different answers** to find what works for all cases.

9. Kathy made 4 pans of brownies. She cut each pan into 6 squares. How many squares of brownies did Kathy make in all?

   A. 6 **B.** 10 **C.** 24 **D.** 28

10. What is the product of $1 \times 5 \times 6$?

    A. 11 **B.** 12 **C.** 25 **D.** 30

11. The ■ stands for what number?

    $7 \times 3 =$ ■

    A. 10 **B.** 21 **C.** 24 **D.** 37

12. Kendra has 4 brothers. She gave each brother 3 apples. How many apples did Kendra give to her brothers in all?

A. 3   **B.** 7   **C.** 12   **D.** 14

FREE RESPONSE

13. Look for a pattern in the table to help you find the product.

$$\begin{array}{r} 11 \\ \times\ 5 \\ \hline \end{array}$$

X	10	11	12
0	0	0	0
1	10	11	12
2	20	22	24
3	30	33	36
4	40	44	48
5	50		60
6	60	66	72

14. 7×3 **15.** 4×4

16. 9×2 **17.** 6×8

18. $\begin{array}{r} 9 \\ \times\ 5 \\ \hline \end{array}$ **19.** $\begin{array}{r} 8 \\ \times\ 7 \\ \hline \end{array}$

20. $\begin{array}{r} 3 \\ \times\ 5 \\ \hline \end{array}$ **21.** $\begin{array}{r} 4 \\ \times\ 9 \\ \hline \end{array}$

22. $\begin{array}{r} 6 \\ \times\ 6 \\ \hline \end{array}$ **23.** $\begin{array}{r} 7 \\ \times\ 6 \\ \hline \end{array}$

24. $3 \times 3 \times 4$ **25.** $2 \times 3 \times 6$

26. $9 \times 3 \times 1$ **27.** $5 \times 8 \times 0$

28. At the bookstore, book covers cost $6. Gary bought 3 book covers. How much did Gary spend in all?

Write a rule for the table. Copy and complete the table.

29.

In	4	5	6	7	8
Out	12	15	18		

30. Write three ways to find $4 \times 3 \times 2$.

31. Draw an array to show 7×6.

Writing in Math

32. Janice is making cookies. She made a table to show how many peanuts she will need. Describe the pattern. Then, copy and complete the table.

Number of cookies	4	5	6	7	8
Number of peanuts	16	20	24		

33. Clark made 3 times as many sandcastles as Judy. Judy made 4 sandcastles. Draw a picture to show the main idea. How many sandcastles did Clark make? Explain how you know.

Think It Through
- I can **draw a picture** to help solve the problem.
- I need to **check to be sure my answer is complete and clear.**

34. Trisha says that you can find 8×9 by finding 3×9 and doubling it. Do you agree? Explain.

Number and Operation

MULTIPLE CHOICE

1. What is the difference of 150 and 79?

　A. 59　　**B.** 71　　**C.** 79　　**D.** 100

2. What is the value of the underlined digit in 5̲10,901?

　A. 5　　　　　　**C.** 5,000

　B. 500　　　　　**D.** 500,000

3. Which product is NOT the same as $5 \times 2 \times 4$?

　A. 10×4

　B. 5×8

　C. 7×4

　D. 20×2

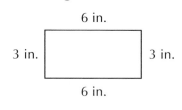

TEST TALK

Think It Through
- I should **watch for words like NOT or EXCEPT**.
- I need to **read each answer choice carefully**.

FREE RESPONSE

4. Find $160 + 27 + 391$.

5. Draw an array to show 6×5.

6. Clair made 40 beaded necklaces. She used 5 blue beads and 10 green beads on each necklace. Clair gave her sister 12 of the beaded necklaces. How many beaded necklaces does Clair have left?

Writing in Math

7. Explain how to find the product of 7 and 4.

Geometry and Measurement

MULTIPLE CHOICE

8. About how long is a dollar bill?

　A. 6 inches　　　**C.** 6 feet

　B. 6 centimeters　**D.** 6 yards

9. What is the name of the solid figure at the right?

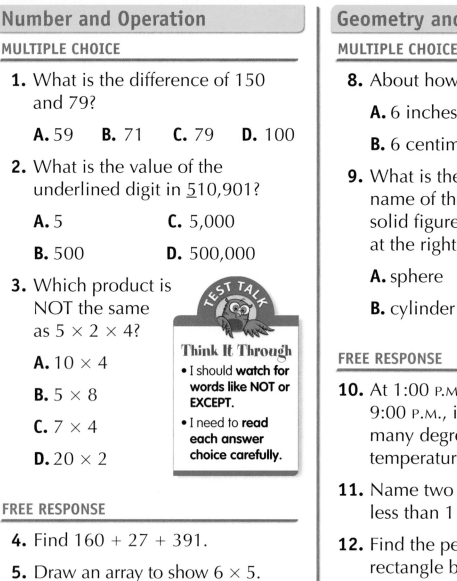

　A. sphere　　　**C.** cone

　B. cylinder　　**D.** pyramid

FREE RESPONSE

10. At 1:00 P.M., it was 78°F. At 9:00 P.M., it was 63°F. How many degrees did the temperature drop?

11. Name two objects that weigh less than 1 pound.

12. Find the perimeter of the rectangle below.

6 in.

3 in.　　　　　　3 in.

6 in.

Writing in Math

13. Jake says the two figures below are congruent. Is he correct? Explain why or why not.

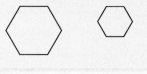

Data Analysis and Probability

MULTIPLE CHOICE

Use the pictograph for Items 14–15.

Cans of Vegetables Sold

Potatoes	🥫🥫
Corn	🥫🥫🥫🥫🥫🥫🥫
Green beans	🥫🥫🥫🥫🥫
Peas	🥫🥫🥫

Each 🥫 = 10 cans.

14. How many cans of peas were sold?

A. 30   **B.** 35   **C.** 40   **D.** 45

15. How many more cans of green beans than cans of peas were sold?

A. 5   **B.** 10   **C.** 20   **D.** 30

FREE RESPONSE

Use the picture below for Items 16–17. Suppose you picked one cube from the bag without looking.

16. Which color are you most likely to pick?

17. Which color are you least likely to pick?

Writing in Math

18. Using the pictograph above, explain how to find the total number of cans that were sold.

Algebra

MULTIPLE CHOICE

19. Find the missing number.

$57 - \blacksquare = 39$

A. 8   **B.** 18   **C.** 28   **D.** 96

20. Find the number that makes the number sentence true.

$4 + x > 14$

A. $x = 4$ **C.** $x = 10$

B. $x = 8$ **D.** $x = 12$

21. Which two numbers come next in the pattern?

25, 29, 33, 37, ▪, ▪

A. 39, 43   **C.** 41, 45

B. 40, 44   **D.** 45, 49

FREE RESPONSE

22. Write a rule for the table. Complete the table.

In	3	4	5	6	7
Out	9	12	15		

23. Mary bought 24 new pencils for school. She gave her friend Tammy 8 pencils, and her friend Cynthia 5 pencils. How many pencils does Mary have left?

Writing in Math

24. Brian says that $y = 18$ can make the number sentence $3 + y < 20$ true. Is he correct? Explain.

Set 6-1 (pages 316–317)

Find 3×7.

You can break apart an array into facts you already know.

$3 \times 7 = 3$ groups of 7

That's 2 sevens plus 1 more seven.

■ ■ ■ ■ ■ ■ ■ $2 \times 7 = 14$
■ ■ ■ ■ ■ ■ ■ $1 \times 7 = 7$

$14 + 7 = 21$

So, $3 \times 7 = 21$.

Remember that you can use facts you already know to help you multiply.

1. 3×8	**2.** 6×3
3. 4×3	**4.** 2×3
5. $\begin{array}{r} 9 \\ \times\, 3 \\ \hline \end{array}$	**6.** $\begin{array}{r} 3 \\ \times\, 3 \\ \hline \end{array}$
7. $\begin{array}{r} 3 \\ \times\, 5 \\ \hline \end{array}$	**8.** $\begin{array}{r} 10 \\ \times\,\ 3 \\ \hline \end{array}$

Set 6-2 (pages 318–319)

Find 4×9.

Think of a 2s fact, then double the product.

$4 \times 9 = 4$ groups of 9.

★ ★ ★ ★ ★ ★ ★ ★ ★
★ ★ ★ ★ ★ ★ ★ ★ ★ $2 \times 9 = 18$

★ ★ ★ ★ ★ ★ ★ ★ ★
★ ★ ★ ★ ★ ★ ★ ★ ★ $2 \times 9 = 18$

$18 + 18 = 36$

So, $4 \times 9 = 36$.

Remember that you can draw arrays to solve multiplication facts.

1. 4×10	**2.** 3×4
3. 6×4	**4.** 4×5
5. $\begin{array}{r} 4 \\ \times\, 4 \\ \hline \end{array}$	**6.** $\begin{array}{r} 7 \\ \times\, 4 \\ \hline \end{array}$
7. $\begin{array}{r} 8 \\ \times\, 4 \\ \hline \end{array}$	**8.** $\begin{array}{r} 4 \\ \times\, 2 \\ \hline \end{array}$

Set 6-3 (pages 320–323)

Find 7×9.

Use 5s facts and 2s facts to help multiply with 7.

● ● ● ● ● ● ● ● ●
● ● ● ● ● ● ● ● ●
● ● ● ● ● ● ● ● ●
● ● ● ● ● ● ● ● ●
● ● ● ● ● ● ● ● ● $5 \times 9 = 45$

● ● ● ● ● ● ● ● ●
● ● ● ● ● ● ● ● ● $2 \times 9 = 18$

$45 + 18 = 63$

So, $7 \times 9 = 63$.

Remember that you can use facts you already know to multiply with 6 and 7.

1. 6×7	**2.** $8 \times \$7$
3. 6×9	**4.** $6 \times \$3$
5. 7×4	**6.** 6×8
7. $\begin{array}{r} 7 \\ \times\, 7 \\ \hline \end{array}$	**8.** $\begin{array}{r} 6 \\ \times\, 2 \\ \hline \end{array}$

Find 8×6.

You can double a 4s fact to multiply with 8.

Find 4×6. Then double the product.

●●●●●●
●●●●●●
●●●●●● $4 \times 6 = 24$

●●●●●●
●●●●●●
●●●●●● $4 \times 6 = 24$

$24 + 24 = 48$

So, $8 \times 6 = 48$.

Remember to check that your picture accurately shows the arrays for the numbers that are being multiplied.

1. 8×7 **2.** $8 \times \$8$

3. $8 \times \$9$ **4.** 6×8

5. $\quad 5$ **6.** $\quad 2$
$\quad \underline{\times 8}$ $\underline{\times 8}$

7. $\quad 3$ **8.** $\quad 9$
$\quad \underline{\times 8}$ $\underline{\times 8}$

Find 6×9.

Use the Commutative Property of Multiplication.

$6 \times 9 = 9 \times 6$

$9 \times 6 = 54$

So, $6 \times 9 = 54$.

Remember that fact strategies can help you find the products for multiplication facts.

1. 9×8 **2.** 7×9

3. 5×8 **4.** 4×7

5. $\quad 3$ **6.** $\quad 9$
$\quad \underline{\times 6}$ $\underline{\times 4}$

When you look for a pattern to solve a problem, follow these steps:

Step 1: Show what you know.

Step 2: Look for what repeats or changes.

Step 3: Check that what repeats or changes works for all cases.

Step 4: Describe the pattern or patterns.

Remember that a pattern exists only if it works for all cases.

    13, 20, 27, 34, ▨, ▨

1. What are the next two numbers in the pattern above?

2. Describe the pattern above. Write the answer in a complete sentence.

Set 6-7 (pages 338–339)

Jamie has 3 times as many toy cars as his brother Frank. Frank has 4 toy cars. How many toy cars does Jamie have?

To find *3 times as many,* multiply by 3.

4		
4	4	4

→ 4 toy cars

→ 3 × 4 = 12 toy cars

Jamie has 12 toy cars.

Remember that to find *twice as many,* or *two times as many,* multiply by 2.

1. Melissa has 5 stickers. Clark has 5 times as many stickers as Melissa. How many stickers does Clark have?

2. Cory lives twice as far from school as Josh. Josh lives 4 miles from school. How far from school does Cory live?

Set 6-8 (pages 340–341)

Find 4 × 6.

Find the product on a fact table.

The yellow lines show 4 × 6 = 24.

4 × 6 = 24

X	0	1	2	3	4	5	6
0	0	0	0	0	0	0	0
1	0	1	2	3	4	5	6
2	0	2	4	6	8	10	12
3	0	3	6	9	12	15	18
4	0	4	8	12	16	20	24
5	0	5	10	15	20	25	30
6	0	6	12	18	24	30	36

Remember you can use a pattern to help you find the product for a multiplication fact.

1. 12 × 4
2. 6 × 8
3. 11 × 9
4. 5 × 7
5. 3 × 11
6. 5 × 12

Set 6-9 (pages 342–343)

Find 4 × 5 × 2.

One Way: (4 × 5) × 2

(4 × 5) × 2

20 × 2 = 40

So, 4 × 5 × 2 = 40

Another Way: 4 × (5 × 2)

4 × (5 × 2)

4 × 10 = 40

So, 4 × 5 × 2 = 40

Remember that the Associative Property of Multiplication says you can change the grouping of the factors, and the product will be the same.

1. 2 × 6 × 4
2. 1 × 8 × 9
3. 5 × 7 × 0
4. 3 × 6 × 2
5. 2 × 2 × 1
6. 3 × 3 × 3
7. 4 × 3 × 4
8. 5 × 3 × 2
9. 6 × 3 × 3
10. 7 × 2 × 5
11. 1 × 9 × 8
12. 9 × 2 × 2

Set 6-10 (pages 344–345)

Write a rule for the table. Complete the table.

In	3	4	5	6	7
Out	6	8	10		

Look for a pattern in the table.

The rule for the table is:
Multiply by 2.

In	3	4	5	6	7
Out	6	8	10	12	14

Remember that the rule must work for all the sets of numbers in a table.

Find a rule for each table. Complete the tables.

1.

In	1	2	3	4	5
Out	3	6	9		

2.

In	3	4	5	6	7
Out	15	20	25		

3.

In	1	2	3	4	5
Out	9	18	27		

Set 6-11 (pages 346–347)

Liz won 3 packages of rubber stamps. Each package contained 8 stamps. How many rubber stamps did Liz win in all?

Show the main idea.

Choose an operation.

Multiply to find the total when you put together equal groups.

$3 \times 8 = 24$

Liz won 24 rubber stamps in all.

Remember that drawing a picture of the main idea can help you choose an operation.

Draw a picture to show the main idea. Choose an operation and solve the problem.

1. Tina earned $12 washing cars and $18 mowing lawns. How much did she earn in all?

2. Joseph is mailing 6 packages that will need 4 stamps each. How many stamps does Joseph need all together?

3. Caroline and Jason rode in a bike-a-thon. Caroline rode 24 miles and Jason rode 18 miles. How many more miles did Caroline ride than Jason?

Set 6-1 (pages 316–317)

1. 3×3 **2.** 4×3 **3.** 3×10

4. $\begin{array}{r} 5 \\ \times\, 3 \\ \hline \end{array}$ **5.** $\begin{array}{r} 3 \\ \times\, 2 \\ \hline \end{array}$ **6.** $\begin{array}{r} 9 \\ \times\, 3 \\ \hline \end{array}$

7. $\begin{array}{r} 7 \\ \times\, 3 \\ \hline \end{array}$ **8.** $\begin{array}{r} 3 \\ \times\, 6 \\ \hline \end{array}$ **9.** $\begin{array}{r} 3 \\ \times\, 8 \\ \hline \end{array}$

10. Mr. Nash divided his class into 8 equal groups. Each group had 3 students. How many total students are in the class?

Set 6-2 (pages 318–319)

1. 4×9 **2.** 3×4 **3.** 4×4

4. $\begin{array}{r} 10 \\ \times\, 4 \\ \hline \end{array}$ **5.** $\begin{array}{r} 0 \\ \times\, 4 \\ \hline \end{array}$ **6.** $\begin{array}{r} 4 \\ \times\, 1 \\ \hline \end{array}$

7. $\begin{array}{r} 4 \\ \times\, 7 \\ \hline \end{array}$ **8.** $\begin{array}{r} 8 \\ \times\, 4 \\ \hline \end{array}$ **9.** $\begin{array}{r} 4 \\ \times\, 5 \\ \hline \end{array}$

10. Continue the pattern below.

24, 28, 32, ▩, ▩, ▩

11. Greg has 6 boxes with 4 pencils in each. How many pencils does Greg have in all?

Set 6-3 (pages 320–323)

1. 6×5 **2.** $2 \times \$7$ **3.** 9×7

4. $8 \times \$6$ **5.** 6×3 **6.** 7×8

7. 0×7 **8.** 6×9 **9.** 10×6

10. $\begin{array}{r} 2 \\ \times\, 6 \\ \hline \end{array}$ **11.** $\begin{array}{r} 7 \\ \times\, 6 \\ \hline \end{array}$ **12.** $\begin{array}{r} 7 \\ \times\, 7 \\ \hline \end{array}$

13. Find the product of 6 and 4. **14.** Find 5 times 7.

15. Kendra's Café has 6 large tables. Each table can seat 6 people. How many people all together can sit at the large tables in Kendra's Café?

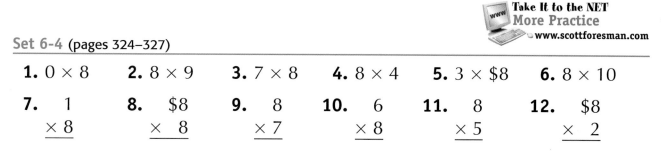
Take It to the NET
More Practice
www.scottforesman.com

Set 6-4 (pages 324–327)

1. 0×8 **2.** 8×9 **3.** 7×8 **4.** 8×4 **5.** $3 \times \$8$ **6.** 8×10

7. $\begin{array}{r} 1 \\ \times 8 \\ \hline \end{array}$ **8.** $\begin{array}{r} \$8 \\ \times\ 8 \\ \hline \end{array}$ **9.** $\begin{array}{r} 8 \\ \times 7 \\ \hline \end{array}$ **10.** $\begin{array}{r} 6 \\ \times 8 \\ \hline \end{array}$ **11.** $\begin{array}{r} 8 \\ \times 5 \\ \hline \end{array}$ **12.** $\begin{array}{r} \$8 \\ \times\ 2 \\ \hline \end{array}$

13. Jennifer has 8 pencil cases with 6 pencils in each. Melissa says this is the same as having 2 pencil cases with 6 pencils in each, plus 6 pencil cases with 6 pencils in each. Is Melissa correct? Explain.

Set 6-5 (pages 328–329)

1. 8×9 **2.** 6×7 **3.** $4 \times \$6$ **4.** 7×10 **5.** $8 \times \$4$ **6.** 5×7

7. $\begin{array}{r} \$3 \\ \times\ 6 \\ \hline \end{array}$ **8.** $\begin{array}{r} 0 \\ \times 7 \\ \hline \end{array}$ **9.** $\begin{array}{r} 3 \\ \times 9 \\ \hline \end{array}$ **10.** $\begin{array}{r} 4 \\ \times 4 \\ \hline \end{array}$ **11.** $\begin{array}{r} 7 \\ \times 8 \\ \hline \end{array}$ **12.** $\begin{array}{r} 8 \\ \times 8 \\ \hline \end{array}$

13. Jeffrey bought 9 packs of rolls. Each pack had 6 rolls. How many rolls did Jeffrey buy in all?

Set 6-6 (pages 332–335)

Describe patterns you see. Write the answers in complete sentences.

1. The school buses of Glenwood School District are numbered following a pattern. What are the numbers of the next two buses in line?

Bus 3   Bus 9   Bus 15   Bus   Bus

2. Briana made three figures with square tiles by following a pattern. How many square tiles will be in the next figure that Briana draws? Draw the next figure.

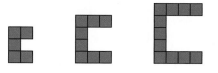

Set 6-7 (pages 338–339)

1. Jason drew 3 times as many pictures as Kevin for the art show. Kevin drew 3 pictures. How many pictures did Jason draw?

2. Melinda has earned 5 scout badges. Casey has earned twice as many scout badges as Melinda. How many scout badges has Casey earned?

3. Darren has saved 5 times as much money as Shawn. Shawn has saved $10. How much money has Darren saved?

4. Jamal caught 7 fireflies. Sam caught 4 times as many fireflies as Jamal. How many fireflies did Sam catch?

Set 6-8 (pages 340–341)

Copy and complete the table. Use the table to find multiplication facts.

X	0	1	2	3	4	5	6	7	8	9	10	11	12
0	0	0	0	0	0	0	0				0	0	0	
1	0	1		3	4		6	7					12
2		2			8	10		14			20		
3			6	9		15			24	27			36
4	0				16	20	24					44	
5		5	10				30			45			
6	0			18		30			48	54			72
7					28	35			56				
8	0	8	16	24		40		56			80		96
9					36		54			81		99	
10	0			30			60			90			120
11		11				55			88			121	
12	0				48			84			120		

1. 3×11 **2.** 7×12 **3.** 4×8 **4.** 11×2 **5.** 8×9 **6.** 2×12

7. $\begin{array}{r} 6 \\ \times\,7 \\ \hline \end{array}$ **8.** $\begin{array}{r} 10 \\ \times\,4 \\ \hline \end{array}$ **9.** $\begin{array}{r} 12 \\ \times\,5 \\ \hline \end{array}$ **10.** $\begin{array}{r} 11 \\ \times\,9 \\ \hline \end{array}$ **11.** $\begin{array}{r} 12 \\ \times\,12 \\ \hline \end{array}$ **12.** $\begin{array}{r} 11 \\ \times\,11 \\ \hline \end{array}$

13. Frances bought 3 bags of oranges with 8 oranges in each bag. She bought 2 more bags with 3 oranges in each. How many oranges did Frances buy in all?

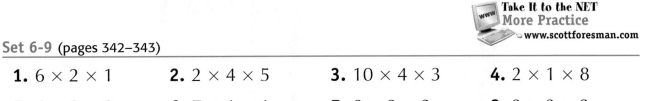
Take It to the NET
More Practice
www.scottforesman.com

Set 6-9 (pages 342–343)

1. $6 \times 2 \times 1$ **2.** $2 \times 4 \times 5$ **3.** $10 \times 4 \times 3$ **4.** $2 \times 1 \times 8$

5. $6 \times 0 \times 9$ **6.** $7 \times 1 \times 1$ **7.** $8 \times 3 \times 2$ **8.** $3 \times 3 \times 3$

9. $4 \times 6 \times 1$ **10.** $5 \times 5 \times 2$ **11.** $6 \times 2 \times 2$ **12.** $2 \times 4 \times 4$

13. $1 \times 1 \times 1$ **14.** $9 \times 9 \times 0$ **15.** $6 \times 3 \times 2$ **16.** $3 \times 2 \times 5$

17. Write three ways to find $4 \times 2 \times 5$. Find the product.

Set 6-10 (pages 344–345)

Write a rule for each table. Complete the tables.

1.

In	4	6	7	8	9
Out	20		35		45

2.

In	2	3	4	5	6
Out	20	30	40		

3.

In	3	4	5	6	7
Out	9	12	15		

4.

In	5	6	7	8	9
Out	20	24	28		

5. Kyle earned 12 bonus points for completing three extra problems. If each extra problem is worth the same number of bonus points, how many bonus points would Kyle earn for completing only one extra problem?

Set 6-11 (pages 346–347)

Draw a picture to show the main idea. Then choose an operation and solve the problem.

1. Jan earns $7 an hour at her job. If she works for 8 hours, how much money will she earn?

2. During swimming practice, Carol swam 10 laps and Terry swam 7 laps. It took Carol 3 minutes to swim each lap. How many more laps did Carol swim than Terry?

3. Ron spends 4 hours each day delivering newspapers. He delivers newspapers 6 days a week. How many hours a week does Ron spend delivering newspapers?

4. Andrea planted 12 flowers in pots and 8 flowers in baskets. She planted 4 times as many daisies as pansies. How many flowers did Andrea plant altogether?

Division Concepts and Facts

DIAGNOSING READINESS

A Vocabulary

(Grade 2 and pages 260, 262)

Choose the best term from the box below.

1. An __?__ shows objects arranged in equal rows.

2. The pattern 2, 4, 6, 8 shows __?__ by 2s.

3. In 2 × 3 = 6, the 2 and 3 are __?__.

Vocabulary

- **array** *(p. 262)*
- **factors** *(p. 260)*
- **products** *(p. 260)*
- **skip counting** *(Grade 2)*

B Subtraction

(Grade 2 and pages 148–149)

4. 16 − 8   5. 9 − 3   6. 32 − 4

7. 18 − 9   8. 28 − 7   9. 42 − 3

10. 25 − 5   11. 36 − 9   12. 24 − 6

13. 14 − 7   14. 12 − 6   15. 42 − 7

16. 15 − 8   17. 11 − 8   18. 17 − 9

19. Kyle had 24 toy airplanes. He sold 18 of them at a garage sale. Then he bought 8 new ones. How many toy airplanes does he have now?

C Meanings of Multiplication

(pages 260–265)

Write a multiplication sentence for each addition sentence or array.

20. 5 + 5 + 5 + 5 = 20

21. 4 + 4 + 4 + 4 + 4 + 4 = 24

22.

23.

D Multiplication Facts

(pages 276–335)

24. 3×4	**25.** 4×6	**26.** 5×5
27. 7×3	**28.** 6×8	**29.** 6×9
30. 8×3	**31.** 5×2	**32.** 4×4
33. 2×3	**34.** 6×7	**35.** 8×8
36. 9×8	**37.** 5×4	**38.** 7×9

39. Nancy bought 4 boxes of crackers with 8 crackers in each box. How many crackers did she buy?

369

Key Idea
You can think of division as sharing equally.

Vocabulary
• division

Materials
• counters

Think It Through
I can **use objects** or **draw pictures** to show the main idea.

Division as Sharing

LEARN

✓ **WARM UP**
1. 2×6 2. 3×9
3. 5×7 4. 6×4
5. 8×2 6. 4×5

How many are in each group?

Ann, John, and Toni have 12 toy cars to share equally. How many will each get?

To decide, think of putting the 12 cars into 3 equal groups. One car at a time is put into each group. When all the cars are grouped, there will be 4 in each group.

You can also use **division** to find the number in each group. The division number sentence below describes the problem.

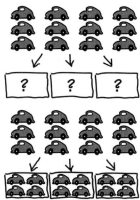

Total number	Number of equal groups	Number in each group

$$12 \div 3 = 4$$ Twelve divided by 3 equals 4.

Ann, John, and Toni each get 4 cars.

Activity

Copy the chart below. Use counters or draw pictures to help you complete it.

	Total Number of Counters	Number of Equal Groups	Number in Each Group	Number Sentence
a.	12	2	___ counters	$12 \div 2 =$ ☐
b.	18	3	___ counters	$18 \div 3 =$ ☐
c.	15	5	___ counters	$15 \div 5 =$ ☐
d.	10	2	___ counters	$10 \div 2 =$ ☐
e.	8	2	___ counters	$8 \div 2 =$ ☐

f. Reasoning Can you separate 12 counters into 5 equal groups with none left over? Explain.

Use counters or draw a picture to solve.

1. 16 crayons
2 boxes
How many crayons in each box?

2. 6 soaps
3 dishes
How many soaps in each dish?

3. Number Sense Brian has 24 apples. He wants to put the same number of apples in each of 3 boxes. He puts 10 apples in one box. Does this make sense? Explain.

PRACTICE

For more practice, see Set 7-1 on p. 422.

A Skills and Understanding

Use counters or draw a picture to solve.

4. 9 flowers
3 vases
How many flowers in each vase?

5. 10 goldfish
2 bowls
How many goldfish in each bowl?

6. Number Sense Linda has 24 ribbons to put into equal groups. She says that 3 equal groups will have more in each group than 4 equal groups. Does this make sense? Explain.

B Reasoning and Problem Solving

7. Draw a picture of counters to show 16 ÷ 2. Write the number sentence.

8. **Writing in Math** Helen has 8 markers, but 2 of them do not write. She and Jeff will share the rest equally. Explain how to find the number each person gets. Then give the answer.

Mixed Review and Test Prep

Take It to the NET
Test Prep
www.scottforesman.com

9. A table has the rule *Multiply by 3*. If the In number is 6, what is the Out number?

10. Cal has 428 stamps in his collection. Joan has 373 stamps. How many more stamps does Cal have?

11. Laura has read 10 pages every day for 6 days. How many pages has she read?

A. 6 **B.** 10 **C.** 16 **D.** 60

 All text pages available online and on CD-ROM.

Key Idea
You can think of division as repeated subtraction.

Materials
• counters

Think It Through
I can **use objects** or **draw pictures** to show the main idea.

Division as Repeated Subtraction

LEARN

How many equal groups?

Marty has 12 plants to put into clay pots. She wants to put 2 plants in each pot. How many clay pots does she need?

You can use repeated subtraction to find how many groups of 2 are in 12.

Start with 12 plants and subtract 2 at a time until there are no plants left. Then count the subtractions.

$12 - 2 = 10$
$10 - 2 = 8$
$8 - 2 = 6$
$6 - 2 = 4$
$4 - 2 = 2$
$2 - 2 = 0$

I can subtract 2 six times. Then there are zero plants left.

You can also use division to solve the problem.

$12 ÷ 2 = 6$ Twelve divided by 2 equals 6.

Marty needs 6 clay pots.

Activity

Use counters or draw pictures to find the number of groups for each problem. Then complete the division sentence.

	Total Number of Items	Number in Each Group	Number of Groups	Division Number Sentence
a.	12 flowers	3 in each vase	___ vases	12 ÷ 3 = ___
b.	20 dolls	5 on each shelf	___ shelves	20 ÷ 5 = ___
c.	10 marbles	2 in each bag	___ bags	10 ÷ 2 = ___
d.	15 pens	5 in each cup	___ cups	15 ÷ 5 = ___
e.	16 beads	4 in each bag	___ bags	16 ÷ 4 = ___

Use counters or draw a picture to solve.

1. 8 stamps
2 stamps on each envelope
How many envelopes?

2. 18 buttons
3 buttons on each pocket
How many pockets?

3. Number Sense Show how you can use repeated subtraction to find how many groups of 5 are in 15. Then write the division sentence for the problem.

PRACTICE *For more practice, see Set 7-2 on p. 422.*

A Skills and Understanding

Use counters or draw a picture to solve.

4. 12 shoes
2 shoes in each pair
How many pairs?

5. 18 eggs
6 eggs in each pan
How many pans?

6. 10 pens
5 pens in each box
How many boxes?

7. Number Sense Pam has 18 pens. Will she need more cases if she puts 2 in each case or 3 in each case?

B Reasoning and Problem Solving

The chart shows how many people played checkers each day. There were 2 people playing each game. How many games were played on

8. Monday?　　**9.** Wednesday?　　**10.** Friday?

11. How many games were played in all?

12. Joy has $14. She will buy sunglasses for $8 and spend the rest on sand toys for $2 each. How many sand toys can she buy?

13. **Writing in Math** Explain how you can use repeated subtraction to find $9 \div 3$. Give the answer.

Day	People
Monday	18
Tuesday	14
Wednesday	20
Thursday	16
Friday	8

Mixed Review and Test Prep

Take It to the NET
Test Prep
www.scottforesman.com

14. Draw 6 dots separated into 2 equal groups. How many are in each group?

15. What is the value of the 6 in 6,253?

A. 60　　**B.** 600　　**C.** 6,000　　**D.** 6

Materials
• counters

Think It Through
I can **divide** to find the number in each group or the number of equal groups.

Writing Division Stories

LEARN

✓ **WARM UP**

1. 3×8 2. 4×3
3. 7×6 4. 5×5
5. 2×9 6. 8×4

What is the main idea of a division story?

Mr. Chan asked his third-grade students to write division stories for the number sentence $18 \div 3 = n$. Mona and Ali decided to write stories about the goldfish in their classroom.

Mona's Story	Ali's Story
I have 3 fish bowls for 18 goldfish. If I want the same number of goldfish in each bowl, how many can I put in each?	I have 18 goldfish and want to put 3 in each fish bowl. How many fish bowls will I need?

✓ **Talk About It**

1. Which picture below shows the main idea in Mona's story? Explain.

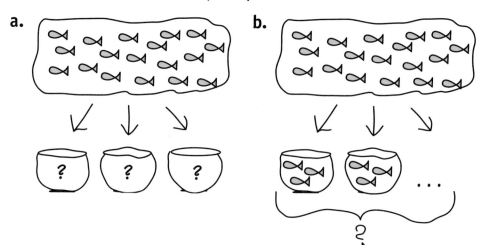

a.

b.

2. Draw a picture to find the answer for Mona's story. Then draw a picture to find the answer for Ali's story.

3. **Number Sense** How are Mona and Ali's stories alike? How are they different?

For 3–6, use the problem below and the picture at the right.

There are 6 more cartons of chocolate milk than white milk in the crate. How many cartons of chocolate milk are there?

3. Make a prediction for the number of cartons of chocolate milk.

4. **Writing in Math** Explain how you can verify your prediction.

5. Do you need to revise your first prediction? If so, make a second prediction.

6. What is the answer to the problem?

For 7–11, use the problem below and the table at the right.

At the arcade, Caryn earned 17 tickets. She used all of her tickets to get three prizes. What three prizes did Caryn get?

7. Make a prediction for the three prizes Caryn got.

8. Verify your prediction.

9. Do you need to revise your first prediction? If so, make a second prediction.

10. What is the answer to the problem?

11. **Writing in Math** Could Caryn's three prizes have been the ball, the whistle, and the ring? Explain.

Arcade Prizes

Prize	Number of Tickets
Airplane	8
Ball	5
Whistle	3
Ring	6

Problem-Solving Strategy

Key Idea
The strategy Try, Check, and Revise can help you solve problems.

Think It Through
I may need to **make several predictions** about the scores before I find the right ones.

Try, Check, and Revise

LEARN

How can you try, check, and revise to solve a problem?

Target Game Naomi played the target game at the fair. She scored exactly 20 points with 3 darts. Where might her darts have landed?

Read and Understand

What do you know?	Three darts hit the target. Twenty points were scored.
What are you trying to find?	Find what numbers the darts landed on.

Plan and Solve

What strategy will you use?   Strategy: **Try, Check, and Revise**

Steps for Using Try, Check, and Revise

Step 1 Make a reasonable first try.
Step 2 Check using data given in the problem.
Step 3 Revise. Use your first try to make a reasonable second try. Check.
Step 4 Continue trying and checking until you get the answer.

Try: 8 + 6 + 4 = 18
Check: Too low, so I need 2 more.

Revise: 10 + 6 + 4 = 20
Check: This is it!

Answer: Naomi's darts could have landed on 10, 6, and 4.

Look Back and Check

Is your answer reasonable?   Yes, 3 numbers were added and the sum is 20.

✓ **Talk About It**

1. Why was one number increased for the second try?

2. Number Sense Could all three numbers be the same? Explain.

For another example, see Set 7-4 on p. 419.

Try, check, and revise to solve each problem. Write each answer in a sentence.

1. Use the target on page 380. Find another way Naomi could score 20 points using three darts.

2. Anna needs 26 juice boxes. She can buy packs of 5, 6, or 8 juice boxes. What kinds of packs should she buy to have exactly 26 boxes?

PRACTICE

For another example, see Set 7-4 on p. 422.

Solve. Write each answer in a sentence.

3. Eddie can make 4-wheel or 6-wheel trucks with his building set. He has 14 wheels in all. How many of each kind of truck can he make?

4. All of Abby's 8 sports cards are either hockey cards or football cards. She has 4 more hockey cards than football cards. How many football cards does Abby have?

5. Emma can choose chocolate or vanilla ice cream. For the topping, she can choose fudge, butterscotch, or strawberries. How many kinds of sundaes can Emma choose from?

6. Chad had 12 football cards and 8 baseball cards. He bought 3 more packs of baseball cards with 4 cards in each pack. How many baseball cards does Chad have in all?

7. Four people are in line. Amy is behind Kay. Rob is first. If Ben is last, who is third?

8. In one circus act, each clown wears red or blue. Twice as many clowns wear blue as red. If 33 clowns are in the act, how many wear blue? How many wear red?

9. <u>Writing in Math</u> Use the target on page 380. Could Naomi get a score of 11 using 3 darts? Explain why or why not.

STRATEGIES

- **Show What You Know**
  Draw a Picture
  Make an Organized List
  Make a Table
  Make a Graph
  Act It Out or Use Objects
- **Look for a Pattern**
- **Try, Check, and Revise**
- **Write a Number Sentence**
- **Use Logical Reasoning**
- **Solve a Simpler Problem**
- **Work Backward**

All text pages available online and on CD-ROM.

Do You Know How?

Do You Understand?

Division as Sharing (7-1)

Use counters or draw a picture to solve.

1. 6 orange slices
3 plates
How many slices on each plate?

A In Exercise 1, does the answer tell the number of equal groups or the number in each group?

Division as Repeated Subtraction (7-2)

Use counters or draw a picture to solve.

2. 10 pennies
2 pennies in each pocket
How many pockets?

B In Exercise 2, how do you know how many equal groups of pennies to make?

Writing Division Stories (7-3)

Write a division story for each. Use counters or draw a picture to solve.

3. 15 ÷ 5   **4.** 24 ÷ 6

C Explain how each story you wrote shows division.

Problem-Solving Strategy: Try, Check, and Revise (7-4)

Try, check, and revise to solve the problem. Write the answer in a sentence.

5. Mathew can buy muffins in packages of 5, 8, or 12. He needs 18 muffins. What kinds of packages should he buy to have exactly 18 muffins?

D If Mathew bought one package of each kind would he have more than he needs or fewer than he needs?

E Would three 12-muffin packages be a reasonable first try at solving this problem? Explain.

MULTIPLE CHOICE

1. 6 strawberries
2 bowls
How many strawberries in each bowl?

A. 6   **B.** 3   **C.** 2   **D.** 1

2. 12 eggs
4 eggs in each bowl
How many bowls? (7-2)

A. 6   **B.** 4   **C.** 3   **D.** 2

FREE RESPONSE

Use counters or draw a picture to solve. (7-1, 7-2)

3. 14 crayons
2 students
How many crayons for each student?

4. 15 cherries
5 bowls
How many cherries in each bowl?

5. 20 stickers
4 on each page
How many pages?

6. 9 apples,
3 apples in each bag
How many bags?

Write a division story for each. Use counters or draw a picture to solve. (7-3)

7. 24 ÷ 8   **8.** 21 ÷ 3   **9.** 16 ÷ 8

Try, check, and revise to solve the problem. Write the answer in a sentence. (7-4)

10. In basketball, a basket can be worth 1, 2, or 3 points. Yoko made 3 baskets and scored a total of 9 points. What kind of baskets did she make?

Writing in Math

11. Explain two ways you could separate 12 counters into equal groups. (7-3)

Algebra

Key Idea
Fact families show how multiplication and division are connected.

Vocabulary
- array (p. 262)
- fact family (p. 70)
- factor (p. 260)
- product (p. 260)
- dividend
- divisor
- quotient

Think It Through
I can use **what I know** about multiplication to understand division.

Relating Multiplication and Division

LEARN

How does an array show division?

In 1818, there were only 20 stars on the United States flag.

There were 4 equal rows of stars.

How many stars were in each row?

The **array** shows:

Multiplication	*Division*
4 rows of **5** stars = 20 stars	20 stars in 4 equal rows = **5** stars in each row
$4 \times 5 = 20$	$20 \div 4 = 5$
	So, there were 5 stars in each row.

How can a fact family help you divide?

A **fact family** shows how multiplication and division are related.

Fact family for 4, 5, and 20:

$$4 \times 5 = 20 \qquad 20 \div 4 = 5$$
$$5 \times 4 = 20 \qquad 20 \div 5 = 4$$

factor × factor = product   dividend ÷ divisor = quotient

✓ Talk About It

1. Skip count by 5s to find 4 × 5. Then start at 20 and skip count by 5s backward to 0. The number of times you count back is the quotient for 20 ÷ 5.

2. How can you use the fact 3 × 6 = 18 to find 18 ÷ 3?

3. **Number Sense** Is 3 × 5 = 15 part of the fact family for 3, 4, and 12? Explain.

Copy and complete. Use counters or draw a picture to help.

1. 5 × ▢ = 30
30 ÷ 5 = ▢

2. 2 × ▢ = 18
18 ÷ 2 = ▢

3. 5 × ▢ = 35
35 ÷ 5 = ▢

4. Number Sense What multiplication fact can help you find 40 ÷ 8?

PRACTICE

For more practice, see Set 7-5 on p. 423.

A Skills and Understanding

Copy and complete. Use counters or draw a picture to help.

5. 2 × ▢ = 8
8 ÷ 2 = ▢

6. 5 × ▢ = 10
10 ÷ 5 = ▢

7. 2 × ▢ = 16
16 ÷ 2 = ▢

8. 3 × ▢ = 12
12 ÷ 3 = ▢

9. 5 × ▢ = 25
25 ÷ 5 = ▢

10. 6 × ▢ = 12
12 ÷ 6 = ▢

11. Number Sense Write the fact family for 2, 7, and 14.

B Reasoning and Problem Solving

12. Al had $15 to spend on making a school flag. He spent $7.45 on fabric and $3.55 for thread. How much money did he have left?

13. There are 15 students in Maria's class. They need to make teams of 5 to play basketball. How many teams can they make?

14. Writing in Math Draw an array. Write a fact family with 2 multiplication and 2 division sentences to go with your array.

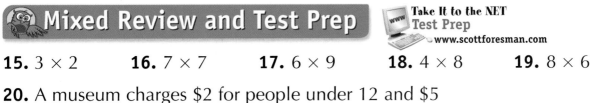

Mixed Review and Test Prep

Take It to the NET
Test Prep
www.scottforesman.com

15. 3 × 2

16. 7 × 7

17. 6 × 9

18. 4 × 8

19. 8 × 6

20. A museum charges $2 for people under 12 and $5 for people over 12. A group of 6 people paid a total of $18. How many of the people were under 12?

A. 6

B. 5

C. 4

D. 3

All text pages available online and on CD-ROM.

Think It Through
Since you want to **share equally,** you can divide.

Dividing with 2 and 5

LEARN

How can you use multiplication to divide by 2 and 5?

Example A

Betsy and Jack are sharing a pizza that is cut into 6 pieces. Each will get the same number of pieces. How many pieces will each get?

Find 6 ÷ 2.

What You **Think**	What You **Write**
2 times what number equals 6? 2 × **3** = 6	6 ÷ 2 = **3** So, Betsy and Jack will each get 3 pieces.

Example B

Lars must read 40 pages of his book in 5 days. How many pages should he read each day?

Find 40 ÷ 5.

What You **Think**	What You **Write**
5 times what number equals 40? 5 × **8** = 40	40 ÷ 5 = **8** He should read 8 pages each day.

✔ **Talk About It**

1. What multiplication fact can help you find 12 ÷ 2?

2. **Reasoning** To find 18 ÷ 2, Jay thinks: "18 times what number equals 2." Do you agree? Explain.

3. How could you skip count backward by 5s to find 40 ÷ 5?

**Take It to the NET
More Examples**
www.scottforesman.com

386

For another example, see Set 7-6 on p. 419.

1. 10 ÷ 2   **2.** 6 ÷ 2   **3.** 25 ÷ 5   **4.** 40 ÷ 5   **5.** 16 ÷ 2

6. Number Sense How can you use multiplication to help you find 14 divided by 2?

PRACTICE

For more practice, see Set 7-6 on p. 423.

A Skills and Understanding

7. 18 ÷ 2   **8.** 4 ÷ 2   **9.** 35 ÷ 5   **10.** 45 ÷ 5   **11.** 12 ÷ 2

12. 15 ÷ 5   **13.** 14 ÷ 2   **14.** 20 ÷ 5   **15.** 8 ÷ 2   **16.** 10 ÷ 5

17. Find 30 divided by 5.   **18.** Divide 20 by 2.   **19.** Divide 50 by 5.

20. Number Sense Ryan says, "I can solve 8 ÷ 2 by using the fact 2 × 8 = 16." Do you agree or disagree? Explain.

B Reasoning and Problem Solving

21. Rex has 30 tiles. He wants to make an array with 5 tiles in each row. How many rows will he have?

22. Alice wants to make one array with 2 rows of 8 tiles and another array with 3 rows of 5 tiles. How many tiles does she need all together?

23. Don has 15 pennies and 3 dimes. Olivia has the same amount of money, but she has only nickels. How many nickels does Olivia have?

24. **Writing in Math** Write a word problem that uses one of the division facts below. Then solve your problem.

20 ÷ 5 = ▮   16 ÷ 2 = ▮

Mixed Review and Test Prep

Take It to the NET
Test Prep
www.scottforesman.com

25. 4 × 8   **26.** 4 × 7   **27.** 3 × 9   **28.** 6 × 3   **29.** 4 × 9

30. 7 × 8   **31.** 5 × 9   **32.** 4 × 6   **33.** 8 × 8   **34.** 9 × 6

35. Which fact is not in the same family of facts as 2 × 9 = 18?

A. 9 × 2 = 18   **C.** 18 ÷ 2 = 9

B. 18 ÷ 9 = 2   **D.** 3 × 6 = 18

36. Jeff bought 3 packs of stickers with 5 stickers in each pack. He gave 4 stickers to Julie. How many stickers did he have left?

A. 11   **C.** 15

B. 19   **D.** 21

All text pages available online and on CD-ROM.

Key Idea
Think about multiplication to help you divide with 3 and 4.

Think It Through
I should divide because I need to **separate the cost into equal groups.**

Dividing with 3 and 4

LEARN

How do you divide by 3 and 4?

Example A	Example B
Three students will buy a pack of erasers for 24 cents at the school store and share the cost. How much should each pay?	At the school store a pack of colored pencils costs 36 cents. Four students will share the cost. How much should each pay?
Find $24 \div 3$.	Find $36 \div 4$.
What You **Think**	What You **Think**
3 times what number equals 24?	4 times what number equals 36?
$3 \times \mathbf{8} = 24$	$4 \times \mathbf{9} = 36$
What You **Write**	What You **Write**
$24 \div 3 = 8$ Each should pay 8 cents.	$36 \div 4 = \mathbf{9}$ Each should pay 9 cents.

There are two ways to write a division problem.

$$36 \div 4 = 9$$
dividend   divisor   quotient

or

$9 \leftarrow$ quotient
divisor $\rightarrow 4\overline{)36} \leftarrow$ dividend

✔ **Talk About It**

1. How does the fact $3 \times 9 = 27$ help you find $27 \div 3$?

2. What multiplication fact can help you find $12 \div 4$?

Take It to the NET
More Examples
www.scottforesman.com

1. 9 ÷ 3   **2.** 12 ÷ 4   **3.** 18 ÷ 3   **4.** 4)‾28   **5.** 3)‾6

6. Number Sense How can you tell without dividing that 24 ÷ 3 is greater than 24 ÷ 4?

PRACTICE

For more practice, see Set 7-7 on p. 423.

Ⓐ Skills and Understanding

7. 12 ÷ 3   **8.** 15 ÷ 3   **9.** 16 ÷ 4   **10.** 21 ÷ 3   **11.** 30 ÷ 3

12. 36 ÷ 4   **13.** 8 ÷ 4   **14.** 40 ÷ 4   **15.** 24 ÷ 3   **16.** 15 ÷ 5

17. 3)‾27   **18.** 2)‾18   **19.** 4)‾24   **20.** 5)‾35   **21.** 4)‾20

22. Divide 32 by 4.   **23.** Divide 12 by 2.   **24.** Find 25 divided by 5.

25. Number Sense Can you use 6 × 6 = 36 to help you find 36 ÷ 4? Explain.

Ⓑ Reasoning and Problem Solving

For 26 and 27, use the picture of stamps.

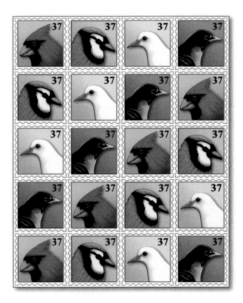

26. Representations Caitlyn bought a sheet of bird stamps. Draw a picture to show another way the stamps could be in equal rows.

27. Suppose Caitlyn gave 6 stamps to her brother. How many stamps would she have left?

28. Kelly and 3 friends want to share a package of 12 pencils equally. How many pencils will each person get?

29. **Writing in Math** Write a word problem that can be solved by finding 21 ÷ 3. Then solve it.

🦉 Mixed Review and Test Prep

Take It to the NET
Test Prep
www.scottforesman.com

30. 45 ÷ 5   **31.** 16 ÷ 2   **32.** 30 ÷ 5   **33.** 4 ÷ 2   **34.** 10 ÷ 5

35. Which number is equal to 40 tens?

    A. 4   **B.** 40   **C.** 400   **D.** 4,000

Dividing with 6 and 7

Think It Through
I can **choose division** when I separate into equal rows or groups.

✔ **WARM UP**
1. 6 × 8   2. 7 × 9
3. 7 × 6   4. 6 × 6
5. 4 × 7   6. 7 × 2

LEARN

What multiplication fact can you use?

Example A	Example B
Julia made 48 squares for a quilt. She wants to put the squares in 6 equal rows. How many squares should be in each row?	Tucker puts 7 squares in each row of a quilt. He has 42 squares in all. How many rows of squares should he make?
Find 48 ÷ 6.	Find 42 ÷ 7.
What You Think	**What You Think**
6 times what number equals 48?	7 times what number equals 42?
$6 \times \mathbf{8} = 48$	$7 \times \mathbf{6} = 42$
What You Write	**What You Write**
$48 \div 6 = 8$ or $6\overline{)48}$ with 8 on top	$42 \div 7 = 6$ or $7\overline{)42}$ with 6 on top
Julia needs 8 squares in each row.	Tucker should make 6 rows of squares.

✔ **Talk About It**

1. What multiplication fact can help you find 24 ÷ 6?

2. How can you use 7 × 9 = 63 to find 63 ÷ 7?

3. Write the fact family for 6, 7, and 42.

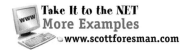

Take It to the NET
www **More Examples**
www.scottforesman.com

390

1. 12 ÷ 6   **2.** 35 ÷ 7   **3.** 7)$\overline{56}$ **4.** 6)$\overline{36}$

5. Number Sense How can you tell without dividing that 42 ÷ 6 is greater than 42 ÷ 7? Explain.

PRACTICE

For more practice, see Set 7-8 on p. 424.

Ⓐ Skills and Understanding

6. 54 ÷ 6   **7.** 49 ÷ 7   **8.** 18 ÷ 6   **9.** 21 ÷ 7   **10.** 24 ÷ 6

11. 20 ÷ 5   **12.** 63 ÷ 7   **13.** 30 ÷ 6   **14.** 28 ÷ 7   **15.** 16 ÷ 4

16. 2)$\overline{18}$ **17.** 6)$\overline{42}$ **18.** 7)$\overline{42}$ **19.** 6)$\overline{54}$ **20.** 6)$\overline{48}$

21. Divide 28 by 4.   **22.** Find 9 divided by 3.   **23.** Divide 32 by 4.

24. Number Sense What is the fact family that shows there are 3 groups of 7 in 21?

Ⓑ Reasoning and Problem Solving

25. Jan's wall hanging has 35 quilt squares in 7 equal rows. How many squares are in each row?

26. Carol paid 5 cents for each day her library book was late. If she paid 40 cents, how many days late was the book?

27. Three pizzas were cut into 8 slices each. Six friends ate all of the pizza, and each person had the same number of slices. How many slices did each person have?

28. Bob wants to buy a remote control truck for $47 and 3 small cars for $7 each. What will the total cost be?

29. **Writing in Math** Write a division story for 49 ÷ 7.

🦉 Mixed Review and Test Prep

Take It to the NET
Test Prep
www.scottforesman.com

30. 24 ÷ 3   **31.** 20 ÷ 4   **32.** 27 ÷ 3   **33.** 16 ÷ 2   **34.** 15 ÷ 5

35. Hannah bought ice cream for $1.25 and paid with a $5 bill. How much change did she get?

   A. $0.75   **B.** $3.75   **C.** $2.75   **D.** $4.75

All text pages available online and on CD-ROM.

Dividing with 8 and 9

LEARN

WARM UP

1. 8×5 2. 4×9
3. 9×9 4. 8×3
5. 8×9 6. 8×8

How can you divide by 8 and 9?

Think It Through
I can think about **fact families** to find division facts.

Example A

The students at Valley School made 72 posters of animals. They want to put them on the wall of the library in 8 equal rows. How many posters should be in each row?

Find $72 \div 8$.

What You **Think**	What You **Write**
8 times what number equals 72? $8 \times \mathbf{9} = 72$	$72 \div 8 = 9$ or $8 \overline{)72}$ with quotient 9 They should put 9 posters in each row.

Example B

Ms. Emerson's third grade class has 27 students. They were divided into groups of 9 students to work on posters. How many groups of students were there?

Find $27 \div 9$.

What You **Think**	What You **Write**
9 times what number equals 27? $9 \times \mathbf{3} = 27$	$27 \div 9 = \mathbf{3}$ or $9 \overline{)27}$ with quotient 3 There were 3 groups of students.

✔ **Talk About It**

1. Explain why it makes sense to divide to find the number of posters in each row.

Take It to the NET
www More Examples
www.scottforesman.com

1. 48 ÷ 8　　**2.** 27 ÷ 9　　**3.** 9)̄81　　**4.** 8)̄56　　**5.** 8)̄16

6. Number Sense What multiplication fact could you use to help find 8)̄32?

PRACTICE

For more practice, see Set 7-9 on p. 424.

Ⓐ Skills and Understanding

7. 45 ÷ 5　　**8.** 54 ÷ 9　　**9.** 36 ÷ 9　　**10.** 21 ÷ 7　　**11.** 32 ÷ 8

12. 72 ÷ 9　　**13.** 42 ÷ 6　　**14.** 64 ÷ 8　　**15.** 30 ÷ 5　　**16.** 24 ÷ 4

17. 7)̄14　　**18.** 8)̄24　　**19.** 7)̄49　　**20.** 9)̄63　　**21.** 8)̄40

22. 7)̄28　　**23.** 9)̄18　　**24.** 8)̄72　　**25.** 6)̄36　　**26.** 5)̄35

27. Divide 12 by 6.　　**28.** Divide 27 by 3.　　**29.** How many 6s in 48?

30. Number Sense What division sentence shows that there are 8 groups of 7 in 56?

Ⓑ Reasoning and Problem Solving

31. Mark had 36 balloons. He gave an equal number to each of 9 friends. How many balloons did each get?

32. A stop sign has 8 sides. How many sides do 6 stop signs have?

33. **Writing in Math** On Tuesday, Sam baked 24 cookies. On Wednesday, he baked 48 more. If he puts 8 cookies in each bag, how many bags can he fill? Explain how you found your answer.

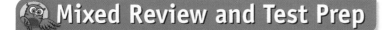

🦉 Mixed Review and Test Prep

Take It to the NET
Test Prep
www.scottforesman.com

34. 48 ÷ 6　　**35.** 35 ÷ 7　　**36.** 54 ÷ 6　　**37.** 56 ÷ 7　　**38.** 28 ÷ 4

39. James bought 32 bagels and 19 donuts. He gave 16 bagels to his teacher. How many bagels did James have left?

A. 51　　　　**B.** 35　　　　**C.** 16　　　　**D.** 3

Do You Know How?	Do You Understand?

Relating Multiplication and Division (7-5)

Copy and complete. Use counters or draw a picture to help.

1. $4 \times \blacksquare = 8$
$8 \div 4 = \blacksquare$

2. $3 \times \blacksquare = 15$
$15 \div 3 = \blacksquare$

Ⓐ Explain how an array could show the facts in Exercise 1.

Ⓑ Write the fact family for Exercise 2.

Dividing with 2 and 5 (7-6)

3. $45 \div 5$

4. $10 \div 2$

5. $30 \div 5$

6. $25 \div 5$

Ⓒ What multiplication fact can you use to help solve Exercise 3?

Dividing with 3 and 4 (7-7)

7. $16 \div 4$

8. $24 \div 4$

9. $4\overline{)36}$

10. $3\overline{)21}$

Ⓓ How many facts are in the fact family for Exercise 7? Explain.

Dividing with 6 and 7 (7-8)

11. $36 \div 6$

12. $14 \div 7$

13. $7\overline{)63}$

14. $6\overline{)18}$

15. There are 56 days until Theresa's birthday. How many weeks is that?

Ⓔ Explain how multiplication can help you solve Exercise 14.

Ⓕ In Exercise 15, what hidden question do you need to answer?

Dividing with 8 and 9 (7-9)

16. $72 \div 8$

17. $32 \div 8$

18. $9\overline{)54}$

19. $8\overline{)64}$

20. $8\overline{)16}$

21. $9\overline{)63}$

Ⓖ What number has 4 groups of 9?

Ⓗ Choose two facts from Exercises 16–21 and explain how you remember them.

MULTIPLE CHOICE

1. Jackie has 12 eggs. She puts an equal number of eggs in 2 bowls. How many eggs are in each bowl? (7-6)

A. 14 **B.** 10 **C.** 8 **D.** 6

2. Lee made 3 sandwiches. She cut each sandwich into 4 pieces. She put an equal number of pieces in 6 bags. How many pieces are in each bag? (7-8)

A. 2 **B.** 5 **C.** 12 **D.** 13

FREE RESPONSE

Copy and complete. Use counters or draw a picture to help. (7-5)

3. $3 \times \blacksquare = 21$
$21 \div 3 = \blacksquare$

4. $4 \times \blacksquare = 16$
$16 \div 4 = \blacksquare$

5. $2 \times \blacksquare = 16$
$16 \div 2 = \blacksquare$

Divide. (7-6, 7-7, 7-8, 7-9)

6. $81 \div 9$ **7.** $32 \div 4$ **8.** $10 \div 5$ **9.** $49 \div 7$ **10.** $15 \div 3$

11. $28 \div 7$ **12.** $54 \div 9$ **13.** $36 \div 4$ **14.** $9 \div 3$ **15.** $4 \div 2$

16. $6\overline{)48}$ **17.** $4\overline{)12}$ **18.** $6\overline{)36}$ **19.** $3\overline{)27}$ **20.** $5\overline{)20}$

21. Ms. Chang bought 4 packs of stickers with 6 stickers in each pack. She wants to give an equal number of stickers to 8 students. How many stickers will each student get? (7-9)

22. Jackie, Jaycee, and Eric want to buy a CD for $9. They will share the cost equally. How much should each person pay? (7-7)

Think It Through
I need to **look back and check** my answer.

Writing in Math

23. Explain how you could use a multiplication fact to help you find $63 \div 7$. (7-8)

24. Draw a picture to show two ways you could arrange 14 counters into equal groups. Write a division sentence under each drawing. (7-8)

Dividing with 0 and 1

✓ **WARM UP**
1. 0×3 2. 8×1
3. 2×0 4. 1×9

LEARN

What are the division rules for 0 and 1?

Example A

	What You **Think**	What You **Write**
Divide a number by 1. $4 \div 1 = \blacksquare$	1 times what number = 4? $1 \times 4 = 4$ So, $4 \div 1 = 4$.	$4 \div 1 = 4$ or $1\overline{)4}$ with quotient 4

Rule: When any number is divided by 1, the quotient is that number.

Example B

	What You Think	What You Write
Divide a number by itself. $7 \div 7 = \blacksquare$	7 times what number = 7? $7 \times 1 = 7$ So, $7 \div 7 = 1$.	$7 \div 7 = 1$ or $7\overline{)7}$ with quotient 1

Rule: When any number (except 0) is divided by itself, the quotient is 1.

Example C

	What You Think	What You Write
Divide zero by a number. $0 \div 2 = \blacksquare$	2 times what number = 0? $2 \times 0 = 0$ So, $0 \div 2 = 0$.	$0 \div 2 = 0$ or $2\overline{)0}$ with quotient 0

Rule: When zero is divided by a number (except 0) the quotient is 0.

Example D

	What You Think	What You Write
Divide a number by zero. $3 \div 0 = \blacksquare$	0 times what number = 3? There is no number that works, so, $3 \div 0$ cannot be done.	$3 \div 0$ cannot be done.

Rule: You cannot divide a number by 0.

✔ **Talk About It**

1. How can you tell without dividing that $427 \div 1 = 427$?

1. $0 \div 6$ **2.** $0 \div 1$ **3.** $4 \div 4$ **4.** $1\overline{)9}$ **5.** $2\overline{)2}$

6. Number Sense Explain how you would use the rules in this lesson to find $0 \div 999$ and $987 \div 987$.

PRACTICE

For more practice, see Set 7-10 on p. 424.

Ⓐ Skills and Understanding

7. $5 \div 1$ **8.** $8 \div 8$ **9.** $6 \div 6$ **10.** $0 \div 7$ **11.** $0 \div 3$

12. $5 \div 5$ **13.** $0 \div 5$ **14.** $0 \div 4$ **15.** $6 \div 1$ **16.** $8 \div 1$

17. $2\overline{)18}$ **18.** $1\overline{)7}$ **19.** $7\overline{)42}$ **20.** $9\overline{)9}$ **21.** $8\overline{)48}$

22. Divide 0 by 8.   **23.** Divide 9 by 3.   **24.** Divide 3 by 3.

25. Number Sense Explain how you would use the rules in this lesson to find $504 \div 1$, $504 \div 504$, and $0 \div 504$.

Ⓑ Reasoning and Problem Solving

Compare. Use $<$, $>$, or $=$.

26. $9 \div 9 \bigcirc 2 \div 2$ **27.** $8 \div 1 \bigcirc 3 \div 1$ **28.** $0 \div 9 \bigcirc 0 \div 2$

Use the table at the right for 29–32.

29. Ted has 35 tickets. How many times can he ride the bumper cars?

30. Mandy rides the merry-go-round twice and the Ferris wheel 3 times. How many tickets does she use?

31. Would 50 tickets be enough to ride the roller coaster 3 times and the bumper cars twice? Explain.

32. <u>Writing in Math</u> Write your own division word problem using the data in the table.

Rides and Attractions	
Petting Zoo	Free
Merry-go-round	2 tickets
Ferris Wheel	3 tickets
Bumper Cars	5 tickets
Roller Coaster	8 tickets

Mixed Review and Test Prep

Take It to the NET
Test Prep
www.scottforesman.com

33. $32 \div 8$ **34.** $54 \div 9$ **35.** Find $48 \div 8$.

A. 4   **B.** 6   **C.** 7   **D.** 8

Key Idea
Sometimes when you divide, there is something left over.

Materials
• counters

Vocabulary
• remainder

Think It Through
I can **draw a picture** to show the main idea.

Remainders

LEARN

How many are left over?

Margie is packing 25 stuffed animals into boxes for a garage sale. Each box will hold 8 stuffed animals. How many boxes will she fill? Are there any animals left over?

You want to separate 25 into equal groups of 8, so you can divide. Any number left over is the **remainder.**

Example

Find 25 ÷ 8.

What You **Do**	What You **Write**
Draw a picture to show the main idea of the problem.	$25 \div 8 = 3\,R1$

What You Do:

(diagram showing 25 separating into 8, 8, . . . with ?)

If you separate 25 objects into groups of 8, you will have 3 groups of 8 with 1 left over. The number left over is called the remainder.

What You Write:

3 R1 is read: "three remainder one."

Margie fills 3 boxes. She has 1 stuffed animal left over.

✓ Talk About It

1. If Margie had 35 stuffed animals and could put 8 in each box, how many boxes could she fill? How many stuffed animals would be left over?

2. Draw a picture to find 14 ÷ 3. Then complete the division sentence.

   14 ÷ 3 = ▨ with ▨ left over, or ▨ R ▨

Activity

How many can be left over?

Copy the table below. For each row, use counters to find the number of groups and the number left over. Then complete the table.

Total Number of Counters (Dividend)	Number in Each Group (Divisor)	Number of Groups (Quotient)	Number Left Over (Remainder)
24	5		
23	5		
22	5		
21	5		
20	5		
19	5		

a. Look at your answers in the table. What pattern do you see in the remainders when the total number of counters decreases by 1? If you continued the table, what would the next four remainders be?

b. If you separate counters into groups of 2, what is the greatest number that will be left over? Find the answer by separating 10 counters into groups of 2. Then use 9 counters, then 8, and so on, until you can no longer make groups of 2.

c. Is the remainder always greater than or less than the divisor? Explain.

d. Choose a 2-digit dividend less than 90. Choose a 1-digit divisor. Make a table like the one above and use counters to help you fill in the table.

TEST TALK

Think It Through

I can **use objects** and **make a table** to show the main idea.

CHECK ✓

For another example, see Set 7-11 on p. 421.

Use counters or draw a picture to find each quotient and remainder.

1. $7 \div 3$ **2.** $11 \div 4$ **3.** $8 \div 3$ **4.** $16 \div 5$ **5.** $13 \div 3$

6. Number Sense Can the remainder ever be equal to the divisor? Explain.

Skills and Understanding

Use counters or draw a picture to find each quotient and remainder.

7. $15 \div 7$ **8.** $13 \div 5$ **9.** $8 \div 6$ **10.** $18 \div 5$ **11.** $5 \div 3$

12. $7 \div 4$ **13.** $10 \div 9$ **14.** $12 \div 5$ **15.** $17 \div 3$ **16.** $9 \div 3$

17. Number Sense What is the largest remainder you can have if you divide a number by 7? Explain.

B **Reasoning and Problem Solving**

18. Pat bought a box of 8 stuffed animals. She and her 3 sisters will share the animals equally. How many will each girl get? Will there be any left over? If so, how many?

19. Jan and Fran have 9 sandwiches to make. Jan thinks they will have enough if they each make 4 sandwiches. Do you agree? Explain.

Math and Social Studies

A team is going to Central America to collect information about birds. The same number of people will go to each of seven countries.

20. The list of birds to be studied is 3 pages long. Each page lists 9 types of birds. How many types will be studied?

21. There are 40 people who want to go. How many can go to each country? How many will be left over?

Use the graph to solve 22 and 23.

22. Which country has the highest point of all 7 countries?

23. List the 7 countries in order of their highest points, from least to greatest.

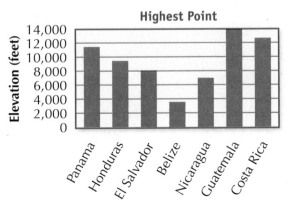

24. <u>Writing in Math</u> Is Matthew's answer correct? If not, explain why and write the correct answer.

$29 \div 4 = 6 \, R5$

C Extensions

25. Mr. Cox is taking his family to the movies. There are 2 adults and 3 children. Mr. Cox has $45. After buying movie tickets, does he have enough money left to buy 3 boxes of popcorn and 5 soft drinks? If not, how much more does he need?

MOVIE THEATER PRICES

ADULTS	$8
CHILDREN	$5
POPCORN	$3
SOFT DRINK	$2

Mixed Review and Test Prep

Take It to the NET
Test Prep
www.scottforesman.com

26. $8 \div 1$ **27.** $5 \div 5$ **28.** $0 \div 6$ **29.** $24 \div 6$ **30.** $35 \div 5$

31. Find $123 + 456 + 275$.

    A. 744   **B.** 754   **C.** 854   **D.** 71,414

Learning with Technology

Using a Calculator to Show Patterns
Copy the table below.

For rows 1–4, add each number in column A to itself until you reach the number in column B. Then write a multiplication sentence to represent the additions. Subtract the number in column A from the number in column B until you reach 0. Then write a division sentence to represent the subtractions.

For row 5, find the pattern in columns A and B, and write the numbers that come next. Fill in the other columns without using your calculator.

	A	B	Multiplication Sentence	Division Sentence
	5	20	$4 \times 5 = 20$	$20 \div 5 = 4$
1.	6	24		
2.	7	28		
3.	8	32		
4.	9	36		
5.				

Division Patterns with 10, 11, and 12

LEARN

When you divide a number by 10 and the remainder is 0, you say that the number is **divisible** by 10 or can be evenly divided by 10. You can also say that the number is a **multiple** of 10.

Activity

What's the pattern?

×	0	1	2	3	4	5	6	7	8	9	10	11	12
0	0	0	0	0	0	0	0	0	0	0	0	0	0
1	0	1	2	3	4	5	6	7	8	9	10	11	12
2	0	2	4	6	8	10	12	14	16	18	20	22	24
3	0	3	6	9	12	15	18	21	24	27	30	33	36
4	0	4	8	12	16	20	24	28	32	36	40	44	48
5	0	5	10	15	20	25	30	35	40	45	50	55	60
6	0	6	12	18	24	30	36	42	48	54	60	66	72
7	0	7	14	21	28	35	42	49	56	63	(70)	77	84
8	0	8	16	24	32	40	48	56	64	72	80	88	96
9	0	9	18	27	36	45	54	63	72	81	90	99	108
10	0	10	20	30	40	50	60	70	80	90	100	110	120
11	0	11	22	33	44	55	66	77	88	99	110	121	132
12	0	12	24	36	48	60	72	84	96	108	120	132	144

a. Copy the table. Find 70 ÷ 10. Color the 10s column blue, circle 70, and follow that row all the way to the left. (70 ÷ 10 = 7)

Use counters or multiply to check. 7 × 10 = 70

b. Color the 11s column, circle 55, and find 55 ÷ 11. Then color the 12s column and find 96 ÷ 12. What multiplication fact can you use to check each answer?

c. Read the 10s column from bottom to top. What pattern do you see in the digits in the ones place? Do the same for the 11s column and the 12s column. What is the pattern?

Find each quotient. You may use a multiplication table, use counters, or draw a picture to help.

1. 48 ÷ 12   **2.** 88 ÷ 11   **3.** 60 ÷ 10   **4.** 110 ÷ 11   **5.** 120 ÷ 12

6. Number Sense Give the pattern for multiplying by 10 and explain how it is like the pattern for dividing evenly by 10.

PRACTICE

For more practice, see Set 7-12 on p. 425.

A Skills and Understanding

Find each quotient. You may use a multiplication table, use counters, or draw a picture to help.

7. 100 ÷ 10   **8.** 33 ÷ 11   **9.** 60 ÷ 12   **10.** 120 ÷ 10   **11.** 132 ÷ 12

12. 99 ÷ 9   **13.** 55 ÷ 5   **14.** 80 ÷ 8   **15.** 30 ÷ 3   **16.** 144 ÷ 12

17. 8)‾72   **18.** 4)‾16   **19.** 6)‾42   **20.** 8)‾24   **21.** 9)‾45

22. Number Sense Eric says that any number that ends in a 0 is divisible by 10. Do you agree? Explain.

B Reasoning and Problem Solving

23. How many dozen roses are in a display of 60 roses? Use a multiplication table to help. (Hint: 1 dozen = 12.)

24. <u>**Writing in Math**</u> Describe any pattern you see in the 5s column on the multiplication table. Explain how the pattern can help you know if a number is divisible by 5.

Mixed Review and Test Prep

Take It to the NET
Test Prep
www.scottforesman.com

Use counters or draw a picture to help find each quotient and remainder.

25. 28 ÷ 5 = ▮ R ▮   **26.** 45 ÷ 6 = ▮ R ▮   **27.** 30 ÷ 4 = ▮ R ▮

28. Find 1,245 + 2,356.

    A. 3,601   **B.** 3,591   **C.** 3,581   **D.** 1,111

Problem-Solving Skill

Algebra

Key Idea
Translating words to a numerical expression can help you solve a problem.

Vocabulary
• numerical expression (p. 168)

TEST TALK

Think It Through
Since I need to make equal groups, I can **conclude** that I need to write a division expression.

Translating Words to Expressions

LEARN

How can you translate words to numerical expressions?

Remember, a **numerical expression** contains numbers and at least one operation. Some examples are:

$$34 + 52 \qquad 8 \div 2 \qquad (12 \div 4) + 3 \qquad 165 - 14 \qquad 3 \times 2 \times 1$$

Take a Hike Kara and her father went on a 21-day hiking trip. Write a numerical expression that shows the number of weeks they hiked.

Read and Understand

Identify key facts and details.   They hiked for 21 days. Each week is 7 days.

Plan and Solve

Translate words into expressions.

What You **Think**	What You **Write**
Word Phrase	*Numerical Expression*
"21 days separated into groups of 7 days"	$21 \div 7$

Other Examples

Word Phrase	Numerical Expression
23 boys; 9 fewer girls than boys	$23 - 9$
twice 8	2×8
the total of 10, 18, and 31	$10 + 18 + 31$
half of 8	$8 \div 2$

✔ Talk About It

1. How many weeks did Kara and her father hike?

For another example, see Set 7-13 on p. 421.

CHECK ✓

Write a numerical expression for each word phrase.

1. the product of 4 and 8

2. 17 more than 20

3. 15 children separated into 3 equal groups

4. the difference when 3 is subtracted from 12

5. Reasoning Does the word *more* always go with subtraction? Explain.

PRACTICE

For more practice, see Set 7-13 on p. 425.

Ⓐ Skills and Understanding

Write a numerical expression for each word phrase.

6. $18 less than $25

7. twice as old as 9 years old

8. the total of 17 students, 8 teachers, and 12 parents

9. 15 apples shared equally by 5 people

10. 3 times as long as 4 inches

11. 32 people minus 14 people

There are 8 bicycles in a rack. Write a numerical expression for how many there will be when there are:

12. 4 times as many bicycles

13. half the number of bicycles

14. 5 more bicycles

15. 3 fewer bicycles

Choose the numerical expression that matches the situation.

16. Fifteen children were on the playground. Then 12 more children came.

    A. 15 − 12   **B.** 15 + 12

17. Tickets for 7 children cost a total of $28. Each ticket costs the same amount.

    A. $28 ÷ 7   **B.** 7 × $28

Writing in Math Write two word phrases for each numerical expression.

18. 5 × 6

19. 24 ÷ 8

20. 24 − 6

21. 8 + 3 + 4 + 5

Problem-Solving Applications

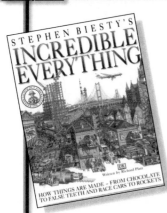

Tunnels Long ago, shovels and dynamite were used to slowly dig tunnels. Now, huge machines chew through rock more quickly and safely.

Trivia In the 1880s, engineers started digging a tunnel beneath the English Channel. That effort was stopped due to fears that the tunnel would be used by invading armies.

1 A tunnel under the English Channel was planned in 1802. Such a tunnel was actually completed 192 years later. When was the tunnel completed?

Using Key Facts

2 The stroke distance is how far the machine can "step" at one time. Using the longest stroke distance, how many steps would the machine take when drilling forward 40 feet?

Key Facts Tunnel-Boring Machines	
Dimension	**Typical Measure**
• Diameter	8–38 feet
• Weight	100–500 tons
• Drill rotation	2–8 times per minute
• Stroke distance	up to 5 feet

Good News/Bad News *Using tunnel-boring machines is often the best way to dig, as long as you do not need to make sharp corners. When turning around, some machines make curves over 300 meters wide.*

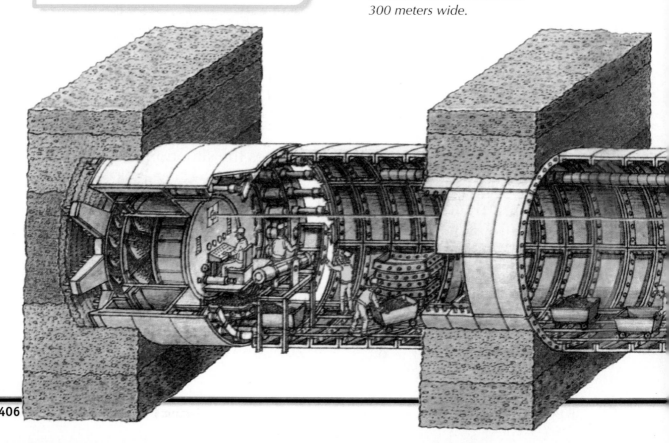

3 The longest tunnel of any type is an aqueduct. It is about 90 miles longer than the longest road tunnel. This road tunnel is 18 miles shorter than the longest railway tunnel. If this railway tunnel is about 33 miles long, what is the length of the world's longest tunnel?

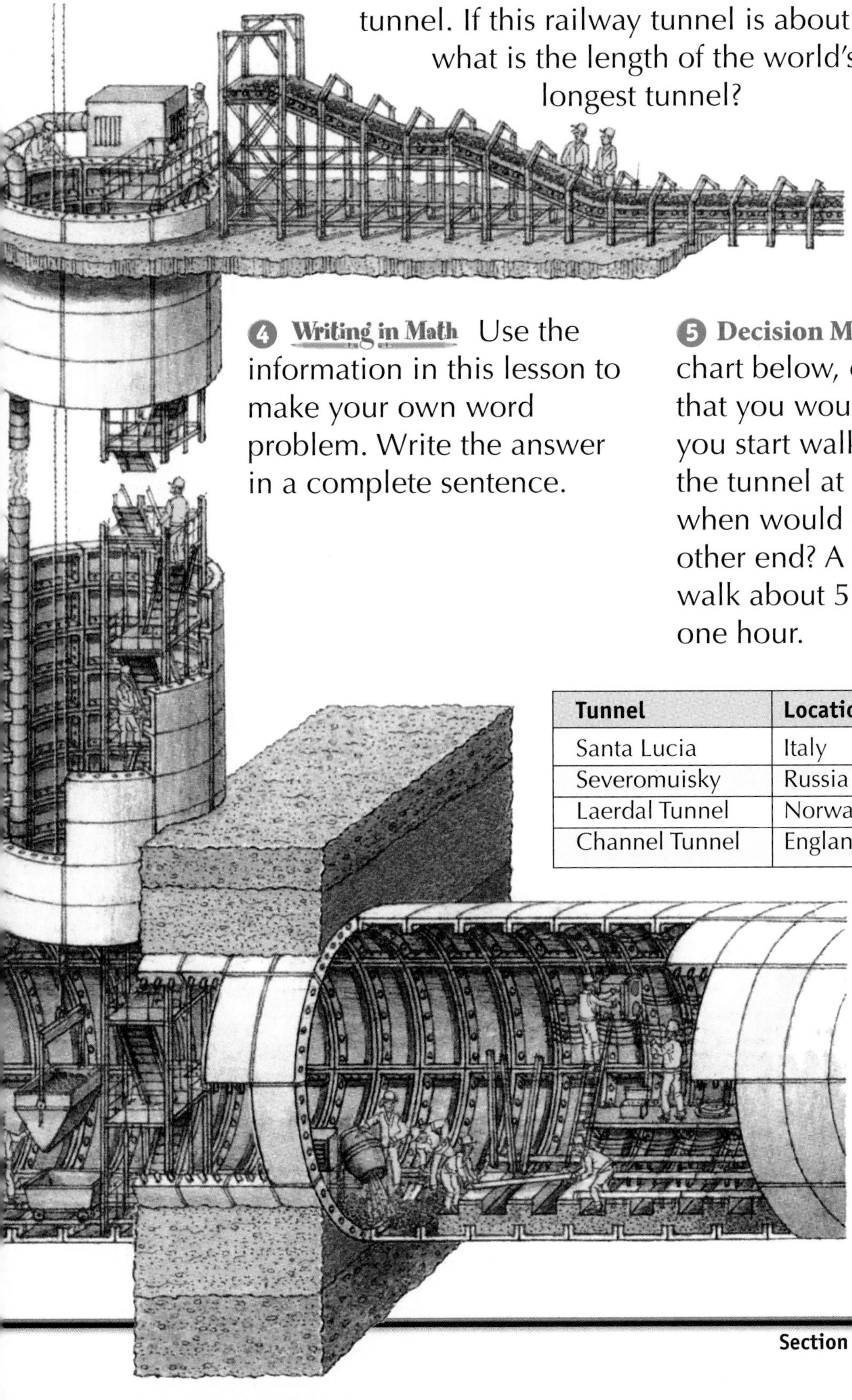

4 <u>Writing in Math</u> Use the information in this lesson to make your own word problem. Write the answer in a complete sentence.

5 Decision Making From the chart below, choose a tunnel that you would like to see. If you start walking through the tunnel at 11:00 A.M., when would you get to the other end? A person can walk about 5 kilometers in one hour.

Tunnel	Location	Length
Santa Lucia	Italy	10 km
Severomuisky	Russia	15 km
Laerdal Tunnel	Norway	25 km
Channel Tunnel	England/France	50 km

Do You Know How?

Do You Understand?

Dividing with 0 and 1 (7-10)

1. $9 \div 1$ **2.** $0 \div 9$

3. $9 \div 9$ **4.** $3 \div 1$

5. $0 \div 3$ **6.** $3 \div 3$

Ⓐ What rule did you use to find each quotient in Exercises 1–6?

Ⓑ Can you find $2 \div 0$? Explain

Remainders (7-11)

Use counters or draw a picture to help you find each answer.

7. $17 \div 8 = $ ▢ with ▢ left over

8. What is the remainder for $7 \div 3$?

Ⓒ Explain how you found your answer for Exercise 8.

Division Patterns with 10, 11, and 12 (7-12)

Use a multiplication table, use counters, or draw a picture to help you find each answer.

9. $24 \div 12$ **10.** $50 \div 10$

11. $44 \div 11$ **12.** $90 \div 9$

Ⓓ How can you tell if a 2-digit number is divisible by 11?

Ⓔ Explain how knowing how to multiply by 10 can help you with dividing by 10.

Problem-Solving Skill: Translating Words to Expressions (7-13)

Write a numerical expression for each phrase or situation.

13. the sum of 48 and 23

14. 3 teams with 8 players each

15. 24 children in 3 equal groups

16. the difference when 8 is subtracted from 20

Ⓕ How did you know what operation to use in Exercise 13?

Ⓖ Draw a picture showing each situation in Exercises 14 and 15. How are the situations alike? How are they different?

TEST TALK

Think It Through
I need to **read each answer choice carefully.**

MULTIPLE CHOICE

1. There are 8 muffins to be shared equally by 8 friends. How many will each person get? (7-10)

A. 64 **B.** 16 **C.** 8 **D.** 1

2. Which numerical expression matches the situation given? (7-13)

45 students separated into 5 equal teams

A. 45×5 **B.** $45 \div 5$ **C.** $45 - 5$ **D.** $45 + 5$

FREE RESPONSE

Copy and complete. You may use counters or draw a picture to help. (7-12)

3. $30 \div 10 = $ ▨
   $30 \div 3 = $ ▨

4. $44 \div 11 = $ ▨
   $44 \div 4 = $ ▨

5. $36 \div 12 = $ ▨
   $36 \div 3 = $ ▨

You may use counters or draw a picture to help find each answer. (7-11)

6. $38 \div 9 = $ ▨ with ▨ left over

7. $28 \div 9 = $ ▨ R ▨

8. $45 \div 8 = $ ▨ R ▨

You may use counters or draw a picture to help find each answer. (7-12)

9. For a field trip, 88 students were separated into 8 equal groups. How many were in each group?

10. Mrs. Chan bought 48 eggs for her cooking class students to use. How many dozen eggs did she buy? (Remember: 1 dozen = 12)

Writing in Math

11. Write a word problem that could be solved using the numerical expression $54 \div 9$. (7-13, 7-14)

12. Draw a picture to show two ways you could arrange 22 counters into equal groups. Write a division sentence under each drawing. (7-12)

CHAPTER 7
Test Talk

Test-Taking Strategies

Understand the question.

Get information for the answer.

Plan how to find the answer.

Make smart choices.

Use writing in math.

Improve written answers.

Plan How to Find the Answer

After you understand a test question and get needed information, you need to plan how to find the answer. Think about problem-solving skills and strategies and computation methods you know.

1. Lee bought a bag of 32 dog biscuits for his 4 puppies.

Lee wants each puppy to get the same number of biscuits. How many biscuits should each puppy get?

A. 36

B. 28

C. 8

D. 6

Understand the question.

I need to find the number of dog biscuits Lee should give each puppy.

Get information for the answer.

*The picture does not give me information I need to solve the problem. I'll need to **get information from the text.***

Plan how to find the answer.

- Think about problem-solving skills and strategies.

   *I need to make equal groups of dog biscuits, so I can **write a number sentence** that involves division.*

- Choose a computation method.

   *Since I know my division facts, I can **use mental math** to find the answer.*

2. To solve this problem, you must ESTIMATE. Do NOT find the exact answer.

This cake is topped with jelly beans. ESTIMATE the number of jelly beans on the whole cake.

Estimate: _____

Think It Through

I need to estimate the number of jelly beans on the whole cake and explain how I made my estimate. The picture shows that each slice of cake has about the same number of jelly beans. So I can **count** *the jelly beans on one slice of cake and use mental math to* **multiply** *by 6, which is the total number of slices.*

Now it's your turn.

For each problem, describe a plan for finding the answer.

3. There are 163 boys and 148 girls signed up for Sunny Days Day Camp. How many children all together are signed up for the camp?

  A. 15

  B. 211

  C. 311

  D. 321

4. To solve this problem, you must ESTIMATE. Do NOT find the exact answer.

ESTIMATE the number of windows on the side of the building shown in the picture.

Estimate: _____

My mom's group at work is the Sales Division.

*When you split things up evenly, **division** is used to find how many equal groups you can make or how many are in each group. (p. 370)*

Self Check

Use division to show how to share equally. (Lessons 7-1, 7-2, 7-3)

Bill, Quan, and Anna have 15 stickers to share equally. How many stickers will each one get?

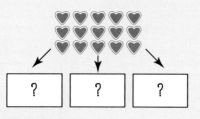

Use **division** to find how many in each group.

Total number		Number of equal groups		Number in each group
15	÷	3	=	5

Bill, Quan, and Anna each get 5 stickers.

There are 24 crayons. Each box has 6 of the crayons. How many boxes are there?

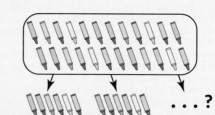

Use division to find how many groups.

Total number		Number in each group		Number of equal groups
24	÷	6	=	4

There are 4 boxes.

1. Write a division story for 18 ÷ 2. Use counters or draw a picture to solve.

Self Check

Use multiplication to help you divide. (Lesson 7-5, 7-6, 7-7, 7-8, 7-9, 7-10)

Find 42 ÷ 7.

What You Think: 7 times what number equals 42?

$7 \times \mathbf{6} = 42$

What You Write: 42 ÷ 7 = 6

A fact family shows how multiplication and division are related.

Fact family for 7, 6, and 42:

$7 \times 6 = 42$ $42 \div 7 = 6$

$6 \times 7 = 42$ $42 \div 6 = 7$

factor factor product   **dividend divisor quotient**

2. Find 40 ÷ 8, 4)28, 0 ÷ 9, and 3 ÷ 1.

We put the remainder of our dinner, or leftovers, in the refrigerator.

When two numbers cannot be evenly divided, there will be a **remainder,** or an amount left over. (p. 398)

Self Check

Sometimes there is something left over when you divide. (Lessons 7-11, 7-12)

Find 30 ÷ 7.

There are 4 equal groups of 7 with a **remainder** of 2.

30 ÷ 7 = 4 **R2**

Find 30 ÷ 10.

There are 3 equal groups of 10. 30 is **divisible** by 10.

30 ÷ 10 = 3

3. Find 36 ÷ 5 and 28 ÷ 7.

Our nation is indivisible. It can't be split up.

A number is **divisible** by another number if there is no remainder when you divide. (p. 402)

Self Check

I can express myself in lots of ways, such as drawings, music, and stories.

A **numerical expression** contains numbers and at least one operation. (p. 404)

Try, check, and revise, or translate words to expressions to solve problems. (Lessons 7-4, 7-13)

Make a reasonable try. Check, revise, and continue until you get the answer.

Sue and Lisa have 11 dolls in all. Sue has 3 more dolls than Lisa. How many dolls does each girl have?

Try: 8 + 3 = 11
Check: 8 − 3 = 5 Too high.
Revise: 7 + 4 = 11
Check: 7 − 4 = 3 That's right!

Sue has 7 dolls and Lisa has 4 dolls.

Translate the words into a **numerical expression.**

Brian had $16. He spent half of it on lunch. How much did Brian spend on lunch?

Think: "half of" means divided by 2.

Numerical Expression: 16 ÷ 2

Solve: 16 ÷ 2 = 8

Brian spent $8 on lunch.

4. Amy and Jim have $12 altogether. Amy has twice as much money as Jim. How much money does each one have?

Answers: 1. Accept all reasonable stories. 2. 5; 7; 0 3. 7 R1; 4 4. Amy has $8, and Jim has $4.

MULTIPLE CHOICE

Choose the correct letter for each answer.

1. What number completes the division sentence shown in this picture?

   A. 6

   B. 10

   C. 14

   D. 24

   $12 \div 2 = \blacksquare$

2. Tom subtracted 3 from 18 six times. What division could he do instead?

   A. $18 \div 3$ C. $6 \div 3$

   B. $3 \div 18$ D. $18 \div 9$

3. Find $45 \div 5$.

   A. 7   B. 8   C. 9   D. 40

4. Find $3\overline{)24}$.

   A. 6   B. 7   C. 8   D. 9

5. Caroline bought 42 stickers to give to her friends. She has 7 friends. If each friend gets the same number of stickers, how many stickers will each friend get?

   A. 9   B. 8   C. 7   D. 6

6. There are 63 players in the volleyball league. Each team will have 9 players. How many teams will there be?

   A. 8   B. 7   C. 6   D. 5

7. What is 48 divided by 8?

   A. 56   B. 40   C. 8   D. 6

8. Which number sentence does NOT belong to the same fact family?

   A. $4 \times 3 = 12$

   B. $12 \div 6 = 2$

   C. $12 \div 3 = 4$

   D. $3 \times 4 = 12$

Think It Through
- I should **watch for highlighted** words in the question, like **NOT** or **CANNOT**.
- I can **eliminate unreasonable** answer choices.

9. Which division CANNOT be done?

   A. $4 \div 1$ C. $4 \div 0$

   B. $0 \div 4$ D. $4 \div 4$

10. Find $25 \div 6$.

    A. 5   C. 4

    B. 4 R1   D. 3 R1

11. What is the quotient of 36 divided by 6?

    A. 6   B. 8   C. 9   D. 12

12. There are 10 students on the debate team. There are twice as many students in the school play. Which numerical expression shows the number of students in the play?

    A. $10 + 2$ C. 2×10

    B. $10 \div 2$ D. $10 - 2$

13. Four friends equally shared 24 pencils. How many pencils did each person have?

    A. 3   **B.** 6   **C.** 8   **D.** 12

14. Find $48 \div 12$.

    A. 4   **B.** 8   **C.** 12   **D.** 24

15. Find $10 \div 2$.

    A. 2   **B.** 5   **C.** 20   **D.** 100

FREE RESPONSE

Find each quotient.

16. $4\overline{)16}$ **17.** $6\overline{)42}$

18. $9\overline{)54}$ **19.** $7\overline{)14}$

20. $90 \div 10$ **21.** $2 \div 2$

22. $20 \div 6$ **23.** $0 \div 6$

Copy and complete.

24. $8 \times \blacksquare = 40$ **25.** $\blacksquare \times 9 = 18$

    $40 \div 8 = \blacksquare$ $18 \div 9 = \blacksquare$

26. $\blacksquare \times 6 = 42$ **27.** $4 \times \blacksquare = 12$

    $42 \div 6 = \blacksquare$ $12 \div 4 = \blacksquare$

28. Write the fact family for 3, 7, and 21.

29. What are the divisor, dividend, and quotient in this division sentence?

    $72 \div 8 = 9$

30. Amy made 45 cookies. She separated them into five equal groups. How many cookies were in each group?

Writing in Math

Think It Through
- I should **check if my answer is complete.**
- I should **look for important words or phrases** that tell what the problem is about.

31. Tina worked 32 hours at the library. She worked 8 hours each day. Write a numerical expression for how many days Tina worked at the library. Explain how your answer would change if Tina had worked 4 hours each day.

32. Write a division story for the number sentence $35 \div 5 = n$. Then draw a picture to solve.

33. Try, check, and revise to solve this problem.

Blank videotapes come in packs of 3, 5, or 6. Mr. Calvin wants to buy 22 tapes for a class project. What kinds of packs should he buy to have exactly 22 videotapes? Explain how you revised your answer after your first try.

Number and Operation

MULTIPLE CHOICE

1. Which number completes the division sentence shown in this picture?

   A. 6

   B. 7

   C. 12

   D. 16

   $14 \div 2 = \blacksquare$

2. Which number sentence is NOT part of the same fact family?

   A. $30 \div 6 = 5$

   B. $30 \div 5 = 6$

   C. $5 + 6 = 11$

   D. $5 \times 6 = 30$

FREE RESPONSE

3. Kim has 14 red pens and 11 blue pens. Bill has 17 red pens and 9 blue pens. Who has more pens in all? Explain.

4. Thomas put 24 tennis balls into 8 cans. He put the same number of balls into each can. How many tennis balls are in each can?

5. Jeff has 3 times as many baseball cards as Matt. Matt has 6 baseball cards. How many baseball cards does Jeff have?

Writing in Math

6. Explain how thinking about multiplication can help you find $20 \div 5$. Then find the quotient.

Geometry and Measurement

MULTIPLE CHOICE

7. What time is shown on the clock?

   A. 2:45

   B. 3:15

   C. 3:45

   D. 9:15

8. Which of the following is NOT a unit to measure length?

   A. yard   C. ounce

   B. inch   D. mile

FREE RESPONSE

9. Angie used all of her string to make jewelry. She used 8 inches of string to make a bracelet. She used 14 inches to make a necklace. How much string did Angie start with?

   Think It Through
   I can try **working backward** to solve the problem.

Writing in Math

10. This thermometer shows the temperature outside. Explain what kind of clothes you should wear outside.

Data Analysis and Probability

MULTIPLE CHOICE

11. Which color marble are you most likely to pick from this bag?

A. red

B. green

C. black

D. yellow

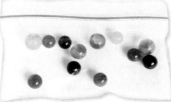

12. How many students voted in all?

A. 16

B. 32

C. 22

D. 38

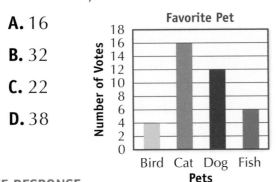

FREE RESPONSE

Use the pictograph for Items 13–15.

Train Ride Tickets Sold

Thursday	▌▌▌▌
Friday	▌▌▌▌▌
Saturday	▌▌▌▌▌▌
Sunday	▌▌▌▌▌▌▌

Each ▌ = 5 tickets.

13. On which day were the most tickets sold? the least?

14. How many tickets were sold on Saturday and Sunday combined?

Writing in Math

15. Fifteen tickets were sold on Wednesday. Explain how you would show this data on the pictograph.

Algebra

MULTIPLE CHOICE

16. Which number goes in the ▊ to complete the pattern?

27, 24, 21, ▊, 15

A. 16   **B.** 17   **C.** 18   **D.** 20

17. Find the missing number.

$24 \div ▊ = 8$

A. 2   **B.** 3   **C.** 4   **D.** 6

18. Solve ▊ $\times 6 = 18$.

A. 2   **B.** 3   **C.** 12   **D.** 24

FREE RESPONSE

19. What is the rule for this table?

In	3	4	5	6
Out	33	44	55	66

20. Linda is playing a counting game. She counts 50, 45, 40, 35, 30. What are the next three numbers she will count?

Think It Through
I should **look for a pattern** to solve the problem.

Writing in Math

21. Write a division story for $32 \div 8$.

Set 7-1 (pages 370–371)

Kim has 12 stickers. She wants to divide them equally on 2 pages in her sticker book. How many stickers will be on each page?

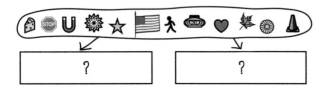

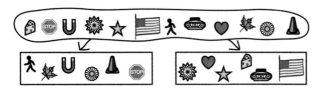

There will be 6 stickers on each page.

Remember that you can think of division as sharing equally.

Use counters or draw a picture to solve.

1. 6 books
2 shelves
How many books on each shelf?

2. 15 buttons
3 shirts
How many buttons on each shirt?

3. 18 students
2 groups
How many students in each group?

Set 7-2 (pages 372–373)

Brad wants to give 12 paintings to 4 aunts. If each aunt receives the same number, how many does each receive?

One Way	Another Way
Subtract 4 until you get zero	Use division to solve.
12 – 4 = 8 I can	12 ÷ 4 = 3
8 – 4 = 4 subtract 4	
4 – 4 = 0 three times.	

Each aunt receives 3 paintings.

Remember that division is another way to do repeated subtraction.

Use counters or draw a picture to solve.

1. 8 earrings
2 in each pair
How many pairs?

2. 15 oranges
5 in each bag
How many bags?

Set 7-3 (pages 374–377)

Write a division story for 20 ÷ 5.

Jenn has 20 chairs. She will put the same number of chairs at 5 tables. How many chairs will be at each table?

20 ÷ 5 = 4

There will be 4 chairs at each table.

Remember that division stories can ask for the number in each group or the number of equal groups.

Write a division story for each. Use counters or draw a picture to solve.

1. 18 ÷ 9   **2.** 12 ÷ 3   **3.** 6 ÷ 2

Here are some steps for using Try, Check, and Revise.

Step 1: Think to make a reasonable first try.

Step 2: Check using information given in the problem.

Step 3: Revise. Use your first try to make a reasonable second try. Check.

Step 4: Continue trying and checking until you get the answer.

Remember to check each try.

1. Kay needs 28 paintbrushes. They come in packages of 4, 6, or 9 paintbrushes. Which packs could she buy?

2. Andy has 7 sweaters in all. He has 3 more solid-colored sweaters than striped sweaters. How many solid-colored sweaters does he have?

Draw the array and find the fact family for 3, 7, and 21.

Factor × Factor = Product	Dividend ÷ Divisor = Quotient
$3 \times 7 = 21$	$21 \div 3 = 7$
$7 \times 3 = 21$	$21 \div 7 = 3$

Remember that a fact family shows multiplication and division using the same numbers.

1. $4 \times \blacksquare = 16$
   $16 \div 4 = \blacksquare$

2. $6 \times \blacksquare = 30$
   $30 \div 6 = \blacksquare$

3. $2 \times \blacksquare = 14$
   $14 \div 2 = \blacksquare$

4. $\blacksquare \times 3 = 27$
   $27 \div 3 = \blacksquare$

Mackenzie walked her dog 15 times during the past 5 days. How many times a day did she walk her dog if it was the same each day?

Find $15 \div 5$.

What You **Think**	What You **Write**
5 times what number equals 15? $5 \times \mathbf{3} = 15$	$15 \div 5 = 3$

Mackenzie walked her dog three times a day.

Remember to think of a related multiplication fact to solve a division problem.

1. $15 \div 5$
2. $10 \div 2$
3. $8 \div 2$
4. $30 \div 5$
5. $16 \div 2$
6. $45 \div 5$
7. $20 \div 5$
8. $6 \div 2$
9. $14 \div 2$
10. $35 \div 5$

Set 7-7 (pages 388–389)

Janine must read 21 pages of her book in 3 days. How many pages must Janine read each day?

Find 21 ÷ 3.

What You **Think**	What You **Write**
3 times what number equals 21? $3 \times 7 = 21$	$21 \div 3 = 7$

Janine must read 7 pages each day.

Remember that division problems can be written in two ways.

1. $8 \div 4$ **2.** $24 \div 3$

3. $9 \div 3$ **4.** $12 \div 4$

5. $3\overline{)27}$ **6.** $4\overline{)24}$

7. $4\overline{)16}$ **8.** $3\overline{)18}$

9. $36 \div 4$ **10.** $15 \div 3$

Set 7-8 (pages 390–391)

Hanna has 56 books to put on 7 shelves. If each shelf is to have an equal number of books, how many books will be on each shelf?

Find 56 ÷ 7.

What You **Think**	What You **Write**
7 times what number equals 56? $7 \times 8 = 56$	$56 \div 7 = 8$

There will be 8 books on each shelf.

Remember that you can use an array to help you visualize the problem.

1. $42 \div 7$ **2.** $12 \div 6$

3. $6\overline{)36}$ **4.** $7\overline{)28}$

5. Divide 49 by 7.

6. Divide 54 by 6.

7. Find 35 divided by 7.

Set 7-9 (pages 392–393)

The third-grade classes are having a kickball tournament. There are 54 students and each team needs 9 players. How many teams will there be?

Find 54 ÷ 9.

What You **Think**	What You **Write**
9 times what number equals 54? $9 \times 6 = 54$	$54 \div 9 = 6$

There will be 6 teams.

Remember that division means separating into equal groups.

1. $40 \div 8$ **2.** $81 \div 9$

3. $64 \div 8$ **4.** $27 \div 9$

5. $16 \div 8$ **6.** $18 \div 9$

7. $9\overline{)72}$ **8.** $8\overline{)56}$

9. $8\overline{)48}$ **10.** $9\overline{)54}$

Set 7-10 (pages 396–397)

Find $8 \div 1$, $8 \div 8$, and $0 \div 8$.

When any number is divided by 1, the quotient is that number. **$8 \div 1 = 8$**

When any number (except 0) is divided by itself, the quotient is 1. **$8 \div 8 = 1$**

When zero is divided by any number (except 0), the quotient is zero. **$0 \div 8 = 0$**

Remember that you cannot divide any number by zero.

1. $4 \div 1$ **2.** $0 \div 7$

3. $6 \div 6$ **4.** $0 \div 1$

5. $0 \div 3$ **6.** $0 \div 4$

7. $5 \div 1$ **8.** $9 \div 9$

9. $6 \div 1$ **10.** $2 \div 2$

Set 7-11 (pages 398–401)

Doug made 38 cupcakes for a bake sale. How many packages of 5 can he make? How many will be left over?

Find $38 \div 5$.

$38 \div 5 = 7$ R3

He can make 7 packages with 3 left over.

Remember that when you divide, if there is something left over, this is the remainder.

Use counters or draw a picture to find each quotient and remainder.

1. $16 \div 5 = $ ▢ with ▢ left over

2. $14 \div 3 = $ ▢ with ▢ left over

3. $21 \div 6 = $ ▢ R ▢

4. $9 \div 2$ **5.** $30 \div 7$

Set 7-12 (pages 402–403)

Find $22 \div 11$.

Think: 11 times what number equals 22?
$11 \times \mathbf{2} = 22$

$22 \div 11 = \mathbf{2}$

Remember that all numbers divisible by 10 will end in a zero.

1. $48 \div 12$ **2.** $77 \div 11$

3. $50 \div 10$ **4.** $96 \div 12$

Set 7-13 (pages 404–405)

Write a numerical expression for "the total of 2, 1, and 3."

$2 + 1 + 3$

Remember to read the problem carefully before translating.

Write a numerical expression for each.

1. twice as much as 12

2. 13 more than 21

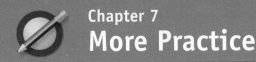

Chapter 7
More Practice

Set 7-1 (pages 370–371)

Use counters or draw a picture to solve.

1. 9 toy boats
3 puddles
How many toy boats in
each puddle?

2. 10 bananas
5 monkeys
How many bananas for
each monkey?

3. Ken needs to put 27 apples in 3 bowls, with the same number in each. How many apples will he put in each bowl?

4. Five children will share 15 grapes equally. How many grapes will each child get?

Set 7-2 (pages 372–373)

Use counters or draw a picture to solve.

1. 12 children
3 in each game
How many games?

2. 8 socks
2 in each pair
How many pairs?

3. 20 chairs
4 chairs at each table
How many tables?

4. Lucas made dinner for 6 people. If he made 12 dinner rolls, how many rolls will each person get?

Set 7-3 (pages 374–377)

Write a division story for each number sentence. Use counters or draw a picture to solve.

1. $18 \div 9 = $ ▓ **2.** $16 \div 8 = $ ▓ **3.** $24 \div 4 = n$ **4.** $6 \div 2 = x$

Set 7-4 (pages 380–381)

Try, check, and revise to solve each problem.

1. Earl played the beanbag toss game. On each throw, he could make 0, 2, 4, or 6 points. He scored 12 points after throwing 3 beanbags. Where might his beanbags have landed?

2. Mrs. Choi needs to buy 28 sandwich buns. They come in packages of 8 or 12. What packages should she buy?

Take It to the NET
More Practice
www.scottforesman.com

Set 7-5 (pages 384–385)

Copy and complete. Use counters or draw a picture to help.

1. $2 \times \square = 6$
$6 \div 2 = \square$

2. $7 \times \square = 28$
$28 \div 7 = \square$

3. $5 \times \square = 40$
$40 \div 5 = \square$

4. $4 \times \square = 12$
$12 \div 4 = \square$

5. $9 \times \square = 54$
$54 \div 9 = \square$

6. $2 \times \square = 18$
$18 \div 2 = \square$

7. $7 \times \square = 35$
$35 \div 7 = \square$

8. $\square \times 8 = 56$
$56 \div 8 = \square$

9. Reasoning Hunter wants to frame his 24 basketball cards. He wants to arrange the cards in an array with at least 3 rows. To fit in the frame he can not have more than 8 rows. Write the fact families for the arrays he could use.

Set 7-6 (pages 386–387)

Divide.

1. $4 \div 2$
2. $16 \div 2$
3. $30 \div 5$
4. $10 \div 5$
5. $12 \div 2$

6. $45 \div 5$
7. $14 \div 2$
8. $15 \div 5$
9. $18 \div 2$
10. $20 \div 5$

11. $40 \div 5$
12. $25 \div 5$
13. $6 \div 2$
14. $10 \div 2$
15. $35 \div 5$

16. Pierce and his brother were told to share 8 sand toys equally. How many sand toys did each boy get?

17. Karen and her brother earned $8 baby-sitting and $10 gardening. If they shared the money equally, how much did each get?

Set 7-7 (pages 388–389)

Divide.

1. $20 \div 4$
2. $3\overline{)18}$
3. $4\overline{)28}$
4. $24 \div 3$
5. $15 \div 3$

6. $27 \div 3$
7. $21 \div 3$
8. $9 \div 3$
9. $36 \div 4$
10. $6 \div 3$

11. $4\overline{)24}$
12. $4\overline{)32}$
13. $3\overline{)12}$
14. $4\overline{)8}$
15. $4\overline{)16}$

16. Randy has 4 cats. He has 12 cat snacks. If each cat gets the same number of snacks, how many snacks will each cat get?

17. There are 8 juice boxes in one package and 4 in another. If 3 children share the juice boxes equally, how many will each child get?

Set 7-8 (pages 390–391)

Divide.

1. $21 \div 7$ 2. $35 \div 7$ 3. $18 \div 6$ 4. $56 \div 7$ 5. $28 \div 7$

6. $12 \div 6$ 7. $36 \div 6$ 8. $63 \div 7$ 9. $42 \div 7$ 10. $54 \div 6$

11. $7\overline{)49}$ 12. $6\overline{)24}$ 13. $7\overline{)14}$ 14. $6\overline{)30}$ 15. $6\overline{)48}$

16. Wendy and Jim and 4 friends are having dinner together. There are 42 baby carrots for all of them to share. If each person gets the same number of carrots, how many carrots will each person get?

Set 7-9 (pages 392–393)

Divide.

1. $27 \div 9$ 2. $16 \div 8$ 3. $40 \div 8$ 4. $72 \div 9$ 5. $54 \div 9$

6. $45 \div 9$ 7. $81 \div 9$ 8. $56 \div 8$ 9. $36 \div 9$ 10. $32 \div 8$

11. $8\overline{)24}$ 12. $8\overline{)72}$ 13. $9\overline{)18}$ 14. $8\overline{)48}$ 15. $9\overline{)63}$

16. Mason is making snow globes. He has 64 snowflakes. If he puts 8 snowflakes in each snow globe, how many snow globes will he make?

17. A meeting room has 24 chairs. Eight chairs are placed at each table. How many tables are there?

Set 7-10 (pages 396–397)

Divide.

1. $2 \div 1$ 2. $3 \div 3$ 3. $6 \div 6$ 4. $0 \div 2$ 5. $4 \div 4$

6. $0 \div 7$ 7. $12 \div 1$ 8. $8 \div 8$ 9. $4 \div 1$ 10. $0 \div 9$

11. $5 \div 5$ 12. $1 \div 1$ 13. $0 \div 5$ 14. $3 \div 1$ 15. $2 \div 2$

16. $7\overline{)7}$ 17. $4\overline{)0}$ 18. $1\overline{)8}$ 19. $3\overline{)0}$ 20. $9\overline{)9}$

21. Mrs. Weber made 12 sandwiches for her students. If there are 12 children in her class, how many sandwiches will each child receive?

Take It to the NET
More Practice
www www.scottforesman.com

Set 7-11 (pages 398–401)

Use counters or draw a picture to find each quotient and remainder.

1. 9 ÷ 6   **2.** 44 ÷ 5   **3.** 16 ÷ 7   **4.** 21 ÷ 4   **5.** 13 ÷ 2

6. 8 ÷ 3   **7.** 12 ÷ 7   **8.** 29 ÷ 3   **9.** 23 ÷ 3   **10.** 14 ÷ 6

11. 17 ÷ 5   **12.** 27 ÷ 6   **13.** 11 ÷ 3   **14.** 8 ÷ 5   **15.** 32 ÷ 6

16. Marcy has 35 pages to read. If she reads 8 pages each day, will she finish in 4 days? If not, how many pages will she have left to read?

Set 7-12 (pages 402–403)

Use a multiplication table, use counters, or draw a picture to help find each quotient.

1. 72 ÷ 12   **2.** 121 ÷ 11   **3.** 120 ÷ 10   **4.** 110 ÷ 11   **5.** 36 ÷ 12

6. 88 ÷ 11   **7.** 100 ÷ 10   **8.** 33 ÷ 11   **9.** 120 ÷ 12   **10.** 50 ÷ 10

11. 96 ÷ 12   **12.** 70 ÷ 10   **13.** 110 ÷ 10   **14.** 60 ÷ 12   **15.** 30 ÷ 10

16. 55 ÷ 11   **17.** 60 ÷ 10   **18.** 77 ÷ 11   **19.** 80 ÷ 10   **20.** 99 ÷ 11

21. There are 144 items in a gross. How many dozen are in a gross? Remember: 1 dozen equals 12.

Set 7-13 (pages 404–405)

Write a numerical expression for each.

1. 15 more than 12

2. the product of 6 and 10

3. the total of 56 and 23

4. 15 divided by 3

5. 21 less than 67

6. twice as many as 12

7. 3 more than 14

8. 16 pens shared equally by 4 children

9. the difference when 9 is subtracted from 98

10. 36 books separated into 4 equal groups

11. 5 times as much as $8

12. 8 rows with 9 in each row

13. $14 minus $8

14. 8 children join 6 children on a playground

Geometry and Measurement

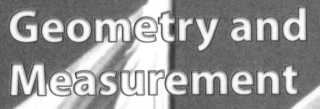

  DIAGNOSING READINESS

A Vocabulary
(Grade 2)

Choose the best term from the box.

1. The red shape is a ___?___.

2. The blue shape is a ___?___.

3. The green shape is a ___?___.

Vocabulary
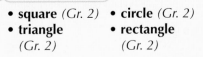
- square *(Gr. 2)*   - circle *(Gr. 2)*
- triangle   - rectangle
  (Gr. 2)   *(Gr. 2)*

B Solid Figures
(Grade 2)

Sphere   Cube   Cylinder

Name the solid figure that each object looks like.

4.   5.   6.

7. Which of the solid figures above can roll?

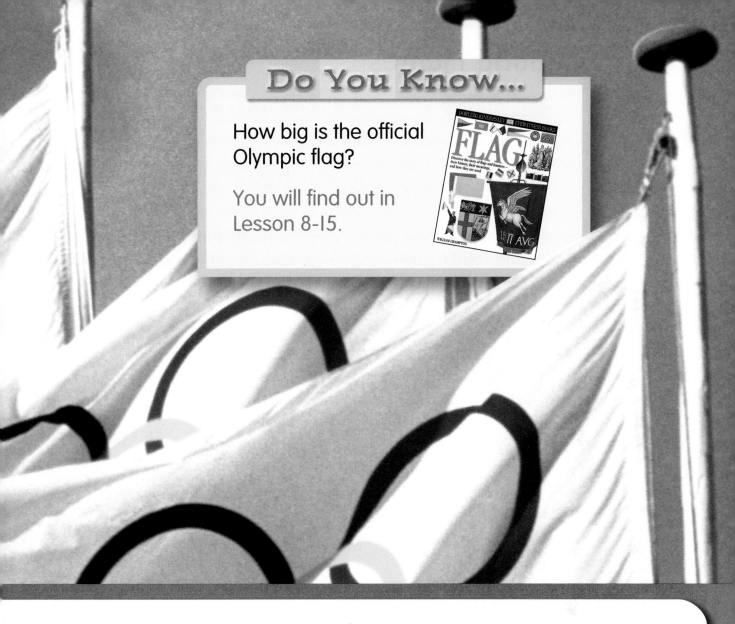

Do You Know...

How big is the official Olympic flag?

You will find out in Lesson 8-15.

C Counting Sides
(Grade 2)

Write the number of sides on each shape.

8.

9. △

10. ⬠

11. ⬡

12. Draw a picture of a shape that has 4 sides.

D Adding More Than 2 Numbers
(pages 136–137)

13. 2 + 5 + 2 + 5

14. 4 + 4 + 6 + 6

15. 6 + 12 + 6

16. How can you solve Exercise 14 by making tens?

17. In three games Dale made the following number of points: 12, 9, and 8. What was his total number of points?

Key Idea
Solid figures in the world around us come in many shapes and sizes.

Vocabulary
• solid figure
• sphere
• cube
• rectangular prism
• pyramid
• cone
• cylinder

Materials
• Set of Solids

Solid Figures

LEARN

Activity

What are some of the solid figures in the world around you?

Objects that have length, width, and height are called **solid figures.** Buildings you see and objects you use every day look like the solid figures shown below.

Here are some solid figures.

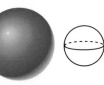  

Sphere   **Cube**   **Rectangular prism**

Pyramid   **Cone**   **Cylinder**

Find an object in the classroom or a solid that matches each of the figures shown above.

a. Which of the solid figures above roll? Which ones do not roll?

b. Compare the cube and the rectangular prism. Tell how they are alike and how they are different.

c. Compare the cone and the cylinder. Tell how they are alike and how they are different.

d. Which solid figure has no flat surfaces?

✓ WARM UP

Name each shape.

1. [rectangle]   2. [circle]

3. [triangle]   4. [square]

TEST TALK

Think It Through
• I can **act it out** by exploring solids.
• I can **compare and contrast** to find how solids are alike and different.

428

What happens when you combine or split solid figures?

This puppet was made by combining solid figures.

a. Copy and complete the table below.

Puppet Part	Solid Figure
Green	Rectangular prism
Yellow	
Red	
Blue	
Orange	
Purple	
Pink	

b. Put two cubes together end-to-end. Then draw or describe the solid figure you made.

c. What solid figures would you get if you cut a cylinder as shown?

TEST TALK

Think It Through

I can **use objects** to show how to combine solid figures.

CHECK ✓

For another example, see Set 8-1 on p. 488.

Name the solid figure or figures each object looks like.

1.

2.

3.

4.

5. Reasoning Which solid figures can be stacked to make a tower with a flat top?

A Skills and Understanding

Name the solid figure or figures each object looks like.

6. **7.** **8.** **9.**

10. Reasoning If you put two cylinders together, flat end to flat end, what solid figure would you make?

B Reasoning and Problem Solving

Name an object in your classroom or your home that is shaped like each solid figure.

11. Sphere   **12.** Cube   **13.** Cylinder   **14.** Rectangular prism

15. What solid figures would you get if you cut a cube as shown?

 Math and Social Studies

Here are two of the world's most famous buildings. What solid figure does each building look like?

16.

Giza, Egypt

17.

Pisa, Italy

18. <u>Writing in Math</u> Draw and describe the solid figure you make if you stack two rectangular prisms.

C Extensions

Artists use **perspective** to make a flat drawing look like a solid figure.

19. Copy these 3 pictures of solids. Then label each one with its name.

20. Try to draw a soup can using perspective.

Mixed Review and Test Prep

Take It to the NET
Test Prep
www.scottforesman.com

Multiply or divide.

21. $42 \div 6$ **22.** 5×8 **23.** 3×9 **24.** $25 \div 5$ **25.** $81 \div 9$

26. There were 95 girls and 82 boys at a school picnic. Which expression shows how many children were at the picnic?

A. $95 - 82$ **B.** $95 \div 82$ **C.** $95 + 82$ **D.** 95×82

Enrichment

Nets

A **net** is a flat pattern that can be folded to make a solid figure. The pictures below show how the net at the right can be folded into a cube.

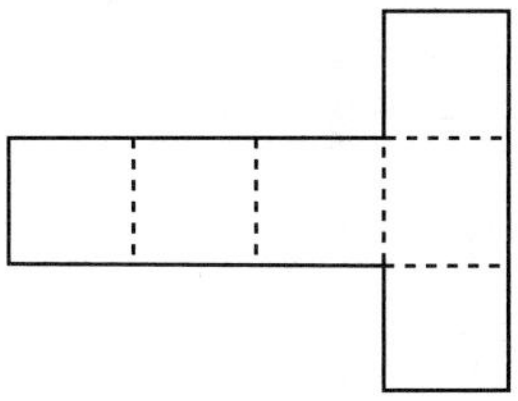

A net for a cube

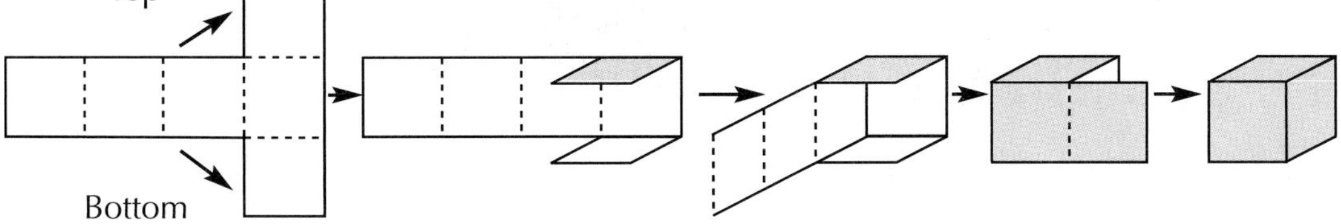

Top

Bottom

Match each net with a solid figure below.

1.

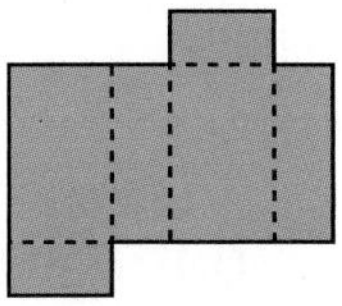

2.

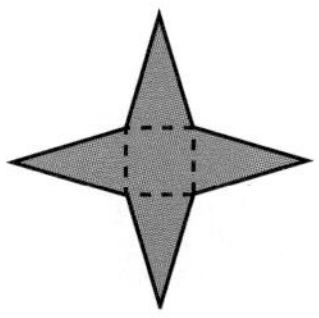

3.

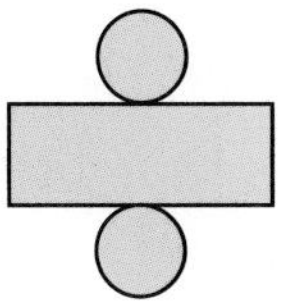

a.

b.

c.

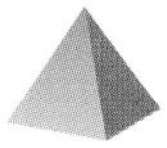

All text pages available online and on CD-ROM.

Section A Lesson 8-1 431

Key Idea
You can describe a solid figure by telling about its parts.

Vocabulary
• face
• edge
• corner
• vertex
• vertices

Materials
• Set of Solids

TEST TALK

Think It Through
I can **draw a picture** to help describe solid figures.

Relating Solids and Shapes

LEARN

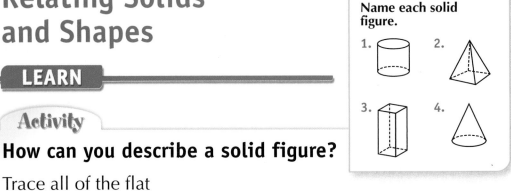
Activity

How can you describe a solid figure?

Trace all of the flat surfaces of each solid figure shown. Describe your tracings as rectangles, squares, circles, or triangles.

a.   b.   c.   d.   e.

What are the parts of solid figures that do not roll?

An **edge** is a line segment where 2 faces meet.

A **corner**, or **vertex**, is where 3 or more edges meet. This solid figure has 8 corners, or **vertices**.

Each flat surface is a **face.**

The flat surfaces of figures that roll are NOT called faces.

✔ Talk About It

1. How many faces does a cube have? What is the shape of each face?

2. What do you notice about the edges of a cube?

3. Is the flat surface of a cone called a face? Explain.

For another example, see Set 8-2 on p. 488.

1. How many edges and vertices does a cube have?

2. Are the flat surfaces of a cylinder called faces? Explain.

3. Which two solid figures have the same number of faces?

PRACTICE

For more practice, see Set 8-2 on p. 492.

A Skills and Understanding

Use the pyramid pictured on page 432 for 4–7.

4. How many edges does the pyramid have?

5. How many vertices does it have?

6. How many faces are there?

7. What are the shapes of the faces?

B Reasoning and Problem Solving

8. How many corners does a juice box have? a juice can?

9. Describe the faces of this wedge of cheese.

10. **Writing in Math** Choose two solid figures. Tell how the two solids are alike. Then tell how the two solids are different.

Mixed Review and Test Prep

Take It to the NET
Test Prep
www.scottforesman.com

Describe a real-world object that is shaped like each solid.

11. Cone   **12.** Cylinder   **13.** Sphere   **14.** Rectangular prism

15. What is the value of 4 dimes, 3 nickels, and 1 penny?

    A. 36¢   **B.** 46¢   **C.** 56¢   **D.** 71¢

Visualize

Visualizing when you read in math can help you use the **problem-solving strategy,** *Act it Out or Use Objects,* in the next lesson.

In reading, visualizing can help you "see" what is happening in a story. In math, visualizing can help you "see" what is happening in a problem and act it out or use objects to solve the problem.

*I'll **act it out and use objects.** I'll use cubes and stack them on my desk.*

*When I **visualize** the problem, I see two cubes joined together.*

Consuela wants to stack two cubes and glue them together. Then she wants to paint the faces that are not glued together. Altogether, how many faces will she paint?

Then I'll count the faces that aren't joined together.

1. How many faces will be glued together?

2. Could you use squares to act out the problem? Explain.

For 3–5, use the problem below.

Michael has 24 pennies. He wants to arrange them in equal stacks. He also wants the number of stacks to be 2 more than the number of pennies in each stack. How should he do this?

3. Visualize the problem. Describe what you see.

4. Now act it out and use objects by representing the problem with 24 plastic or paper circles.

5. Writing in Math Could Michael use 2 stacks with 12 pennies in each stack? Why or why not?

For 6–8, use the problem below.

Mrs. Matzen is making a square quilt by sewing together square pieces of fabric. All of the squares are the same size. There will be 4 squares along each edge of the quilt. The squares around the edge of the quilt will be blue, and the rest will be yellow. How many yellow squares will she use?

6. Visualize the problem. Describe what you see.

7. Now act it out and use objects by representing the problem with plastic or paper squares.

8. How many squares did you need to act out the problem?

For 9–11, use the problem below.

Dorothy has 6 coins. Their total value is 38¢. What coins does she have?

9. Visualize the problem. Describe what you see.

10. Now act it out and use objects by representing the problem with plastic coins or make play money out of paper.

11. Writing in Math Does Dorothy have any pennies? How do you know?

Problem-Solving Strategy

Visualizing
can help you with...
the problem-solving strategy, *Act It Out.*

Act It Out

LEARN

How can you act out a problem to solve it?

Building Blocks How many cubes are needed to build the house shown at the right, including the chimney? The building is completely filled with cubes.

Read and Understand

What do you know?

The bottom part of the house is 5 cubes long, 4 cubes wide, and 3 cubes high. The chimney is 2 cubes long, 2 cubes wide, and 3 cubes tall.

What are you trying to find?

Find the number of cubes needed all together to build the house.

Plan and Solve

What strategy will you use?

Strategy: Act It Out

I will use cubes to act it out.

Step 1 Choose objects if needed to act it out.

Step 2 Show what you know.

Step 3 Act out the problem.

Step 4 Find the answer in your work.

Answer: Seventy-two cubes are needed.

Look Back and Check

Is your answer reasonable?

Yes. The house has 3 layers of 20 cubes each. 20 + 20 + 20 = 60

The chimney has 3 layers of 4 cubes each.

4 + 4 + 4 = 12 and 60 + 12 = 72

Key Idea
Learning how and when to act it out can help you solve problems.

Materials
• color cubes

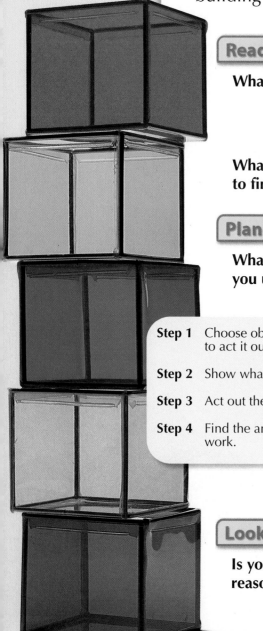

✔ Talk About It

1. Why is it important to know that the building is completely filled with cubes?

2. Explain why acting out the Building Blocks problem might be a better strategy than drawing a picture.

When might you solve a problem by acting it out?

Bridges The three bridges below are made of cubes. There is a pattern in the number of cubes used. How many cubes are needed to build the fifth bridge in the pattern?

> **When to Act it Out**
>
> Think about acting it out when:
> • The numbers in the problem are small.
> • There is some action in the problem that you can do or that you can show with objects.

Solution

Nine cubes are needed to build the fifth bridge.

✔ Talk About It

3. How was "acting it out" used to solve the Bridges problem?

4. What patterns do you see in the solution to the Bridges problem?

CHECK ✔

For another example, see Set 8-3 on p. 488.

Solve this problem by acting it out. Write the answer in a complete sentence.

1. There is a pattern in the number of squares used to make each set of steps shown at the right. How many squares are used to make 6 steps?

1 step   2 steps   3 steps

A Using the Strategy

Solve this problem by acting it out.
Write the answer in a complete
sentence.

1 row   2 rows   3 rows

2. The picture at the right shows how
Brian saw paint cans stacked at the
paint store. How many cans would
be in a stack with 5 rows?

Use the Beach Walk problem for 3–5. Solve
each problem by acting it out. Write the
answer in a complete sentence.

3. When Ryan had taken 8 steps, how many
steps had his father taken?

4. When Ryan had taken 20 steps, how many
had his father taken?

> **Beach Walk** Ryan and his
> father went for a walk on
> the beach. Ryan took
> 4 short steps for every
> 2 long steps his father took.

5. **Decision Making** Ryan wants to take the
same number of steps as his father and cover the same
distance. Should Ryan's steps be twice as long as they
are now or half as long?

Math and Social Studies

The Diaz family took part in an international
doll fair. Dolls from many different countries
were displayed.

6. Two sets of Russian stacking dolls on
display each have 5 dolls that stack
together. The other three sets each have
7 dolls. How many dolls are in all 5 sets?

7. Mrs. Diaz placed dolls from four countries
on a table. The dolls from Guatemala were
behind all the other dolls. The dolls from
Russia were behind the dolls from Portugal
and in front of the dolls from Thailand.
Which dolls were displayed in front?

B Mixed Strategy Practice

Solve each problem. Write the answer in a complete sentence.

8. Carla made some gifts. She gave 1 to her teacher and 2 to each of 5 friends. She then had 2 gifts left. How many gifts did Carla make in the beginning?

9. Dan has 40 cents. All of the coins are nickels. How many nickels does Dan have?

10. **Writing in Math** Four solid shapes are needed to build the new city tower: a cylinder, a rectangular prism, a sphere, and a cube. Use the clues below to describe the tower from bottom to top. Then draw a picture of the tower.

- The cylinder will not touch the ground.

- The rectangular prism will not touch the sphere.

- The cube is under the cylinder and above the rectangular prism.

- The sphere is above the cylinder.

Mixed Review and Test Prep

**Take It to the NET
Test Prep**
www.scottforesman.com

11. What solid figure has a flat surface that is a circle?

12. How many faces does a cube have?

13. Ruth did 63 extra math problems in 7 days. She did the same number of problems each day. Which number sentence would you use to find the number of problems she did each day?

A. $63 + 7 = $ ▨   **C.** $63 \times 7 = $ ▨

B. $63 - 7 = $ ▨   **D.** $63 \div 7 = $ ▨

14. **Writing in Math** Ken has 8 quarters, 5 dimes, 5 nickels, and 5 pennies. This is all the money he has. Explain why the total value of all of Ken's coins could not be $2.81. Then find the correct amount of money he had.

TEST TALK

Think It Through
Stuck? I won't give up. I can:
• Reread the problem.
• Tell what I know.
• Identify key facts and details.
• Tell the problem in my own words.
• Show the main idea.
• Try a different strategy.
• Retrace my steps.

STRATEGIES

- **Show What You Know**
Draw a Picture
Make an Organized List
Make a Table
Make a Graph
Act It Out or Use Objects
- **Look for a Pattern**
- **Try, Check, and Revise**
- **Write a Number Sentence**
- **Use Logical Reasoning**
- **Solve a Simpler Problem**
- **Work Backward**

All text pages available online and on CD-ROM.

Do You Know How?

Do You Understand?

Solid Figures (8-1)

Name the solid figure that each object looks like.

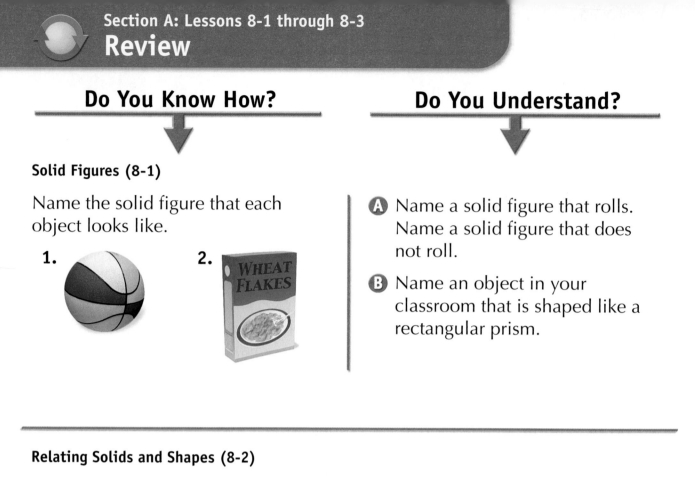

1.

2.

Ⓐ Name a solid figure that rolls. Name a solid figure that does not roll.

Ⓑ Name an object in your classroom that is shaped like a rectangular prism.

Relating Solids and Shapes (8-2)

Write the number of faces on each solid figure.

3.

4.

Ⓒ How many vertices are on a cube?

Ⓓ Name two solid figures that have the same number of faces.

Problem-Solving Strategy: Act it Out (8-3)

Solve this problem by acting it out. Write the answer in a complete sentence.

5. Andy has 16 seashells. He wants to arrange them in 1 or more rows, with the same number in each row. How many different ways can he arrange them?

Ⓔ If you use counters to act out Exercise 5, will one of the arrangements form a square? Explain.

Ⓕ How many rows of 16 shells would there be?

MULTIPLE CHOICE

1. What is the name of the solid figure? (8-1)

  A. cone   **C.** cylinder

  B. cube   **D.** pyramid

2. How many faces does a cube have? (8-2)

  A. 4   **C.** 6

  B. 8   **D.** 12

FREE RESPONSE

Name the solid figure that each object looks like. (8-1)

3.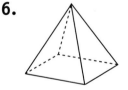

4.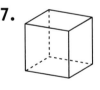

5.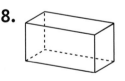

Write the number of edges on each solid figure. (8-2)

6.

7.

8.

9. Mrs. Owen wants her 24 students to form equal groups
with more than 1, but fewer than 12, in each group. How
many different ways could they be grouped? Write the
answer in a complete sentence. (8-3)

Writing in Math

10. Can you make a stack of two spheres? Explain. (8-1)

11. I am a solid figure with two flat surfaces. They are both
circles. Am I a cone? Explain. (8-2)

Key Idea
You can find lines and line segments in shapes and objects.

Vocabulary
• point
• line
• line segment
• ray
• intersecting lines
• parallel lines

Materials
• ruler

Lines and Line Segments

LEARN

What is important to know about lines?

Lines and parts of lines are used in building shapes and solid figures.

A **point** is an exact position.

A **line** is a set of points that is endless in both directions.

A **line segment** is part of a line. It has two endpoints.

A **ray** is part of a line that is endless in one direction. It has one endpoint.

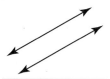

Intersecting lines cross at one point.

Parallel lines never cross.

What are some real-world examples of lines?

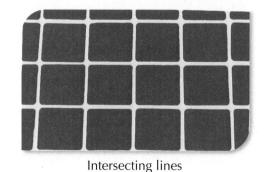

Intersecting lines

Parallel lines

✔ Talk About It

1. Can two line segments intersect? Two rays? Explain.

2. **Reasoning** Find an example of parallel lines and intersecting lines in your classroom.

 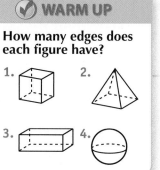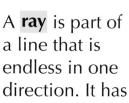

Write the name for each.

1. •

2.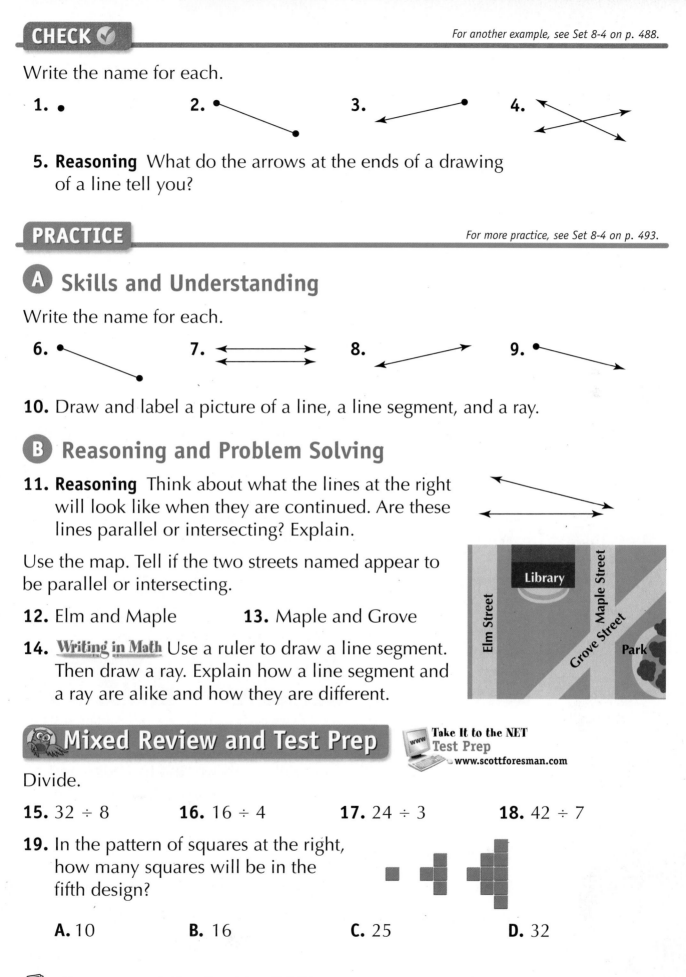

3.

4.

5. **Reasoning** What do the arrows at the ends of a drawing of a line tell you?

PRACTICE
For more practice, see Set 8-4 on p. 493.

A Skills and Understanding

Write the name for each.

6. •

7. ←⟷→

8.

9. •

10. Draw and label a picture of a line, a line segment, and a ray.

B Reasoning and Problem Solving

11. **Reasoning** Think about what the lines at the right will look like when they are continued. Are these lines parallel or intersecting? Explain.

Use the map. Tell if the two streets named appear to be parallel or intersecting.

12. Elm and Maple

13. Maple and Grove

14. **Writing in Math** Use a ruler to draw a line segment. Then draw a ray. Explain how a line segment and a ray are alike and how they are different.

Mixed Review and Test Prep

Take It to the NET
Test Prep
www.scottforesman.com

Divide.

15. 32 ÷ 8

16. 16 ÷ 4

17. 24 ÷ 3

18. 42 ÷ 7

19. In the pattern of squares at the right, how many squares will be in the fifth design?

A. 10

B. 16

C. 25

D. 32

Vocabulary
• angle
• vertex (p. 432)
• right angle
• acute angle
• obtuse angle
• perpendicular

Angles

LEARN

How do you describe angles?

An **angle** is made by two rays that have the same endpoint. That endpoint is called the **vertex** of the angle.

vertex

Different angles have different-sized openings.

 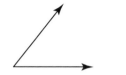

A **right angle** makes a square corner. It is also called a *90-degree angle*.

An **acute angle** is less than a right angle.

An **obtuse angle** is greater than a right angle.

What are some real-world examples of angles?

Right angle

Acute angle

Obtuse angle

Lines, line segments, or rays that form right angles are **perpendicular.** In the first picture above, the top edge and the side edge of the kitchen counter are perpendicular line segments.

Talk About It

1. How can you use the corner of an index card or sheet of paper to decide if an angle is right, acute, or obtuse?

Tell if each angle is right, acute, or obtuse.

1. 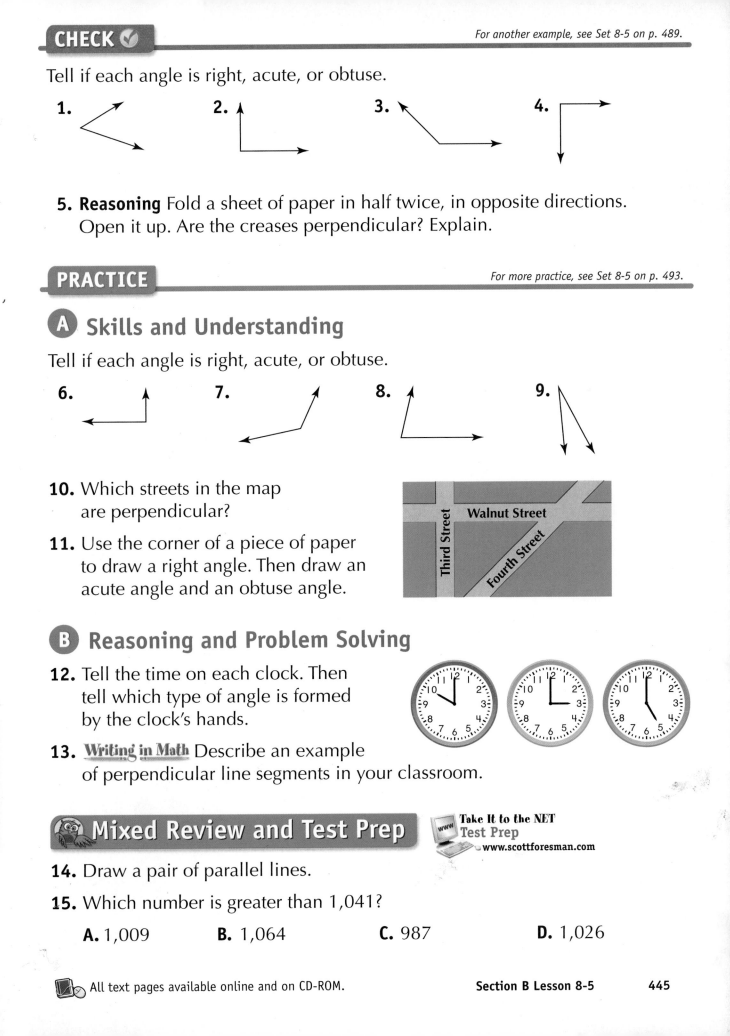   **2.**   **3.**   **4.**

5. Reasoning Fold a sheet of paper in half twice, in opposite directions. Open it up. Are the creases perpendicular? Explain.

PRACTICE

For more practice, see Set 8-5 on p. 493.

Ⓐ Skills and Understanding

Tell if each angle is right, acute, or obtuse.

6.   **7.**   **8.**   **9.**

10. Which streets in the map are perpendicular?

11. Use the corner of a piece of paper to draw a right angle. Then draw an acute angle and an obtuse angle.

Walnut Street
Third Street
Fourth Street

Ⓑ Reasoning and Problem Solving

12. Tell the time on each clock. Then tell which type of angle is formed by the clock's hands.

13. **Writing in Math** Describe an example of perpendicular line segments in your classroom.

Mixed Review and Test Prep

Take It to the NET
Test Prep
www.scottforesman.com

14. Draw a pair of parallel lines.

15. Which number is greater than 1,041?

A. 1,009   **B.** 1,064   **C.** 987   **D.** 1,026

Key Idea
Polygons have straight sides and are named by the number of sides they have.

Vocabulary
• polygon
• side
• triangle
• quadrilateral
• pentagon
• hexagon
• octagon

Materials
• geoboards or dot paper or  tools

Polygons

LEARN

Activity

What is a polygon?

A **polygon** is a closed figure made up of straight line segments. Each line segment on a polygon is a **side.** Each corner, or vertex, of a polygon forms an angle.

Polygon

corner or vertex ⟶ side

Is each figure below a polygon? If not, explain why not.

a.

b.

c.

d.

e.

f.

g.

h.

i.

j. How many sides are there in the polygon shown on the geoboard? How many angles?

Use a geoboard or dot paper.

k. Make a polygon with 3 sides. How many angles are there?

l. Try to make a polygon with 2 sides. Is it possible? Explain.

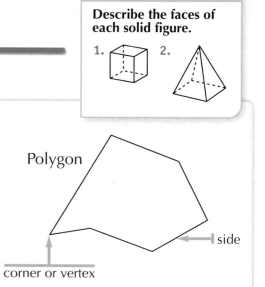
446

Activity

How are polygons named?

Polygons are named by the number of sides they have.

a. Use a geoboard or dot paper to make each polygon listed in the table. Count the angles. Then copy and complete the table.

b. Suppose a polygon has 10 sides. Predict how many angles it has.

Polygon	Number of Sides	Number of Angles
Triangle	3	
Quadrilateral	4	
Pentagon	5	
Hexagon	6	
Octagon	8	

TEST TALK

Think It Through

I can **look for a pattern** to help make a prediction.

CHECK ✓

For another example, see Set 8-6 on p. 489.

Is each figure below a polygon? If it is a polygon, give its name. If not, explain why.

1.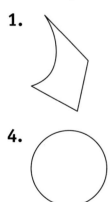

2.

3.

4.

5.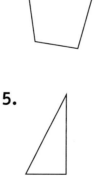

6.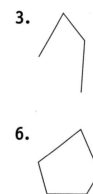

7. Reasoning Tell which polygon comes next in the pattern. Explain why.

A Skills and Understanding

Is each figure below a polygon? If it is a polygon, give its name.
If not, explain why.

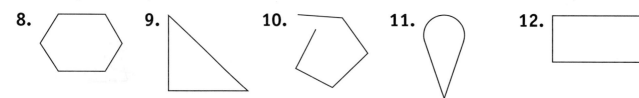

8.   9.   10.   11.   12.

13. **Reasoning** Tell which polygon comes next in the pattern.
Explain why.

B Reasoning and Problem Solving

Answer each riddle in Exercises 14–16 with the
name of a polygon shown at the right.

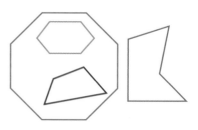

14. I am outside the red polygon. What am I?

15. I am inside the red polygon, but I am not a
hexagon. What am I?

16. I have 2 fewer sides than the red polygon. What am I?

17. Jessie used straws to make a separate triangle, octagon,
and quadrilateral. How many straws did she use?

Math and Everyday Life

Many signs are shaped like polygons.

18. What polygon describes the shape of
each traffic sign?

19. Which traffic signs have right angles?

20. **Writing in Math** Pick any two signs.
Explain how their shapes are alike
and how are they different.

C Extensions

Some special tile patterns, called **tessellations,** are made up of polygons arranged in a special way. What polygons do you see in each tile pattern below?

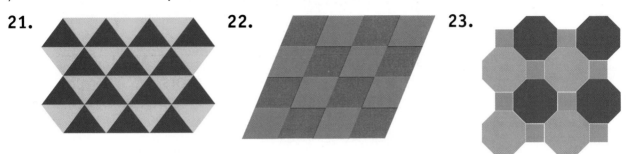

21. **22.** **23.**

24. Draw your own tile pattern. You may trace objects to help.

Mixed Review and Test Prep

Take It to the NET
Test Prep
www.scottforesman.com

25. Draw an obtuse angle.

26. Draw a ray.

27. Find 509 − 64.

A. 445 **C.** 565

B. 545 **D.** 573

28. 27 ÷ 9 = ▮

A. 9 **C.** 4

B. 6 **D.** 3

Learning with Technology

Geometry Shapes eTool

Use the Geometry Shapes eTool to create tessellations. Arrange several triangles together to form a tessellation. Then create a tessellation of hexagons near the triangles.

Now break apart both tessellations and use the two shapes to create one large tessellation. You may add or remove triangles and hexagons for this new tessellation.

Vocabulary
• equilateral triangle
• isosceles triangle
• scalene triangle
• right triangle
• acute triangle
• obtuse triangle

Materials
• grid paper
• scissors
• crayons
• tape or glue

Think It Through
I can **make a model** to help understand triangles.

Triangles

LEARN

Activity

How can you describe triangles by their sides?

a. Use grid paper. Color three sets of paper strips with the lengths and colors shown. Cut out the strips.

8 units	8 units	8 units	3 equal lengths
10 units	10 units	6 units	2 equal lengths, 1 different length
7 units	9 units	11 units	All 3 different lengths

b. Use the strips to make a red triangle, a purple triangle, and an orange triangle. Tape or glue the strips in place on a sheet of paper.

Triangles can be named by the lengths of their sides.

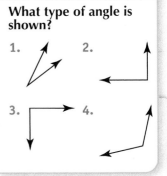

Equilateral triangle
All sides are the same length.

Isosceles triangle
At least two sides are the same length.

Scalene triangle
No sides are the same length.

c. Label each of your triangles with the correct name.

d. How can you use a strip of grid paper to help you decide if a triangle is equilateral, isosceles, or scalene?

How can you describe triangles by their angles?

Another way to describe triangles is by their angles.

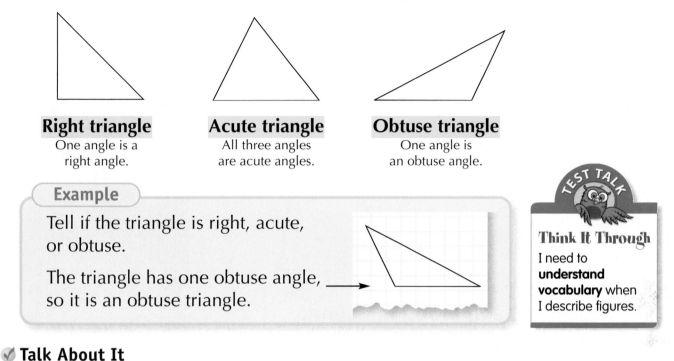

Right triangle
One angle is a
right angle.

Acute triangle
All three angles
are acute angles.

Obtuse triangle
One angle is
an obtuse angle.

Example

Tell if the triangle is right, acute,
or obtuse.

The triangle has one obtuse angle,
so it is an obtuse triangle.

Think It Through
I need to
**understand
vocabulary** when
I describe figures.

✔ **Talk About It**

1. Are all three angles in an obtuse triangle obtuse?

2. How could you use grid paper to decide if a triangle is
   right, acute, or obtuse?

3. **Reasoning** How could you make one straight cut in a
   sheet of rectangular paper to form two right triangles?

CHECK ✓

For another example, see Set 8-7 on p. 489.

You may use grid paper for 1–6.

Tell if each triangle is equilateral, isosceles, or scalene.

1.   2. 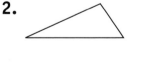   3.

Tell if each triangle is right, acute, or obtuse.

4.    5. 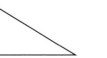   6.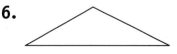

7. **Reasoning** Describe the triangle at the right by its sides and
   by its angles. (Hint: Give it two names.)

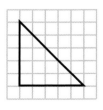

A Skills and Understanding

You may use grid paper for 8–13.

Tell if each triangle is equilateral, isosceles, or scalene.

8.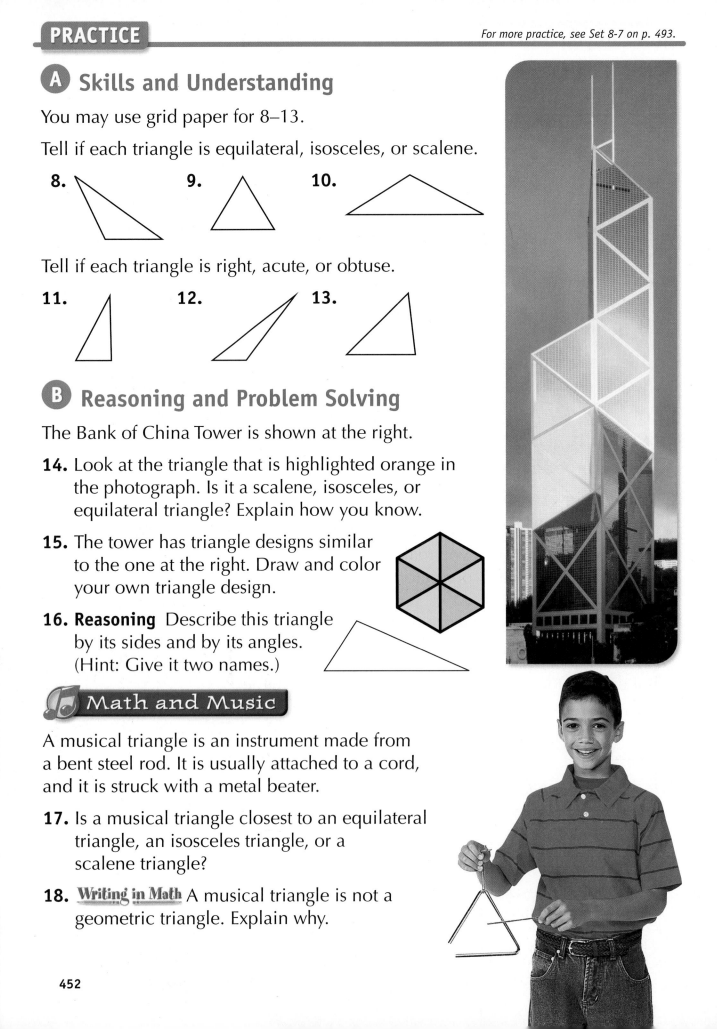

9.

10.

Tell if each triangle is right, acute, or obtuse.

11.

12.

13.

B Reasoning and Problem Solving

The Bank of China Tower is shown at the right.

14. Look at the triangle that is highlighted orange in the photograph. Is it a scalene, isosceles, or equilateral triangle? Explain how you know.

15. The tower has triangle designs similar to the one at the right. Draw and color your own triangle design.

16. Reasoning Describe this triangle by its sides and by its angles. (Hint: Give it two names.)

Math and Music

A musical triangle is an instrument made from a bent steel rod. It is usually attached to a cord, and it is struck with a metal beater.

17. Is a musical triangle closest to an equilateral triangle, an isosceles triangle, or a scalene triangle?

18. Writing in Math A musical triangle is not a geometric triangle. Explain why.

C Extensions

On grid paper, draw a coordinate grid as shown. Then draw line segments to show the paths described.

19. Start at (1, 1). Move up 5 units. Then move to the right 4 units. Then return to the starting point. Is the triangle you formed right, acute, or obtuse? Is it equilateral, isosceles, or scalene?

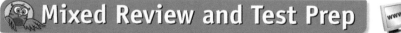

Mixed Review and Test Prep

Take It to the NET
Test Prep
www.scottforesman.com

20. 438 + 118   **21.** 13 + 22 + 47   **22.** $1.66 + 0.27   **23.** 42 + 30

24. The shape of which sign has only right angles?

A. ONE WAY   B.   C.   D. EXIT

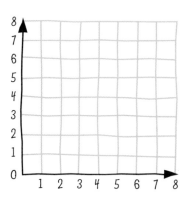

Discovery CHANNEL SCHOOL

Discover Math in Your World

It's in the Stars

Have you ever gone out at night and found a group of stars that look like a big dipper? Many ancient people were sky watchers. They named groups of stars, called constellations, after animals and imaginary people. The Big Dipper is part of the constellation named Ursa Major, the Great Bear.

1. Trace the part of Ursa Major that forms the bowl of the Big Dipper. What polygon do you see?

2. Trace another polygon you see in Ursa Major. Name the polygon.

Take It to the NET
Video and Activities
www.scottforesman.com

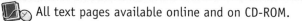

Key Idea
There are different kinds of quadrilaterals. Some have special names.

Vocabulary
• rectangle
• square
• parallelogram
• rhombus
• trapezoid

Materials
• grid paper

Think It Through
I need to look carefully at all the definitions before I name a quadrilateral.

Quadrilaterals

What are some special quadrilaterals?

The top of the table in Gina's classroom is the shape of a special quadrilateral. Here are the names of some quadrilaterals with special names.

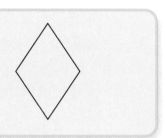

Rectangle
Four right angles and opposite sides are the same length.

Square
Four right angles and all sides are the same length.

Notice that a square is a special rectangle.

Parallelogram
Opposite sides are parallel and the same length.

Rhombus
Opposite sides are parallel and all sides are the same length.

Trapezoid
There is only one pair of parallel sides.

Example

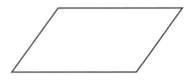

Name the quadrilateral.

Opposite sides are parallel, and the sides all have the same length, so the figure is a rhombus.

✔ **Talk About It**

1. What is the shape of the tabletop shown at the top of the page?

2. If the quadrilateral in the example also had 4 right angles, what would you call it?

Write at least one special name for each quadrilateral.

1. 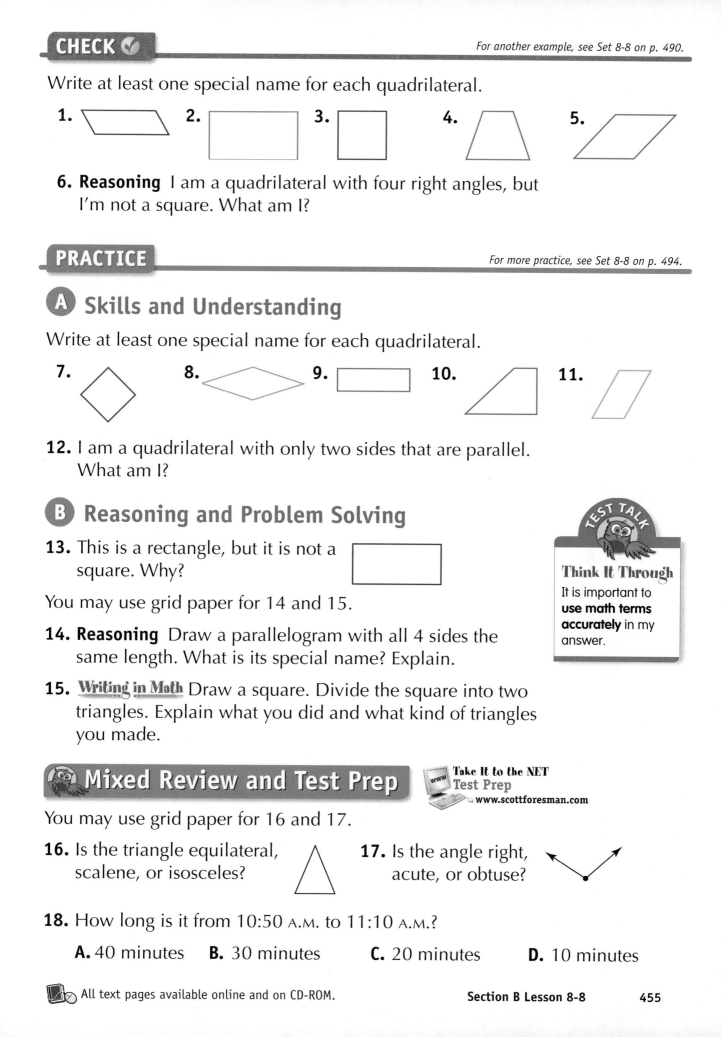 **2.** **3.** **4.** **5.**

6. Reasoning I am a quadrilateral with four right angles, but I'm not a square. What am I?

PRACTICE

For more practice, see Set 8-8 on p. 494.

A Skills and Understanding

Write at least one special name for each quadrilateral.

7. **8.** **9.** **10.** **11.**

12. I am a quadrilateral with only two sides that are parallel. What am I?

B Reasoning and Problem Solving

13. This is a rectangle, but it is not a square. Why?

You may use grid paper for 14 and 15.

14. Reasoning Draw a parallelogram with all 4 sides the same length. What is its special name? Explain.

15. Writing in Math Draw a square. Divide the square into two triangles. Explain what you did and what kind of triangles you made.

TEST TALK

Think It Through
It is important to **use math terms accurately** in my answer.

Mixed Review and Test Prep

Take It to the NET
Test Prep
www.scottforesman.com

You may use grid paper for 16 and 17.

16. Is the triangle equilateral, scalene, or isosceles?

17. Is the angle right, acute, or obtuse?

18. How long is it from 10:50 A.M. to 11:10 A.M.?

A. 40 minutes   **B.** 30 minutes   **C.** 20 minutes   **D.** 10 minutes

All text pages available online and on CD-ROM.

Think It Through
Using grid paper to **draw a picture** can help when drawing a congruent figure.

Congruent Figures and Motion

LEARN

Activity

How do you flip a figure?

A **flip,** or **reflection,** of a figure gives its mirror image.

a. Fold a piece of tracing paper in half. Trace a polygon on one side of the folded paper.

b. Flip the folded paper to the unused side. Trace your figure.

c. Open up the paper and compare the two figures.

The two figures are **congruent.** This means they have the same size and shape.

Trace the first figure on tracing paper. Then place the drawing over the second figure. Tell whether the figures are congruent.

d.

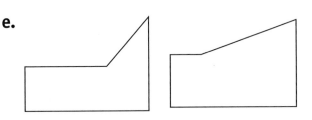

e.

f. Draw a polygon on grid paper. Have a classmate draw a polygon that is congruent to yours. Repeat with several more examples.

Activity

What are some other ways to move figures?

You can **slide,** or **translate,** a figure. You can also **turn,** or **rotate,** a figure. When you slide, turn, or flip a figure you make a congruent figure.

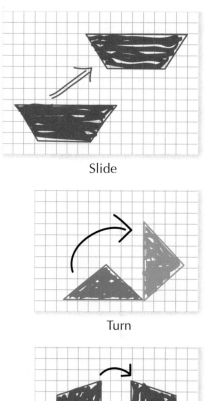

Slide

Turn

Flip

a. On a sheet of grid paper, trace a polygon and color it. Slide it. Then trace it again. Label your picture *Slide.*

b. Trace another polygon. Turn it. Then trace it again. Label your picture *Turn.*

c. Trace a different polygon and color it, flip it over, and then trace it again. Label your picture *Flip.*

d. Work with a partner. On a fresh sheet of grid paper, trace a polygon. Without showing your partner, flip it, slide it, or turn it. Trace it again. Ask your partner to tell what motion you used.

CHECK ✓

For another example, see Set 8-9 on p. 490.

Are the figures congruent? Write *yes* or *no.* You may use tracing paper to decide.

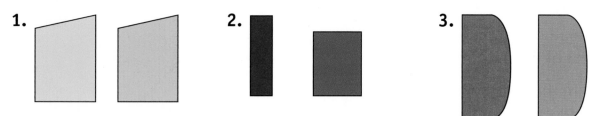

Write *flip, slide,* or *turn* for each. You may use tracing paper.

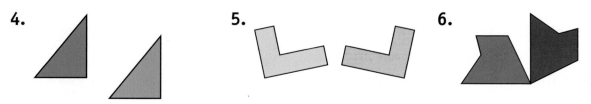

7. Reasoning Could a triangle and a square ever be congruent? Explain.

A Skills and Understanding

Are the figures congruent? Write *yes* or *no*. You may use tracing paper to decide.

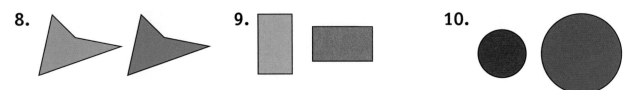

8.

9.

10.

Write *flip, slide,* or *turn* for each. You may use tracing paper to decide.

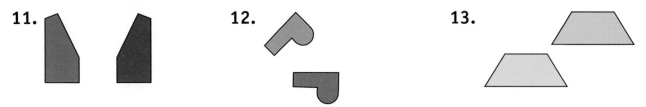

11.

12.

13.

14. Reasoning Are all triangles congruent? Explain.

B Reasoning and Problem Solving

15. Draw a rectangle. Then draw a line that divides the rectangle into two congruent figures. Describe the figures.

16. Find two congruent shapes in your classroom.

 Math and Art

Many interesting designs can be made with the tangram pieces shown. Trace the pieces and cut them out.

17. Use all of the pieces to make each of the 3 animals shown.

18. More than the seven pieces are required for this camel. Which additional piece or pieces are needed for the blue region?

19. **Writing in Math** Which tangram pieces are congruent? How can you show that they are congruent?

Tangram puzzle: According to Chinese legend, a man named Tan dropped a square tile which broke into these seven pieces.

C Extensions

Figures that have the same shape are **similar** figures. If they also have the same size, then they are congruent.

Not similar

Similar

Write whether the figures look like they are similar. Write *yes* or *no*.

20.

21.

22.

23.

Mixed Review and Test Prep

Take It to the NET
Test Prep
www.scottforesman.com

24. How many sides does a rhombus have?

25. 44 ÷ 6 =

A. 6 R4   **B.** 7   **C.** 7 R2   **D.** 8 R4

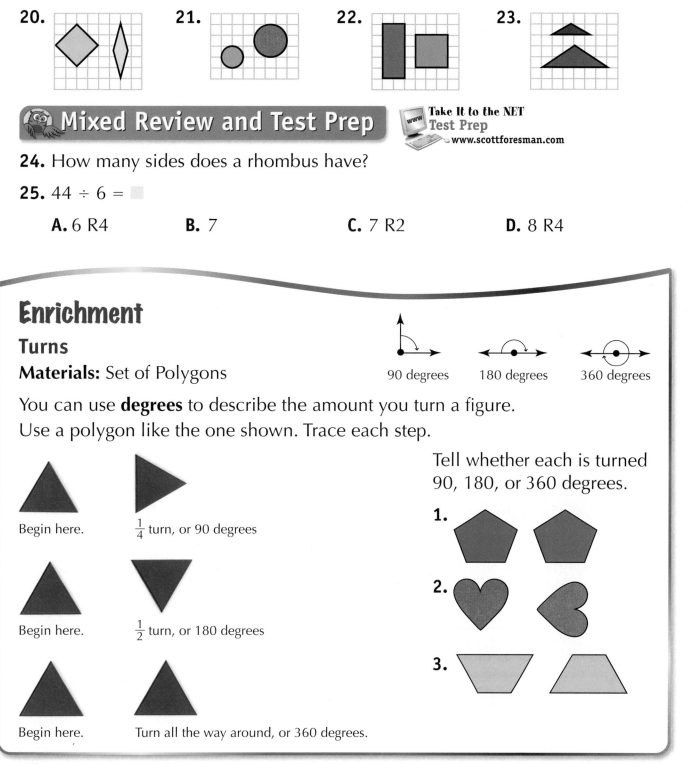

Enrichment

Turns

Materials: Set of Polygons

90 degrees   180 degrees   360 degrees

You can use **degrees** to describe the amount you turn a figure.
Use a polygon like the one shown. Trace each step.

Begin here. $\frac{1}{4}$ turn, or 90 degrees

Begin here. $\frac{1}{2}$ turn, or 180 degrees

Begin here.   Turn all the way around, or 360 degrees.

Tell whether each is turned 90, 180, or 360 degrees.

1.

2.

3.

All text pages available online and on CD-ROM.

Think It Through
I can **draw a picture** to help understand symmetry.

Symmetry

LEARN

Activity

What are symmetric figures?

a. Fold a piece of paper in half.

b. Draw a curve that begins and ends at the fold.

c. With the paper still folded, cut along the curve.

d. Open the paper.

Your figure is **symmetric** because the two halves of the figure match. The fold line is the **line of symmetry.**

Can a shape have more than one line of symmetry?

Some figures are not symmetric. Some have more than one line of symmetry.

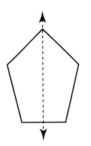

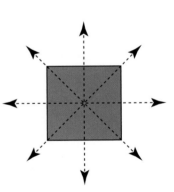

This figure has one line of symmetry.

This figure is not symmetric. It has no lines of symmetry.

This figure has four lines of symmetry.

✓ **Talk About It**

1. How many lines of symmetry does the rectangle shown have? To decide, trace the rectangle and fold the tracing paper.

Tell whether each figure is symmetric. Write *yes* or *no*.
You may use tracing paper to decide.

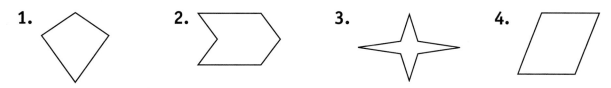

1.

2.

3.

4.

5. **Reasoning** Which figure above has more than one line of symmetry?

PRACTICE

For more practice, see Set 8-10 on p. 494.

Ⓐ Skills and Understanding

Tell whether each figure is symmetric. Write *yes* or *no*.
You may use tracing paper to decide.

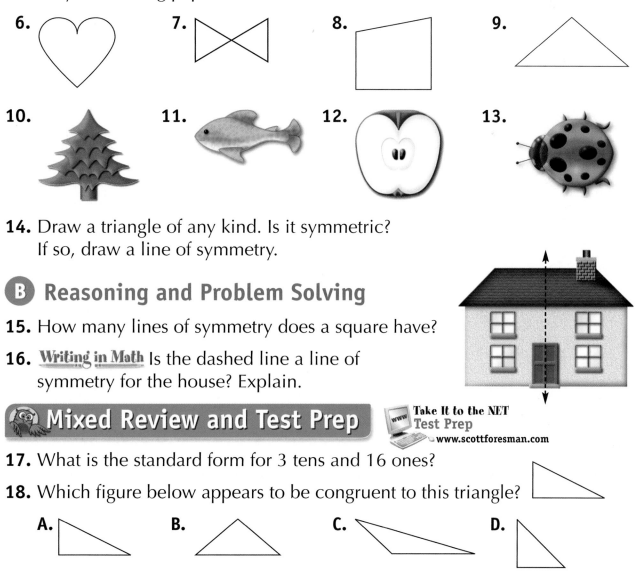

6.

7.

8.

9.

10.

11.

12.

13.

14. Draw a triangle of any kind. Is it symmetric?
If so, draw a line of symmetry.

Ⓑ Reasoning and Problem Solving

15. How many lines of symmetry does a square have?

16. **Writing in Math** Is the dashed line a line of
symmetry for the house? Explain.

Mixed Review and Test Prep

Take It to the NET
Test Prep
www.scottforesman.com

17. What is the standard form for 3 tens and 16 ones?

18. Which figure below appears to be congruent to this triangle?

A.

B.

C.

D.

Do You Know How?

Do You Understand?

Lines and Line Segments (8-4)

Write the name for each.

1.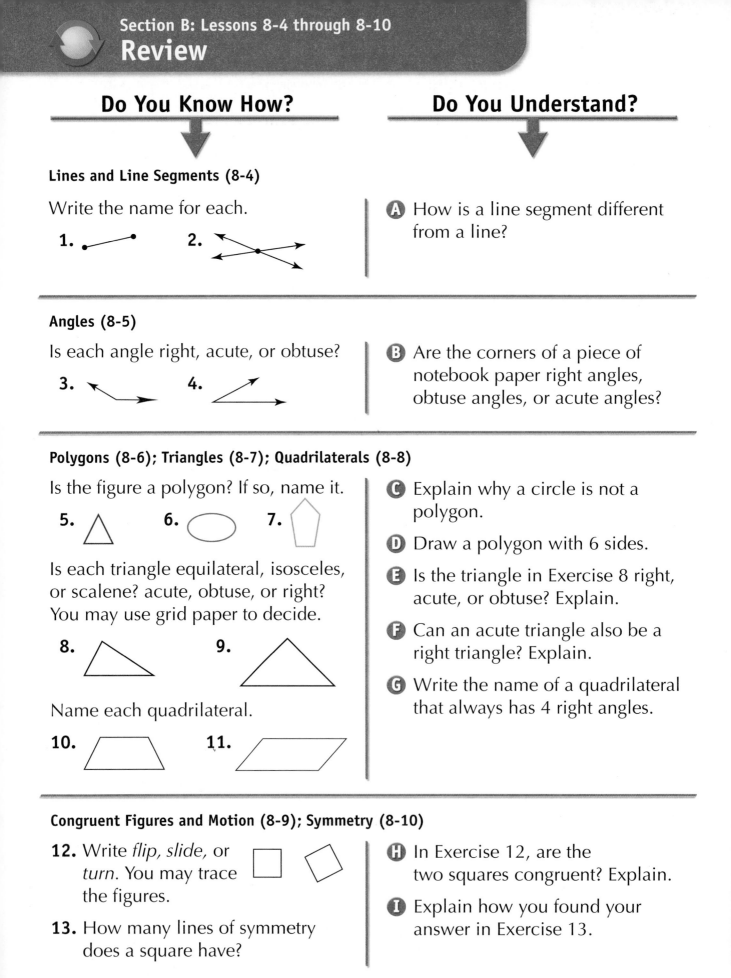

2.

Ⓐ How is a line segment different from a line?

Angles (8-5)

Is each angle right, acute, or obtuse?

3.

4.

Ⓑ Are the corners of a piece of notebook paper right angles, obtuse angles, or acute angles?

Polygons (8-6); Triangles (8-7); Quadrilaterals (8-8)

Is the figure a polygon? If so, name it.

5.

6.

7.

Is each triangle equilateral, isosceles, or scalene? acute, obtuse, or right? You may use grid paper to decide.

8.

9.

Name each quadrilateral.

10.

11.

Ⓒ Explain why a circle is not a polygon.

Ⓓ Draw a polygon with 6 sides.

Ⓔ Is the triangle in Exercise 8 right, acute, or obtuse? Explain.

Ⓕ Can an acute triangle also be a right triangle? Explain.

Ⓖ Write the name of a quadrilateral that always has 4 right angles.

Congruent Figures and Motion (8-9); Symmetry (8-10)

12. Write *flip, slide,* or *turn.* You may trace the figures.

13. How many lines of symmetry does a square have?

Ⓗ In Exercise 12, are the two squares congruent? Explain.

Ⓘ Explain how you found your answer in Exercise 13.

MULTIPLE CHOICE

1. Which is an obtuse triangle? (8-7)

A.   C.

B.   D.

2. Which is a pentagon? (8-6)

A.   C.

B.   D.

FREE RESPONSE

Write the name for each. (8-4)

3.

4.

Name each quadrilateral. (8–8)

5.

6.

Tell whether each angle is right, acute, or obtuse. (8-5)

7.

8.

9.

Is each figure a polygon? If so, give its name. (8-6)

10.

11.

12.

Tell if each triangle is equilateral, isosceles, or scalene. (8-7)

13.

14.

15.

Write *flip, slide,* or *turn* for each. (8-9)

16.   **17.**

Is the figure symmetric? (8-10)

18.   **19.**

Writing in Math

20. Can an obtuse triangle also be a scalene triangle? Explain. Draw a picture if it helps. (8-7)

TEST TALK

Think It Through
I can **draw a picture to explain** my answer.

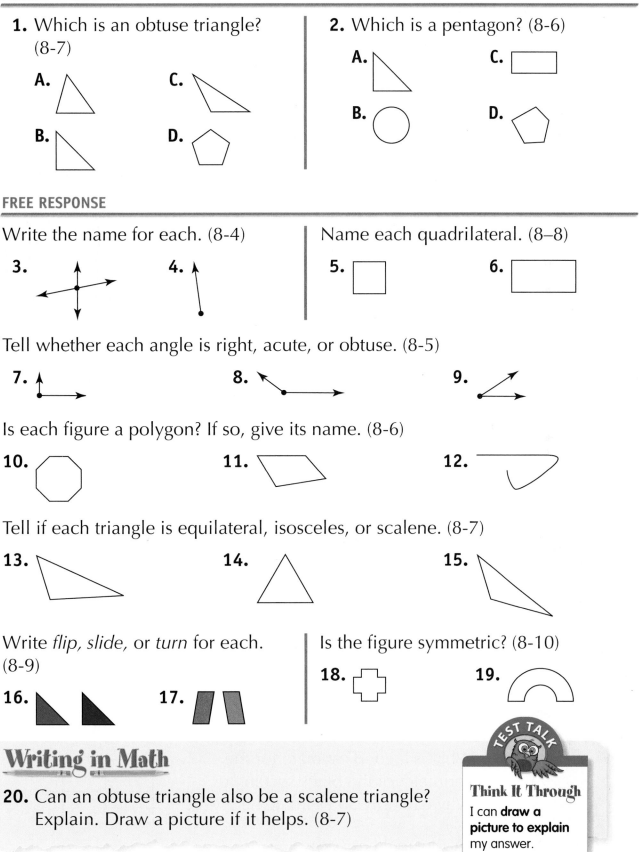

Key Idea
You can find the distance around a figure.

Vocabulary
• perimeter

Materials
• paper clips
• crayons
• grid paper
  or  tools

TEST TALK

Think It Through
I can **use objects** to measure perimeter.

Perimeter

LEARN

Activity

What is the perimeter of a figure?

The distance around a figure is its **perimeter.** Find the perimeter of the cover of your math book by measuring with paper clips.

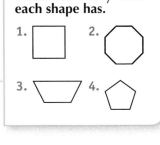

a. Place paper clips around the edges of your book. How many did you use?

b. Find the perimeter again using crayons.

c. Did you use more crayons or paper clips? Explain why it took more or fewer crayons to find the perimeter.

The perimeter of the orange rectangle below is 18 units. You can find the perimeter by counting the units along the outside of the rectangle.

Find the perimeter of each.

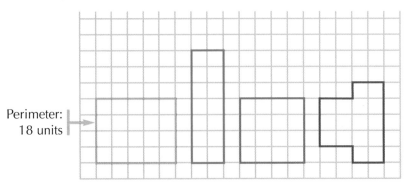

Perimeter: 18 units

d. Green rectangle   **e.** Purple square   **f.** Blue octagon

g. What is a good estimate for the perimeter of the black rectangle? Why can only an estimate be given?

How do you find perimeter using measurements?

Example A

Find the perimeter of this pentagon.

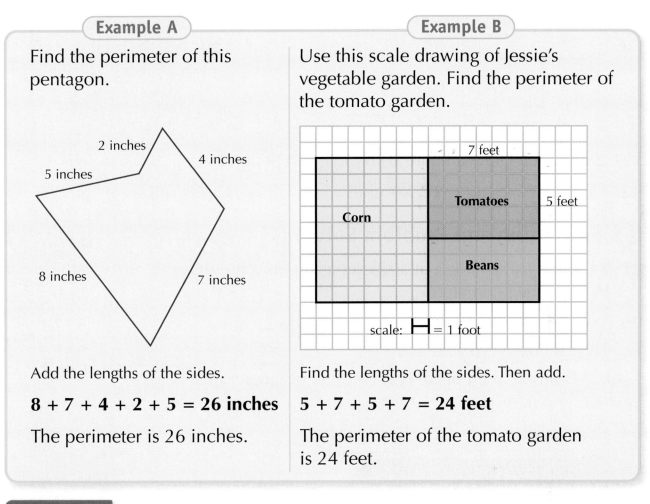

2 inches
4 inches
5 inches
8 inches
7 inches

Add the lengths of the sides.

8 + 7 + 4 + 2 + 5 = 26 inches

The perimeter is 26 inches.

Example B

Use this scale drawing of Jessie's vegetable garden. Find the perimeter of the tomato garden.

7 feet
Tomatoes   5 feet
Corn
Beans

scale: ⊢ = 1 foot

Find the lengths of the sides. Then add.

5 + 7 + 5 + 7 = 24 feet

The perimeter of the tomato garden is 24 feet.

CHECK ✓

For another example, see Set 8-11 on p. 491.

Find the perimeter of each polygon.

1.

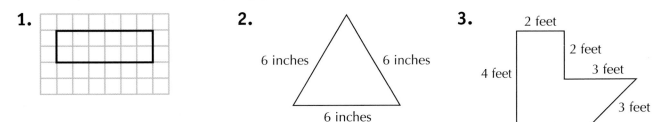

2.

6 inches   6 inches

6 inches

3.

2 feet
2 feet
4 feet   3 feet
3 feet
3 feet

Use grid paper. Draw a figure with each perimeter.

4. 12 units

5. 4 units

6. 22 units

7. Reasoning Can different shapes have the same perimeter? Draw a picture on grid paper to help explain.

Find the perimeter of each polygon.

8.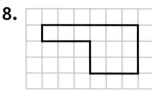

9.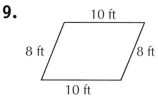

10.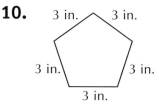

Use grid paper. Draw a figure with the given perimeter.

11. 8 units

12. 14 units

13. 24 units

B Reasoning and Problem Solving

14. Reasoning The length of a side of a square is 8 units. What is the perimeter?

15. The perimeter of an equilateral triangle is 21 units. How long is each side?

Look at Example B on page 465. Find the perimeter of each garden named.

16. Bean garden

17. Corn garden

18. Whole vegetable garden

Math and Science

How would you like to take a close-up picture of a shark?

19. What is the perimeter of the floor in the shark cage shown at the right?

20. **Writing in Math** Ari wants to put rope around the poster of a shark below. He figured out how much rope he needs using paper and pencil. Is his work correct? If not, correct his work.

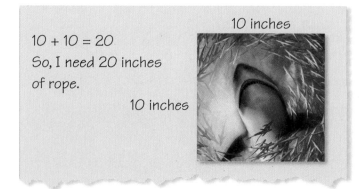

10 + 10 = 20.
So, I need 20 inches of rope.

10 inches

10 inches

Scientists study and photograph sharks from the safety of an underwater shark cage. The floor of this shark cage is shaped like a rectangle, 5 feet by 6 feet.

C Extensions

The perimeter of a circle has a special name—**circumference.**

21. Look around your classroom for an object shaped like a cylinder. Use it to trace a circle on a sheet of paper. Measure the circumference of the circle using crayons or paper clips.

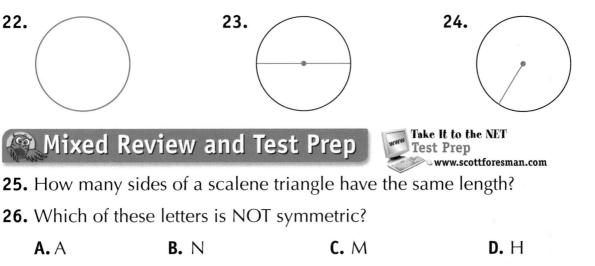

Some of the special parts of a circle are shown at the right. For each circle below, tell whether the red part is the **radius, diameter,** or **circumference.**

22. **23.** **24.**

Mixed Review and Test Prep

25. How many sides of a scalene triangle have the same length?

26. Which of these letters is NOT symmetric?

A. A   **B.** N   **C.** M   **D.** H

Learning with Technology

Geometry Drawing eTool

Use the Geometry Drawing eTool to draw symmetric figures. Draw a rectangle.

1. How many lines of symmetry does your rectangle have? Find the perimeter of the rectangle. If the rectangle was cut across its vertical line of symmetry, what would the perimeters of each of the two rectangles be?

2. Draw an equilateral triangle. How many lines of symmetry does your triangle have? Draw line segments to represent the lines of symmetry.

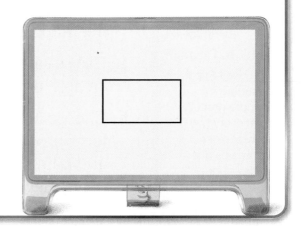

All text pages available online and on CD-ROM.

Key Idea
Square units are used to measure the space inside a figure.

Vocabulary
• square unit
• area

Materials
• paper clips
• square tiles
• grid paper
or **tools**

Area

LEARN

Activity

How do you measure area?

You found the perimeter of your math book cover in paper clips. Now use paper clips to find the area of your math book cover.

a. Place paper clips over the surface of your math book cover. How many did you use?

b. Repeat Part a using square tiles. Did you use more paper clips or square tiles? Explain.

A **square unit** is a square with sides that are each 1 unit long. The number of square units needed to cover the region inside a figure is its **area.**

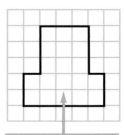
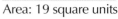

Area: 19 square units

1 square unit

1 square unit

c. Count the square units to find the area of each figure at the right.

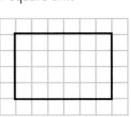

d. Estimate the number of square units in the triangle at the right.

e. Use square tiles to make a figure with an area of 16 square units.

f. Choose an object from your classroom, for example, a crayon box. Set the object on a piece of grid paper and trace around the object. Then remove the object and estimate the area of the shape you traced.

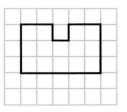

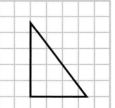

Think It Through

I can **use logical reasoning** to estimate area. I'll count every two partly covered squares as one whole square.

How can you multiply to find area?

When you find the area of a rectangle or square, you can think of the grid squares as an array.

This rectangle shows 4 rows of squares with 6 squares in each row.

4 rows

6 square units in each row

To find the area of the rectangle, you can multiply.

4 × 6 = 24 square units

The area of the rectangle is 24 square units.

Think It Through
I can **use what I know** about multiplication to find area.

✔ Talk About It

1. How could you count squares to find the area of the rectangle above?

2. Could you multiply to find the area of the figure below? Explain.

CHECK ✔

For another example, see Set 8-12 on p. 491.

Find the area of each figure. Write your answer in square units.

1.

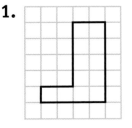

2.

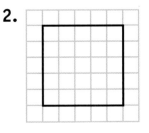

3.

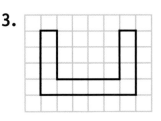

4. Reasoning Use grid paper. Draw a figure that has an area of 12 square units. What is the perimeter of the figure?

A Skills and Understanding

Find the area of each figure. Write your answer in square units.

5.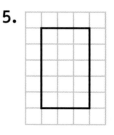

6.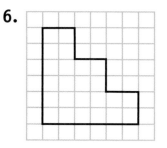

7.

8. In the figures above, which figure has the greatest area? the greatest perimeter?

B Reasoning and Problem Solving

9. Reasoning Use grid paper. Make two different figures that each have an area of 16 square units. Find each perimeter.

10. How can you multiply to find the area of the figure in Exercise 5?

11. Estimate the area of the figure to the right.

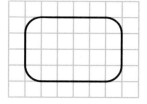

 Math and Art

A gallery is planning a display of animal photographs.

12. What is the area of each photo?

13. Use grid paper. Draw a rectangle that has a smaller area than the giraffe photo and a greater area than the monkey photo.

14. <u>Writing in Math</u> Is Amy's work correct? If not, tell why and correct her work.

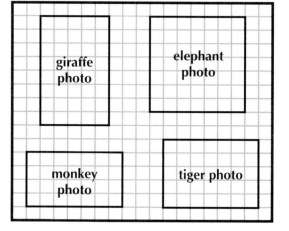

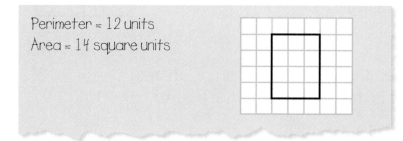

Perimeter = 12 units
Area = 14 square units

C Extensions

A **square inch** is a square with one-inch sides.

A **square centimeter** is a square with one-centimeter sides.

A **square foot** is a square with one-foot sides.

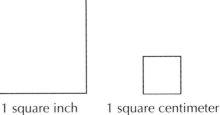

1 square inch   1 square centimeter

15. Is the area of a book cover closer to 1 square foot or 1 square inch?

16. If you found the area of a sheet of paper in square inches and then in square centimeters, which would have more units? How do you know?

Mixed Review and Test Prep

Take It to the NET
Test Prep
www.scottforesman.com

17. Write from least to greatest: 652, 625, 637

18. How many feet of fencing are needed for Ollie's garden?

    A. 11 feet   **C.** 24 feet

    B. 22 feet   **D.** 30 feet

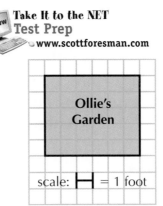

Ollie's Garden

scale: ⊢ = 1 foot

Enrichment

Circle Graphs

Anita spent $18 on materials to make a kite. The **circle graph** at the right shows the three items she bought and what part of the total cost was spent on each.

Notice that the section for nylon is the largest. This means that the nylon cost more than either of the other two items.

1. Which item cost the least? How do you know?

2. One of the items cost $9. Which item do you think that was? Why?

3. If the frame cost twice as much as the string, how much did each one cost? Hint: Use what you learned in Exercise 2 to help solve this problem.

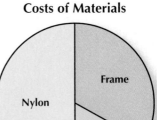

Costs of Materials

Frame

Nylon

String

Key Idea
The space inside a solid figure can be measured with cubic units.

Vocabulary
• cubic unit
• volume

Materials
• small cubes
• small box

Think It Through
I can **use objects** to help find the volume of a solid figure.

Volume

LEARN

Activity

How can we measure the space inside a solid figure?

a. Use a small box. How many small cubes do you think it will take to fill your box?

b. Fill the box with as many small cubes as possible. How many did you use?

A **cubic unit** is a cube with edges that are 1 unit long. The number of cubic units needed to fill a solid figure is its **volume.**

Build each solid figure with cubes. Then count the cubic units to find the volume.

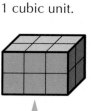

Each small cube is 1 cubic unit.

Volume:
12 cubic units

c.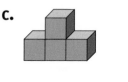

d.

e.

CHECK ✓   *For another example, see Set 8-13 on p. 491.*

Find the volume of each figure. Write your answer in cubic units.

1.

2.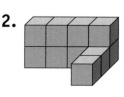

3.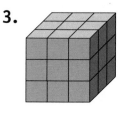

4. Reasoning Draw or build two different solids each with a volume of 8 cubic units.

A Skills and Understanding

Find the volume of each figure. Write your answer in cubic units.

5.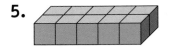

6.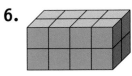

7.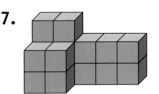

8. Reasoning Draw or build two different solids, each with a volume of 12 cubic units.

B Reasoning and Problem Solving

9. Estimate the volume of the rectangular prism at the right.

10. Maddy made a rectangular prism with 5 layers of cubes. There are 6 cubes in each layer. What is the volume of the rectangular prism?

11. **Writing in Math** Tell how the two figures at the right are the same. Then tell how they are different.

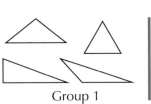

Mixed Review and Test Prep

Take It to the NET
Test Prep
www.scottforesman.com

Find each answer.

12. 7×7 **13.** $15 \div 3$ **14.** $24 \div 4$ **15.** 8×0 **16.** 6×10

17. **Writing in Math** Kiko sorted some geometric shapes into two groups. Describe a rule Kiko used to sort the shapes.

Group 1   Group 2

18. Use grid paper. Draw a rectangle with an area of 24 square units.

19. In the morning, Ray painted 12 windows. By the end of the day he had painted all 26 windows in the house. Which expression could you use to find how many windows he painted in the afternoon?

   A. $26 + 12$ **B.** $26 - 12$ **C.** 26×12 **D.** $26 \div 12$

Problem-Solving Skill

Reading Helps!

Brainstorming
can help you with...
writing to describe.

Key Idea
There are specific things you can do to write a good description in math.

Writing to Describe

⎯ LEARN ⎯

How do you write a good description?

When you **write to describe** geometric figures, you need to use geometric terms.

Shapes Use geometric terms to describe two ways the square and the rectangle shown below are alike.

Square	Rectangle

Think It Through
I should **list the characteristics** of squares and rectangles to help me decide how they are alike.

Writing a Math Description

- Write down all the geometric terms that tell about the shapes in the group.

- Look for the geometric terms that tell how the shapes are alike.

- Use these geometric terms to tell about or describe how the shapes are alike.

Geometric terms that describe how the square and rectangle are alike:
    4 sides
    4 right angles

A square and a rectangle both have 4 right angles and 4 sides.

✔ Talk About It

1. What geometric terms did you use in your descriptions?

2. Write a statement that tells how the square and the rectangle shown are different.

A pencil can be used to write about 45,000 words!

Use geometric terms in your descriptions.

1. Write a statement that describes how the figures at the right are alike.

2. Write a statement that describes how the figures at the right are different.

Write to describe.

3. Write a statement to describe how triangles A and B are alike.

4. Write a statement describing how triangles A and B are different.

5. a. How are a pyramid and a cone alike?

    b. How are a pyramid and a cone different?

6. a. How are a square and a rectangle alike?

    b. How are a square and a rectangle different?

7. Clare traced a trapezoid. Then she flipped it over and traced it again.

    a. How are the two trapezoids the same?

    b. How are they different?

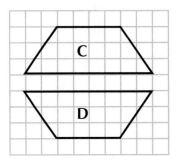

8. Reasoning I am a cone. My friend has two flat surfaces that are the same shape as my flat surface. My friend has no vertices. What kind of solid figure is my friend?

9. How are figures A and B alike? How are they different? Hint: Include perimeter and area in your descriptions.

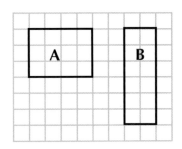

10. How are a trapezoid and a rhombus alike? How are they different?

11. How is multiplication like addition? How is multiplication different from addition?

DK

Problem-Solving Applications

Sports Flags Flags used in sports come in many shapes and sizes. They can be used as signals or as markers to indicate boundaries and directions. Fans wildly wave flags to cheer on their teams!

FLAG
Discover the story of flags and banners –
their history, their meanings,
and how they are used
WILLIAM CRAMPTON

Trivia Although the first modern Olympics were held in 1896, the Olympic flag was not designed until 1913 and was not used until the 1920 games.

Marker flags

1 Playing fields and race courses may be marked with flags. What kind of angles are seen in the marker flags? in the soccer linesmen's flags?

2 In some gymnastics competitions, a wand is used to gracefully move a long ribbon. The wand may be about 2 feet long. The ribbon must be about 10 times this length. How long is the ribbon?

Using Key Facts

3 What is the perimeter of the official Olympic flag? What is its area?

Key Facts
Official Olympic Flag
• Height   about 7 feet
• Width   about 10 feet
• Number of rings   5
• Ring diameter   about 2 feet

Gymnastics ribbon

Bunting

④ Look at the two-colored bunting flag above. Is the line between the yellow and red parts of this bunting flag a line of symmetry? If not, describe any line of symmetry that can be drawn.

Checkered flag

⑤ Checkered flags may vary from race to race. One checkered flag has five rows of squares that are 4 inches wide. Each row has 6 squares. How many squares are on this checkered flag? What is the flag's perimeter?

Good News/Bad News *If a racecar driver sees the checkered flag waving, it means that the driver has won the race. If a driver sees the flag held still, it means that someone else has won the race.*

⑥ **Decision Making** Design and draw a flag you could use to cheer on a sports team. It must have at least 2 different polygons. Label each polygon.

⑦ <u>Writing in Math</u> Describe the flag you made in Question 6 with enough detail so that a person could draw it without seeing your picture.

Soccer linesmen's flag

Do You Know How?

Do You Understand?

Perimeter (8-11)

Find the perimeter of the polygon.

1.
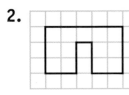

Ⓐ How can you count units to find the perimeter?

Ⓑ Use grid paper. Draw a figure with a perimeter of 12 units.

Area (8-12)

Find the area of each figure. Write your answer in square units.

2. **3.**
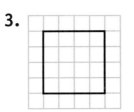

Ⓒ What is the perimeter of the figure in Exercise 2?

Ⓓ Can you multiply to find the area of the figure in Exercise 3? Explain.

Volume (8-13)

4. Find the volume of the figure. Write your answer in cubic units.

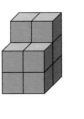

Ⓔ How many cubes are completely hidden in the figure for Exercise 4?

Ⓕ Lisa filled a box with 3 layers of 10 cubes. What is the volume of the box?

Problem-Solving Skill: Writing to Describe (8-14)

5. Write two statements that describe how the rectangle and the parallelogram are alike. Use geometric terms.

Ⓖ What geometric terms did you use to describe how a rectangle and a parallelogram are alike?

MULTIPLE CHOICE

1. What is the area of the figure? (8-12)

    A. 16 square units   **C.** 10 square units

    B. 12 square units   **D.** 6 square units

2. What is the perimeter of the triangle? (8-11)

    A. 10 inches   **C.** 25 inches

    B. 15 inches   **D.** 30 inches

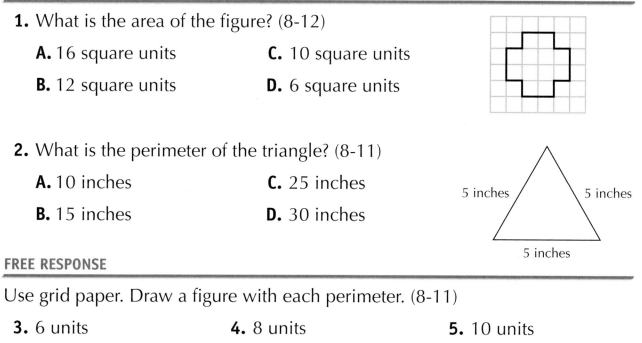

FREE RESPONSE

Use grid paper. Draw a figure with each perimeter. (8-11)

3. 6 units   **4.** 8 units   **5.** 10 units

Find the area of each figure. Write your answer in square units. (8-12)

6.
     7.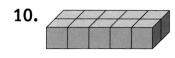
     8.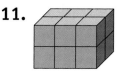

Find the volume of each figure. Write your answer in cubic units. (8-13)

9.   **10.**   **11.**

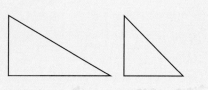

Writing in Math

12. Can a square have the same perimeter as a rectangle? Draw a picture to help explain. (8-11)

13. Describe how the triangles at the right are alike. Use geometric terms. (8-14, 8-15)

Test-Taking Strategies

Understand the question.
Get information for the answer.
Plan how to find the answer.
Make smart choices.
Use writing in math.
Improve written answers.

Plan How to Find the Answer

After you understand a test question and get needed information, you need to plan how to find the answer. Think about problem-solving skills and strategies and computation methods you know.

1. On a grid like the one below, draw a rectangle that has an area of 24 square units.

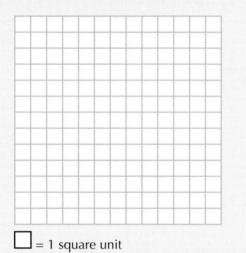

☐ = 1 square unit

What is the perimeter of the rectangle you drew?

_____ units

Understand the question.

I need to draw a rectangle. Then I need to find the perimeter.

Get information for the answer.

*The grid has no information. I'll need to **get information from the text**.*

Plan how to find the answer.

• Think about problem-solving skills and strategies.

*I can **try, check, and revise** my drawing until I have a rectangle whose area is 24 square units. Then I can **use addition** to find the perimeter.*

• Choose computation methods.

*Since I know my multiplication facts, I can **use mental math** to check that the area is 24 square units. Then I can use **paper and pencil** to add the lengths of the sides to find the perimeter.*

2. Look at the quadrilateral below.

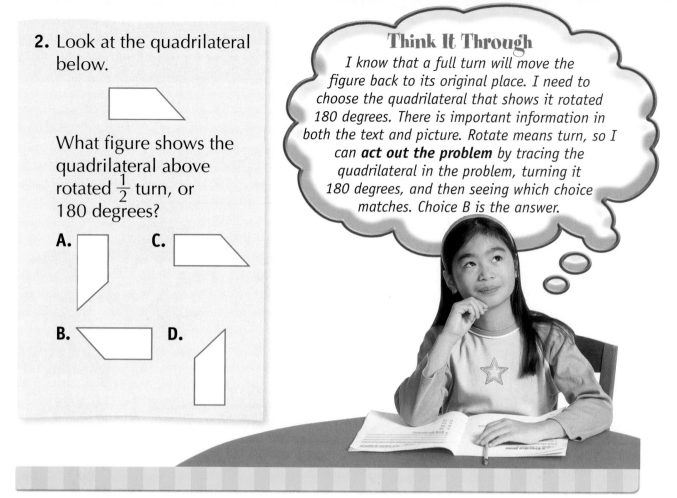

What figure shows the quadrilateral above rotated $\frac{1}{2}$ turn, or 180 degrees?

A.

B.

C.

D.

Think It Through

*I know that a full turn will move the figure back to its original place. I need to choose the quadrilateral that shows it rotated 180 degrees. There is important information in both the text and picture. Rotate means turn, so I can **act out the problem** by tracing the quadrilateral in the problem, turning it 180 degrees, and then seeing which choice matches. Choice B is the answer.*

Now it's your turn.

For each problem, describe a plan for finding the answer.

3. On the grid below, draw a rectangle that has a perimeter of 14 units.

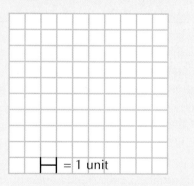

= 1 unit

What is the area in square units of the rectangle you drew?

4. Look at the triangle below.

What figure shows the triangle above reflected?

A.

C.

B.

D.

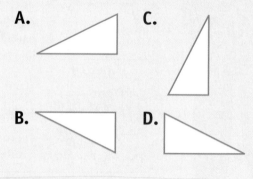

Self Check

Streets cross at intersections.

Intersecting lines cross each other. (p. 442)

Use geometric terms to describe figures. (Lessons 8-4, 8-5)

Lines and Parts of Lines

Point:

Line:

Line segment:

Ray:

Pairs of Lines

Parallel

Intersecting

Perpendicular

Angles

vertex

right

acute

obtuse

1. Write the name for each figure at the right.

(a)　(b)　(c)

"Poly-" means more than one.

A **polygon** has 3 or more sides. (p. 446)

Self Check

Identify geometric figures. (Lessons 8-1, 8-2, 8-6, 8-7, 8-8)

You can use the classifications shown at the right to identify a figure.

Trapezoid

A **polygon** is a closed flat figure made up of line segments.

face
edge
corner or vertex

A **solid figure** has 3 dimensions.

Rectangular prism

Flat Figures

polygons: triangle, quadrilateral, pentagon, hexagon, octagon
triangles: equilateral, isosceles, scalene, right, acute, obtuse
quadrilaterals: rectangle, square, parallelogram, rhombus, trapezoid

Solid Figures

all flat surfaces: cube, rectangular prism, pyramid
curved surfaces: sphere, cylinder, cone

2. Identify each figure.

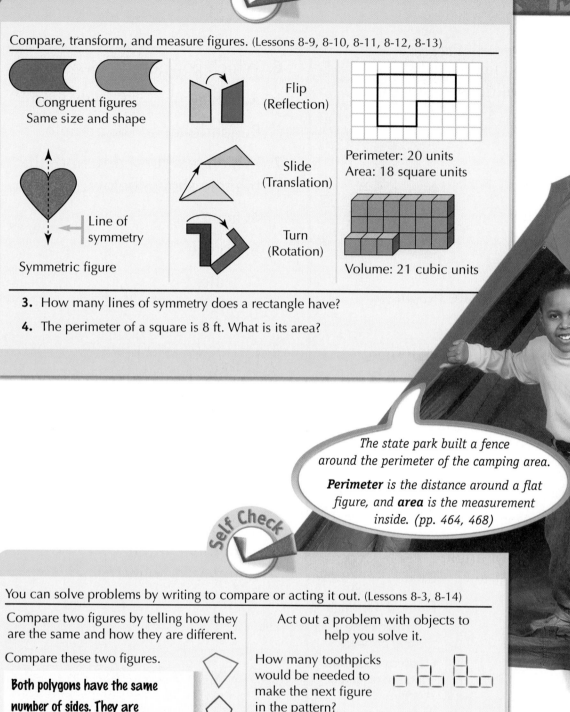

Compare, transform, and measure figures. (Lessons 8-9, 8-10, 8-11, 8-12, 8-13)

Congruent figures
Same size and shape

Line of symmetry

Symmetric figure

Flip (Reflection)

Slide (Translation)

Turn (Rotation)

Perimeter: 20 units
Area: 18 square units

Volume: 21 cubic units

3. How many lines of symmetry does a rectangle have?

4. The perimeter of a square is 8 ft. What is its area?

The state park built a fence around the perimeter of the camping area.

Perimeter is the distance around a flat figure, and **area** is the measurement inside. (pp. 464, 468)

You can solve problems by writing to compare or acting it out. (Lessons 8-3, 8-14)

Compare two figures by telling how they are the same and how they are different.

Compare these two figures.

Both polygons have the same number of sides. They are quadrilaterals. The bottom quadrilateral is a symmetric figure, but the top one is not symmetric.

Act out a problem with objects to help you solve it.

How many toothpicks would be needed to make the next figure in the pattern?

Use toothpicks to make the next figure.

22 toothpicks

5. How many toothpicks would be in the next (5th) figure in the pattern above?

Answers: 1. (a) intersecting lines, (b) ray, (c) right angle 2. right scalene triangle; rectangle; octagon; cube 3. 2 4. 4 square feet 5. 28 toothpicks

MULTIPLE CHOICE

1. Which solid figure does the building look like?

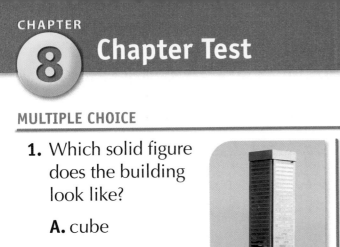

A. cube

B. pyramid

C. rectangular prism

D. cylinder

2. Which solid figure has no flat surfaces?

A. cone **C.** cylinder

B. cube **D.** sphere

3. What is the name for the figure below?

A. point **C.** line segment

B. line **D.** ray

4. What kind of angle is shown below?

A. acute

B. vertex

C. right

D. obtuse

TEST TALK

Think It Through
- I can **eliminate wrong answers.**
- I can **compare** the angle to a square corner.

5. Which figure is NOT a polygon?

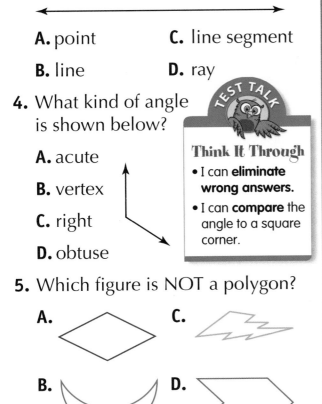

A. **C.**

B. **D.**

6. Which polygon has 5 sides?

A. hexagon **C.** pentagon

B. quadrilateral **D.** triangle

7. Which term best describes the triangle shown below?

A. acute

B. obtuse

C. scalene

D. right

8. Name the quadrilateral shown below.

A. parallelogram

B. rectangle

C. rhombus

D. trapezoid

9. Which figure is congruent to the figure at the right?

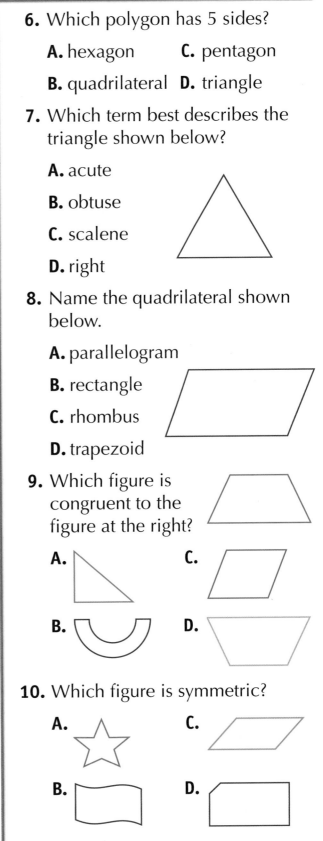

A. **C.**

B. **D.**

10. Which figure is symmetric?

A. **C.**

B. **D.**

11. What is the perimeter of this rectangular swimming pool?

A. 8 feet

B. 14 feet

C. 28 feet

D. 32 feet

8 feet

6 feet

12. Find the volume of this figure.

A. 3 cubic units

B. 4 square units

C. 7 cubic units

D. 8 cubic units

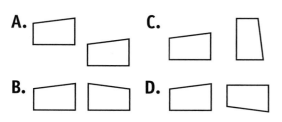

13. Which of the following shows a turn?

A.

C.

B.

D.

FREE RESPONSE

14. How many faces, edges, and vertices does this solid figure have?

15. How many square yards of carpet will be needed to cover the floor in Jessica's room?

Jessica's Room

☐ = 1 sq. yard

16. The perimeter of an equilateral triangle is 24 feet. What is the length of each side of the triangle?

Writing in Math

17. A. How are quadrilaterals A and B alike?

B. How are quadrilaterals A and B different?

A   B

18. Solve this problem by acting it out.

How many sides would be used to make the fifth polygon if you follow the pattern below? Explain how you know.

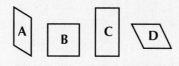

TEST TALK

Think It Through
- Before I choose objects to act it out, I need to **understand the pictures.**
- I need to **check if my answer makes sense.**

19. Sort these quadrilaterals into two groups. Explain the rule you used.

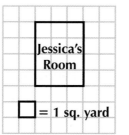

A   B   C   D

Number and Operation

MULTIPLE CHOICE

1. What is the sum of 472 and 319?

   Think It Through
   I can **use estimation to eliminate wrong answers**.

   A. 153

   B. 761

   C. 781

   D. 791

2. Carol has 56 beads. She will use 8 beads to make each necklace. How many necklaces can she make?

   A. 7   **B.** 8   **C.** 48   **D.** 448

3. Which number sentence is NOT part of the same fact family?

   A. $42 \div 7 = 6$ **C.** $42 \div 6 = 7$

   B. $6 + 7 = 13$ **D.** $7 \times 6 = 42$

FREE RESPONSE

4. Mark bought a bag of pretzels for $2.35 and a sandwich for $4.98. How much change did he get back from $10?

Writing in Math

5. Mrs. Coleman bought 3 boxes of pencils. What do you need to know to find how many pencils she bought in all? Explain your answer.

Geometry and Measurement

MULTIPLE CHOICE

6. Name the quadrilateral shown below.

   A. parallelogram

   B. rectangle

   C. pentagon

   D. square

7. What is the area of the figure?

   A. 12 square units

   B. 18 square units

   C. 20 square units

   D. 28 square units

   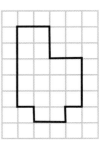

FREE RESPONSE

8. A square has a perimeter of 24 meters. What is the length of each side of the square?

9. Math class started at 10:50 A.M. and ended at 11:35 A.M. How long was the class?

Writing in Math

10. **A.** How are figures A and B the same?

    B. How are figures A and B different?

    A   B

Data Analysis and Probability

Use the line plot for Items 11 and 12.

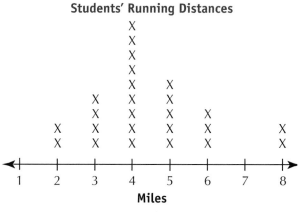

Students' Running Distances

11. What is the mode of the data?

   A. 4   **B.** 5   **C.** 7   **D.** 8

12. How many students ran exactly 5 miles?

   A. 4   **B.** 5   **C.** 6   **D.** 8

Use the coordinate grid for 13–15.

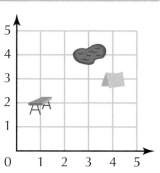

13. What is located at (3, 4)?

14. Name the ordered pair to describe the location of the picnic table.

Writing in Math

15. Explain how to plot and label a point for a basketball court that is located at (4, 2).

Algebra

16. What number sentence does this array show?

   A. 3 + 5 = 8

   B. 3 × 5 = 15

   C. 3 × 3 = 9

   D. 5 × 5 = 25

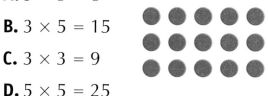

17. Which number goes in the ▨ to complete the pattern?

   21, 17, 13, ▨, 5

   A. 10   **B.** 9   **C.** 8   **D.** 7

18. Write a numerical expression for the phrase below.

   9 less than 28

Think It Through
I need to **choose an operation** that matches the words in the problem.

19. Copy and complete.

   6 × ▨ = 48   48 ÷ 6 = ▨

Writing in Math

20. Mr. Flynn will donate $2 for every book that his son reads in the school read-a-thon. How many books will his son have to read for Mr. Flynn to donate $22? Explain how you found your answer.

Set 8-1 (pages 428–431)

Name this solid figure.

The figure has all flat surfaces and a point at the top. The figure is a pyramid.

Remember that some solid figures roll and some do not.

Name the solid figure or figures each object looks like.

1.    2.

Set 8-2 (pages 432–433)

How many faces, edges, and vertices does the following solid figure have?

A rectangular prism has 6 faces, 12 edges, and 8 vertices.

Remember that a corner, or vertex, is where 3 or more edges meet.

Tell how many faces, edges, and vertices each solid figure has.

1. 2.

Set 8-3 (pages 436–439)

When you solve a problem by acting it out, follow these steps.

Step 1: Choose objects to act it out.

Step 2: Show what you know.

Step 3: Act out the problem.

Step 4: Find the answer.

Remember, decide what the objects represent before you act out the problem.

1. How many cans would be used in the 5th stack?

1st stack   2nd stack   3rd stack

Set 8-4 (pages 442–443)

Write the name for the following.

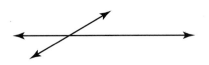

The lines cross at one point. They are intersecting lines.

Remember that parallel lines never cross.

Write the name for each.

1. ←——→   2. •——→

3. •——•   4.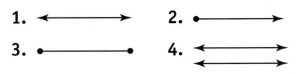

Set 8-5 (pages 444–445)

Tell whether the angle is right, acute, or obtuse.

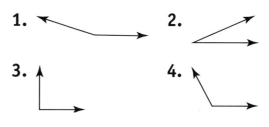

The angle makes a square corner.

The angle is a right angle.

Remember that the opening of an acute angle is less than that of a right angle.

Describe each angle.

1. 2.

3. 4.

Set 8-6 (pages 446–449)

Is the figure at the right a polygon? If it is a polygon, give its name. If not, explain why.

The figure is closed and is made up of straight line segments. The figure is a polygon.

The figure has 5 sides and 5 corners. The figure is a pentagon.

Remember that a polygon is made up of line segments.

Is each figure a polygon? If it is a polygon, give its name. If not, explain why.

1. 2.

3. 4.

Set 8-7 (pages 450–453)

Tell if the triangle is equilateral, isosceles, or scalene.

None of the sides are the same length. The triangle is a scalene triangle.

Tell if the triangle is right, acute, or obtuse.

One angle is an obtuse angle.

The triangle is an obtuse triangle.

Remember that all the sides in an equilateral triangle are the same length.

Describe each triangle by its angles and sides. You may use grid paper to decide.

1. 2.

3. 4.

Set 8-8 (pages 454–455)

Name the following quadrilateral.

Opposite sides are parallel, and opposite sides have the same length.

The figure is a parallelogram.

Remember that all quadrilaterals have four sides.

Name each quadrilateral.

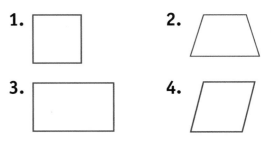

1.   2.

3.   4.

Set 8-9 (pages 456–459)

Are the figures congruent?

The two figures are the same size and shape. They are congruent.

Write *flip, slide,* or *turn.*

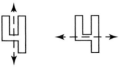

The shaded figure is a mirror image. The figures show a flip.

Remember that you can trace figures to check if they are congruent.

Are the figures congruent?

1.   2.

Write *flip, slide,* or *turn.*

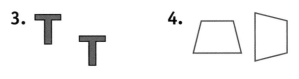

3.   4.

Set 8-10 (pages 460–461)

Tell if the figure is symmetric.

The two halves of the figure do not match.

The figure is not symmetric.

Remember that a symmetric figure has two halves that are congruent.

Tell whether each figure is symmetric. Write *yes* or *no.* You may trace to decide.

1.   2.

Find the
perimeter of
this polygon.

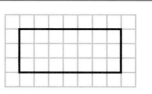

$3 + 7 + 3 + 7 = 20$ feet

The perimeter is 20 feet.

Remember to add the lengths of all
the sides to find the perimeter.

Find the perimeter of each polygon.

1. 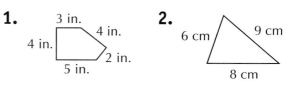 **2.**

Find the area of this figure.

Eighteen square units
are needed to cover
the region inside
the figure.

The area of the figure
is 18 square units.

Remember that you can multiply to
find the area of a rectangle.

Find the area of each figure.

1. 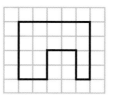 **2.**

Find the volume
of this figure.

Eight cubic units are
needed to fill the solid figure.

The volume of the figure is 8 cubic units.

Remember to count all the cubes.

Find the volume of each figure.

1. 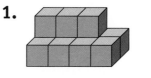 **2.**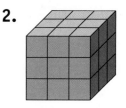

When you write to describe, follow
these tips.

1. Use pictures to show how
   the objects or ideas are alike
   and how they are different.

2. Make lists of ways the objects or
   ideas are alike and different.

Remember to use your pictures to
help you make your lists.

1. How are a pyramid and a
   cone alike?

2. How are a pyramid and a cone
   different?

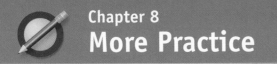
Set 8-1 (pages 428–431)

Name the solid figure or figures each object looks like.

1.   **2.**   **3.**   **4.**

5. Toby glued two cubes together. What solid figure did he make?

Set 8-2 (pages 432–433)

Tell how many faces, edges, and vertices each solid figure has.

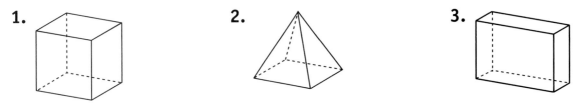

1.   **2.**   **3.**

4. Aleesha is holding two different solid figures that do not roll. The two solid figures have the same number of faces, same number of edges, and same number of vertices. What two solid figures is Aleesha holding?

Set 8-3 (pages 436–439)

Solve each problem by acting it out. Write the answer in a complete sentence.

1. The figures below are made of cubes. There is a pattern in the number of cubes used. How many cubes are needed to build the fifth figure in the pattern?

 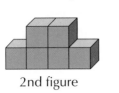 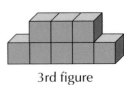

1st figure   2nd figure   3rd figure

2. Phil and Tabitha were building towers out of connecting cubes. For every 3 cubes that Phil stacked, Tabitha stacked 4 cubes. When Phil had stacked 12 cubes, how many cubes had Tabitha stacked?

Take It to the NET
More Practice
www.scottforesman.com

Set 8-4 (pages 442–443)

Write the name for each.

1. 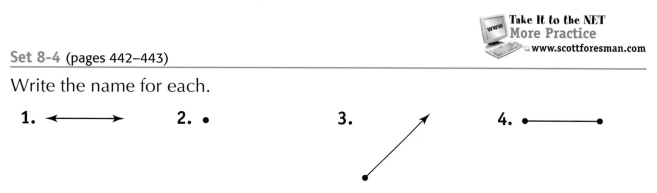   **2.**   **3.**   **4.**

5. The Town Hall is on the corner where Main Street crosses First Street. Tell if the streets are parallel or intersecting.

Set 8-5 (pages 444–445)

Tell if each angle is right, acute, or obtuse.

1.   **2.**   **3.**   **4.**

5. Describe the center lines in the picture.

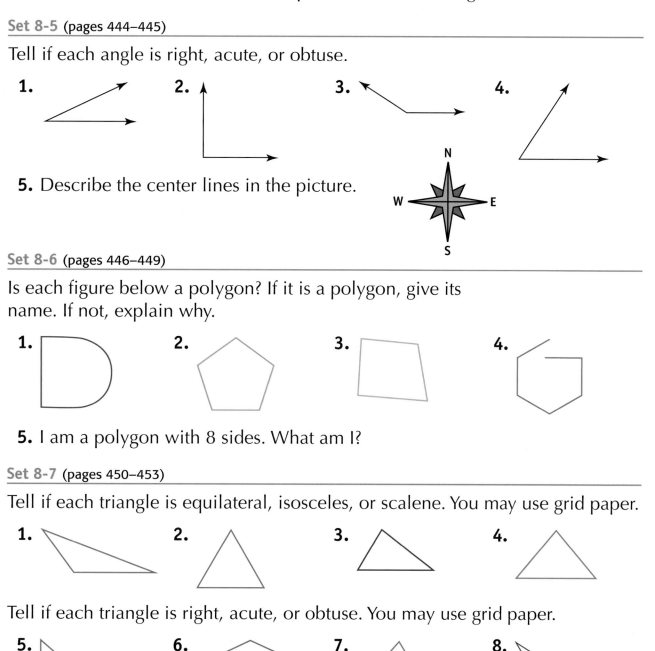

Set 8-6 (pages 446–449)

Is each figure below a polygon? If it is a polygon, give its name. If not, explain why.

1.   **2.**   **3.**   **4.**

5. I am a polygon with 8 sides. What am I?

Set 8-7 (pages 450–453)

Tell if each triangle is equilateral, isosceles, or scalene. You may use grid paper.

1.   **2.**   **3.**   **4.**

Tell if each triangle is right, acute, or obtuse. You may use grid paper.

5.   **6.**   **7.**   **8.**

Set 8-8 (pages 454–455)

Write the name of each quadrilateral.

1.   2.   3.   4.

5.   6.   7.   8.

9. Kelly drew two squares side by side to make another quadrilateral. What quadrilateral did Kelly draw?

Set 8-9 (pages 456–459)

Are the figures congruent? Write yes or no. You may trace to decide.

1.   2.   3.

Write *flip, slide,* or *turn* for each. You may trace to decide.

4.   5.   6.

7. Draw a square. Then draw a line that divides the square into two congruent figures. Describe the figures.

Set 8-10 (pages 460–461)

Tell whether each figure is symmetric. Write *yes* or *no*. You may trace to decide.

1.   2.   3.   4.

5. How many lines of symmetry does this letter H have?

Take It to the NET
More Practice
www.scottforesman.com

Set 8-11 (pages 464–467)

Find the perimeter of each polygon.

1.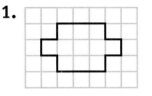

2.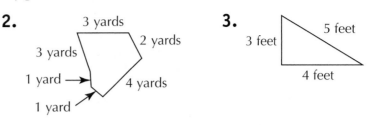
3 yards
2 yards
3 yards
1 yard →
4 yards
1 yard →

3.
3 feet
5 feet
4 feet

4. The perimeter of an equilateral triangle is 18 inches. How long is each side?

Set 8-12 (pages 468–471)

Find the area of each figure. Write your answer in square units.

1.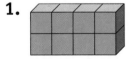

2.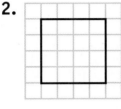

3.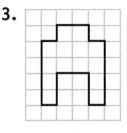

4. How can you multiply to find the area in Exercise 2?

Set 8-13 (pages 472–473)

Find the volume of each figure. Write your answer in cubic units.

1.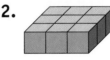

2.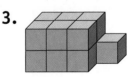

3.

4. Anna made a rectangular prism using 3 layers with 4 cubes in each layer. Find the volume.

Set 8-14 (pages 474–475)

Write to describe. You may draw a picture to help.

1. A. How are a rectangle and a parallelogram alike?

   B. How are a rectangle and a parallelogram different?

2. A. How are figures A and B alike?

   B. How are figures A and B different?

A   B

CHAPTER 9

Fractions and Measurement

 DIAGNOSING READINESS

A Vocabulary

(Grade 2 and page 464)

Choose the best term from the box.

1. When a shape has two equal parts each is called one __?__.

2. The __?__ can be used to measure length.

3. To find the __?__ of a polygon, add the lengths of its sides.

Vocabulary
- **fourth** *(Gr. 2)*
- **half** *(Gr. 2)*
- **inch** *(Gr. 2)*
- **perimeter** *(p. 464)*

B Division Facts

(Pages 386–393)

4. 36 ÷ 6

5. 12 ÷ 3

6. 15 ÷ 5

7. 8 ÷ 2

8. 10 ÷ 5

9. 16 ÷ 2

10. 30 ÷ 6

11. 24 ÷ 4

12. Sam has 18 marbles to share equally with a friend. How many marbles will each person get?

13. Twelve students will be placed in teams of 2. How many teams will there be?

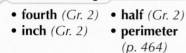

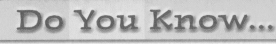

Do You Know...

When was the first button-making machine patented?

You'll find out in Lesson 9-17.

THE BOOK OF
BUTTONS
A practical and creative guide to the decorative use of buttons
Joyce Whittemore
DK

C Fraction Concepts
(Grade 2)

For each picture, tell how many equal parts are red. Then tell how many equal parts there are in all.

14.

15.
16.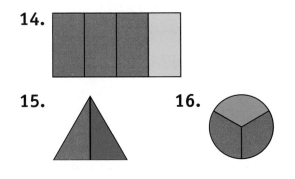

D Customary Linear Measurement
(Grade 2)

17. Would you measure the width of your hand in inches or feet?

18. How many inches are in 1 foot?

19. Which is longer, a foot or a yard?

20. Is the length of a caterpillar closer to 3 inches or 3 feet?

21. Is the width of a doorway about 3 feet or 3 yards?

Key Idea
A whole can be divided into equal parts in different ways.

Materials
• grid paper
• crayons
• scissors

Think It Through
I can **draw a picture** to show equal parts.

Equal Parts of a Whole

LEARN

✓ WARM UP

1. $12 \div 2$ 2. $15 \div 5$

3. $16 \div 4$ 4. $14 \div 2$

5. $18 \div 6$ 6. $9 \div 3$

Activity

How can you divide a whole into equal parts?

David and Sonja must divide a piece of grid paper into 2 equal parts. They found different ways to make equal parts.

I know that the two parts are equal because each part is 8 square units.

If I fold the paper on the green line, the parts will match.

So, I know that the two parts are equal.

Use square pieces of grid paper and crayons.

a. Show another way to divide the grid paper into 2 equal parts.

b. Show two ways to divide the grid paper into 4 equal parts.

c. Can you divide the grid paper into 8 equal parts? Explain.

d. Do equal parts have to be the same shape? Explain.

What do you call the equal parts of a whole?

Example

Here are some names of equal parts of a whole.

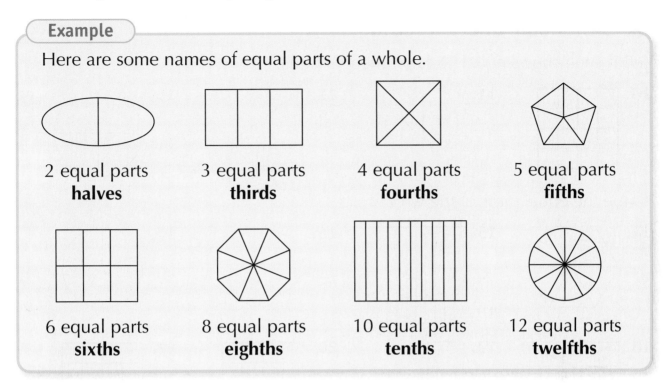

2 equal parts
halves

3 equal parts
thirds

4 equal parts
fourths

5 equal parts
fifths

6 equal parts
sixths

8 equal parts
eighths

10 equal parts
tenths

12 equal parts
twelfths

✔ Talk About It

1. How many equal parts are there when you divide a whole into halves? fourths? sixths? twelfths?

2. Could you divide a circle into 4 equal parts? Explain.

CHECK ✔

For another example, see Set 9-1 on p. 554.

Tell if each shows equal parts or unequal parts.

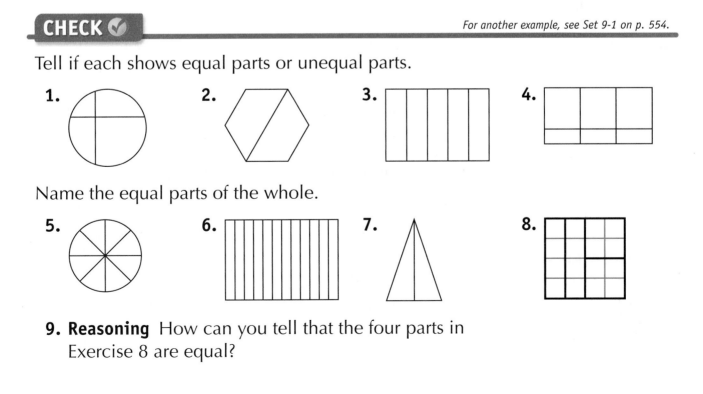

1.

2.

3.

4.

Name the equal parts of the whole.

5.

6.

7.

8.

9. Reasoning How can you tell that the four parts in Exercise 8 are equal?

A Skills and Understanding

Tell if each shows equal parts or unequal parts.

10. 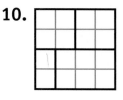 **11.**  **12.** 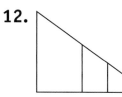 **13.**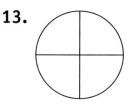

Name the equal parts of the whole.

14. 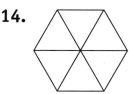 **15.** 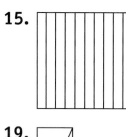 **16.** **17.**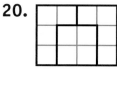

18. 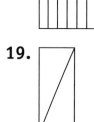 **19.** **20.** **21.**

Use grid paper. Draw a picture to show each.

22. fourths   **23.** thirds   **24.** sixths

B Reasoning and Problem Solving

Math and Everyday Life

A football field is 160 feet wide.
Each end zone is 30 feet long.

The playing area of a football field is 100 yards long. It is divided into 10 equal parts.

25. How long is each equal part of the football field? Hint: 100 ÷ 10 = ▨

26. What is the name of the parts when a whole is divided into 10 equal parts?

27. **Writing in Math** Did Jason divide the grid paper into fifths? Explain.

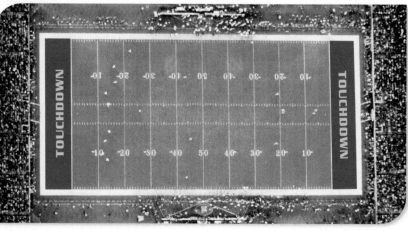

C Extensions

28. Trace the figure at the right and cut it out. Fold your cutout shape in half. Fold it in half again to make 4 equal parts. Label your figure by writing the name of the equal parts.

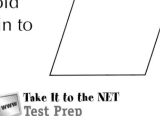

Mixed Review and Test Prep

Take It to the NET
Test Prep
www.scottforesman.com

29. Write a statement describing how a square and an equilateral triangle are alike. Then write a statement describing how they are different.

Multiply or divide.

30. 6×10 **31.** 8×9 **32.** 8×7 **33.** $42 \div 6$ **34.** $14 \div 2$

35. Find the volume of the solid figure.

A. 16 cubic units   **C.** 10 cubic units

B. 12 cubic units   **D.** 8 cubic units

Learning with Technology

Fractions eTool

You can use the Fractions eTool to divide a whole into equal parts.

- Select the denominators mode in the Strips workspace.

- Select 10 for the denominator.

- This will divide the rectangle into 10 equal parts.

Divide the rectangle into the number of equal parts shown. Then name the equal parts of the whole.

1. 10   **2.** 3   **3.** 5   **4.** 12

Divide the rectangle into the equal parts shown.

5. halves   **6.** fourths

7. eighths   **8.** sixths

Key Idea
You can write
a fraction to
describe the
equal parts of
a whole.

Vocabulary
• fraction
• numerator
• denominator

Naming Fractional Parts

LEARN

WARM UP
Tell if each shows
equal parts.

1.

2.

What is a fraction?

You can use **fractions** to name equal parts of a whole.

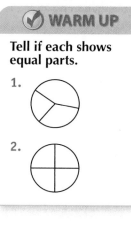

Example

The flag of Nigeria has 3 equal parts. What fraction of the flag is green?

Numerator ——→ $\frac{2}{3}$ ←— 2 equal parts are green
Denominator —→ ←— 3 equal parts **in all**

What You **Write**	What You **Say**
$\frac{2}{3}$ of the flag is green.	*Two thirds* of the flag is green.

✔ **Talk About It**

1. What fraction of Nigeria's flag is not green?

2. What fraction of each square is blue?

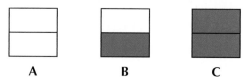

A   B   C

3. Reggie cut an apple into 4 equal pieces. He ate 1 piece. What fraction tells how much of the apple he ate?

Take It to the NET
More Examples
www.scottforesman.com

CHECK ✓

Write the fraction of each figure that is red.

1.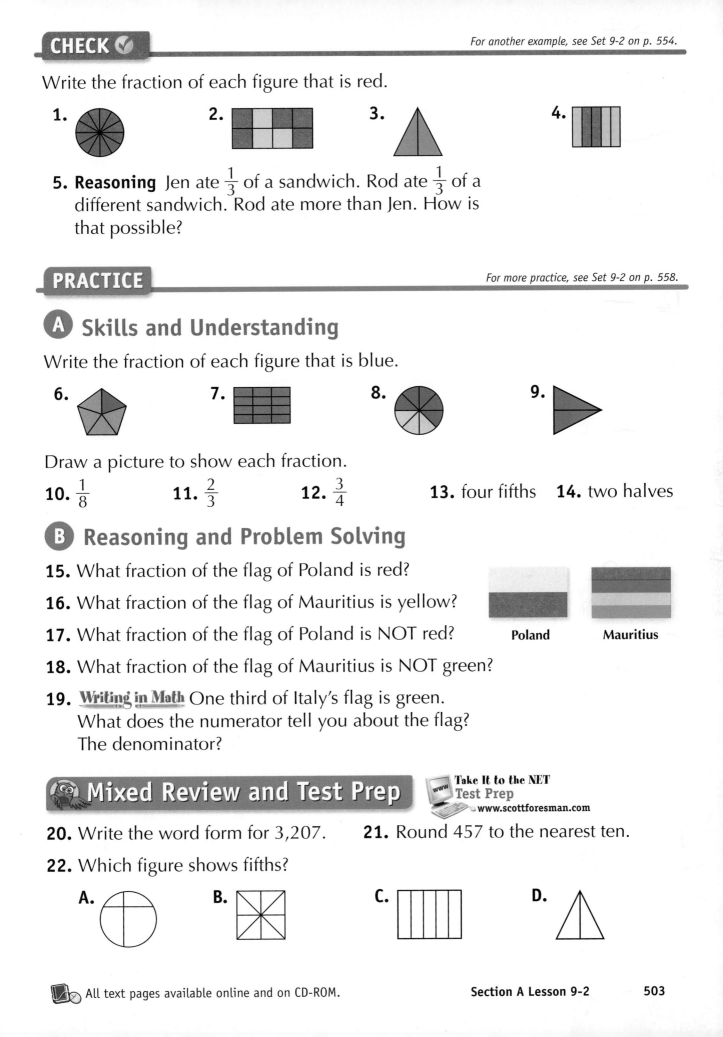

2.

3.

4.

5. **Reasoning** Jen ate $\frac{1}{3}$ of a sandwich. Rod ate $\frac{1}{3}$ of a different sandwich. Rod ate more than Jen. How is that possible?

PRACTICE

For more practice, see Set 9-2 on p. 558.

A Skills and Understanding

Write the fraction of each figure that is blue.

6.

7.

8.

9.

Draw a picture to show each fraction.

10. $\frac{1}{8}$ 11. $\frac{2}{3}$ 12. $\frac{3}{4}$ 13. four fifths   14. two halves

B Reasoning and Problem Solving

15. What fraction of the flag of Poland is red?

16. What fraction of the flag of Mauritius is yellow?

17. What fraction of the flag of Poland is NOT red?

18. What fraction of the flag of Mauritius is NOT green?

Poland   **Mauritius**

19. **Writing in Math** One third of Italy's flag is green. What does the numerator tell you about the flag? The denominator?

Mixed Review and Test Prep

Take It to the NET
Test Prep
www.scottforesman.com

20. Write the word form for 3,207.

21. Round 457 to the nearest ten.

22. Which figure shows fifths?

A.   B.   C.   D.

Key Idea
The same fractional amount can be named in different ways.

Vocabulary
• equivalent fractions

Materials
• fraction strips or  tools

Think It Through
I can **use objects** to find equivalent fractions.

Equivalent Fractions

LEARN

WARM UP
Continue the pattern.
1. 2, 4, 6, 8, ▪, ▪,
2. 3, 6, 9, 12, ▪, ▪,
3. 4, 8, 12, 16, ▪, ▪,

Activity

How can different fractions have the same value?

Fractions that name the same amount are called **equivalent fractions.**

$\frac{1}{2}$ names the same amount as $\frac{3}{6}$.

$$\frac{1}{2} = \frac{3}{6}$$

$\frac{1}{2}$ and $\frac{3}{6}$ are **equivalent fractions.**

Use a $\frac{1}{2}$ fraction strip.

a. Line up $\frac{1}{4}$ strips until they match the $\frac{1}{2}$ strip. How many fourths are the same as $\frac{1}{2}$?

b. Copy and complete: $\frac{1}{2} = \frac{▪}{4}$

c. Line up $\frac{1}{8}$ strips until they match the $\frac{1}{2}$ strip. How many eighths are the same as $\frac{1}{2}$?

d. Copy and complete: $\frac{1}{2} = \frac{▪}{8}$

Use a $\frac{1}{3}$ strip.

e. Line up $\frac{1}{6}$ strips until they match the $\frac{1}{3}$ strip. Write a fraction with 6 in the denominator that is the same as $\frac{1}{3}$.

f. Put together two $\frac{1}{3}$ fraction strips. How many $\frac{1}{6}$ strips do you need to match $\frac{2}{3}$ exactly? Write a fraction that shows how many sixths equal $\frac{2}{3}$.

For another example, see Set 9-3 on p. 554.

CHECK ✓

Copy and complete each number sentence.

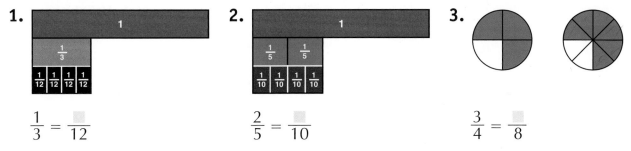

1.
$$\frac{1}{3} = \frac{\blacksquare}{12}$$

2.
$$\frac{2}{5} = \frac{\blacksquare}{10}$$

3.
$$\frac{3}{4} = \frac{\blacksquare}{8}$$

4. Number Sense Name two fractions that are equivalent to one half.

PRACTICE

For more practice, see Set 9-3 on p. 558.

Ⓐ Skills and Understanding

Copy and complete each number sentence.

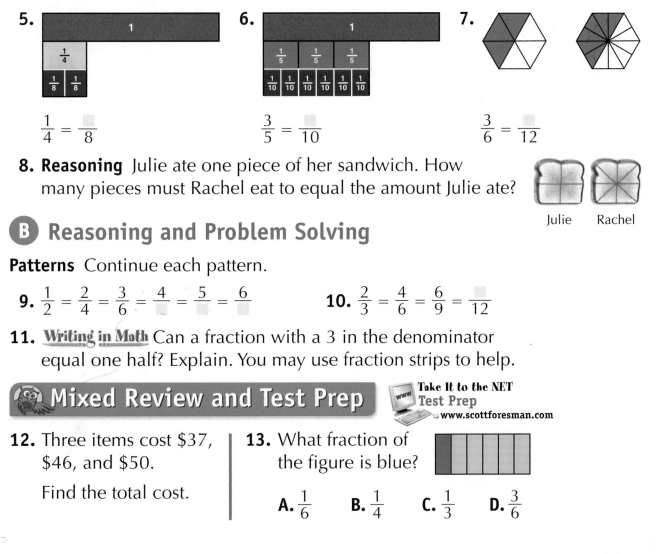

5.
$$\frac{1}{4} = \frac{\blacksquare}{8}$$

6.
$$\frac{3}{5} = \frac{\blacksquare}{10}$$

7.
$$\frac{3}{6} = \frac{\blacksquare}{12}$$

8. Reasoning Julie ate one piece of her sandwich. How many pieces must Rachel eat to equal the amount Julie ate?

Julie   Rachel

Ⓑ Reasoning and Problem Solving

Patterns Continue each pattern.

9. $\frac{1}{2} = \frac{2}{4} = \frac{3}{6} = \frac{4}{\blacksquare} = \frac{5}{\blacksquare} = \frac{6}{\blacksquare}$

10. $\frac{2}{3} = \frac{4}{6} = \frac{6}{9} = \frac{\blacksquare}{12}$

11. Writing in Math Can a fraction with a 3 in the denominator equal one half? Explain. You may use fraction strips to help.

🦉 Mixed Review and Test Prep

Take It to the NET
Test Prep
www.scottforesman.com

12. Three items cost $37, $46, and $50.

Find the total cost.

13. What fraction of the figure is blue?

A. $\frac{1}{6}$ **B.** $\frac{1}{4}$ **C.** $\frac{1}{3}$ **D.** $\frac{3}{6}$

Key Idea
There are different ways to compare and order fractions.

Vocabulary
•unit fractions

Materials
• fraction strips
or  tools

Think It Through
I can **use objects** to compare fractions.

Comparing and Ordering Fractions

WARM UP

Compare. Write <, >, or =.

1. 41 ⬤ 14
2. 199 ⬤ 203
3. 810 ⬤ 805
4. 1,409 ⬤ 1,490

LEARN

Activity

How can you compare unit fraction strips?

A **unit fraction** is a fraction with a numerator of 1.

a. Use the 7 unit fraction strips shown here. Arrange them in order from longest to shortest.

b. Which unit fraction strip is longest?

c. Which unit fraction strip is shortest?

d. Which unit fraction strips are longer than $\frac{1}{6}$? Which are shorter?

e. Do you agree with Jackson's statement at the left? Give an example to help explain.

$\frac{1}{2}$ $\frac{1}{3}$ $\frac{1}{6}$ $\frac{1}{4}$ $\frac{1}{8}$ $\frac{1}{12}$ $\frac{1}{10}$

> When two fractions have the same numerator, the fraction with the greater denominator is less than the other.

How do you compare fractions?

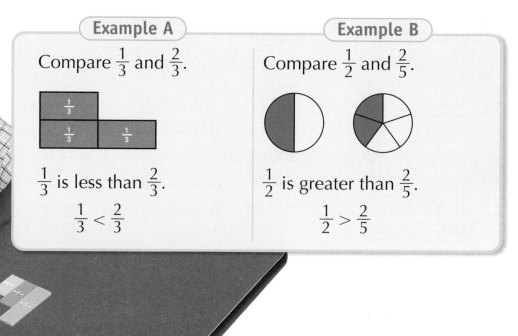

Example A

Compare $\frac{1}{3}$ and $\frac{2}{3}$.

$\frac{1}{3}$ is less than $\frac{2}{3}$.

$$\frac{1}{3} < \frac{2}{3}$$

Example B

Compare $\frac{1}{2}$ and $\frac{2}{5}$.

$\frac{1}{2}$ is greater than $\frac{2}{5}$.

$$\frac{1}{2} > \frac{2}{5}$$

✔ Talk About It

1. Explain how you know that $\frac{3}{4}$ is greater than $\frac{1}{4}$.

2. Number Sense A cheese pizza is cut into 12 equal slices and a vegetable pizza of the same size is cut into 8 equal slices. Which pizza has the larger slices? Explain.

How do you order fractions?

Example C

Write $\frac{1}{4}$, $\frac{3}{8}$, and $\frac{1}{2}$ in order from greatest to least.

$\frac{1}{2} > \frac{3}{8}$ and $\frac{3}{8} > \frac{1}{4}$.

$\frac{1}{2}, \frac{3}{8}, \frac{1}{4}$

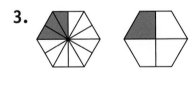

✔ Talk About It

3. Explain how to order $\frac{1}{5}$, $\frac{1}{2}$, and $\frac{1}{10}$ from least to greatest.

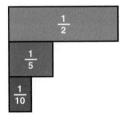

CHECK ✔

For another example, see Set 9-4 on p. 554.

Compare. Write >, <, or =.

1.

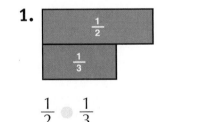

$\frac{1}{2}$ ● $\frac{1}{3}$

2.

$\frac{3}{8}$ ● $\frac{4}{8}$

3.

$\frac{3}{12}$ ● $\frac{1}{4}$

4. Order $\frac{2}{4}$, $\frac{1}{3}$, and $\frac{1}{6}$ from least to greatest.

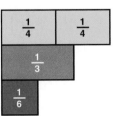

5. Number Sense Can two different unit fractions be equal? Why or why not?

A Skills and Understanding

Compare. Write >, <, or =.

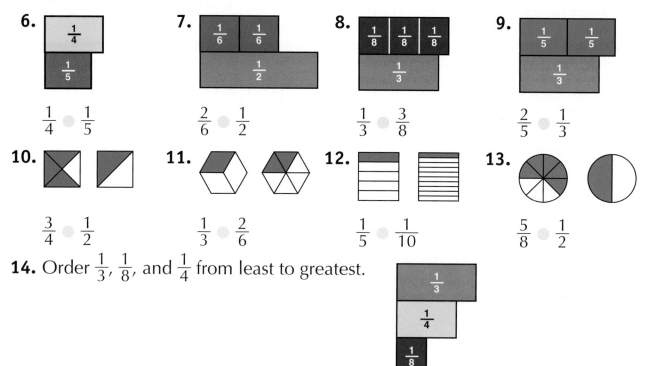

6. $\dfrac{1}{4}$ ● $\dfrac{1}{5}$

7. $\dfrac{2}{6}$ ● $\dfrac{1}{2}$

8. $\dfrac{1}{3}$ ● $\dfrac{3}{8}$

9. $\dfrac{2}{5}$ ● $\dfrac{1}{3}$

10. $\dfrac{3}{4}$ ● $\dfrac{1}{2}$

11. $\dfrac{1}{3}$ ● $\dfrac{2}{6}$

12. $\dfrac{1}{5}$ ● $\dfrac{1}{10}$

13. $\dfrac{5}{8}$ ● $\dfrac{1}{2}$

14. Order $\dfrac{1}{3}$, $\dfrac{1}{8}$, and $\dfrac{1}{4}$ from least to greatest.

15. Number Sense Is $\dfrac{1}{2}$ of Circle A the same amount as $\dfrac{1}{2}$ of Circle B? Explain.

B Reasoning and Problem Solving

Math and Social Studies

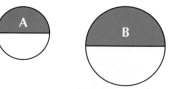

Oceans cover more than $\dfrac{7}{10}$ of the Earth's surface. North America makes up about $\dfrac{1}{6}$ of the Earth's land area.

16. Is more than $\dfrac{1}{2}$ of the Earth's surface covered with ocean? Explain.

17. Writing in Math What fraction of the Earth's land area is not North America? Draw a picture of a circle divided into 6 equal parts to help.

C Extensions

18. Write a fraction that is greater than $\frac{3}{4}$ and has a denominator of 12. Use fraction strips or trace the picture at the right.

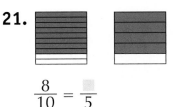

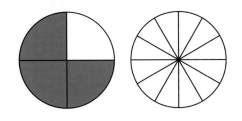
Take It to the NET
Test Prep
www.scottforesman.com

Mixed Review and Test Prep

Copy and complete each number sentence.

19.

$$\frac{4}{8} = \frac{\square}{4}$$

20.

$$\frac{1}{3} = \frac{\square}{12}$$

21.

$$\frac{8}{10} = \frac{\square}{5}$$

22. How much would it cost for 10 students and 3 teachers to get into Funland Park?

    A. $24   **C.** $74

    B. $50   **D.** $116

FUNLAND PARK	
Park Admission charges	
Children (under 6 years)	$2
Students (6 to 17 years)	$5
Adults (over 17 years)	$8

Practice Game

Fraction Building

Number of Players: 2
Materials: Fraction Action Game Board, 1 for each player
Fraction Cards

- Players take turns picking a card, then shading in the fraction on his or her game board.

- Shade any combination to make the fraction shown. For example, to show $\frac{3}{4}$, you may shade $\frac{3}{4}$ or $\frac{1}{2}$ and $\frac{1}{4}$.

- If you cannot shade in the fraction picked, the turn is over.

- The winner is the first player to shade in all three rows.

Think It Through
When I **estimate**, I do not have to give the exact amount.

Estimating Fractional Amounts

LEARN

How do you compare fractions to estimate?

Haley is giving lemonade to her brother. She wants to give him a glass that is about half full. Which glass should she give him?

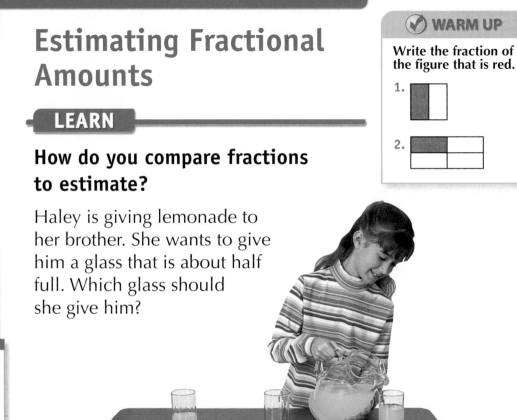

A — About $\frac{1}{2}$ full   B — Less than $\frac{1}{4}$ full   C — About $\frac{3}{4}$ full

Glass A is about half full. She should give him Glass A.

Example A

Estimate the fraction of a whole pizza that is left.

About $\frac{1}{4}$ of the pizza is left.

Example B

Estimate the fraction of the yard that is grass.

About $\frac{2}{3}$ of the yard is grass.

✓ Talk About It

1. In Example A, is there less than or more than one half of the pizza left? How can you tell?

2. **Reasoning** Look at the shaded part of the clock. About what fraction of an hour has passed since 9:00?

CHECK ✓

Estimate the amount that is shaded.

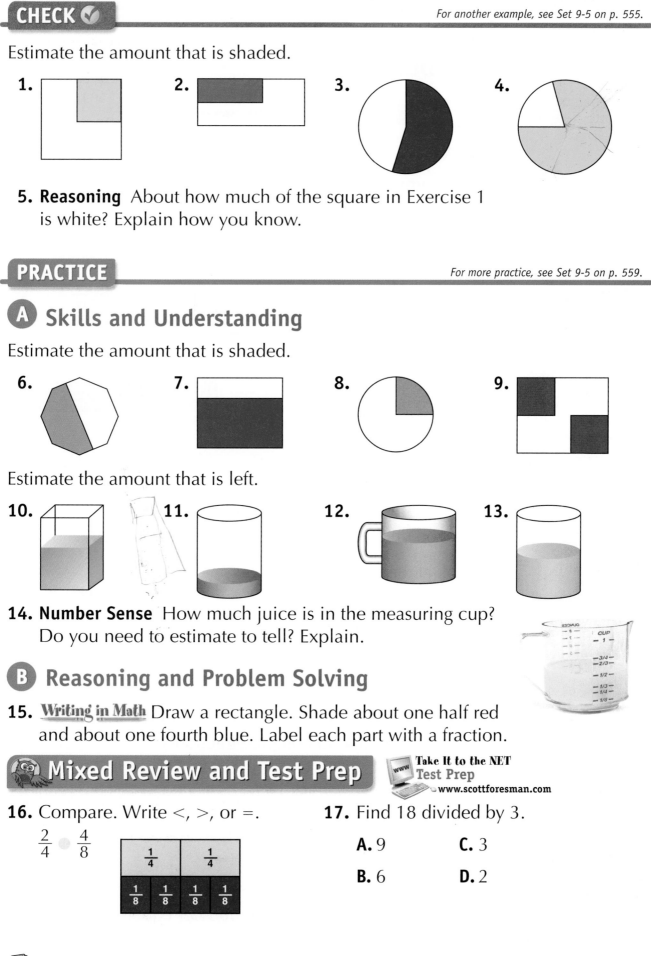

1.

2.

3.

4.

5. Reasoning About how much of the square in Exercise 1 is white? Explain how you know.

PRACTICE

For more practice, see Set 9-5 on p. 559.

Ⓐ Skills and Understanding

Estimate the amount that is shaded.

6.

7.

8.

9.

Estimate the amount that is left.

10.

11.

12.

13.

14. Number Sense How much juice is in the measuring cup? Do you need to estimate to tell? Explain.

Ⓑ Reasoning and Problem Solving

15. Writing in Math Draw a rectangle. Shade about one half red and about one fourth blue. Label each part with a fraction.

Mixed Review and Test Prep

Take It to the NET
Test Prep
www.scottforesman.com

16. Compare. Write <, >, or =.

$\frac{2}{4}$ ● $\frac{4}{8}$

$\frac{1}{4}$		$\frac{1}{4}$	
$\frac{1}{8}$	$\frac{1}{8}$	$\frac{1}{8}$	$\frac{1}{8}$

17. Find 18 divided by 3.

A. 9   **C.** 3

B. 6   **D.** 2

All text pages available online and on CD-ROM.

Key Idea
You can locate fractions on a number line.

Materials
• fraction strips
or  **e** tools

Fractions on the Number Line

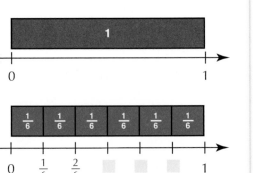
LEARN

Activity

How do you find fractions on a number line?

You can use fractions to name points on a number line.

Use fraction strips.

a. Use the 1 strip to draw a number line from 0 to 1.

b. Use the $\frac{1}{6}$ strips to divide the distance between 0 and 1 into sixths. Label $\frac{1}{6}$, $\frac{2}{6}$, $\frac{3}{6}$, $\frac{4}{6}$, and $\frac{5}{6}$.

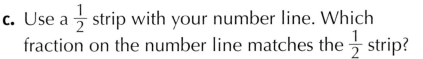

c. Use a $\frac{1}{2}$ strip with your number line. Which fraction on the number line matches the $\frac{1}{2}$ strip?

d. Look at the pattern in the fractions on your number line. How many sixths are the same as 1?

e. Use a 1 strip to draw another number line from 0 to 1. Use $\frac{1}{5}$ strips to label $\frac{1}{5}$, $\frac{2}{5}$, $\frac{3}{5}$, $\frac{4}{5}$. How many fifths are the same as 1?

f. Which is greater, $\frac{2}{5}$ or $\frac{4}{5}$? How can you use your number line to compare fractions?

CHECK ✓

For another example, see Set 9-6 on p. 555.

1. Write the missing fractions for the number line.

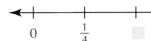
0    $\frac{1}{4}$ ▢   ▢   1

2. **Number Sense** What whole number equals $\frac{4}{4}$?

Think It Through
I can **use objects** to see how fractions relate to one another.

A Skills and Understanding

Write the missing fractions for each number line.

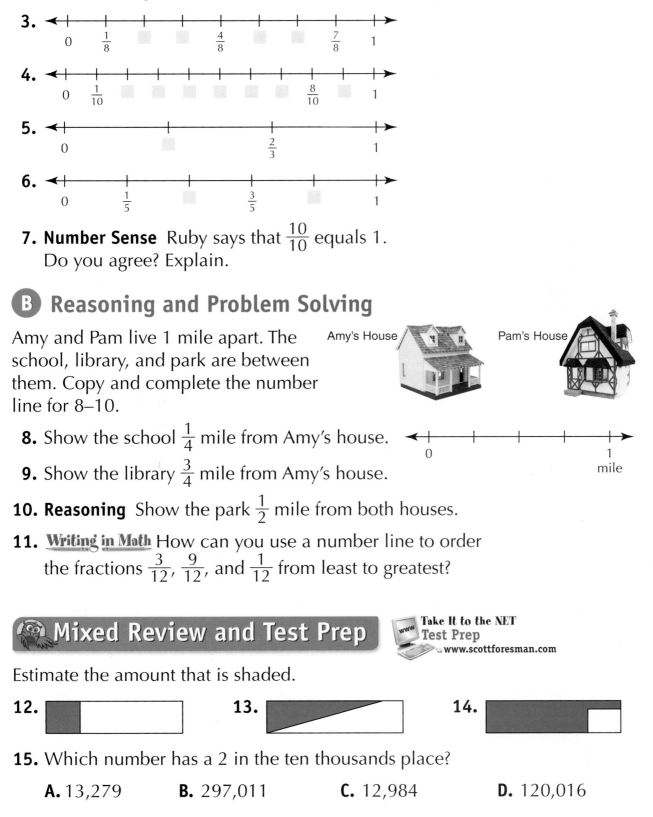

3. 0 $\frac{1}{8}$ ▢   ▢ $\frac{4}{8}$ ▢   ▢ $\frac{7}{8}$ 1

4. 0 $\frac{1}{10}$ ▢ ▢ ▢ ▢ ▢ $\frac{8}{10}$ ▢   1

5. 0   ▢ $\frac{2}{3}$ 1

6. 0 $\frac{1}{5}$ ▢ $\frac{3}{5}$ ▢   1

7. Number Sense Ruby says that $\frac{10}{10}$ equals 1. Do you agree? Explain.

B Reasoning and Problem Solving

Amy and Pam live 1 mile apart. The school, library, and park are between them. Copy and complete the number line for 8–10.

Amy's House   Pam's House

8. Show the school $\frac{1}{4}$ mile from Amy's house.

9. Show the library $\frac{3}{4}$ mile from Amy's house.

0   1 mile

10. Reasoning Show the park $\frac{1}{2}$ mile from both houses.

11. Writing in Math How can you use a number line to order the fractions $\frac{3}{12}$, $\frac{9}{12}$, and $\frac{1}{12}$ from least to greatest?

Mixed Review and Test Prep

Take It to the NET
Test Prep
www.scottforesman.com

Estimate the amount that is shaded.

12. **13.** **14.**

15. Which number has a 2 in the ten thousands place?

    A. 13,279   **B.** 297,011   **C.** 12,984   **D.** 120,016

Do You Know How?

Do You Understand?

Equal Parts of a Whole (9-1); Naming Fractional Parts (9-2)

1. Name the equal parts of the circle.

2. Write the fraction of the circle that is blue.

Ⓐ If the circle had 3 equal parts, what would they be called?

Ⓑ What fraction of the circle is not blue?

Equivalent Fractions (9-3)

3. Copy and complete.

$\frac{1}{2} = \frac{\blacksquare}{6}$

Ⓒ In Exercise 3, how can you tell how many sixths equal $\frac{1}{2}$?

Ⓓ Can a fraction with a denominator of 8 equal $\frac{1}{2}$? Explain.

Comparing and Ordering Fractions (9-4)

4. Order $\frac{1}{2}$, $\frac{1}{4}$, and $\frac{2}{3}$ from least to greatest.

Ⓔ In Exercise 4, how do you know which fraction comes first?

Estimating Fractional Amounts (9-5)

5. Estimate the amount that is left.

Ⓕ About how much of the pizza was eaten? Explain.

Fractions on the Number Line (9-6)

6. Write the missing numbers.

0    $\frac{1}{6}$ ▨   ▨   ▨ $\frac{5}{6}$ 1

Ⓖ What whole number equals $\frac{6}{6}$?

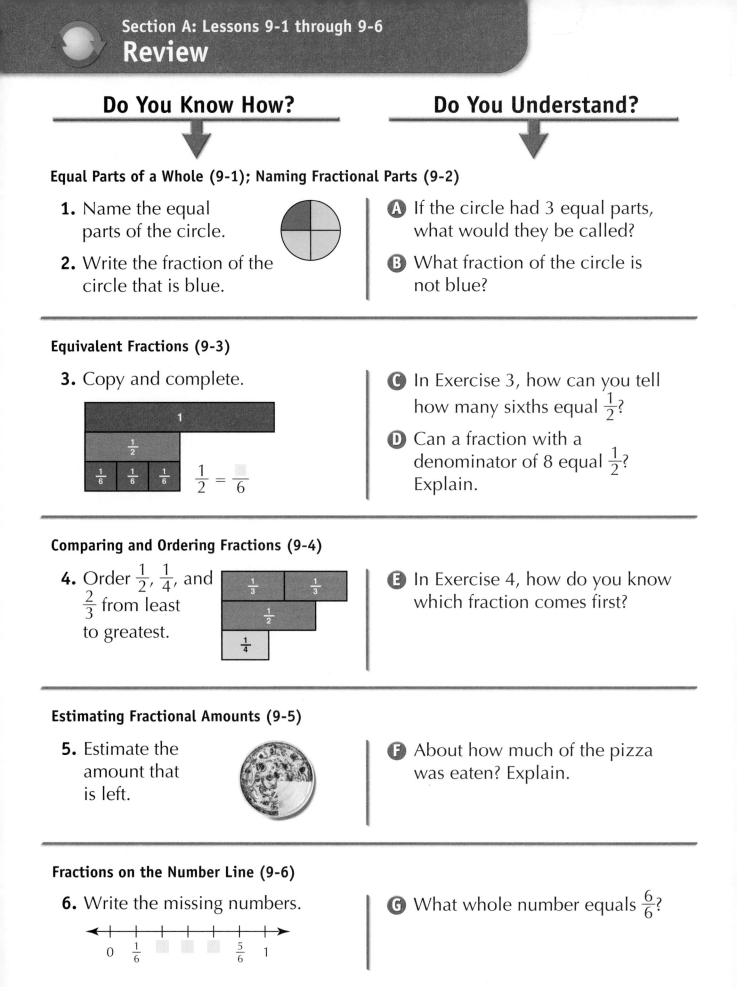

Think It Through

I should **eliminate wrong answer choices.**

MULTIPLE CHOICE

1. What fraction of the rectangle is blue? (9-2)

A. $\frac{1}{2}$　　C. $\frac{1}{4}$

B. $\frac{1}{3}$　　D. $\frac{1}{5}$

2. What are the missing fractions for the number line? (9-6)

A. $\frac{2}{5}, \frac{4}{5}$　　C. $\frac{0}{5}, \frac{2}{5}$

B. $\frac{3}{5}, \frac{4}{5}$　　D. $\frac{4}{5}, \frac{5}{5}$

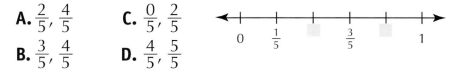

FREE RESPONSE

Name the equal parts of each figure. Then write the fraction of each figure that is green. (9-1, 9-2)

3. **4.** **5.** **6.**

7. Copy and complete. (9-3)

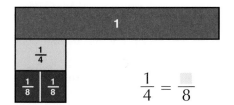

$\frac{1}{4} = \frac{\blacksquare}{8}$

8. Compare. Write >, <, or =. (9-4)

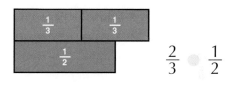

$\frac{2}{3}$ ⬤ $\frac{1}{2}$

Write the missing fractions for each number line. (9-6)

9.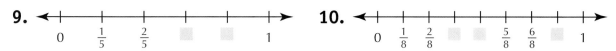

10.

Estimate the amount that is shaded. (9-5)

11.

12.

Writing in Math

13. In a fraction that tells what part of a shape is shaded, what does the numerator tell you? The denominator? (9-2)

Think It Through
I can **draw a picture** to help find a fraction of a set.

Fractions and Sets

LEARN

How do fractions name part of a set?

A fraction can name part of a set, or group, of objects.

Example

Eight boys and four girls went on a science field trip. What fraction of the students are boys?

$\dfrac{8}{12}$ ← Number of boys
$\phantom{\dfrac{8}{12}}$ ← Total number of students

G   G   B   B   B   B

$\dfrac{8}{12}$ of the students are boys.

G   G   B   B   B   B

✔ Talk About It

1. Why do you need to know the total number of students to answer the problem?

2. What fraction of the students are girls?

3. **Reasoning** Jason said that $\frac{1}{3}$ of the students are girls. Is he correct? Explain.

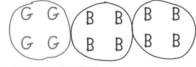

Take It to the NET
More Examples
www.scottforesman.com

For another example, see Set 9-7 on p. 555.

CHECK ✔✔

1. What fraction of the pieces of fruit are pears?

2. What fraction of the balls are yellow?

3. What fraction of the checkers are red?

4. **Number Sense** Jim has 4 red marbles and some blue marbles. If $\frac{4}{7}$ of his marbles are red, how many blue marbles does he have?

A Skills and Understanding

5. What fraction of the balls are footballs?

6. What fraction of the animals are dogs?

7. What fraction of the cars are red?

8. Number Sense Catherine has 2 hamsters, 1 cat, and 2 dogs at her house. What fraction of her pets are dogs?

B Reasoning and Problem Solving

Draw a picture to show each fraction of a set.

9. $\frac{2}{3}$ of the cupcakes are chocolate

10. $\frac{1}{2}$ of the pieces of fruit are red apples

11. In the book *Roadrunner's Dance,* 10 different gifts are given to Roadrunner. Quail gives one of the gifts. What fraction of all the gifts did Quail give?

12. Reasoning Troy cut an orange into 4 sections. Then he cut each section in half. He ate one piece. What fraction of the orange was left?

13. Writing in Math Write a problem about the fruit shown at the right. Use a fraction in your problem. Trade with a partner and solve.

Mixed Review and Test Prep

Take It to the NET
Test Prep
www.scottforesman.com

14. Mark has 7 toy planes. George has twice as many. How many toy planes does George have?

15. Write the missing fraction for the number line.

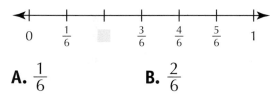

A. $\frac{1}{6}$ **B.** $\frac{2}{6}$ **C.** $\frac{1}{2}$ **D.** $\frac{2}{3}$

Think It Through

I can **draw a picture** to help find a fraction of a set.

Finding Fractional Parts of a Set

LEARN

How can you divide to find a fraction of a set?

Example A

Sam used $\frac{1}{3}$ of a carton of eggs to make muffins. There were 12 eggs in the carton. How many eggs did he use?

Find $\frac{1}{3}$ of 12.

Remember, the denominator tells you how many equal parts to make,

What You **Show**	What You **Think**	What You **Write**
	Divide 12 into 3 equal groups. $12 \div 3 = 4$	$\frac{1}{3}$ of 12 = 4

Sam used 4 eggs.

Example B

Find $\frac{1}{4}$ of 20.

What You **Show**	What You **Think**	What You **Write**
	Divide 20 into 4 equal groups. $20 \div 4 = 5$	$\frac{1}{4}$ of 20 = 5

✔ Talk About It

1. In example B, why do you divide 20 into 4 equal groups?

2. How could you draw a picture to find $\frac{1}{3}$ of 15?

Take It to the NET More Examples
www.scottforesman.com

For another example, see Set 9-8 on p. 555.

1. Find $\frac{1}{3}$ of 15 grapes.

$$15 \div 3 = \blacksquare$$

$$\frac{1}{3} \text{ of } 15 = \blacksquare$$

2. Find $\frac{1}{2}$ of 12 peanuts.

$$12 \div 2 = \blacksquare$$

$$\frac{1}{2} \text{ of } 12 = \blacksquare$$

3. Number Sense To find one third of 21, what two numbers should you divide? Find the answer.

PRACTICE

For more practice, see Set 9-8 on p. 559.

Ⓐ Skills and Understanding

4. Find $\frac{1}{2}$ of 8 apples.

$$8 \div 2 = \blacksquare$$

$$\frac{1}{2} \text{ of } 8 = \blacksquare$$

5. Find $\frac{1}{5}$ of 10 cherries.

$$10 \div 5 = \blacksquare$$

$$\frac{1}{5} \text{ of } 10 = \blacksquare$$

6. Find $\frac{1}{2}$ of 14.

7. Find $\frac{1}{3}$ of 18.

8. Find $\frac{1}{8}$ of 32.

9. Number Sense If you divide 36 by 4, what fraction of 36 are you finding? Find the answer.

Ⓑ Reasoning and Problem Solving

10. Reasoning Explain how you know that $\frac{1}{8}$ of 26 is greater than 3.

11. Summer lasts for $\frac{1}{4}$ of a year. How many months does summer last? (Hint: A year has 12 months.)

12. ~~Writing in Math~~ Write a problem about the oranges. Use the fraction $\frac{1}{3}$ in your problem. Solve.

Mixed Review and Test Prep

www **Take It to the NET**
Test Prep
www.scottforesman.com

13. $17 \div 5 = \blacksquare$ R $\blacksquare$

14. What fraction of the letters in the word FUNNY are Ns?

  A. $\frac{3}{5}$ **B.** $\frac{2}{5}$ **C.** $\frac{2}{3}$ **D.** $\frac{5}{5}$

Key Idea
You can use what you know about adding and subtracting whole numbers to add and subtract fractions with like denominators.

Materials
• fraction strips or 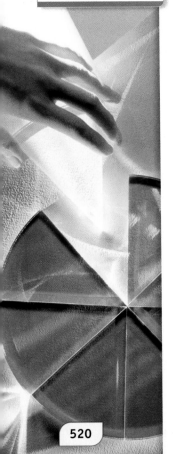 tools

TEST TALK

Think It Through

When the denominators are the same. I can **think about adding or subtracting whole numbers.**

3 eighths +
2 eighths =
5 eighths

Adding and Subtracting Fractions

LEARN

Activity

How do you use fraction strips to add or subtract fractions?

Use fraction strips.

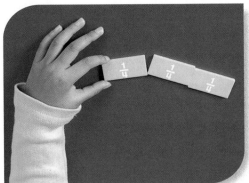

a. Join $\frac{1}{4}$ and $\frac{2}{4}$.

$$\frac{1}{4} + \frac{2}{4} = \frac{\blacksquare}{4}$$

b. Join $\frac{1}{5}$ and $\frac{3}{5}$.

$$\frac{1}{5} + \frac{3}{5} = \frac{\blacksquare}{5}$$

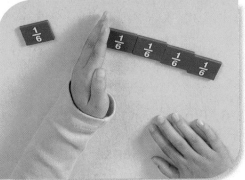

c. Show $\frac{5}{6}$. Take away $\frac{4}{6}$.

$$\frac{5}{6} - \frac{4}{6} = \frac{\blacksquare}{6}$$

d. Show $\frac{3}{3}$. Take away $\frac{1}{3}$.

$$\frac{3}{3} - \frac{1}{3} = \frac{\blacksquare}{3}$$

e. What patterns do you see for adding and subtracting fractions?

What's the rule?

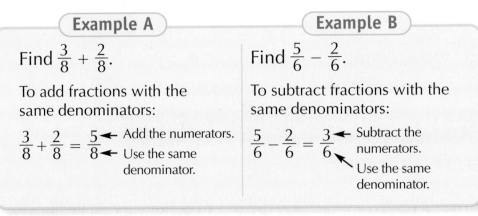

Example A

Find $\frac{3}{8} + \frac{2}{8}$.

To add fractions with the same denominators:

$$\frac{3}{8} + \frac{2}{8} = \frac{5}{8}$$ ← Add the numerators.
← Use the same denominator.

Example B

Find $\frac{5}{6} - \frac{2}{6}$.

To subtract fractions with the same denominators:

$$\frac{5}{6} - \frac{2}{6} = \frac{3}{6}$$ ← Subtract the numerators.
↖ Use the same denominator.

✔ **Talk About It**

1. Could you use the rule to add $\frac{3}{8}$ and $\frac{2}{6}$? Explain.

For another example, see Set 9-9 on p. 556.

CHECK ✓

Add or subtract. You may use fraction strips or draw a picture to help.

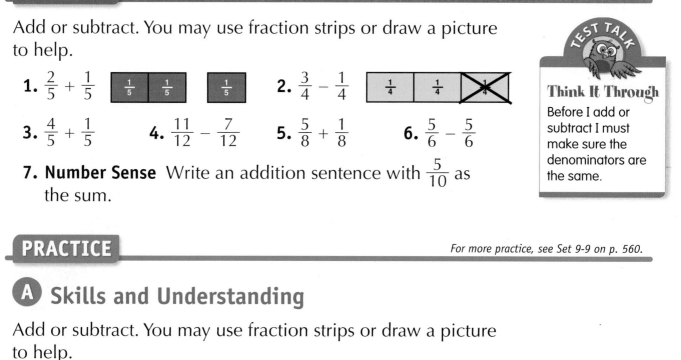

1. $\frac{2}{5} + \frac{1}{5}$

2. $\frac{3}{4} - \frac{1}{4}$

3. $\frac{4}{5} + \frac{1}{5}$　　**4.** $\frac{11}{12} - \frac{7}{12}$　　**5.** $\frac{5}{8} + \frac{1}{8}$　　**6.** $\frac{5}{6} - \frac{5}{6}$

7. Number Sense Write an addition sentence with $\frac{5}{10}$ as the sum.

Think It Through
Before I add or subtract I must make sure the denominators are the same.

PRACTICE

For more practice, see Set 9-9 on p. 560.

A Skills and Understanding

Add or subtract. You may use fraction strips or draw a picture to help.

8. $\frac{1}{6} + \frac{2}{6}$

9. $\frac{4}{8} - \frac{1}{8}$

10. $\frac{3}{8} - \frac{2}{8}$　　**11.** $\frac{3}{10} + \frac{5}{10}$　　**12.** $\frac{1}{4} + \frac{2}{4}$　　**13.** $\frac{5}{12} - \frac{4}{12}$

14. Reasoning Bud ate $\frac{2}{8}$ of the sandwich and Lea ate $\frac{1}{8}$ of it. Write an addition sentence that shows what fraction of the sandwich they ate all together.

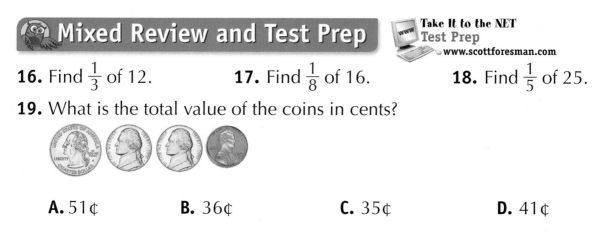

B Reasoning and Problem Solving

15. Writing in Math Write a subtraction problem about a pizza that was cut into 5 equal pieces. Use fractions. Trade with a partner and solve.

🦉 Mixed Review and Test Prep

Take It to the NET
Test Prep
www.scottforesman.com

16. Find $\frac{1}{3}$ of 12.　　**17.** Find $\frac{1}{8}$ of 16.　　**18.** Find $\frac{1}{5}$ of 25.

19. What is the total value of the coins in cents?

A. 51¢　　**B.** 36¢　　**C.** 35¢　　**D.** 41¢

 All text pages available online and on CD-ROM.

Key Idea
Numbers greater
than 1 that are
not whole
numbers can be
named using
fractions.

Vocabulary
• mixed number

Materials
• 6 rectangular
  pieces of paper
• scissors

Mixed Numbers

LEARN

Activity

How can you use fractions to share equally?

Four friends have 6 fruit bars to share equally.

Use 6 rectangles of paper for fruit bars.

a. Draw 4 circles to show the 4 friends.

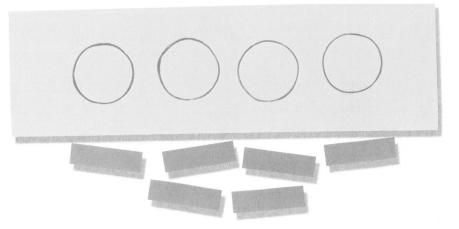

b. Do you think each person will get more than or less than 1 whole fruit bar? Explain.

c. Place a rectangle in each circle.

d. Cut the 2 leftover rectangles in half.

e. Continue to share the fruit bars equally. How many whole fruit bars does each friend get? How many halves?

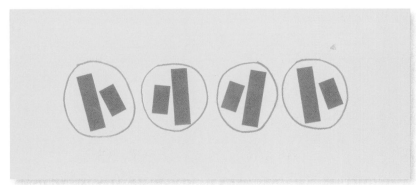

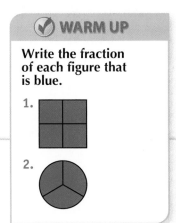

WARM UP

Write the fraction of each figure that is blue.

1.

2.

What are mixed numbers?

When you have a fraction that is greater than 1, you can use a **mixed number** to name the amount. A mixed number has a whole number and a fraction.

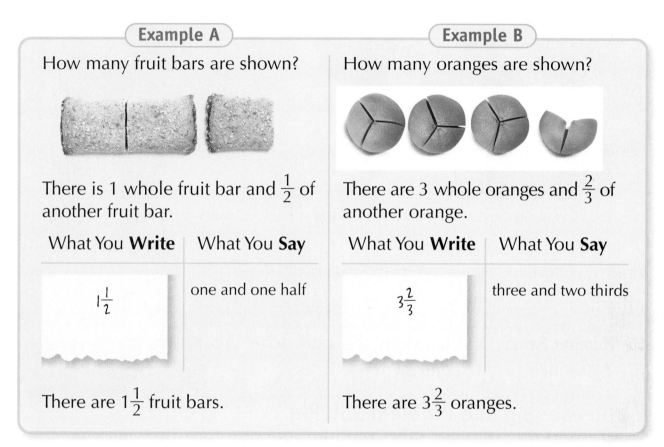

Example A

How many fruit bars are shown?

There is 1 whole fruit bar and $\frac{1}{2}$ of another fruit bar.

What You **Write**	What You **Say**
$1\frac{1}{2}$	one and one half

There are $1\frac{1}{2}$ fruit bars.

Example B

How many oranges are shown?

There are 3 whole oranges and $\frac{2}{3}$ of another orange.

What You **Write**	What You **Say**
$3\frac{2}{3}$	three and two thirds

There are $3\frac{2}{3}$ oranges.

✔ Talk About It

1. Look at Example A. How many halves are in $1\frac{1}{2}$?

2. Look at Example B. Is $3\frac{2}{3}$ greater than or less than $3\frac{1}{2}$? Explain.

CHECK ✓

For another example, see Set 9-10 on p. 556.

Write a mixed number for each picture.

1. **2.** **3.**

4. Reasoning Two pizzas were each cut into 4 pieces. All together, three pieces were eaten. Write a mixed number to tell how much pizza was left.

A Skills and Understanding

Write a mixed number for each picture.

5.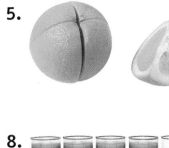

6.

7.

8.

9.

10.

1 cup $\frac{2}{3}$ cup

Draw a picture to show each mixed number.

11. $1\frac{1}{3}$ **12.** $2\frac{1}{4}$ **13.** $3\frac{2}{3}$ **14.** $3\frac{1}{2}$

15. Number Sense Which is more, $2\frac{1}{2}$ sandwiches or $2\frac{1}{4}$ sandwiches? Use the picture to help.

B Reasoning and Problem Solving

Math and Science

An Arabian camel can grow to be as tall as $7\frac{1}{2}$ feet at the hump.

16. There are 12 inches in a foot. How many inches are in $\frac{1}{2}$ foot?

17. How many inches are in 7 feet? Add the number of inches in 7 feet and the number of inches in $\frac{1}{2}$ foot. How many inches are $7\frac{1}{2}$ feet?

18. Writing in Math A mother camel waits about 13 months for her baby to be born. Bill wrote a mixed number to show how many years this is. Is he right? Explain.

13 months = $1\frac{1}{12}$ years

C Extensions

19. Copy and complete the number line. (Hint: Each missing number is a mixed number.)

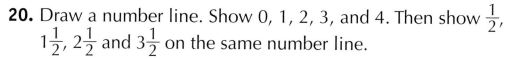

20. Draw a number line. Show 0, 1, 2, 3, and 4. Then show $\frac{1}{2}$, $1\frac{1}{2}$, $2\frac{1}{2}$ and $3\frac{1}{2}$ on the same number line.

Mixed Review and Test Prep

Take It to the NET
Test Prep
www.scottforesman.com

21. Use the picture. Find $\frac{4}{5} - \frac{2}{5}$.

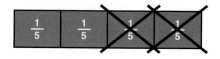

22. Find $502 - 246$.

    A. 256   **C.** 356

    B. 366   **D.** 344

DISCOVERY CHANNEL SCHOOL

Discover Math in Your World

Still Standing Tall

If you go to Athens, Greece, you will see the ruins of the Parthenon. This temple to the goddess Athena was completed in 432 B.C., so it is very likely that Alexander the Great visited the Parthenon. If you go to Nashville, Tennessee, you can see an exact copy of the Parthenon.

1. The statue of Athena in Nashville is about 42 feet tall. She is holding another statue that is about $\frac{1}{7}$ her height. About how tall is the statue that Athena is holding?

2. The room in Nashville that houses the statue of Athena is 93 feet long and 63 feet wide. What is the perimeter of the room?

Take It to the NET
Video and Activities
www.scottforesman.com

Activate Prior Knowledge

Activating prior knowledge when you read in math can help you use the **problem-solving strategy, *Solve a Simpler Problem,*** in the next lesson.

In reading, activating prior knowledge can help you connect new ideas to what you know. In math, activating prior knowledge can help you connect a new problem to one you know how to solve.

How many different line segments can you find in the figure?

The segment connecting *A* and *B* is 1 unit long.

So I'll start with ***simpler problems*** *like finding the number of segments that are 1 unit long, the number that are 2 units long, and the number that are 3 units long.*

Then I'll use the answers to the simpler problems to find the answer to the original problem.

1. How many different line segments can you name that are 1 unit long? 2 units long? 3 units long?

2. How can you use the answers to these simpler problems to solve the original problem?

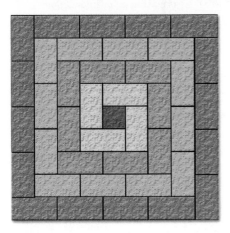

For 3–4, use the problem below.

How many full-size bricks are there in the patio shown at the left?

3. How many yellow bricks are there? orange bricks? tan bricks? brown bricks?

4. **Writing in Math** How can you use the answers to the simpler problems to solve the original problem?

For 5–8, use the problem below.

Jeffrey Louis Randall is writing his initials, *JLR*. How many different arrangements of the three letters are possible?

5. If *J* is the first letter, how many ways can the other two letters be written after the *J*?

6. If *L* is the first letter, how many ways can the other two letters be written after the *L*?

7. If *R* is the first letter, how many ways can the other two letters be written after the *R*?

8. **Writing in Math** Suppose the problem involved four different initials, *J, R, L,* and *T*. What simpler problems could you solve to help you find how many different arrangements of the four letters are possible?

For 9–10, use the problem below.

Cory has the coins shown. He asked his mom to exchange them for all nickels. How many nickels will he get?

9. How many nickels would Cory get for 1 quarter?

10. **Writing in Math** What simpler problems could you solve to help you solve the original problem.

Problem-Solving Strategy

Reading Helps!

Activating prior knowledge

can help you with...

the problem-solving strategy, *Solve a Simpler Problem.*

Key Idea
Learning how and when to solve a simpler problem can help you solve problems.

Solve a Simpler Problem

LEARN

How do you solve a simpler problem?

Shapes Within Shapes You can find large squares made up of small squares in this quilt. How many squares are in the quilt?

Read and Understand

What do you know?

A square has 4 sides of the same length. Squares can be different sizes.

What are you trying to find?

Find the number of squares in the quilt.

Plan and Solve

What strategy will you use?

How to Solve a Simpler Problem

Step 1 Break apart or change the problem into ones that are easier to solve.

Step 2 Solve the simpler problems.

Step 3 Use the answers to the simpler problems to solve the original problem.

Strategy: Solve a Simpler Problem

I can look for squares inside squares.

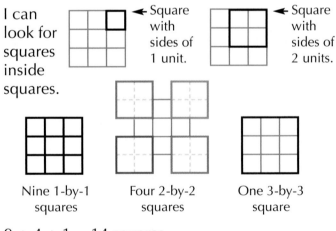

← Square with sides of 1 unit.

← Square with sides of 2 units.

Nine 1-by-1 squares

Four 2-by-2 squares

One 3-by-3 square

$9 + 4 + 1 = 14$ squares

Answer: There are 14 squares in the quilt.

Look Back and Check

Is your work correct?

Yes. I counted all possible squares. I added correctly.

✔ **Talk About It**

1. Why do you add to solve this problem?

Solve. Write the answer in a complete sentence.

1. Eric's notebook has 30 pages. He wants to write a number on each page. How many digits will he write when he numbers all the pages in the notebook?

   a. How many digits are needed for pages 1 through 9?

   b. How many digits are needed for pages 10 through 19?

   c. How many digits are needed for pages 20 through 29? for page 30?

   d. How can you find the total number of digits? Solve the problem.

PRACTICE

For more practice, see Set 9-11 on p. 560.

Solve. Write the answer in a complete sentence.

2. How many triangles are in the figure?

 (Hint: Look for a large triangle as well as small triangles.)

3. Rachel had an apple. She cut it in half, then cut each piece in half again. She ate one piece of the apple. How many pieces did Rachel have left?

4. Carter made a paper chain. He used this pattern.

He ended with a yellow link. If he used 10 blue links, how many yellow links did he use?

5. Chris made 9 pancakes. He took 3 and then gave an equal number to each of his two sisters. There were no pancakes left. How many pancakes did each sister get?

6. **Writing in Math** Jake is in line with 3 other students. Anne is second in line. Rod is behind Anne. If Carlo is last in line, who is first? Explain how you solved the problem.

STRATEGIES

- **Show What You Know**
  Draw a Picture
  Make an Organized List
  Make a Table
  Make a Graph
  Act It Out or Use Objects
- **Look for a Pattern**
- **Try, Check, and Revise**
- **Write a Number Sentence**
- **Use Logical Reasoning**
- **Solve a Simpler Problem**
- **Work Backward**

Choose a tool

Mental Math

Do You Know How?

Do You Understand?

Fractions and Sets (9-7)

1. What fraction of the apples are green?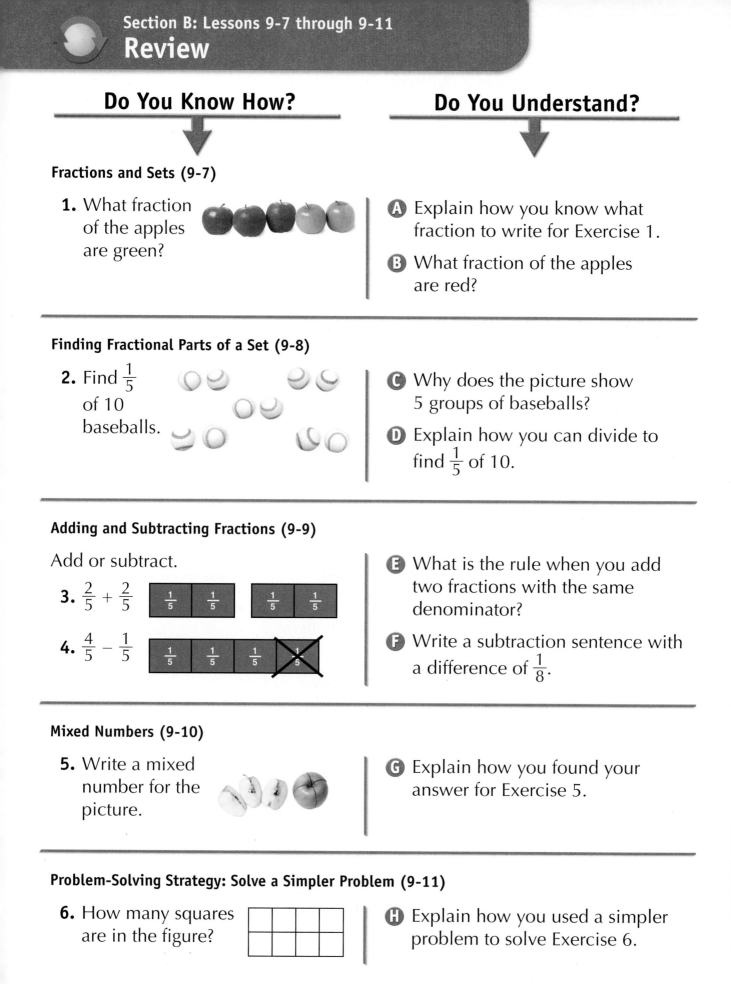

(A) Explain how you know what fraction to write for Exercise 1.

(B) What fraction of the apples are red?

Finding Fractional Parts of a Set (9-8)

2. Find $\frac{1}{5}$ of 10 baseballs.

(C) Why does the picture show 5 groups of baseballs?

(D) Explain how you can divide to find $\frac{1}{5}$ of 10.

Adding and Subtracting Fractions (9-9)

Add or subtract.

3. $\frac{2}{5} + \frac{2}{5}$ | $\frac{1}{5}$ | $\frac{1}{5}$ | | $\frac{1}{5}$ | $\frac{1}{5}$ |

4. $\frac{4}{5} - \frac{1}{5}$ | $\frac{1}{5}$ | $\frac{1}{5}$ | $\frac{1}{5}$ | $\frac{1}{5}$ |

(E) What is the rule when you add two fractions with the same denominator?

(F) Write a subtraction sentence with a difference of $\frac{1}{8}$.

Mixed Numbers (9-10)

5. Write a mixed number for the picture.

(G) Explain how you found your answer for Exercise 5.

Problem-Solving Strategy: Solve a Simpler Problem (9-11)

6. How many squares are in the figure?

(H) Explain how you used a simpler problem to solve Exercise 6.

MULTIPLE CHOICE

1. There are 6 boys and 4 girls in the school chorus. What fraction of the chorus members are boys? (9-7)

A. $\frac{4}{6}$ **B.** $\frac{6}{10}$ **C.** $\frac{4}{10}$ **D.** $\frac{2}{10}$

2. What mixed number is shown? (9-10)

A. $\frac{1}{3}$ **C.** $1\frac{1}{4}$

B. $\frac{3}{4}$ **D.** $1\frac{3}{6}$

FREE RESPONSE

3. What fraction of the eggs are brown? (9-7)

4. What fraction of the insects are ants? (9-7)

5. Find $\frac{1}{2}$ of 16 peanuts. (9-8)

6. Find $\frac{1}{3}$ of 12 cars. (9-8)

Add or subtract. (9-9)

7. $\frac{2}{4} - \frac{1}{4}$

8. $\frac{5}{8} + \frac{2}{8}$

Draw a picture to show each mixed number. (9-10)

9. $2\frac{1}{2}$ **10.** $1\frac{1}{5}$ **11.** $1\frac{2}{3}$

12. Kayla is numbering pages 7 through 35 in her photo album. How many digits will she use to number these pages? (9-11)

Writing in Math

13. Draw a picture to show $1\frac{1}{4}$ oranges. How many fourths is this? (9-10)

Key Idea
You can measure length using different units of measurement.

Vocabulary
• inch (in.)

Materials
• large paper clips
• small paper clips
• crayons
• inch ruler

Think It Through
I can **use objects** to measure length.

Length

LEARN

Activity

Can an object have two different lengths?

a. Copy the table.

b. Measure the length of your math book using each object.

c. Record each measurement in the table.

Length of My Math Book

Length in small paper clips	
Length in large paper clips	
Length in crayons	

d. Why does it take fewer crayons to measure the book than small paper clips?

Why do you use inches to measure?

An **inch (in.)** is a standard unit of measure.

├────────────┤
1 inch

To use a ruler, line up the object with the 0 mark.

INCHES

The pencil is 4 inches long to the nearest inch.

The crayon is 3 inches long to the nearest inch.

✔ **Talk About It**

1. How could you estimate the width of your hand in inches?

Take It to the NET
More Examples
www.scottforesman.com

Estimate each length. Then measure to the nearest inch.

1.

2.

3. Reasoning Jane's hand is 8 small paper clips long. Doug's hand is 3 large paper clips long. Could their hands be the same size? Explain.

PRACTICE   *For more practice, see Set 9-12 on p. 560.*

A Skills and Understanding

Estimate each length. Then measure to the nearest inch.

4.

5.

6.

7.

8. Without using a ruler, draw a line segment about 5 inches long. Then measure it to the nearest inch.

B Reasoning and Problem Solving

9. Find the perimeter of the green square to the nearest inch.

10. **Writing in Math** How could you use a string to decide if the red curve is longer than the blue curve?

Mixed Review and Test Prep

Take It to the NET
www **Test Prep**
www.scottforesman.com

11. How many rectangles are in the figure?

12. What mixed number is shown by the blue shading?

A. $1\frac{1}{3}$ **B.** $1\frac{2}{3}$ **C.** $2\frac{1}{3}$ **D.** $3\frac{1}{2}$

Measuring to the Nearest $\frac{1}{2}$ and $\frac{1}{4}$ Inch

LEARN

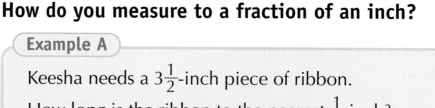
How do you measure to a fraction of an inch?

Example A

Keesha needs a $3\frac{1}{2}$-inch piece of ribbon.

How long is the ribbon to the nearest $\frac{1}{2}$ inch?

0   1   2   3   4

INCHES

The ribbon is $3\frac{1}{2}$ inches long to the nearest $\frac{1}{2}$ inch.

Example B

Cameron must measure a cricket for her science report. How long is the cricket to the nearest $\frac{1}{4}$ inch?

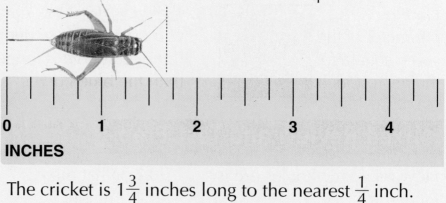

0   1   2   3   4

INCHES

The cricket is $1\frac{3}{4}$ inches long to the nearest $\frac{1}{4}$ inch.

✓ **Talk About It**

1. How long is the cricket to the nearest $\frac{1}{2}$ inch?

CHECK ✓

Write each measurement in inches. You may make a table to help.

1. 2 feet

2. 4 feet, 2 inches

3. 1 foot, 6 inches

4. Number Sense Find $\frac{1}{2}$ of 12. How many inches are in $\frac{1}{2}$ foot?

PRACTICE

For more practice, see Set 9-14 on p. 561.

A Skills and Understanding

Write each measurement in inches. You may make a table to help.

5. 5 feet

6. 2 feet, 2 inches

7. 3 feet, 4 inches

8. 6 feet

9. 4 feet, 1 inch

10. 1 foot, 1 inch

11. Number Sense Name 3 things you would measure in feet and inches. Name 3 things you would NOT measure in feet and inches.

B Reasoning and Problem Solving

12. List the long-jump distances for Stella, Mason, and Jack in order from shortest to longest.

Oakbend School Long Jump

Stella	2 feet, 4 inches
Mason	23 inches
Jack	2 feet

13. **Writing in Math** Ramie found how many inches are in 5 feet, 8 inches. Is her work shown at the right correct? If not, write what she did wrong.

Feet	1	2	3	4	5
Inches	12	24	36	48	60

60 inches + 8 inches = 68 inches
There are 68 inches in 5 feet, 8 inches.

🦉 Mixed Review and Test Prep

 Take It to the NET
Test Prep
www.scottforesman.com

Measure the length of each object to the nearest $\frac{1}{2}$ inch and nearest $\frac{1}{4}$ inch.

14.

15.

16. Find 498 + 87.

A. 695   **B.** 585   **C.** 487   **D.** 455

Key Idea
You can measure distance in feet, yards, and miles.

Vocabulary
• yard (yd)
• mile (mi)

Feet, Yards, and Miles

LEARN

What are some ways you can measure distance?

A **yard (yd)** is 3 feet. A baseball bat is about a yard long.

WARM UP

Copy and complete the table.

Feet	1	2	3	4	5
Inches	12			48	

Customary Units of Length

12 inches = 1 foot (ft)
3 feet = 1 yard (yd)
36 inches = 1 yard
5,280 feet = 1 mile (mi)
1,760 yards = 1 mile

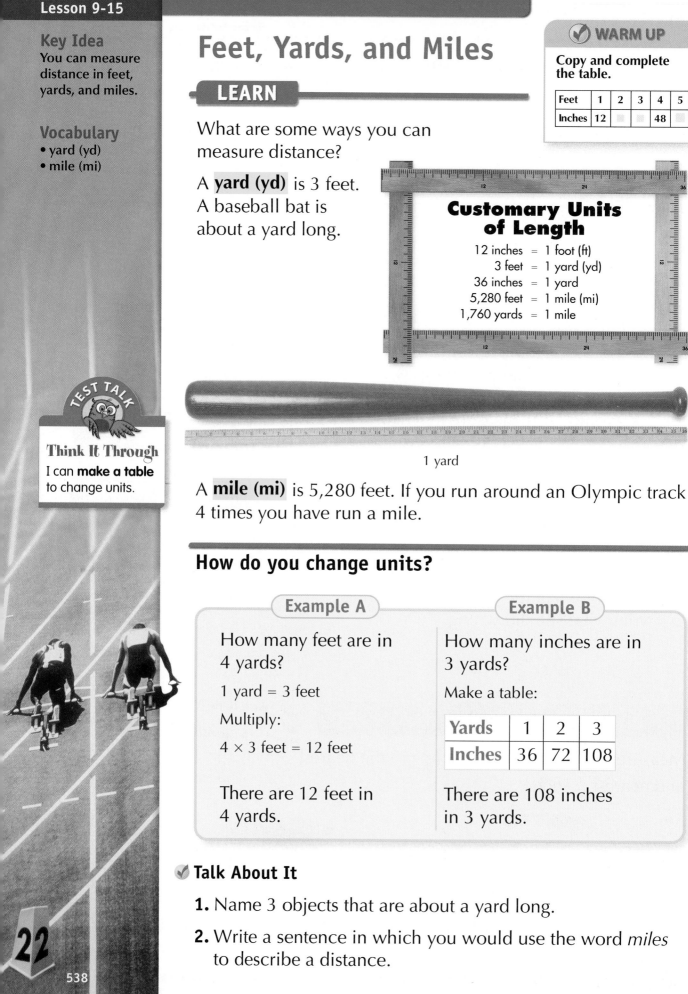

1 yard

A **mile (mi)** is 5,280 feet. If you run around an Olympic track 4 times you have run a mile.

How do you change units?

Example A

How many feet are in 4 yards?

1 yard = 3 feet

Multiply:

4 × 3 feet = 12 feet

There are 12 feet in 4 yards.

Example B

How many inches are in 3 yards?

Make a table:

Yards	1	2	3
Inches	36	72	108

There are 108 inches in 3 yards.

Think It Through
I can **make a table** to change units.

✔ Talk About It

1. Name 3 objects that are about a yard long.

2. Write a sentence in which you would use the word *miles* to describe a distance.

Change the units. You may make a table to help.

1. How many feet are in 2 yards?   **2.** How many inches are in 4 yards?

3. Number Sense Would you measure the length of a parking lot in yards or inches? Explain.

PRACTICE

For more practice, see Set 9-15 on p. 561.

Ⓐ Skills and Understanding

Change the units. You may make a table to help.

4. How many inches are in 1 yard?   **5.** How many feet are in 6 yards?

6. How many feet are in 10 yards?   **7.** How many inches are in 2 yards?

Compare. Write $<$, $>$, or $=$.

8. 1,000 feet ⬤ 1 mile   **9.** 2 feet ⬤ 1 yard   **10.** 70 inches ⬤ 2 yards

Choose the better estimate.

11. A man's height:
6 feet or 6 yards

12. The distance you travel on an airplane: 700 yards or 700 miles

13. Number Sense Name a distance you would measure in miles.

Ⓑ Reasoning and Problem Solving

14. Reasoning The rim of a basketball hoop is 3 yards, 1 foot above the floor. How many feet is this?

15. **Writing in Math** Carlo wants to find how many yards are in 12 feet. Complete the table. Then explain how to solve.

Yards	1	2	3
Feet	3		

🦉 Mixed Review and Test Prep

Take It to the NET
Test Prep
www.scottforesman.com

Write each measurement in inches. You may make a table to help.

16. 2 feet   **17.** 1 foot, 7 inches   **18.** 4 feet

19. Find 500 − 409.

A. 109   **B.** 99   **C.** 91   **D.** 89

Problem-Solving Skill

Key Idea
Some problems have extra information, and some do not have enough information to solve them.

Think It Through

I need to **identify supporting details** about the dimensions of the frame to solve the problem.

Extra or Missing Information

LEARN

How can you decide what information you need?

Picture Frame Jack wants to paint a picture to go in this frame. How long should his painting be? How wide should it be?

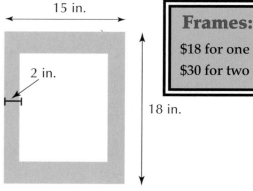

15 in.

2 in.

18 in.

Frames:
$18 for one
$30 for two

Read and Understand

Tell what the question is asking.

The inside of the frame has a shorter length and width than the outside. I need to know the inside length and width.

Identify key facts and details.

The outside of the frame has a length of 18 inches and a width of 15 inches. The frame is 2 inches wide. One frame costs $18 and 2 cost $30.

Plan and Solve

Find the extra or missing information.

I don't need to know how much the frame costs.

Inside width:
$(15 - 2) - 2 = 11$ in.

Inside length:
$(18 - 2) - 2 = 14$ in.

✓ Talk About It

1. Give the answer to the question in a complete sentence.

For another example, see Set 9-16 on p. 557.

CHECK ✓

Decide if each problem has extra information or missing information. Solve if you have enough information.

Grapes . . . $1.99 per pound
Bananas. . $1.09 per pound
Melons. . . $1.50 each

1. There will be 12 people at Katie's party. Each person will get one piece of melon. If she cuts each melon into 4 pieces, how much money will Katie need for melons?

2. Katie spent $13.08 on party supplies. She needs to buy one pound of grapes for a fruit salad. Does Katie have enough money left for the grapes? Explain.

PRACTICE

For more practice, see Set 9-16 on p. 561.

Decide if each problem has extra information or missing information. Solve if you have enough information.

For 3–4, use the graph.

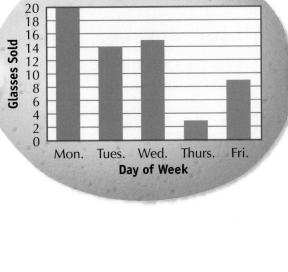

Number of Glasses of Lemonade Sold

3. Todd sold twice as many glasses of lemonade on Saturday as he sold all together on Thursday and Friday. How many glasses did he sell on Saturday?

4. Todd sold large lemonades for $2 and small lemonades for $1. If he sold a total of 16 large lemonades on Monday through Friday, how many small lemonades did Todd sell?

5. Lara earns $4 for an hour of pulling weeds. She pulled weeds in 3 lawns on Monday and 2 lawns on Wednesday. How much money did she earn?

6. **Writing in Math** Write a story problem that uses extra information. Use information from the sign at the right. Trade with a partner and solve.

Tickets:

Adults:	$13.50
12 and under:	$9.00

(You must be 45 inches tall to ride all rides.)

All text pages available online and on CD-ROM.

📖 Problem-Solving Applications

THE BOOK OF
BUTTONS
A practical and creative guide to
the decorative use of buttons

Joyce Whittemore [DK]

Buttons No one is sure who first invented them, but buttons have been used by many cultures through history. They come in all shapes, sizes, materials and colors. Around the world, button collecting is a popular and profitable pastime.

Trivia In 1520, King Francis I of France owned a velvet suit that had 13,600 gold buttons on it!

❶ Read the trivia. Write the word form for the number of buttons on the king's suit.

❷ What fraction of the triangle-shaped buttons pictured below are pointing down? are purple?

❸ The first button-collecting club was formed in 1938. The first button-making machine was patented 87 years before that time. When was the first button-making machine patented?

Good News/Bad News In the 1800s, glittering buttons became more affordable when diamonds on buttons were replaced with polished cut steel. Unfortunately, the steel rusted easily.

Using Key Facts

4 How would a button collector classify a button that is $1\frac{3}{4}$ inches across? $\frac{1}{8}$ inch across?

Key Facts
Classifying Buttons

Class	Size
•Large	$1\frac{1}{4}$ inches or over
•Medium	$\frac{3}{4}$ inch up to $1\frac{1}{4}$ inches
•Small	$\frac{3}{8}$ inch up to $\frac{3}{4}$ inch
•Diminutive	Less than $\frac{3}{8}$ inch

5  Use the pictures in this lesson to write your own problem involving buttons and fractions. Write the answer to your question in a complete sentence.

6 **Decision Making** Choose 3 buttons from the chart below and list them in order from smallest to largest.

Button	Silver	Gold	Gray	Purple
Size	$\frac{7}{8}$ inch	$\frac{3}{8}$ inch	$\frac{1}{2}$ inch	$\frac{5}{8}$ inch

Do You Know How?

Do You Understand?

Length (9-12)

1. Estimate the length. Then measure to the nearest inch.

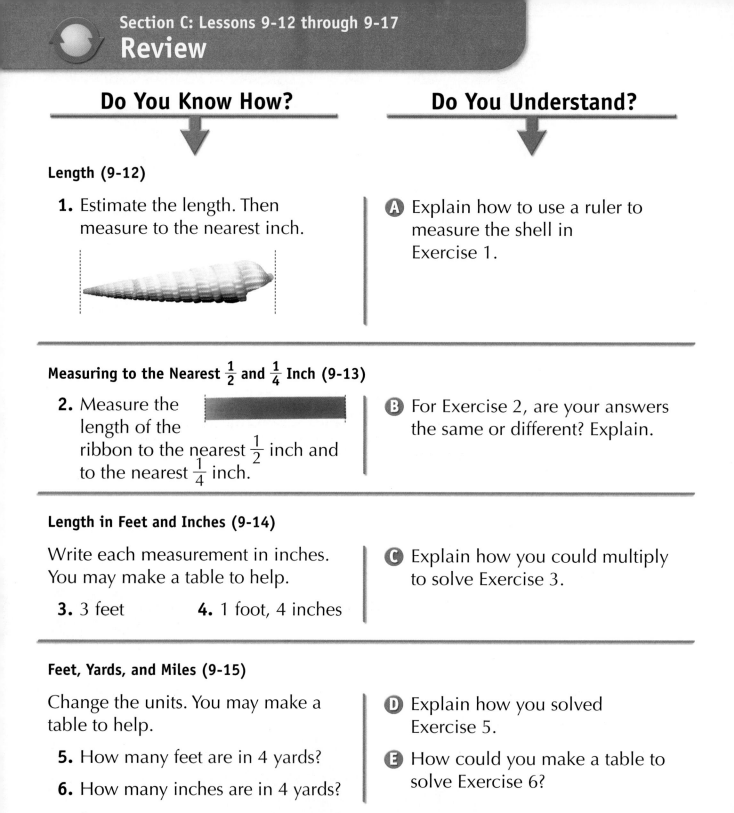

A Explain how to use a ruler to measure the shell in Exercise 1.

Measuring to the Nearest $\frac{1}{2}$ and $\frac{1}{4}$ Inch (9-13)

2. Measure the length of the ribbon to the nearest $\frac{1}{2}$ inch and to the nearest $\frac{1}{4}$ inch.

B For Exercise 2, are your answers the same or different? Explain.

Length in Feet and Inches (9-14)

Write each measurement in inches. You may make a table to help.

3. 3 feet

4. 1 foot, 4 inches

C Explain how you could multiply to solve Exercise 3.

Feet, Yards, and Miles (9-15)

Change the units. You may make a table to help.

5. How many feet are in 4 yards?

6. How many inches are in 4 yards?

D Explain how you solved Exercise 5.

E How could you make a table to solve Exercise 6?

Problem-Solving Skill: Extra or Missing Information (9-16)

7. Joyce bought 6 apples and cut each one into 4 pieces. She paid $0.50 for each apple. How many pieces were there?

F Is there any missing information that is needed to solve Exercise 7? Is there extra information? Explain.

MULTIPLE CHOICE

1. Elizabeth jumped 2 feet, 7 inches. How many inches is this? (9-14)

A. 9 inches   **B.** 14 inches   **C.** 24 inches   **D.** 31 inches

2. Tomas has a piece of wood that is 1 yard long. How much should he cut off to get a piece that is 25 inches long? (9-15)

A. 9 inches   **B.** 11 inches   **C.** 1 foot   **D.** 24 inches

FREE RESPONSE

Estimate the length. Then measure to the nearest inch. (9-12)

3.

Think It Through

I need to **check** my measurement carefully.

Measure each length to the nearest $\frac{1}{2}$ and $\frac{1}{4}$ inch. (9-13)

4.

5.

Write each measurement in inches. You may make a table to help. (9-14)

6. 1 foot, 1 inch   **7.** 6 feet   **8.** 2 feet, 6 inches

Change the units. You may make a table to help. (9-15)

9. How many inches are in 2 yards?   **10.** How many feet are in 9 yards?

Solve. (9-16, 9-17)

11. Ryan fed his aunt's dog for 4 days. He used 2 cups of food 2 times a day. How much food did he use each day?

Writing in Math

12. Grady says the grasshopper is $2\frac{1}{2}$ inches long to the nearest inch. Do you agree? Explain. (9-13)

0   1   2

INCHES

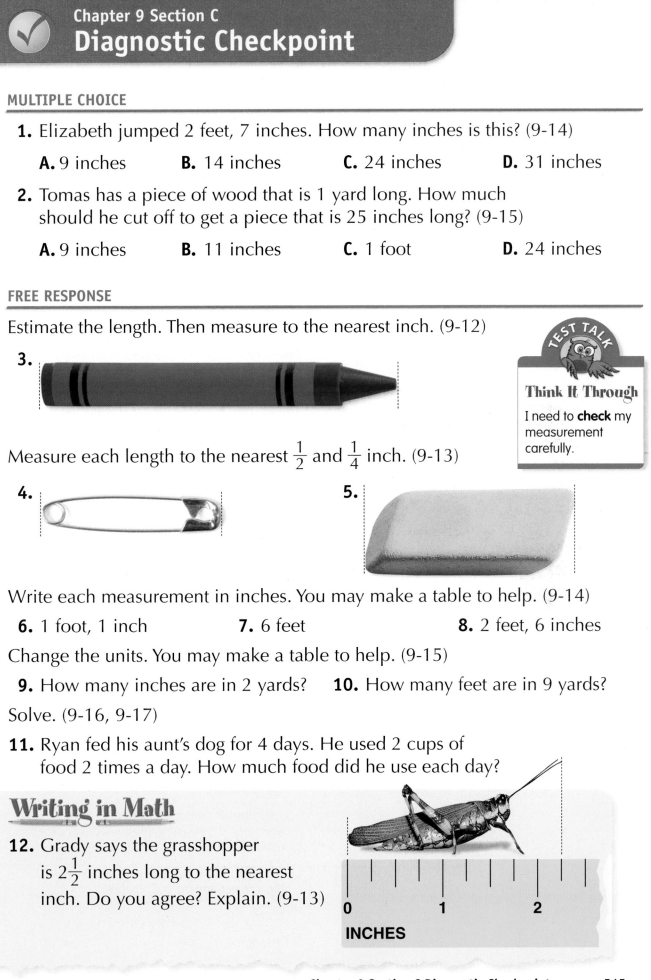

Test-Taking Strategies

Understand the question.

Get information for the answer.

Plan how to find the answer.

→ **Make smart choices.**

Use writing in math.

Improve written answers.

Make Smart Choices

To answer a multiple-choice test question, you need to choose an answer from answer choices. The steps below will help you make a smart choice.

1. What units of measure would be the most appropriate to find the length of the screwdriver?

A. pounds

B. miles

C. inches

D. feet

Understand the question.

I need to choose the best units of measure.

Get information for the answer.

*The **picture** shows the item that would be measured.*

Plan how to find the answer.

As I think about units that are used to measure length, I should look at the choices and eliminate those that do not make sense.

Make Smart Choices.

- Eliminate wrong answers.

  Pounds are used to measure weight, not length. Answer choice A, pounds, is wrong.

- Check answers for reasonableness.

  I live 3 miles from school. Miles are very long. Answer choice B, miles, is unreasonable.

  I am almost 4 feet tall. The screwdriver looks shorter than a foot. Answer choice D, feet, is unreasonable.

  Only answer choice C is left. It would be reasonable to measure the screwdriver in inches because an inch is about the length of a stamp.

  The correct answer is C, inches.

2. Janine has a window shade on her window. What fraction below best describes the part of the window covered by the window shade?

> **Think It Through**
>
> *I need to choose the best fraction for the part of the window covered by the shade. I can **check the reasonableness** of the answer choices. Less than $\frac{1}{2}$ of the window is covered, so answer choices B and D are not reasonable. That leaves A and C. If it's A, $\frac{1}{8}$, then 8 pieces the size of the shade shown should fit in the window. That doesn't look right. So it must be C, $\frac{1}{3}$. That seems reasonable. I can picture 3 pieces fitting in the window.*

A. $\frac{1}{8}$ **B.** $\frac{2}{3}$ **C.** $\frac{1}{3}$ **D.** $\frac{1}{2}$

Now it's your turn.

For each problem, give the answer and explain how you made your choice.

3. What units of measure would be the most appropriate to find the length of a car?

A. miles

B. feet

C. gallons

D. inches

4. After dinner, Fred had some pie. What fraction below best describes the amount that is left?

A. $\frac{1}{2}$ **C.** $\frac{1}{3}$

B. $\frac{3}{4}$ **D.** $\frac{1}{6}$

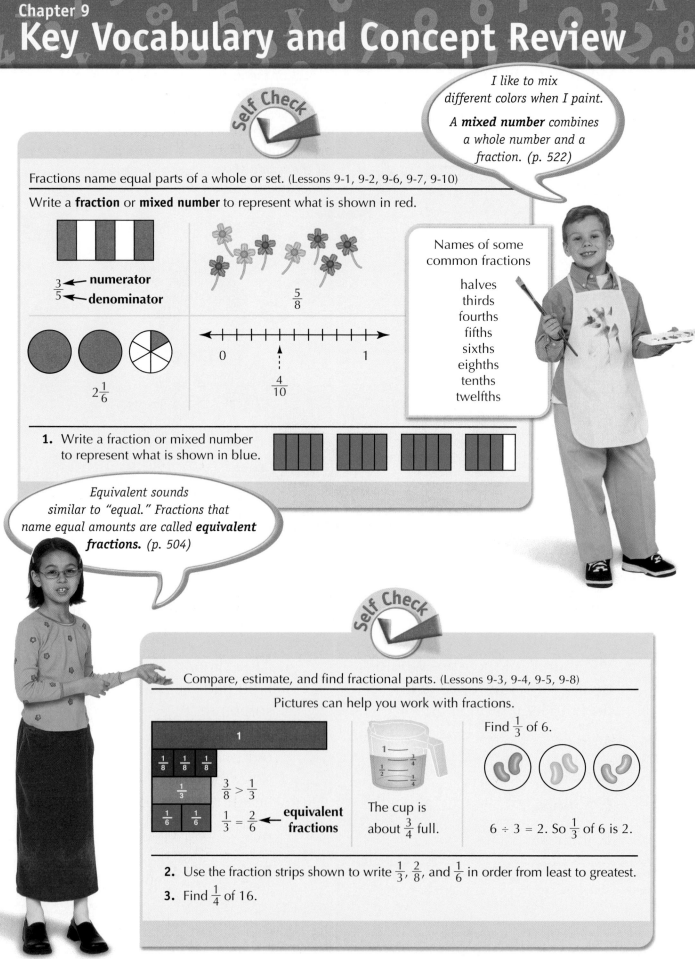

Self Check

I like to mix different colors when I paint.

*A **mixed number** combines a whole number and a fraction. (p. 522)*

Fractions name equal parts of a whole or set. (Lessons 9-1, 9-2, 9-6, 9-7, 9-10)

Write a **fraction** or **mixed number** to represent what is shown in red.

$\frac{3}{5}$ ← **numerator**
← **denominator**

$\frac{5}{8}$

$2\frac{1}{6}$

$\frac{4}{10}$

Names of some common fractions

halves
thirds
fourths
fifths
sixths
eighths
tenths
twelfths

1. Write a fraction or mixed number to represent what is shown in blue.

*Equivalent sounds similar to "equal." Fractions that name equal amounts are called **equivalent fractions.** (p. 504)*

Self Check

Compare, estimate, and find fractional parts. (Lessons 9-3, 9-4, 9-5, 9-8)

Pictures can help you work with fractions.

| 1 |
| $\frac{1}{8}$ | $\frac{1}{8}$ | $\frac{1}{8}$ |
| $\frac{1}{3}$ |
| $\frac{1}{6}$ | $\frac{1}{6}$ |

$\frac{3}{8} > \frac{1}{3}$

$\frac{1}{3} = \frac{2}{6}$ ← **equivalent fractions**

The cup is about $\frac{3}{4}$ full.

Find $\frac{1}{3}$ of 6.

$6 \div 3 = 2$. So $\frac{1}{3}$ of 6 is 2.

2. Use the fraction strips shown to write $\frac{1}{3}$, $\frac{2}{8}$, and $\frac{1}{6}$ in order from least to greatest.

3. Find $\frac{1}{4}$ of 16.

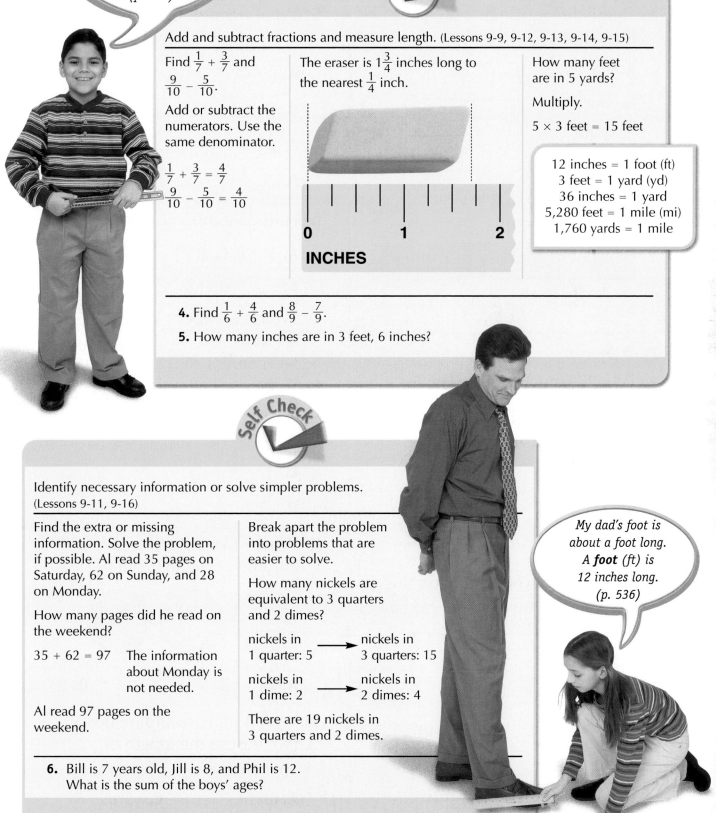

My thumb is about 1 inch long from the knuckle to the tip.

An **inch** (in.) is a standard unit of measure. (p. 532)

Add and subtract fractions and measure length. (Lessons 9-9, 9-12, 9-13, 9-14, 9-15)

Find $\frac{1}{7} + \frac{3}{7}$ and $\frac{9}{10} - \frac{5}{10}$.

Add or subtract the numerators. Use the same denominator.

$\frac{1}{7} + \frac{3}{7} = \frac{4}{7}$

$\frac{9}{10} - \frac{5}{10} = \frac{4}{10}$

The eraser is $1\frac{3}{4}$ inches long to the nearest $\frac{1}{4}$ inch.

```
0          1          2
INCHES
```

How many feet are in 5 yards?

Multiply.

5×3 feet = 15 feet

12 inches = 1 foot (ft)
3 feet = 1 yard (yd)
36 inches = 1 yard
5,280 feet = 1 mile (mi)
1,760 yards = 1 mile

4. Find $\frac{1}{6} + \frac{4}{6}$ and $\frac{8}{9} - \frac{7}{9}$.

5. How many inches are in 3 feet, 6 inches?

Identify necessary information or solve simpler problems. (Lessons 9-11, 9-16)

Find the extra or missing information. Solve the problem, if possible. Al read 35 pages on Saturday, 62 on Sunday, and 28 on Monday.

How many pages did he read on the weekend?

$35 + 62 = 97$ The information about Monday is not needed.

Al read 97 pages on the weekend.

Break apart the problem into problems that are easier to solve.

How many nickels are equivalent to 3 quarters and 2 dimes?

nickels in 1 quarter: 5 → nickels in 3 quarters: 15

nickels in 1 dime: 2 → nickels in 2 dimes: 4

There are 19 nickels in 3 quarters and 2 dimes.

My dad's foot is about a foot long. A **foot** (ft) is 12 inches long. (p. 536)

6. Bill is 7 years old, Jill is 8, and Phil is 12. What is the sum of the boys' ages?

Answers: 1. $3\frac{3}{4}$ 2. $1\frac{1}{2}$ 3. $\frac{6}{8}, \frac{1}{3}$ 4. $\frac{5}{6}, \frac{1}{9}$ 5. 42 inches 6. 19

MULTIPLE CHOICE

1. Name the equal parts of this whole.

A. halves

B. fourths

C. sixths

D. eighths

2. What fraction of this figure is red?

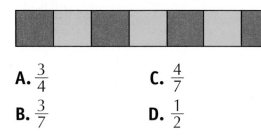

A. $\frac{3}{4}$

B. $\frac{3}{7}$

C. $\frac{4}{7}$

D. $\frac{1}{2}$

3. Which is the best estimate for the amount that is green?

A. about $\frac{1}{4}$

B. about $\frac{1}{2}$

C. about $\frac{3}{4}$

D. about 1

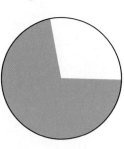

4. What fraction is missing on this number line?

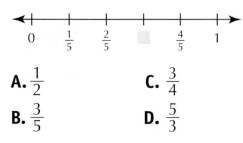

A. $\frac{1}{2}$

B. $\frac{3}{5}$

C. $\frac{3}{4}$

D. $\frac{5}{3}$

5. What fraction of the balls are yellow?

A. $\frac{2}{7}$

B. $\frac{7}{9}$

C. $\frac{2}{9}$

D. $\frac{9}{7}$

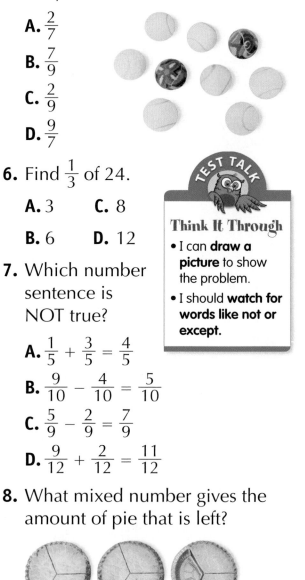

6. Find $\frac{1}{3}$ of 24.

A. 3   C. 8

B. 6   D. 12

Think It Through
- I can **draw a picture** to show the problem.
- I should **watch for words like not or except.**

7. Which number sentence is NOT true?

A. $\frac{1}{5} + \frac{3}{5} = \frac{4}{5}$

B. $\frac{9}{10} - \frac{4}{10} = \frac{5}{10}$

C. $\frac{5}{9} - \frac{2}{9} = \frac{7}{9}$

D. $\frac{9}{12} + \frac{2}{12} = \frac{11}{12}$

8. What mixed number gives the amount of pie that is left?

A. $\frac{2}{3}$ B. $2\frac{1}{3}$ C. $2\frac{2}{3}$ D. $3\frac{1}{3}$

9. Which units would be best to measure the length of your pencil?

A. inches   C. yards

B. feet   D. miles

10. What is the length of this pin to the nearest $\frac{1}{4}$ inch?

A. $\frac{1}{4}$ inch

B. $\frac{3}{4}$ inch

C. $1\frac{1}{4}$ inches

D. $1\frac{3}{4}$ inches

11. How many inches are in 2 feet?

A. 12   **C.** 24

B. 18   **D.** 72

12. How many feet are in 5 yards?

A. 3   **C.** 20

B. 15   **D.** 25

FREE RESPONSE

Draw a picture to show each fraction or mixed number.

13. $\frac{4}{5}$ **14.** $1\frac{1}{3}$

15. $2\frac{1}{2}$ **16.** $\frac{3}{7}$

Compare. Use >, <, or =.

17.

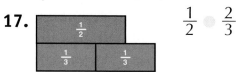

$\frac{1}{2}$ ● $\frac{2}{3}$

18. Al had 20 baseball cards. He gave $\frac{1}{4}$ of his cards to Mack. How many cards did Al give Mack?

Copy and complete the number sentence.

19.

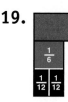

$\frac{1}{6} = \frac{\blacksquare}{12}$

20. Solve a simpler problem to answer this question.

Kim had 2 bananas. She cut each into 4 equal pieces. Then she cut each piece into thirds. How many banana pieces did she have?

Think It Through
• I can **break apart** or change the problem into ones that are easier to solve.

Writing in Math

21. Decide if the problem has extra or missing information. Explain. Solve if you have enough information.

Alan made a plain pizza and a pepperoni pizza. He cut each pizza into 8 equal slices. His friends ate 5 slices of the plain pizza and 7 slices of the pepperoni pizza. What fraction of the plain pizza was left?

22. Explain how you can tell how many fourths are in $1\frac{3}{4}$.

23. Describe how you can use a number line to order the fractions $\frac{3}{7}$, $\frac{5}{7}$, and $\frac{1}{7}$ from least to greatest.

Number and Operation

MULTIPLE CHOICE

1. What fraction of the marbles are blue?

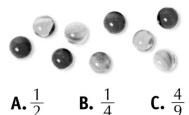

A. $\frac{1}{2}$ **B.** $\frac{1}{4}$ **C.** $\frac{4}{9}$ **D.** $\frac{5}{9}$

2. Which of the following numbers are written in order from least to greatest?

A. 1,797   1,979   1,977

B. 1,977   1,797   1,979

C. 1,797   1,977   1,979

D. 1,979   1,977   1,797

3. Karen bought 12 muffins at the bakery. Each muffin cost $2. How much money did Karen spend in all?

A. $6   **B.** $10   **C.** $14   **D.** $24

FREE RESPONSE

4. What fraction of this figure is shaded red?

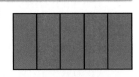

Writing in Math

5. On a number line, which fraction is closer to 0, $\frac{1}{4}$ or $\frac{3}{4}$? Explain.

Think It Through
I can **draw a picture** to show my thinking.

Geometry and Measurement

MULTIPLE CHOICE

6. What is the perimeter of this park?

A. 25 yards

B. 50 yards

C. 100 yards

D. 150 yards

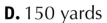
10 yards

15 yards

7. How many inches are in 3 feet, 4 inches?

A. 7 inches   **C.** 36 inches

B. 16 inches   **D.** 40 inches

8. What time will it be 2 hours after 9:30 A.M.?

A. 7:30 A.M.   **C.** 9:32 A.M.

B. 11:30 A.M.   **D.** 11:30 P.M.

FREE RESPONSE

9. I am a quadrilateral with all equal sides. My corners are right angles. What kind of quadrilateral am I?

10. The perimeter of an equilateral triangle is 21 feet. What is the length of each of its sides?

Writing in Math

11. Explain why this rectangular prism is NOT a cube.

Data Analysis and Probability

12. Which is **certain** to happen?

A. It will rain tomorrow.

B. Next week will have 7 days.

C. A flipped coin will land on heads.

D. The bus will be on time.

13. Which describes the number in a data set that occurs most often?

A. mean   **C.** mode

B. range   **D.** median

Use the pictograph for 14–16.

School Car Wash

Friday	
Saturday	
Sunday	

Each 🚗 = 5 cars washed.

14. On which day were the most cars washed?

15. How many cars were washed on Friday?

Writing in Math

16. Thomas says the total number of cars washed was 11. Do you agree? Explain why or why not.

Algebra

17. Which property of multiplication states that $3 \times 4 = 4 \times 3$?

A. Commutative **C.** Zero

B. Identity   **D.** Associative

18. Which fraction is next in the pattern?

$$\frac{1}{2} = \frac{2}{4} = \frac{3}{6} = \blacksquare$$

A. $\frac{4}{6}$ **B.** $\frac{4}{7}$ **C.** $\frac{4}{8}$ **D.** $\frac{4}{9}$

19. What is the rule for this table?

In	25	20	15	10
Out	18	13	8	3

20. There is a pattern in the squares used to make each set of steps below. How many squares are used to make 5 steps?

1 step   2 steps   3 steps

Writing in Math

21. A hospital must have 2 nurses on duty for every 10 patients. If there are 70 patients in the hospital, how many nurses must be on duty? Explain how you found your answer.

Think It Through
- I can **draw a picture** to help.
- I will make my answer **brief, but complete.**

Set 9-1 (pages 498–501)

Name the equal parts of the whole.

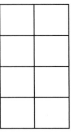

There are 8 equal parts.

The equal parts are called **eighths.**

Remember that, to show eighths, you must have 8 *equal* parts.

1. Name the equal parts of the whole.

Set 9-2 (pages 502–503)

What fraction of this figure is green?

$\dfrac{\text{numerator}}{\text{denominator}} = \dfrac{\text{green equal parts}}{\text{equal parts in all}} = \dfrac{3}{7}$

$\dfrac{3}{7}$ of the figure is green.

Remember the numerator goes above and the denominator goes below the fraction bar.

Write the fraction of each figure that is red.

1. 　　**2.**

Set 9-3 (pages 504–505)

Complete the number sentence.

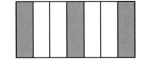

$\dfrac{2}{3} = \dfrac{\blacksquare}{6}$.

$\dfrac{2}{3} = \dfrac{4}{6}$.

$\dfrac{2}{3}$ and $\dfrac{4}{6}$ are equivalent fractions.

Remember that equivalent fractions name the same amount.

Copy and complete the number sentence.

1. $\dfrac{3}{4} = \dfrac{\blacksquare}{8}$

Set 9-4 (pages 506–509)

Compare $\dfrac{3}{8}$ and $\dfrac{1}{2}$.

$\dfrac{3}{8} \,\bullet\, \dfrac{1}{2}$

$\dfrac{3}{8}$ is less than $\dfrac{1}{2}$.　　$\dfrac{3}{8} < \dfrac{1}{2}$

Remember you can use fraction strips to compare fractions.

1.

$\dfrac{1}{3} \,\bullet\, \dfrac{1}{5}$

2. Order $\dfrac{1}{2}$, $\dfrac{1}{3}$, and $\dfrac{1}{5}$ from least to greatest.

Estimate the fraction of the pizza that is left.

Compare the pizza to a fraction you know.

 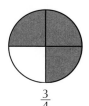

$\frac{3}{4}$

About $\frac{3}{4}$ of the pizza is left.

Remember that you can compare fractions to $\frac{1}{4}$, $\frac{1}{2}$, and $\frac{3}{4}$ to estimate fractional amounts.

Estimate the fraction that is left.

1.  **2.**

What fractions are missing in the number line?

Each section of the number line is $\frac{1}{5}$.

The missing fractions are $\frac{2}{5}$ and $\frac{4}{5}$.

Remember to look for a pattern in the fractions on your number line.

Write the missing fractions for each number line.

1.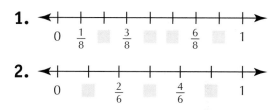

0   $\frac{1}{8}$ ▢ $\frac{3}{8}$ ▢   ▢ $\frac{6}{8}$ ▢   1

2.

0   ▢ $\frac{2}{6}$ ▢ $\frac{4}{6}$ ▢   1

What fraction of the triangles are pink?

$$\frac{\text{numerator}}{\text{denominator}} = \frac{\textbf{number of pink triangles}}{\textbf{total number of triangles}} = \frac{5}{8}$$

$\frac{5}{8}$ of the triangles are pink.

Remember to count all the objects in a set to find the denominator.

1. What fraction of the balls are yellow?

Find $\frac{1}{3}$ of 12 marbles.

$12 \div 3 = 4$

$\frac{1}{3}$ of 12 = 4

Remember that you can draw a picture to help you divide a set into equal groups.

1. Find $\frac{1}{5}$ of 15.

Set 9-9 (pages 520–521)

Find $\frac{1}{6} + \frac{4}{6}$.

Add the numerators.
Use the same denominator.

$$\frac{1}{6} + \frac{4}{6} = \frac{5}{6}$$

Remember when fractions have the same denominator, add or subtract the numerators and use the same denominator.

1. $\frac{5}{8} - \frac{3}{8}$

2. $\frac{3}{5} + \frac{1}{5}$ **3.** $\frac{6}{7} - \frac{4}{7}$ **4.** $\frac{4}{10} + \frac{2}{10}$

Set 9-10 (pages 522–525)

How many pies are shown?

There is 1 whole pie and $\frac{2}{5}$ of another pie.

There are $1\frac{2}{5}$ pies.

Remember that a mixed number has a whole number and a fraction.

1. How many sandwiches are shown?

Set 9-11 (pages 528–529)

When you solve a simpler problem, follow these steps.

Step 1: Change the problem into problems that are easier to solve.

Step 2: Solve the simpler problems.

Step 3: Use the answers to the simpler problems to solve the original problem.

Remember to check that you include the answers to all of the simpler problems in your final answer.

1. How many squares are in the figure?

Set 9-12 (pages 532–533)

Measure the length of the ribbon to the nearest inch.

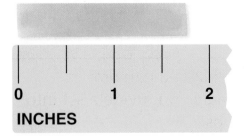

The ribbon is 2 inches long to the nearest inch.

Remember to line up one side of the object with the zero mark on the ruler.

Measure the length of each object to the nearest inch.

1.

2.

Measure the length to the nearest $\frac{1}{2}$ inch and nearest $\frac{1}{4}$ inch.

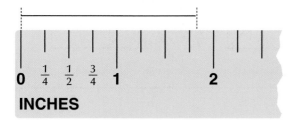

INCHES

To the nearest $\frac{1}{2}$ inch, the length is 2 inches.

To the nearest $\frac{1}{4}$ inch, the length is $1\frac{3}{4}$ inches.

Remember a measurement to the nearest $\frac{1}{2}$ or $\frac{1}{4}$ inch can be a whole number, a fraction, or a mixed number.

Measure to the nearest $\frac{1}{2}$ inch and nearest $\frac{1}{4}$ inch.

1.

2.

Set 9-14 (pages 536–537)

How many inches are in 4 feet, 2 inches?

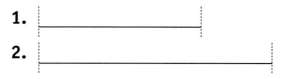

Think: 1 foot = 12 inches

4×12 inches = 48 inches

48 inches + 2 inches = 50 inches

There are 50 inches in 4 feet, 2 inches.

Remember that you can also make a table to change from feet to inches.

Write each measurement in inches.

1. 5 feet   **2.** 3 feet, 4 inches

3. 1 foot, 7 inches **4.** 8 feet

Set 9-15 (pages 538–539)

How many feet are in 7 yards?

Think: 1 yard = 3 feet

7×3 feet = 21 feet

There are 21 feet in 7 yards.

Remember that 1 yard = 36 inches and that 1 mile = 5,280 feet.

1. How many inches are in 3 yards?

Set 9-16 (pages 540–541)

To solve a problem with a lot of information, follow these steps.

Step 1: Find the main idea and the key facts and details.

Step 2: Cross out any extra information.

Step 3: Solve if you have enough information.

Remember to make sure you understand what you need to find.

Solve if you have enough information.

1. Jenna bought 4 yards of cloth for $3.50 per yard. She needs 3 feet of the cloth to make each pillow. How many pillows can she make?

Set 9-1 (pages 498–501)

Name the equal parts of the whole.

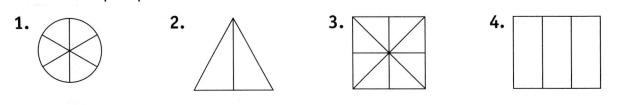

1.   **2.**   **3.**   **4.**

Set 9-2 (pages 502–503)

Write the fraction of each figure that is blue.

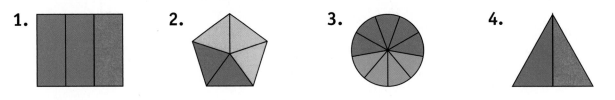

1.   **2.**   **3.**   **4.**

Set 9-3 (pages 504–505)

Copy and complete each number sentence.

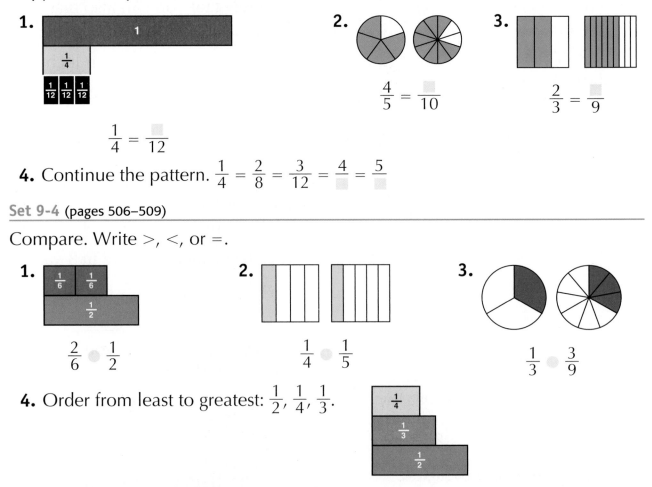

1.

$\dfrac{1}{4} = \dfrac{\blacksquare}{12}$

2.

$\dfrac{4}{5} = \dfrac{\blacksquare}{10}$

3.

$\dfrac{2}{3} = \dfrac{\blacksquare}{9}$

4. Continue the pattern. $\dfrac{1}{4} = \dfrac{2}{8} = \dfrac{3}{12} = \dfrac{4}{\blacksquare} = \dfrac{5}{\blacksquare}$

Set 9-4 (pages 506–509)

Compare. Write >, <, or =.

1.

$\dfrac{2}{6} \; \bullet \; \dfrac{1}{2}$

2.

$\dfrac{1}{4} \; \bullet \; \dfrac{1}{5}$

3.

$\dfrac{1}{3} \; \bullet \; \dfrac{3}{9}$

4. Order from least to greatest: $\dfrac{1}{2}, \dfrac{1}{4}, \dfrac{1}{3}.$

Take It to the NET
More Practice
www.scottforesman.com

Set 9-5 (pages 510–511)

Estimate the amount that is shaded.

1. **2.** **3.** **4.**

5. Draw a square. Shade about three fourths green.

Set 9-6 (pages 512–513)

Write the missing fractions on each number line.

1.

0   $\frac{1}{5}$ ▪ $\frac{3}{5}$ ▪   1

2.
0   $\frac{1}{9}$ ▪   ▪ $\frac{4}{9}$ $\frac{5}{9}$ ▪ $\frac{7}{9}$ ▪   1

3. On the number line in Exercise 2, what fraction could you write instead of 1?

Set 9-7 (pages 516–517)

1. What fraction of the balls are blue?

2. What fraction of the fruit are oranges?

3. What fraction of the crayons are red?

4. Draw a picture to show that $\frac{1}{2}$ of some crayons are green.

Set 9-8 (pages 518–519)

1. Find $\frac{1}{4}$ of 12 checkers.

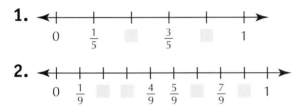

$12 \div 4 = $ ▪

$\frac{1}{4}$ of 12 = ▪

2. Find $\frac{1}{5}$ of 10 marbles.

$10 \div 5 = $ ▪

$\frac{1}{5}$ of 10 = ▪

3. Sara gave $\frac{1}{2}$ of her 6 stickers to her sister. How many stickers did Sara give to her sister?

Set 9-9 (pages 520–521)

Add or subtract. You may use fraction strips or draw a picture to help.

1. $\frac{3}{7} + \frac{2}{7}$ **2.** $\frac{6}{10} - \frac{5}{10}$ **3.** $\frac{1}{4} + \frac{2}{4}$ **4.** $\frac{1}{2} - \frac{1}{2}$

5. $\frac{4}{11} + \frac{6}{11}$ **6.** $\frac{4}{5} - \frac{2}{5}$ **7.** $\frac{1}{8} + \frac{1}{8}$ **8.** $\frac{2}{9} + \frac{2}{9}$

9. Andrew ate $\frac{1}{6}$ of a sub sandwich, and Tammy ate $\frac{4}{6}$ of the sub sandwich. Write an addition sentence that shows what fraction of the sandwich they ate all together.

Set 9-10 (pages 522–525)

Write a mixed number for each picture.

1. 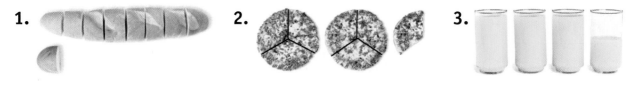 **2.** **3.**

4. Bill has $1\frac{1}{2}$ sandwiches left. How many halves are in $1\frac{1}{2}$?

Set 9-11 (pages 528–529)

Write the answer in a complete sentence.

1. Haley is at the top of page 6 in her library book. The book ends at the bottom of page 40. How many pages does Haley have left to read in her library book?

2. How many triangles can you find in the figure?

Set 9-12 (pages 532–533)

Estimate each length. Then measure to the nearest inch.

1. **2.**

3. Without using a ruler, draw a line segment about 4 inches long. Then measure it to check. Record the measurement to the nearest inch.

Take It to the NET
More Practice
www.scottforesman.com

Set 9-13 (pages 534–535)

Measure the length of each object to the nearest $\frac{1}{2}$ inch and $\frac{1}{4}$ inch.

1.

2.

3. Paul says that this screw is 2 inches long. Did he measure it to the nearest $\frac{1}{2}$ inch or to the nearest $\frac{1}{4}$ inch? Explain.

Set 9-14 (pages 536–537)

Write each measurement in inches. You may make a table to help.

1. 3 feet

2. 3 feet 1 inch

3. 4 feet

4. 2 feet 6 inches

5. 10 feet

6. 1 foot 9 inches

7. In one month, Plant A grew 20 inches. Plant B grew 1 foot 6 inches. Which plant grew more? Explain.

Set 9-15 (pages 538–539)

Change the units. You may make a table to help.

1. How many inches are in 2 yards?

2. How many feet are in 12 yards?

3. How many feet are in 7 yards?

4. How many inches are in 5 yards?

5. A park is 2,000 feet wide and 1 mile long. Which measurement of the park is larger? Explain.

Set 9-16 (pages 540–541)

Decide if each problem has extra or missing information. Solve if you have enough information.

1. Samuel bought 2 pounds of turkey and 3 pounds of ham. He will use $\frac{1}{5}$ of a pound of turkey for each sandwich. How many turkey sandwiches can Samuel make?

2. Carla spent $9.50 on school supplies. She needs to buy 2 more folders. Does she have enough money left for the folders? Explain.

CHAPTER 10

Decimals and Measurement

DIAGNOSING READINESS

A Vocabulary
(pages 22, 86, 498)

Choose the best term from the box.

1. One of ten equal parts is called a __?__.

2. When you say that 6 is greater than 5, you are __?__ the numbers.

3. If you say you are about 4 feet tall, you are __?__ your height.

Vocabulary
- **tenth** *(p. 498)*
- **third** *(p. 499)*
- **comparing** *(p. 18)*
- **estimating** *(p. 86)*

B Naming Fractions
(pages 502–503)

Write the fraction of each figure that is blue.

4.

5. 6.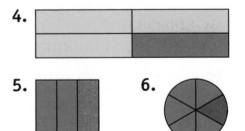

7. Grant had a pizza with 10 equal pieces. He ate 3 pieces. What fraction of the pizza did he eat?

Do You Know...

How long can a beaver hold its breath?

You'll find out in Lesson 10-9.

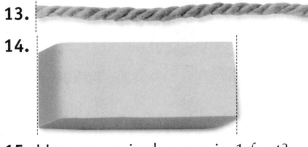

C Money
(pages 162–165)

Add or subtract.

8. $3.28
   $+ \ 4.11$

9. $5.09
   $+ \ 2.25$

10. $6.55
   $- \ 3.38$

11. $2.25
   $- \ 1.99$

12. John bought a notebook for $1.29. He bought a pen for $0.89. How much did he spend in all?

D Length in Inches
(pages 532–533, 536–537)

Measure each object to the nearest inch.

13.

14.

15. How many inches are in 1 foot?

Key Idea
You can use what you know about fractions to name decimals.

Vocabulary
• tenths
• decimal
• fraction (p. 502)
• mixed number (p. 522)

Materials
• tenths grids
or 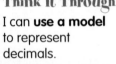 tools

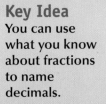

Think It Through
I can **use a model** to represent decimals.

Tenths

 **LEARN**

Activity

How are decimals and fractions alike?

You know that **tenths** show 10 equal parts of a whole. Tenths can be written as **fractions** or as **decimals.**

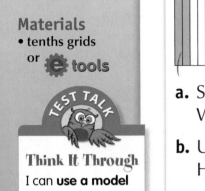

Word Form	Fraction	Decimal
two tenths	$\frac{2}{10}$	0.2

decimal point

a. Shade 7 parts on a tenths grid.
Write a fraction and a decimal for the shaded part.

b. Use another tenths grid. Shade 0.4 of the grid.
How many parts did you shade?

Shade a tenths grid to show each decimal.

c. 0.5   **d.** 0.9   **e.** 0.1

What if the amount is greater than 1?

You can write a **mixed number** as a decimal.

Example

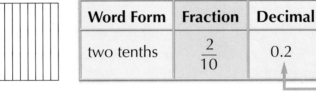

Word Form	Fraction	Decimal
one and three tenths	$1\frac{3}{10}$	1.3

✔ Talk About It

1. How is one whole shown in the tenths grids above?

2. How many tenths grids would be needed to show 4.8?

3. What number is shown if 3 whole grids are shaded?

Take It to the NET
More Examples
www.scottforesman.com

Write a fraction and a decimal for each shaded part.

1.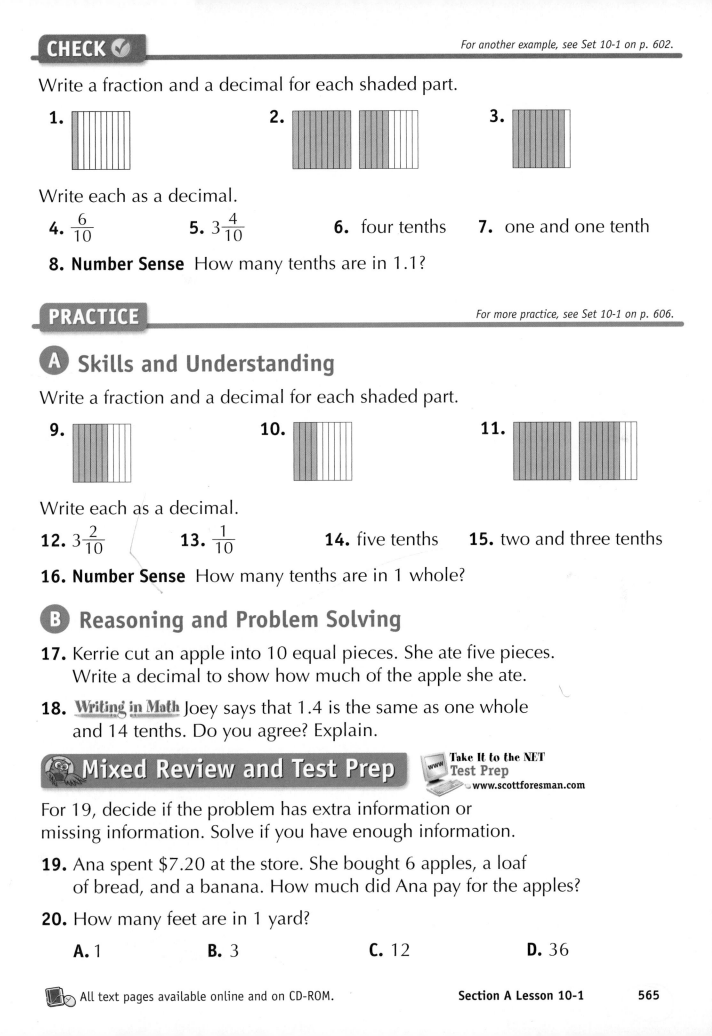

2.

3.

Write each as a decimal.

4. $\frac{6}{10}$

5. $3\frac{4}{10}$

6. four tenths

7. one and one tenth

8. Number Sense How many tenths are in 1.1?

PRACTICE

For more practice, see Set 10-1 on p. 606.

A Skills and Understanding

Write a fraction and a decimal for each shaded part.

9.

10.

11.

Write each as a decimal.

12. $3\frac{2}{10}$

13. $\frac{1}{10}$

14. five tenths

15. two and three tenths

16. Number Sense How many tenths are in 1 whole?

B Reasoning and Problem Solving

17. Kerrie cut an apple into 10 equal pieces. She ate five pieces. Write a decimal to show how much of the apple she ate.

18. Writing in Math Joey says that 1.4 is the same as one whole and 14 tenths. Do you agree? Explain.

Mixed Review and Test Prep

Take It to the NET
Test Prep
www.scottforesman.com

For 19, decide if the problem has extra information or missing information. Solve if you have enough information.

19. Ana spent $7.20 at the store. She bought 6 apples, a loaf of bread, and a banana. How much did Ana pay for the apples?

20. How many feet are in 1 yard?

A. 1   **B.** 3   **C.** 12   **D.** 36

Key Idea
You can use
what you
know about
fractions to read
and write
hundredths.

Vocabulary
• hundredth

Think It Through
I can **use a model**
to show hundredths.

Hundredths

LEARN

How do you show hundredths?

A **hundredth** is one of 100 equal parts of
a whole. Like tenths, hundredths can be
written as fractions or as decimals.

In a track meet, a runner won a race by
97 hundredths of a second. Another race was
won by one and two hundredths seconds.

✓ WARM UP
Write each as a
decimal.
1. four tenths
2. one and 9 tenths
3. three tenths

	Word Form	Fraction	Decimal
	ninety-seven hundredths	$\frac{97}{100}$	0.97
	one and two hundredths	$1\frac{2}{100}$	1.02

✓ Talk About It

1. How can you write $\frac{4}{100}$ as a decimal?

How can you read and write decimals using place value?

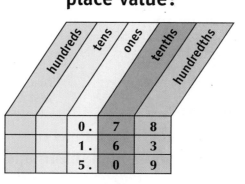

hundreds	tens	ones	tenths	hundredths
		0.	7	8
		1.	6	3
		5.	0	9

What You **Say**	What You **Write**
Seventy-eight hundredths	0.78
One and sixty-three hundredths	1.63
Five and nine hundredths	5.09

✓ Talk About It

2. Why is there a zero in the tenths place in 5.09?

3. How do you write 1.63 as a
mixed number?

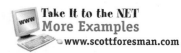

Take It to the NET
More Examples
www.scottforesman.com

Write a fraction or mixed number and a decimal for each shaded part.

1. **2.** **3.**

Write each as a decimal.

4. $\frac{23}{100}$ **5.** $2\frac{55}{100}$ **6.** 40 hundredths

7. Number Sense How many tenths are in 0.07?

PRACTICE

For more practice, see Set 10-2 on p. 606.

Ⓐ Skills and Understanding

Write a fraction or mixed number and a decimal for each shaded part.

8. **9.** **10.**

Write each as a decimal.

11. $\frac{19}{100}$ **12.** $1\frac{6}{100}$ **13.** 70 hundredths

14. Number Sense Is 0.50 the same as $\frac{1}{2}$? Explain.

Ⓑ Reasoning and Problem Solving

Mrs. Miller packed a snack box for a class field trip.

15. How many snacks did she pack in all?

16. Write a fraction and a decimal to show what part of the snacks are granola bars.

17. Writing in Math Explain how 0.09 is different from 0.90.

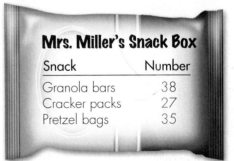

Mrs. Miller's Snack Box

Snack	Number
Granola bars	38
Cracker packs	27
Pretzel bags	35

 Mixed Review and Test Prep

Take It to the NET
Test Prep
www.scottforesman.com

18. 454 + 786   **19.** 889 + 972   **20.** 14 + 67 + 12

21. Which shows three tenths?

A. 0.03   **B.** 0.3   **C.** 3.0   **D.** 30.0

Think It Through
I can **use a number line to compare decimals.**

Comparing and Ordering Decimals

✓ **WARM UP**
Write each as a decimal.
1. seven tenths
2. forty hundredths
3. $\frac{15}{100}$ 4. $\frac{9}{10}$

LEARN

How can you use models to compare and order decimals?

Julie bought 0.43 pounds of cheese and 0.36 pounds of ham. Did Julie buy more or less cheese than ham?

Example A

Compare 0.43 and 0.36. Use <, =, or >.

0.43 ● 0.36

One Way: Use hundredths grids.

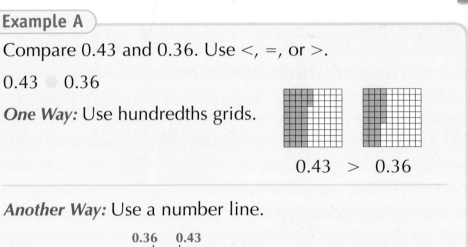

0.43 > 0.36

Another Way: Use a number line.

Julie bought more cheese than ham.

Example B

Order 0.65, 0.78, and 0.37 from least to greatest.

On a number line, the numbers increase as you move from left to right.

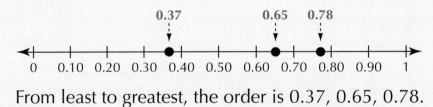

From least to greatest, the order is 0.37, 0.65, 0.78.

✓ **Talk About It**

1. **Number Sense** On a number line, where would 1.3 appear? Is 1.3 greater than or less than 0.3? Explain.

Can tenths and hundredths name the same amount?

Example C

0.20 and 0.2 name the same amount.

In decimal form, tenths can be written as hundredths by writing a zero in the hundredths place.

0.4 = 0.40
1.6 = 1.60
4.9 = 4.90

	Word Form	Fraction	Decimal
	twenty hundredths	$\frac{20}{100}$	0.20
	two tenths	$\frac{2}{10}$	0.2

In decimal form, hundredths can be written as tenths if there is a zero in the hundredths place. Just take off the zero.

0.20 = 0.2   7.80 = 7.8

✔ Talk About It

2. How could you use grids to show that 0.30 = 0.3?

3. Can 0.45 be written as tenths? Explain.

CHECK ✔

For another example, see Set 10-3 on p. 603.

Compare. Use <, >, or =.

1.

0.07 ● 0.70

2.

0.6 ● 0.2

Use a number line to order the decimals from least to greatest.

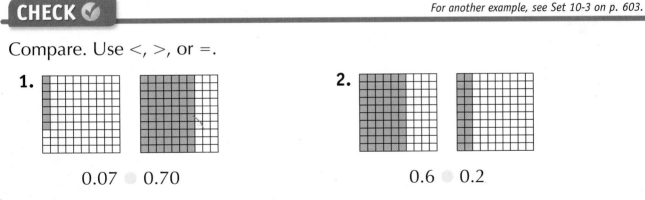

3. 0.40   0.25   0.15

4. 0.34   0.20   0.46

5. Number Sense How could you use the number line above to order 0.2, 0.5, and 0.4 from least to greatest?

A Skills and Understanding

Compare. Use <, >, or =.

6.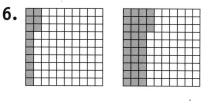

0.13 ● 0.33

7.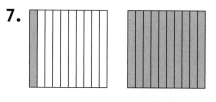

0.1 ● 1.0

Use the number line to order the decimals from least to greatest.

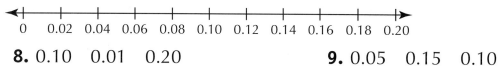

0   0.02   0.04   0.06   0.08   0.10   0.12   0.14   0.16   0.18   0.20

8. 0.10   0.01   0.20

9. 0.05   0.15   0.10

10. **Number Sense** On the number line above, 0.03 would come between which two given decimals?

B Reasoning and Problem Solving

Math and Science

Data File	
Weights of Bats	
Name	Weight (ounces)
Banana bat	0.11
Lesser horseshoe bat	0.18
Kitti's hognosed bat	0.07
Proboscis bat	0.09
Smoky bat	0.11

The bats listed in the table at the right are among the smallest bats in the world. The weights of individual bats of the same kind might be very different.

11. Which bat weighs the most?

12. Which bat weighs the least?

Compare the weights of the bats in the order named. Use <, >, or =.

13. Banana bat ● Proboscis bat

14. Smoky bat ● Lesser horseshoe bat

15. **Writing in Math** Explain how to order the weights of the bats from greatest to least.

Mixed Review and Test Prep

Take It to the NET
Test Prep
www.scottforesman.com

16. 4 × 6   17. 5 × 8   18. 7 × 3   19. 6 × 8   20. 3 × 9

21. Which decimal is the same as $\frac{5}{100}$?

   A. 5.0   **B.** 0.5   **C.** 0.50   **D.** 0.05

Learning with Technology

Using a Calculator to Write Fractions as Decimals

You can use your calculator to write a fraction or mixed number as a decimal.

To write $\frac{3}{4}$ as a decimal, enter 3 $\boxed{\text{/}}$ 4. Press $\boxed{\text{F⊃D}}$. The display will show $\boxed{0.75}$, so the decimal name for $\frac{3}{4}$ is 0.75.

To write 1.8 as a mixed number, enter 1.8. Press $\boxed{\text{F⊃D}}$. The display will show $\boxed{1\text{u}8/10}$, so the mixed number is $1\frac{8}{10}$.

Copy and complete each table.

	Fraction	Decimal
1.	$\frac{1}{4}$	
2.	$\frac{3}{5}$	
3.	$\frac{85}{100}$	

	Decimal	Mixed Number
4.	1.37	
5.	1.7	
6.	3.05	

Enrichment

Connecting Fractions and Decimals to Money

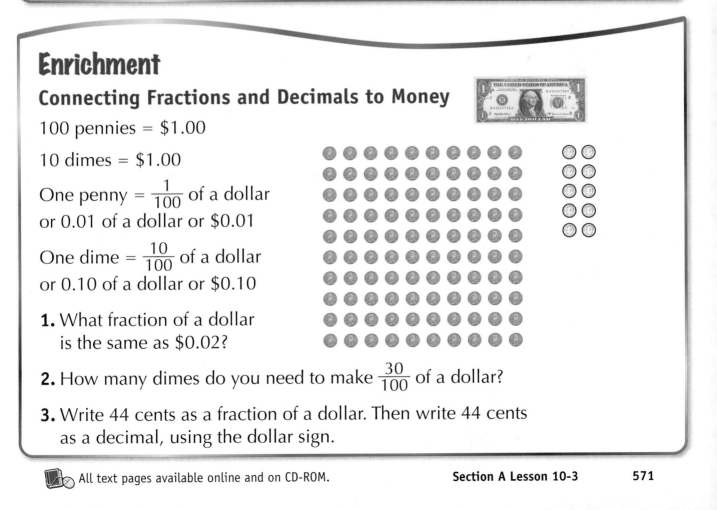

100 pennies = $1.00

10 dimes = $1.00

One penny = $\frac{1}{100}$ of a dollar or 0.01 of a dollar or $0.01

One dime = $\frac{10}{100}$ of a dollar or 0.10 of a dollar or $0.10

1. What fraction of a dollar is the same as $0.02?

2. How many dimes do you need to make $\frac{30}{100}$ of a dollar?

3. Write 44 cents as a fraction of a dollar. Then write 44 cents as a decimal, using the dollar sign.

Adding and Subtracting Decimals

LEARN

How can you find the total?

Tyler wears a pedometer to keep a record of distances when he walks his dog. Last Saturday, he walked 2.85 miles to the lake and then 1.74 miles on a shortcut home. How far did he walk?

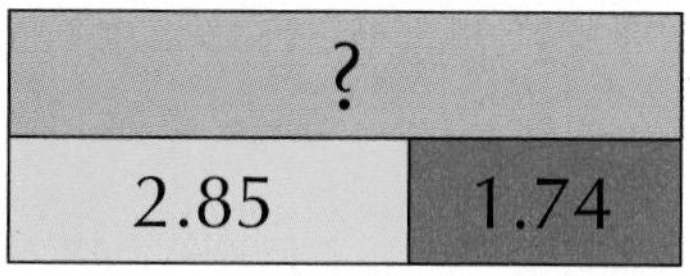

?
Total Miles Walked

| 2.85 | 1.74 |

I need to put together 2 groups, so I will add.

How do you add decimals?

Example A

Find 2.85 + 1.74.

STEP 1	STEP 2	STEP 3	STEP 4
Line up the decimal points.	Add hundredths. Regroup if needed.	Add tenths. Regroup if needed.	Add ones. Write a decimal point in the sum.
2.85 + 1.74	2.85 + 1.74 ——— 9	¹ 2.85 + 1.74 ——— 59	¹ 2.85 + 1.74 ——— 4.59

Tyler walked 4.59 miles.

✓ **Talk About It**

1. How is adding decimals like adding whole numbers? How is it different?

2. How could estimation help you with Example A?

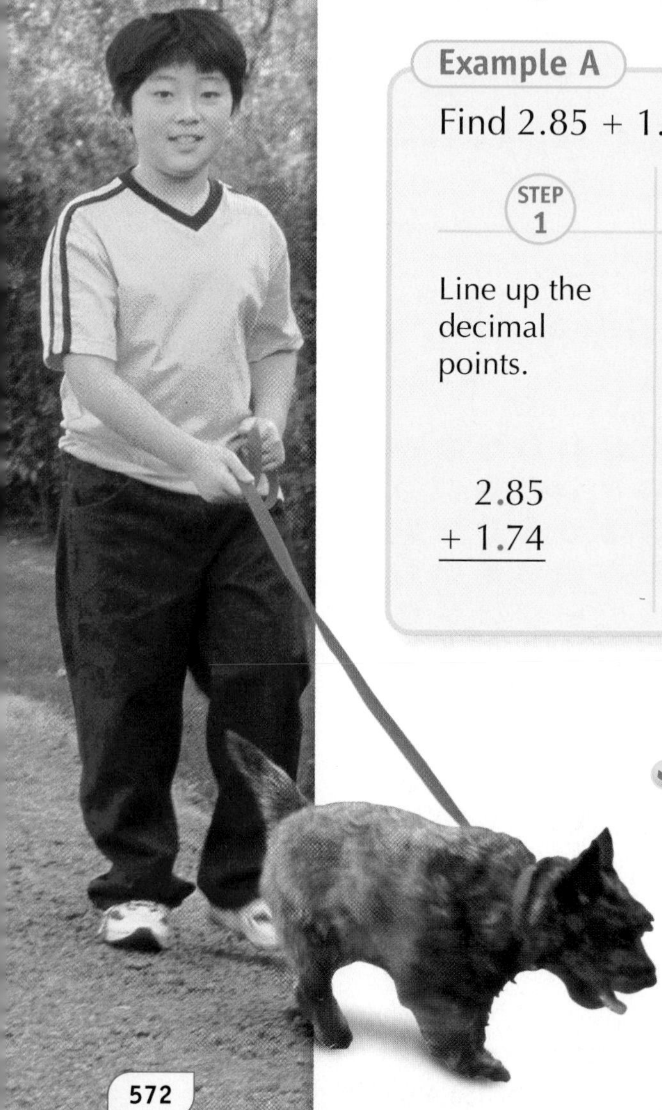

How is subtracting decimals like subtracting whole numbers?

Olivia's pedometer shows that she ran 5.47 miles on Saturday and 3.94 miles on Sunday. How many more miles did Olivia run on Saturday than on Sunday?

Example B

Find 5.47 − 3.94.

STEP 1	STEP 2	STEP 3	STEP 4
Line up the decimal points.	Subtract the hundredths. Regroup if needed.	Subtract the tenths. Regroup if needed.	Subtract the ones. Write a decimal point in the difference.
5.47 − 3.94	5.47 − 3.94 3	4 14 5.47 − 3.94 5 3	4 14 5.47 − 3.94 1.53

Olivia ran 1.53 miles more on Saturday than on Sunday.

✔ Talk About It

3. How is subtracting decimals like subtracting whole numbers? How is it different?

4. Harvey subtracted 7.8 − 5.9 and gave 19 as his answer. How do you know his answer is wrong? What was his mistake?

CHECK ✔

For another example, see Set 10-4 on p. 603.

Add.

1. 3.41 + 2.58	**2.** 6.60 + 1.92	**3.** 4.1 + 5.7	**4.** 7.0 + 3.9

Subtract.

5. 5.81 − 2.55	**6.** 8.33 − 4.61	**7.** 6.7 − 3.1	**8.** 7.1 − 1.8

9. **Number Sense** How can you tell without adding that 0.5 + 0.7 is greater than 1?

A Skills and Understanding

Add.

10. 8.29
      + 9.31

11. 3.45
      + 6.72

12. 8.8
      + 3.1

13. 1.8
      + 7.5

Subtract.

14. 3.72
      − 2.94

15. 6.10
      − 5.41

16. 7.2
      − 4.4

17. 5.3
      − 1.1

18. Number Sense Write an addition number sentence using decimals that have a sum equal to 1.

B Reasoning and Problem Solving

 Math and Social Studies

In the year 2000, the construction of the longest road tunnel was completed in Laerdal, Norway, at a length of 15.2 miles. Use the data file to answer the following questions.

19. How much longer is the St. Gotthard tunnel than the Gran Sasso tunnel?

20. If the Arlberg and the Gran Sasso tunnels were placed end-to-end, how long would the combined tunnel be?

21. If the Gran Sasso and Mt. Blanc tunnels were placed end-to-end, would the combined tunnel be longer than the Laerdal tunnel? Explain.

22. **Writing in Math** Is Alice's work below correct? If not, tell why and correct her work.

Data File

Road Tunnels	
Tunnel	Length (Miles)
St. Gotthard	10.14
Arlberg	8.69
Mt. Blanc	7.21
Gran Sasso	6.32

Find 4.53 − 2.91.

$$\overset{3}{\cancel{4}}.\overset{15}{\cancel{5}}3$$
$$-\ 2.91$$
$$\overline{\quad.162}$$

C Extensions

Sometimes you need to round amounts of money to the nearest dollar. For example, $15.23 is between $15 and $16. The halfway point between $15 and $16 is $15.50. Since $15.23 is less than $15.50, it rounds to $15.

Round each amount to the nearest dollar. For Exercise 26, think of the rules for rounding whole numbers.

23. $38.86   **24.** $9.56   **25.** $73.42   **26.** $7.50

Mixed Review and Test Prep

Take It to the NET
Test Prep
www.scottforesman.com

27. 40 ÷ 5   **28.** 18 ÷ 3   **29.** 35 ÷ 7   **30.** 24 ÷ 4

31. Order the decimals 2.28, 2.40, and 2.06 from least to greatest.

```
◄──┼────┼────┼────┼────┼────┼────┼────┼────┼────┼──►
  2.0  2.05  2.10  2.15  2.20  2.25  2.30  2.35  2.40  2.45  2.50
```

A. 2.06   2.40   2.28   **C.** 2.40   2.06   2.28

B. 2.28   2.40   2.06   **D.** 2.06   2.28   2.40

Discovery CHANNEL SCHOOL   Discover Math in Your World

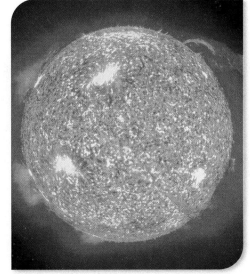

Sun Up

Although the sun is 93 million miles away, it provides all of the heat and light on Earth. Of the part of the sun's energy that reaches Earth,

> 0.15 is absorbed by the atmosphere,
> 0.42 is reflected back into space, and
> 0.43 is absorbed by Earth's surface.

1. What fraction of the sun's energy is absorbed by Earth's surface?

2. Add the three decimals. What is the sum?

Take It to the NET
Video and Activities
www.scottforesman.com

Understand Graphic Sources: Lists

Understanding graphic sources such as lists when you read in math can help you use the **problem-solving strategy,** *Make an Organized List,* in the next lesson.

In reading, understanding lists can help you understand what you read. In math, understanding lists can help you solve problems.

Jamie made an organized list to show all the possible sandwiches he could make.

*The labels at the top of the **list** tell me what items are being combined.*

Each row describes a different combination of bread and filling.

Bread	Filling
wheat	chicken salad
wheat	tuna salad
wheat	shrimp salad
white	chicken salad
white	tuna salad
white	shrimp salad

There are 6 different combinations.

The number of rows tells the number of different combinations.

1. How many different fillings did Jamie have to choose from?

2. Why did Jamie write *chicken salad* twice?

3. How could Jamie have organized his list in a different way?

For 4–6, use the problem below and the list at the right.

Doreen has a quarter, a dime, a nickel, and a penny. She told her little sister to pick any 2 coins. Doreen made a list to show all the possible pairs of coins.

Coin 1	Coin 2
penny	nickel
penny	dime
penny	quarter
nickel	dime
nickel	quarter
dime	quarter

4. How many different pairs are possible?

5. How many of these pairs include a dime?

6. **Writing in Math** When Doreen made her list, why didn't she add another row listing *quarter* first?

For 7–10, use the problem below and the list at the right.

Carol made this packing list for a trip.

Pants	Shirts	Shoes
jeans	red T-shirt	sneakers
jeans	yellow T-shirt	sneakers
jeans	red T-shirt	sandals
jeans	yellow T-shirt	sandals

7. How many different t-shirts is Carol packing? different pants? different shoes?

8. How many different outfits can Carol wear?

9. If Carol forgets to pack her sandals, how many different outfits will she be able to wear?

10. **Writing in Math** How could Carol have organized her list in a different way?

For 11–12, use the problem below and the diagram and list at the right. A line can be named using two points on it.

Abe drew a line and labeled 3 points. Then he made this list to show all the different names for the line.

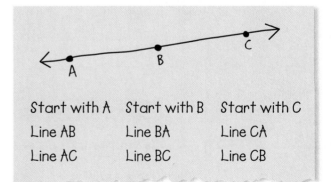

Start with A	Start with B	Start with C
Line AB	Line BA	Line CA
Line AC	Line BC	Line CB

11. How many different names are possible?

12. **Writing in Math** Describe how Abe organized his list.

Problem-Solving Strategy

Key Idea
Learning how and when to make an organized list can help you solve problems.

Vocabulary
• diagonal

Make an Organized List

LEARN

How do you make an organized list?

The red line segment *AC* is called a **diagonal.** Segment *CA* is the same diagonal. The blue line segment *BD* (or *DB*) is also a diagonal. How many diagonals are in a pentagon?

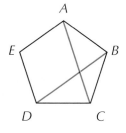

Read and Understand

What do you know?

A pentagon has 5 corners.

A diagonal connects 2 corners that are not next to each other.

What are you trying to find?

Find the number of diagonals in a pentagon.

Plan and Solve

What strategy will you use?

Strategy: Make an Organized List

Show all possible diagonals.

Start at *A*.
Draw segments **AC** and **AD**.

Start at *B*.
Draw segments **BD** and **BE**.

Continue. Start at *C*, then *D*, then *E*.

Answer: There are 5 diagonals.

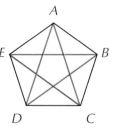

How to Make an Organized List

Step 1 Identify the items to be combined.

Step 2 Choose one of the items. Find combinations keeping that item the same.

Step 3 Repeat Step 2 as often as needed.

Look Back and Check

Is your work correct? Yes, there are no repeats.

✔ Talk About It

1. Did you draw any lines when you started at *D*? Explain.

Solve. Write the answer in a complete sentence.

1. How many different ways can you order lunch for $1.99? Continue the list to find all the ways.

Soup and sandwich

Soup and salad

Soup and chili

PICK ANY TWO ITEMS FOR $1.99

Cup of soup
Turkey sandwich
Salad
Bowl of chili

PRACTICE

For more practice, see Set 10-5 on p. 608.

Solve. Write the answer in a complete sentence.

2. How many diagonals does a hexagon have? Continue the list to find all the diagonals.

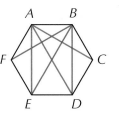

Start with A:
Segments
AC, AD, AE

Start with B:
Segments
BD, BE, BF

STRATEGIES

- **Show What You Know**
  Draw a Picture
  Make an Organized List
  Make a Table
  Make a Graph
  Act It Out or Use Objects
- **Look for a Pattern**
- **Try, Check, and Revise**
- **Write a Number Sentence**
- **Use Logical Reasoning**
- **Solve a Simpler Problem**
- **Work Backward**

Choose a tool

Mental Math

3. Frankie used 4 cups of flour and $1\frac{1}{2}$ cups of sugar for cookies. He used 3 cups of flour and $\frac{1}{2}$ cup of sugar for muffins. How many cups of flour did he use in all?

4. Jodie used beads to make this pattern. If she makes 6 rows of the pattern, how many red beads will she use?

1st row
2nd row
3rd row
4th row

5. <u>Writing in Math</u> How many different sandwiches can you choose? How would your answer change if rye bread were another choice? Explain your answer.

Sandwich Choices

White or wheat bread

Turkey or ham

Do You Know How?

Do You Understand?

Tenths (10-1)

Write each as a decimal.

1. $1\frac{1}{10}$ **2.** $\frac{7}{10}$ **3.** eight tenths

A In Exercise 1, how many tenths are there in all?

Hundredths (10-2)

Write a fraction and a decimal for the shaded part.

4.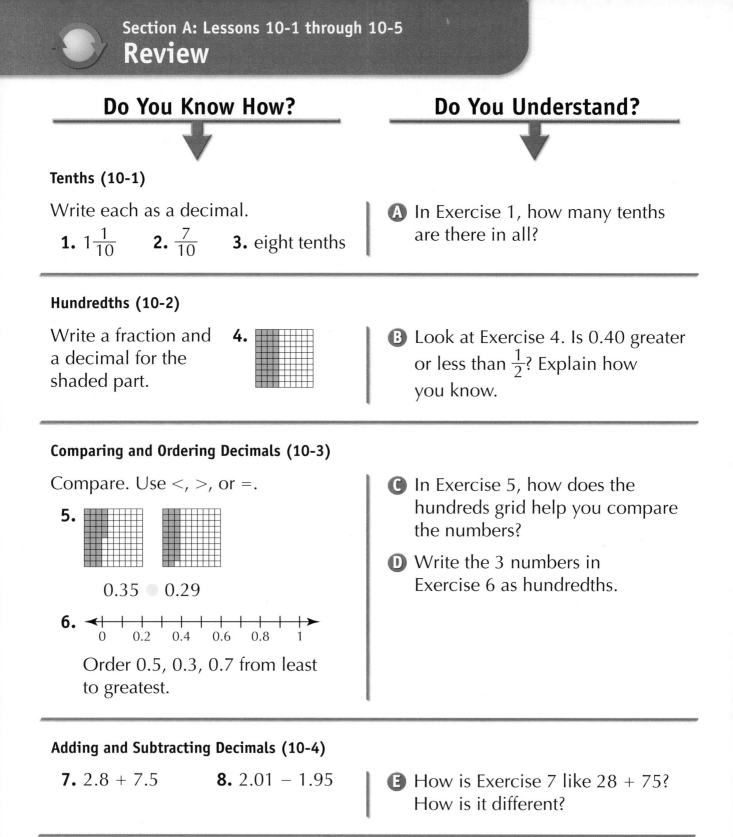

B Look at Exercise 4. Is 0.40 greater or less than $\frac{1}{2}$? Explain how you know.

Comparing and Ordering Decimals (10-3)

Compare. Use <, >, or =.

5.

0.35 ● 0.29

6.

0 0.2 0.4 0.6 0.8 1

Order 0.5, 0.3, 0.7 from least to greatest.

C In Exercise 5, how does the hundreds grid help you compare the numbers?

D Write the 3 numbers in Exercise 6 as hundredths.

Adding and Subtracting Decimals (10-4)

7. 2.8 + 7.5   **8.** 2.01 − 1.95

E How is Exercise 7 like 28 + 75? How is it different?

Problem-Solving Strategy: Make an Organized List (10-5)

9. Ray can have crackers or pretzels with cheese or peanut butter. How many different snack choices does he have?

F Explain how an organized list can help solve Exercise 9.

MULTIPLE CHOICE

1. What decimal is shown in the tenths grid? (10-1)

   A. 0.01   **B.** 0.1   **C.** 1.0   **D.** 10.0

2. What decimal names the same amount as $\frac{21}{100}$? (10-2)

   A. 2.1   **B.** 0.21   **C.** 0.12   **D.** 0.02

FREE RESPONSE

Write each as a decimal. (10-1, 10-2)

3. $\frac{4}{10}$ **4.** $2\frac{5}{100}$ **5.** twenty-three hundredths

Compare. Use <, >, or =. (10-3)

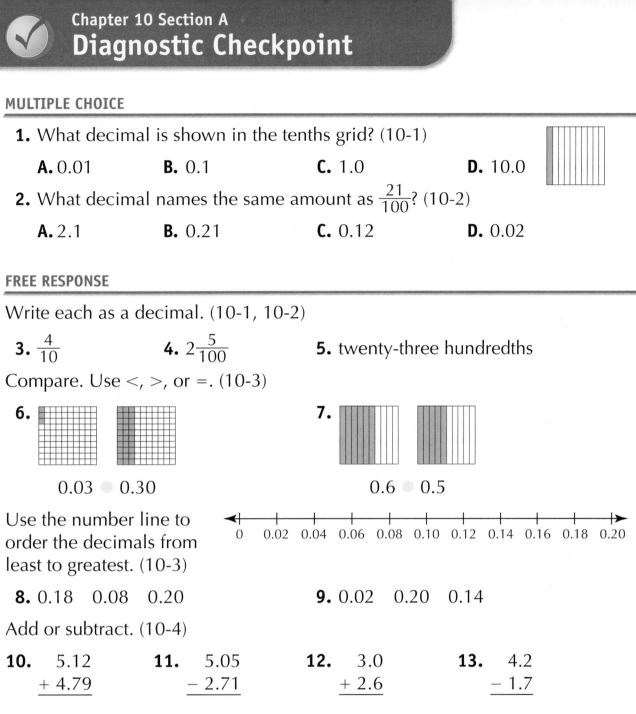

6.   0.03 ● 0.30   **7.**   0.6 ● 0.5

Use the number line to order the decimals from least to greatest. (10-3)

8. 0.18   0.08   0.20   **9.** 0.02   0.20   0.14

Add or subtract. (10-4)

10.   5.12
      + 4.79

11.   5.05
      − 2.71

12.   3.0
      + 2.6

13.   4.2
      − 1.7

Solve. Write the answer in a complete sentence. (10-5)

14. How many kinds of pizzas can you order for $8.99?

$8.99 Pizza Special!

Thin or thick crust
Mushroom or sausage topping

Writing in Math

15. Explain how you know that 0.09 is less than 0.10. (10-3)

TEST TALK

Think It Through
I should make my answer **brief but complete.**

Key Idea
You can measure using metric units.

Vocabulary
• centimeter (cm)
• decimeter (dm)

Materials
• centimeter ruler

Centimeters and Decimeters

LEARN

WARM UP
1. Name something you would measure in inches.
2. Name something you would measure in feet.

Activity

How do you use a centimeter ruler?

The **centimeter (cm)** is a metric unit of length. It is about the width of your finger. A **decimeter (dm)** is another metric unit of length.

1 cm

1 dm = 10 cm

CENTIMETERS
1 2 3 4 5 6 7 8 9 10 11 12

The eraser is 6 cm long, to the nearest centimeter.
The marker is 10 cm long, to the nearest centimeter.
You can also say that the marker is about 1 dm long.

a. Copy the table below.

b. Estimate the length of each object in centimeters. Record each estimate.

c. Find the length of each object to the nearest centimeter using a centimeter ruler. Record each measure.

Object	Estimated Length	Length to the Nearest Centimeter
A paper clip		
Your math book		
A pencil		

Estimate each length. Then measure to the nearest centimeter.

1.

2.

3. Number Sense Without using a ruler, draw a line that is about 7 cm long. Check your estimate by measuring.

PRACTICE

For more practice, see Set 10-6 on p. 608.

Ⓐ Skills and Understanding

Estimate each length. Then measure to the nearest centimeter.

4.

5.

6. Number Sense Estimate the length of your hand and your foot. Then measure each to check your estimate.

Ⓑ Reasoning and Problem Solving

7. Measure the length and width of your math book to the nearest centimeter. Then estimate the perimeter to the nearest 10 cm.

8. Writing in Math Tasha says, "A centimeter is a little longer than an inch." Do you agree? Explain.

Mixed Review and Test Prep

Take It to the NET
www Test Prep
www.scottforesman.com

9. 1.38
     + 5.31

10. 3.11
      − 2.67

11. 0.56
      + 3.87

12. Peter has a red shirt and a white shirt, black shorts and green shorts. How many different outfits can he make?

A. 2   **B.** 4   **C.** 6   **D.** 8

Vocabulary
• meter (m)
• kilometer (km)

Materials
• meter stick

Meters and Kilometers

LEARN

In the Olympics, platform divers use a platform that is 10 **meters (m)** above the water.

✓ **WARM UP**

1. Name something that is about 1 cm long.
2. About how long is your pencil in centimeters?

Think It Through
I can **use objects** to get an idea of how long a meter is.

Activity

How long is a meter?

A meter is 100 centimeters. It is a little longer than a yard.

a. Copy the table below.

b. Estimate whether each object is greater than, less than, or about 1 meter. Record your estimate.

c. Use a meter stick to check your estimate. Record each measure.

Object	Estimate: Greater than, less than, or about 1 meter	Measure (to the nearest meter)
Height of your desk		
Length of the chalkboard		
Length of your foot		
Width of your classroom		
Height of a classmate		
Width of a window		

d. List some things at home that you think are about 1 meter long. Compare your list with a classmate's list.

e. Mr. O'Leary is 2 meters tall. What is his height in centimeters?

Take It to the NET
More Examples
www.scottforesman.com

How long is a kilometer?

A **kilometer (km)** is 1,000 meters.

In most cars, the speedometer shows the speed in miles per hour and in kilometers per hour. This is because some countries measure highway distances in kilometers.

A kilometer is a little more than half a mile.

Most people can walk about 1 km in 10 minutes or less.

On the highway, a car can travel about 100 kilometers in an hour.

✔ Talk About It

1. Would you measure a parking lot in meters or kilometers?

2. Which distance is greater, 850 meters or 1 kilometer? How do you know?

3. **Reasoning** Do you think an athlete could run a 10 km race in an hour or less? Explain.

CHECK ✓

For another example, see Set 10-7 on p. 605.

Choose the best estimate for each measurement.

1. length of a hiking trail   **A.** 3 m

2. length of a picnic bench   **B.** 3 km

3. length of a beetle   **C.** 3 cm

Tell if you would use meters or kilometers for each measurement.

4. The length of your backyard

5. The distance across Canada

6. The distance from your home to school

7. **Number Sense** Which is longer, 100 kilometers or 100 miles? How do you know?

A Skills and Understanding

Choose the best estimate for each.

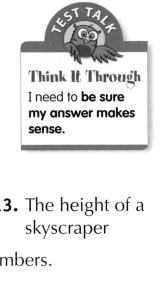

8. distance you drive to the mall   **A.** 12 cm

9. length of a classroom   **B.** 12 m

10. length of compact disk case   **C.** 12 km

Tell if you would use meters or kilometers for each.

11. The length of
your bedroom

12. The distance between
two towns

13. The height of a
skyscraper

Copy and complete. Use patterns to find the missing numbers.

14.

cm	100	200	300	400	500
m	1	2			

15.

M	1,000	2,000	3,000	4,000	5,000
km	1		3		

16. Number Sense Which race is longer,
500 m or 5 km? Explain your answer.

B Reasoning and Problem Solving

Math and Everyday Life

In many parts of the world, snow is a normal
part of life in the winter months. The table
shows the total snowfall for one season in
three different cities.

17. How much more snow fell in Burlington
than in Lander?

18. How much more snow fell in Juneau than
in Lander?

19. Writing in Math In a letter to a friend, Bryce
wrote the sentence at the right. Do you
agree with him? Explain.

Snowfall

City	Amount
Burlington	200 cm
Juneau	280 cm
Lander	168 cm

Burlington had more than
3 meters of snow.

C Extensions

You know that a centimeter is a part of a meter and also that a centimeter is part of a decimeter. Copy and complete each pair of statements. In each pair, use the first one to help you with the second. Some answers will be decimals.

20. 1 m = ☐ cm

    1 cm = ☐ m

21. 3 m = ☐ cm

    3 cm = ☐ m

22. 1 dm = ☐ cm

    5 cm = ☐ dm

Mixed Review and Test Prep

Take It to the NET
Test Prep
www.scottforesman.com

Measure each to the nearest centimeter.

23.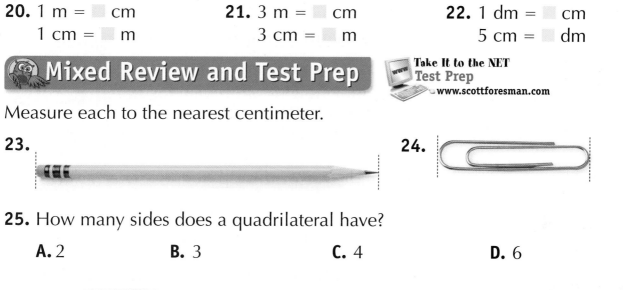

24.

25. How many sides does a quadrilateral have?

    A. 2   **B.** 3   **C.** 4   **D.** 6

Enrichment Material
Measuring with Your Hands and Feet

At one time people used parts of their body to measure. In ancient Egypt, the *cubit* was a standard unit of length. A cubit was the length of a person's forearm from the elbow to the tip of the middle finger. The foot and span were also used as units of length.

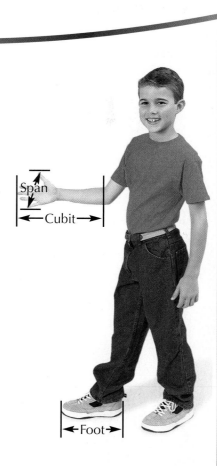

Measure the length of each object in the units given.

1. The bulletin board in your cubits

2. The classroom in your feet

3. Your desk in your span

4. Compare each of the measurements you found with those of a classmate. Are they the same?

5. **Writing in Math** Why do you think hands, arms, and feet are not used to measure today?

Problem-Solving Skill

Key Idea
There are specific things you can do to write a good explanation in math.

Writing to Explain

How do you write a good explanation?

When you explain a pattern, you need to tell how the numbers change to make the pattern.

Walking Patterns Sally prepared for a 5 km walk by writing how far she walked each day in a notebook. The distances she walked on the first three days are shown in the table below. Use the pattern to complete the table for Day 4 and Day 5.

Distance Walked

Mon.	1.0 km
Tues.	1.5 km
Wed.	2.0 km

Day	1	2	3	4	5
Distance walked	1.0 km	1.5 km	2.0 km	2.5 km	3.0 km

Explain how the number of kilometers Sally walked changes as the number of days changes.

Think It Through
When I write to explain a pattern, I should think about **steps in the process** of finding the next number in the pattern.

Writing a Math Explanation

- First, find a pattern.
- Tell how the pattern changes the number for each day.
- Use specific numbers as part of your explanation.
- Use words such as "increased" or "decreased."

Each day Sally increased the distance she walked by 0.5 km.

As each day increases by 1, the number of kilometers increases by 0.5 km.

On day 4 Sally will walk 2.0 + 0.5 = 2.5 km.

On day 5, Sally will walk 2.5 + 0.5 = 3.0 km.

✔ Talk About It

1. How does the table help you explain the pattern?

2. If Sally continued the pattern, on what day will she have walked 5.0 km? Explain.

For another example, see Set 10-8 on p. 605.

1. The pictures at the right show arrangements of card tables. Each table is 1 meter long and 1 meter wide.

Complete the pattern below to show the perimeter of arrangements of 4 tables and 5 tables.

Number of tables	1	2	3	4	5
Perimeter	4 m	6 m	8 m		

Explain how the perimeter of the arrangement changes as the number of tables changes.

For more practice, see Set 10-8 on p. 609.

Write to explain.

2. Bobby has a wooden pole that is 1 meter long. He is cutting the pole into pegs that are each 20 centimeters long. Copy and complete the table to show how much of the pole is left after Bobby has cut 3 pegs and 4 pegs.

Number of pegs	0	1	2	3	4
Length of the pole	100 cm	80 cm	60 cm		

Explain how the length of the pole changes as the number of pegs cut from the pole changes.

3. Name an object that has a length of about 1 meter. Explain why you think the object is about a meter long.

4. Explain how a decimal and a fraction are related. Use examples as part of your explanation.

5. Tell what part of the whole is shaded in the grid at the right. Use *tenths* and *hundredths* in your explanation.

6. Can you multiply to solve the problem below? Explain why or why not.

Maddie bought 3 packs of pencils. Each pack had 6 pencils. How many pencils did Maddie buy?

Problem-Solving Applications

Beavers When beavers build dams, they create ponds and swamps that help many animals in the woodlands. Unfortunately, they may also cause roads, golf courses, and pastures to be flooded. Not many animals can change the environment as much as beavers.

Trivia Fossils of giant beavers have been discovered. These extinct animals were about 8 feet long and possibly weighed over 800 pounds!

❶ In 2001, the record for a person holding one's breath was 486 seconds, which is a little more than 8 minutes. Beavers can stay underwater for about 414 seconds longer. For how many seconds can a beaver stay underwater?

❷ Beavers can chew through a 6-inch tree in 15 minutes. That is about 15.24 centimeters of wood. Write the word form for this number of centimeters.

❸ Most beaver lodges are home to about 7 beavers. If a pond had 4 lodges, about how many beavers live at the pond?

Using Key Facts

❹ The body length of the beaver in the Key Facts chart is only from its nose to the base of its tail. It does not include the length of the tail. How long is the entire beaver?

Key Facts Typical Beavers	
• Tail length	30 cm
• Tail width	18 cm
• Tail thickness	2 cm
• Body length	90 cm
• Back feet length	17 cm
• Fur length	2–7 cm
• Life span	12 years

5 <u>Writing in Math</u> Use the information in this lesson to write your own word problem. Write the answer in a complete sentence.

6 Decision Making For several years, the number of beavers in a pond was recorded. In 2001, there were 6 beavers. In 2002, there were 12 beavers. In 2003, there were 18 beavers. In 2004, there were 15 beavers. Make a graph that would best show this information.

7 One of the largest beaver dams was about 1 kilometer long. Was this dam longer or shorter than a mile?

Good News/Bad News A beaver's soft fur keeps it warm throughout the winter, but it also became very appealing to the clothing industry. Fur traders almost hunted the beaver to extinction in the 1800s.

Do You Know How?

Do You Understand?

Centimeters and Decimeters (10-6)

Estimate each length. Then measure to the nearest centimeter.

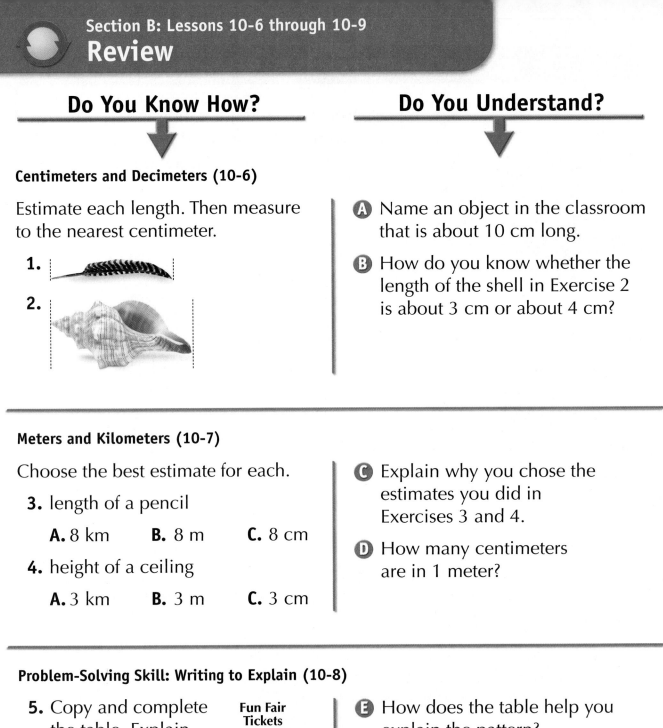

1.

2.

Ⓐ Name an object in the classroom that is about 10 cm long.

Ⓑ How do you know whether the length of the shell in Exercise 2 is about 3 cm or about 4 cm?

Meters and Kilometers (10-7)

Choose the best estimate for each.

3. length of a pencil

   A. 8 km   **B.** 8 m   **C.** 8 cm

4. height of a ceiling

   A. 3 km   **B.** 3 m   **C.** 3 cm

Ⓒ Explain why you chose the estimates you did in Exercises 3 and 4.

Ⓓ How many centimeters are in 1 meter?

Problem-Solving Skill: Writing to Explain (10-8)

5. Copy and complete the table. Explain how the cost of the tickets changes as the number of tickets changes.

Fun Fair Tickets

Number of Tickets	Cost
1	15¢
2	30¢
3	45¢
4	
5	

Ⓔ How does the table help you explain the pattern?

Ⓕ How much would 10 Fun Fair tickets cost?

MULTIPLE CHOICE

1. What is the length to the nearest centimeter? (10-6)

CENTIMETERS

A. 4 cm　　　**B.** 5 cm　　　**C.** 6 cm　　　**D.** 7 cm

2. How many meters are in 1 kilometer? (10-7)

A. 10 m　　　**B.** 100 m　　　**C.** 1,000 m　　　**D.** 10,000 m

FREE RESPONSE

Estimate each length. Then measure to the nearest centimeter. (10-6)

3.　　　　　**4.**

Choose the best estimate for each measurement. (10-7)

5. length of a grasshopper　　　**A.** 4 m

6. height of a lamppost　　　　　**B.** 4 km

7. distance you might ride a bike　**C.** 4 cm

8. Copy and complete the table to show the number of months in 1, 2, 3, and 4 years. Explain how the number of months changes as the number of years changes. (10-8, 10-9)

Years	1	2	3	4
Months	12	24		

TEST TALK

Think It Through
I need to **check that my answers are reasonable.**

Writing in Math

9. Alex says the caterpillar is 6 cm long to the nearest centimeter. Do you agree? Explain. (10-6)

CENTIMETERS

Test-Taking Strategies

Understand the question.

Get information for the answer.

Plan how to find the answer.

Make smart choices.

Use writing in math.

Improve written answers.

Make Smart Choices

To answer a multiple-choice test question, you need to choose an answer from answer choices. The steps below will help you make a smart choice.

1. The crayon is 8 centimeters long. About how long is the pencil?

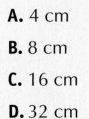

A. 4 cm

B. 8 cm

C. 16 cm

D. 32 cm

Understand the question.

I need to find the length of the pencil.

Get information for the answer.

*The **text** tells me the length of the crayon. The **picture** shows the items I should compare.*

Plan how to find the answer.

As I compare the pencil to the crayon, I should look at the choices and eliminate those that do not make sense.

Make Smart Choices.

• Eliminate wrong answers.

The pencil is longer than the crayon, so answer choices A and B are wrong.

• Check answers for reasonableness.

Answer choices C and D are left. Sixteen centimeters is twice the length of the crayon, and the pencil looks about twice as long as the crayon, so C seems reasonable. Thirty-two centimeters is four times the length of the crayon, so D does not seem reasonable.

The correct answer is C, 16 centimeters.

2. What unit of measure would be the most appropriate to measure the distance between Cleveland and Pittsburgh?

A. meter

B. centimeter

C. kilometer

D. decimeter

Think It Through

I need to choose the best unit for measuring the distance between two cities. My uncle is about 2 m tall, so meters wouldn't be good for measuring big distances. Answer choice A is wrong. A piece of chalk is about a centimeter thick and a toothbrush is about a decimeter long, so those units are too small. Choices B and D are wrong. The only choice left is C. That's reasonable because kilometers are used to measure long distances.

Now it's your turn.

For each problem, give the answer and explain how you made your choice.

3. What unit of measure would be the most appropriate to measure the length of a built-in swimming pool?

A. centimeter

B. kilometer

C. decimeter

D. meter

4. The safety pin is 3 cm long. About how long is the glue stick?

A. 1 cm

B. 3 cm

C. 9 cm

D. 15 cm

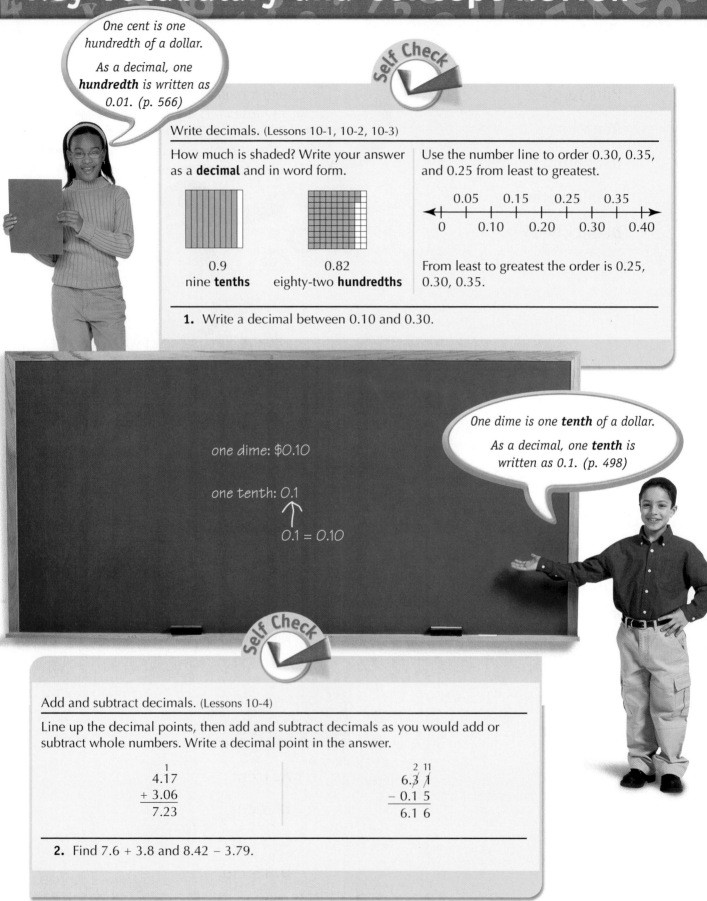

One cent is one hundredth of a dollar.

As a decimal, one **hundredth** is written as 0.01. (p. 566)

Self Check

Write decimals. (Lessons 10-1, 10-2, 10-3)

How much is shaded? Write your answer as a **decimal** and in word form.

0.9
nine **tenths**

0.82
eighty-two **hundredths**

Use the number line to order 0.30, 0.35, and 0.25 from least to greatest.

From least to greatest the order is 0.25, 0.30, 0.35.

1. Write a decimal between 0.10 and 0.30.

one dime: $0.10

one tenth: 0.1

0.1 = 0.10

One dime is one **tenth** of a dollar.

As a decimal, one **tenth** is written as 0.1. (p. 498)

Self Check

Add and subtract decimals. (Lessons 10-4)

Line up the decimal points, then add and subtract decimals as you would add or subtract whole numbers. Write a decimal point in the answer.

$$\begin{array}{r} \overset{1}{4.17} \\ +\ 3.06 \\ \hline 7.23 \end{array}$$

$$\begin{array}{r} \overset{2\ 11}{6.\cancel{3}\,\cancel{1}} \\ -\ 0.1\ 5 \\ \hline 6.1\ 6 \end{array}$$

2. Find 7.6 + 3.8 and 8.42 − 3.79.

There are 100 cents in a dollar.

There are 100 **centimeters** in a meter. (p. 582)

This is 1 **centimeter** (cm): |———|

1 **decimeter** (dm) = 10 cm
1 **meter** (m) = 100 cm
1 **kilometer** (km) = 1,000 m

Use metric lengths (Lessons 10-6, 10-7)

Measure to the nearest centimeter.

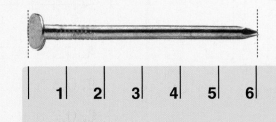

CENTIMETERS

The nail is about 6 cm long.

Would you measure the distance between cities in meters or kilometers?

Use kilometers. A kilometer is a little more than half a mile, but a meter is about the height of a preschooler.

3. Do you think a bed is 2 cm, 2 m, or 2 km long?

The flag of the Republic of the Congo has a yellow diagonal stripe.

In a polygon, a **diagonal** connects 2 corners that are not next to each other. (p. 578)

Make an organized list or write to explain to solve problems. (Lessons 10-5, 10-8)

Make an organized list to show all the ways items can be combined.

How many ways can Paul choose 2 drinks from a choice of water, milk, juice, and cocoa?

water, milk
water, juice
water, cocoa
milk, juice
milk, cocoa
juice, cocoa

There are 6 ways.

Use geometric terms accurately when you write to explain.

Explain the use of line segments in this figure.

The 8 outer line segments are the sides of an octagon. The 5 line segments inside the octagon are diagonals.

4. How many ways can you choose 3 drinks from the 4 choices given above?

Answers: 1. Sample answer: 0.15 2. 11.4; 4.63 3. 2 m 4. 4 ways

MULTIPLE CHOICE

1. Which decimal names the shaded part of this whole?

A. 0.3

B. 0.7

C. 3.0

D. 7.0

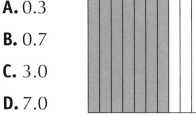

2. Which mixed number equals 1.9?

A. $1\frac{1}{9}$

C. $1\frac{9}{10}$

B. $1\frac{9}{1}$

D. $9\frac{1}{10}$

3. Which is six hundredths written as a decimal?

A. 0.06

C. 6.00

B. 0.6

D. 600

4. Which decimal names the shaded part of this whole?

A. 0.21

B. 0.79

C. 2.1

D. 7.9

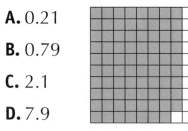

5. Which of the following statements is NOT correct?

A. 0.69 < 0.96

B. 0.30 = 0.3

C. 0.80 = 0.08

D. 0.54 > 0.45

Think It Through
I can **use grids or a number line** to **compare decimals.**

6. Use the number line to choose the decimals that are written in order from least to greatest.

```
      0.10   0.30   0.50   0.70   0.90
  ◄──┼──┼──┼──┼──┼──┼──┼──┼──┼──┼──►
     0    0.20   0.40   0.60   0.80   1
```

A. 0.37   0.73   0.30

B. 0.37   0.30   0.73

C. 0.73   0.37   0.30

D. 0.30   0.37   0.73

7. Find 4.17 + 1.08.

A. 3.09

C. 5.25

B. 5.15

D. 5.97

8. What is 3.6 subtracted from 5.0?

A. 1.4   **B.** 2.6   **C.** 2.4   **D.** 8.6

9. You want to find the sum of 2.49 and 1.85. Arrange the steps below in the correct order to solve the problem.

> **Step A:** Add the tenths. Regroup.
> **Step B:** Line up the decimal points.
> **Step C:** Add the ones.
> **Step D:** Write the decimal point in the sum.
> **Step E:** Add the hundredths. Regroup.

A. A, E, C, B, D

B. B, C, A, E, D

C. B, E, A, C, D

D. B, D, E, A, C

10. Which is the best estimate for the length of this nail to the nearest centimeter?

A. 1 cm **B.** 5 cm **C.** 8 dm **D.** 5 m

11. Which item's length could be estimated at about 8 meters?

A. a stapler   **C.** a garage

B. a refrigerator   **D.** a mountain range

12. Which unit would be best to measure the length of a caterpillar?

A. centimeter   **C.** meter

B. decimeter   **D.** kilometer

FREE RESPONSE

Write each as a decimal.

13. $\frac{9}{100}$ **14.** $1\frac{8}{10}$

15. $2\frac{53}{100}$ **16.** $\frac{1}{10}$

Compare. Use >, <, or =.

17.

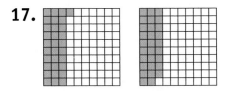

0.31 ● 0.29

18.

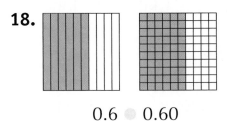

0.6 ● 0.60

Add or subtract.

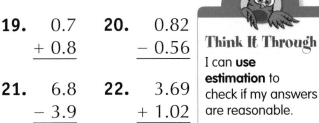

19.   0.7
    + 0.8

20.   0.82
    − 0.56

21.   6.8
    − 3.9

22.   3.69
    + 1.02

23. Brenda bought 2.8 meters of denim cloth and 4.6 meters of velvet cloth. How much cloth did she buy in all? How much more velvet cloth did she buy than denim cloth?

24. Copy and complete the organized list to solve this problem. How many different sandwiches can you choose?

Turkey on White

Turkey on Wheat

Sandwich Choices
Fillers: Turkey or Ham
Breads: White or Wheat

Writing in Math

25. Draw a picture of tenths grids to compare 0.5 and 0.3. Use >, <, or = to compare.

26. Explain how you would measure your pencil to the nearest centimeter.

27. What is this mixed number? Explain how you know.

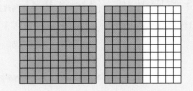

Number and Operation

MULTIPLE CHOICE

1. Which numbers are written in order from least to greatest?

   A. 0.17 0.71 0.70

   B. 0.71 0.70 0.17

   C. 0.17 0.70 0.71

   D. 0.70 0.71 0.17

2. Mrs. Bryant wants to divide all the students going on the field trip into equal groups. Which of the following group sizes will NOT work if there are 42 students going on the field trip?

   A. 2 students   **C.** 7 students

   B. 6 students   **D.** 10 students

FREE RESPONSE

3. Write one and seventeen hundredths as a decimal and a mixed number.

4. Paper plates come in packages of 10. If you buy 9 packages, how many paper plates will you have in all?

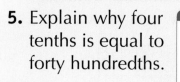

5. Explain why four tenths is equal to forty hundredths.

Think It Through
I can **draw a picture** to show my thinking.

Geometry and Measurement

MULTIPLE CHOICE

6. Which is the best estimate for the length of this ribbon?

   A. 5 centimeters **C.** 5 meters

   B. 5 decimeters **D.** 5 kilometers

7. Each side of an equilateral triangle is 4 cm long. What is the perimeter of the triangle?

   A. 8 cm   **C.** 16 cm

   B. 12 cm   **D.** 20 cm

8. Which of these solid figures does NOT have curved surfaces?

   A. sphere   **C.** cylinder

   B. cone   **D.** pyramid

FREE RESPONSE

9. Write the time shown on this clock in two different ways.

10. Each section of fencing is 1 meter long. How many sections do you need to build a fence that is 1 kilometer long?

Writing in Math

11. How many ways can you make $0.11 using pennies, nickels, and dimes? Make an organized list to solve.

Take It to the NET
More Practice
www.scottforesman.com

Set 10-7 (pages 584–587)

Choose the best estimate of each measure.

1. Length of a fish pond   **A.** 7 km

2. Length of a nature trail   **B.** 7 m

3. Length of a twig   **C.** 7 cm

4. Length of a truck   **A.** 5 m

5. Distance you might drive   **B.** 5 cm

6. Width of a driver's license   **C.** 5 km

7. Length of an adult's leg   **A.** 1 cm

8. Width of your fingernail   **B.** 1 m

9. Distance you might walk to school   **C.** 1 km

10. Cameron is measuring his bedroom floor to decide how much carpet to buy. Should he use centimeters, meters, or kilometers? Explain.

Set 10-8 (pages 588–589)

Write your answers in complete sentences.

1. The triangles below were made with craft sticks. Copy the table and use the pattern to complete it.

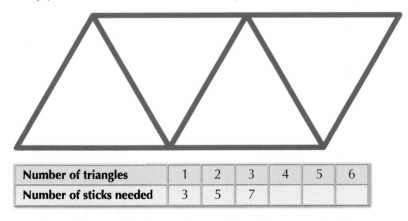

Number of triangles	1	2	3	4	5	6
Number of sticks needed	3	5	7			

Explain how the number of sticks needed changes as the number of triangles changes.

Multiplying and Dividing Greater Numbers

 DIAGNOSING READINESS

A Vocabulary
(pages 260, 384, 398)

Choose the best term from the box.

1. The answer in a division problem is a __?__.

2. The answer in a multiplication problem is a __?__.

3. When dividing, any number left over is the __?__.

Vocabulary
- **product** *(p. 260)*
- **quotient** *(p. 384)*
- **factor** *(p. 260)*
- **remainder** *(p. 398)*

B Multiplication Facts
(pages 260–329)

4. 8×5 **5.** 5×7

6. 6×4 **7.** 6×9

8. 4×10 **9.** 7×2

10. 3×4 **11.** 9×9

12. 8×7 **13.** 7×6

14. Jeanne bought 3 packs of juice boxes. Each pack has 6 juice boxes. How many juice boxes did she buy?

How many times as fast as the first steam trains are today's trains?

You'll find out in Lesson 11-16.

STEPHEN BIESTY'S
INCREDIBLE
CROSS-SECTIONS

FEATURING TWO FOLD-OUT PICTURES NEARLY 3 FEET LONG!

C Division Facts
(pages 370–403)

15. 16 ÷ 4   **16.** 15 ÷ 3

17. 24 ÷ 6   **18.** 27 ÷ 9

19. 42 ÷ 7   **20.** 56 ÷ 8

21. 63 ÷ 9   **22.** 36 ÷ 4

23. 18 ÷ 2   **24.** 64 ÷ 8

25. Sheri and her brother shared 14 crackers equally. How many crackers did each person get?

D Rounding
(pages 28–29)

Round to the nearest ten.

26. 18   **27.** 65   **28.** 51

29. 588   **30.** 632   **31.** 225

Round to the nearest hundred.

32. 322   **33.** 450   **34.** 207

35. 155   **36.** 731   **37.** 692

38. Round 1,099 to the nearest hundred.

Mental Math: Multiplication Patterns

LEARN

Activity

How do you multiply with 100 and 1,000?

a. Think about the 10s facts you've already learned.
Find 5 × 10, 7 × 10, 4 × 10, and 3 × 10.

Use place-value blocks.

b. Show 5 groups of 1 hundred.

> 5 × 1 hundred = **5 hundreds**
> 5 × 100 = **500**

c. Show 5 groups of
1 thousand.

> 5 × 1 thousand = **5 thousands**
> 5 × 1,000 = **5,000**

d. Use place-value blocks to find the missing numbers.

4 × 100 =	7 × 100 =	3 × 100 =
4 × 1,000 =	7 × 1,000 =	3 × 1,000 =

e. What pattern do you see when you multiply a number
by 10? by 100? by 1,000?

Activity

How can you multiply by multiples of 10, 100, and 1,000?

> 4 groups of 3 hundreds = **12 hundreds**
> 4 × 300 = **1,200**

a. Use place-value blocks to complete.

3 × 2 =	4 × 3 =	6 × 4 =
3 × 20 =	4 × 30 =	6 × 40 =
3 × 200 =	4 × 300 =	6 × 400 =
3 × 2,000 =	4 × 3,000 =	6 × 4,000 =

b. Use patterns to find each product.

2 × 7 =	5 × 4 =	6 × 9 =
2 × 70 =	5 × 40 =	6 × 90 =
2 × 700 =	5 × 400 =	6 × 900 =
2 × 7,000 =	5 × 4,000 =	6 × 9,000 =

What's the rule?

Helen used a multiplication pattern and Pete used a rule to find 3×800.

> *I know the basic fact*
> $3 \times 8 = 24$.
>
> $3 \times 800 = 24$ with
> 2 more zeros or 2,400

> 3×8 ones = 24 ones, or 24
> 3×8 tens = 24 tens, or 240
> So, 3×8 hundreds =
> 24 hundreds or 2,400.

✔ Talk About It

1. Why does Pete place 2 zeros at the end of the product?

2. How could you use Helen's pattern to find 6×500?

3. Bobby says, "6×5 is 30, so 6×500 is 300." Do you agree? Explain.

TEST TALK

Think It Through
I can **look for a pattern** to find a rule.

CHECK ✓

For another example, see Set 11-1 on p. 670.

Use mental math to find each product.

1. 8×100 2. $3 \times 1,000$ 3. 1×100

4. 5×200 5. 3×20 6. 6×800

7. 9×300 8. $4 \times 4,000$ 9. $3 \times 9,000$

10. **Number Sense** What basic fact can you use to find 2×900? Find the product.

A Skills and Understanding

Use mental math to find each product.

11. 3 × 10   **12.** 4 × 1,000   **13.** 5 × 100   **14.** 9 × 500

15. 40 × 6   **16.** 600 × 7   **17.** 5 × 500   **18.** 5 × 8,000

19. 4 × 800   **20.** 8 × 2,000   **21.** 8,000 × 7   **22.** 900 × 7

23. Number Sense Jerry says, "4 × 2 = 8, so 4 × 2,000 = 80,000." Do you agree? Explain.

B Reasoning and Problem Solving

Algebra Find the missing number in each number sentence.

24. ▨ × 10 = 40   **25.** 7 × ▨ = 140   **26.** ▨ × 300 = 2,100

 Math and Everyday Life

Most people in the United States use about 100 gallons of water every day.

27. If you wash 3 loads of laundry in a washing machine, how much water will you use?

28. How much water would you save if you took a 10-minute shower each day for 5 days instead of a bath?

29. Reasoning How many gallons of water would you use if you took a 5-minute shower?

30. **Writing in Math** Is Brent's explanation below correct? If not, tell why and write the correct explanation.

Data File

How Much Water?	
Activity	**Estimated Number of Gallons**
Flushing a toilet	5
Running 1 dishwasher load	10
Taking a 10-minute shower	20
Running 1 washing machine load	60
Taking a bath	50

> Explain how to use mental math to find 2 × 500.
>
> Think: 2 x 5 hundreds = 10 hundreds.
> 10 hundreds is the same as 100.
> So, the product is 100.

C Extensions

Find two possible factors for each product.

31. 160 **32.** 3,200 **33.** 250 **34.** 3,600

Mixed Review and Test Prep

Take It to the NET
Test Prep
www.scottforesman.com

Write each as a decimal.

35. $\frac{43}{100}$ **36.** seven tenths **37.** one and fifteen hundredths

38. Describe how to measure the safety pin to the nearest centimeter.

CENTIMETERS

39. Which unit would be best for measuring the distance from Florida to Maine?

A. centimeters **B.** meters **C.** decimeters **D.** kilometers

Enrichment

Relating Multiplication to Place Value

You know how to write 3,465 in expanded form. You can also use multiplication to show a number in expanded form.

Expanded form:

$$3,000 \quad + \quad 400 \quad + \quad 60 \quad + \quad 5$$

$$(3 \times 1,000) + (4 \times 100) + (6 \times 10) + (5 \times 1)$$

1. Copy and complete.

$$5,609 = 5,000 \quad + \quad 600 \quad + \quad 9$$

$$(5 \times \blacksquare) + (6 \times \blacksquare) + (9 \times \blacksquare)$$

Use multiplication to show each number in expanded form.

2. 3,721 **3.** 519 **4.** 2,092 **5.** 4,490

Key Idea
You can round to estimate products.

TEST TALK

Think It Through
- I can **draw a picture** to show the main idea.
- I can **multiply** because equal groups are being combined.

Estimating Products

LEARN

Exact answer or estimate?

Giant kelp is a water plant that grows about 18 inches a day. Does it grow more than 100 inches in a week?

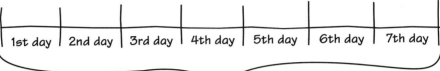

| 1st day | 2nd day | 3rd day | 4th day | 5th day | 6th day | 7th day |

18 in. + 18 in. + 18 in. + 18 in. + 18 in. + 18 in. + 18 in.

I only need an **estimate** because I just need to know if the plant grows **more than** 100 inches in a week.

How can you estimate products?

Example A

Does giant kelp grow more than 100 inches in a week?

Estimate 7 × 18. Then compare your estimate to 100.

Round 18 to the nearest ten.

7 × 18
  ↓ 18 rounds to 20.
7 × 20 = 140

7 × 18 is about 140. 140 > 100

Giant kelp grows more than 100 inches in a week.

Example B

Jason earned $214 each week. About how much did he earn in 5 weeks?

Estimate 5 × 214.

Round 214 to the nearest hundred.

5 × 214
  ↓ 214 rounds to 200.
5 × 200 = 1,000

5 × 214 is about 1,000.

Jason earned about $1,000 in 5 weeks.

✔ **Talk About It**

1. Is the exact answer in Example A more than or less than 140? In Example B, is the exact answer more than or less than $1,000? In each case, how do you know?

2. **Number Sense** Explain how you would use rounding to estimate 6 × 408.

For another example, see Set 11-2 on p. 670.

CHECK ✓

Estimate each product.

1. 3×87 **2.** 5×65 **3.** 8×303 **4.** 4×287

5. Number Sense How can you estimate to find if 4×38 is greater than 3×88?

PRACTICE

For more practice, see Set 11-2 on p. 674.

A Skills and Understanding

Estimate each product.

6. 7×29 **7.** 5×36 **8.** 9×82 **9.** 3×45 **10.** 7×77

11. 6×305 **12.** 4×271 **13.** 8×114 **14.** 2×926 **15.** 6×575

16. Number Sense How can you estimate to find whether 4×319 is greater than 1,100?

B Reasoning and Problem Solving

Use the graph for 17–19.

17. About how many inches will a giant bamboo plant grow in 8 weeks?

18. Reasoning Will a eucalyptus tree grow more than or less than 10 feet in a year? Explain. (Remember: There are 52 weeks in 1 year.)

19. Writing in Math Is the growth of callie grass in 4 weeks greater than or less than the growth of giant kelp in 1 week? Tell how you decided.

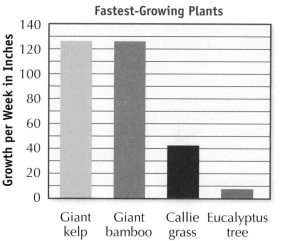

Fastest-Growing Plants

Growth per Week in Inches

Plant: Giant kelp, Giant bamboo, Callie grass, Eucalyptus tree

Mixed Review and Test Prep

 Take It to the NET
Test Prep
www.scottforesman.com

20. 7×200 **21.** 3×50 **22.** 8×600 **23.** 9×40

24. Which of the following is sixty thousand, four hundred two written in standard form?

     A. 642   **B.** 6,402   **C.** 60,402   **D.** 60,420

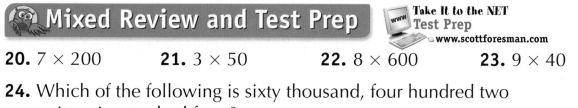 All text pages available online and on CD-ROM.

Key Idea
You can use division patterns to divide multiples of 10 and 100.

Vocabulary
- quotient (p. 384)
- dividend (p. 384)
- divisor (p. 384)

Materials
- place-value blocks or
  e tools

Think It Through
I can **use objects** and **look for a pattern** to divide with multiples of 10 and 100.

Mental Math: Division Patterns

LEARN

Activity

Can you find the pattern?

You can use division facts to divide greater numbers.

$12 \div 4 = 3$

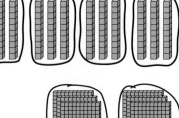

$12 \text{ tens} \div 4 = \mathbf{3} \text{ tens}$

$120 \div 4 = \mathbf{30}$

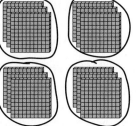

$12 \text{ hundreds} \div 4 = \mathbf{3} \text{ hundreds}$

$1{,}200 \div 4 = \mathbf{3}00.$

a. Copy and complete each basic fact. Then use place-value blocks to find the other quotients.

$18 \div 2 = \blacksquare$ $9 \div 3 = \blacksquare$ $24 \div 4 = \blacksquare$
$180 \div 2 = \blacksquare$ $90 \div 3 = \blacksquare$ $240 \div 4 = \blacksquare$
$1{,}800 \div 2 = \blacksquare$ $900 \div 3 = \blacksquare$ $2{,}400 \div 4 = \blacksquare$

b. How does knowing $12 \div 4$ help you find $120 \div 4$ and $1{,}200 \div 4$?

c. What pattern do you see in the zeros in each dividend and quotient in Part a?

d. You know that $10 \div 5 = 2$. Use place-value blocks to find $100 \div 5$ and $1{,}000 \div 5$. Does the pattern work? Explain.

How can you use mental math to divide with multiples of 10 and 100?

To find the quotient 1,800 ÷ 3 mentally, Tony used a division pattern and Mary used a rule.

> 18 ones ÷ 3 = 6 ones, or 6
> 18 tens ÷ 3 = 6 tens, or 60
> 18 hundreds ÷ 3 =
> 6 hundreds, or 600

> 18 ÷ 3 = 6
> 1,800 ÷ 3 = 6 with
> 2 more zeros,
> or 600

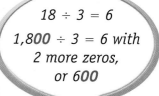

✔ Talk About It

1. What basic fact do Tony and Mary both use to find the quotient 1,800 ÷ 3?

2. Why does Mary place 2 zeros at the end of the basic fact quotient?

3. When you divide 2,500 by 5, how many zeros are written after the 5 in the quotient? Explain.

CHECK ✓

For another example, see Set 11-3 on p. 670.

Use patterns and mental math to find each quotient.

1. 36 ÷ 6
360 ÷ 6
3,600 ÷ 6

2. 27 ÷ 3
270 ÷ 3
2,700 ÷ 3

3. 40 ÷ 8
400 ÷ 8
4,000 ÷ 8

Use mental math to find each quotient.

4. 6,400 ÷ 8

5. 320 ÷ 4

6. 4,000 ÷ 5

7. Number Sense Brian says "36 ÷ 4 is 9, so 3,600 ÷ 4 is 900."
Do you agree? Explain.

Ⓐ Skills and Understanding

Use patterns to find each quotient.

8. 6 ÷ 3	**9.** 81 ÷ 9	**10.** 30 ÷ 5	**11.** 27 ÷ 9
60 ÷ 3	810 ÷ 9	300 ÷ 5	270 ÷ 9
600 ÷ 3	8,100 ÷ 9	3,000 ÷ 5	2,700 ÷ 9

Use mental math to find each quotient.

12. 200 ÷ 4   **13.** 80 ÷ 4   **14.** 400 ÷ 8   **15.** 1,500 ÷ 5

16. 2,400 ÷ 8   **17.** 4,900 ÷ 7   **18.** 120 ÷ 6   **19.** 1,600 ÷ 4

20. Number Sense How many $5 bills make $200?

Ⓑ Reasoning and Problem Solving

Math and Science

Every time your heart beats, it is pumping blood throughout your body. Animals' hearts do the same job, but at different rates. How many times does each animal's heart beat in one minute?

21. Mouse   **22.** Horse   **23.** Bat

24. Frog   **25.** Chicken

26. Writing in Math Is Jacob's work at the right correct? If not, tell why and write a correct answer.

Data File

Animal Heart Rates	
Animal	**Heartbeats Every 5 Minutes**
Bat	3,500
Mouse	2,500
Chicken	1,500
Horse	200
Frog	150

Find 3,000 ÷ 6.

I know that 30 ÷ 6 = 5.
So, 30 hundreds ÷ 6 = 5 hundreds.
3,000 ÷ 6 = 500.

Mixed Review and Test Prep

Take It to the NET
Test Prep
www.scottforesman.com

Estimate each product.

27. 8 × 17   **28.** 9 × 125   **29.** 4 × 675   **30.** 5 × 243

31. What is 2,657 rounded to the nearest hundred?

    A. 2,600   **B.** 2,660   **C.** 2,700   **D.** 3,000

Learning with Technology

Using a Calculator to Find the Average by Dividing

Karen, Juanita, and Alec each bought a pack of markers at a different store. You can describe the cost of a pack of markers by finding the **average** cost. The average is the same as the *mean*. You can use a calculator to find the average cost of a pack of markers.

Karen: $2.95
Juanita: $2.50
Alec: $1.99

Step 1: Add the cost of each pack of markers.

Press: 2.95 [+] 2.50 [+] 1.99 [=]

Display: | 7.44 |

Step 2: Divide by the number of items you have added.

Press: [÷] 3 [=]

Display: | 2.48 |

So, the average cost of a pack of markers is $2.48.

1. Jeannie, Emma, Lynnette, and Kyle each paid a different price for modeling clay. Find the average cost of the modeling clay.

   Jeannie: $0.99   Emma: $1.05   Lynnette: $1.60   Kyle: $1.16

Enrichment

Predicting the Size of the Answer

You can use number sense to describe an answer without solving the problem.

Find 345 + 143.

A. 152   **B.** 188   **C.** 488   **D.** 501

Find 41 ÷ 5.

F. 8   **G.** 8 R1   **H.** 46   **J.** 205

The sum of whole numbers will always be greater than either addend. Choose C or D.

The quotient of two whole numbers is always less than the dividend. So, the answer must be F or G.

1. Write a rule that tells why the answer must be **A** or **B**.

   Find 3 × 24.

   A. 75   **B.** 72   **C.** 24   **D.** 21

Key Idea
You can use
basic division
facts to help you
estimate
quotients.

Estimating Quotients

LEARN

Think It Through
- I can **draw a picture** to show the main idea.
- I only need an **estimate** because I just need to know **about** how many cups each person will get.

Exact answer or estimate?

Tamara bought a bag of pretzels for snacks for a club meeting. The bag holds 14 cups of pretzels. If there will be 5 people at the meeting, about how many cups of pretzels will each person get?

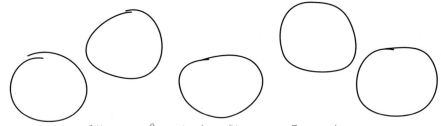

14 cups of pretzels split among 5 people

I just need to know about how many cups, so an estimate is enough.

How can you estimate quotients?

Example

Estimate 14 ÷ 5.

Use a **basic division fact.**

$$14 ÷ 5$$

Think: 14 is close to 15.

$$15 ÷ 5 = 3$$

So 14 ÷ 5 is about 3.

Each person will get about 3 cups of pretzels.

✓ **Talk About It**

1. Will each person get more than or less than 3 cups of pretzels? How do you know?

Estimate each quotient.

1. 37 ÷ 9
2. 60 ÷ 7
3. 44 ÷ 5
4. 28 ÷ 3

5. Number Sense What basic fact could you use to estimate 25 ÷ 4?

PRACTICE

For more practice, see Set 11-4 on p. 674.

A Skills and Understanding

Estimate each quotient.

6. 17 ÷ 4
7. 65 ÷ 9
8. 50 ÷ 8
9. 25 ÷ 3
10. 33 ÷ 4

11. 79 ÷ 9
12. 49 ÷ 5
13. 15 ÷ 7
14. 33 ÷ 8
15. 55 ÷ 6

16. Number Sense Which is greater, 49 ÷ 7 or 50 ÷ 7? How do you know without finding the exact answer?

B Reasoning and Problem Solving

17. A grasshopper can jump about 10 times the length of its body. About how many inches can a grasshopper jump?

18. Reasoning Candace filled a watering can with 2 gallons of water. She watered 6 large plants. About how many cups of water did each plant get? (Hint: There are 16 cups in a gallon.)

The body of a grasshopper is about 2 inches long.

19. **Writing in Math** Write two basic facts you could use to estimate 17 ÷ 2. Tell whether each estimate is greater than or less than the actual quotient.

🦉 Mixed Review and Test Prep

Take It to the NET
Test Prep
www.scottforesman.com

Find each quotient.

20. 1,400 ÷ 2
21. 810 ÷ 9
22. 4,500 ÷ 5
23. 600 ÷ 3

24. Which fraction is the same as 0.01?

A. $\frac{1}{2}$
B. $\frac{1}{4}$
C. $\frac{1}{10}$
D. $\frac{1}{100}$

Do You Know How? | ## Do You Understand?

Mental Math: Multiplication Patterns (11-1)

Use mental math to find each product.

1. 5×30 **2.** $8 \times 2,000$

3. 7×20 **4.** 300×4

5. $6 \times 1,000$ **6.** $5,000 \times 5$

Ⓐ Tell what basic fact you used to find the product in each of Exercises 1–6.

Ⓑ How can 5×4 help you find 5×400?

Estimating Products (11-2)

Estimate each product.

7. 4×109 **8.** 6×78

9. 467×3 **10.** 5×29

11. 2×97 **12.** 8×81

Ⓒ Will the actual product in Exercise 7 be greater than or less than your estimate? How do you know?

Mental Math: Division Patterns (11-3)

Use mental math to find each quotient.

13. $630 \div 7$ **14.** $1,200 \div 4$

15. $300 \div 3$ **16.** $3,600 \div 6$

17. $240 \div 8$ **18.** $2,000 \div 5$

Ⓓ Tell what basic fact you used to find each quotient in Exercises 13–18.

Ⓔ How can $45 \div 9$ help you find $4,500 \div 9$?

Estimating Quotients (11-4)

Estimate each quotient.

19. $16 \div 5$ **20.** $80 \div 9$

21. $43 \div 6$ **22.** $29 \div 4$

23. $38 \div 9$ **24.** $54 \div 7$

Ⓕ Will the actual quotient in Exercise 24 be greater than or less than your estimate? How do you know?

MULTIPLE CHOICE

1. Use mental math to find $6 \times 3{,}000$. (11-1)

    A. 18,000   **B.** 1,800   **C.** 180   **D.** 18

2. Which is the best estimate for $47 \div 9$? (11-4)

    A. 6   **B.** 5   **C.** 4   **D.** 3

FREE RESPONSE

Use mental math to find each product. (11-1)

3. 7×100 **4.** 5×80 **5.** $9 \times 6{,}000$

6. 500×3 **7.** 4×300 **8.** $4{,}000 \times 8$

9. 9×30 **10.** 700×8 **11.** $2 \times 5{,}000$

Use mental math to find each quotient. (11-3)

12. $240 \div 6$ **13.** $270 \div 9$ **14.** $600 \div 2$

15. $1{,}500 \div 3$ **16.** $800 \div 4$ **17.** $1{,}600 \div 8$

Estimate each product or quotient. (11-2, 11-4)

18. 4×844 **19.** 6×92 **20.** 5×693

21. 9×76 **22.** 3×37 **23.** 2×516

24. $70 \div 9$ **25.** $59 \div 8$ **26.** $26 \div 7$

27. $13 \div 5$ **28.** $35 \div 9$ **29.** $43 \div 6$

Writing in Math

Think It Through

I should make my answer brief but complete.

30. Explain how to use a basic fact to estimate $64 \div 9$.

31. Explain how you can use 6×7 to find $6 \times 7{,}000$.

32. Is Ray's work correct? If not, explain what he did wrong and solve the problem.

> $3{,}000 \div 6 = ?$ $30 \div 6 = 5$
> 30 hundreds $\div 6 = 5$ hundreds
> $3{,}000 \div 6 = 50$

Key Idea
You can use an array to show multiplication with greater numbers.

Vocabulary
• array (p. 262)

Materials
• place-value blocks or

 tools

TEST TALK

Think It Through

• I can **make a model** to show multiplication.

• I can **solve a simpler problem** when I multiply with greater numbers.

Multiplication and Arrays

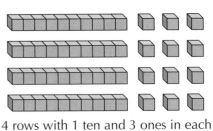
✓ WARM UP
1. 3 × 40   2. 5 × 20
3. 7 × 90   4. 8 × 70
5. 6 × 80   6. 9 × 40

LEARN

A good place to find an array is in a parking lot, where cars are found in equal rows.

Activity

How can you use an array to show how to multiply with greater numbers?

Show 4 × 13 using place-value blocks and an array.

Step 1: Use place-value blocks to build the array.

4 rows with 1 ten and 3 ones in each

Step 2: Break apart the array into tens and ones. Find how many tens in all. Find how many ones in all.

4 tens   12 ones

Step 3: Add the tens and ones to find the product.

$40 + 12 = 52$
$4 \times 13 = 52$

a. Use place-value blocks to build each array. Follow the steps above to find each product.

3 × 14   2 × 26   5 × 31

b. For each array you made in Part a, how many tens and how many ones did you have?

c. Explain how finding the total number of tens, then the total number of ones, is like solving two simpler problems. Use 3 × 14 as an example.

How do you draw a picture to help multiply?

You can draw a picture of an array to show multiplication.

Find 3 × 24.

What You **Show**	What You **Think**
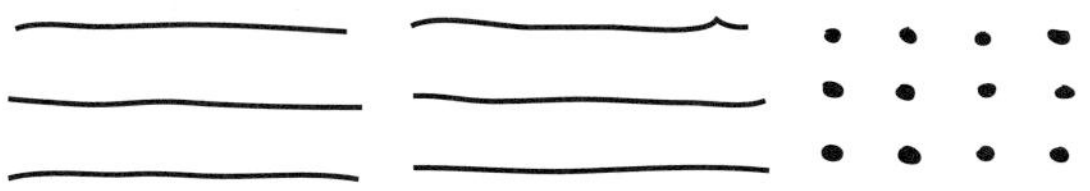	3 rows of 2 tens = 6 tens 3 rows of 4 ones = 12 ones 60 + 12 = 72

a. What does each —— show? What does each • show?

b. Draw a picture of an array for each. Find each product.

  6 × 13   5 × 41   4 × 24   9 × 12

c. What multiplication sentence could you write for this array?

d. How many ones blocks would you draw to show 3 × 18?

CHECK ✓

For another example, see Set 11-5 on p. 671.

Find each product. You may draw a picture to help.

1. 3 × 22

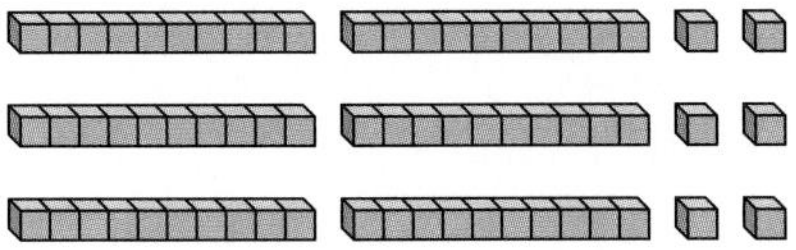

2. 4 × 36

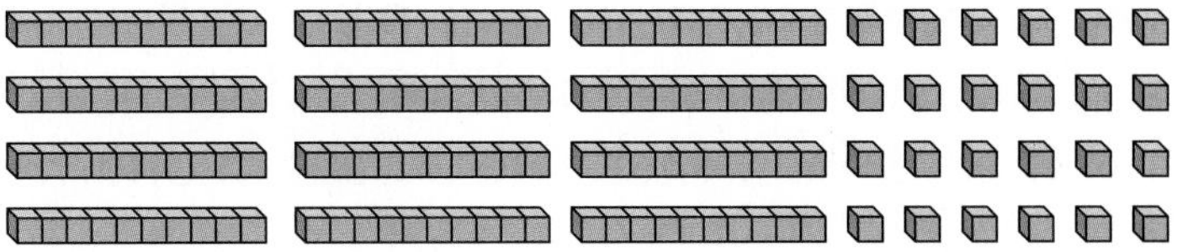

3. 4 × 24   **4.** 5 × 17   **5.** 3 × 35

6. Number Sense Kurt started to draw a picture to show
5 × 42. Copy and complete the picture. What is the product?

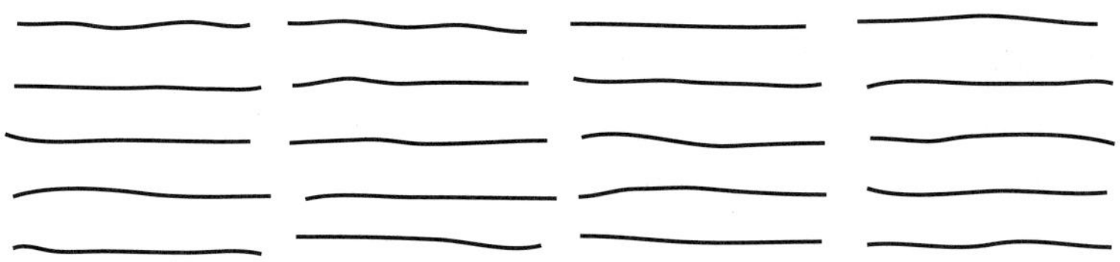

A Skills and Understanding

Find each product. You may draw a picture to help.

7. 2×34

8. 3×16

9. 6×18 **10.** 2×41 **11.** 3×29 **12.** 4×25

13. Reasoning Write a multiplication sentence with a product greater than 100. Draw an array to show your problem.

B Reasoning and Problem Solving

Math and Social Studies

The average person will walk 75,000 miles by the time he or she is 50 years old. That is like walking 3 times around Earth at the equator. Some people walk even more because of their jobs. How many miles would each person normally walk in 4 weeks? You may draw a picture to help.

Data File

Jobs That Require the Most Walking	
Job	Number of Miles Normally Walked in 1 Week
Police officer	32
Mail carrier	21
TV reporter	19
Nurse	18
Doctor	16

14. Police officer **15.** TV reporter

16. Nurse **17.** Mail carrier

18. Estimation About how many miles does a doctor normally walk in one day? (Remember: There are 7 days in one week.)

19. Writing in Math Miranda drew an array to show 2×38. Is her work correct? If not, draw a correct array and solve the problem.

Find 2×38.

2 rows of 3 tens = 6 tens or 60.
2 rows of 5 ones = 10 ones.
60 + 10 = 70.
So, $2 \times 38 = 70$.

PRACTICE

C Extensions

Algebra Write the missing number. You may draw a picture to help.

20. 22 × ▢ = 66 **21.** 32 × ▢ = 96 **22.** 27 × ▢ = 54 **23.** 19 × ▢ = 57

Mixed Review and Test Prep

Take It to the NET
Test Prep
www.scottforesman.com

Estimate each quotient.

24. 25 ÷ 6 **25.** 80 ÷ 9 **26.** 13 ÷ 4 **27.** 48 ÷ 7

28. What is the value of the underlined digit in 5<u>5</u>,555?

A. 50 **B.** 500 **C.** 5,000 **D.** 50,000

Discovery Channel School

Discover Math in Your World

Don't Work Too Hard

The llama (say LAH muh) has been used in the South American Andes Mountains for hundreds of years as a pack animal. A llama is about 4 feet tall. It can carry about 130 pounds and can travel up to 20 miles a day. If a llama thinks its pack is too heavy or that it has worked too hard, it will sit down and refuse to move.

1. How many pounds can 2 llamas carry?

2. How many miles can a llama travel in 5 days?

3. Is a llama taller than a yardstick? Explain.

4. If a bag of potatoes weighs 10 pounds, how many bags could a llama carry?

Take It to the NET
Video and Activities
www.scottforesman.com

Key Idea
To multiply
larger numbers,
you can break
numbers apart
by place value.

Breaking Numbers Apart to Multiply

LEARN

How can you use place value to multiply?

Electric power is measured in units called watts. Jeff has learned that his laptop computer uses 27 watts for each hour of use. If Jeff works on his computer for 3 hours, how much electricity will he use?

Example

Find 3 × 27.

What You **Show**	What You **Write**
Multiply ones: 3 × 7 = **21** Multiply tens: 3 × 20 = **60**	27 × 3 **21** + **60** 81

Jeff will use 81 watts.

✓ Talk About It

1. In the example, could you multiply the tens first and then the ones? Explain.

2. Draw a picture and show what you would write for 2 × 17.

3. **Estimation** Explain how you could use estimation to check if your answer is reasonable.

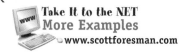
Take It to the NET
More Examples
www.scottforesman.com

Find each product.

1. 16
× 3
‾‾‾‾
18

2. 43
× 3

3. $67
× 2

4. 14
× 7

5. 31 × 5

6. Number Sense Jennifer says, "To find 4 × 16, I can add 24 and 60." Do you agree? Why or why not?

Ⓐ Skills and Understanding

Find each product.

7. 29
× 4

8. 46
× 5

9. $38
× 4

10. 35
× 7

11. 57
× 4

12. 3 × 45   **13.** 6 × 71   **14.** 8 × 14   **15.** 2 × 92   **16.** 7 × $63

17. Number Sense Explain why 7 × 25 is the same as 35 + 140.

Ⓑ Reasoning and Problem Solving

Use the table for 18–19.

18. How many watts does a CD player use in 2 hours?

19. Reasoning Darius used his computer printer for 30 minutes. How many watts of electricity were used?

20. Writing in Math Explain how you can break apart 38 into tens and ones to find 3 × 38. Give the product.

Electricity Use

Appliance	Watts Used in an Hour
Desktop computer	115
Computer printer	100
VCR	40
CD player	35
DVD player	23

Mixed Review and Test Prep

Take It to the NET
Test Prep
www.scottforesman.com

21. 87 + 92   **22.** 119 + 48   **23.** 620 + 75   **24.** 342 + 816

25. Four rows of 2 tens and 3 ones shows which product?

A. 2 × 3   **B.** 4 × 32   **C.** 4 × 23   **D.** 2 × 34

All text pages available online and on CD-ROM.

A Skills and Understanding

Find each product. Decide if your answer is reasonable.

7.   27
   × 4

8.   18
   × 9

9. $43
   × 5

10.   65
   × 3

11.   74
   × 2

12.   13
   × 8

13.   56
   × 7

14.   24
   × 8

15.   31
   × 9

16.   82
   × 3

17.   49
   × 2

18.   15
   × 9

19.   63
   × 4

20. $84
   × 2

21.   51
   × 3

22. 5×47

23. 72×3

24. $2 \times \$99$

25. 61×8

26. 23×6

27. **Number Sense** Write a multiplication sentence for which you need to regroup ones to solve.

28. **Mental Math** Without solving the problem, how can you tell whether 54×9 is greater or less than 450?

B Reasoning and Problem Solving

Math and Science

Many animals can run much faster than people can.

29. What is the farthest a cheetah can run in 3 seconds?

30. What is the farthest a greyhound can run in 4 seconds?

31. In 5 seconds, how much farther can a gazelle run than a greyhound?

32. **Writing in Math** Is Phil's explanation below correct? If not, tell why and write a correct response.

Data File

Fastest Animals	
Animal	Maximum Speed (feet per second)
Cheetah	95
Gazelle	69
Horse	63
Greyhound	62

Explain the steps for finding 3×37.

  ¹
  37   3 × 7 ones is 21 ones, or 2 tens and 1 one.
× 3   Write the 1 in the ones column.
―――
  91   3 × 3 = 9 tens
       The answer is 91.

C Extensions

33. Write a question that can be answered from the data file on page 634 and that uses multiplication with regrouping. Estimate to check your answer.

Mixed Review and Test Prep

Take It to the NET
Test Prep
www.scottforesman.com

Find each product.

34.   36
       ×   7

35.   53
       ×   4

36. 19×6

37. 24×9

38. Kelly earned $509 babysitting this summer. She put all but $225 in the bank. How much did Kelly put in the bank?

A. $284   **C.** $384

B. $324   **D.** $734

39. Paul brought $50 to the state fair. He spent $18 to get in and bought lunch for $9. How much money did Paul have when he left the fair?

A. $32   **C.** $41

B. $27   **D.** $23

Practice Game

Climb Division Mountain

Number of Players: 2–4

Materials: Division Mountain Game Board
Counter or game piece for each player
Division Cards

$13 \div 6$

$27 \div 9$

Place the cards face down in a pile next to the game board. Players take turns drawing a card and giving the quotient and remainder. Remember, the remainder might be 0. Other players check the answer. If the answer is correct, the player moves the marker the number of spaces equal to the remainder. If the answer is incorrect, the player moves the marker back one space. Play continues until one player reaches Division Mountain.

Think It Through

I can multiply another way.

$$\begin{array}{r} 921 \\ \times\ \ \ 5 \\ \hline 5 \\ 100 \\ 4500 \\ \hline 4,605 \end{array}$$

Multiplying Three-Digit Numbers

✔ WARM UP

1. 5×300 2. 9×200
3. 8×500 4. 6×400
5. 200×3 6. 700×2

LEARN

How do you multiply hundreds?

The Pentagon Building has 5 sides. Each side is 921 feet long. What is the perimeter of the Pentagon?

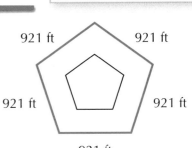

921 ft   921 ft
921 ft   921 ft
921 ft

Example A

Find 5×921.

STEP 1	STEP 2	STEP 3
Multiply the ones. Regroup if needed.	Multiply the tens. Add any regrouped tens. Regroup if needed.	Multiply the hundreds. Add any regrouped hundreds.
$$\begin{array}{r} 921 \\ \times\ \ \ 5 \\ \hline 5 \end{array}$$	$$\begin{array}{r} {}^1\ \ \ \\ 921 \\ \times\ \ \ 5 \\ \hline 05 \end{array}$$	$$\begin{array}{r} {}^1\ \ \ \\ 921 \\ \times\ \ \ 5 \\ \hline 4{,}605 \end{array}$$

Estimate to check. $5 \times 900 = 4{,}500$

The product 4,605 is close to 4,500, so the answer is reasonable.

The perimeter of the Pentagon is 4,605 feet.

Example B	**Example C**
3-digit product, no regrouping	4-digit product, 2 regroupings
$$\begin{array}{r} 132 \\ \times\ \ \ 3 \\ \hline 396 \end{array}$$	$$\begin{array}{r} {}^{2\,4}\ \ \\ 547 \\ \times\ \ \ 6 \\ \hline 3{,}282 \end{array}$$

✔ Talk About It

1. In Example C, what does the small 4 mean?

Take It to the NET
More Examples
www.scottforesman.com

CHECK ✓

Find each product. Estimate to check reasonableness.

1. 213
× 3

2. 408
× 2

3. 450
× 7

4. 614
× 9

5. 762
× 8

6. Reasoning Ruby thinks 3 × 297 is greater than 1,000. Estimate to decide if she is correct.

PRACTICE

For more practice, see Set 11-8 on p. 676.

A Skills and Understanding

Find each answer. Estimate to check reasonableness.

7. 142
× 4

8. 308
× 5

9. 417
× 2

10. 821
× 6

11. 119
× 3

12. 351
× 5

13. 145
× 6

14. 306
× 7

15. 454
× 4

16. 289
× 5

17. 2 × 239

18. 4 × 562

19. 4 × 775

20. 250 × 8

21. Number Sense Write a multiplication sentence with a 3-digit number for which you must regroup to solve.

B Reasoning and Problem Solving

22. The Great Pyramid of Khufu is square at the bottom. Each side of the square is 751 feet long. What is the perimeter of the pyramid at the bottom?

23. A hippopotamus can eat 130 pounds of vegetable matter a day. How many pounds of vegetable matter can a hippopotamus eat in a week?

24. Writing in Math Show that you can find the answer to 8 × 263 by finding 8 × 200, 8 × 60, and 8 × 3.

Mixed Review and Test Prep

Take It to the NET
Test Prep
www.scottforesman.com

25. 6,029 − 1,416

26. 5,520 + 715

27. 2,641 + 3,173

28. Which is the product 6 × 59?

A. 3,054

B. 354

C. 304

D. 65

Think It Through
I can **multiply** when I join equal groups.

Multiplying Money

LEARN

When do you multiply money?

Tina is taking her brothers to the movies. How much will Tina pay for 3 children's tickets?

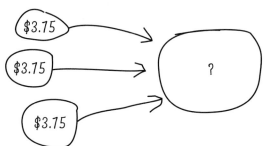

$3.75

$3.75

$3.75

?

Find 3 × $3.75.

Matinee Admission	
Adults	**$7.25**
Students	**$5.50**
(12–18 years old)	
Children	**$3.75**
(Under 12 years old)	

How do you multiply money?

Example

STEP 1

Multiply the same way as with whole numbers.

$$\begin{array}{r} \overset{2\ 1}{\$3.75} \\ \times\quad 3 \\ \hline 1125 \end{array}$$

STEP 2

Write the answer in dollars and cents.

$$\begin{array}{r} \overset{2\ 1}{\$3.75} \\ \times\quad 3 \\ \hline \$11.25 \end{array}$$

Estimate to check. 3 × $3.75

3 × $4 = $12

The product $11.25 is close to $12, so the answer is reasonable.
Tina will pay $11.25.

✔ Talk About It

1. How do you know where to put the decimal point in the answer for the example?

Find each product. Estimate to check reasonableness.

1.	2.	3.	4.	5.
$1.05	$0.13	$6.34	$7.80	$4.28
× 9	× 2	× 8	× 3	× 3

6. Number Sense Is $25 enough for 3 adult movie tickets? Explain.

PRACTICE

For more practice, see Set 11-9 on p. 676.

A Skills and Understanding

Find each product. Estimate to check reasonableness.

7.	8.	9.	10.	11.
$1.56	$0.02	$0.27	$5.13	$3.11
× 6	× 2	× 9	× 8	× 9

12.	13.	14.	15.	16.
$1.33	$4.07	$5.98	$4.06	$2.60
× 6	× 5	× 8	× 5	× 5

17. 6 × $0.43   **18.** 4 × $6.29   **19.** 8 × $1.07   **20.** 4 × $2.50

21. Reasoning Explain how the product 3 × $4.20 is like the product 3 × 420. How is it different?

B Reasoning and Problem Solving

When the drama club performed at the local theater, treats were sold as shown at the right. Find each cost.

Popcorn
Small $1.29
Medium $2.29
Large $3.00

Lemonade
Small $0.99
Medium $1.25
Large $1.59

22. 4 medium popcorns   **23.** 5 small popcorns

24. 3 large lemonades   **25.** 4 small lemonades

26. 2 small popcorns and 2 small lemonades

27. Writing in Math Explain how you could find the cost of 2 small popcorns and 1 medium lemonade.

Mixed Review and Test Prep

Take It to the NET
Test Prep
www.scottforesman.com

28. 2 × 429   **29.** 367 × 3   **30.** 7 × 601

31. Which angle is an acute angle?

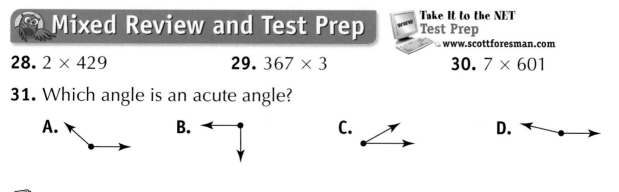

A.   B.   C.   D.

All text pages available online and on CD-ROM.

Materials
• calculator

Think It Through
Before I do a calculation, I should **decide which method makes sense.**

Choose a Computation Method

✓ **WARM UP**
1. 105 × 3 2. 240 × 4
3. 5 × 117 4. 6 × 333

LEARN

When do you use different methods to solve a problem?

When you multiply, first try mental math. Next, think about using paper and pencil. For large numbers that are difficult to multiply, you can use a calculator.

Students in the History Club at Valley High School are earning money for a trip to England.

Global Travel Trip Deals

Ten-day Trip Deal	$2,000
Seven-day Trip Deal	$1,389
Plane tickets	$231
Hyde Park Hotel (one night)	$159

Example A	Example B	Example C
How much do 9 Ten-Day Trip Deals cost?	How much do 4 plane tickets cost?	How much do 9 Seven-Day Trip Deals cost?
9 × 2,000 = ▨	**4 × 231 =** ▨	**9 × 1,389 =** ▨
This is easy to do in my head. I'll use **mental math.**	There are not a lot of regroupings. I'll use **paper and pencil.**	There are lots of regroupings. I'll use a **calculator.**

Example A:
9 × 2 = 18
9 × 2,000 = 18,000

Example B:
$$\begin{array}{r} \overset{1}{231} \\ \times\ 4 \\ \hline 924 \end{array}$$

Example C:
9 × 1389
= 12501

Cost: $18,000   Cost: $924   Cost: $12,501

✓ **Talk About It**

1. How could you estimate to check the answer in Example C?

2. Which method is best to find the cost of 7 nights at the Hyde Park Hotel? Explain.

Find each product. Tell which computation method you used.

1.	200	**2.**	96	**3.**	389	**4.**	1,500
	× 3		× 7		× 3		× 2

5. Number Sense Manuel used paper and pencil to find 8 × $500. Could he have found the answer a faster way? Explain.

PRACTICE

For more practice, see Set 11-10 on p. 676.

Ⓐ Skills and Understanding

Find each product. Tell which computation method you used.

6.	$456	**7.**	3,883	**8.**	604	**9.**	$1,200	**10.**	400
	× 9		× 7		× 2		× 4		× 4

11. 9 × 1,000   **12.** 6 × 270   **13.** 326 × 8   **14.** 5,699 × 5

15. Reasoning Why is using a calculator not the best method for finding 4 × 22?

Ⓑ Reasoning and Problem Solving

The London Eye in England is the world's largest Ferris wheel. It takes 30 minutes to make one full circle. Each car on the London Eye holds 25 people.

16. How long would the London Eye take to go around 4 times?

17. If 6 cars are still empty, how many more people can get on the London Eye?

18. **Writing in Math** What method would you use to find how many people 9 cars would hold? Explain.

Mixed Review and Test Prep

Take It to the NET
Test Prep
www.scottforesman.com

Find each product. Estimate to check reasonableness.

19. 5 × $2.91   **20.** 7 × $6.40   **21.** 8 × $1.15

22. What is the next number in this pattern? 24, 36, 48, ▨

A. 68   **B.** 54   **C.** 56   **D.** 60

 All text pages available online and on CD-ROM.

Draw Conclusions

Drawing conclusions when you read in math can help you use the **problem-solving strategy, _Use Logical Reasoning,_** in the next lesson.

In reading, drawing conclusions can help you make sense of things as you think through a story. In math, drawing conclusions can help you use logical reasoning as you think through a problem.

First I'll make a chart to record the information given in the problem.

Three pets are named Fluff, Zippy, and Ginger. They are a cat, a dog, and a hamster. Fluff is the cat, and Zippy is not the dog. Find the name that goes with each pet.

*To fill in the chart, I need to look at each column and row and **draw conclusions.***

Pet Names

	Cat	Dog	Hamster
Fluff	Yes		
Zippy		No	
Ginger			

If there is a *Yes,* then you can conclude that the other cells in that row and column have to be *No.*

*Continue using the facts and **logical reasoning** to fill in all the cells in the chart and solve the problem.*

1. Why can you draw the conclusion Ginger is the dog?

2. In each row and column, how many cells can say *Yes?*

For 3–5, use the problem below.

Four players on the basketball team had their 10th, 11th, 12th, and 13th birthdays this month. Debbie is the youngest. Sharon is not 12 years old. Tamika is the oldest.

	10th	11th	12th	13th
Debbie	Yes			
Sharon			No	
Tamika				Yes
Kelly				

3. Why can you draw the conclusion that Debbie is not 13 years old?

4. Why can you draw the conclusion that Sharon did not turn 10 this month?

5. Writing in Math Could Kelly have had her 12th birthday this month? Why or why not?

For 6–10, use the problem below.

The picture at the right shows the lockers that Dan, Ari, Jake, and Mei use at school.

6. Dan has an even numbered locker. What conclusion can you draw?

7. Mei's locker number is a multiple of 10. What conclusion can you draw?

8. Writing in Math Based on the information in Exercises 6 and 7, what is Dan's locker number? How did you draw this conclusion?

9. Jake's locker number is divisible by 3. What is Jake's locker number?

10. Writing in Math Could Ari's locker number be an even number? Why or why not?

Problem-Solving Strategy

Reading Helps!

Drawing conclusions

can help you with...

the problem-solving strategy, *Use Logical Reasoning*.

Key Idea
Learning how and when to use logical reasoning can help you solve problems.

Use Logical Reasoning

LEARN

How do you make an organized list?

Birthday Puzzle What is the date of Ella's birthday in July? Use these clues to decide.

1. The date has 2 digits.

2. The sum of the digits is 8.

3. The date is an even number.

July						
S	M	T	W	T	F	S
	1	2	3	4	5	6
7	8	9	10	11	12	13
14	15	16	17	18	19	20
21	22	23	24	25	26	27
28	29	30	31			

Read and Understand

What do you know?

The date has 2 digits with a sum of 8. It is an even number.

What are you trying to find?

Find the date of Ella's birthday.

Plan and Solve

What strategy will you use?

Strategy: Use Logical Reasoning

Draw a calendar to show what you know.

Even number

How to Use Logical Reasoning

Step 1 Draw a picture to help organize the information.

Step 2 Fill in the information you are given.

Step 3 Use the picture and reasoning to draw conclusions.

Answer: Ella's birthday is on the 26th.

Look Back and Check

Is your work correct?

Yes. All the clues match my answer.

✔ Talk About It

1. Why are the 17th and the 26th circled?

Solve. Write the answer in a complete sentence.

1. Copy the table. Then finish filling in the table to decide who came in first in the running race.

- Al was second.
- Cheri was NOT third.
- Phil was last.

	Diane	Cheri	Phil	Al
1st				No
2nd	No	No	No	Yes
3rd				No
4th				No

A Using the Strategy

Solve. Write the answer in a complete sentence.

2. Copy and complete the picture to find who is tallest: Ellie, Maddie, Reggie, or Nick.

- Ellie is shorter than Maddie.
- Maddie is taller than Reggie.
- Nick is the shortest.

STRATEGIES

- **Show What You Know**
  Draw a Picture
  Make an Organized List
  Make a Table
  Make a Graph
  Act It Out or Use Objects
- **Look for a Pattern**
- **Try, Check, and Revise**
- **Write a Number Sentence**
- **Use Logical Reasoning**
- **Solve a Simpler Problem**
- **Work Backward**

Choose a tool

Mental Math

3. The school fair will be in May. Copy the calendar and finish marking it to find when the fair will be.

- The fair will not be on a weekend.
- The date of the fair has 2 digits.
- The sum of the digits is 5.

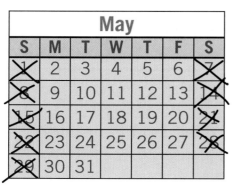

May						
S	M	T	W	T	F	S
✗	2	3	4	5	6	✗
✗	9	10	11	12	13	✗
✗	16	17	18	19	20	✗
✗	23	24	25	26	27	✗
✗	30	31				

4. How many different kinds of pizzas can you choose for $8.99?

Tony's Pizza Deal

Choose: Thin Crust or Thick Crust

Then choose one of these toppings: Green peppers, Meatballs, or Olives

$8.99

Do You Know How?

Do You Understand?

Multiplication and Arrays (11-5)

Find each product. You may draw a picture to help.

1. 5 × 31   **2.** 8 × 13   **3.** 24 × 6

A How can you tell without solving that the answer for Exercise 1 is greater than 100?

Breaking Numbers Apart to Multiply (11-6); Multiplying Two-Digit Numbers (11-7)

Find each product.

4. 3 × 13   **5.** 4 × 48   **6.** 67 × 3

7. 15 × 7   **8.** 4 × 86   **9.** 6 × 36

B How can you check that your answer to Exercise 9 is reasonable?

Multiplying Three-Digit Numbers (11-8); Multiplying Money (11-9)

Find each product. Estimate to check reasonableness.

10. 2 × 103   **11.** 5 × 118

12. $1.67 × 3   **13.** 2 × $2.53

14. 3 × $1.20   **15.** 4 × 289

C Show how to solve Exercise 11 by finding 5 × 100, 5 × 10, and 5 × 8.

D How do you know where to put the decimal point in the product of Exercise 12?

Choose a Computation Method (11-10)

Find each product. Tell which computation method you used.

16. 5 × 189   **17.** 5 × 119

18. 2 × 3,000   **19.** 3 × 221

E Explain why you chose the method you did for finding each product in Exercises 16–19.

Problem-Solving Strategy: Use Logical Reasoning (11-11)

20. I am a 3-digit odd number less than 115. The sum of my digits is 4. What number am I?

F Explain how you solved Exercise 20.

MULTIPLE CHOICE

1. What multiplication sentence is shown by the array? (11-5)

A. $3 \times 37 = 111$ **C.** $3 \times 7 = 21$

B. $2 \times 37 = 74$ **D.** $2 \times 23 = 46$

2. Find $2 \times \$3.50$. (11-9)

A. $7.75   **B.** $7.00   **C.** $5.50   **D.** $3.75

FREE RESPONSE

Find each product. (11-5)

3. 3×26

4. 2×45

Find each product. Estimate to check reasonableness. (11-6, 11-7, 11-8, 11-9)

5. 27	**6.** 33	**7.** 45	**8.** 76	**9.** 67
× 8	× 6	× 9	× 2	× 3

10. 25	**11.** 54	**12.** 137	**13.** 145	**14.** $1.60
× 2	× 5	× 5	× 2	× 3

15. 4×66 **16.** 93×3 **17.** $2 \times \$1.91$ **18.** $\$1.21 \times 3$

Find each product. Tell which computation method you used. (11-10)

19. 6×547 **20.** 3×300 **21.** $1,298 \times 4$ **22.** $4,000 \times 3$

23. Copy and complete the table to decide who came in second in the swim race. (11-11)

- Alec was first.
- Grace was not last.
- Rick was third.

	Grace	Alec	Kim	Rick
1st	No	Yes	No	No
2nd		No		
3rd		No		
4th		No		

Writing in Math

24. Explain how you can estimate to check $\$3.98 \times 2 = \$7.96$. (11-9)

TEST TALK

Think It Through
• I can **choose division** when I'm separating into equal groups.
• I can **make a model** to show division.

Using Objects to Divide

WARM UP
1. $40 \div 5$ 2. $24 \div 6$
3. $80 \div 2$ 4. $56 \div 7$
5. $32 \div 4$ 6. $27 \div 3$

Activity

How can you model division with greater numbers?

Follow these steps to find $64 \div 4$.

a. Use place-value blocks to show 64. Draw 4 circles to show how many equal groups you will make.

b. Divide the tens. Put an equal number of tens in each circle. There are 2 tens left over.

c. Regroup the leftover tens as ones.
2 tens = 20 ones
Combine them with the 4 ones that were already there, so there are 24 ones. Place an equal number of ones in each circle.

$64 \div 4 = 16$

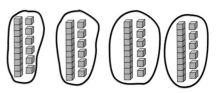

I can put 1 ten and 6 ones in each group.
1 ten 6 ones = 16

d. Use place-value blocks to find each quotient.

$42 \div 3$ $52 \div 4$ $75 \div 5$

Use place-value blocks or draw a picture to find each quotient.

1. 32 ÷ 2   **2.** 54 ÷ 3   **3.** 42 ÷ 3

4. 76 ÷ 4   **5.** 80 ÷ 5   **6.** 28 ÷ 2

7. Number Sense How can you tell whether 78 ÷ 2 is greater than 30 without dividing?

Think It Through
I'll keep my pictures simple.

PRACTICE

For more practice, see Set 11-12 on p. 677.

Use place-value blocks or draw a picture to find each quotient.

8. 65 ÷ 5   **9.** 48 ÷ 3   **10.** 72 ÷ 6   **11.** 56 ÷ 4   **12.** 84 ÷ 7

13. 57 ÷ 3   **14.** 68 ÷ 4   **15.** 98 ÷ 7   **16.** 76 ÷ 2   **17.** 90 ÷ 6

18. Number Sense How could you estimate to check that 57 ÷ 3 = 19 has a reasonable answer?

B Reasoning and Problem Solving

On Earth, objects weigh 6 times as much as they weigh on the moon. How much does each object weigh on the moon?

19. Communication system

20. Space suit

21. Photography supplies

22. Rock samples

ASTRONAUTS' CARGO	
Object	**Earth Weight (pounds)**
Communication system	84
Space suit	180
Photography supplies	72
Moon rock samples	48

23. Writing in Math On Earth, objects weigh about 3 times as much as they weigh on Mars. Explain how you can find the weight of a space suit on Mars.

Mixed Review and Test Prep

 **Take It to the NET**
Test Prep
www.scottforesman.com

Find each product. Tell which computation method you used.

24. 102 × 4   **25.** 719 × 3   **26.** 2 × 804

27. I am a 2-digit number less than 30. The sum of my digits is 5. I am an odd number. What number am I?

A. 41   **B.** 23   **C.** 14   **D.** 5

 All text pages available online and on CD-ROM.

Breaking Numbers Apart to Divide

✓ **WARM UP**

Estimate each quotient.

1. $74 \div 8$ 2. $40 \div 9$

3. $50 \div 6$ 4. $41 \div 4$

LEARN

How can you use place value to divide?

Sometimes you can break apart a number into tens and ones to divide.

Greg, Sally, and Mark need to make 96 party favors. If they each make the same number, how many should each person make?

Example

Find $96 \div 3$.

What You **Think**	What You **Show**
Think about 96 as tens and ones. $96 = 90 + 6$ Divide the tens: $90 \div 3 = 30$ Divide the ones: $6 \div 3 = 2$ Add the two quotients: $30 + 2 = 32$	

Think It Through

I can **draw a picture** to show how I break numbers apart to divide.

Greg, Sally, and Mark should each make 32 party favors.

✓ Talk About It

1. How does the picture help you solve the problem?

2. How could you use the break-apart method to divide 68 by 2?

CHECK ✓   *For another example, see Set 11-13 on p. 673.*

Use the break-apart method to find each quotient. You may draw a picture to help.

  1. $26 \div 2$ **2.** $84 \div 4$ **3.** $63 \div 3$ **4.** $77 \div 7$ **5.** $50 \div 5$

  6. Number Sense Micah says that $48 \div 2 = 20 + 4$. Is he correct? Explain.

A Skills and Understanding

Use the break-apart method to find each quotient. You may draw a picture to help.

7. $69 \div 3$ **8.** $86 \div 2$ **9.** $88 \div 2$ **10.** $39 \div 3$ **11.** $44 \div 4$

12. $36 \div 3$ **13.** $42 \div 2$ **14.** $63 \div 3$ **15.** $64 \div 2$ **16.** $82 \div 2$

17. $2\overline{)64}$ **18.** $4\overline{)48}$ **19.** $5\overline{)55}$ **20.** $3\overline{)99}$ **21.** $6\overline{)60}$

22. Reasoning What division sentence is shown in the drawing?

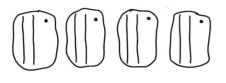

B Reasoning and Problem Solving

Algebra Compare. Write $<$, $>$, or $=$.

23. $28 \div 2 \ \bullet \ 84 \div 4$ **24.** $36 \div 3 \ \bullet \ 48 \div 4$ **25.** $90 \div 3 \ \bullet \ 60 \div 6$

26. $26 \div 2 \ \bullet \ 28 \div 2$ **27.** $35 \div 7 \ \bullet \ 50 \div 5$ **28.** $88 \div 4 \ \bullet \ 66 \div 3$

29. Number Sense How could you solve Exercise 26 without dividing?

30. Writing in Math Explain how to use the break-apart method to find $42 \div 2$. Draw a picture to show the problem.

Mixed Review and Test Prep

Take It to the NET
Test Prep
www.scottforesman.com

31. Find the sum: $\$38.51 + \$27.93$

32. Find the difference: $\$85.63 - \$27.45$

Choose the division sentence that matches each model.

33.

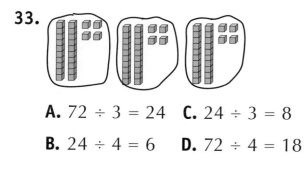

A. $72 \div 3 = 24$ **C.** $24 \div 3 = 8$

B. $24 \div 4 = 6$ **D.** $72 \div 4 = 18$

34.

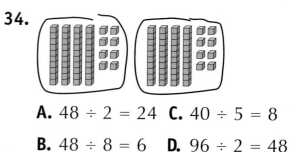

A. $48 \div 2 = 24$ **C.** $40 \div 5 = 8$

B. $48 \div 8 = 6$ **D.** $96 \div 2 = 48$

Key Idea
You can divide greater numbers using paper and pencil.

Vocabulary
• remainder (p. 398)

Dividing

LEARN

How do you record division?

Four scout troops want to sell 72 cartons of popcorn. Each troop will get the same number of cartons to sell. How many will each troop get? Will there be any left over?

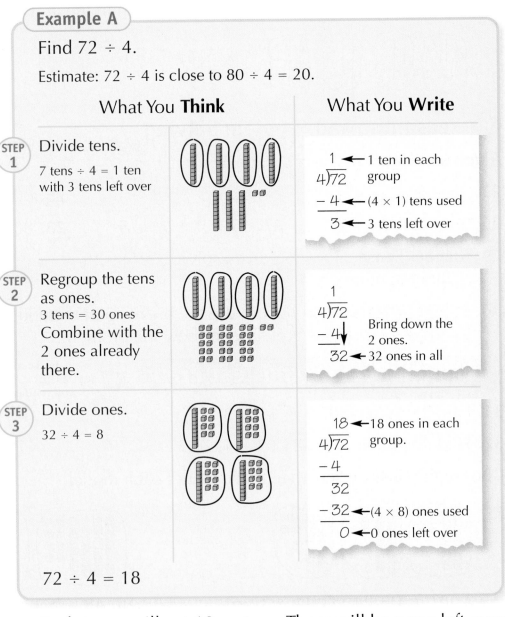

Example A

Find 72 ÷ 4.

Estimate: 72 ÷ 4 is close to 80 ÷ 4 = 20.

What You **Think**		What You **Write**
STEP 1 Divide tens. 7 tens ÷ 4 = 1 ten with 3 tens left over		1 ← 1 ten in each group 4)72 − 4 ← (4 × 1) tens used 3 ← 3 tens left over
STEP 2 Regroup the tens as ones. 3 tens = 30 ones. Combine with the 2 ones already there.		1 4)72 − 4↓ Bring down the 2 ones. 32 ← 32 ones in all
STEP 3 Divide ones. 32 ÷ 4 = 8		18 ← 18 ones in each group. 4)72 − 4 32 − 32 ← (4 × 8) ones used 0 ← 0 ones left over

72 ÷ 4 = 18

Each troop will get 18 cartons. There will be none left over.

✓ **Talk About It**

1. In Step 2, why do you rename 3 tens as 30 ones?

Where do you start dividing?

For another example, see Set 11-14 on p. 673.

Example B

Find $43 \div 5$.

Estimate: $43 \div 5$ is about $40 \div 5 = 8$.

STEP 1

Decide where to start. You can't divide tens.

$5)\overline{43}$

STEP 2

Divide ones.

$$\begin{array}{r} 8 \\ 5)\overline{43} \\ \underline{40} \\ 3 \end{array}$$

Multiply: 5×8

Subtract.

STEP 3

Compare.

$$\begin{array}{r} 8 \text{ R3} \\ 5)\overline{43} \\ \underline{40} \\ 3 \end{array}$$

$3 < 5$. The remainder is less than the divisor. There are no more digits to bring down.

Check that $43 \div 5 = 8$ R3 is correct.

STEP 1

Multiply the quotient by the divisor.

$$\begin{array}{r} \mathbf{8} \text{ R3} \\ 5)\overline{43} \end{array}$$

$\mathbf{8 \times 5 = 40}$

STEP 2

Add the remainder. The result should be the dividend.

$$\begin{array}{r} \mathbf{8} \text{ R}\mathbf{3} \\ 5)\overline{43} \end{array}$$

$\mathbf{40 + 3 = 43}$ The answer checks.

✔ **Talk About It**

2. Check the answer for Example A by multiplying.

Take It to the NET
More Examples
www.scottforesman.com

CHECK ✓

Copy and complete. Check your answers.

1.
$$\begin{array}{r} 1\blacksquare \\ 3)\overline{45} \\ \underline{-3} \\ 1\blacksquare \\ \underline{\blacksquare\blacksquare} \\ 0 \end{array}$$

2.
$$\begin{array}{r} 1\blacksquare \\ 6)\overline{84} \\ \underline{-6} \\ 2\blacksquare \\ \underline{-\blacksquare\blacksquare} \\ \blacksquare \end{array}$$

3.
$$\begin{array}{r} 7 \text{ R}\blacksquare \\ 7)\overline{51} \\ \underline{-\blacksquare\blacksquare} \\ \blacksquare \end{array}$$

4.
$$\begin{array}{r} \blacksquare \text{ R}\blacksquare \\ 6)\overline{38} \\ \underline{-\blacksquare\blacksquare} \\ \blacksquare \end{array}$$

5.
$$\begin{array}{r} \blacksquare\blacksquare \text{ R}\blacksquare \\ 5)\overline{56} \\ \underline{-\blacksquare} \\ 06 \\ \underline{-\blacksquare} \\ \blacksquare \end{array}$$

6. **Number Sense** Charlie says that $35 \div 4 = 3$ R5. Multiply and add to tell whether he is correct.

A Skills and Understanding

Copy and complete. Check your answer.

7.
$$
\begin{array}{r}
3\blacksquare \\
2\overline{)76} \\
-6 \\
\hline
\blacksquare6 \\
-\blacksquare\blacksquare \\
\hline
\blacksquare
\end{array}
$$

8.
$$
\begin{array}{r}
7\ \text{R}\blacksquare \\
7\overline{)55} \\
-49 \\
\hline
\blacksquare
\end{array}
$$

9.
$$
\begin{array}{r}
\blacksquare\blacksquare \\
6\overline{)78} \\
-\blacksquare \\
\hline
\blacksquare8 \\
-\blacksquare\blacksquare \\
\hline
\blacksquare
\end{array}
$$

10.
$$
\begin{array}{r}
\blacksquare\ \text{R}\blacksquare \\
9\overline{)30} \\
-\blacksquare\blacksquare \\
\hline
\blacksquare
\end{array}
$$

11.
$$
\begin{array}{r}
\blacksquare\blacksquare\ \text{R}\blacksquare \\
4\overline{)65} \\
-\blacksquare \\
\hline
\blacksquare\blacksquare \\
-\blacksquare\blacksquare \\
\hline
\blacksquare
\end{array}
$$

Divide. Check your answers.

12. $3\overline{)57}$ **13.** $9\overline{)82}$ **14.** $2\overline{)33}$ **15.** $6\overline{)77}$ **16.** $2\overline{)25}$

17. Reasoning Marilyn says that when you divide a number by 7, the remainder will always be less than 7. Do you agree? Explain.

B Reasoning and Problem Solving

Math and Everyday Life

Seventy students are going on a school picnic. The pictograph shows how many passengers can ride in each type of vehicle.

18. How many minivans would be needed to drive all the students going on the picnic?

19. Will 7 vans be enough to drive them all?

20. How many more station wagons than minivans would be needed to drive all the students?

21. Writing in Math Is Collette's work below correct? If not, tell why and correct her work.

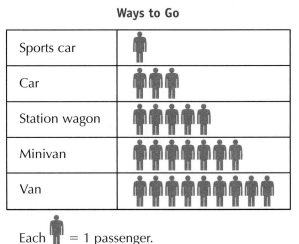

Ways to Go

Each 🧍 = 1 passenger.

> Find 41 ÷ 6.
>
> First I will estimate. $\begin{array}{r} 5 \\ 6\overline{)41} \\ 30 \\ \hline 11 \end{array}$
> 30 ÷ 6 = 5.
>
> So, 41 ÷ 6 = 5 R11.

C Extensions

Copy and complete to divide 3-digit numbers.

22.

```
   2 ▢▢ R ▢
3)731       Divide hundreds: 7 ÷ 3 = 2
  6↓
  13        Multiply: 3 × 2
 -▢▢↓       Subtract. Compare. 1 < 3
  ▢▢1
  -▢
  ▢▢
```

23.

```
  ▢▢▢
4)548
 -▢▢
  ▢4
 -▢▢
  ▢8
  ▢▢
  ▢▢
```

24.

```
  ▢▢ R ▢
6)129
 -▢▢
  ▢9
 -▢
  ▢
```

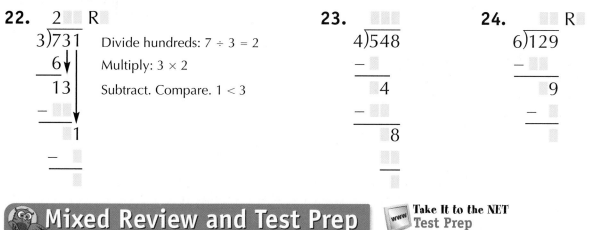

Mixed Review and Test Prep

Take It to the NET
Test Prep
www.scottforesman.com

25. Break apart tens and ones to find 48 ÷ 4. You may draw a picture.

26. Algebra Which number makes this sentence true? $5 \times \boxed{} = 70$

A. 75   **B.** 14   **C.** 15   **D.** 85

Enrichment

Dividing Money

Materials: bills and coins

How much should each person pay if 3 people share the cost of the paints?

Find $3.45 ÷ 3.

Paint Set $3.45

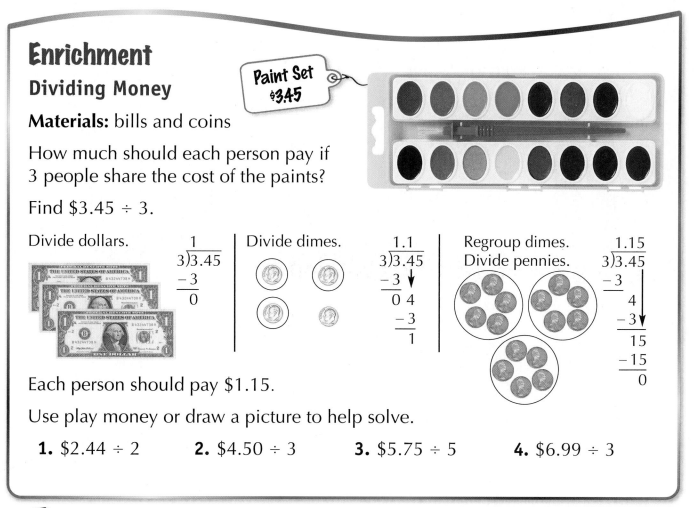

Divide dollars.

```
    1
3)3.45
 -3
  0
```

Divide dimes.

```
    1.1
3)3.45
 -3 ↓
  0 4
   -3
    1
```

Regroup dimes.
Divide pennies.

```
    1.15
3)3.45
 -3
  4↓
 -3↓
  15
 -15
   0
```

Each person should pay $1.15.

Use play money or draw a picture to help solve.

1. $2.44 ÷ 2   **2.** $4.50 ÷ 3   **3.** $5.75 ÷ 5   **4.** $6.99 ÷ 3

Problem-Solving Skill

Key Idea
The real-world situation tells how to interpret the remainder.

Think It Through
I can **use the information in the problem** to help me interpret the meaning of the 4 hours that are left over.

Interpreting Remainders

LEARN

How do you know what to do with a remainder?

When you solve a problem using division, you can look at the real-world situation to interpret the remainder.

Henry Ford In 1913, Henry Ford started an assembly line to make cars. It took about 6 hours to make 1 car. A work week had 40 hours.

Example A	Example B	Example C
How many cars could be completed in one work week?	How many cars would be worked on in one work week?	How many hours would have been spent working on the 7th car in one work week?

Plan and Solve

$\begin{array}{r} 6\text{ R4} \\ 6\overline{)40} \\ -36 \\ \hline 4 \end{array}$	$\begin{array}{r} 6\text{ R4} \\ 6\overline{)40} \\ -36 \\ \hline 4 \end{array}$	$\begin{array}{r} 6\text{ R4} \\ 6\overline{)40} \\ -36 \\ \hline 4 \end{array}$
Six cars could be completed.	Seven cars would be worked on.	Four hours would have been spent on the 7th car.

Look Back and Check

The 4 hours left over were not enough to complete a car.	Workers would begin making a 7th car in the remaining 4 hours.	Six cars were completed in 36 hours. There were 4 more hours in the work week.

✔ **Talk About It**

1. Why is the answer to each of the three examples different?

656

For another example, see Set 11-15 on p. 673.

CHECK ✓

Solve. Write the answer in a complete sentence.

1. There are 38 students going to a museum. Each van can hold 8 students. How many vans will be needed?

2. Jack is making gingerbread cookies. He needs 5 raisins to decorate each cookie. If he has 26 raisins, how many cookies can Jack make?

PRACTICE

For more practice, see Set 11-15 on p. 677.

Use the table for 3 and 4.

3. Sheila has 45 prize tickets. How many marbles can she get?

4. Mark got 3 rings and 2 stickers. How many tickets did he use?

5. It takes Emory 3 minutes to make a friendship bracelet. If he works for 17 minutes, how many bracelets did Emory work on?

6. Keiko makes necklaces like the one on the right. She has 29 blue beads and 20 red beads.

    a. How many necklaces can Keiko make?

    b. How many more blue beads does she need to make one more necklace?

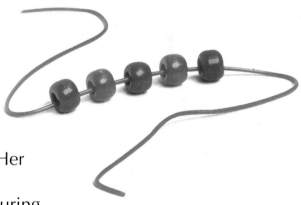

7. Jen needs 10 cups of water to make soup. Her measuring cup holds 4 cups of water. How many times must Jen put water in the measuring cup to measure 10 cups of water?

8. Ms. Wallace's class must sit in 4 equal rows in the gym. If there are 24 students in Ms. Wallace's class, how many students are in each row?

9. **Writing in Math** Write a story problem that can be solved using $22 \div 3 = 7$ R1. Write and explain what the remainder means in your story problem.

Problem-Solving Applications

Steam Trains In the early 1800s, Britain was the first country to use steam trains. By 1870, railroads crossed many countries and they changed society in many ways. The task of moving people and products became faster, easier, and cheaper. Railroads are still very important to our lives today.

STEPHEN BIESTY'S
INCREDIBLE
CROSS-SECTIONS

FEATURING TWO FOLD-OUT PICTURES NEARLY 3 FEET LONG?

Trivia Steam trains not only transported passengers, they also transported mail. In fact, most trains had a traveling post office where mail was sorted to shorten delivery time. That was efficient!

FLYING SCOTSMAN

❶ One of the first steam-powered passenger trains traveled 8 miles per hour. Today, one of the fastest passenger trains can travel 320 miles per hour. Today's train is how many times as fast as the steam-powered train?

❷ The first public railroad in England was 20 miles long. The first public railroad in the United States was 21 kilometers long. Which railroad was longer?

❸ When the train *Flying Scotsman* was built in 1923, many said it was the best train ever built. After 76 years of use, it was restored to its original greatness. When was it restored?

Good News/Bad News In many ways, steam trains were the best means of traveling during the 1800s, but many people did not like them. Some people were so frightened by speeding trains that they tried to pass laws that would limit trains to traveling at a top speed of 9 miles per hour.

Key Facts
Flying Scotsman

- About 9 feet wide and 13 feet high
- Uses 45 pounds of coal every mile
- Uses 40 pounds of water every mile
- First steam train to go 100 mph

Using Key Facts

④ After traveling 5 miles, how much more coal than water would *Flying Scotsman* use?

⑤ **Writing in Math** Write your own word problem that involves trains. Write the answer in a complete sentence.

⑥ After its restoration, *Flying Scotsman* left London at 8:55 A.M. and was scheduled to arrive at York 5 hours 40 minutes later. It actually arrived at York 15 minutes late. When did it arrive at York?

Car	Seats
1st class	36
2nd class	44
Dining	24
Observation	60

⑦ **Decision Making** Suppose you could combine 10 cars from the table above to make one steam train. How many of each type of car would you use? How many seats would your train have?

Do You Know How?

Do You Understand?

Using Objects to Divide (11-12)

Draw a picture to find each quotient.

1. 58 ÷ 2   **2.** 87 ÷ 3

3. 65 ÷ 5   **4.** 52 ÷ 4

Ⓐ In Exercise 1, how can you tell that the quotient is greater than 20 without dividing?

Breaking Numbers Apart to Divide (11-13)

Use the break-apart method to divide. You may draw a picture to help.

5. 84 ÷ 4   **6.** 88 ÷ 2

7. 3)63   **8.** 4)88

9. 2)86   **10.** 3)99

Ⓑ In Exercise 6, how many tens are in each group? How many ones?

Ⓒ Is it true that 46 ÷ 2 = 20 + 3? Explain.

Dividing (11-14)

Divide. Check your answers.

11. 2)92   **12.** 5)87   **13.** 3)74

14. 6)53   **15.** 7)83   **16.** 4)64

17. 9)48   **18.** 8)96   **19.** 3)41

Ⓓ In Exercise 11, what steps did you take to check your answer?

Ⓔ In Exercise 17, what basic fact could you use to estimate the quotient?

Problem-Solving Skill: Interpreting Remainders (11-15)

There are 85 people coming to the auditorium for a school play. There are 9 chairs in each row.

20. How many rows of chairs are needed?

21. How many rows of chairs can be filled?

22. How many chairs will be empty?

Ⓕ Explain how you found your answer for Exercise 20.

Ⓖ To answer Exercise 21, did you use the quotient, the remainder, or neither? Explain.

Ⓗ To answer Exercise 22 did you use the quotient, the remainder, or neither? Explain.

TEST TALK

Think It Through
For multiple-choice items, I should **eliminate unreasonable answers.**

MULTIPLE CHOICE

1. Divide. $3\overline{)87}$ (11-14)

   A. 23 R1   **B.** 29   **C.** 29 R3   **D.** 37

2. Divide. $8\overline{)76}$ (11-14)

   A. 8 R 12   **B.** 9   **C.** 9 R4   **D.** 94

FREE RESPONSE

Draw a picture to find each quotient. (11-12)

3. 58 ÷ 2   4. 63 ÷ 3   5. 98 ÷ 7   6. 72 ÷ 6

Use the break-apart method to find each quotient. You may draw a picture to help. (11-13)

7. 84 ÷ 4   8. 63 ÷ 3   9. 48 ÷ 4   10. 88 ÷ 2

Divide. Check your answers. (11-14)

11. $3\overline{)87}$ 12. $9\overline{)73}$ 13. $4\overline{)65}$ 14. $7\overline{)91}$

15. $5\overline{)68}$ 16. $8\overline{)27}$ 17. $2\overline{)98}$ 18. $6\overline{)39}$

Solve each problem. (11-15, 11-16)

Fifty-six students are going on a field trip. They will ride in minivans. Each van can carry 9 passsengers.

19. How many vans are needed?

20. How many vans can be filled?

21. After as many vans as possible are filled, how many students will be in the last van?

Writing in Math

22. Draw a picture to find 36 ÷ 2. Explain your picture. (11-12)

23. Explain how you would use the break-apart method to find 39 ÷ 3. (11-13)

Test-Taking Strategies

Understand the question.

Get information for the answer.

Plan how to find the answer.

→ Make smart choices.

Use writing in math.

Improve written answers.

Make Smart Choices

To answer a multiple-choice test question, you need to choose an answer from answer choices. The steps below will help you make a smart choice.

1. Jason bought posters for his room for $6 each including sales tax. He spent $48. How many posters did he buy?

A. 4

B. 7

C. 8

D. 12

Understand the question.

I need to find the number of posters Jason bought.

Get information for the answer.

*The **text** gives me all the information I need.*

Plan how to find the answer.

I can use a number sentence.

$6 \times \blacksquare = 48$

Make Smart Choices.

• Try working backward from an answer.

I'll use each answer choice to replace the ■.

Try 4: $6 \times 4 = 24$. That's not right.

Try 7: $6 \times 7 = 42$. That's not right.

Try 8: $6 \times 8 = 48$. That works.

The correct answer is C, 8.

2. Lily had 36 square tiles. She noticed she could make an array of 4 rows with 9 tiles in each row.

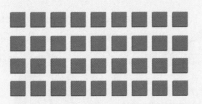

Which other array could Lily make with all of the tiles?

A. 4 rows with 8 tiles in a row

B. 3 rows with 10 tiles in a row

C. 8 rows with 6 tiles in a row

D. 6 rows with 6 tiles in a row

Think It Through

I need to find an array that uses 36 tiles. Arrays can be used to show multiplication, so I can use a multiplication number sentence for this array: ☐ × ☐ = 36. I'll **work backward** from each answer and replace the missing numbers.

4 × 8 = 32 That's not right.

3 × 10 = 30 That's not right.

8 × 6 = 48 That's not right.

6 × 6 = 36 That works. The answer is D.

Now it's your turn.

For each problem, give the answer and explain how you made your choice.

3. Sara gets paid $5 per hour doing lawn work. Last Saturday she earned $35. How many hours did she work?

A. 3   **B.** 7   **C.** 9   **D.** 32

4. Art arranged 48 thumbtacks in an array of 4 rows with 12 thumbtacks in each row.

Which other array could Art make with all of the tacks?

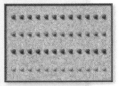

A. 7 rows with 7 tacks in a row

B. 6 rows with 8 tacks in a row

C. 5 rows with 10 tacks in a row

D. 9 rows with 6 tacks in a row

My mom estimates that we live about 20 miles from town.

You can **estimate** an answer if you don't need an exact amount. (p. 616)

Self Check ✓

Mentally find products and quotients and make estimates. (Lessons 11-1, 11-2, 11-3, 11-4)

Find 4 × 700.

4 × 7 = 28
4 × 70 = 280

4 × **7**00 = 2,**8**00   4 × 7 hundreds = 28 hundreds

Find 4,800 ÷ 6.

48 ÷ 6 = 8
480 ÷ 6 = 80

4,**8**00 ÷ 6 = **8**00   48 hundreds ÷ 6 = 8 hundreds

Estimate 8 × 365.

8 × 365
↓   Round 365 to the nearest hundred.
8 × 400 = 3,200

8 × 365 is about 3,200.

Estimate 38 ÷ 9.

38 ÷ 9   Use basic facts.
↓   Think: 38 is close to 36.
36 ÷ 9 = 4

38 ÷ 9 is about 4.

1. Find 7 × 6,000 and 250 ÷ 5, and estimate 9 × 39 and 50 ÷ 6.

Array sounds like "arrangement."

Remember, an **array** is an arrangement of objects in equal rows. (p. 626)

Self Check ✓

Follow steps in order when you multiply. (Lessons 11-5, 11-6, 11-7, 11-8, 11-9)

Draw an **array.** Then break numbers apart to multiply. Add the tens and ones.

```
——— ———   • • •    23
——— ———   • • •  ×  4
——— ———   • • •    12
——— ———   • • •  + 80
                   92
```

Multiply tens:
4 × 20 = 80

Multiply ones:
3 × 4 = 12

Record your work by multiplying the ones, then tens, then hundreds.

```
  1
  23
×  4
  92
```

```
  2
  341
×   7
2,387
```

Multiply money like whole numbers.

```
   3
 $4.61
×    5
$23.05
```

Put the dollar sign and decimal point in the product.

2. Find 18 × 3, 425 × 6, and $1.69 × 4.

Use models or paper and pencil to divide. (Lessons 11-12, 11-13, 11-14)

Find 84 ÷ 4.

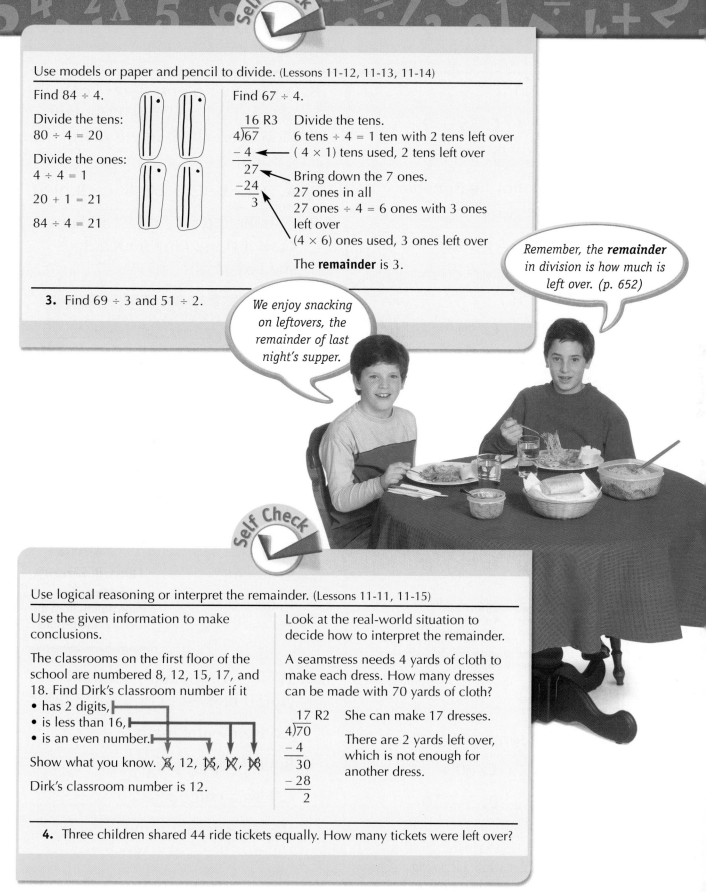

Divide the tens:
80 ÷ 4 = 20

Divide the ones:
4 ÷ 4 = 1

20 + 1 = 21

84 ÷ 4 = 21

Find 67 ÷ 4.

$$16 \text{ R}3$$
$$4\overline{)67}$$
$$-\ 4$$
$$\overline{\ \ 27}$$
$$-24$$
$$\overline{\ \ \ 3}$$

Divide the tens.
6 tens ÷ 4 = 1 ten with 2 tens left over
(4 × 1) tens used, 2 tens left over

Bring down the 7 ones.
27 ones in all
27 ones ÷ 4 = 6 ones with 3 ones left over
(4 × 6) ones used, 3 ones left over

The **remainder** is 3.

*Remember, the **remainder** in division is how much is left over. (p. 652)*

3. Find 69 ÷ 3 and 51 ÷ 2.

We enjoy snacking on leftovers, the remainder of last night's supper.

Use logical reasoning or interpret the remainder. (Lessons 11-11, 11-15)

Use the given information to make conclusions.

The classrooms on the first floor of the school are numbered 8, 12, 15, 17, and 18. Find Dirk's classroom number if it
• has 2 digits,
• is less than 16,
• is an even number.

Show what you know. 8, 12, 15, 17, 18

Dirk's classroom number is 12.

Look at the real-world situation to decide how to interpret the remainder.

A seamstress needs 4 yards of cloth to make each dress. How many dresses can be made with 70 yards of cloth?

$$17 \text{ R}2$$
$$4\overline{)70}$$
$$-\ 4$$
$$\overline{\ \ 30}$$
$$-28$$
$$\overline{\ \ \ 2}$$

She can make 17 dresses.

There are 2 yards left over, which is not enough for another dress.

4. Three children shared 44 ride tickets equally. How many tickets were left over?

Answers: 1. 42,000; 50; sample estimates: 360; 8 2. 54; 2,550; $6.76 3. 23; 25 R1
4. 2 tickets

MULTIPLE CHOICE

1. Find $7 \times 8,000$.

   A. 560   **C.** 56,000

   B. 5,600   **D.** 560,000

2. Which is the most reasonable estimate for 4×87?

   A. 280   **B.** 320   **C.** 360   **D.** 800

3. What basic fact can you use to find $3,000 \div 5$?

   A. $3 + 5 = 8$ **C.** $30 \div 5 = 6$

   B. $3 \times 5 = 15$ **D.** $5 - 3 = 2$

4. Which is the most reasonable estimate for $49 \div 6$?

   A. 5   **C.** 9

   B. 8   **D.** 11

5. Which array shows the product 3×28?

   A.

   B.

   C.

   D.

6. Which is the same as 6×19?

   A. $60 + 54$ **C.** $60 + 540$

   B. $6 + 54$ **D.** $6 + 19$

7. Find 47×5.

   A. 42   **B.** 52   **C.** 125   **D.** 235

8. A gardener plants 8 rows of herb plants. Each row has 115 plants. How many herb plants are in the garden?

   A. 107   **B.** 123   **C.** 800   **D.** 920

9. Camille buys 4 folders at the school store. How much does she pay in all?

School Store
——— *Price List* ———

Pens . . . . **$1.25** each

Folders . . . . . **$2.75** each

Pencils . . . . . **$0.55** each

   A. $1.10

   B. $8.00

   C. $11.00

   D. $12.00

TEST TALK

Think It Through
I need to **gather information** from the text and the picture.

10. Which computation method would be best to find $6 \times 3,000$?

   A. Use mental math.

   B. Use paper and pencil.

   C. Use a calculator.

   D. Use a number line.

11. Which model shows 48 ÷ 3?

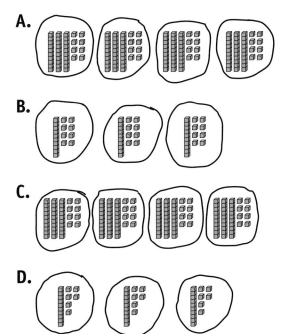

12. Which is the same as 93 ÷ 3?

A. 3 + 1   **C.** 30 + 1

B. 30 + 3   **D.** 33 + 3

13. Find 43 ÷ 4.

A. 10   **C.** 11

B. 10 R3   **D.** 11 R1

FREE RESPONSE

Find each product or quotient.

14. $\begin{array}{r} \$0.47 \\ \times \quad\quad 5 \\ \hline \end{array}$

Think It Through

I can **use estimation** to check if my answers are reasonable.

15. $\begin{array}{r} 64 \\ \times \quad 8 \\ \hline \end{array}$

16. 4)‾59‾   **17.** 7)‾84‾

18. 80 ÷ 5   **19.** 3 × 207

20. Copy and complete the table to decide who won first place in the science fair.

- Tim won third place.

- Brian did NOT win fourth place.

- Ellen won second place.

	Tim	Brian	Ellen	Kari
1st	No			
2nd	No			
3rd	Yes	No	No	No
4th	No			

Writing in Math

21. Solve the problem. Then explain how you interpreted the remainder to find the answer.

It takes Sharon 3 hours to make each gift basket. How many baskets can she make in 40 hours?

22. How can you decide which computation method to use to solve a multiplication problem?

23. Why is it helpful to estimate your answer before you multiply or divide greater numbers?

Number and Operation

MULTIPLE CHOICE

1. Which of the following is NOT another way to write 2,500?

   A. 2,000 + 500

   B. 2 thousands 5 hundreds

   C. 2,000 + 50

   D. 25 hundreds

2. There are 65 students signed up for Field Day. How many students should be on each team so that the teams are equal and every student is on a team?

   A. 4 students   **C.** 6 students

   B. 5 students   **D.** 10 students

FREE RESPONSE

3. Tabitha earns $9.75 an hour at her job at a kennel. If she works 4 hours on Monday, how much will she earn?

4. Show two different ways to find 28 × 7. Give the product.

Writing in Math

5. Explain how you can use mental math to find 6,400 ÷ 8. Give the quotient.

Think It Through
- I will **write my steps in order.**
- I can **draw pictures** to show my thinking.

Geometry and Measurement

MULTIPLE CHOICE

6. Which tool would be best to measure the weight of a person?

   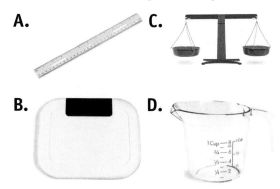

   A.   **C.**

   B.   **D.**

7. Which is the best estimate for the length of your textbook?

   A. 3 cm   **C.** 3 m

   B. 30 cm   **D.** 3 km

FREE RESPONSE

8. The perimeter of a square is 20 feet. What is the length of each side?

9. Kevin woke up at 7:30 A.M. It took him 45 minutes to get dressed and eat breakfast. At what time did he finish eating breakfast?

Writing in Math

10. Explain why this figure is a quadrilateral and a square.

Data Analysis and Probability

MULTIPLE CHOICE

11. On which of the following is this spinner most likely to land?

A. A number less than 5

B. An even number

C. An odd number

D. A number greater than 5

12. You spin the spinner above once. How many possible outcomes are there?

A. 3   **B.** 4   **C.** 5   **D.** 10

FREE RESPONSE

Use the line graph for 13–15.

Book Club Membership

Number of Members (y-axis: 0, 5, 10, 15, 20)
Year (x-axis: 1997, 1998, 1999, 2000)

13. Which year had the most club members?

14. In which year did 14 people belong to the book club?

Writing in Math

15. Explain why a line graph is a good way to display this data.

Algebra

MULTIPLE CHOICE

16. If $x > 5$ and $x < 9$, which of the following could be true?

A. $x = 5$ **C.** $x = 9$

B. $x = 7$ **D.** $x = 10$

17. Which operation sign goes in the ● to make the number sentence true?

$4 ● 17 = 68$

A. +   **B.** −   **C.** ×   **D.** ÷

FREE RESPONSE

18. What is the rule for this table?

In	2	20	200	2,000
Out	8	80	800	8,000

19. Write a number sentence for "4 more than p is 10."

20. Two pens cost $4. Three pens cost $6. Four pens cost $8. How much will nine pens cost?

Writing in Math

TEST TALK

21. How many dots will be in the sixth figure in this pattern? Explain how you found your answer.

Think It Through
I need to **find a pattern** and continue it to find the answer.

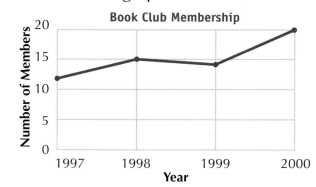

1st   2nd   3rd   4th

Set 11-1 (pages 612–615)

Find $7 \times 4,000$.

Use basic facts and patterns.

$7 \times 4 = 28$ ← **Basic fact**

$\left. \begin{array}{l} 7 \times 40 = 280 \\ 7 \times 400 = 2,800 \\ 7 \times 4,000 = 28,000 \end{array} \right\}$ **Pattern of zeros**

Remember when the product of a basic fact contains a zero, that zero is not part of the pattern.

1. 7×300 **2.** $9 \times 6,000$

3. $4 \times 5,000$ **4.** 5×200

5. 8×900 **6.** $3 \times 3,000$

Set 11-2 (pages 616–617)

Estimate 7×56.

Round 56 to the nearest ten. Then multiply.

7×56

$7 \times 60 = 420$

So, 7×56 is about 420.

Remember that to estimate the product with a 3-digit factor, round that factor to the nearest hundred.

Estimate each product.

1. 5×319 **2.** 8×67

3. 7×42 **4.** 2×769

5. 4×875 **6.** 6×58

Set 11-3 (pages 618–621)

Find $2,000 \div 5$.

Use basic facts and patterns.

$20 \div 5 = 4$ ← **Basic fact**

$\left. \begin{array}{l} 200 \div 5 = 40 \\ 2,000 \div 5 = 400 \end{array} \right\}$ **Pattern of zeros**

Remember that the number of zeros in the dividend (not including the basic fact) will be the number of zeros in the quotient.

1. $480 \div 6$ **2.** $3,600 \div 9$

3. $2,000 \div 4$ **4.** $720 \div 8$

5. How many $5 bills do you need to make $300?

Set 11-4 (pages 622–623)

Estimate $41 \div 8$.

Use a basic division fact.

$41 \div 8$ Think: 41 is close to 40.

$40 \div 8 = 5$

So, $41 \div 8$ is about 5.

Remember that you can think about basic multiplication facts to remember basic division facts.

Estimate each quotient.

1. $35 \div 4$ **2.** $19 \div 2$

3. $60 \div 9$ **4.** $44 \div 7$

Draw an array to find 4×23.

8 tens in all   12 ones in all

$80 + 12 = 92$ So, $4 \times 23 = 92$.

Remember to keep your drawings simple.

Find each product. You may draw a picture to help.

1. 3×27 **2.** 4×18

3. 5×14 **4.** 3×32

Set 11-6 (pages 630–631)

Break apart numbers to find 58×3.

$$
\begin{array}{r}
58 \\
\times\ \ 3 \\
\hline
24 \leftarrow 3 \times 8 = 24 \\
+\ 150 \leftarrow 3 \times 50 = 150 \\
\hline
174 \leftarrow 24 + 150 = 174
\end{array}
$$

Remember to be sure to include a zero when you multiply the tens.

1. 73   **2.** 59
   $\times\ \ 4$ $\times\ \ 2$

3. $35   **4.** 81
   $\times\ \ 6$ $\times\ \ 3$

Set 11-7 (pages 632–635)

Find 27×6.

1
Multiply the ones. Regroup if needed.

2
Multiply the tens. Add any regrouped tens.

$$
\begin{array}{r}
4 \\
27 \\
\times\ 6 \\
\hline
2
\end{array}
\qquad
\begin{array}{r}
4 \\
27 \\
\times\ 6 \\
\hline
162
\end{array}
$$

Remember you can estimate to check that your answer is reasonable.

1. 29   **2.** 42
   $\times\ \ 8$ $\times\ \ 5$

3. $79   **4.** 16
   $\times\ \ 4$ $\times\ \ 9$

5. Driving at 55 miles per hour, how many miles can you travel in 8 hours?

Set 11-8 (pages 636–637)

Find 237×4.

Multiply ones, then tens, then hundreds. Regroup as needed.

$$
\begin{array}{r}
2 \\
237 \\
\times\ 4 \\
\hline
8
\end{array}
\qquad
\begin{array}{r}
1\ 2 \\
237 \\
\times\ 4 \\
\hline
48
\end{array}
\qquad
\begin{array}{r}
1\ 2 \\
237 \\
\times\ 4 \\
\hline
948
\end{array}
$$

Remember to check your answer with an estimated product.

1. 239   **2.** 117
   $\times\ \ 5$ $\times\ \ 8$

3. 129×7 **4.** 4×390

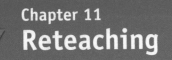

Set 11-9 (pages 638–639)

Find $1.79 × 8.

1	**2**
Multiply the same way as with whole numbers.	Write the answer in dollars and cents.

$$\begin{array}{r} {\scriptstyle 6\ 7} \\ \$1.79 \\ \times \qquad 8 \\ \hline 1432 \end{array}$$

$$\begin{array}{r} {\scriptstyle 6\ 7} \\ \$1.79 \\ \times \qquad 8 \\ \hline \$14.32 \end{array}$$

Remember that multiplication problems with dollars and cents need a dollar sign and a decimal point in the product.

1. $\begin{array}{r} \$4.15 \\ \times \qquad 3 \\ \hline \end{array}$

2. $\begin{array}{r} \$2.08 \\ \times \qquad 6 \\ \hline \end{array}$

3. $2.35 × 8

4. 9 × $0.17

Set 11-10 (pages 640–641)

Find each product.

6 × 3,000
Use mental math.

> 6 × 3 = 18
> 6 × 30 = 180
> 6 × 300 = 1,800
> 6 × 3,000 = 18,000

5 × 104
Use paper and pencil. There are not a lot of regroupings.

$$\begin{array}{r} {\scriptstyle 2} \\ 104 \\ \times \qquad 5 \\ \hline 520 \end{array}$$

9 × 1,468
Use a calculator. There are lots of regroupings.

9 $\boxed{\times}$ 1468 $\boxed{=}$ $\boxed{13212}$

Remember to use the computation method that you think works best for each problem.

1. $\begin{array}{r} 413 \\ \times \quad 2 \\ \hline \end{array}$

2. $\begin{array}{r} 500 \\ \times \quad 9 \\ \hline \end{array}$

3. $\begin{array}{r} 8,000 \\ \times \qquad 7 \\ \hline \end{array}$

4. $\begin{array}{r} 587 \\ \times \quad 6 \\ \hline \end{array}$

5. 340 × 3

6. 8 × 5,409

Set 11-11 (pages 644–645)

When you use logical reasoning to solve a problem, follow these steps.

Step 1: Draw a picture to help organize the information.

Step 2: Fill in the information you are given.

Step 3: Use the picture and reasoning to make conclusions.

Remember that each column and row of your table can have only one YES.

Copy and complete the table to decide who is tallest.

- Tim is the shortest.
- Ben is taller than Ann.

	Tim	Ben	Ann
Tallest	No		
2nd	No		
Shortest	Yes	No	No

Use place-value blocks to find
42 ÷ 3.

Show 42. Draw
3 circles. Put an
equal number of
tens and ones in
each circle.

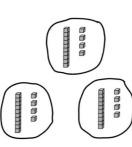

Remember to regroup any leftover
tens as ones.

Use place-value blocks or draw a
picture to find each quotient.

1. 64 ÷ 4   **2.** 36 ÷ 2

3. 78 ÷ 6   **4.** 84 ÷ 7

5. 80 ÷ 5   **6.** 63 ÷ 3

Break numbers apart to find 69 ÷ 3.

Divide the tens: 60 ÷ 3 = 20

Divide the ones: 9 ÷ 3 = 3

Add the two quotients: 20 + 3 = 23

So, 69 ÷ 3 = 23.

Remember to break apart the
dividend into tens and ones.

1. 28 ÷ 2   **2.** 55 ÷ 5

3. 36 ÷ 3   **4.** 84 ÷ 4

5. 64 ÷ 2   **6.** 93 ÷ 3

Find 75 ÷ 4.

1	**2**	**3**	**4**
Divide the tens.	Regroup tens and combine ones.	Divide the ones.	Record the remainder.

$$\begin{array}{r} 1 \\ 4\overline{)75} \\ -4 \\ \hline 3 \end{array}$$

$$\begin{array}{r} 1 \\ 4\overline{)75} \\ -4\downarrow \\ \hline 35 \end{array}$$

$$\begin{array}{r} 18 \\ 4\overline{)75} \\ -4\downarrow \\ \hline 35 \\ -32 \\ \hline 3 \end{array}$$

$$\begin{array}{r} 18\ R3 \\ 4\overline{)75} \\ -4\downarrow \\ \hline 35 \\ -32 \\ \hline 3 \end{array}$$

Remember you can multiply and add
to check your answer.

1. 75 ÷ 5   **2.** 49 ÷ 4

3. 29 ÷ 2   **4.** 80 ÷ 6

5. How do you know when to write
a remainder?

Each ticket costs $5. If Al has $27,
how many tickets can he buy?

$$\begin{array}{r} 5\ R2 \\ 5\overline{)27} \\ -25 \\ \hline 2 \end{array}$$

Interpret the Remainder:
The $2 left over is not enough money
to buy another ticket.

So, Al can buy 5 tickets.

Remember that the real-world
situation will help you decide how
to interpret the remainder.

1. There are 65 dolls to mail. Each
box holds up to 7 dolls. How
many boxes are needed?

Set 11-1 (pages 612–615)

Use mental math to find each product.

1. 6 × 100   **2.** 3 × 1,000   **3.** 8 × 100   **4.** 1 × 1,000

5. 2 × 500   **6.** 7 × 2,000   **7.** 5 × 700   **8.** 3 × 800

9. A century is 100 years. How many years are in 5 centuries?

Set 11-2 (pages 616–617)

Estimate each product.

1. 8 × 17   **2.** 4 × 32   **3.** 9 × 28   **4.** 5 × 64

5. 2 × 45   **6.** 7 × 81   **7.** 3 × 762   **8.** 6 × 304

9. Dana put 18 cheese cubes on each of 4 plates. Did she use more than 100 cubes? Explain.

Set 11-3 (pages 618–621)

Use patterns and mental math to find each quotient.

1. 56 ÷ 8   **2.** 24 ÷ 3   **3.** 40 ÷ 5   **4.** 54 ÷ 9
560 ÷ 8   240 ÷ 3   400 ÷ 5   540 ÷ 9
5,600 ÷ 8   2,400 ÷ 3   4,000 ÷ 5   5,400 ÷ 9

Use mental math to find each quotient.

5. 420 ÷ 7   **6.** 6,300 ÷ 7   **7.** 210 ÷ 3   **8.** 3,000 ÷ 5

9. Jon has 450 fliers to send to 9 stores. If he sends the same number to each store, how many will each get?

Set 11-4 (pages 622–623)

Estimate each quotient.

1. 36 ÷ 5   **2.** 80 ÷ 9   **3.** 52 ÷ 8   **4.** 17 ÷ 2

5. 24 ÷ 9   **6.** 16 ÷ 3   **7.** 48 ÷ 7   **8.** 40 ÷ 6

9. Ben worked 29 hours in 7 days. About how many hours did he work each day?

Take It to the NET
More Practice
www.scottforesman.com

Set 11-5 (pages 626–629)

Find each product. You may draw a picture to help.

1. 4 × 27

2. 3 × 19

3. 6 × 31   **4.** 5 × 24   **5.** 4 × 17   **6.** 7 × 18

7. There are 52 weeks in one year. How many weeks are there in 3 years?

Set 11-6 (pages 630–631)

Find each product.

1. 6 × 58   **2.** 4 × 75   **3.** 3 × 28   **4.** 9 × 17

5. 5 × 32   **6.** 7 × 49   **7.** 6 × 13   **8.** 8 × 64

9. 6 × 27   **10.** 9 × 35   **11.** 4 × 91   **12.** 5 × 68

13. A case contains 24 cans of juice. Bill bought 8 cases of juice for the class picnic. How many cans of juice did he buy?

Set 11-7 (pages 632–635)

Find each product. Decide if your answer is reasonable.

1. 27 × 5   **2.** 84 × 3   **3.** $51 × 9   **4.** 15 × 7   **5.** 48 × 4

6. 54 × 8   **7.** 17 × 9   **8.** 24 × 7   **9.** 92 × 3   **10.** 87 × 2

11. 6 × 51   **12.** 36 × 5   **13.** 62 × 7   **14.** 25 × 9

15. There are 36 inches in 1 yard. Tamika used 5 yards of cloth to make a dress. How many inches of cloth did she use?

Set 11-8 (pages 636–637)

Find each product. Estimate to check reasonableness.

1. 117
  × 8

2. 245
  × 6

3. 504
  × 3

4. 625
  × 4

5. 711
  × 5

6. 4 × 329   **7.** 112 × 8   **8.** 670 × 5   **9.** 3 × 502

10. Will lives 475 miles from his grandparents in Miami. How many miles will he drive in all to visit them and then drive home?

Set 11-9 (pages 638–639)

Find each product. Estimate to check reasonableness.

1. $2.19
  × 5

2. $1.75
  × 4

3. $3.12
  × 8

4. $0.63
  × 6

5. $4.08
  × 9

6. 7 × $1.08   **7.** 3 × $4.25   **8.** 9 × $2.70   **9.** 5 × $0.79

10. Each granola bar costs $1.59. Tim buys 8 granola bars. How much do they cost in all?

Set 11-10 (pages 640–641)

Find each product. Tell which computation method you used.

1. 300
  × 8

2. 75
  × 4

3. 659
  × 6

4. 1,400
  × 2

5. 16
  × 9

6. Which computation method would you use to find 7 × 125? Explain.

Set 11-11 (pages 644–645)

1. Copy and complete the table to decide who is first in line.

- Mei is second.

- Ben is NOT third

- Ali is last.

	Ali	Ben	Joe	Mei
1st				No
2nd	No	No	No	Yes
3rd				No
4th				No

Take It to the NET
More Practice
www.scottforesman.com

Set 11-12 (pages 648–649)

Use place-value blocks or draw a picture to find each quotient.

1. 52 ÷ 4   **2.** 72 ÷ 8   **3.** 48 ÷ 3   **4.** 63 ÷ 3

5. 75 ÷ 5   **6.** 96 ÷ 3   **7.** 108 ÷ 12   **8.** 84 ÷ 4

9. How can you tell that 58 ÷ 2 is greater than 20 without dividing?

Set 11-13 (pages 650–651)

Use the break apart method to find each quotient. You may draw a picture to help.

1. 39 ÷ 3   **2.** 84 ÷ 4   **3.** 48 ÷ 2   **4.** 66 ÷ 3

5. 4)48   **6.** 2)68   **7.** 3)93   **8.** 9)99

9. Kelly says that 82 ÷ 2 = 40 + 2. Is she correct? Explain.

Set 11-14 (pages 652–655)

Copy and complete. Check your answers.

1.
```
    1 ▦
 3)54
 - 3
   2 ▦
 - ▦▦
   0
```
2.
```
    1 ▦
 7)91
 - 7
   2 ▦
 - ▦▦
   0
```
3.
```
    8 R ▦
 6)52
 - ▦▦
   ▦
```
4.
```
   ▦▦ R ▦
 5)73
 - ▦
   ▦▦
 - ▦▦
   ▦
```

Divide. Check your answers.

5. 2)35   **6.** 7)84   **7.** 4)62   **8.** 3)78

9. Karen made 68 cookies for the bake sale. She put 4 cookies in each bag. How many bags did she fill?

Set 11-15 (pages 656–657)

Solve. Write each answer in a complete sentence.

1. There are 52 students going on a field trip. Each van can hold 8 students. How many vans are needed to drive all the students?

Measurement and Probability

DIAGNOSING READINESS

A Vocabulary
(pages 498–502, 532)

Choose the best term from the box.

1. You can use __?__ to name equal parts of a whole.

2. The __?__ of a fraction tells how many equal parts there are in all.

3. Feet and __?__ are two customary units of length.

Vocabulary
- **inches** *(p. 532)*
- **denominator** *(p. 502)*
- **fractions** *(p. 498)*
- **numerator** *(p. 502)*

B Multiplying and Dividing *(pages 612–655)*

4. 5×16

5. 3×24

6. $7 \times 1,000$

7. 6×900

8. $8,000 \div 8$

9. $16 \div 2$

10. $36 \div 3$

11. $50 \div 2$

12. 15×100

13. $3,200 \div 4$

14. Max had a board 12 feet long. He cut it into 3 equal pieces. How long was each piece?

Do You Know...

How much heavier is a person's brain than the brain of a stegosaurus?

You'll find out in Lesson 12-11.

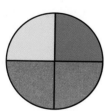

C Writing Fractions

(pages 502–503)

15. What fraction of the circle is red?

16. What fraction of the circle is yellow?

17. Six friends went to a movie. Three of them bought popcorn. What fraction of the group bought popcorn?

D Comparing

(pages 18–21, 506–509, 582–585)

Compare. Use <, >, or =.

18. 3,000 ⬤ 2,500

19. 380 ⬤ 391

20. 2 × 100 ⬤ 200

21. 2,700 ⬤ 3 × 1,000

22. 4 × 12 ⬤ 40

23. $\frac{3}{4}$ ⬤ $\frac{2}{4}$ **24.** $\frac{1}{6}$ ⬤ $\frac{5}{6}$

25. Which is longer, 3 meters or 3 centimeters?

Key Idea
We use special units to tell how much liquid a container will hold.

Vocabulary
• capacity
• cup (c)
• pint (pt)
• quart (qt)
• gallon (gal)

Materials
• measuring cup
• a variety of pint, quart, and gallon containers
• a variety of unmarked containers
• water

Think It Through
• I can **use objects** to compare units of capacity.
• I can **make a table** to record what I find.

Customary Units of Capacity

LEARN

Activity

How much does a container hold?

The **capacity** of a container is the amount a container will hold. Some customary units of capacity are shown below.

cup (c)   **pint (pt)**   **quart (qt)**   **gallon (gal)**

Copy and complete the table below. You will need water and containers for 1 cup, 1 pint, 1 quart, and 1 gallon.

Size of Container	Number of			
	Cups	Pints	Quarts	Gallons
Cup	1	0	0	0
Pint		1	0	0
Quart			1	0
Gallon				1

a. Use a measuring cup and a pint container. Fill the cup with water to the "1 cup" mark. Pour the water into the pint container. Repeat until the pint container is filled. Record the number of cups in a pint.

b. Use cup, pint, and quart containers. Measure to complete the row in the table for quarts.

c. Use cup, pint, quart, and gallon containers. Measure to complete the row in the table for gallons.

d. Copy and complete.

1 pint = ▢ cups   1 quart = ▢ pints   1 gallon = ▢ quarts

e. Use other containers. Estimate how much each will hold. Then measure to check your estimate.

How can you change from one unit of capacity to another?

Example A

Eight quarts is how many gallons?

8 qt = ☐ gal

You know that 4 quarts make a gallon, so **divide** 8 by 4 to find the number of gallons.
$8 \div 4 = 2$, so 8 qt = 2 gal.

8 qt = 2 gal

Example B

Ten gallons is how many quarts?

10 gal = ☐ qt

You know that there are 4 quarts in a gallon, so **multiply** 10 by 4 to find the number of quarts.
$10 \times 4 = 40$, so 10 gal = 40 qt.

10 gal = 40 qt

✔ Talk About It

1. In Examples A and B, how could you check the answers?

2. How many cups are in 3 quarts? Explain how you found your answer.

3. **Reasoning** Why do you divide when changing from a smaller unit to a larger unit? Why do you multiply when changing from a larger unit to a smaller unit?

CHECK ✔

For another example, see Set 12-1 on p. 722.

Estimate Choose the better estimate for each.

1.	2.	3.	4.
1 c or 1 qt	25 qt or 25 gal	3 pt or 3 gal	2 c or 2 qt

Find each missing number.

5. 2 pt = ☐ qt   **6.** 2 c = ☐ pt   **7.** 4 qt = ☐ gal   **8.** 4 pt = ☐ c

9. 16 qt = ☐ gal   **10.** 3 gal = ☐ qt   **11.** 5 qt = ☐ pt   **12.** 10 c = ☐ pt

13. Reasoning Which is more orange juice, 1 quart or 3 pints? Explain.

A Skills and Understanding

Estimate Choose the better estimate for each.

14.

2c or 2 qt

15.

1 c or 1 gal

16.

50 pt or 50 gal

17.

1 c or 1 qt

Find each missing number.

18. 1 gal = ▢ qt   **19.** 2 pt = ▢ qt   **20.** 1 pt = ▢ c

21. 2 gal = ▢ qt   **22.** 8 pt = ▢ qt   **23.** 12 qt = ▢ gal

24. 8 qt = ▢ pt   **25.** 20 pt = ▢ qt   **26.** 16 c = ▢ pt

27. Which is more, 3 cups of juice or 1 pint of juice?

28. Which is less, 5 quarts of milk or 1 gallon of milk?

29. Number Sense How many pints is 3 qt 2 pt?

> **TEST TALK**
>
> **Think It Through**
> - To **change a smaller unit to a larger unit,** I divide.
> - To **change a larger unit to a smaller unit,** I multiply.

B Reasoning and Problem Solving

Math and Science

Water is one of the most important things in our diets. Use the information below the picture to solve each problem.

30. How many cups of water should a child drink in a day?

31. How many pints of water should an adult drink each day?

32. Is the amount of water an adult should drink each day more than, less than, or equal to a quart of water?

33. **Writing in Math** The milk that Jason gets at school comes in a $\frac{1}{2}$-pint carton. Explain how you can find the number of cups in $\frac{1}{2}$ pint.

Adults should drink about 8 cups of water a day. Children should drink about 3 pints of water a day.

C Extensions

Three other units of capacity are shown. Use the relationships to answer the questions.

teaspoon (tsp)    tablespoon (tbsp)

3 tsp = 1 tbsp

fluid ounce (fl oz)

1 c = 8 fl oz

34. Three tablespoons of lemon juice equal how many teaspoons of juice?

35. Two cups of lemonade equal how many fluid ounces of lemonade?

Mixed Review and Test Prep

Take It to the NET
Test Prep
www.scottforesman.com

36. Find 216×5.

37. Find $84 \div 4$.

38. Find $63 \div 8$.

39. Pauline poured 32 cups of soup into bowls that hold 3 cups each. How many cups of soup were left over?

A. 10 cups   **B.** 3 cups   **C.** 2 cups   **D.** 32 cups

Enrichment

Measuring Dry Materials

In this lesson you measured liquids. You can also measure dry materials using some of the same units.

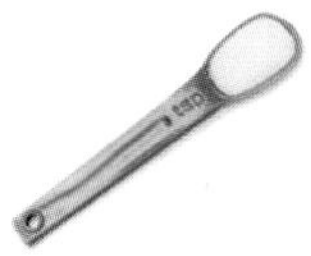

teaspoon of baking powder

tablespoon of butter

cup of flour

pint of blueberries

quart of strawberries

1. In the recipe shown at the right, list the dry ingredients including the butter. Tell what unit is used to measure each of them.

2. In the shortcake recipe, is the amount of baking powder more than or less than 1 tablespoon?

3. List three other dry ingredients that you might measure in teaspoons or tablespoons.

Strawberry Shortcake

2 cups flour
4 teaspoons baking powder
6 tablespoons of butter
1 cup milk
1 quart strawberries, sliced

Key Idea
Capacity can
be measured
using metric
units, as well as
customary units.

Vocabulary
• milliliter (mL)
• liter (L)

Materials
• liter bottles
• eyedropper
 marked in
 milliliters
• measuring
 cups marked
 in milliliters
• liter containers
• spoon and
 drinking glass
• quart container
• water

Milliliters and Liters

LEARN

Activity

How can you measure capacity with metric units?

A **milliliter (mL)** and a **liter (L)** are metric units that measure capacity.

A milliliter is about 20 drops from an eyedropper.

The water bottle holds
1 liter (L) of water.

1 L = 1,000 mL

a. Use an eyedropper, a spoon, and water. Find the capacity of a spoon in milliliters.

b. Use a 100 mL container, a drinking glass, and water. Find the capacity of the glass in milliliters.

c. How many drinking glasses can you fill with 1 liter of water?

d. Use other containers. Estimate how much they will hold. Then measure to check your estimate.

e. Use a liter container and a quart container. Which is more, a liter or a quart?

How do you change between liters and milliliters?

Example A

2,000 mL = ▢ L

You know that
1,000 mL = 1 L
so 2,000 mL = 2 × 1 L

2,000 mL = 2 L

Example B

3 L = ▢ mL

You know that
1 L = 1,000 mL,
so 3 L = 3 × 1,000 mL.

3 L = 3,000 mL

3 × 1,000 mL = 3,000 mL

✔ **Talk About It**

1. Two liters of milk is how many milliliters of milk?

Estimation Choose the better estimate for each.

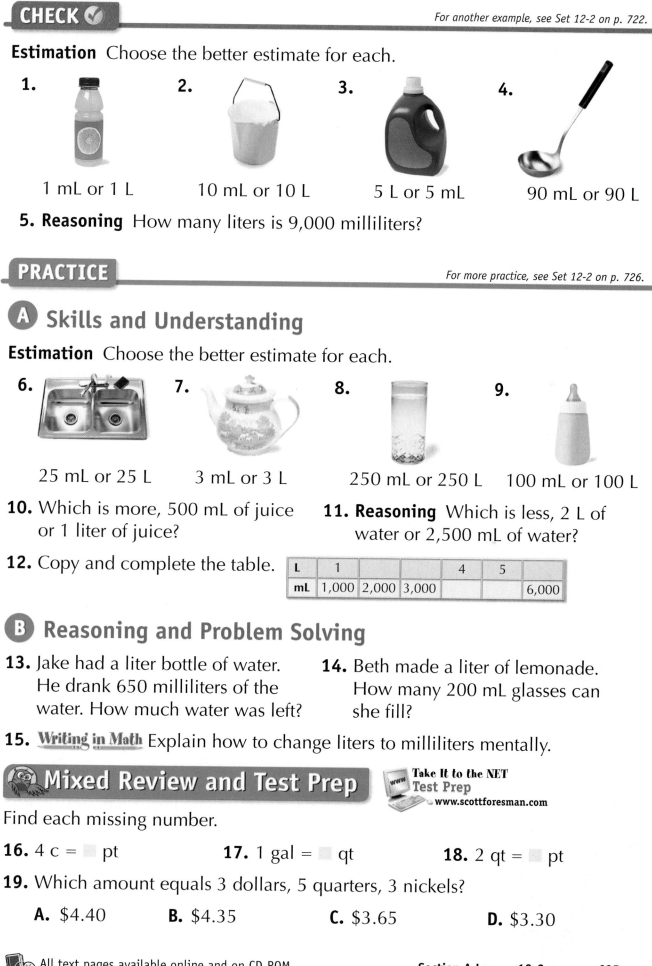

1.

1 mL or 1 L

2.

10 mL or 10 L

3.

5 L or 5 mL

4.

90 mL or 90 L

5. Reasoning How many liters is 9,000 milliliters?

PRACTICE

For more practice, see Set 12-2 on p. 726.

Ⓐ Skills and Understanding

Estimation Choose the better estimate for each.

6.

25 mL or 25 L

7.

3 mL or 3 L

8.

250 mL or 250 L

9.

100 mL or 100 L

10. Which is more, 500 mL of juice or 1 liter of juice?

11. Reasoning Which is less, 2 L of water or 2,500 mL of water?

12. Copy and complete the table.

L	1			4	5	
mL	1,000	2,000	3,000			6,000

Ⓑ Reasoning and Problem Solving

13. Jake had a liter bottle of water. He drank 650 milliliters of the water. How much water was left?

14. Beth made a liter of lemonade. How many 200 mL glasses can she fill?

15. Writing in Math Explain how to change liters to milliliters mentally.

Mixed Review and Test Prep

Take It to the NET
Test Prep
www.scottforesman.com

Find each missing number.

16. 4 c = ▨ pt

17. 1 gal = ▨ qt

18. 2 qt = ▨ pt

19. Which amount equals 3 dollars, 5 quarters, 3 nickels?

    A. $4.40   **B.** $4.35   **C.** $3.65   **D.** $3.30

All text pages available online and on CD-ROM.

Identify Steps in a Process

Identifying the steps in a process when you read in math can help you use the **problem-solving strategy, *Work Backward,*** in the next lesson.

In reading, identifying the steps in a process can help you organize what you read. In math, it can help you work backward to solve problems in which you know the result of a series of steps.

*First I'll **identify the steps** in the problem.*

Andrew's aunt gave him some money for his birthday. He bought a cap for $6 and a puzzle book for $2. He has $7 left. How much money did his aunt give him?

Draw a diagram to show the steps and the result.

Birthday money $? → Cap − $6 → Puzzle book − $2 → Money left $7

Birthday money $? ← Cap + $6 ← Puzzle book + $2 ← Money left $7

*Then **work backward** from the result doing the reverse of each step.*

1. How many steps from the starting number were taken to get the result $7?

2. As you work backward, how do you reverse the step where Andrew bought a puzzle book?

For 3–6, use the problem below.

Jamal's father gave him some spending money for his school trip to the Wisconsin Dells. In the morning he bought a souvenir for $4. Then he spent $6 for a car ride and $5 for lunch. He had $5 left. How much money did his father give him?

3. Draw a diagram to show the steps in the problem.

4. What is the result in this problem? How many steps from the beginning were taken to get the result?

5. Now work backward. How can you reverse the step where Jamal spent $5 for lunch?

6. **Writing in Math** Explain the steps you would take to find out how much money Jamal's father gave him.

For 7–10, use the bus schedule at the right and the problem below.

Dana is taking the Blue Haven Express bus. It takes her 20 minutes to walk to the station. She needs 10 minutes to buy her ticket and 15 minutes to check her luggage. At what time should she leave her house for the bus station?

Cape Loris Buses	
Bus	**Time**
Ambassador	1:30 P.M.
Pioneer Regal	3:45 P.M.
Blue Haven Express	6:15 P.M.
Trailblazer	8:00 P.M.

7. Draw a diagram to show the steps in the problem.

8. What is the result in this problem? How many steps from the beginning were taken to get the result?

9. Now work backward. How can you reverse the step where Dana walks to the station?

10. **Writing in Math** Tony says that Dana should leave for the station at 5:10 P.M. How can you check if Tony's answer is correct?

Problem-Solving Strategy

Key Idea
Learning how and when to work backward can help you solve problems.

Think It Through
I need to **reverse the steps** that end at 8:15 A.M., to find the starting time.

Work Backward

LEARN

How do you work backward to solve a problem?

School Start School starts at 8:15 A.M. It takes Lydia 30 minutes to walk to school, 15 minutes to eat, and 30 minutes to get ready. What time should she get up?

Read and Understand

What do you know?

Lydia needs to be at school by 8:15 A.M. She needs 30 minutes to walk, 15 minutes to eat, and 30 minutes to get ready.

What are you trying to find?

Find the time she should get up.

Plan and Solve

What strategy will you use?

Strategy: **Work Backward**

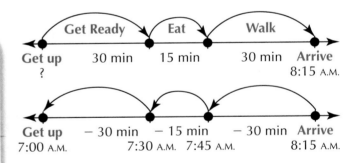

How to Work Backward

Step 1 Identify what is unknown at the beginning.

Step 2 Draw a picture to show each change, starting from the beginning.

Step 3 From the end, work backward, using the opposite of each change.

Answer: Lydia should get up at 7:00 A.M.

Look Back and Check

Is your answer reasonable?

Yes, I worked backward from 8:15 by subtracting the times. I subtracted correctly.

✔ Talk About It

1. What does the "?" on the first number line represent?

2. What do − 30, − 15, and − 30 on the second number line mean?

For another example, see Set 12-3 on p. 723.

Solve the problem by working backward. Write the answer in a complete sentence.

1. It took Ann 45 minutes to hike from camp to Shelter Cove. She stayed at Shelter Cove for 20 minutes. Then it took her 25 minutes to walk to the beach. She arrived at the beach at 11:45 A.M. When did she leave camp?

PRACTICE

For more practice, see Set 12-3 on p. 727.

Solve each problem. Write the answer in a complete sentence.

2. Krista, Howard, and Jo are hiking near camp. Howard is in front of Krista. Jo is between Howard and Krista. Who is first in line?

3. Jose left camp at 12:30 P.M. It took him 15 minutes to walk to the dock. He spent 10 minutes on the dock. Then it took him 40 minutes to paddle a canoe to Lost Island. At what time did he arrive at Lost Island?

4. The coach can pick Jake, Lee, and Ron to be pitcher, catcher, and shortstop. How many different ways can the coach pick the 3 players for the 3 different positions?

5. Lois cut a piece of ribbon into two equal pieces. Then she cut 12 inches off one of the pieces. This piece is now 30 inches long. How long was the original piece of ribbon?

6. After Gwen spent $2.75 for food and $1.25 for bottled water, she had $6.00 left. How much did she have before she bought the food and water?

7. <u>Writing in Math</u> Write and explain how you found the answer to Exercise 4.

STRATEGIES

- **Show What You Know**
  Draw a Picture
  Make an Organized List
  Make a Table
  Make a Graph
  Act It Out or Use Objects
- **Look for a Pattern**
- **Try, Check, and Revise**
- **Write a Number Sentence**
- **Use Logical Reasoning**
- **Solve a Simpler Problem**
- **Work Backward**

Choose a tool

Mental Math

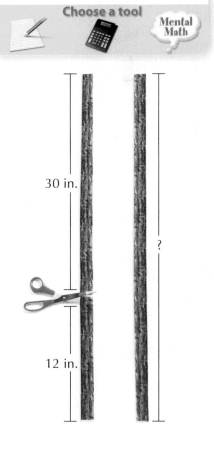

30 in.

?

12 in.

Key Idea
We use special units to tell how heavy an object is.

Vocabulary
• ounce (oz)
• pound (lb)

Materials
• pan balance
• ounce and pound weights
• objects to weigh

Think It Through
• I can **use objects** to compare weights.
• I can **make a table** to record the weights.

Customary Units of Weight

LEARN

Activity

How much does an object weigh?

In the customary system, **ounces (oz)** and **pounds (lb)** are used to measure weight.

Ten pennies weigh about 1 ounce.

One hundred sixty pennies weigh about 1 pound.
1 lb = 16 oz

Copy the table below. Find 4 objects to weigh.

Estimate

Object	Less than 1 lb	1 lb	More than 1 lb	Actual Weight

a. Select an object. Write the name of the object in the table. Hold the object in one hand and a 1-pound weight in the other. Estimate the object's weight as more than 1 pound, about 1 pound, or less than 1 pound. Write your estimate in the table.

b. Now use a balance. Put the object on one side and ounce or pound weights on the other. If the object weighs less than 1 pound, find the weight in ounces. If the object weighs more than 1 pound, give the weight as ▮ lb ▮ oz.

c. Repeat Steps a and b for other objects.

How do you change between pounds and ounces?

Example A

A 2-pound bag of trail mix contains how many ounces?

2 lb = ▨ oz

1 lb = 16 oz
2 × 16 oz = 32 oz

2 lb = 32 oz

A 2-pound bag of trail mix contains 32 ounces.

Example B

An 18-ounce bag of peanuts contains how many pounds and ounces?

18 oz = ▨ lb ▨ oz

You can think of 18 oz as 16 oz + 2 oz.
Then you can replace 16 oz with l lb.

18 oz = 16 oz + 2 oz
18 oz = 1 lb 2 oz

An 18-ounce bag of peanuts contains 1 pound 2 ounces.

✔ Talk About It

1. Write 1 lb 5 oz in ounces.

2. Write 28 oz as pounds and ounces.

3. Number Sense Is 35 ounces more than or less than 2 pounds? Explain.

 CHECK ✔

For another example, see Set 12-4 on p. 723.

Estimation Choose the better estimate for each weight.

1.

1 lb or 6 oz

2.

3 oz or 3 lb

3.

10 oz or 10 lb

4.

2 lb or 2 oz

Find each missing number.

5. 1 lb = ▨ oz   **6.** 3 lb = ▨ oz   **7.** 10 lb = ▨ oz

8. 1 lb 8 oz = ▨ oz   **9.** 1 lb 3 oz = ▨ oz   **10.** 20 oz = 1 lb ▨ oz

11. Number Sense Kara's puppy Skipper weighed 3 lb 10 oz last month. He now weighs 4 lb 2 oz. Did he gain more or less than 1 pound?

Skills and Understanding

Choose the better estimate for each weight.

12. envelope

2 oz or 2 lb

13. turkey

15 oz or 15 lb

14. 3rd-grade boy

60 oz or 60 lb

15. apple

5 oz or 5 lb

Find each missing number.

16. 4 lb = ■ oz

17. 8 lb = ■ oz

18. 1 lb 12 oz = ■ oz

19. 2 lb 3 oz = ■ oz

20. 24 oz = 1 lb ■ oz

21. 17 oz = ■ lb ■ oz

22. Number Sense How many ounces are in $\frac{1}{2}$ pound? Explain.

B **Reasoning and Problem Solving**

Math and Science

Your brain reached full size when you were 6 years old. It weighs about 3 pounds.

23. How much heavier is a dolphin's brain than your brain?

Dolphin's brain: 3 lb 5 oz   *Chimpanzee's brain: 15 oz*

24. A chimpanzee's brain is how much less than one pound?

25. How much heavier is a whale's brain than your brain?

26. **Writing in Math** Is Ryan's statement correct or incorrect? Explain.

A dog's brain weighs more than a kangaroo's brain, but less than a chimpanzee's brain.

Dog's brain: $\frac{1}{4}$ lb

Whale's brain: 17 lb 1 oz   *Kangaroo's brain: 2 oz*

C Extensions

Explain what you would measure and what customary units you would use to find

27. the space the fish tank takes on a tabletop.

28. the amount of water the fish tank holds.

29. how heavy the fish tank is.

Mixed Review and Test Prep

Take It to the NET
Test Prep
www.scottforesman.com

30. Leon bought an eraser for 25¢ and 2 pencils for 20¢ each. After buying these things, he had 10¢ left. How much money did Leon have before he bought the eraser and pencils?

31. Which is the best estimate of the amount of lemonade a pitcher will hold ?

A. 20 L   **B.** 20 mL   **C.** 2 L   **D.** 2 mL

Learning with Technology

Money eTool

Find the amount of money Sam started with, using the Money eTool. Sam bought 1 lb 2 oz of bananas at 6 cents an ounce. He then bought 2 lb 3 oz of lunch meat at 28 cents an ounce. He had $2.15 left over.

1. Change the weights of the bananas and the lunch meat to ounces.

2. Multiply the weight, in ounces, by the price of each item per ounce.

3. Place your two amounts in the workspace with the odometer turned on.

Amount

4. What other amount should you place in the workspace to find out how much money Sam started with? How much money did Sam have before he bought the bananas and lunch meat?

All text pages available online and on CD-ROM.

Key Idea
There are metric units, as well as customary units, to tell how heavy an object is.

Vocabulary
- gram (g)
- kilogram (kg)

Materials
- pan balance
- gram and kilogram weights
- pound weights
- objects to weigh

Think It Through
I can **use objects** to find relationships between units of metric measure.

Grams and Kilograms

LEARN

Activity

How can I tell how heavy an object is using metric measures?

In the metric system, **grams (g)** and **kilograms (kg)** are metric units that tell how heavy an object is.

1 g

1 kg
1,000 g = 1 kg

a. Hold five paper clips in one hand. Find an object that you think is about as heavy as the paper clips. Now use a balance to check your estimate.

b. Find an object that you think is about as heavy as a baseball bat. Check your estimate.

c. Select other objects. Estimate how heavy each is in metric units. Then check your estimate.

d. Use the balance and weights. Find out which is heavier, 1 kilogram or 1 pound.

How do you change between units?

Example A	Example B
Estimation Would 1,000 g or 10 kg better describe how heavy a dog is?	5 kg = ▨ g
1,000 g = 1 kg Most dogs are heavier than a baseball bat.	1 kg = 1,000 g, so 5 kg = 5 × 1,000 g
10 kg is a better estimate.	**5 kg = 5,000 g**

✓ **Talk About It**

1. In Example B, why were 5 and 1,000 multiplied?

Choose the better estimate.

1.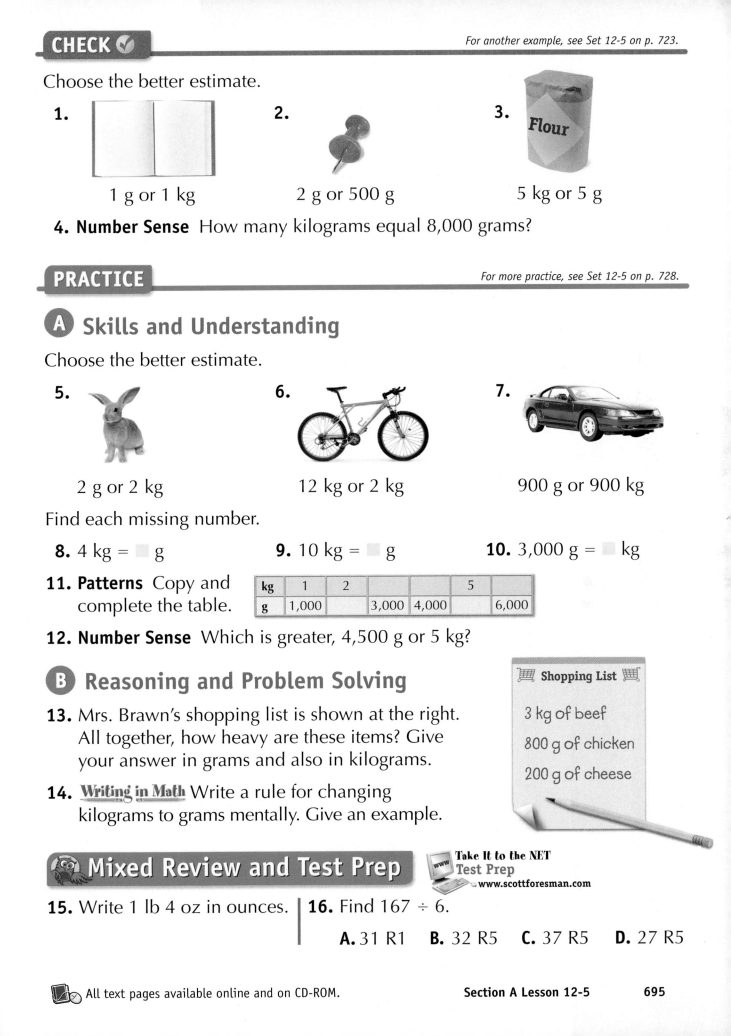

1 g or 1 kg

2.

2 g or 500 g

3.

Flour

5 kg or 5 g

4. Number Sense How many kilograms equal 8,000 grams?

PRACTICE

For more practice, see Set 12-5 on p. 728.

(A) Skills and Understanding

Choose the better estimate.

5.

2 g or 2 kg

6.

12 kg or 2 kg

7.

900 g or 900 kg

Find each missing number.

8. 4 kg = ▮ g

9. 10 kg = ▮ g

10. 3,000 g = ▮ kg

11. Patterns Copy and complete the table.

kg	1	2			5	
g	1,000		3,000	4,000		6,000

12. Number Sense Which is greater, 4,500 g or 5 kg?

(B) Reasoning and Problem Solving

13. Mrs. Brawn's shopping list is shown at the right. All together, how heavy are these items? Give your answer in grams and also in kilograms.

14. **Writing in Math** Write a rule for changing kilograms to grams mentally. Give an example.

🛒 **Shopping List** 🛒

3 kg of beef

800 g of chicken

200 g of cheese

Mixed Review and Test Prep

Take It to the NET
Test Prep
www.scottforesman.com

15. Write 1 lb 4 oz in ounces.

16. Find 167 ÷ 6.

A. 31 R1   **B.** 32 R5   **C.** 37 R5   **D.** 27 R5

Vocabulary
• thermometer
• degrees Fahrenheit (°F)
• degrees Celsius (°C)

Temperature

LEARN

WARM UP
1. $5\overline{)97}$ 2. $3\overline{)119}$
3. $2\overline{)76}$ 4. $2\overline{)38}$

How are temperatures measured?

A **thermometer** measures temperatures in **degrees Fahrenheit (°F)** or in **degrees Celsius (°C).**

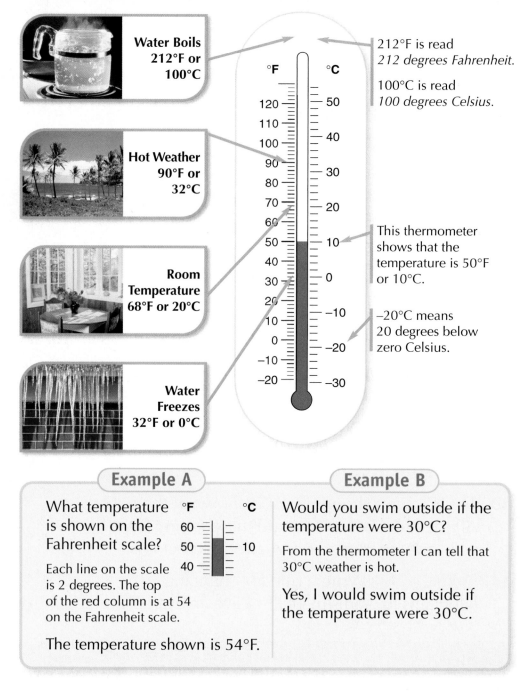

Water Boils
212°F or 100°C

212°F is read *212 degrees Fahrenheit.*

100°C is read *100 degrees Celsius.*

Hot Weather
90°F or 32°C

This thermometer shows that the temperature is 50°F or 10°C.

Room Temperature
68°F or 20°C

−20°C means 20 degrees below zero Celsius.

Water Freezes
32°F or 0°C

Example A

What temperature is shown on the Fahrenheit scale?

Each line on the scale is 2 degrees. The top of the red column is at 54 on the Fahrenheit scale.

The temperature shown is 54°F.

Example B

Would you swim outside if the temperature were 30°C?

From the thermometer I can tell that 30°C weather is hot.

Yes, I would swim outside if the temperature were 30°C.

Talk About It

1. **Estimation** What do you think the temperature is in your classroom, 70°F or 95°F?

696

CHECK ✓

Write each temperature using °C.

1.

2.

3.

4.

5. **Reasoning** Would you wear a winter coat outside if the temperature was 25°C?

PRACTICE

For more practice, see Set 12-6 on p. 728.

A Skills and Understanding

Write each temperature using °F.

6.

7.

8.

9.

Estimate Choose the better temperature for each activity.

10. ice skating
25°F or 45°F

11. raking leaves
10°C or 0°C

12. swimming
80°C or 30°C

13. bicycling
15°F or 50°F

14. In 10–13, describe each temperature as *hot, warm, cool,* or *cold.*

B Reasoning and Problem Solving

15. **Writing in Math** In the book *Sugarbush Spring*, Molly's family collects sap and makes maple syrup. To boil into syrup, the sap must reach a temperature of 219°F. How much hotter is this than the temperature at which water boils? Explain your answer.

Mixed Review and Test Prep

Take It to the NET
Test Prep
www.scottforesman.com

Find each missing number.

16. 1 kg = ▧ g

17. 6 kg = ▧ g

18. 4,000 g = ▧ kg

19. Find $50.83 − $36.58.

A. $14.25

B. $14.35

C. $24.25

D. $24.35

Do You Know How?

Do You Understand?

Customary Units of Capacity (12-1)
Customary Units of Weight (12-4)

Find each missing number.

1. 4 c = ▩ pt   **2.** 2 gal = ▩ qt

3. 6 pt = ▩ qt   **4.** 3 lb = ▩ oz

5. Is the capacity of a large bucket 10 c or 10 qt?

6. Would a letter weigh 4 oz or 4 lb?

Ⓐ Explain how you found your answer for Exercise 2.

Ⓑ In Exercise 6, how did you decide which is the better estimate for the weight of a letter?

Milliliters and Liters (12-2)
Grams and Kilograms (12-5)

Find each missing number.

7. 5 L = ▩ mL   **8.** 3 kg = ▩ g

9. Would a mug hold 200 mL or 2 L?

10. How heavy is a cat, 8 g or 8 kg?

Ⓒ Explain how you found the number of grams in 3 kg.

Ⓓ Compare 200 mL and 2 L. Which is more? How much more?

Temperature (12-6)

Write the temperature shown.

11. in °C   **12.** in °F

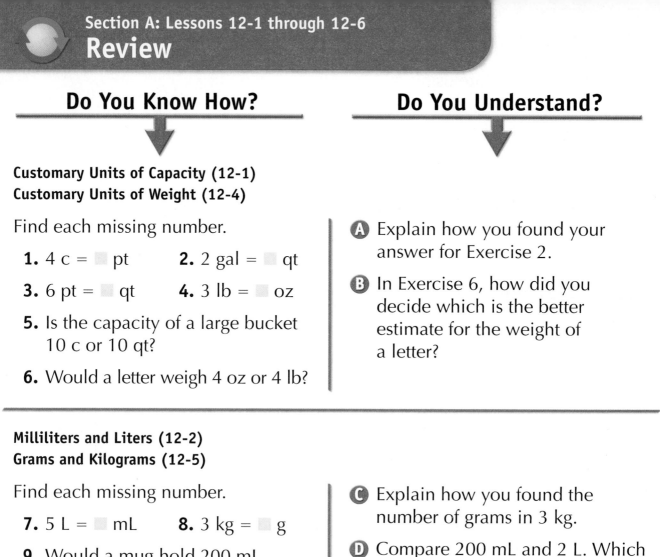

Ⓔ Describe the temperature shown on the thermometer as *hot, warm, cool,* or *cold.*

Problem-Solving Strategy: Work Backward (12-3)

13. Toni spent $0.55 for a folder, $0.39 for a pencil, and $1.25 for paper. Then she had $0.75 left. How much did Toni have before she bought these items?

Ⓕ Explain how you worked backward to find the answer for Exercise 13.

MULTIPLE CHOICE

1. How many ounces are in 1 pound 6 ounces? (12-4)

A. 7 oz   **B.** 112 oz   **C.** 10 oz   **D.** 22 oz

2. Four pints of lemonade will fill how many cups? (12-1)

A. 2 c   **B.** 16 c   **C.** 8 c   **D.** 6 c

FREE RESPONSE

Find each missing number. (12-1, 12-2, 12-4, 12-5)

3. 12 qt = ▢ gal

4. 8 pt = ▢ qt

5. 4 gal = ▢ qt

6. 10 c = ▢ pt

7. 4 qt = ▢ pt

8. 16 oz = ▢ lb

9. 4 lb = ▢ oz

10. 10 lb = ▢ oz

11. 1 kg = ▢ g

12. 4 kg = ▢ g

13. 1 L = ▢ mL

14. 4 L = ▢ mL

15. 34 oz = 2 lb ▢ oz

16. 1 lb 8 oz = ▢ oz

17. Jacob drank 1,300 mL of water. How much more than 1 L of water is this? (12-1)

18. If it is snowing outside, is the temperature closer to 30°C or 0°C? (12-6)

19. Dean got to school at 8:00 A.M. The bus ride took 30 minutes. He waited for the bus for 15 minutes. After he got up, he spent 45 minutes getting ready and eating. What time did Dean get up? (12-3)

Think It Through

- I should **read a problem carefully** and then decide on the strategy I will use.
- I should always **check my answer.**

Writing in Math

20. Write a rule for changing kilograms to grams. Write a rule for changing liters to milliliters. How are the two rules alike? (12-2, 12-5)

Vocabulary
• possible
• likely
• unlikely
• certain
• impossible

Think It Through
• First I will decide if **the event is certain, possible, or impossible.**
• If **the event is possible,** then I will decide if it is **likely or unlikely.**

Describing Chances

LEARN

What are the chances an event will happen?

Many events are **possible.** If the event has a good chance of happening it is **likely.** If an event is possible but probably won't happen, it is **unlikely.**

Example A

Rain is a possible event. It is likely that it is raining somewhere in the world. It is unlikely that it is raining in the desert.

Some events are **certain.** Other events are **impossible.**

Example B

It is certain that the sun will come up in the east.

Example C

It is impossible for a person to fly like a bird.

✔ Talk About It

1. Suppose you toss the number cube. Is the chance of tossing a number less than 7 certain or impossible? Why?

2. Is the chance of tossing a 0 certain or impossible? Why?

This number cube has the numbers 1, 2, 3, 4, 5 and 6 on the sides.

Use *certain*, *likely*, *unlikely*, or *impossible* to describe each event..

1. Tomorrow will have 24 hours.

2. All library books are checked out.

3. The numbers 1 through 6 are on a number cube. You will toss 8.

4. You will toss 1, 2, 3, 4, or 5 on the number cube in Exercise 3.

5. Reasoning Give another number cube event that is likely.

PRACTICE

For more practice, see Set 12-7 on p. 728.

A Skills and Understanding

Ben is in the third grade. Use *certain*, *likely*, *unlikely*, or *impossible* to describe each event.

6. Ben will grow to be 100 feet tall.

7. Ben will watch television tonight.

8. Ben will travel to the moon.

9. Ben will need food to grow.

10. Reasoning Give an example of an event that is unlikely.

B Reasoning and Problem Solving

Suppose you pick one name from those at the right without looking. Use *certain*, *impossible*, *likely*, or *unlikely* to describe each event.

11. Picking a girl's name

12. Picking the name Tim

13. Picking the name Marcia

14. Picking a boy's name

15. **Writing in Math** Explain how your answers for Exercises 11 and 14 would change if "Alice" were "Alan."

Mixed Review and Test Prep

Take It to the NET
Test Prep
www.scottforesman.com

Multiply or divide.

16. 68×7

17. 362×4

18. $79 \div 8$

19. $75 \div 3$

20. 56×6

21. $98 \div 2$

22. Which is the best temperature for snow skiing?

A. 50°F   **B.** 25°F   **C.** 20°C   **D.** 10°C

Key Idea
Fairness of a game depends on the chance each player has of winning.

Vocabulary
- outcomes
- equally likely
- fair

Materials
- spinner divided into four equal sections and labeled 1, 2, 3, and 4

  or  tools

TEST TALK

Think It Through
To solve a problem about the fairness of a game, I can **act it out.**

Fair and Unfair

LEARN

Activity

How do you know if a game is fair?

The spinner is divided into four equal sections. The four possible **outcomes** of a spin are 1, 2, 3, or 4. Since the sections are the same size, the outcomes are **equally likely.**

Make a spinner like the one shown.

a. Predict which player will win Game A. Then play Game A. Are spinning a 4 and spinning a number less than 4 equally likely?

> *Game A is not fair with this spinner. The chance of landing on 4 is 1 out of 4. The chance of landing on a number less than 4 is 3 out of 4.*

> *The chance of landing on an even number is 2 out of 4. The chance of landing on an odd number is the same, so Game B is fair with the spinner.*

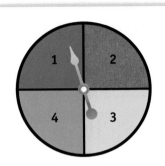

Play each game with a partner. First decide who will be Player 1 and Player 2. Then take turns and spin 20 times. Record who scores the point after each spin.

Spinner Game A
- Player 1 scores a point if the spinner lands on 4.
- Player 2 wins a point if the spinner lands on a number less than 4.

Spinner Game B
- Player 1 scores a point if the spinner lands on an even number.
- Player 2 wins a point if the spinner lands on an odd number.

b. Play Game B. Are spinning an even number and spinning an odd number equally likely?

A game is **fair** if each person has the same chance of winning.

c. Why is Game A unfair?

d. Reasoning How might you change the spinner to make both Games A and B fair?

For another example, see Set 12-8 on p. 725.

For 1 and 2 use the spinner at the right.

1. Give the chance of each outcome.

Yellow	White	Green
▢ out of ▢	▢ out of ▢	▢ out of ▢

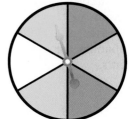

2. Reasoning In a game for 6 players, each player chooses yellow, white, or green. You score a point when the spinner lands on your color. Would this game be fair using this spinner?

PRACTICE

For more practice, see Set 12-8 on p. 729.

A Skills and Understanding

For 3 and 4, use the spinners below. Give the chance of each outcome for the spinner named.

3. Spinner A:

Yellow
▢ out of ▢

White
▢ out of ▢

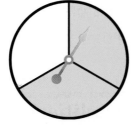

4. Spinner B:

Green
▢ out of ▢

White
▢ out of ▢

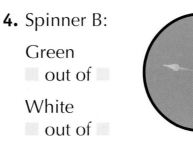

5. Draw a spinner using 4 colors for which all outcomes would be equally likely.

B Reasoning and Problem Solving

6. Bradley drew a spinner with 12 equal sections. Six sections are blue. Landing on blue or green is equally likely. How many sections are green?

7. <u>Writing in Math</u> In a game for 2 players, each player chooses a color and scores a point when the spinner lands on that color. Describe a spinner that would make this game fair.

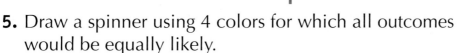

Mixed Review and Test Prep

Take It to the NET
www Test Prep
www.scottforesman.com

8. Find $\frac{1}{2}$ of 8.

9. Find $\frac{1}{3}$ of 9.

10. Find $\frac{1}{5}$ of 15.

11. Which describes this statement: "A tree can walk."

    A. likely   **B.** certain   **C.** impossible   **D.** unlikely

Key Idea
You can use fractions to describe the probability for events.

Vocabulary
• probability

Probability

LEARN

How do you find a probability?

There are 3 yellow and 2 blue tiles in the bag. The possible outcomes for drawing a tile without looking are yellow or blue. Three out of the 5 tiles are yellow.

Probability tells the chance an event will happen. You can write the probability of an event as a fraction.

Chance of drawing a yellow tile: 3 out of 5

Probability of drawing a yellow tile: $\frac{3}{5}$

Chance of drawing a blue tile: 2 out of 5

Probability of drawing a blue tile: $\frac{2}{5}$

How do you compare probabilities?

In the experiment above, the probability of drawing a yellow tile is greater than the probability of drawing a blue tile because $\frac{3}{5} > \frac{2}{5}$.

Example A

The numbers 1 through 6 are on the sides of the number cube. Compare the probabilities of tossing an even number and tossing an odd number.

Tossing an Even Number	Tossing an Odd Number
Outcomes that are even: 2, 4, and 6	Outcomes that are odd: 1, 3, and 5
Probability: 3 out of 6, or $\frac{3}{6}$	Probability: 3 out of 6, or $\frac{3}{6}$

$\frac{3}{6} = \frac{3}{6}$. The probability of tossing an even number is equal to the probability of tossing an odd number.

Ms. Gibbons puts the names of some students in a jar. Each day she draws a name without looking and that student is her helper for the day. The names in the jar today are shown.

Annie
Jim T.
Tom
Jake
Jim G.
Kate
Greg
Joyce

Three out of 8 names are girls. The probability of drawing a girl's name is $\frac{3}{8}$.

Five out of 8 names are boys. The probability of drawing a boy's name is $\frac{5}{8}$.

One out of 8 names is Annie. The probability of drawing the name Annie is $\frac{1}{8}$.

✔ **Talk About It**

1. In Example B, which is greater, the probability of drawing a boy's name or the probability of drawing a girl's name? Why?

2. What is true about the probabilities of two events that are equally likely?

3. What is true about the probabilities of two events that are not equally likely.

CHECK ✓

For another example, see Set 12-9 on p. 725.

For each exercise, give the chance of drawing a green tile. Then give the probability.

1.

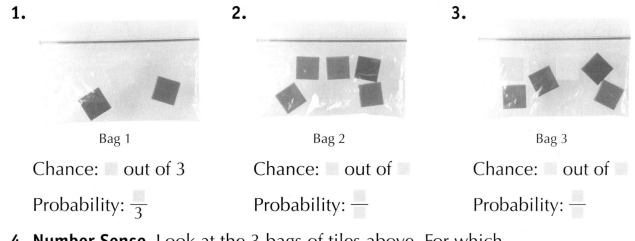

Bag 1

Chance: ▢ out of 3

Probability: $\frac{}{3}$

2.

Bag 2

Chance: ▢ out of ▢

Probability: $\frac{}{}$

3.

Bag 3

Chance: ▢ out of ▢

Probability: $\frac{}{}$

4. **Number Sense** Look at the 3 bags of tiles above. For which bags would the following statement be true?

Probability of drawing a green tile = Probability of drawing a red tile

For more practice, see Set 12-9 on p. 729.

A Skills and Understanding

A number cube has the numbers 1 through 6 on the sides.
Give the chance and the probability of each event.

5. Tossing the
number 1

Chance: ▨ out of 6

Probability: $\dfrac{▨}{6}$

6. Tossing a number
less than 3

Chance: ▨ out of ▨

Probability: $\dfrac{▨}{▨}$

7. Tossing a number
greater than 2

Chance: ▨ out of ▨

Probability: $\dfrac{▨}{▨}$

In 8–11, the slips of paper shown are put into a bag. One slip
of paper will be drawn without looking. Give the probability
it will be a vowel (A, E, I, O, or U).

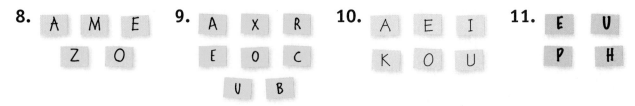

8. A M E
Z O

9. A X R
E O C
U B

10. A E I
K O U

11. E U
P H

12. Number Sense In which bags above is the probability of drawing
a vowel the same as the probability of drawing a consonant?

B Reasoning and Problem Solving

Math and Social Studies

People around the world have enjoyed playing the
game dominoes for hundreds of years.

Suppose the dominoes at the right were put in a
bag and you were to draw one out without
looking. Find the probability of drawing a domino

13. that is red.

14. that is green.

15. on which the total
number of dots is
greater than zero.

16. on which the total
number of dots is 5.

17. Writing in Math In a game, a green spin on this
spinner means you move forward one space. A yellow
spin means you move back one space. Explain whether
you will be ahead or behind after 10 spins.

C Extensions

If an event is certain, the probability that it will happen is 1. If an event is impossible, the probability that it will happen is 0.

18. What is the probability of drawing a green marble?

19. What is the probability of drawing a blue marble?

20. Give two other events with a probability of 1. Give two other events with a probability of 0.

Mixed Review and Test Prep

Take It to the NET
Test Prep
www.scottforesman.com

21. 32×4 **22.** 7×56 **23.** $29 \div 2$ **24.** $78 \div 3$

25. What is the chance of spinning red?

   A. 3 out of 8   **C.** 3 out of 5

   B. 5 out of 8   **D.** 1 out of 8

Discovery CHANNEL SCHOOL

Discover Math in Your World

T. Rex the Terrible

Even though *Tyrannosaurus rex* lived over 70 million years ago, it is one of the best-known animals in the world. *T. rex* was 20 feet tall and 40 to 50 feet long. It weighed as much as 7 tons. The word *dinosaur* means "terrible lizard." With sharp teeth that were 6 inches long, and powerful, curved claws, *T. rex* was one of the most terrible.

1. One ton is 2,000 pounds. How many pounds is 7 tons?

2. Do you think the chance of seeing *T. rex* alive today is certain, likely, unlikely, or impossible?

Take It to the NET
Video and Activities
www.scottforesman.com

Problem-Solving Skill

Reading Helps!

Identifying steps in a process

can help you with...

writing to explain.

Key Idea
There are specific things you can do to write a good explanation in math.

Think It Through

When I write to explain, I should **list the steps** I took, such as describing the spinners and how this affects probability.

Writing to Explain

LEARN

How do you write a good explanation?

When you write to explain a prediction, you need to tell why something happened.

Which spinner? Three friends each took 20 turns on the same spinner. Use the results of their spins to predict which of the two spinners at the right they most likely used. Explain how you made your prediction.

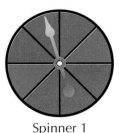

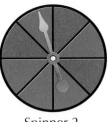

Spinner 1   Spinner 2

Results of Spinner Experiment

Name	Number of Times the Spinner Landed on Red	Number of Times the Spinner Landed on Green
Karen	14	6
Max	15	5
Rosi	13	7

Writing a Math Explanation

- State your prediction.

- Use information from the problem to help explain your prediction.

- When a problem has choices for the answer, explain why some of the choices are not chosen.

- Use specific examples or numbers to explain why something makes sense.

I think the friends used Spinner 1.

The table tells me that most of the spins were red. Spinner 1 has more red than green.

Spinner 2 has more green. More spins would be red using Spinner 1.

✓ Talk About It

1. Spinner 2 was not chosen. Why?

1. Benny drew a marble from a bag, recorded the color, and then replaced the marble. He did this 100 times. The table shows the results.

Green	Orange	Blue
8	63	29

Predict which bag of marbles he used. Explain how you made your prediction.

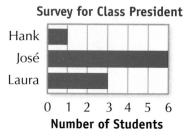

Bag A

Bag B   Bag C

Write to explain.

2. Frank asked 10 classmates if they would vote for Hank, José, or Laura for class president. The results are shown in the graph. Based on this information, predict who will win the election. Explain how you made your prediction.

Survey for Class President

Hank

José

Laura

0 1 2 3 4 5 6
Number of Students

3. Sally drew a spinner with blue and yellow sections. She predicted that in 30 spins she would spin blue more times than she would spin yellow. Draw a spinner that fits Sally's prediction. Explain why it fits the prediction.

4. A number cube shows 1, 2, 3, 4, 5, and 6. Libby predicted that in 100 tosses, she would get an even number about the same number of times as getting an odd number. Do you agree or disagree? Explain.

5. Estimation Are you more than 1 million seconds old? Explain how you know.

6. Tom tossed 2 number cubes at the same time. Make an organized list of the possible outcomes. Then find the probability of tossing one even number and one odd number. Explain your answer. Hint: Since the cubes are tossed at the same time, the order does not matter.

Problem-Solving Applications

Dinosaur Park Fossils are difficult to find because only certain conditions will cause bones to fossilize. Along the banks of the Red Deer River in Alberta, Canada, is one of the best places in the world to look for fossils. The area is now called Dinosaur Provincial Park.

Trivia The *Apatosaurus* was once also known as the *Brontosaurus*. By mistake, scientists gave one dinosaur two different names. When they realized this, they kept the first name given to the dinosaur, *Apatosaurus*.

Euoplocephalus

❶ Fossils of the *Euoplocephalus* are among the most common fossils in Dinosaur Park. This animal may have weighed about 2 tons. How many pounds is this? (1 ton = 2,000 pounds)

❷ A human brain weighs about 3 pounds. The brain of a *Stegosaurus* probably weighed only about 3 ounces. How many ounces heavier is a human brain than the brain of a *Stegosaurus?*

❸ Decision Making Four scientists want to search a field that measures 100 feet by 40 feet. Draw four ways they could divide the field so that each person has an equal chance of finding a fossil. How many square feet will each person have?

Lambeosaurus

4 The *Lambeosaurus* grew to be 45 feet shorter than the full length of a basketball court. If a basketball court is 94 feet long, how long was a *Lambeosaurus*? Is the length of a *Lambeosaurus* more than half the length of the court?

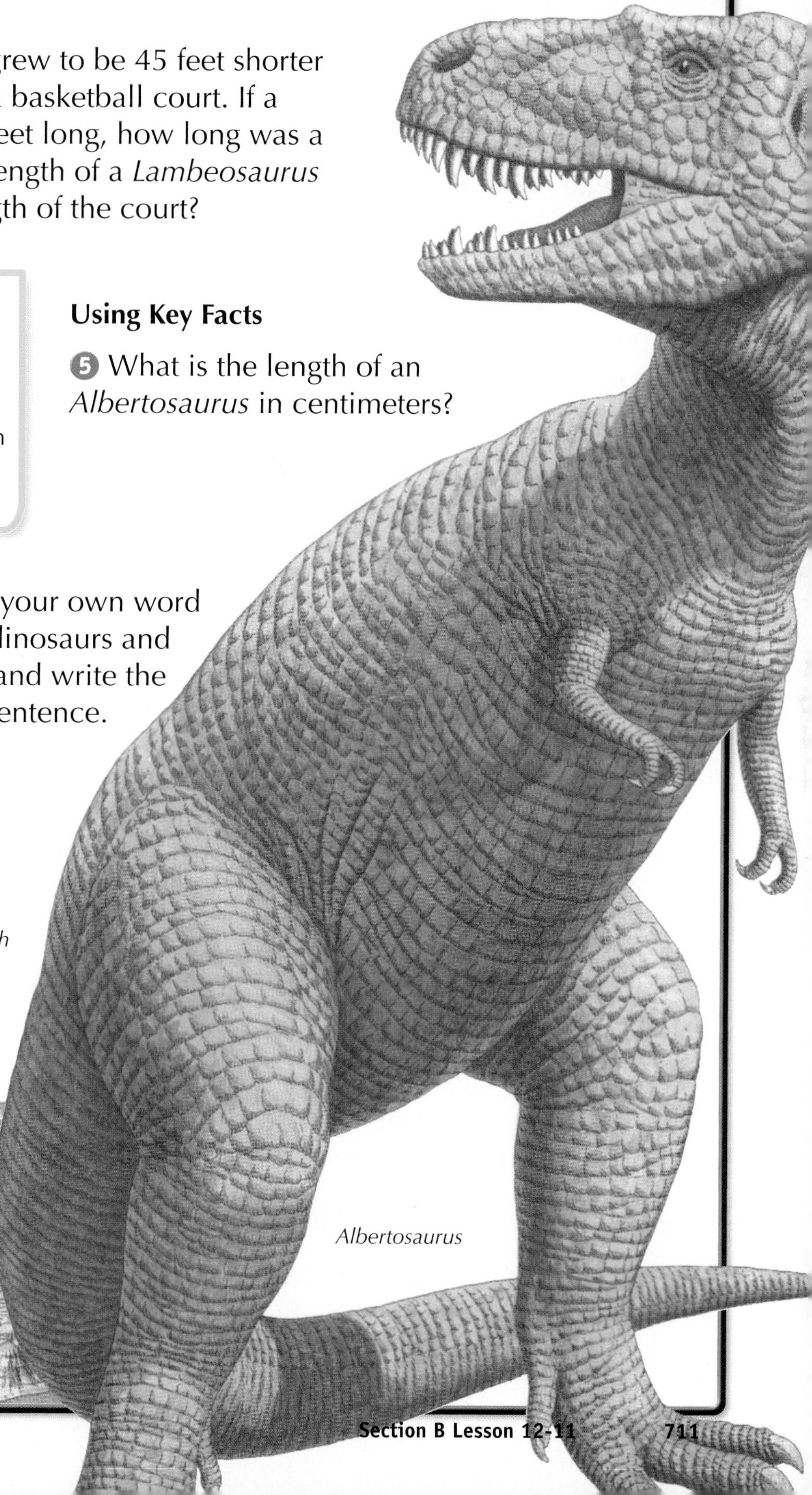

Key Facts
Albertosaurus

- Up to 9 m long
- Up to 3.5 m tall
- Curved, saw-toothed teeth
- 2 fingers on each hand
- Smaller than a *T. rex*

Using Key Facts

5 What is the length of an *Albertosaurus* in centimeters?

6 **Writing in Math** Write your own word problem that involves dinosaurs and measurement. Solve it and write the answer in a complete sentence.

Good News/Bad News
By studying fossils, scientists can learn much about dinosaurs, such as how they may have walked. Unfortunately, there is much that we will never be able to learn, such as the color of their bodies.

Albertosaurus

Do You Know How?

Do You Understand?

Describing Chances (12-7)

Use *certain, likely, unlikely,* or *impossible* to describe each event.

1. The sun will set in the west.

2. A student will be absent today.

Ⓐ If an event is likely to happen is there a chance it will not happen?

Ⓑ Give an example of an impossible event.

Fair and Unfair (12-8)

3. Give the chance of spinning each color.

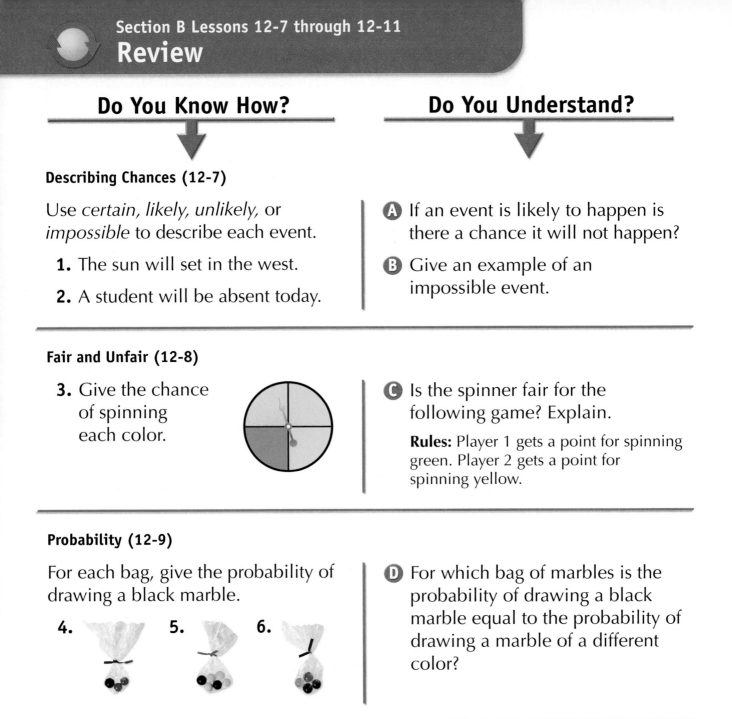

Ⓒ Is the spinner fair for the following game? Explain.

Rules: Player 1 gets a point for spinning green. Player 2 gets a point for spinning yellow.

Probability (12-9)

For each bag, give the probability of drawing a black marble.

4. **5.** **6.**

Ⓓ For which bag of marbles is the probability of drawing a black marble equal to the probability of drawing a marble of a different color?

Problem-Solving Skill: Writing to Explain (12-10)

7. These slips of paper are in a jar. Suppose you draw a slip, record the letter, and replace the slip.

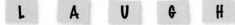

L   A   U   G   H

If you do this 50 times, predict what you will draw more times, a vowel or a consonant. Explain.

Ⓔ Did you use numbers in your explanation? If you did, what numbers did you use?

MULTIPLE CHOICE

1. What is the probability of drawing a red block? (12-9)

   A. $\frac{3}{6}$ **B.** $\frac{3}{3}$ **C.** $\frac{2}{6}$ **D.** $\frac{2}{4}$

2. Which number cube toss is impossible? (12-7)

   A. an even number   **C.** a number less than 6

   B. the number 2   **D.** a number greater than 6

   The numbers 1 though 6 are on the number cube.

FREE RESPONSE

For 3–8, use the number tiles at the right. (12-7)

Suppose these number tiles are in a jar, and you draw one without looking. Describe the chance of each outcome as certain, likely, unlikely, or impossible.

3. Drawing a 5   4. Drawing a 4   5. Drawing a 3

Give the probability of each event. (12-9)

6. Drawing 1   7. Drawing 4   8. Drawing 1, 2, or 3

9. Suppose the spinner at the right is used for a game. Player 1 scores a point if the spinner lands on a vowel. Player 2 scores a point if the spinner lands on a consonant. Is the game a fair game? Why or why not? (12-8)

   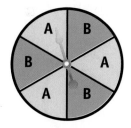

Writing in Math

10. Draw a bag of black and white marbles. Suppose you pick a marble from the bag without looking, record the color, and replace the marble. If you did this 100 times, predict whether you would pick a white marble more times, fewer times, or about the same number of times as you would pick a black marble. Explain how you made your prediction. (12-10, 12-11)

TEST TALK

Think It Through

- I should make my explanation brief but complete.
- I should use "because" to give reasons for something.

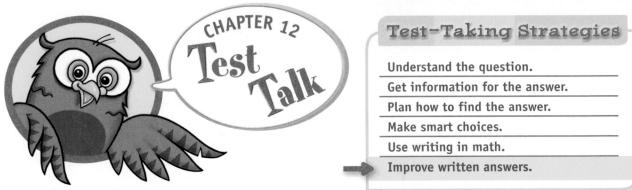

Test-Taking Strategies

Understand the question.

Get information for the answer.

Plan how to find the answer.

Make smart choices.

Use writing in math.

→ Improve written answers.

Improve Written Answers

You can follow the tips below to learn how to improve written answers on a test. It is important to write a clear answer and include only information needed to answer the question.

The rubric below is a scoring guide for Test Question 1.

Scoring Rubric

4 points

Full credit: 4 points
The player and probabilities are correct.

3 points

Partial credit: 3 points
The player is correct, but only one probability is correct.

2 points

Partial credit: 2 points
Either the player is correct, or the probabilities are correct, but not both.

1 point

Partial credit: 1 point
The player is incorrect, and only one probability is correct.

0 points

No credit: 0 points
The players and probabilities are both incorrect.

---

1. Ken and Kathy are playing a game with a number cube labeled 1–6. Ken gets a point for tossing a number less than 5. Kathy gets a point for tossing an even number.

Explain who has the better chance of winning. Then give each player's probability of scoring a point when he or she tosses the number cube.

Improve Written Answers

- Check if your answer is complete.

  *To **get as many points as possible,** I must explain which player has the better chance of winning and find each player's probability of scoring a point.*

- Check if your answer makes sense.

  *I should **compare the probabilities.** It should be greater for the player I chose.*

- Check if your explanation is clear and easy to follow.

  Reread the answer. Did I clearly explain which player has a better chance of winning? Did I give each player's probability of scoring a point? Did I include only necessary information?

Gary used the scoring rubric on page 714 to score a student's answer to Test Question 1. The student's paper is shown below.

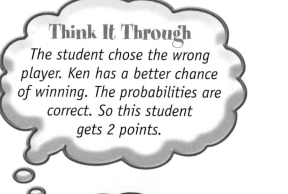

Explain who has the better chance of winning. Then give each player's probability of scoring a point when he or she tosses the number cube.

Kathy has a better chance of

winning. The probability that

Ken will score a point is $\frac{4}{6}$.

The probability that Kathy

will score a point is $\frac{3}{6}$.

Now it's your turn.

Score the student's paper. If it does not get 4 points, rewrite it so that it does.

2. Hannah and Chad are playing a spinner game. Hannah gets a point for spinning a 1-digit number. Chad gets a point for spinning an odd number.

On the lines below, explain who has the better chance of winning. Then give each player's probability of scoring a point when he or she spins the spinner.

Hannah has a better chance of

winning. The probability that

she will score a point is $\frac{4}{8}$.

There are four quarters in a dollar.

*There are 4 **quarts** in a gallon. (p. 680)*

Self Check

Use customary and metric units to measure capacity. (Lessons 12-1, 12-2)

Find each missing number.

12 qt = ☐ gal
12 ÷ 4 = 3   To change to a
12 qt = 3 gal   larger unit, divide.

5 L = ☐ mL
5 × 1,000 = 5,000   To change to a
5 L = 5,000 mL   smaller unit, multiply.

> **Customary Units of Capacity**
> 1 pint (pt) = 2 cups (c)
> 1 quart (qt) = 2 pints
> 1 gallon (gal) = 4 quarts
>
> **Metric Units of Capacity**
> 1 liter (L) = 1,000 milliliters (mL)

1. Give each missing number: 10 pt = ☐ c and 2,000 mL = ☐ L.

I weigh 52 pounds.

*A grapefruit weighs about one **pound (lb).** (p. 690)*

Self Check

Use customary and metric units to tell how heavy an object is. (Lessons 12-4, 12-5)

Find each missing number.

4 lb 10 oz = ☐ oz   Multiply to change
4 × 16 = 64   4 pounds to ounces.
64 + 10 = 74   Then add the extra
4 lb 10 oz = 74 oz   10 ounces.

6,000 g = ☐ kg
6,000 ÷ 1,000 = 6   To change to a
6,000 g = 6 kg   larger unit, divide.

> **How Heavy Is It?**
>
> **Customary Units**
> 1 pound (lb) = 16 ounces (oz)
>
> **Metric Units**
> 1 kilogram (kg) = 1,000 grams (g)

2. Give each missing number: 2 lb 4 oz = ☐ oz and 8 kg = ☐ g.

Self Check

Find probability. (Lessons 12-7, 12-8, 12-9)

Describe the likelihood of events.

Spin a 1: **unlikely**

Spin a number less than 6: **likely**

Spin a number less than 10: **certain**

Spin a 3-digit number: **impossible**

Find the probability of spinning an even number.

Probability of even: 3 out of 7 or $\frac{3}{7}$

If Jill chooses even, and Mel chooses odd, is it a **fair** game?

No. Even and odd on this spinner are not **equally likely.**

3. What is the probability of spinning a number greater than 2?

Self Check

Read temperatures, work backward, and write to explain. (Lessons 12-3, 12-6, 12-10)

Temperature is measured in **degrees Fahrenheit (°F)** or **degrees Celsius (°C).**

Explain how you could use a **thermometer** to solve the following problem.

Between midnight and noon the temperature went up 4°F, then down 2°F, and then up 5°F. It was 46°F at noon. Find the temperature at midnight.

Use a thermometer that shows degrees Fahrenheit. Work backward. Start at the end, 46°F, and use the opposite of each change. Go down 5°F to 41°F. Go up 2°F to 43°F. Go down 4°F to 39°F. The temperature at midnight was 39°F.

4. After Keri read the temperature in the morning, it went up 7°F, then down 4°F, and then up 3°F to 14°F. What was the temperature when Keri read it?

Answers: 1. 20; 2. 36; 8,000 3. 5 out of 7 or $\frac{5}{7}$ 4. 8°F

Chapter 12 Key Vocabulary and Concept Review 717

MULTIPLE CHOICE

1. Which is the best estimate for the capacity of a water glass?

A. 1 gallon

B. 1 quart

C. 1 pint

D. 1 cup

2. Which statement is NOT true?

A. 7 L = 7,000 mL

B. 1,000 mL = 10 L

C. 2,000 mL = 2 L

D. 4 L = 4,000 mL

3. Which temperature below would be best for ice skating outside?

A. 30°F

B. 73°C

C. 37°C

D. 73°F

4. How many ounces are in 1 pound?

A. 4 ounces

B. 12 ounces

C. 16 ounces

D. 24 ounces

5. Which of the following measures is the greatest?

A. 3 kg

B. 5,000 g

C. 3,500 g

D. 25 kg

6. Mr. Jackson bought 1 lb 7 oz of cheese. How many ounces of cheese did he buy in all?

A. 7 oz

B. 17 oz

C. 23 oz

D. 230 oz

7. What temperature is shown on the thermometer below?

A. 10°F

B. 50°C

C. 15°C

D. 50°F

8. In a game, each player chooses red or green. You score a point when the spinner lands on your color. Which spinner would make this game fair?

Think It Through

I need to **gather information** from the text and the pictures.

A. **C.**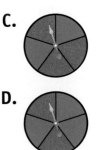

B. **D.**

9. Which of these statements describes an unlikely event?

Think It Through
• I need to **understand math vocabulary.**
• I will **read** the question and each statement **carefully.**

A. It will snow in Key West, FL.

B. You will do math today.

C. Tuesday will follow Monday.

D. You will toss a 7 on a number cube labeled 1 through 6 on its sides.

10. What is the probability of drawing a red tile from this bag without looking?

A. $\frac{2}{7}$

B. $\frac{5}{7}$

C. $\frac{7}{5}$

D. $\frac{7}{2}$

FREE RESPONSE

Find each missing number.

11. 12 gal = ▨ qt

12. 4 kg = ▨ g

13. 2,000 mL = ▨ L

14. 8 c = ▨ pt

15. 7 L = ▨ mL

16. 6,000 g = ▨ kg

17. Write the temperature using °F and °C.

°F   °C
40
30   0
20

18. A number cube has the numbers 1 through 6 on its sides. Give the chance and the probability of tossing the number 2.

Chance: ▨ out of ▨

Probability: $\frac{}{▨}$

19. Work backward to solve this problem.

After Brenda spent $5.75 on a movie ticket and $4.50 on snacks, she had $3.00 left. How much money did she bring to the movie?

Choose the best estimate for each.

20.

6 oz or 6 lb

21.

4 mL or 4 L

Writing in Math

22. Suppose you draw 4 marbles from the bag below. Predict the results. Explain how you made your prediction.

23.

How do you determine whether or not a game is fair?

24. Sharon made 2 gallons of lemonade. How many 1-cup servings did she make? Explain.

Number and Operation

MULTIPLE CHOICE

1. Stella bought 2 gallons of paint. Which operation would be best used to find how many quarts of paint she bought?

  A. addition   **C.** subtraction

  B. division   **D.** multiplication

2. A florist has 28 roses and 4 vases. How many roses should she put in each vase so that each vase has the same number of roses and all of the roses are used?

  A. 3   **B.** 5   **C.** 7   **D.** 8

FREE RESPONSE

3. After Darius spent $6.25 on a book and $2.50 on a magazine, he had $4.00 left. How much money did he have before he bought the items?

4. Write 767, 775, and 756 in order from least to greatest.

Writing in Math

5. Draw a picture to find $\frac{1}{2}$ of 6. Give the answer and explain how you found it.

Think It Through
- I will **write my steps in order.**
- I can **draw pictures** to show my thinking.

Geometry and Measurement

MULTIPLE CHOICE

6. This paper clip is about 1 inch long. About how long is the hair ribbon?

  A. about 3 in.   **C.** about 6 in.

  B. about 4 in.   **D.** about 9 in.

7. Which polygon does NOT always have all congruent sides?

  A. square   **C.** rhombus

  B. rectangle   **D.** equilateral triangle

FREE RESPONSE

8. Kim weighed some pears on a scale. How many pounds did the pears weigh?

9. A pitcher holds 2 liters. How many milliliters does it hold?

Writing in Math

10. An athlete ran around this park 3 times. How far did he run in all? Explain.

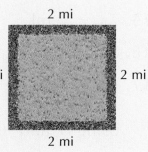

2 mi

2 mi   2 mi

2 mi

Data Analysis and Probability

11. The guests at Amanda's birthday party were the following ages: 7, 8, 11, 6, 7, 9, 10, and 8. What is the range of their ages?

A. 5   **B.** 7   **C.** 8   **D.** 11

12. Which graph is best to display data that changes over time?

A. pictograph   **C.** line graph

B. bar graph   **D.** circle graph

FREE RESPONSE

Use the spinners for 13–15.

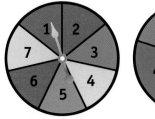 

Spinner A   Spinner B

13. What is the probability that Spinner A will land on a number greater than 2?

14. On which number is Spinner B most likely to land?

Writing in Math

15. In a game, each player is given a number 1 through 4. Players score a point when the spinner lands on their number. Would this game be fair using Spinner B? Explain.

Think It Through
I need to **gather information** from the text and draw a picture.

Algebra

MULTIPLE CHOICE

16. Evan spent $15 on a kite, including tax. He paid with a $20 bill. Which number sentence could be used to find the total amount of change Evan got back?

A. $15 + 20 = n$ **C.** $20 - 15 = n$

B. $20 + n = 15$ **D.** $15 - n = 20$

17. Which number sentence is NOT true if $m = 3$?

A. $21 \div m = 7$ **C.** $m + 9 = 13$

B. $7 \times m = 21$ **D.** $12 - m = 9$

FREE RESPONSE

18. Copy and complete the table.

mL	1,000	2,000			4,000
L	1		3		

19. To keep up with his father, Trent has to take 3 steps for each of his father's steps. How many steps will Trent take if his father takes 24 steps?

Writing in Math

20. Alex is making a border for his bedroom wall using the pattern below.

What is the next figure in his pattern? Explain.

Set 12-1 (pages 680–683)

Find the missing number.

20 qt = ▮ gal

Divide to change from smaller units to larger units.

Think:
1 qt < 1 gal
4 qt = 1 gal

20 qt = ▮ gal
20 ÷ 4 = 5
20 qt = 5 gal

Find the missing number.

6 pt = ▮ c

Multiply to change from larger units to smaller units.

Think:
1 pt > 1 c
1 pt = 2 c

6 pt = ▮ c
6 × 2 = 12
6 pt = 12 c

Remember that, from least to greatest, the customary units of capacity are cup (c), pint (pt), quart (qt), and gallon (gal).

Find each missing number.

1. 5 gal = ▮ qt   **2.** 12 c = ▮ pt

3. 8 pt = ▮ qt   **4.** 7 pt = ▮ c

Choose the better estimate.

5.

1 gal or 1 qt

6. Which is more, 6 quarts of water or 1 gallon of water?

Set 12-2 (pages 684–685)

Choose the better estimate.

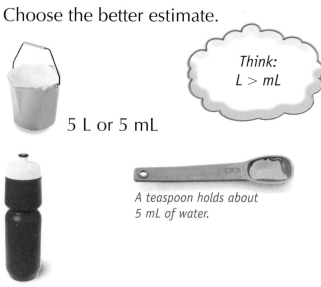

Think:
L > mL

5 L or 5 mL

A teaspoon holds about 5 mL of water.

A sports water bottle holds about 1 L of water.

A teaspoon of water would not fill the bucket, but 5 water bottles might. So, 5 L is a better estimate for the capacity of a bucket than 5 mL.

Remember that 1 liter (L) equals 1,000 milliliters (mL).

Find each missing number.

1. 2 L = ▮ mL

2. 3,000 mL = ▮ L

Choose the better estimate.

3.    **4.**

15 mL or 15 L   4 L or 4 mL

5. Which is more, 1 L of milk, or 450 mL of milk?

When you work backward to solve a problem, follow these steps.

Step 1: Identify what is unknown at the beginning.

Step 2: Draw a picture to show each change, starting from the beginning.

Step 3: From the end, work backward, using the opposite of each change.

Remember that the opposite of addition is subtraction and the opposite of subtraction is addition.

1. After Max spent $8.50 for a pizza and $1.75 for a drink, he had $3.00 left. How much money did Max have before he bought the pizza and drink?

Find the missing number.

21 oz = ▨ lb ▨ oz

21 = 16 + 5

You can think of 21 oz as 16 oz + 5 oz
Since 16 oz = 1 lb, replace
the 16 oz with 1 lb.

So, 21 oz = 1 lb 5 oz

Remember when you want to change pounds to ounces, multiply the number of pounds by 16.

Find each missing number.

1. 2 lb = ▨ oz

2. 19 oz = 1 lb ▨ oz

Choose the better estimate.

3.

10 oz or 10 lb

Find the missing number.

3 kg = ▨ g

3 × 1,000 = 3,000

Think:
1 kg = 1,000 g

3 kg = 3,000 g

Find the missing number.

7,000 g = ▨ kg

7,000 = 7 × 1,000

Think:
1,000 g = 1 kg

7,000 g = 7 kg

Remember that 1 gram (g) tells you about how heavy a paper clip is, and 1 kilogram (kg) tells you about how heavy a baseball bat is.

Find each missing number.

1. 8 kg = ▨ g

2. 5,000 g = ▨ kg

3. Emma caught a 4-kilogram catfish and a 3,500-gram rockfish. Which fish is heavier?

Set 12-6 (pages 696–697)

Write the temperature using °C and °F.

Look at the Fahrenheit scale. The top of the red column is at 50.

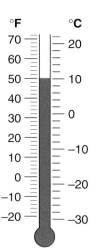

The temperature is 50°F.

Look at the Celsius scale. The top of the red column is at 10.

The temperature is 10°C.

Remember that the same temperature is always a lower number in °C than in °F.

Write each temperature using °F and °C.

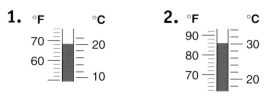

1.   2.

Choose the better temperature for each activity.

3. campfire
45°F or 95°F

4. water skiing
33°C or 3°C

Set 12-7 (pages 700–701)

Without looking, you will pick one number from those below. Describe each pick as certain, likely, unlikely, or impossible.

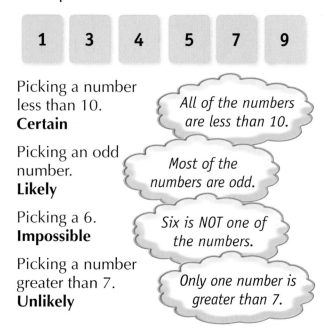

1   3   4   5   7   9

Picking a number less than 10.
Certain

All of the numbers are less than 10.

Picking an odd number.
Likely

Most of the numbers are odd.

Picking a 6.
Impossible

Six is NOT one of the numbers.

Picking a number greater than 7.
Unlikely

Only one number is greater than 7.

Remember that a certain event always happens, an impossible event never happens, a likely event has a good chance of happening, and an unlikely event probably won't happen.

Describe each statement as certain, likely, unlikely, or impossible.

1. February will have 28 days.

2. Next year will have 12 months.

3. It will snow on July 4th, in Florida.

4. You will grow to be 500 feet tall.

Give the chance that the spinner will land on red. Is the spinner fair?

How many equal sections in all? 4

How many red sections? 1

The chance of the spinner landing on red is 1 out of 4.

The spinner is fair because all of the sections are the same size and each section is a different color.

Remember that a game is fair if each person has the same chance of winning.

Give the chance of each outcome.

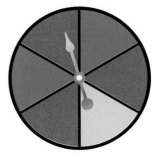

1. Yellow
   ▓ out of ▓

2. Red
   ▓ out of ▓

3. Green
   ▓ out of ▓

Give the chance of drawing a red tile from the bag. Then give the probability.

Count the total number of tiles: 5

Count the total number of red tiles: 2

Chances: 2 out of 5

Probability: $\frac{2}{5}$

Remember that you can write the probability of an event as a fraction.

1. A number cube has the numbers 1 through 6 on its sides. Give the chance and probability of tossing the number 5.

   Chance: ▓ out of ▓

   Probability: $\frac{}{}$

When you write to explain a prediction, follow these steps

Step 1: If you can, use information in tables, graphs, or pictures to help you explain your prediction.

Step 2: When the problem has choices, explain why some of the choices do not make sense.

Step 3: Use specific numbers in your explanation.

Remember to write clear explanations.

1. Jo drew a slip of paper from a bag without looking and then replaced it. In 20 draws, she drew an even number 18 times and an odd number 2 times. Predict which bag Jo most likely used. Explain how you made your prediction.

Bag 1

Bag 2

Bag 3

Chapter 12 Reteaching 725

Set 12-1 (pages 680–683)

Choose the better estimate for each.

1.

Sour Cream

1 gal or 1 pt

2.

40 pt or 40 gal

3.

2 c or 2 gal

Find each missing number.

4. 1 pt = ▦ c   **5.** 1 gal = ▦ qt   **6.** 1 qt = ▦ pt

7. 6 qt = ▦ pt   **8.** 16 qt = ▦ gal   **9.** 14 pt = ▦ qt

10. 2 gal = ▦ qt   **11.** 5 pt = ▦ c   **12.** 8 gal = ▦ qt

13. Carolyn bought 2 gallons of paint. Mike bought 4 quarts of paint. Who bought the most paint?

Set 12-2 (pages 684–685)

Choose the better estimate for each.

1.

1 mL or 1 L

2.

20 mL or 20 L

3.

2 L or 2 mL

Find each missing number.

4. 1 L = ▦ mL   **5.** 12 L = ▦ mL   **6.** 8,000 mL = ▦ L

7. Which is more, 1,500 mL of lemonade or 1 liter of lemonade?   **8.** Which is less, 7 L of gasoline or 17,000 milliliters of gasoline?

9. Aleesha made a liter of fruit punch. How many 500-milliliter pitchers can she fill?

Take It to the NET
More Practice
www.scottforesman.com

Set 12-3 (pages 688–689)

Solve each problem by working backward. Write the answer in a complete sentence.

1. Mr. Simon's flight leaves at 5:15 P.M. It takes him 30 minutes to drive to the airport and 15 minutes to park and walk to the check-in counter. He needs to check in at the airport 1 hour before his flight leaves. At what time should he leave his house?

2. Wendy had $5.00 when she left the county fair. She spent $11.00 on her admission ticket. Then she bought lunch for $6.00. After lunch, she spent $17.00 on games and rides. How much money did Wendy bring to the county fair?

Set 12-4 (pages 690–693)

Choose the better estimate for each.

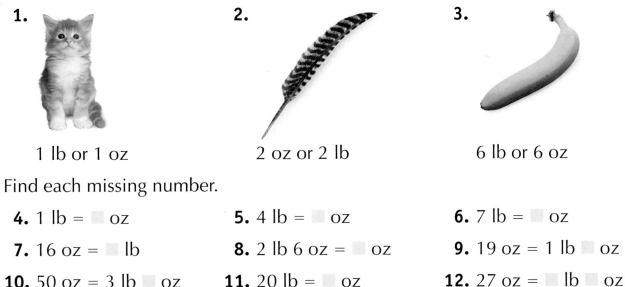

1. 1 lb or 1 oz

2. 2 oz or 2 lb

3. 6 lb or 6 oz

Find each missing number.

4. 1 lb = ▉ oz

5. 4 lb = ▉ oz

6. 7 lb = ▉ oz

7. 16 oz = ▉ lb

8. 2 lb 6 oz = ▉ oz

9. 19 oz = 1 lb ▉ oz

10. 50 oz = 3 lb ▉ oz

11. 20 lb = ▉ oz

12. 27 oz = ▉ lb ▉ oz

13. Timothy bought $\frac{1}{2}$ pound of turkey at the deli. How many ounces of turkey did he buy?

Set 12-5 (pages 694–695)

Choose the better estimate for each.

1.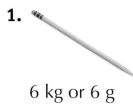

6 kg or 6 g

2.

1 kg or 1 g

3.

10 g or 10 kg

4.

20 kg or 20 g

Find each missing number.

5. 3 kg = ▒ g   **6.** 2,000 g = ▒ kg   **7.** 6 kg = ▒ g   **8.** 5,000 g = ▒ kg

9. At the farmers' market, Ted bought a 3-kilogram container of strawberries. Anita bought a 4,500-gram container of blueberries. Which container of berries is heavier?

Set 12-6 (pages 696–697)

Write each temperature using °F and °C.

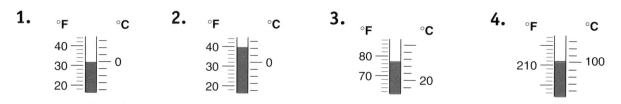

1.
°F   °C
40
30   0
20

2.
°F   °C
40
30   0
20

3.
°F   °C
80
70   20

4.
°F   °C
210   100

Choose the best estimate for each activity.

5. snow boarding
9°C or 39°C

6. scuba diving
58°F or 85°F

7. jogging
52°C or 21°C

8. camping
65°F or 16°F

9. In Exercises 5-8, tell if each temperature is hot, warm, cool, or cold.

Set 12-7 (pages 700–701)

Describe each statement as certain, likely, unlikely, or impossible.

1. Next week will have 7 days.

2. You will find buried treasure.

3. The numbers 1 through 6 are on a a number cube. You will toss 7.

4. A bag is filled with the 5 vowel letter tiles. You pick A, E, or I.

5. Give examples of events in school next week that are certain, likely, unlikely, and impossible to occur.

Take It to the NET
More Practice
www.scottforesman.com

Set 12-8 (pages 702–703)

Use the spinners at the right. Give the chance of each outcome.

1. Spinner A: Yellow
   ▦ out of ▦

3. Spinner B: Red
   ▦ out of ▦

2. Spinner B: Yellow
   ▦ out of ▦

4. Spinner A: Green
   ▦ out of ▦

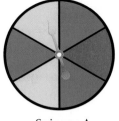

Spinner A

5. In a game, each player is given a color: yellow, green, or red. You score a point when the spinner lands on your color. Is this game fair using Spinner A? Spinner B? Explain your answers.

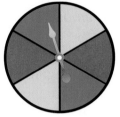

Spinner B

Set 12-9 (pages 704–707)

A number cube has the numbers 1 through 6 on its sides.
Give the chance and the probability of each event.

1. Tossing the number 6.

   Chance: ▦ out of ▦

   Probability: $\frac{▦}{6}$

2. Tossing a number less than 4.

   Chance: ▦ out of ▦

   Probability: $\frac{▦}{▦}$

3. Tossing an even number.

   Chance: ▦ out of ▦

   Probability: $\frac{▦}{▦}$

Give the chance and the probability of drawing a blue tile.

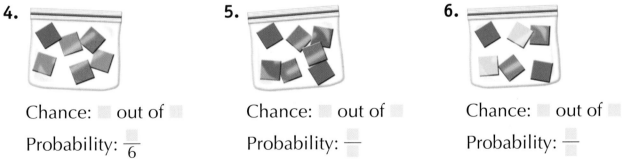

4.

   Chance: ▦ out of ▦

   Probability: $\frac{▦}{6}$

5.

   Chance: ▦ out of ▦

   Probability: $\frac{▦}{▦}$

6.

   Chance: ▦ out of ▦

   Probability: $\frac{▦}{▦}$

7. For which of the bags above is the chance of drawing a blue tile or drawing a red tile equally likely?

Set 12-10 (pages 708–709)

1. Nora put 16 red and blue cubes in a bag. She predicted that in 20 draws, she would draw a red cube and a blue cube about the same number of times. Show 16 cubes that would fit Nora's predictions. Explain why they fit the prediction.

A

A.M. Time between midnight and noon. (p. 192)

acute angle An angle that measures less than a right angle. (p. 444)

acute triangle A triangle with three acute angles. (p. 450)

addends Numbers added together to give a sum. (p. 66)
Example: $2 + 7 = 9$

Addend   Addend

angle A figure formed by two rays that have the same endpoint. (p. 444)

area The number of square units needed to cover a region. (p. 468)

array A way of displaying objects in rows and columns. (p. 262)

Associative (grouping) Property of Addition The grouping of addends can be changed and the sum will be the same. (p. 66)

Associative (grouping) Property of Multiplication The grouping of factors can be changed and the product will be the same. (p. 342)

B

bar graph A graph using bars to show data. (p. 212)

C

capacity The amount a container can hold. (p. 680)

centimeter (cm) A metric unit of length. (p. 582)

century Period of time. One century equals 100 years. (p. 200)

certain event An event that is sure to happen. (p. 700)

Commutative (order) Property of Addition Numbers can be added in any order and the sum will be the same. (p. 66)

Commutative (order) Property of Multiplication Numbers can be multiplied in any order and the product will be the same. (p. 262)

compare To decide if one number is greater than or less than another number. (p. 18)

compatible numbers Numbers that are easy to add, subtract, multiply or divide mentally. (p. 86)

cone A solid figure with a circle as its base and a curved surface that meets at a point. (p. 428)

congruent figures Figures that have the same shape and size. (p. 456)

coordinate grid A grid used to show ordered pairs. (p. 218)

corner Where 3 or more edges meet in a solid figure. (p. 432)

cube A solid figure with 6 faces that are congruent squares. (p. 428)

cubic unit A cube with edges 1 unit long, used to measure volume. (p. 472)

cup A customary unit of capacity. (p. 680)

cylinder A solid figure with two congruent circles as bases. (p. 428)

D

data Pieces of collected information. (p. 204)

decade A unit of time equal to 10 years. (p. 200)

decimal A number with one or more digits to the right of the decimal point. (p. 564)

decimal point A dot used to separate dollars from cents and ones from tenths in a number. (pp. 36, 564)

decimeter (dm) A metric unit of measure. 1 decimeter equals 10 centimeters. (p. 582)

degrees Celsius (°C) A metric unit of temperature. (p. 696)

degrees Fahrenheit (°F) A customary unit of temperature. (p. 696)

denominator The number below the fraction bar in a fraction, the total number of equal parts in all. (p. 502)

diagonal A line segment other than a side that connects two corners of a polygon. (p. 578)

Diagonal

difference The answer when subtracting two numbers. (p. 70)

digits The symbols 0, 1, 2, 3, 4, 5, 6, 7, 8, and 9 used to write numbers. (p. 6)

dividend The number to be divided. (p. 384)
Example: 63 ÷ 9 = 7

Dividend

divisible Can be divided by another number without leaving a remainder. (p. 402)
Example: 10 is divisible by 2.

division An operation that tells how many equal groups there are or how many are in each group. (p. 370)

divisor The number by which another number is divided. (p. 384)
Example: 63 ÷ 9 = 7

Divisor

dollar sign ($) A symbol used to indicate money. (p. 36)

E

edge A line segment where two faces of a solid figure meet. (p. 432)

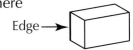

Edge →

elapsed time Total amount of time that passes from the beginning time to the ending time. (p. 198)

equally likely outcomes Outcomes that have the same chance of happening. (p. 702)

equation A number sentence that says two expressions are equal. (p. 168)

equilateral triangle A triangle with all sides the same length. (p. 450)

equivalent fractions Fractions that name the same part of a whole, same part of a set, or same location on a number line. (p. 504)

estimate To give an approximate number or answer. (p. 86)

even number A whole number that has 0, 2, 4, 6, or 8 in the ones place; A number that is a multiple of 2. (p. 24, 276)

expanded form A number written as the sum of the values of its digits. (p. 6)
Example: 2,476 = 2,000 + 400 + 70 + 6

F

face A flat surface of a solid that does not roll. (p. 432)

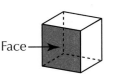

Face →

fact family A group of related facts using the same numbers. (pp. 70, 384)

factors Numbers that are multiplied together to give a product. (p. 260)
Example: 7 × 3 = 21

Factor   Factor

fair game A game in which each player is equally likely to win. (p. 702)

flip (reflection) The change in the position of a figure that is the result of picking it up and turning it over. (p. 456)

Example:

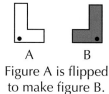

A B

Figure A is flipped
to make figure B.

foot (ft) A customary unit of length. 1 foot equals 12 inches. (p. 536)

fraction A symbol, such as $\frac{2}{8}$, $\frac{5}{1}$, or $\frac{5}{5}$, used to name a part of a whole, a part of a set, or a location on a number line. (p. 502)

front-end estimation A way to estimate a sum or difference by using the first digit of each number. (pp. 86, 98)

G

gallon (gal) A customary unit of capacity. 1 gallon equals 4 quarts. (p. 680)

gram (g) A metric unit used to tell how heavy an object is. (p. 694)

H

half hour A unit of time equal to 30 minutes. (p. 192)

hexagon A polygon with 6 sides. (p. 446)

hour A unit of time equal to 60 minutes. (p. 192)

hundredth One of 100 equal parts of a whole. (p. 566)

I

Identity (one) Property of Multiplication The product of any number and 1 is that number. (p. 286)

Identity (zero) Property of Addition The sum of any number and zero is that same number. (p. 67)

impossible event An event that will never happen. (p. 700)

inch (in.) A customary unit of length. (p. 532)

inequality A number sentence that uses < (less than) or > (greater than). (p. 168)

intersecting lines Lines that cross at one point. (p. 442)

isosceles triangle A triangle with at least two sides the same length. (p. 450)

K

key Explanation of what each symbol represents in a pictograph. (p. 212)

kilogram (kg) A metric unit used to tell how heavy an object is. 1 kilogram equals 1,000 grams. (p. 694)

kilometer (km) A metric unit of length. 1 kilometer equals 1,000 meters. (p. 584)

L

leap year A year that is 366 days long in which February has 29 days. (p. 200)

likely event An event that will probably happen. (p. 700)

line A straight path of points that is endless in both directions. (p. 442)

line graph A graph used to show how data changes over time. (p. 222)

line of symmetry
A line on which a figure can be folded so that both parts match exactly. (p. 460)

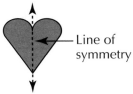
Line of symmetry

line plot A display of data along a number line. (p. 208)

line segment A part of a line that has two endpoints. (p. 442)

liter (L) A metric unit of capacity. 1 liter equals 1,000 milliliters. (p. 684)

meter (m) A metric unit of length. 1 meter equals 100 centimeters. (p. 584)

mile (mi) A customary unit of length. 1 mile equals 5,280 feet. (p. 538)

milliliter (mL) A metric unit of capacity. (p. 684)

minute A unit of time equal to 60 seconds. (p. 192)

mixed number A number with a whole number part and a fraction part. (p. 522)
Example: $2\frac{3}{4}$

mode The number or numbers that occur most often in a group of data. (p. 208)

month One of the twelve parts into which a year is divided. (p. 200)

multiple The product of the number and any other whole number. (p. 276)
Example: 0, 4, 8, 12, and 16 are multiples of 4.

multiplication An operation that gives the total number when you put together equal groups. (p. 260)

N

number line A line that shows numbers in order using a scale. (p. 18)
Example:

numerator The number above the fraction bar in a fraction. (p. 502)

numerical expression An expression that contains numbers and at least one operation. A numerical expression is also called a number expression. (pp.168, 404)

O

obtuse angle An angle that measures more than a right angle. (p. 444)

obtuse triangle A triangle with one obtuse angle. (p. 450)

octagon A polygon with 8 sides. (p. 446)

odd number A whole number that has 1, 3, 5, 7, or 9 in the ones place; A number not divisible by 2. (p. 24)

order To arrange numbers from least to greatest or from greatest to least. (p. 22)

ordered pair Two numbers used to name a point on a coordinate grid. (p. 218)

ordinal numbers Numbers used to tell the order of people or objects. (p. 4)

ounce (oz) A customary unit of weight. (p. 690)

outcome A possible result of a game or experiment. (p. 702)

overestimate An estimate that is greater than the exact answer. (p. 90)

P

P.M. Time between noon and midnight. (p. 193)

parallel lines
Lines that
never intersect.
(p. 442)

parallelogram A quadrilateral in which opposite sides are parallel. (p. 454)

pentagon A polygon with 5 sides. (p. 446)

perimeter The distance around a figure. (p. 464)

period A group of three digits in a number, separated by a comma. (p. 12)

perpendicular lines
Two lines that intersect
to form right angles.
(p. 444)

pictograph A graph using pictures or symbols to show data. (p. 212)

pint (pt) A customary unit of capacity. 1 pint equals 2 cups. (p. 680)

place value The value given to the place a digit has in a number. (p. 6)
Example: In 3,946, the place value of the digit 9 is *hundreds.*

plot Locate and mark a point on a coordinate grid using a given ordered pair. (p. 218)

point An exact position often marked by a dot. (p. 44)

polygon A closed figure made up of straight line segments. (p. 446)

possible event An event that might or might not happen. (p. 700)

pound (lb) A customary unit of weight. 1 pound equals 16 ounces. (p. 690)

probability The chance an event will happen. (p. 704)

product The answer to a multiplication problem. (p. 260)

pyramid A solid figure whose base is a polygon and whose faces are triangles with a common point. (p. 428)

Q

quadrilateral A polygon with 4 sides. (p. 446)

quart (qt) A customary unit of capacity. 1 quart equals 2 pints. (p. 680)

quarter hour A unit of time equal to 15 minutes (p. 192)

quotient The answer to a division problem. (p. 384)

R

range The difference between the greatest value and the least value in a data set. (p. 208)

ray A part of a line that has one endpoint and continues endlessly in one direction. (p. 442)

rectangle A quadrilateral with four right angles. (p. 454)

rectangular prism A solid figure with faces that are rectangles. (p. 428)

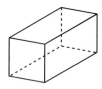

regroup To name a whole number in a different way. (p. 126)
Example: 28 = 1 ten 18 ones.

remainder The number that is left over after dividing. (pp. 398, 652)
Example: 31 ÷ 7 = 4R3
Remainder

rhombus A quadrilateral with opposite sides parallel and all sides the same length. (p. 454)

right angle An angle that forms a square corner. (p. 444)

right triangle A triangle with one right angle. (p. 450)

rounding Replacing a number with a number that tells about how much or how many to the nearest ten, hundred, thousand, and so on. (p. 28)
Example: 42 rounded to the nearest 10 is 40.

S

scale The numbers that show the units used on a graph. (p. 212)

scalene triangle A triangle with no sides the same length. (p. 450)

second A unit of time. Sixty seconds equal 1 minute. (p. 192)

side A line segment forming part of a polygon. (p. 446)

slide (translation) The change in the position of a figure that moves it up, down, or sideways. (p. 457)
Example:

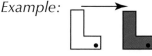

solid figure A figure that has length, width, and height. (p. 428)

sphere A solid figure in the shape of a ball. (p. 428)

square A quadrilateral with four right angles and all sides the same length. (p. 454)

square number The product of a number multiplied by itself. (p. 324)

square unit A square with sides 1 unit long, used to measure area. (p. 468)

standard form A way to write a number showing only its digits. (p. 6)
Example: 3,845

sum The answer when adding two or more addends. (p. 66)
Example: 7 + 9 = 16
Sum

survey Collecting information by asking a number of people the same question and recording their answers. (p. 204)

symmetry A figure has symmetry if it can be folded along a line so that both parts match exactly. (p. 460)

T

tally chart A chart on which data is recorded. (p. 204)

tally mark A mark used to record data on a tally chart. (p. 204)
Example: = 5

tenth One out of 10 equal parts of a whole. (p. 564)

thermometer A device used to measure temperature. (p. 696)

trapezoid A quadrilateral with only one pair of parallel sides. (p. 454)

triangle A polygon with 3 sides. (p. 446)

turn (rotation) The change in the position of a figure that moves it around a point. (p. 456)
Example:

twice Two times a number (p. 338)

U

underestimate An estimate that is less than the exact answer. (p. 90)

unit fraction A fraction with a numerator of 1. (p. 506)

Example: $\frac{1}{2}$

unlikely event An event that probably won't happen. (p. 700)

V

vertex (plural, vertices) The point where two rays meet to form an angle. The points where the sides of a polygon meet. The points where 3 or more edges meet in a solid figure. (pp. 432, 444, 446)

volume The number of cubic units needed to fill a solid figure. (p. 472)

W

week A unit of time equal to 7 days. (p. 20)

word form A number written in words. (p. 6)

Example: 9,325 = nine thousand, three hundred twenty-five

Y

yard (yd) A customary unit of length. 1 yard equals 3 feet or 36 inches. (p. 538)

year A unit of time equal to 365 days, or 52 weeks, or 12 months. (p. 200)

Z

Zero Property of Multiplication The product of any number and zero is zero. (p. 286)

Measures–Customary

Length
1 foot (ft) = 12 inches (in.)
1 yard (yd) = 3 feet, or 36 inches
1 mile = 1,760 yards, or 5,280 feet

Weight
1 pound (lb) = 16 ounces (oz)

Capacity
1 pint (pt) = 2 cups
1 quart (qt) = 2 pints
1 gallon (gal) = 4 quarts

Measures–Metric

Length
1 decimeter (dm) = 10 centimeters (cm)
1 meter (m) = 100 centimeters
1 kilometer (km) = 1,000 meters

Mass/Weight
1 kilogram (kg) = 1,000 grams (g)

Capacity
1 liter (L) = 1,000 milliliters (mL)

Time

1 minute (min) = 60 seconds (s)
1 hour (h) = 60 minutes
1 day (d) = 24 hours
1 week (wk) = 7 days

1 month (mo) = 28 to 31 days, or
                about 4 weeks
1 year (yr) = 12 months, or
                52 weeks, or
                365 days
1 leap year = 366 days

Money

1 penny = 1 cent (¢)
1 nickel = 5 cents
1 dime = 10 cents

1 quarter = 25 cents
1 half dollar = 50 cents
1 dollar ($) = 100 cents

Symbols

=	is equal to	10¢	ten cents
>	is greater than	$1.60	one dollar and sixty cents
<	is less than	6:45	six forty-five
. . .	and so on	°C	degree Celsius
		°F	degree Fahrenheit

quart, 680
square foot, 471
square inch, 471
tablespoon, 683
teaspoon, 683
yard, 538

Cylinder, 428

Data. *See also* Graphs.
collecting, 204–205
describing shape of, 210
ordered pair, 218–221
organizing, 204–211
survey, 204
tally chart, 204–207

Day, 192

Decade, 200

Decimal point, 36

Decimals
adding, 572–575
comparing, 568–571
and fractions, 564, 571
hundredths, 566–567
and money, 571
ordering, 568–571
place value, 564–567
subtracting, 572–575
tenths, 564–565

Decimeter, 582–583

Decision Making, 45, 105, 171, 239, 272, 295, 438, 543, 591, 659, 710

Degrees, 459, 696

Degrees Celsius, 696–697

Degrees Fahrenheit, 696–697

Denominator, 502

Diagnosing Readiness. *See* Assessment

Diagnostic Checkpoint. *See* Assessment

Diameter, 467

Difference, 98–101. *See also* Subtraction

Digit, 6

Dime, 36. *See also* Money.

Discover Math in Your World (Discovery Channel)
Don't Work Too Hard, 629
Heat: Fire, 101
It's in the Stars, 453
The Manu Biosphere Reserve in Peru, 21
No Bones About It, 323
One Leaf At A Time, 155
Reinventing the Wheel, 279
Snow Desert, 215
Still Standing Tall, 525
Sun Up, 575
T. Rex The Terrible, 707
The Tunnel, Chunnel, 377

Divide, 370

Dividend, 384. *See also* Division.

Dividing Money, 655

Divisible, 402

Division
breaking apart numbers, 650–651
concept of, 370–374
dividend, 384
divisor, 384
facts. See Division facts.
interpret remainder, 656–657
patterns in, 402–403
quotient, 384, 622–623
recording, 652–655
related to multiplication, 384–385
remainder, 398–401, 652
as repeated subtraction, 372–373
as sharing, 370–371, 522–523
stories, 374–377
using objects, 648–649
zero, 396–397

Division facts
dividing by 0, 396–397
dividing by 1, 396–397
dividing by 2, 386–387
dividing by 3, 388–389
dividing by 4, 388–389
dividing by 5, 386–387
dividing by 6, 390–391
dividing by 7, 390–391
dividing by 8, 392–393
dividing by 9, 392–393
dividing by 10, 402–403
dividing by 11, 402–403
dividing by 12, 402–403
and multiplication facts, 390

Divisor, 384. *See also* Division.

Dollar, 36

Dollar sign, 36

Doubling, 276, 318

Draw a Picture Strategy, 140–143

Edges, 432

Eighths, 499

Elapsed time, 198–199

Enrichment
At Most, At Least, 31
Benchmark Numbers, 165
Circle Graphs, 471
Connecting Fractions and Decimals to Money, 571
Dividing Money, 655
Mean and Median, 211
Measuring Dry Materials, 683
Measuring with Your Hands and Feet, 587
Nets, 431
Predicting the Size of an Answer, 621

Relating Multiplication to Place Value, 615
Roman Numerals, 27
Turns, 459
Using Objects to Solve Problems, 265
Venn diagram, 69

Equal parts of a whole, 398, 498–501

Equality, 168–169

Equations. *See also* Number sentences.
addition, 168–169
number sentences, 70–71, 76–77, 384–385
subtraction, 168–169

Equilateral triangle, 450

Equally likely, 702

Equivalent fractions, 504–505

Estimation
compatible numbers, 87, 99
data, 214
differences, 98–101
fractional amounts, 510–511
front-end, 87, 99
in measurement. *See* Measurement
overestimate, 90–91
products, 616–617
quotients, 622–623
recognizing, 696
rounding, 86, 98
sums, 86–89, 134, 137
underestimate, 90-91
verify reasonableness of answers, 630

eTools. *See* Learning with Technology

Evaluate an algebraic expression, 168

Even numbers, 24, 258, 276

Evenly divided, 370–371, 398, 402, 522

Event, 700–701

Exact answer or estimate, 160–161, 616, 622

Expanded form, 6

Expressions
addition, 168
evaluating, 168
and missing numbers, 168
numerical, 168
subtraction, 168
translating words to, 404–405

Extra or missing information, 324, 540–541

Face, 432

Fact families
relating addition and subtraction, 70–71
relating multiplication and division, 384–385

Fact table, 340

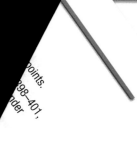

Quarter hour, 192–195

Quarter inch, 534–535

Quotient, 348, 622–623. *See also* Division

Radius, 467

Range, 208

Ray, 442

Readiness. *See* Assessment

Reading Helps, *See the first page of each problem solving lesson.*

Reasonable Answers, 633

Reasonableness
  data, 209
  estimation, 99
  extra information, 14
  mental math, 81, 84
  numbers, 87, 99
  rounding, 30
  skip counting, 25
  time, 197

Reasoning
  addition, 68
  algebra, 72
  calendar, 201
  data, 209, 218, 220, 227, 233, 329
  division, 370, 386, 391, 400, 623, 651, 654
  equal groups, 391
  fractions, 499, 503, 505, 510, 511, 513, 516, 517, 519, 521, 523
  geometry, 429, 430, 433, 442, 443, 445, 447, 448, 451, 452, 455, 457, 458, 461, 465, 466, 469, 470, 472, 473, 475
  measurements, 533, 535, 539, 585, 681, 685, 695, 697
  mental math, 85, 614
  money, 38, 41, 329, 639
  multiplication, 277, 278, 283, 617, 628, 631, 637, 639, 641
  numbers, 5, 19, 23, 134
  patterns, 280
  probability, 701, 702, 703
  problem-solving strategy, 644–645
  remainder, 400
  rounding, 30
  skip counting, 25
  subtraction, 148, 154
  time, 194, 197, 199

Recognizing exact answer or estimate, 160–161, 616, 622

Rectangle, 221, 454–455

Rectangular prism, 428

Reflection (flip), 456

Regroup, 126

Regrouping
  in addition, 67, 126, 132–135, 146–147
  in multiplication, 632–633

  with place-value blocks, 146–147
  in subtraction, 152–153

Relate fractions and decimals, 564

Relating Multiplication to Place Value, 615

Relational symbols, choosing. *See* Compare.

Remainder, 398–401, 656–657. *See also* Division

Repeated addition. *See* Multiplication, as repeated addition.

Represent data, 204–211

Representations
  equal groups, 264, 389
  multiplication, 264
  number line, 23
  patterns, 26
  time, 26, 196

Reteaching, 56–59, 116–119, 182–185, 250–253, 306–309, 360–363, 418–421, 488–491, 554–557, 602–605, 670–673, 722–725

Review. *See* Assessment

Rhombus, 454

Right angle, 444

Right triangle, 451

Roman numerals, 27

Rotation (turn), 457

Rounding
  in estimation. *See* Estimation, rounding
  to nearest dollar, 575
  to nearest ten, 28, 98
  to nearest hundred, 29, 98
  to nearest thousand, 31, 89
  whole numbers, 28–31

Ruler
  centimeter, 582–583
  inch, 532–533

Rules, 72–73, 344–345. *See also* Properties.

Scalene triangle, 450

Scales, 212, 228

Second, 192

Section Review. *See* Assessment

Segment, line, 442–443

Sets, fractional parts of, 516–519

Shapes, 432–433. *See also* Geometry

Side, 446

Similar figures, 459

Similarity, 459

Sixths, 499

Skip counting, 259, 281

Slide (translation), 457

Solid figure
  attributes, 428
  corner, 432
  cube, 428
  cylinder, 428
  edge, 432
  face, 432
  pyramid, 428
  rectangular prism, 428
  relating to shapes, 432–433
  sphere, 428
  vertex, 432
  volume, 472–473

Solve a Simpler Problem strategy, 528–529

Solve problems. *See* Problem solving

Space figure. *See* Solid figure

Sphere, 428

Spreadsheet Tool/Grapher eTool, 231

Spreadsheet Tool/Graphing and Tally Features, 207

Square, 454

Square centimeter, 471

Square foot, 471

Square inch, 471

Square number, 325

Square units, 468

Standard form, 6

Statistics. *See* Data

Subtraction
  across zeros, 156–157
  decimals, 572–575
  fractions, like denominators, 520–521
  money, 162–165
  number sentences, 76
  place-value blocks, 150–151
  regrouping, 152–153
  related to addition, 70–71
  tens, using, 94–95
  three-digit numbers, 150–155
  two-digit numbers, 148–149

Sum, 64, 66, 124

Sums, estimating, 86–89

Survey, 204

Symbols
  choosing operational symbols, 346–347
  choosing relational symbols ($>$ $<$ $=$). *See* Compare
  decimal point, 36

Symmetric, 460

Symmetry, 460–461